NEW HOLLAND FIELD GUIDE TO THE

BIRDS

D1581705

— OF —

SOUTH-EAST ASIA

- THAILAND
- PENINSULAR MALAYSIA
- SINGAPORE
- VIETNAM
- CAMBODIA
- LAOS
- MYANMAR

ILLUSTRATED BY RICHARD ALLEN, TIM WORFOLK,
STEPHEN MESSAGE, JAN WILCZUR, CLIVE BYERS,
MIKE LANGMAN, IAN LEWINGTON, CHRISTOPHER SCHMIDT,
ANDREW MACKAY, JOHN COX, ANTHONY DISLEY,
HILARY BURN, DANIEL COLE AND MARTIN ELLIOTT

CRAIG ROBSON

NEW
HOLLAND

This edition published in 2010 by
New Holland Publishers (UK) Ltd
London • Cape Town • Sydney • Auckland

Garfield House, 86–88 Edgware Road,
London W2 2EA, United Kingdom
www.newhollandpublishers.com

80 McKenzie Street, Cape Town 8001, South Africa

Unit 1, 66 Gibbes Street, Chatswood, NSW 2067, Australia

218 Lake Road, Northcote, Auckland, New Zealand

10 9 8 7 6 5 4

ISBN 978 1 84330 746 4

First published in 2005

Publishing Manager: Jo Hemmings
Senior Editor: Jane Morrow and Charlotte Judet
Editor: Nigel Collar
Design and plate make-up: D & N Publishing, Hungerford, Berkshire
Production: Joan Woodroffe
Index: Janet Dudley

Reproduction by Modern Age Repro Co. Ltd, Hong Kong
Printed and bound in Singapore by Tien Wah Press (Pte) Ltd

CONTENTS

INTRODUCTION

This guide is a condensed version of *A Field Guide to the Birds of South-East Asia* (Robson 2000), and is intended to be as portable as possible, for use in the field. Obviously, in order to save space and therefore weight, the species accounts are relatively short and are intended to be as concise as possible within the publisher's brief. Additionally, the illustrations are spread across an increased number of plates (142 rather than 104), and all of the species text faces the relevant plates. For more detailed information on a given species, consult the above-mentioned guide.

Taxonomy and nomenclature follow *A Field Guide to the Birds of South-East Asia*, with the following exceptions (the references followed for each treatment appear in parentheses): Siamese Partridge *Arborophila diversa* is lumped in **Chestnut-headed Partridge** *A. cambodiana* (Eames *et al.* 2002); Hodgson's Hawk Cuckoo *Hierococcyx fugax* becomes two species, **Malaysian Hawk Cuckoo** *H. fugax* and **Hodgson's Hawk Cuckoo** *H. nisicolor* (King 2002); **Mongolian Gull** *Larus mongolicus* is treated as a distinct species, rather than a race of Herring Gull *L. argentatus* (Yésou 2001, 2002); **Slender-billed Vulture** *Gyps tenuirostris* is split from Long-billed (Indian) Vulture *G. indicus* (Rasmussen and Parry 2001); **Indian Spotted Eagle** *Aquila hastata* is split from Lesser Spotted Eagle *A. pomarina* (Parry *et al.* 2002); **Green-backed Flycatcher** *Ficedula elisae* is split from Narcissus Flycatcher *F. narcissina* (Round 2000); and Common Stonechat *Saxicola torquata* becomes **Siberian Stonechat** *S. maura* (Wink *et al.* 2002). Three species new to science also appear in this guide: **Omei Warbler** *Seicercus omeiensis* (Martens *et al.* 1999), **Chestnut-eared Laughingthrush** *Garrulax konkakinhensis* (Eames and Eames 2001), and **Mekong Wagtail** *Motacilla samveasnae* (Duckworth *et al.* 2001). Additionally, the generic name ***Houbaropsis*** is reinstated for Bengal Florican, rather than *Eupodotis* (Inskipp *et al.* 1996), and the common name **Ludlow's Fulvetta** is used for *Alcippe ludlowi*, as the alternative (Brown-throated Fulvetta) is so misleading. Unfortunately, however, in order to balance out the plates, and compare some similar species, it has not been possible to follow the exact (correct) species order.

Eleven species that were not illustrated in the original work (**Wandering Whistling-duck** *Dendrocygna arcuata*, **Swan Goose** *Anser cygnoides*, **Sacred Kingfisher** *Todirhamphus sanctus*, **Stilt Sandpiper** *Micropalama himantopus*, **Aleutian Tern** *Sterna aleutica*, **Black Tern** *Chlidonias niger*, **Red-tailed Tropicbird** *Phaethon rubricauda*, **Chinese Penduline Tit** *Remiz consobrinus*, **Snowy-throated Babbler** *Stachyris oglei*, **Chaffinch** *Fringilla coelebs* and **Reed Bunting** *Emberiza schoeniclus*) are now fully illustrated, as are 16 species that have been recorded as new to the region since publication of the original work (**Red-breasted Merganser** *Mergus serrator*, **Alpine Swift** *Tachymarptis melba*, **White-headed Stilt** *Himantopus leucocephalus*, **Laughing Gull** *Larus atricilla*, **Black-legged Kittiwake** *Rissa tridactyla*, **Arctic Tern** *Sterna paradisaea*, **Horned Grebe** *Podiceps auritus*, **Yellow-billed Loon** *Gavia adamsii*, **Rusty-bellied Shortwing** *Brachypteryx hyperythra*, **Wallcreeper** *Tichodroma muraria*, **Pleske's Warbler** *Locustella pleskei*, **Common Chiffchaff** *Phylloscopus collybita*, **Chestnut-eared Laughingthrush**, **Ludlow's Fulvetta**, **Mekong Wagtail** and **Rustic Bunting** *Emberiza rustica*). A single new subspecies (or species, depending on your viewpoint) now recorded from the region, White Wagtail *Motacilla alba lugens* (aka 'Black-backed Wagtail'), is also illustrated. Significantly, it has also been possible to have more than 120 illustrations from the original guide improved or corrected.

Two species (**Vega Gull** *L. vegae* and **Saunders's Tern** *S. saundersi*) that were included in the original work, but have not been recorded from the region, are now deleted.

All species known to have been recorded in the region by the author up to spring 2003 are dealt with and illustrated, and distribution and other texts have been widely updated. Two new species for South-East Asia have been recorded between this date and the book going to press: **Little Gull** *Larus minutus* at Bang Pu, Samut Prakan, C Thailand, in November 2001, and **Eurasian Golden Oriole** *Oriolus oriolus* at Pulau Langkawi, Kedah, Peninsular Malaysia in January 2001.

If readers find any errors or omissions, the author (c/o New Holland Publishers) would be pleased to receive any information that updates or corrects that presented herein, in the hope that an improved edition may appear in the future.

SPECIES ACCOUNT/PLATE INFORMATION

- The **total length** of each species appears after the species name.
- A **comparative approach** has been adopted with species descriptions, where scarcer species are generally compared to commoner or more widespread species. In general, those species considered to be **easily identifiable** have been afforded less coverage than the more difficult species.
- **Comparisons between similar species** are dealt with directly and separately under the various sex/age or other headings.
- **Males** are described first (except in polyandrous species) and female plumage compared directly to the male plumage.
- Names of illustrated **subspecies** are only given after the first sex/age class dealt with. It can be assumed that the following illustrations are of the same race, until another one is mentioned. The ornithological regions of South-East Asia (see inside back cover) where a given subspecies has been recorded (e.g. NW Thailand, S Annam) appear in parentheses after its name – though generally not in the case of the first subspecies listed, the range of which can be deduced by consulting the map and then subtracting the ranges of other subspecies. Subspecies given as 'ssp.' are currently undescribed or in the process of being described.

Details of **non-illustrated** sex/age classes refer to the last named subspecies in the sequence. The subspecies listed under '**Other subspecies**' are generally not considered to differ markedly from the first subspecies mentioned.

- **Altitude ranges** refer to South-East Asia only.
- References to 6°, 9° and 12° N etc. refer to the 'Malay Peninsular' only, unless stated.
- Species depicted on any one plate have been illustrated to the same **scale** (smaller in the case of flight figures) unless stated.
- Readers will notice that some regularly used words in the **range texts**, and the **generic names** of a few species have been abbreviated. These were necessary space-saving measures.

ACKNOWLEDGEMENTS

I am grateful to a number of people for their valuable assistance during the preparation of this work. In particular, I would like to thank those artists who painted new figures and made amendments to some of the original ones.

During visits to the bird collections at the Natural History Museum, Tring, I was greatly assisted again by staff there (Mark Adams, Robert Prys-Jones and F.E 'Effie' Warr).

Others who helped me in updating the text were Philip Round, Pamela Rasmussen, Per Alström, Bill Clark, Peter Davidson, Will Duckworth, Jonathan Eames, Tim Inskipp, Mikhail Kalyakin, Peter Kennerley, Ben King, Le Hai Quang, Paul Leader, Yoshimitsu Shigeta and David Wells.

I am also very grateful to Nigel Collar for his painstaking work in editing the manuscript, and the designer at D & N Publishing for the difficult task of rearranging the plates. Jo Hemmings, Jane Morrow and Charlotte Judet at New Holland showed a high level of commitment to the project.

ABBREVIATIONS & CONVENTIONS

Co	Common	**WV**	Winter visitor
Fc	Fairly common	**FWV**	Former winter visitor
Lc	Locally common	**PM**	Passage migrant
Lfc	Locally fairly common	**NBV**	Non-breeding visitor
Un	Uncommon	**FNBV**	Former non-breeding visitor
Ul	Uncommon local	**VS**	Visits/visiting/visitor
Lo	Local	**V**	Vagrant
Sc	Scarce	**Fo**	Formerly occurred
Sl	Scarce local	**Frc**	Formerly recorded
Vl	Very local	**Rc**	Recorded
Ra	Rare	**E**	Extinct
Rl	Rare local		
		>	More than
R	Resident	<	Less than (up to)
FER	Feral resident	ssp.	subspecies currently undescribed
FR	Former resident	Syn.	Synonym
BV	Breeding visitor	M	Male
B	Breeds	f	Female
FB	Formerly bred		

GLOSSARY

Axillaries: the feathers at the base of the underwing.

Bird-wave: mixed-species feeding flock.

Casque: an enlargement of the upper mandible, as in many hornbill species.

Cere: a fleshy structure at the base of the bill which contains the nostrils.

Clang: loud ringing sound.

Clangour: clanging noise.

Comb: erect unfeathered fleshy growth, situated lengthwise on crown.

Crest: tuft of feathers on crown of head, sometimes erectile.

Distal: (of the part) further from the body.

Dorsal: of or on the back

Eclipse: a dull short-term post-nuptial plumage.

Face: informal term for the front part of the head, usually including the forehead, lores, cheeks and often the chin.

Flight feathers: in this work, a space-saving collective term for primaries and secondaries.

Fringe: complete feather margin.

Frugivorous: fruit-eating.

Graduated tail: tail on which each feather, starting outermost, is shorter than the adjacent inner feather.

Gregarious: living in flocks or communities.

Gular: pertaining to the throat.

Gunung: Malay word for mountain.

Hackles: long, pointed neck feathers.

Hepatic: brownish-red (applied to the rufous morph of some cuckoos).

Knob: a fleshy protrusion on the upper mandible of the bill.

Lappet: a fold of skin (wattle) hanging or protruding from the head.

Lateral: on or along the side.

Leading edge: the front edge (usually of the forewing in flight).

Local: occurring or relatively common within a small or restricted area.

Mask: informal term for the area of the head around the eye, often extending back from the bill and covering (part of) the ear-coverts.

Mesial: down the middle (applied to streak on chin/throat, mostly of raptors); interchangeable with gular.

Morph: a permanent alternative plumage exhibited by a species, having no taxonomic standing and usually involving base colour, not pattern.

Nomadic: prone to wandering, or occurring erratically, with no fixed territory outside breeding season.

Nuchal: pertaining to the nape and hindneck.

Ocelli: eye-like spots, often iridescent.

Orbital: surrounding the eye.

Pelagic: of the open sea.

Polyandrous: mating with more than one male (usually associated with sex-role reversal).

Post-ocular: behind the eye.

Race: *see* Subspecies.

Rami: barbs of feathers.

Shaft-streak: a pale or dark line in the plumage produced by the feather shaft.

Subspecies: a geographical population whose members all show constant differences, in plumage and/or size etc., from those of other populations of the same species.

Subterminal: immediately before the tip.

Terminal: at the tip.

Terrestrial: living or occurring mainly on the ground.

Tibia: upper half of often visible avian leg (above the reverse 'knee').

Trailing edge: the rear edge (usually of the wing in flight).

Underparts: the lower parts of the body (loosely applied).

Underside: the entire lower surface of the body.

Upperparts: the upper parts of the body, usually excluding the head, tail and wings (loosely applied).

Upperside: the entire upper surface of the body, tail and wings.

Vagrant: a status for a species nationally or regionally when it is accidental (rare and irregular) in occurrence.

Vermiculated: marked with narrow wavy lines, often only visible at close range.

Web: a vane (to one side of the shaft) of a feather.

Wing-bar: a line across a closed wing formed by different-coloured tips to the greater or median coverts, or both.

Wing-panel: a lengthwise strip on closed wing formed by coloured fringes (usually on flight feathers).

AVIAN TOPOGRAPHY

The figures below illustrate the main plumage tracts and bare-part features. This terminology for bird topography has been used extensively in the species descriptions, and a full understanding of these terms is important if the reader is to make full use of this book; they are a starting point in putting together a description.

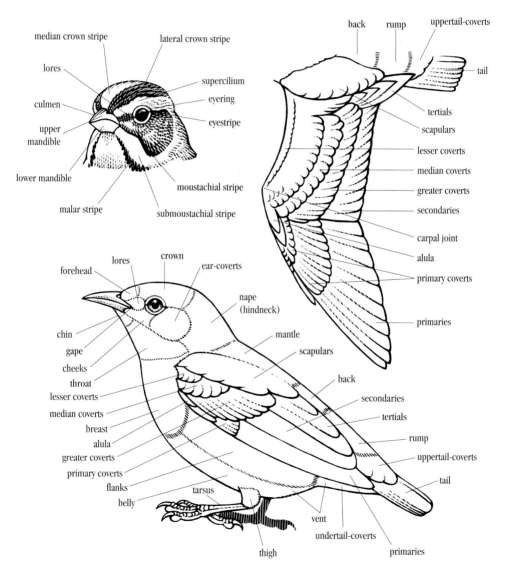

PLATE 1 SCRUBFOWL, FRANCOLINS, PARTRIDGES, QUAILS & BUTTONQUAILS

1 NICOBAR SCRUBFOWL *Megapodius nicobariensis* 39 cm
(**a**) **Adult** *nicobariensis*: Plain brown and greyish, red facial skin. **Juvenile**: Brown below, facial skin smaller/paler, initially buffier facial area. VOICE *kyouououou-kyou-kou-kouk-oukoukoukou* (first note rising, rest decreasing in staccato series) from males. Cackling *kuk-a-kuk-kuk* call. HABITAT & BEHAVIOUR Island forest understorey, nearby sandy beaches. Runs from danger. RANGE FR (still?) Coco Is, S Myanmar.

2 CHINESE FRANCOLIN *Francolinus pintadeanus* 31–33 cm
(**a**) **Male** *phayrei*: Blackish with whitish spots/bars, ear-coverts white with black surround, throat white. Crown-sides rufous, scapulars chestnut. (**b**) **Female**: Duller/browner, less black on crown-centre, little chestnut on scapulars, more barred than spotted below. (**c**) **Juvenile**: Duller than female, less rufous on crown, pale streaks above, eyestripe and moustachial streak almost lacking or latter reduced to spots. VOICE Male territorial call is loud harsh metallic *wi-ta-tak-takaa*. HABITAT Open forest and woodland, grass and scrub; up to 1,800 m. RANGE Fc/co R (except Tenasserim, S Thailand, Pen Malaysia, Singapore).

3 BLACK PARTRIDGE *Melanoperdix nigra* 24–27 cm
(**a**) **Male** *nigra*: Glossy black with slightly browner wings. (**b**) **Female**: Dark chestnut; buffier head-sides/throat/vent, black scapulars spots. Chestnut scales/bars on head-sides/throat (may be blacker on cheeks). (**c**) **Juvenile**: As female but fine pale and dark vermiculations and some pale spots above; less black on scapular, large whitish spots and dark bars down breast-sides/flanks, whiter vent. HABITAT & BEHAVIOUR Broadleaved evergreen forest; up to 610 m. Very shy. RANGE Sc R Pen Malaysia.

4 COMMON QUAIL *Coturnix coturnix* 20–20.5 cm
(**a**) **Male** *coturnix*: Possibly tends to have less chestnut base colour to breast/flanks and browner upperparts than non-breeding male Japanese; slightly larger (wing >105 mm). (**b**) **Female/first winter**: No dark gular stripe. May be inseparable in field (either sex) from Japanese. VOICE Male territorial call is rhythmic whistled *pit pil-it*. May give slightly ringing *pik-kreee* when flushed. HABITAT Lowland grassy areas, cultivation. RANGE Ra WV/V W,S Myanmar.

5 JAPANESE QUAIL *Coturnix japonica* 19 cm
(**a**) **Male non-breeding** *japonica*: As female but throat with blackish to chestnut gular-line and bar, breast warmer (often more chestnut and less blackish streaks. (**b**) **Male breeding**: Pinkish-chestnut head-sides/throat diagnostic. Often has dark throat-bands. (**c,d**) **Female/first winter**: Brownish above with whitish/buff streaks and speckles, rufescent to chestnut breast/flanks, with black and whitish streaks. Pale buff/whitish throat with double dark bar at side (often short moustachial line almost joining first bar). Base colour of breast and flanks tends to more chestnut than Common (broad chestnut streaks may be distinctive if present), typically somewhat darker/greyer above; wing <105 mm. Sharply pointed feathers on throat-sides distinctive if visible. VOICE Males utter a loud *choo-peet-trrr* or *guku kr-r-r-r-r*. HABITAT Grassy areas, cultivation; up to 500 m. RANGE Sc/un WV Myanmar, NW Thailand, N Laos, W,E Tonkin. V Cambodia, C Annam. ? B N Myanmar, E Tonkin.

6 RAIN QUAIL *Coturnix coromandelica* 16.5–18.5 cm
(**a**) **Male**: Black on breast and flanks. (**b**) **Female/juvenile**: Duller/more uniform breast than Japanese (often greyish), with more irregular dark spots and bolder whitish streaks; primaries unbarred. Juvenile breast perhaps initially more heavily speckled. VOICE Males give 3–5 sharp metallic *whit-whit* couplets. HABITAT Dry grassland and cultivation, scrub; up to 1,525 m (mainly lowlands). RANGE Sc/lc R (local movements) Myanmar (except Tenasserim), Thailand (except S), Cambodia, S Annam.

7 BLUE-BREASTED QUAIL *Coturnix chinensis* 13–15 cm
(**a**) **Male** *chinensis*: Face and breast slaty-blue, throat black and white, vent chestnut. (**b,c**) **Female**: Quite dull/uniform above, buff supercilium, blackish barred breast/flanks. **Juvenile**: As female but perhaps initially duller with dark mottling and whitish streaks on breast/flanks. Males soon show some adult plumage. VOICE Sweet whistled *ti-yu ti-yu* (sometimes 3 notes) from male. HABITAT Dry/slightly marshy grassland, scrub, cultivation; up to 1,300 m. RANGE Un/co R (except W Myanmar, S Laos, N,S Annam). Local movements in Pen Malaysia at least.

8 SMALL BUTTONQUAIL *Turnix sylvatica* 13–14 cm
(**a,b**) **Female** *mikado*: Buff-and-black-streaked chestnut wing-coverts, paler breast than Yellow-legged, bluish/blackish bill, greyish-pinkish legs. **Male**: Mantle less rufous. (**c**) **Juvenile**: Breast duller than female, blackish spots across breast. **Other subspecies** *T.s.dussumier* (Myanmar): Paler above, more obvious buff and rufous-chestnut on hindneck/upper mantle. *T.s.davidi* (Cochinchina). VOICE Female territorial call is series of 1 s long *booo* notes. Recalls Barred, but notes more mournful, longer, slower, and more slowly repeated. HABITAT Dry grassland, thickets bordering cultivation; up to 1,150 m. RANGE Sc/lo R C,S,E Myanmar, NW,C Thailand, Cambodia, N,C Laos, E Tonkin, C Annam, Cochinchina.

9 YELLOW-LEGGED BUTTONQUAIL *T.tanki* 16.5–18 cm
(**a,b**) **Female** *blanfordii*: Yellow legs, black spots on sandy-buff coverts, deep buff breast-patch, round black upper flank spots, mostly yellowish bill. Shows the most contrasting wing-coverts. **Male**: Lacks female's rufous nuchal collar. (**c**) **Juvenile**: Duller breast-patch than male, faint dark bars on lower throat/breast, duller wing-covert spots. VOICE Females apparently utter low hooting notes, which increase in strength and turn into human-like moan. HABITAT Grassland, scrub, cultivation, secondary growth; up to 2,135 m. RANGE Un/co R (except southern S Thailand, Pen Malaysia, Singapore). Un PM E Tonkin, N Annam.

10 BARRED BUTTONQUAIL *Turnix suscitator* 15–17.5 cm
(**a,b**) **Female** *thai*: Black throat-patch and breast/flank bars, black-and-buff-barred coverts, rufous-buff vent. Quite greyish above. (**c**) **Male/juvenile**: No black on throat/breast. (**d**) **Female** *blakistoni* (**rc** NW Thailand, N Indochina): Rufous-chestnut above (both sexes). **Other subspecies** *T.s.atrogularis* (S Thailand southwards): Richer buff below. *T.s.plumbipes* (SW,W Myanmar); *pallescens* (C,S Myanmar). VOICE Females give soft, quickly repeated, ventriloquial series of rising *ooo* notes (increasing in volume before ending abruptly). HABITAT Dry grassy areas, thickets, cultivation; to 1,650 m. RANGE Co R throughout.

PLATE 2 *ARBOROPHILA* PARTRIDGES & FERRUGINOUS PARTRIDGE

1 HILL PARTRIDGE *Arborophila torqueola* 27.5–30.5 cm
(**a**) **Male** *batemani*: Chestnut crown, rufescent ear-coverts, narrow white upper breast-band, wavy blackish mantle-barring. (**b**) **Female**: Head-sides, throat and foreneck buffy/rufous, breast scaled rufous-brown and grey, much chestnut on flanks. (**c**) **Juvenile**: Like female, but breast spotted buff/whitish. **Other subspecies** *A.t.griseata* (W Tonkin): Greyer above, more rufescent crown, slatier breast. **VOICE** Territorial call is mournful whistle, lasting c. 1.5 s. **HABITAT** Broadleaved evergreen forest; 2,135–3,005 m. **RANGE** Lc **R** W,N Myanmar, W Tonkin.

2 RUFOUS-THROATED PARTRIDGE *A.rufogularis* 26–29 cm
(**a**) **Adult** *tickelli*: Black-streaked rufous throat/neck, grey breast, chestnut flank-streaks. (**b**) **Female**: Plainer/buffier throat, white spots/streaks below, small black markings but no broad pale grey to buffish-grey markings on scapulars/coverts. (**c**) **Adult** *intermedia* (SW,W,N,S Myanmar): Mostly black throat. (**d**) **Adult** *annamensis* (S Annam): Whitish throat, often a black necklace. **Other subspecies** *A.r.euroa* (N Indochina); *guttata* (C Annam). **VOICE** Territorial call is long clear whistle followed by whistled couplets: *whu-whu whu-whu..*, gradually ascending scale and increasing in pitch. Partner may add monotonous *kew-kew-kew...* **HABITAT** Broadleaved evergreen forest; 1,000–2,590 m. **RANGE** Co **R** Myanmar (except C), W,NW,NE Thailand, Laos, W,E Tonkin, N,C,S Annam.

3 WHITE-CHEEKED PARTRIDGE *A.atrogularis* 25.5–27 cm
(**a**) **Adult**: Black throat, brownish crown, greyish breast, small flank markings. **VOICE** Accelerating ascending, throaty, quavering *prrrer* notes, usually followed by emphatic *wi-bu* or *wa-bu* couplets (*wi/wa*). Partner often adds monotonous *chew-chew-chew...* **HABITAT** Broadleaved evergreen forest, secondary growth; 610–1,220 m. **RANGE** Un **R** SW,W,N,E(north) Myanmar.

4 BAR-BACKED PARTRIDGE *A.brunneopectus* 26.5–29.5 cm
(**a**) **Adult** *brunneopectus*: Pale buffish supercilium/upper throat, black mantle-bars, brown breast, black-and-white flank markings. (**b**) **Adult** *henrici* (N,C Indochina): Pale of head richer buff. (**c**) **Adult** *albigula* (S Annam): Head whiter. **VOICE** Males give loud *brr* notes (increasing in volume), then *wi-wu* couplets (also becoming louder before ending abruptly). Partner often adds *chew-chew-chew...* **HABITAT** Broadleaved evergreen forest; 500–1,525 m; rarely to 1,850 m in S Annam. **RANGE** Un/lc **R** C,E,S Myanmar, Tenasserim, W,NW,NE Thailand, northeast Cambodia, Laos, Vietnam (except Cochinchina).

5 MALAYAN PARTRIDGE *Arborophila campbelli* 28 cm
(**a**) **Adult**: Largely black head/neck, grey upper mantle/breast, pale rufous-and-black flank markings. **Juvenile**: More chestnut-tinged above, breast barred blackish, grey and dull rufous, flanks more heavily marked chestnut, black and buff. **VOICE** Like Bar-backed; *oii* notes, usually followed by shrill, whistled *pi-bor* couplets. **HABITAT** Broadleaved evergreen forest; 1,000–1,600 m. **RANGE** Un/fc **R** extreme S Thailand, Pen Malaysia.

6 ORANGE-NECKED PARTRIDGE *Arborophila davidi* 27 cm
(**a**) **Adult**: Black band down neck and across lower foreneck, rest of neck mostly orange, throat whitish, breast brown rather

grey. **VOICE** Accelerating *prruu* notes, soon running to rapid, gradually higher series of <70 *pwi* notes. Also rapid piping *tutututututututututu...* (<60 notes). Partner often adds stressed *tchew-tchew-tchew-tchew...* **HABITAT** Broadleaved evergreen/semi-evergreen forest, bamboo; 140–250 m. **RANGE** Lfc/co **R** east Cambodia, north-east Cochinchina.

7 CHESTNUT-HEADED PARTRIDGE *A.cambodiana* 28 cm
(**a**) **Adult** *cambodiana*: Chestnut head/breast, blackish crown/eyestripe, heavily barred/mostly black above, large black-and-white flank markings. Variable white and black markings across breast. (**b**) **Adult** *diversa* (SE Thailand): Head, neck and upperparts recall Bar-backed, breast chestnut, has more black-and-white below than *cambodiana*. (**c**) **Adult**: Less well-marked individual. **Juvenile** Chestnut of breast washed-out, head pattern less contrasting (*diversa*). **Other subspecies** *A.c.chandamonyi* (west Cambodia): Roughly intermediate. **HABITAT** Broadleaved evergreen forest; 400–1,000 m (700–1,500 m in Thailand). **RANGE** Co/ul **R** SE Thailand, west and south-west Cambodia.

8 SCALY-BREASTED PARTRIDGE *A. chloropus* 27–31.5 cm
(**a**) **Adult** *chloropus*: Plain; greenish legs, reddish bill with dull yellowish tip, indistinct flank markings. **Juvenile**: Whitish shafts and tips on breast/flank feathers. (**b**) **Adult** *cognacqi* (S Indochina, except Cambodia): Duller. **Other subspecies** *A.c.peninsularis* (south W Thailand): Similar to *cognacqi* below. *A.c.olivacea* (Cambodia, N,C Laos, W Tonkin). **VOICE** Slowy accelerating clear notes (often doubled), then 5–7 loud, harsh, undulating couplets: *tu-tu....tu-tu-tu..tu-tu. tu-tu-tu-tutututututututu TCHIRRA-TCHWIU-TCHIRRA-TCHWIU-TCHIRRA-TCHWIU...* **HABITAT** Broadleaved forest, secondary growth, bamboo; up to 1,000 m. **RANGE** Co **R** N,C,S Myanmar, north Tenasserim, W,NW,NE,SE Thailand, Indochina (except E Tonkin, N,C Annam).

9 ANNAM PARTRIDGE *Arborophila merlini* 29 cm
(**a**) **Adult**: Yellow legs and feet, warm buff base colour to foreneck, large blackish markings on lower breast/flanks. **VOICE** Possibly not distinguishable from Scaly-breasted. **HABITAT** Broadleaved evergreen forest, secondary growth; up to 600 m. **RANGE** Lo **R** C Annam.

10 CHESTNUT-NECKLACED PARTRIDGE *A.charltonii* 26–32 cm
(**a**) **Adult** *charltonii*: Chestnut breast-band and ear-patch. (**b**) **Adult** *tonkinensis* (E Tonkin, N Annam): Narrower breast-band/ear-patch. **VOICE** Like Scaly-breasted. **HABITAT** Broadleaved evergreen forest; up to 500 m. **RANGE** Ra **R** south Tenasserim, S Thailand, Pen Malaysia. Lc **R** E Tonkin, N Annam.

11 FERRUGINOUS PARTRIDGE *Caloperdix oculea* 28–32 cm
(**a**) **Male** *oculea*: Chestnut head/breast, pale-scaled black mantle and body-sides, black covert-spots. 1 or 2 spurs. **Female**: No spurs or one short one. **Juvenile** Black-barred nape, blackish spotted/barred breast. **VOICE** Ascending accelerating high notes, terminated abruptly with harsh couplets: *p-pi-pi-pipipipipipi dit-duit dit-duit*. **HABITAT** Broadleaved evergreen forest, bamboo; up to 915 m. **RANGE** Sc/un **R** Tenasserim, W,S Thailand, Pen Malaysia.

PLATE 3 PARTRIDGES, PHEASANTS, TRAGOPANS, MONALS & JUNGLEFOWL

1 LONG-BILLED PARTRIDGE *Rhizothera longirostris* 38 cm
(**a**) **Male** *longirostris*: Long stout bill, yellow legs, light chestnut head-sides/underparts, with grey foreneck and upper breast. Complex chestnut, brown, black and buff markings above. (**b**) **Female**: No grey on neck/breast. (**c**) **Juvenile**: Paler-faced and more chestnut above than female, dark marks and buff streaks on breast and mantle. VOICE Far-carrying double whistle with higher second note; usually in repetitive duet, producing rising, four-note sequence. HABITAT Broadleaved evergreen forest, bamboo; up to 1,500 m. RANGE Sc/un R south Tenasserim, W (south), S Thailand, Pen Malaysia.

2 CRESTED PARTRIDGE *Rollulus rouloul* 24–29.5 cm
(**a**) **Male**: Glossy blackish; fan-like chestnut-maroon crest, red soft parts. (**b**) **Female**: Deep green, with dark grey hood, blackish nape, chestnut scapulars and rusty-brown wings with darker vermiculations. No crest, but soft parts/forehead-plumes recall male. (**c**) **Juvenile**: Greyer than female, rufescent crown-sides, buffish covert-spots. VOICE Melancholy upslurred whistled *su-il*. HABITAT Broadleaved evergreen forest; up to 1,220 m. RANGE Sc/lc R south Tenasserim, W (south), S Thailand, Pen Malaysia.

3 MOUNTAIN BAMBOO PARTRIDGE *Bambusicola fytchii* 35 cm
(**a**) **Male** *fytchii*: Long-tailed, pale supercilium, blackish postocular stripe, chestnut-streaked neck/breast, large black markings below. Flight feathers distinctly chestnut. (**b**) **Female**: Postocular stripe brown. **Juvenile**: Buffier above than female, with larger dark markings, less chestnut and some dark bars on breast. **Other subspecies** *B.f.hopkinsoni* (SW,W Myanmar). VOICE Explosive shrill chattering, which slows then dies away. Harsh *tch-hherrrr* calls. HABITAT Grass, scrub, bamboo, secondary growth; 1,200–2,135 m. RANGE Co R W,N,E Myanmar, NW Thailand, N Laos, W Tonkin.

4 BLOOD PHEASANT *Ithaginis cruentus* M 44–48, f 40–42 cm
(**a**) **Male** *marionae*: Black head-sides, red forehead/throat, greyish above with whitish streaks, green on coverts/tertials, red breast with black then pale green streaks, grey belly with greenish streaks, red undertail-coverts with whitish markings, pale red tail-fringes. (**b**) **Female** Brown with fine dark barring, grey nape. **Juvenile** As female but may be buff-speckled above and buff-streaked below. Males soon show some adult plumage. VOICE Shrill high hissing *huewerrrr...hieu-hieu-hieu-hieu*. Sharp *tchwik*. HABITAT Broadleaf and mixed broadleaf/coniferous forest, bamboo; 2,590–3,355 m. RANGE Un/lfc R N Myanmar.

5 BLYTH'S TRAGOPAN *Tragopan blythii* M 65–70, f 58–59 cm
(**a,b**) **Male** *blythii*: Orange-red and black head pattern, naked yellow face/throat, orange-red neck/upper breast, round white and chestnut-red spots and buff-and-black bars above/on vent; dull brownish-grey breast-/belly-patch. Blue-bordered yellow throat-lappet extended in display. (**c**) **Female**: Greyish-brown (warmer coverts/tail) with cryptic whitish, buff and blackish markings; yellowish eyering. **Juvenile**: As female. Males attain red on neck during first year. VOICE Males give loud, moaning *ohh ohhah ohaah ohaaah ohaaaha ohaaaha ohaaaha...* HABITAT Oak and oak/rhododendron forest, bamboo; 1,830–2,600 m, locally to 1,525 m. RANGE Sc/un R W,N Myanmar.

6 TEMMINCK'S TRAGOPAN *T.temminckii* M 62–64, f 55–58 cm
(**a,b**) **Male** Crimson; bold greyish-white spots below, black above eye, naked blue skin on face/throat. Throat-lappet blue with paler spots in centre and row of red bars down each side. (**c**) **Female**: Eyering blue, more distinctly streaked lower throat/breast than Blyth's, bolder whitish spots/streaks below, usually distinctly rufescent-tinged throat/neck; crown perhaps blacker with bolder rufous streaks. **Juvenile**: As female but may be warmer with buff throat and buff streaks on body. Males attain orange-red on neck during first year. VOICE 6–9 eerie moaning notes, terminated by short nasal note: *woh woah woaah   waaah waaah waaah waaah griiik*. HABITAT Broadleaved evergreen forest, secondary growth; 2,135–3,050 m. RANGE Sc/un R N Myanmar, W Tonkin.

7 HIMALAYAN MONAL *Lophophorus impejanus* 63–72 cm
(**a**) **Male**: Long crest, rufous tail, largely purplish/turquoise above, with white restricted to large back-patch. (**b**) **Female**: Short crest, plainer head than Sclater's, contrasting all-white throat, variable whitish streaks below, narrow whitish uppertail-covert band, narrower/buffier pale tail-tip. **Juvenile**: Darker above than female, and streaked buff (crown almost uniform), more barred and less streaked below (including lower throat). **First-winter male**: Similar pattern of adult features to Sclater's. VOICE Loud curlew-like upward-inflected whistles: *kur-leiu*; *kleeh-vick* etc., and higher *kleeh* notes. Similar *kleeh-wick-kleeh-wick..*, mixed with urgent *kwick-kwick..* when alarmed. HABITAT As Sclater's; recorded at 3,050 m (occurs higher elsewhere). RANGE Ra R extreme N Myanmar.

8 SCLATER'S MONAL *Lophophorus sclateri* 63–68 cm
(**a**) **Male**: White back to uppertail-coverts, white-tipped chestnut tail, short crest, green/purple above, reddish-copper shoulders. (**b**) **Female**: Dark base colour to plumage, contrasting pale area (blackish and whitish vermiculations) on back to uppertail-coverts (often washed buffish); blackish tail with whitish bars and rather broad whitish tip; crown/head-sides distinctly speckled and streaked, throat-centre whitish. **Juvenile**: Darker above than female with buff streaks. **First-winter male**: Some black on throat/undertail-coverts, paler back to uppertail-coverts, sometimes a few odd glossy feathers above. HABITAT Open broadleaved and broadleaved/coniferous forest, forest edge, scrub, cliffs, alpine meadows; 2,630–3,960 m. RANGE Un/lo R east N Myanmar.

9 RED JUNGLEFOWL *Gallus gallus* M 65–78, f 41–46 cm
(**a**) **Male** *spadiceus*: Maroon to golden-yellow hackles, maroon scapulars/lesser coverts, arched dark green tail. Red comb, facial skin and lappets. (**b**) **Male eclipse**: Loses hackles after breeding, tail shorter, comb and lappets reduced. (**c**) **Female**: Quite uniform brown, short hackles, rather short/blunt dark tail, bare pinkish face. **Juvenile**: Like female, but males are blacker below and darker/plainer above. (**d**) **Male** *gallus* (NE [eastern], SE Thailand, S Indochina): White 'ear-patch' (smaller on female). **Other subspecies** *G.g.jabouillei* (east N Laos, W,E Tonkin, N Annam). VOICE Higher than domestic fowl, with last syllable cut short. HABITAT Forest edge, open woodland; up to 1,830 m. RANGE Co R (except C Thailand), sc/un Singapore.

PLATE 4 *LOPHURA* PHEASANTS

1 KALIJ PHEASANT *Lophura leucomelanos* M 63–74, f 50–60 cm
(**a**) **Male** *lathami*: Blue-black; white-scaled lower back to uppertail-coverts, greyish/greenish legs. (**b**) **Female**: Dark, with greyish-olive scales above (whiter on coverts), black outertail, chestnut-brown central tail, warm buff/whitish shaft-streaks below, brown/greenish-grey legs. **Juvenile**: Differs as in Silver. (**c**) **Male** *williamsi* (W,C,S[north-west] Myanmar): Whitish vermiculations above, less obvious rump/uppertail-covert scales. (**d**) **Female**: Paler; pale brownish central tail, black outertail with white vermiculations. **Other subspecies** *L.l.oatesi* (SW [south-east], S Myanmar west of Irrawaddy): Only faint grey scales on lower back to uppertail-coverts; resembles Silver (*lineata*). Female resembles *williamsi* but less distinct scales above, central tail may be browner with heavier markings, outertail mid-brown (or chestnut-tinged) with dark brown to blackish vermiculations, may have broader whitish streaks below (can also show dark either side of streaks) and some blackish vermiculations; may exhibit features approaching Silver (*lineata*). **VOICE** Repeated high **WHiiii** in alarm, and subdued but quite sharp **whit-whit-whit...** **HABITAT** Broadleaved forests, bamboo; up to 2,590 m. **RANGE** Co **R** SW,W,N Myanmar and C,S Myanmar west of Irrawaddy R.

2 SILVER PHEASANT *L.nycthemera* M c.80–127, f 56–71 cm
(**a**) **Male** *nycthemera* (inc. *rufipes, occidentalis, ripponi, jonesi, beaulieui; ?berliozi*): White above with black chevrons/lines, red legs. Whitest in north-east. (**b**) **Female**: Plain-looking brown (sometimes warmish) above, blackish-and-whitish-barred outertail, broad blackish and white scales below (duller/buffier with browner scales to west/south-west). In E Tonkin, underparts like upperparts (tinged greyer) with whitish shaft-streaks and paler throat; tail may be rather plain with finer vermiculations on outer feathers. **Other subspecies**: **Group 1** (**c**) **Male** *lineata* (S Myanmar east of Irrawaddy, south E Myanmar, W, western NW Thailand) and *crawfurdii* (Tenasserim, south W Thailand): Much denser markings above, legs often dark grey/pinkish-brown (particularly *lineata*). (**d**) **Female**: Light scaling above, black-and-white V-shapes on hindneck, mostly dull chestnut breast/belly (blackish on *crawfurdii*) with white streaks, paler central tail. **Group 2** (**e**) **Male** *lewisi* (SE Thailand, SW Cambodia), *engelbachi* (S Laos), *beli* (C Annam), and *annamensis* (C[southern], S Annam): Bolder markings above than *lineata*, red legs. (**f**) **Female** *lewisi*: Chestnut-tinged above with greyish scaling, greyer and relatively plain below. Females of other races in this group have underparts like upperparts (warmer on *engelbachi*) with whitish shaft-streaks and paler throat (*beli* and *engelbachi* may have blackish and whitish vermiculations on lower breast to vent); tail may be rather plain compared to *nycthemera*. **Juvenile**: As female but may have black spots/bars on scapulars/coverts; males soon obvious. **VOICE** Grunting **WWERK** in alarm, and **WWERK wuk-uk-uk-uk..**, with sharp **HSSiik**. Rising **swii-ieeik**. Throaty **wutch-wutch-wutch..** and **UWH. HABITAT & BEHAVIOUR** Broadleaved forests; up to 2,020 m. Often in small flocks; usually shy. **RANGE** Un/lc **R** N(south-east),E,C & S (east of Irrawaddy) Myanmar, north Tenasserim, Thailand (except C,S), Indochina (except Cochinchina?).

3 IMPERIAL PHEASANT *Lophura imperialis* M 75, f c.60 cm
(**a**) **Male**: Large, long-tailed, dark crest. (**b**) **Female**: Like Silver (*annamensis*) but dark chestnut above, with greyish feather-tips/-centres (looks mottled), tail blackish-chestnut, centre of underparts warmer-tinged; short crest. **Juvenile**: As female but may have black spots on scapulars; males with patches of adult plumage (fully adult after c.16 months). **HABITAT** Broadleaved evergreen forest; below 200 m. **RANGE** Ra **R** N,C(north) Annam. **NOTE** Thought to be of hybrid origin (Edwards's or Vietnamese x Silver Pheasant).

4 EDWARDS'S PHEASANT *Lophura edwardsi* 58–65 cm
(**a**) **Male**: Glossy dark blue; white crest, shorish tail, greenish-blue covert-fringes. (**b**) **Female**: Quite plain greyish-brown with warmer scapulars and wings, blackish tail with dark brown (slightly warm) central feathers. **Juvenile male**: As female, but patches of adult plumage; assumes complete plumage during first year. **Juvenile female**: As adult but may have black spots/bars on mantle and coverts. **VOICE** Low guttural **uk uk uk uk uk..** in alarm. **HABITAT** Broadleaved evergreen forest; below 300 m. **RANGE** Rl **R** C Annam.

5 VIETNAMESE PHEASANT *Lophura hatinhensis* 58–65 cm
(**a**) **Male**: White central tail. **Female**: Like Edwards's. **VOICE** Like Edwards's. **HABITAT** As Edwards's; below 200 m. **RANGE** Sl **R** N,C(north) Annam. **NOTE** Probably conspecific with Edwards's.

6 CRESTLESS FIREBACK *L.erythrophthalma* M 47–51, f 42–44 cm
(**a**) **Male** *erythrophthalma*: Blackish-blue/-purplish, fine whitish vermiculations above/on breast-sides, shortish caramel-coloured tail with dark base, greyish legs. (**b**) **Female**: Blackish-bluish/-purplish with browner head, paler throat. **Juvenile**: As female but body tipped rusty-brown. **VOICE** Low **tak-takrau**. Vibrating throaty **purr**; loud **kak** in alarm. **HABITAT** Broadleaved evergreen forest; lowlands. **RANGE** Un/lfc **R** Pen Malaysia.

7 CRESTED FIREBACK *L.ignita* M 65–73.5, f 56–59 cm
(**a**) **Male** *rufa*: White-streaked flanks, white central tail, blue facial skin, reddish legs. (**b**) **Female**: Dull rufous-chestnut; white-streaked breast, white-scaled blackish belly/vent. **Juvenile female**: No crest, may have black-barred nape to scapulars/coverts. **Subadult male**: As adult but chestnut central tail, rufous flank-streaks. **VOICE** Guttural **UKHH-UKHH-UKHH..** in alarm. (**HH** more metallic), mixed with lower **uur** notes. **HABITAT** Broadleaved evergreen forest; up to 200 m, locally to 1,200 m. **RANGE** Ra/lc **R** south Tenasserim, S Thailand, Pen Malaysia.

8 SIAMESE FIREBACK *L. diardi* M c.70–80, f 53–60 cm
(**a**) **Male**: Long crest, mostly grey body, black-and-white barred scapulars/coverts, golden-buff back-patch, bluish-barred maroon rump/uppertail-coverts and on purplish-black belly, blackish-green tail. (**b**) **Female**: Boldly barred wings/tail, largely rufous-chestnut body and outertail, white-scaled belly/flanks. **Juvenile**: As female but may have duller mantle with dark vermiculations, duller base colour below; males lack rufous/chestnut tones, and soon attain adult patches. **VOICE** Metallic **tsik tik-tik tik tik tik..**, grunting **UKHT..UKHT..UKHT..** **HABITAT** Broadleaved evergreen/semi-evergreen forest, secondary growth; up to 800 m. **RANGE** Un/lc **R** NW(eastern),NE,SE Thailand, Indochina (except W,E Tonkin).

PLATE 5 PHEASANTS & GREEN PEAFOWL

1 MRS HUME'S PHEASANT *Syrmaticus humiae* M 91, f 60 cm
(**a**) **Male** *burmanicus*: Chestnut with greyish-purple hood, white wing-bars, dark-barred grey tail. (**b**) **Female**: Warm brown; whitish wing-bars/underpart-scales/tail-tip. **Other subspecies** *S.h.humiae* (west of Irrawaddy R). **VOICE** Males give crowing *cher-a-per, cher-a-per, cher cher, cheria, cheria*. Sharp *tuk tuk*. **HABITAT** Open broadleaved evergreen and oak/pine forest; 1,200–2,285 m. **RANGE** Un/lfc **R** W,N,C,E,S(east) Myanmar, NW Thailand.

2 COMMON PHEASANT *Phasianus colchicus* M 75–91, f 57 cm
(**a**) **Male** *elegans*: Purple-green neck/breast, chestnut body with black streaks/bars, dark-barred brown tail, green-grey coverts, back and rump. (**b**) **Female**: Rufous/buffish above with blackish markings, buffy below with blackish-scaled breast/flanks. **Juvenile**: Like female. (**c**) **Male** *takatsukasae* (north-east E Tonkin): White collar, copper-maroon breast. Female plainer/buffier below than *elegans*. **Other subspecies** *P.c.rothschildi* (north-west E Tonkin): Male's neck/breast more purple. **VOICE** Explosive *korrk-kok* from males. Loud *gogOK gogOK...* alarm. **HABITAT** Clearings, secondary growth, grass; 1,220–1,830 m. **RANGE** Lo **R** N,E Myanmar, E Tonkin.

3 LADY AMHERST'S PHEASANT *Chrysolophus amherstiae* M 130–173 cm, f 63.5–68 cm
(**a**) **Male**: Black-scaled white ruff, green mantle/breast, white belly, long black-barred white tail. (**b**) **Female**: Boldly dark-barred. **Juvenile**: Duller crown and barring than female, buff and dark grey tail-bars, narrower buff flight feather barring. Males attain adult plumage from first autumn. **VOICE** Males utter loud grating *hirk hik-ik*, interspersed with 1–3 quick *hwik* notes (introduction or encore?). **HABITAT** Open broadleaved evergreen forest; 1,525–2,440 m. **RANGE** Un/lo **R** N,E Myanmar.

4 MOUNTAIN PEACOCK PHEASANT *Polyplectron inopinatum* M 65, f 46 cm
(**a**) **Male**: No crest or pale facial skin, very chestnut above, with small bluish ocelli, blackish below, whitish-speckled head/neck. (**b**) **Female/juvenile**: Ocelli smaller and black, tail shorter. **VOICE** 1–4 fairly loud harsh clucks/squawks (c.0.5 s apart), every 5–6 s. **HABITAT** Broadleaved evergreen forest; 800–1,600 m, rarely 600 m. **RANGE** Un **R** extreme S Thailand, Pen Malaysia.

5 GERMAIN'S PEACOCK PHEASANT *P.germaini* M 58, f 48 cm
(**a**) **Male**: Smaller/darker than Grey, darker ocelli (more greenish-blue but often look darker purple), red facial skin. (**b**) **Female**: Darker/plainer than Grey, more defined ocelli, no obvious pale scales above, reddish facial skin. **Juvenile**: Ocelli blacker/fainter than female; faintly pale-scaled coverts, plainer below. **VOICE** Faster and higher than Grey: *erraarrrrr....erraarrrrrakak....aarrrr-akh-akh-akh-akh...AKH-AKH-AKH-AKH...* **HABITAT** Broadleaf evergreen and semi-evergreen forest, bamboo; up to 1,400 m. **RANGE** Lc **R** east Cambodia, C(south), S Annam, Cochinchina.

6 GREY PEACOCK PHEASANT *P.bicalcaratum* M 56–76, f 50 cm
(**a**) **Male** *bicalcaratum*: Greyish; white throat, green/purple ocelli above, pink face-skin. (**b**) **Female**: Darker/plainer; less distinct ocelli. **Juvenile**: As female. **Other subspecies**

P.b.ghigii (Vietnam). **VOICE** Loud airy *PU PWOI* (*PWOI* drawn/rising) from male. Growling rattles, then harsh/loud notes: *uhrrrrr uhrrrrr uhrrrruk orrokhokhokh OKH-OKH-OKH-OKH ORKH-ORKH-ORKH ORKH-ORKH-ORKH...* **HABITAT** Broadleaved evergreen forest; up to 2,320 m. **RANGE** Un/lfc **R** Myanmar, W,NW,NE,S(north) Thailand, northeast Cambodia, Laos, W,E Tonkin, N,C(north) Annam.

7 MALAYAN PEACOCK PHEASANT *P.malacense* M 52, f 42 cm
(**a**) **Male**: Warmish brown; greenish ocelli, long crest, pale orange face-skin, dark ear-coverts. (**b**) **Female**: Less distinct ocelli, no obvious crest, indistinct paler scales above. **Juvenile**: As female. Male as adult by first summer but with darker ocelli, plainer breast and glossless crest. **VOICE** Loud slow *PUU PWORR*. Explosive cackle, then throaty clucks: *TCHI-TCHI-TCHAO-THAO..wuk-wuk-wuk-wuk-wuk...* Loud harsh *TCHOWW*. **HABITAT** Broadleaved evergreen forest; up to 305 m. **RANGE** Un/lc **R** south Tenasserim, S Thailand (E?), Pen Malaysia.

8 CRESTED ARGUS *Rheinardia ocellata* M 190–239, f 75 cm
(**a**) **Male** *nigrescens*: Dark brown, speckled whitish; brown-and-white eyebrow/crest. (**b**) **Female**: Warm brown; black bars above, shorter crest. (**c**) **Male** *ocellata* (Indochina): Crest shorter/browner; eyebrow white, foreneck chestnut, tail more chestnut/grey. Female greyer than *nigrescens*; finer/more intricate markings, white eyebrow. **Juvenile**: Initially as female. Male soon shows some adult features (full plumage in third year). **VOICE** *R.o.ocellata*: Territorial call at dancing ground is loud *WOO'O-WAO* (rising then louder). Also repeated far-carrying disyllabic *oowaaaa* etc. Yelping *pook* alarm. **HABITAT** Broadleaved evergreen forest; 790–1,100 m; 0–1,500 m in Indochina (1,700–1,900 m S Annam). **RANGE** Sc/vl **R** Pen Malaysia. Sc/lc **R** C,S(east) Laos, N,C,S Annam.

9 GREAT ARGUS *Argusianus argus* M 160–203, f 72–76 cm
(**a**) **Male** *argus*: Naked blue on head/neck, warm brown above with fine pale speckles/mottling, mostly dark chestnut below, very long secondaries and very long white-spotted tail. (**b**) **Female** Head and neck like male, complete rufous-chestnut collar, less distinct markings above, duller and plainer below, much shorter barred tail, much shorter secondaries. **Juvenile** As female. Male soon develops longer speckled tail. **VOICE** Male territorial call is loud *KWAH-WAU* (*WAU* louder/longer). Female gives 25–35 loud *WAU* notes, latterly longer, more upward-inflected. **HABITAT** Broadleaved evergreen forest; up to 950 m. **RANGE** Un/lc **R** south Tenasserim, S Thailand, Pen Malaysia.

10 GREEN PEAFOWL *Pavo muticus* M 180–250, f 100–110 cm
(**a**) **Male** *imperator*: Green, scaled blackish, long neck, tall crest, extremely long train with colourful ocelli. (**b**) **Female**: Duller, lacks train. **Juvenile**: Duller than female. Second-year male similar to adult but lacks ocelli on train. **Other subspecies** *P.m.spicifer* (west of Irrawaddy R), *muticus* (Tenasserim/S Thailand southward). **VOICE** Territorial males utter loud *KI-WAO*; females loud *AOW-AA* (*AOW* stressed). **HABITAT** Open forest (mainly by rivers/wetlands); up to 915 m. **RANGE** Vl **R** N,C,S Myanmar, W,NW Thailand, Cambodia, N,S Laos, N,C,S Annam, Cochinchina. **FR** (currently?) SW,W,E Myanmar, Tenasserim, C Laos. **FR** (E) NE,S Thailand, Pen Malaysia.

8–10 to different scale

PLATE 6 GEESE, SHELDUCKS, WHITE-WINGED DUCK & COMB DUCK

1 SWAN GOOSE *Anser cygnoides* 81–94 cm
(**a,b**) **Adult**: Bill thick-based, blackish; dark brown crown and hindneck, contrasting pale creamy-brownish lower head-sides, throat and foreneck, narrow whitish frontal band (borders bill-base). Wing pattern recalls Greater White-fronted. (**c**) **Juvenile**: Crown/hindneck duller, no frontal band. **VOICE** Prolonged resounding honks, ending at higher pitch. 2–3 short harsh notes in alarm. **HABITAT** Banks of large rivers, marshy freshwater wetland margins; recorded at 450 m. **RANGE** V NW Thailand, N Laos.

2 BEAN GOOSE *Anser fabalis* 75–90 cm
(**a,b**) **Adult** *middendorffii*: Black bill with pale orange subterminal band, rather dark head/neck, orangey legs. In flight shows darker upperwing-coverts than Greylag, uniform dark underwing. **Juvenile**: Duller orange bill-band and legs. **VOICE** May give fairly deep *hank-hank* or *wink-wink* in flight. **HABITAT** Large rivers, lakes; recorded in lowlands. **RANGE** V N Myanmar.

3 GREATER WHITE-FRONTED GOOSE *Anser albifrons* 65–75 cm
(**a,b**) **Adult** *albifrons*: Pinkish bill, broad white frontal patch, irregular black belly-patches, orangey legs. In flight, darker upperwing-coverts than Greylag, all-dark underwing. (**c**) **Juvenile**: No frontal patch or belly-patches. Smaller/smaller-billed than Greylag, darker (particularly head/neck), more orangey legs. **VOICE** In flight, repeated musical *lyo-lyok* (pitch varies), higher than Greylag and Bean. **HABITAT** Lakes, rivers, grain fields, grassy areas; lowlands. **RANGE** V W,E Myanmar.

4 LESSER WHITE-FRONTED GOOSE *Anser erythropus* 53–66 cm
(**a,b**) **Adult**: Smaller than Greater, shorter body, neck and legs, smaller and brighter pink bill, yellow eyering, rounder head (forecrown steeper/higher), white frontal patch extends further onto crown and ends in more of a point. Wings project noticeably beyond tail-tip at rest (not or only slightly projecting in Greater); rather darker overall (mainly head/neck) with smaller black belly-patches (usually) and clearer white line along inner edge of flanks. (**c**) **Juvenile**: From Greater by proportions, primary projection, darker coloration. **VOICE** Flight calls quicker/squeakier than Greater, typically repeated *kyu-yu-yu*. **HABITAT & BEHAVIOUR** Freshwater lakes, marshes; recorded at c.800 m. Walks/feeds faster than Greater. **RANGE** V E Myanmar.

5 GREYLAG GOOSE *Anser anser* 78–90 cm
(**a,b**) **Adult** *rubrirostris*: Pink bill/legs, quite pale plumage, plain head/neck, no belly-patches (only speckles). Pale coverts in flight. **Juvenile**: Duller bill and legs, no dark belly-speckles. **VOICE** Deeper than other geese. Loud clanging honking *aahng-ahng-ung* in flight. **HABITAT & BEHAVIOUR** Lakes, rivers, estuaries, arable fields, grassy areas; lowlands. Usually in flocks; may associate with other geese. **RANGE** Ra/lo **WV** N,C Myanmar, E Tonkin; formerly N,C Annam. **V** NW Thailand, C Laos.

6 BAR-HEADED GOOSE *Anser indicus* 71–76 cm
(**a,b**) **Adult**: Striking black-and-white pattern on head and neck, yellow bill and legs; pale wing-coverts contrast with dark flight feathers above and below. (**c**) **Juvenile**: Rather uniform

brownish-grey hindcrown to hindneck, greyish lores and upper foreneck. **VOICE** Soft nasal, repeated, honking *oh-wa*, *aah-aah* and *ooh-ah* etc. Notes somewhat lower, more nasal and wider-spaced than other geese. **HABITAT** Large rivers, lakes, arable fields, grassy areas; up to 400 m. **RANGE** Ra/sc **WV** W,N(lc),C,S Myanmar. **V** north Tenasserim, NW Thailand, N Laos, E Tonkin.

7 RUDDY SHELDUCK *Tadorna ferruginea* 61–67 cm
(**a,b**) **Male breeding**: Largely orange-rufous, mostly creamy-buff head, narrow black collar. Blackish wings with contrasting whitish coverts. **Male non-breeding**: Collar faint/absent. (**c**) **Female**: No collar, head buffier with whiter face. **Juvenile**: As female but head/upperparts strongly washed greyish-brown, duller below. **VOICE** Typically, rolling, honking *aakh* and trumpeted *pok-pok-pok-pok...* **HABITAT & BEHAVIOUR** Large rivers, lakes; up to 900 m. Normally in flocks. **RANGE** Lc **WV** Myanmar. **V** W(coastal),NW,C,NE Thailand, N Laos, E Tonkin, N Annam.

8 COMMON SHELDUCK *Tadorna tadorna* 58–67 cm
(**a,b**) **Male**: Looks black-and-white; green-glossed hood, chestnut breast-band, red bill with large basal knob. **Male eclipse**: Bill knob smaller, face mottled whitish, less defined breast-band. (**c**) **Female**: Smaller, bill duller with no knob, head/neck duller, face marked with white, breast-band thinner/duller. **Female eclipse**: Duller/greyer; more white face markings, even less distinct breast-band. May resemble juvenile. **Juvenile**: Largely brownish head, neck and upperparts, whitish face, eyering and foreneck, no breast-band, all whitish below, white-tipped flight feathers, dull pinkish bill. **VOICE** Female utters rapid *gag-ag-ag-ag-ag...*; male thin low whistles. **HABITAT** Large rivers, lakes, coastal mudflats; up to 400 m. **RANGE** V SW,N,C,S Myanmar, NW,C Thailand, N Laos, E Tonkin, C Annam.

Cambodia – group in pods

9 WHITE-WINGED DUCK *Cairina scutulata* 66–81 cm
(**a,b**) **Male**: All dark with black-speckled whitish hood (can be mainly white), mostly yellowish bill; white coverts contrast with black primaries. **Female**: Smaller/slightly duller, usually denser-mottled hood. **Juvenile**: Duller/browner, initially pale brownish head/neck. **VOICE** Vibrant honks in flight, often ending with nasal whistle. Single short harsh honks. **HABITAT & BEHAVIOUR** Pools and rivers in forest, freshwater swamp forest; up to 800, rarely 1,500 m. Not gregarious; mostly nocturnal feeder. **RANGE** Ra/lo **R** N Myanmar, W,NE,S Thailand, Cambodia, C,S Laos, N,S Annam, Cochinchina; formerly NW Thailand. **FR** (currently?) SW,W,C,E,S Myanmar, Tenasserim, Pen Malaysia.

10 COMB DUCK *Sarkidiornis melanotos* 56–76 cm
(**a**) **Male non-breeding** *melanotos*: Black-speckled hood, grey flanks, broad knob (comb) on dark bill; dark wings. **Male breeding**: Much larger comb, buffy head-/neck-sides. (**b,c**) **Female**: Smaller; duller above, no comb. (**d**) **Juvenile**: Mostly dark brown upperside, dark brown eyestripe, rest of head, neck and underparts washed brownish-buff with some dark markings on breast-sides/flanks. **VOICE** Occasional low croaks. Wheezy whistles and grunts when breeding. **HABITAT** Freshwater lakes and marshes; lowlands. **RANGE** Ra/sc **R** (some movements) N,C,S Myanmar, Cambodia. Ra **WV** NW,NE,C Thailand, Cochinchina. **V** C Laos, E Tonkin. **FR** (currently?) SW,E Myanmar.

PLATE 7 WHISTLING-DUCKS, COTTON PYGMY-GOOSE & TYPICAL DUCKS

1 FULVOUS WHISTLING-DUCK *Dendrocygna bicolor* 45–53 cm (**a,b**) **Adult**: Rich dark rufous head/underparts, crown hardly darker than head-sides, bold streaked neck-patch, blackish line down hindneck, bold white flank-streaks, white uppertail-coverts; uniform-looking upperwing. **Juvenile**: Duller/greyer; greyish uppertail-coverts, less obvious neck/flank markings. **VOICE** Repeated thin whistled *k-weeoo*. Harsh *kee*. **HABITAT** Lowland lakes, large rivers, marshes. **RANGE** Ra **R** (local movements) S Myanmar. **FR** (currently?) C Myanmar. **Rc** (status?) N,SW,E Myanmar, Tenasserim, Cochinchina.

2 LESSER WHISTLING-DUCK *Dendrocygna javanica* 38–41 cm (**a,b**) **Adult**: Brown head, dark cap, brownish-rufous below, reddish-chestnut lesser wing-/uppertail-coverts, centre of hindneck only slightly darker than neck-sides, faint flank-streaks. **Juvenile**: Duller; crown often paler, more greyish-brown. **VOICE** Incessantly whistled *whi-whee*, usually when flying (wings also make whistling sound). **HABITAT & BEHAVIOUR** Lakes, marshes; up to 1,450 m. Often in large flocks. **RANGE** Lc **R**, subject to some movements (except W Tonkin, N Annam); sc Singapore.

3 WANDERING WHISTLING-DUCK *D.arcuata* 40–45 cm (**a,b**) **Adult** *arcuata*: Larger than Lesser, blackish-brown of forecrown reaches eye-level, prominent blackish line down hindneck, richer chestnut flanks with large black-and-white markings, white outer uppertail-coverts, duller upperwing-coverts. **Juvenile**: Duller; paler belly, less distinct flank pattern. **VOICE** High twittering *pwit-wit-ti-t-t..* and high whistles. **HABITAT** Freshwater lakes/marshes. **RANGE** Sc **FER** Singapore.

4 COTTON PYGMY-GOOSE *Nettapus coromandelianus* 35 cm (**a,b**) **Male** *coromandelianus*: Small; blackish cap, breast-band/collar, upperparts (glossed green) and vent, white head-sides/neck and underparts. grey-washed flanks; rounded wings with broad white band. **Male eclipse**: Greyish-washed head-sides/neck, darker eyestripe, greyish-mottled breast/flanks, no obvious breast-band/collar. Retains wing pattern. (**c,d**) **Female**: Black eyestripe, duller/browner above, duller neck and underparts with darker mottling (mainly breast), vague breast-band/collar, pale vent; narrow white trailing edge to secondaries. **Juvenile**: As female but head-sides duller, eyestripe broader, looks unglossed above. **VOICE** Male gives cackling *WUK-wirrar-rakWUK-wirrarrakWUK-wirrarrak..*; female a weak *quack*. **HABITAT** Freshwater lakes/marshes; up to 800 m. **RANGE** Sc/lc **R**, subject to local movements (except SE Thailand, Singapore, W Tonkin, N Annam). Sc **NBV** Singapore.

5 MANDARIN DUCK *Aix galericulata* 41–49 cm (**a**) **Male** Bulky head, reddish bill, long pale supercilium, erect orange-rufous wing-sails. **Male eclipse**: As female but reddish bill, less obvious 'spectacles', shaggier neck, more glossy above. (**b,c**) **Female**: Greyish head, white spectacles, whitish streaks/spots on breast/flanks, pinkish-greyish bill; upperwing quite uniform with white-tipped greenish secondaries. (**d**) **Juvenile**: Browner than female, faint spectacles, diffuse breast/flank markings. **HABITAT** Freshwater lakes and pools; up to 400 m. **RANGE** V C Myanmar, NW,C Thailand, W Tonkin.

6 SUNDA TEAL *Anas gibberifrons* 36–43 cm (**a,b**) **Adult** *albogularis*: Dark brown; white eye-patch and throat-patch (or just a white eyering), dark grey bill (sometimes some pink); darker underwing than female Common. (**c**) **Adult variant**: Much white on head/neck. **VOICE** Male gives clear low *preep*; female loud high laughing quacks. **HABITAT** Lakes, marshes, coastal wetlands; lowlands. **RANGE** Fo (currently?) Coco Is, S Myanmar. **V** mainland S Myanmar.

7 GARGANEY *Anas querquedula* 36–41 cm (**a,b**) **Male**: Bold white supercilium, pale grey, dark-vermiculated flanks, elongated grey, black and white scapulars. Mostly bluish-grey upperwing-coverts, secondaries bordered by broad white bands. **Male eclipse**: As female but no defined white line below eyestripe, throat whiter; retains wing colour and pattern. (**c,d**) **Female**: Bold head pattern. Dark crown, narrow whitish supercilium, large whitish loral patch extending in line below blackish eyestripe, dark cheek-bar, whitish throat. In flight, grey tinged upperwing-coverts, secondaries with little green gloss and narrower white borders; distinctly dark leading edge to underwing-coverts (also male). (**e**) **Juvenile**: Darker than female with less defined head pattern; dark markings on belly. **VOICE** Male utters a dry rattling *knerek*, female a short high *quack*. **HABITAT** Lakes, marshes, various wetlands; up to 800 m. **RANGE** Sc/lc **WV** (except W Tonkin).

8 BAIKAL TEAL *Anas formosa* 39–43 cm (**a**) **Male**: Striking buff, green, white and black head, pinkish breast, grey flanks with white band at front/rear, black undertail-coverts. (**b**) **Male eclipse**: As female but darker/warmer mantle-fringing, warmer breast and flanks, duller loral spot. (**c,d**) **Female**: From Garganey by isolated round loral spot, whitish band from below/behind eye to throat, broken supercilium (buffier behind eye), buffish-white line at side of undertail-coverts. In flight (both sexes), warm-tipped greater coverts, blacker leading edge to underwing than Common. (**e**) **Juvenile**: As female but buffier/larger loral spot; dark mottled (not plain) whitish belly-centre. **VOICE** Deep *wot-wot-wot..* from males; low *quack* from females. **HABITAT** Freshwater lakes; lowlands. **RANGE** V N Myanmar, NW,C Thailand.

9 COMMON TEAL *Anas crecca* 34–38 cm (**a**) **Male** *crecca*: Chestnut head with buff-edged dark green eye-patch, buffish patch on blackish vent; horizontal white scapular line. (**b,c**) **Female**: Relatively plain-headed; narrow buffish-white line on side of undertail-coverts. In flight, secondaries have broad white band at front and narrow band at rear, underwing extensively white, with darker leading edge (male has greyer upperwing-coverts). **Male eclipse**: As female but darker/more uniform above, larger markings below, eyestripe faint/absent. **Juvenile**: As female but plainer above, belly speckled dark; may show darker ear-coverts. **VOICE** Liquid *preep-preep..* from males; sharp high *quack* from females when flushed. **HABITAT** Lakes, large rivers, marshes, various wetlands; up to 1,830 m. **RANGE** Un/lc **WV** (except Tenasserim, SE,S Thailand, Pen Malaysia, Singapore, S Laos, S Annam, Cochinchina). **V** Pen Malaysia, Singapore.

PLATE 8 DABBLING DUCKS

1 GADWALL *Anas strepera* 46–56 cm
(**a**) **Male:** Greyish; black vent, blackish bill. Square white patch on inner secondaries. **Male eclipse:** Like female but greyer and more uniform above; retains tertial and upperwing colour and pattern. Bill can be all dark (see female Falcated). (**b,c**) **Female:** Smaller/more compact than Mallard, head squarer with less contrasting pattern, bill finer and blackish with orange sides. White patch on secondaries obvious in flight. **Juvenile:** As female but richer brown below, breast more distinctly streaked; contrasts more with grey head and neck. White patch on secondaries may be faint on females. **VOICE** Courting males utter short **nheck** and low whistle; females a repeated **gag-ag-ag-ag...** **HABITAT** Freshwater lakes, marshes; up to 800 m. **RANGE** Sc/un **WV** W,N(lc/c),C,E,S Myanmar, north Tenasserim, NW Thailand, E Tonkin. **V** C,W(coastal) Thailand, Singapore.

2 FALCATED DUCK *Anas falcata* 48–54 cm
(**a**) **Male:** Mostly greyish; glossy green and purple head, white throat/foreneck with black band, long black and whitish tertials, black-bordered yellowish-white patch on vent-side; grey upperwing-coverts contrast with greenish-black secondaries. **Male eclipse:** Darker above than female, breast/flanks richer brown; wing pattern retained but tertials shorter. (**b,c**) **Female:** Dark grey bill, quite plain greyish-brown head, rather 'full' nape, dark-scaled rich brown breast/flanks, white-bordered dark secondaries, white underwing-coverts. **Juvenile:** As female but buffier, greyer tips to greater coverts. **VOICE** Short low whistle followed by wavering **uit-trr**, and deep nasal **bep**. **HABITAT** Lowland lakes and marshes. **RANGE** Ra/un **WV** SW,N,C,E Myanmar, NW,NE,C Thailand, N Laos, E Tonkin, C Annam.

3 EURASIAN WIGEON *Anas penelope* 45–51 cm
(**a,b**) **Male:** Bright chestnut head with yellowish median stripe, pinkish breast, black vent, white centre of abdomen and rear flanks, black-tipped pale grey bill. Large white patch on wing-coverts, greyish underwing with whiter greater/primary coverts. **Male eclipse:** Head and breast warmer than female; keeps white wing-patch. (**c,d**) **Female:** Rather plain brown (breast and flanks more chestnut), rounded head, black-tipped pale grey bill. In flight, looks uniform below with contrasting white belly/vent; upperwing-coverts paler and greyer than rest of wing. **Juvenile:** As female but almost glossless secondaries, brown mottling on belly. **VOICE** Piercing whistled **wheeooo** and more subdued **whut-whittoo** from males; growling **krrr** from females. **HABITAT** Lakes, marshes, large rivers; up to 800 m. **RANGE** Sc/un **WV** Myanmar (except Tenasserim), NW,NE,C Thailand, N Laos, E Tonkin. **V** S Thailand, Pen Malaysia, Singapore, Cambodia, C Annam, Cochinchina.

4 MALLARD *Anas platyrhynchos* 50–65 cm
(**a**) **Male** *platyrhynchos*: Yellowish bill, purplish-green head, white collar, purplish-brown breast; greyish upperwing-coverts. (**b**) **Male eclipse:** Like female but breast more chestnut, bill dull yellowish. (**c,d**) **Female:** Dull orange bill with uneven dark markings, contrasting dark eyestripe. Darkish wing-coverts, white-bordered dark blue secondaries, pale underwing. **Juvenile:** As female but crown/eyestripe blackish, breast neatly

streaked, flanks more streaked (less scaled), bill initially mostly dull reddish/orange. **VOICE** Male gives rasping **kreep**; female mocking **QUACK-QUACK-QUACK-quack-quack-quack...** **HABITAT** Lakes, large rivers, marshes; up to 420 m. **RANGE** Ra **WV** N(un/lc),C,E Myanmar, NW Thailand. **V** E Tonkin.

5 SPOT-BILLED DUCK *Anas poecilorhyncha* 55–63 cm
(**a,b**) **Male** *haringtoni*: Yellow-tipped black bill, red loral spot, pale head with blackish crown and eyestripe, spotted breast/flanks. White-bordered dark green secondaries, largely white tertials, demarcated white underwing-coverts. **Female:** Loral spot indistinct/absent, usually smaller markings below. **Juvenile:** Browner/less distinctly marked below than female, no loral spot. (**c,d**) **Adult** *zonorhyncha* (**rc** N Myanmar?): No loral spot, dark cheek-band, dark body, mostly dark tertials, usually dark bluish secondaries with indistinct white border. **Other subspecies** *A.p.poecilorhyncha* (SW,W Myanmar?): Male has larger red loral spot, paler head-sides, neck and breast, bolder underpart markings. Female differs as male but normally shows small red loral spot. **VOICE** Descending **quark** notes. **HABITAT** Lakes, large rivers, marshes; up to 800 m. **RANGE** Un/lfc **R** (some movements) N,C,E,S Myanmar, Cambodia, S Laos, E Tonkin, Cochinchina. Sc/un **WV** NW,NE,C,SE Thailand, N Laos; ? N Myanmar. **Rc** (status?) N,C Annam.

6 NORTHERN SHOVELER *Anas clypeata* 43–52 cm
(**a,b**) **Male:** Huge bill, dark glossy green head, white underparts with chestnut sides; largely blue upperwing-coverts, bold white underwing-coverts. (**c**) **Male eclipse:** Flanks/belly more rufous than female, body markings blacker, upperwing-coverts bluer. (**d,e**) **Female:** Huge orange-edged bill; crown and eyestripe not sharply contrasting; bluish-grey on upperwing-coverts. **Juvenile male:** As female but upperwing similar to adult. Immatures can resemble sub-eclipse adults. **Juvenile female:** Darker crown than female, paler and more spotted below, faint greater covert bar, glossless secondaries. **VOICE** Hollow liquid **sluk-uk** or **g'dunk** from courting males; descending **gak-gak-gak-ga-ga** from females. **HABITAT** Lakes, large rivers, marshes; up to 800 m. **RANGE** Un **WV** Myanmar (except W), Thailand (except SE,S), E Tonkin. **V** Pen Malaysia, Singapore, Cambodia, C Annam, Cochinchina.

7 NORTHERN PINTAIL *Anas acuta* 51–56 cm
(**a,b**) **Male:** Dark chocolate-brown head, white of breast extending in line up and behind ear-coverts, long forming single point tail-streamers; extensively dark underwing-coverts. **Male eclipse:** Greyer above than female, grey tertials; retains bill and wing colour/pattern. (**c,d**) **Female:** Slender grey bill, plain head, longish neck; extensively dark underwing-coverts. Upperwing-coverts duller than male, secondaries much duller/browner, greater covert tips whiter. **Juvenile:** Darker above than female, bolder flank pattern. **VOICE** Low **preep-preep** from males; weak descending quacks and low croaks from females. **HABITAT** Lakes, large rivers, marshes; up to 800 m. **RANGE** Un/lc **WV** SW,W,N,E,C,S Myanmar, north Tenasserim, W,NW,NE,C Thailand, Cambodia, N,C Laos, E Tonkin, N,C Annam, Cochinchina. **V** S Thailand, Pen Malaysia, Singapore.

PLATE 9 RED-CRESTED POCHARD & DIVING DUCKS

1 RED-CRESTED POCHARD *Rhodonessa rufina* 53–57 cm
(**a**) **Male**: Red bill, bulky orange-rufous head, black breast and tail-coverts, white on flanks. **Male eclipse**: As female but bill red, eyes reddish. (**b,c**) **Female**: Plain brownish; dark crown (extends around eye), contrasting whitish head-sides and fore-neck, pink-tipped dark bill; quite pale brown wing-coverts, broad whitish band across flight feathers, largely whitish under-wing (male similar but upperwing-coverts darker). **Juvenile**: As female but bill all dark. **VOICE** Usually silent. Courting male gives rasping wheeze; female utters a grating chatter. **HABITAT & BEHAVIOUR** Freshwater lakes and marshes, large rivers; up to 800 m. Mainly feeds by diving, sometimes by up-ending and head-dipping. **RANGE** Sc/un **WV** N,C,E Myanmar. **V** C Thailand, E Tonkin.

2 COMMON POCHARD *Aythya ferina* 42–49 cm
(**a**) **Male**: Grey with chestnut hood, and black lower neck, breast and tail-coverts. Bill blackish with pale bluish-grey band. Upperwing-coverts purer grey than female. (**b**) **Male eclipse**: Duller/browner overall. (**c,d**) **Female non-breeding**: Mottled greyish-brown; dark undertail-coverts, peaked head, pale spectacles and facial/throat markings, dark eyes; greyish upperwing without white band. **Female breeding**: Body somewhat plainer/browner, head-sides somewhat plainer. **Juvenile**: Duller than female, more uniform above, all-dark bill, much plainer head (may lack obvious spectacles). **VOICE** Repeated soft wheezy *pee* from courting males; harsh *krrr* from females. **HABITAT** Freshwater lakes; up to 800 m. **RANGE** Ra/sc **WV** N(lc),C,E Myanmar, NW Thailand, E Tonkin. **V** C Thailand.

3 FERRUGINOUS POCHARD *Aythya nyroca* 38–42 cm
(**a**) **Male**: Rich chestnut; blackish above, white eyes, domed head, white undertail-coverts. More white on upperwing-bar than other *Aythya* ducks, defined white on belly. **Male eclipse**: Only slightly brighter than female, eyes white. (**b,c**) **Female**: More chestnut-brown, eyes dark. **Juvenile**: Head-sides, foreneck, flanks and upperparts paler than female, belly and sides of undertail-coverts mottled brown. **VOICE** Short *chuk* and soft *wheeoo* from courting males; snoring *err err err..* and harsh *gaaa* from females. **HABITAT** Freshwater lakes, marshes, large rivers; up to 800 m. **RANGE** Ra/un **WV** SW,W,N(lc),C,E,S Myanmar, W,NW,NE,C Thailand, E Tonkin. **V** W Thailand.

4 BAER'S POCHARD *Aythya baeri* 41–46 cm
(**a**) **Male**: Greenish-black hood, whitish eyes, rich chestnut-brown breast, chestnut-brown sides with white on foreflanks, white undertail-coverts. In flight, white upperwing-band extends less onto outer primaries than on Ferruginous. **Male eclipse**: As female but eyes whitish. (**b,c**) **Female**: Dark brown hood (contrasts with warm brown breast), no nuchal tuft, usually a diffuse dark chestnut loral patch, dark eyes, often some whitish throat-mottling, duller breast and flanks, less white on foreflanks (may be hidden when swimming). **Juvenile**: Head more chestnut-tinged than female with darker crown and hindneck; lacks defined loral patch. **HABITAT** Lakes, large rivers and their deltas; up to 800 m. **RANGE** Sc/lo **WV** Myanmar (except Tenasserim), NW,C Thailand, E Tonkin. **V** S Thailand.

5 TUFTED DUCK *Aythya fuligula* 40–47 cm
(**a**) **Male**: Blackish with white flanks, purplish-glossed head, drooping crest, grey bill with whitish band and black tip. (**b**) **Male eclipse**: Browner black; greyish flanks, small crest, duller bill. (**c–e**) **Female**: Dark brown with paler flanks, slight nuchal tuft/bump, yellow eyes, often some white on face at sides of bill-base; less extensive white upperwing-band than other *Aythya* ducks (same on male). Undertail-coverts can be white. **Juvenile**: As female but somewhat paler head/upperparts (crown dark), pale area on lores, little or no crest, browner eyes (particularly female). **VOICE** Low vibrant whistled *wheep-wee-whew* from courting males; growling *err err err..* from females. **HABITAT** Lakes, large rivers; up to 1,300 m. **RANGE** Sc/un **WV** W,N(lfc),C,E,S Myanmar, NW,NE,C Thailand, E Tonkin. **V** S Thailand, Pen Malaysia, Singapore, C Annam.

6 GREATER SCAUP *Aythya marila* 42–51 cm
(**a**) **Male** *marila*: Bluish-grey bill with small black tip, rounded green-glossed head, pale grey above; greyish upperwing-coverts. **Male eclipse**: Browner head, neck and breast, darker/browner vermiculations above, faintly grey and brown vermiculated flanks; may show whitish patch on lores and/or ear-coverts. (**b,c**) **Female**: Broad white face-patch (encircling bill-base), usually some grey vermiculations on upperparts and flanks, undertail-coverts always dark. Broader white upperwing-band than Tufted (also male). (**d**) **Female worn** (summer): Pale patch on ear-coverts. **Juvenile**: Initially less white on face than female, but usually a whitish patch on ear-coverts, no grey vermiculations on upperparts and flanks, flanks buffier. **VOICE** Courting male utters soft cooing and whistling; female gives a harsh gruff *arr arr arr...* **HABITAT** Lowland lakes, coastal waters. **RANGE** **V** N Myanmar, NW Thailand, E Tonkin.

7 COMMON GOLDENEYE *Bucephala clangula* 42–50 cm
(**a,b**) **Male** *clangula*: Greenish-black head, white loral spot, breast and underparts; large white upperwing-patch, small white patch on underside of secondaries. **Male eclipse**: Head a little darker than female, usually a trace of loral spot; retains bill and wing colour/pattern. (**c,d**) **Female**: Rather dark greyish; whitish collar, dark brown head, yellow eyes, blackish bill with pale yellowish band. Upperwing-patch bisected by two narrow black bands. **Juvenile**: Duller/browner body than female, no collar, all-dark bill. Males attain white on lores during first winter. **VOICE** Whistles and grating notes from courting males; *be-beeezh* (when head-tossing), followed by low rattle. Harsh *berr* or *graa* from females. **HABITAT** Lowland lakes, large rivers; found in plains. **RANGE** Ra/sc **WV** N,C Myanmar.

8 SMEW *Mergellus albellus* 38–44 cm
(**a**) **Male**: Mostly white, black face- and nape-patches, black lines above/on breast-sides. **Male eclipse**: As female but keeps wing pattern. (**b,c**) **Female/juvenile**: Small size/bill, greyish with chestnut crown/nape, blackish lores, white lower head-sides/throat. Broad white upperwing-covert band, narrower bands bordering secondaries. **VOICE** Courting male utters low croaks and whistles; female low growling notes. **HABITAT** Lakes, large rivers; up to 450 m. **RANGE** **V** W,N Myanmar.

PLATE 10 PINK-HEADED DUCK, MERGANSERS, GREBES & LOONS

1 PINK-HEADED DUCK *Rhodonessa caryophyllacea* 60 cm
(**a,b**) **Male**: Large and long-necked, peaked crown, deep pink head/neck, blackish-brown throat-centre, foreneck and most of remaining plumage, pinkish bill. Pale brownish-buff secondaries, whitish leading edge to wing-coverts, largely pale pink underwing. (**c**) **Female**: Duller; head/neck pale greyish-pink, crown/hindneck washed brownish, bill duller. **Juvenile**: Body duller brown than female with fine whitish fringing. **VOICE** Male utters weak whizzy whistle, female a low ***quack***. **HABITAT & BEHAVIOUR** Pools and swamps in open forest/grassland; lowlands. Shy; sometimes flocks when not breeding. Dabbles and dives. **RANGE** Rc SW,N,C Myanmar. Last confirmed sighting 1908.

2 RED-BREASTED MERGANSER *Mergus serrator* 52–58 cm
(**a,b**) **Male**: Thin-based slender bill, red eyes, shaggy crest, white collar, black-streaked rufescent lower neck/breast, white-spotted black breast-sides. Large white upperwing-patch bisected by two black lines. **Male eclipse**: Mantle blacker than female, retains wing pattern and red eyes. (**c,d**) **Female**: Rufescent hood with untidy crested appearance, paler throat/foreneck (not demarcated), pale and dark loral lines, variable pale eyering; reddish-brown eyes, brownish-grey body with vaguely pale-scaled flanks. Smaller white upperwing-patch bisected by single line. **Juvenile**: As female but bill duller, crest shorter, breast and central underparts greyer. **VOICE** Males display-call is weak ***chika...pitchee***; female gives grating ***prrak prrak prrak...*** **HABITAT** Sea coasts. **RANGE** V E Tonkin.

3 SCALY-SIDED MERGANSER *Mergus squamatus* 52–58 cm
(**a,b**) **Male**: Like Red-breasted but longer crest, brown eyes, white breast and flanks with dark grey scales on latter; shows more white on lesser upperwing-coverts. Nostrils almost midway along bill (rather than near base). **Male eclipse**: Darker above than female, retains wing pattern. (**c,d**) **Female**: Longer crest than Red-breasted, brown eyes, unmarked lores and orbital area, grey scales on whitish lower breast-sides/flanks; purer grey above. **Juvenile**: Flanks may be more uniformly grey than female. **VOICE** Similar to Red-breasted. **HABITAT** Large rivers, lakes; up to 500 m. **RANGE** V NW Thailand, W,E Tonkin.

4 COMMON MERGANSER *Mergus merganser* 61–72 cm
(**a,b**) **Male** *comatus*: Long slender red bill (thicker-based than other *Mergus*), dark eyes, greenish-black hood, 'full' nape, white below with pinkish flush. Large plain white upperwing-patch. **Male eclipse**: Mantle darker than female, flanks whiter; keeps wing pattern. (**c,d**) **Female**: Rufous-chestnut hood, demarcated white throat, slightly shaggier nape than male; otherwise greyish, with white central underparts. Upperwing-patch smaller. **Juvenile**: Duller than female; pale loral stripe, slightly less demarcated throat. **VOICE** Courting male repeats a soft frog-like ***kuoorrp kuoorrp...*** and similar ***drruu-drro***; female gives harsh ***skrrak skrrak*** etc. **HABITAT** Large rivers, rarely lakes; up to 1,135 m. **RANGE** Un/fc **WV** east N Myanmar.

5 LITTLE GREBE *Tachybaptus ruficollis* 25–29 cm
(**a,b**) **Adult non-breeding** *poggei*: Stocky and duck-like, ruffed rear end, mostly pale bill, mostly brownish-buff head-sides/

underparts, dark eyes. Only narrow whitish tips to secondaries. (**c**) **Adult breeding**: Head-sides, throat and foreneck dark rufous-chestnut, flanks rich dark brown, eyes yellow, bill blackish with prominent yellow gape. **Juvenile**: As adult non-breeding but dark-striped head-side. **Other subspecies** *capensis* (Myanmar): More white on secondaries. **VOICE** Shrill whinnying trill on breeding grounds. Sharp ***bee-eep*** and ***wit*** or ***bit*** notes. **HABITAT** Lakes, pools, various wetlands; up to 1,450 m. **RANGE** Un/c R (local movements) throughout.

6 GREAT CRESTED GREBE *Podiceps cristatus* 46–51 cm
(**a,b**) **Adult non-breeding**: Long neck, rather long pink bill, white head-sides/foreneck and underparts, black loral stripe, grey-brown flanks. In flight, neck extends forwards, feet protrude backwards, white leading edge to upperwing, scapular band and secondaries. (**c**) **Adult breeding**: Blackish crest, rufous-chestnut and blackish 'head-frills', rufescent flanks. **Juvenile**: As adult non-breeding but head-sides striped brown. **VOICE** Harsh, rolling ***aooorrr*** and chattering ***kek-kek-kek..*** on breeding grounds. **HABITAT** Lakes, large rivers; up to 1,000 m. **RANGE** Ra/un **WV** N,C,E Myanmar. **V** NW Thailand.

7 HORNED GREBE *Podiceps auritus* 31–38 cm
(**a,b**) **Adult non-breeding**: Flatter-crowned than Black-necked, thicker/straighter bill (tip often pale), black cap demarcated from white head-sides at eye-level, thinner line down hindneck, pale loral spot. Upperwing shows small white shoulder-patch and white secondaries. (**c**) **Adult breeding**: Outstanding black and gold 'head-frills', reddish-chestnut foreneck/underparts. **Juvenile**: Browner than adult non-breeding, dusky facial band. **VOICE** Feeble trembling ***hii-arrr*** or nasal rattling ***joarrrh***. Whinnying trill in diminishing pulses, during display. **HABITAT** Large rivers; lowlands. **RANGE** V N Myanmar.

8 BLACK-NECKED GREBE *Podiceps nigricollis* 28–34 cm
(**a,b**) **Adult non-breeding** *nigricollis*: Pointed, uptilted dark bill, peaked crown, blackish around red eye, white nape-sides/throat, greyish neck-band and flanks; white secondaries/inner primaries. (**c**) **Adult breeding**: Black head/neck, golden flash from eye, chestnut flanks. **Juvenile**: As adult non-breeding but head-sides/foreneck may be washed buffish. **VOICE** Fluty rising ***poo-eeet*** and short whistled ***wit***. Shrill trilled ***tsssrrrooooeep*** in display. **HABITAT** Large rivers, lakes, coastal waters; lowlands. **RANGE** Ra **WV** N Myanmar. **V** E Tonkin.

9 YELLOW-BILLED LOON *Gavia adamsii* 77–90 cm
(**a,b**) **Adult non-breeding**: Could be confused with swimming juvenile cormorants. Thick pointed ivory-/yellowish-white bill (usually held upward) with dark on culmen, thick head/neck, very steep forehead, blackish-brown crown/hindneck, shadowy half-collar, white below. Greyish-brown above/along flanks, with blackish mottling. (**c**) **Adult breeding**: Black head/neck with black-striped white patches, black above with white chequers and spots; yellower-tinged more uniformly pale bill. (**d**) **Juvenile**: Paler/browner than adult non-breeding, neatly scaled above/along flanks. **HABITAT** Large rivers; recorded in plains. **RANGE** V N Myanmar (one sight record).

PLATE 11 WRYNECKS, PICULETS & SMALLER TYPICAL WOODPECKERS

1 EURASIAN WRYNECK *Jynx torquilla* 16–18 cm
(**a**) **Adult** *torquilla*: Cryptic pattern; grey-brown with dark central stripe above, buffy-white with dark bars below, heavily barred wings/tail. **Juvenile**: Duller, darker, more barred above, fainter bars below. **VOICE** Ringing ***quee-quee-quee-quee-quee...*** (notes fall in pitch) from males. Repeated ***tak*** or ***kek*** notes. **HABITAT & BEHAVIOUR** Dry open areas, secondary growth, scrub, grass, cultivation; up to 2,285 m. Often feeds on ground. **RANGE** Un/fc **WV** Myanmar, Thailand (except S), N,C,S(sc) Laos, W,E Tonkin, Cochinchina(sc). Also **PM** N Myanmar.

2 SPECKLED PICULET *Picumnus innominatus* 9–10.5 cm — Arakan Cambodia
(**a**) **Male** *malayorum*: Bold olive-slate and white head-pattern, black-barred rufous-buff forehead, whitish below with blackish spots/bars. (**b**) **Female**: Olive-slate forehead. **Juvenile**: As respective adults but bill pale. (**c**) **Male** *chinensis* (Tonkin): Crown, ear-coverts and submoustachial cinnamon-brown. **VOICE** Territorial call is high ***ti-ti-ti-ti-ti***. Tinny drumming. Sharp ***tsit*** and squeaky ***sik-sik-sik***. **HABITAT** Broadleaved evergreen and mixed deciduous forest, secondary growth, bamboo; up to 1,935 m (915–1,370 m in Pen Malaysia). **RANGE** Co **R** (except SW Myanmar, C,SE Thailand, Singapore).

3 RUFOUS PICULET *Sasia abnormis* 8–9.5 cm
(**a**) **Male** *abnormis*: Yellowish forehead, pink eyering, greenish-olive above, rufous head/below. (**b**) **Female**: Forehead rufous. (**c**) **Juvenile**: Dull olive above (mantle washed slaty), brownish-slate below; dark bill. May show rufous on chin, belly and vent. **VOICE** High ***kik-ik-ik-ik-ik..*** from male. Drums like White-browed. Sharp ***tic*** or ***tsit***. **HABITAT** Bamboo, broadleaved evergreen forest, secondary growth; up to 1,370 m. **RANGE** Fc/c **R** south Tenasserim, S Thailand, Pen Malaysia.

4 WHITE-BROWED PICULET *Sasia ochracea* 8–9.5 cm
(**a**) **Male** *reichenowi*: White supercilium, rufescent-olive mantle/scapulars, buffish-rufous below. (**b**) **Female**: Forehead rufous. **Juvenile**: Like Rufous. (**c**) **Male** *hasbroucki* (Tenasserim, S Thailand): Blackish eyering. **Other subspecies** *S.o.ochracea* (N,E Myanmar to N Indochina): More dark olive crown/mantle (looks collared), deeper rufous below. **VOICE** High trilled ***chi rrrrrrrra*** from male. Tinny drumming: ***tit trrrrrrrrit***. Sharp ***chi***. **HABITAT** Bamboo, broadleaved forest, secondary growth; up to 1,910 m. **RANGE** Fc/c **R** (except C,SE,southern S Thailand, Pen Malaysia, Singapore).

5 PALE-HEADED WOODPECKER *Gecinulus grantia* 25 cm
(**a**) **Male** *indochinensis*: Maroon-chestnut above, pinkish-red crown-patch, barred wings. (**b**) **Female**: No crown-patch. **Juvenile**: As female but mostly dark brown above, darker/greyer below. (**c**) **Male** *grantia* (Myanmar): Redder crown-patch/upperparts, yellower head-sides, more olive below, less wing-barring. **VOICE** Strident laughing *YI* ***wee-wee-wee*** from males. Shortish, quite loud, full, even drumming. Harsh ***grrrit-grrrit-grrrit*** etc. **HABITAT** Bamboo, broadleaved evergreen and semi-deciduous forest; up to 1,900 m. **RANGE** Ra/un **R** SW,W,N,C Myanmar, north NW Thailand (ra), north-east Cambodia, Laos, Vietnam.

6 BAMBOO WOODPECKER *Gecinulus viridis* 25–26 cm
(**a**) **Male** *viridis*: Greyish-olive above, red crown/nape, red rump/uppertail-covert tips, olive-brown below. (**b**) **Female**: No red on head. **Juvenile**: Darker/browner than female, often greyish-tinged below. **Other subspecies** *G.v.robinsoni* (S Thailand southwards). **VOICE** Shrill ***kyeek-kyeek-kyeek-kyeek..*** etc. from male. Short loud drums. Dry cackle, slower than Bay; occasionally ***bik*** notes. **HABITAT** Bamboo, broadleaved forest; up to 1,400 m. **RANGE** Un **R** S,E Myanmar, Tenasserim, Thailand (except C), Pen Malaysia, south-west N Laos.

7 BUFF-RUMPED WOODPECKER *Meiglyptes tristis* 17 cm
(**a**) **Male** *grammithorax*: Densely barred; whitish-buff lower back/rump. (**b**) **Female**: No red submoustachial. **Juvenile**: Darker; narrower pale body-barring, obscurely marked below. **VOICE** Male utters trilled ***ki-i-i-i-i-i***. Weak drumming. Sharp ***pit***, longer ***pee***. **HABITAT** Broadleaved evergreen forest, secondary growth; up to 760 m. **RANGE** Co **R** south Tenasserim, S Thailand, Pen Malaysia; formerly Singapore.

8 BLACK-AND-BUFF WOODPECKER *M.jugularis* 17–19 cm
(**a**) **Male**: White nuchal-patch, dark throat. (**b**) **Female**: No red submoustachial. **Juvenile**: Duller; clearer head-barring. **VOICE** Males give rattling ***titititititit'weerk'weerk'weerk..***, sometimes mixed with nasal ***ki'yew***. **HABITAT** More open broadleaved evergreen/semi-evergreen forest, bamboo; up to 915 m. **RANGE** Un/lfc **R** SW,S,E Myanmar, Tenasserim, W,NW,NE,SE Thailand, Indochina (except W,E Tonkin).

9 BUFF-NECKED WOODPECKER *Meiglyptes tukki* 21 cm
(**a**) **Male** *tukki*: Narrowly barred, plain head, pale buff neck-patch. (**b**) **Female**: No red submoustachial. **Juvenile**: Pale bars broader, upper breast paler. Male may show red on crown or forehead. **VOICE** High trilled ***kirr-r-r*** from male. Both sexes drum. High ***ti ti ti ti..***, single ***pee***. **HABITAT** Broadleaved evergreen forest; up to 1,100 m. **RANGE** Un/fc **R** south Tenasserim, S Thailand, Pen Malaysia; formerly Singapore.

10 GREY-AND-BUFF WOODPECKER *Hemicircus concretus* 14 cm
(**a**) **Male** *sordidus*: Very small; short tail; red crown, pointed crest, sooty-greyish, whitish-buff scales above. (**b**) **Female**: Greyish crown. **Juvenile**: Scaling buffier and more prominent, black-tipped cinnamon-rufous crown; some red on crown. **VOICE** Drums weakly. Calls with high drawn-out ***kee-yew***, sharp ***pit*** notes, vibrating ***chitterr***. **HABITAT** Broadleaved evergreen forest; up to 1,130 m. **RANGE** Un **R** south Tenasserim, W(south), S Thailand, Pen Malaysia; formerly Singapore.

11 HEART-SPOTTED WOODPECKER *H.canente* 15–17 cm
(**a**) **Male**: Very small; short tail; pointed crest, white lower scapulars/tertials with black heart-shapes. (**b**) **Female**: White forecrown. **Juvenile**: As female but whitish parts buffier, often some black bars on forehead. **VOICE** Drums weakly. Calls with nasal ***ki-YEW***, high ***kee-kee-kee..***, grating ***chur-r***, squeaky ***chirrick*** etc. **HABITAT** Broadleaved forests, bamboo; up to 915 m. **RANGE** Fc **R** Myanmar (except W,N,C), Thailand (except C and southern S), Cambodia, Laos, S Annam, Cochinchina.

PLATE 12 *DENDROCOPOS* WOODPECKERS

1 SUNDA PYGMY WOODPECKER *D.moluccensis* 13 cm
(a) Male *moluccensis*: Browner above than Grey-capped, dull brownish crown, broad dark greyish-brown ear-covert band and defined submoustachial, broader but more diffuse streaks below. **Female**: No red on crown. **Juvenile**: Duller/browner and less obviously streaked below, mostly pale lower mandible. Male has more orangey crown-streak. **VOICE** Male territorial call is sharp trilled *kikikikikiki* or whirring *trrrrr-i-i*. **HABITAT** Mangroves, coastal scrub, locally parks/gardens. **RANGE** Un/lc **R** (mostly coastal) Pen Malaysia, Singapore (also inland).

2 GREY-CAPPED PYGMY WOODPECKER *D.canicapillus* 14 cm
(a) Male *canicapillus*: Small; brownish-grey crown (black-edged), ear-covert band and faint submoustachial, dark-streaks below, short red streak on rear crown-side. **(b) Female:** No red on crown. **Juvenile**: Darker; heavier streaks below. Male often has more extensive orange-red on head. **(c) Male** *kaleensis* (N Myanmar, N Indochina): Larger; blacker mantle, buffier below. **Other subspecies** *D.c.delacouri* (south-eastern Thailand, Cambodia, Cochinchina); *auritus* (S Thailand southwards). **VOICE** Rattling *tit-tit-erb-r-r-r-r-b* (usually preceded by call) from males. Subdued drumming. Short *kik* or *pit*, squeaky *kweek-kweek-kweek*. **HABITAT** Broadleaf forests, secondary growth, coastal scrub; up to 1,830 m (lowlands Pen Malaysia). **RANGE** Co **R** (except Singapore).

3 FULVOUS-BREASTED WOODPECKER *D.macei* 17–18 cm
(a) Male *longipennis*: Red crown, extensively barred above, streaks/bars on whitish underparts, pinkish vent. **(b) Female**: Black crown. **Juvenile**: Duller; pink/red of undertail-coverts paler/less extensive, red on crown-centre (more on male). **(c) Male** *macei* (W,N Myanmar): 18.5–21 cm; buffish below, redder vent, darker flank-bars, black central tail. **(d) Female**: As male but black crown/nape. **VOICE** Male territorial call is *pik pipipipipipipipipi*. Drums weakly. Loud *tchik* or *pik*, soft *chik-a-chik-a-chit*. **HABITAT** Deciduous woodland, scattered trees in open country, gardens, plantations; up to 600 m, locally 1,220 m. **RANGE** Un/fc **R** Myanmar, NW,W,C Thailand, Cambodia, C,S Laos, S Annam, Cochinchina.

4 STRIPE-BREASTED WOODPECKER *D.atratus* 20.5–22 cm
(a) Male: Like Fulvous-breasted (race *macei*) but upper mantle unbarred, uniform distinct streaks below. **(b) Female**: Black crown and nape. **Juvenile**: Paler/greyer and less distinctly streaked below, more flame-red undertail-coverts; some red on crown (more on male but paler). **VOICE** Whinnying rattle from territorial males. Loud *tchik*, similar to Great Spotted. **HABITAT** Broadleaved evergreen forest; 800–2,200 m, locally down to 230 m. **RANGE** Fc/c **R** SW,W,S,E Myanmar, Tenasserim, W,NW,NE Thailand, Laos, southern C Annam.

5 YELLOW-CROWNED WOODPECKER *D.mahrattensis* 18 cm
(a) Male *aurocristatus*: Forecrown brownish-yellow, hindcrown red; dense white bars/spots above, no black on head, brown streaks below, red belly-centre. **(b) Female**: Yellowish-brown hindcrown. **Juvenile**: Browner above, diffuse streaks below, pinker belly-patch. Male has some orange-red on hind-

crown, female some on crown-centre. **VOICE** Rapid *kik-kik-kik-r-r-r-r-b* from males. Drums. Sharp *click-click*, feeble *peek* notes. **HABITAT** Deciduous woodland, scattered trees in open country; up to 915 m. **RANGE** Ra/un **R** SW,W,C,S Myanmar, C Thailand, east Cambodia, S Laos, S Annam.

6 RUFOUS-BELLIED WOODPECKER *D.hyperythrus* 19–23 cm
(a) Male *hyperythrus*: Red crown/nape, white face, deep rufous below, red undertail-coverts. **(b) Female**: White-spotted black crown/nape. **Juvenile**: Dark-streaked head-sides, duller/paler below with blackish bars; orange-red on crown (male more). Subadult has blackish-barred, whitish-mottled throat/breast. **Other subspecies** *D.h.subrufinus* (Tonkin): 25 cm; paler/browner below, pinker vent. *D.h.annamensis* (NE Thailand, S Indochina): Paler rufous below. **VOICE** Rattling *chit-chit-chit-r-r-r-r-b* from males. Both sexes drum. Fast *ptiki-titiit...* **HABITAT** Broadleaved and coniferous, locally deciduous forest; 600–3,100 m. **RANGE** Sc/un **R** W,N,C,E Myanmar, W,NW,NE Thailand, Cambodia, S Annam. Sc **WV** W,E Tonkin.

7 CRIMSON-BREASTED WOODPECKER *D.cathpharius* 17 cm
(a) Male *tenebrosus*: Black above, white wing-patch, red hindcrown/nape, heavy streaks below, red on breast and vent. **(b) Female**: No red on head, smaller/duller breast-patch. **Juvenile**: Duller above, whiter below with diffuse streaks and no red, red of vent paler/lacking; orange-red on hindcrown and nape (more on male). **(c) Male** *pyrrbothorax* (W Myanmar): All-red nape, more black on neck. **(d) Female** *pyrrbothorax*: More black on neck. **VOICE** Fast descending rattle from males. Also drums. High *tchik*, shrill *kee-kee-kee*. **HABITAT** Broadleaved evergreen forest; 1,200–2,800 m. **RANGE** Sc/un **R** W,C,N,E Myanmar, NW Thailand, N Laos, W Tonkin.

8 DARJEELING WOODPECKER *D.darjellensis* 23.5–25.5 cm
(a) Male: Long bill, little red on crown, black above, white wing-patch, rich buff below with bold streaks. **(b) Female**: All-black crown. **Juvenile**: No golden-buff on neck-side, duller below with faint throat-streaks, paler/duller red undertail-coverts. Male has pale flame-red on most of crown, female some on centre or none. **VOICE** Fast rattled *di-di-di-d-dddddt* from male. Both sexes drum (like Great Spotted). Loud *tsik*, like Great Spotted. **HABITAT** Broadleaved evergreen forest; 1,525–2,800 m. **RANGE** Un **R** W,N Myanmar, north W Tonkin.

9 GREAT SPOTTED WOODPECKER *D.major* 25.5–28 cm
(a) Male *cabanisi*: Black above, white wing-patch, brownish-white below, red on hindcrown/vent. **(b) Female**: Black crown. **Juvenile**: Duller above, crown red with black edgings, submoustachial ill-defined, band behind ear-coverts may be broken, duller below, flanks often streaked, lower flanks may be barred, pinker vent (can be buffy/whitish). **Other subspecies** *D.m.stresemanni* (W,N Myanmar): Darker/browner head-sides/underparts, may show red on breast. **VOICE** Male territorial call is a *kix-krrarraarr*. Both sexes drum. Call is a sharp *kix*. **HABITAT** Broadleaved evergreen forest; 1,000–2,745 m, sometimes down to 450 m in winter. **RANGE** Sc/un **R** W,N,E Myanmar, N Laos, W,E Tonkin. **WV** only in parts of E Tonkin.

PLATE 13 *PICUS* WOODPECKERS

1 BANDED WOODPECKER *Picus miniaceus* 25.5–27 cm
(**a**) **Male** *malaccensis*: Red-rufous ear-coverts, warm-washed neck/breast, barred body and primaries. (**b**) **Female**: Browner head-side with whitish speckles. **Juvenile**: Dull brown crown (red rear), plainer body. **Other subspecies** *P.m.perlutus* (W Thailand): Narrower dark bars below. **VOICE** Falling *peew* or *kwee* notes from male. Short *keek*. **HABITAT** Broadleaved evergreen forest, secondary growth; up to 915 m. **RANGE** Un/fc **R** south Tenasserim, W,S Thailand, Pen Malaysia, Singapore.

2 LESSER YELLOWNAPE *Picus chlorolophus* 25–28 cm
(**a**) **Male** *chlorolophus*: Red crown-side and submoustachial, white moustachial, bars below. (**b**) **Female**: Red on hindcrown only. **Juvenile**: Crown/nape duller, bolder breast-bars; male without submoustachial. (**c**) **Male** *rodgeri* (Pen Malaysia): Red crown (blackish-tipped centre), darker below, narrow pale bars. (**d**) **Male** *krempfi* (Cochinchina): Mostly red crown, darker above, whiter belly/vent. **Other subspecies** *P.c.laotianus* (east NW,north NE Thailand, N Laos)/*citrinocristatus* (Tonkin, N Annam): Males redder-crowned; latter almost lacks submoustachial, darker below, bars on flanks only. *P.c.annamensis* (south NE,SE Thailand, southern Laos, C,S Annam): Like *krempfi*. **VOICE** Far-carrying *peee-ah* from males. <10 slightly descending *kwee* or *kee* notes. May drum. Short *chak*. **HABITAT** Broadleaved forest; up to 1,830 m (above 1,065 m in Pen Malaysia). **RANGE** Co **R** (except C,S Thailand, Singapore).

3 CRIMSON-WINGED WOODPECKER *Picus puniceus* 24–28 cm
(**a**) **Male** *observandus*: Red crown/submoustachial/wings, plain mantle and breast, blue eyering. (**b**) **Female**: No submoustachial, paler/plainer below. **Juvenile**: Duller/greyer; red of head restricted to hindcrown, white-speckled head-sides/underparts. Males submoustachial much smaller/lacking. **VOICE** *PEE-bee* or *PEE-bee-bee-bee* from territorial males. Also *peep* or falling *pi-eew*. Weak drums. **HABITAT** Broadleaved evergreen forest, secondary growth, plantations; up to 825 m (below 600 m in Thailand). **RANGE** Fc/co **R** south Tenasserim, W(south),S Thailand, Pen Malaysia; formerly Singapore.

4 GREATER YELLOWNAPE *Picus flavinucha* 31.5–35 cm
(**a**) **Male** *lylei*: Rufescent crown, yellow throat, streaked foreneck, barred primaries. (**b**) **Female**: Olive hindcrown, rufescent chin/submoustachial, streaked/mottled throat. **Juvenile**: Duller below, may show faint belly-bars. Male initially has olive-scaled crown, more buffy-whitish throat. (**c**) **Male** *wrayi* (Pen Malaysia): Smaller/darker, defined yellow chin/submoustachial, crown duller with olive at rear, crest shorter with less yellow. (**d**) **Female**: Darker, more uniform below, crest differs as male. (**e**) **Male** *flavinucha* (Myanmar, W Thailand): Rufescent forecrown, darker neck-/breast-sides. **Other subspecies** *P.f.archon* (east NW,north NE Thailand, Laos, W Tonkin, N,C,S Annam) and *pierrei* (south NE,SE Thailand, Cambodia, Cochinchina): Black streaks go further up throat on males. *P.f.styani* (E Tonkin). **VOICE** Drums infrequently. Loud disyllabic *kyaa* or *kiyaep*. **HABITAT** Broadleaved forest, locally pine forest; up to 2,745 m (above 915 m in Pen Malaysia). **RANGE** Co **R** (except C,S Thailand, Singapore).

5 CHECKER-THROATED WOODPECKER *P.mentalis* 28 cm
(**a**) **Male** *humii*: Olive crown, chestnut neck/upper breast, rufous-red wings, barred primaries. (**b**) **Female**: Dull chestnut neck and upper breast. **Juvenile**: Browner on crown and below, duller wings. **VOICE** Male utters series of *wi* notes. Short drums; *kyick* and *Klyee..Klyee..Klyee...* **HABITAT** Broadleaf evergreen forest; up to 1,220 m. **RANGE & STATUS** Un/co **R** south Tenasserim, S Thailand, Pen Malaysia; formerly Singapore.

6 STREAK-BREASTED WOODPECKER *P.viridanus* 31–32 cm
(**a**) **Male** *viridanus*: Neck-sides and throat duller olive than Laced, throat and upper breast streaked. (**b**) **Female**: Black crown and nape. **Juvenile**: Duller; fainter markings below, more scaled-looking flanks/belly; male's crown more orangey. **Other subspecies** *P.v.weberi* (south of c.12°N): 28–31 cm; darker body. **VOICE** Explosive *kirrr*. Series of 4 or more *tcheu* notes. **HABITAT** Lowland broadleaved evergreen forest, mangroves. **RANGE** Un/lfc **R** SW,S,C,south E Myanmar, Tenasserim, W,S Thailand, extreme north-west Pen Malaysia.

7 LACED WOODPECKER *Picus vittatus* 27–33 cm
(**a**) **Male**: Red crown, blackish submoustachial, plain yellowish-olive neck/throat/upper breast, dark streaks/loops on belly. (**b**) **Female**: Black crown/nape. **Juvenile**: Duller; scalier belly, can have faint throat/breast-streaks; male crown with less, paler red. **VOICE** Male's call faster than Grey-headed (notes shorter/lower). Steady drum. Abrupt *ik*. **HABITAT** Broadleaved forest, mangroves, plantations, bamboo; up to 1,525 m (lowlands Pen Malaysia, Singapore). **RANGE** Un/co **R** E Myanmar, Tenasserim, Thailand (except S), southern Pen Malaysia (and Langkawi Is), Singapore, Indochina (except W,E Tonkin).

8 STREAK-THROATED WOODPECKER *P.xanthopygaeus* 29 cm
(**a**) **Male**: Pale eyes, white supercilium, little black on submoustachial, streaked ear-coverts/neck/throat/breast. (**b**) **Female**: Black crown/nape, grey-streaked crown. **Juvenile**: Duller; fainter markings below (more scaled/barred belly); male has less red on crown/nape, female fainter crown-streaks. **VOICE** Drums. Sharp *queemp*. **HABITAT** Deciduous forest, scattered trees; up to 500 m, locally higher in Myanmar. **RANGE** Sc/co **R** W,C,E,S Myanmar, W,NW(west),NE(south-west) Thailand, Cambodia, S Laos, Cochinchina.

9 GREY-HEADED WOODPECKER *Picus canus* 30.5–34.5 cm
(**a**) **Male** *hessei*: Red forecrown, black hindcrown, grey head-sides, black loral/submoustachial stripes. (**b**) **Female**: Grey-streaked black crown. **Juvenile**: Duller body; vaguely mottled mantle/scapulars, less defined submoustachial; sometimes bars/mottling on belly; male has less red on forecrown. **Other subspecies** *P.c.robinsoni* (Pen Malaysia): Much darker body, darker grey head-sides, longer/thinner bill. *P.c.sobrinus* (E Tonkin): Golden-tinged above, greener below. *P.c.sordidior* (north E Myanmar). **VOICE** Male territorial call is descending >3 note *kieu... kieu...kieu...* Long drums. Short *kik* and *keek..kak-kak-kak*. **HABITAT** All kinds of open forest; up to 2,135 m (915–1,830 m in Pen Malaysia). **RANGE** Sc/fc **R** (except C,S Thailand, Singapore, N Annam).

PLATE 14 MISCELLANEOUS WOODPECKERS

1 RUFOUS WOODPECKER *Celeus brachyurus* 25 cm
(a) **Male** *phaioceps*: Red cheek-patch; short black bill, speckled throat. (b) **Female:** No cheek-patch. (c) **Male** *squamigularis* (S Thailand southwards): Heavier marked throat, barred belly. (d) **Male** *fokiensis* (Tonkin, N Annam): Creamy head, heavy crown/throat-streaks, darker body. Female creamier-headed and darker below than *phaioceps*. (e) **Male** *annamensis* (southern Indochina, N Laos): Darker-headed than *fokiensis*. **VOICE** Laughing *kweep-kweep-kweep* from males. Also, slightly descending and accelerating series of notes. Drumming slowly grinds to halt: *bddddddd d d dt*. **HABITAT** Broadleaved forest, secondary growth; up to 1,450 m (below 1,050 m in Thailand/Pen Malaysia). **RANGE** Un/co **R** throughout.

2 RED-COLLARED WOODPECKER *Picus rabieri* 30–32 cm
(a) **Male**: Red hood with olive-greyish head-sides/throat, whitish belly-bars. (b) **Female**: Forehead/crown blackish, less red on submoustachial. **Juvenile**: Duller than female; immature male with orange-red on head/upper breast, crown mixed black. **VOICE** Drums in short, fast, rattling rolls. **HABITAT** Broadleaved evergreen forest, secondary growth; up to 1,050 m. **RANGE** Sc/un **R** north-east Cambodia, Laos, W,E Tonkin, N,C Annam.

3 BLACK-HEADED WOODPECKER *Picus erythropygius* 33 cm
(a) **Male** *nigrigenis*: Black head, red crown-patch, yellow neck/throat, red rump. (b) **Female**: Black crown. **Juvenile**: Duller above, paler throat, buffier upper breast, diffusely scaled below; male's crown-patch washed out. **Other subspecies** *P.e.erythropygius* (NE Thailand, Indochina): Male has smaller crown-patch. **VOICE** Undulating yelping *ka-tek-a-tek-a-tek-a-tek..* from male. Loud double call. **HABITAT** Dry dipterocarp, deciduous and pine forest; up to 1,000 m. **RANGE** Sc/un **R** C,S,E Myanmar, north Tenasserim, W,NW,NE Thailand, Cambodia, C,S Laos, C(south-west),S Annam, north Cochinchina.

4 OLIVE-BACKED WOODPECKER *Dinopium rafflesii* 28 cm
(a) **Male** *rafflesii*: Like flamebacks but body olive. (b) **Female**: Black crown. **Juvenile**: Duller; red on male's head only on crest, forehead can be spotted red. **VOICE** Male utters slow, varied *chak chak chak chak chak-chak..* (6–30+ notes) or faster, more regular 10–50 note series. Single *chak*, soft trilled *ti-i-i-i-i*, squeaky *tiririt*. **HABITAT** Broadleaf evergreen forest; up to 1,200 m. **RANGE** Sc/un **R** south Tenasserim, W(south),S Thailand, Pen Malaysia; formerly Singapore.

5 HIMALAYAN FLAMEBACK *Dinopium shorii* 30 cm
(a) **Male** *anguste*: As Common but redder mantle, brownish submoustachial, lighter breast markings. (b) **Female**: From Common by submoustachial loop; from Greater by streaked crown, black hindneck. **Juvenile**: Browner; more obscurely marked below. Red of male's head only on crest, forehead/crown brown, streaked paler; female has broadly pale-streaked brown crown. **VOICE** Similar to Greater, but somewhat slower and quieter. **HABITAT** Deciduous and semi-evergreen forest; up to 1,220 m. **RANGE** Un **R** SW,W,N,C,S Myanmar.

6 COMMON FLAMEBACK *Dinopium javanense* 28–30 cm
(a,b) **Male** *intermedium*: Single black submoustachial, all-black hindneck, no black on lores/crown-side. (c) **Female**: White-streaked black crown. **Juvenile**: Blacker-brown breast with white spots, fainter belly-scales. Male mostly black on forehead/crown, red crest; female more spotted than streaked crown. **Other subspecies** *D.j.javanense* (S Thailand southwards). **VOICE** Long, trilled *ka-di-di-di-di-di-di..* (faster/less metallic than Greater). Softer drums than Greater. 1–2 *kow* notes, *kowp-owp-owp-owp* in flight. **HABITAT** Open deciduous forest, gardens, plantations, mangroves; up to 800 m (locally higher Myanmar). **RANGE** Un/co **R** (except N Myanmar).

7 BLACK-RUMPED FLAMEBACK *D.benghalense* 26–29 cm
(a) **Male** *benghalense*: Black throat/rump/forehead-streaks. (b) **Female**: White-streaked black forecrown. **Juvenile**: Dull; fainter markings below. Male has red-tipped crown, sometimes white spots; female little/no forecrown spotting. **VOICE** Whinnying *kyi-kyi-kyi-kyi...* Strident *kierk*. **HABITAT** Open woodland, plantations; lowlands. **RANGE** Co **R** SW Myanmar.

8 GREATER FLAMEBACK *Chrysocolaptes lucidus* 29–32 cm
(a,b) **Male** *guttacristatus*: Long bill, submoustachial loop, white centre of hindneck. (c) **Female**: White-spotted black crown. **Juvenile**: More olive above, duller/more obscurely marked below; male has less red and pale spotting on crown. **Other subspecies** *C.l.chersonesus* (Pen Malaysia): Smaller, slightly more olive above, more red on back, broader supercilium/underpart markings. **VOICE** Rapid metallic monotone *tititi-tititit...* Loud drums. Single *kik* notes. **HABITAT** Broadleaved forests, mangroves, old plantations; up to 1,200 m. **RANGE** Co **R** (except C Thailand); local/coastal Pen Malaysia.

9 MAROON WOODPECKER *Blythipicus rubiginosus* 24 cm
(a) **Male**: Plain maroon-chestnut upperparts, blackish tail with faint pale bars. Red neck-patch, often red on submoustachial. (b) **Female**: No red on head. **Juvenile**: Warmer above; may show red on crown. **VOICE** Shrill descending *keek-eek-eek-eek-eek-eek* from males. High wavering *kik-kik-kik-kik-kik-kik...* Nervous *kik* notes, or *kik-ik...kik-ik*. **HABITAT** Broadleaved evergreen forest, secondary growth, bamboo; up to 1,525 m (below 900 m in Thailand). **RANGE** Co **R** south Tenasserim, W(south),S Thailand, Pen Malaysia; formerly Singapore (one recent unconfirmed record).

10 BAY WOODPECKER *Blythipicus pyrrhotis* 26.5–29 cm
(a) **Male** *pyrrhotis*: Long bill; paler head, black bars above, red neck-patch. (b) **Female**: No red on neck. **Juvenile**: Head darker with paler crown-streaks, bolder bars above, darker below with faint rufous bars; male with less (duller) red on neck. (c) **Male** *cameroni* (Pen Malaysia): Darker; smaller neck-patch. **Other subspecies** *B.p.annamensis* (S Annam): Similar to *cameroni*. **VOICE** Harsh descending laughter: *keek keek-keek-keek-keek-keek*. Cackling *dit-d-d-di-di-di-di-dit-d-d-di-di..*, squirrel-like *kecker-rak-kecker-rak..*, loud chattering *kerere-kerere-kerere..* in alarm. **HABITAT** Broadleaved forest; to 2,745 m (above 1,065 m Pen Malaysia). **RANGE** Co **R** (except C Myanmar, C,SE,S Thailand, Singapore).

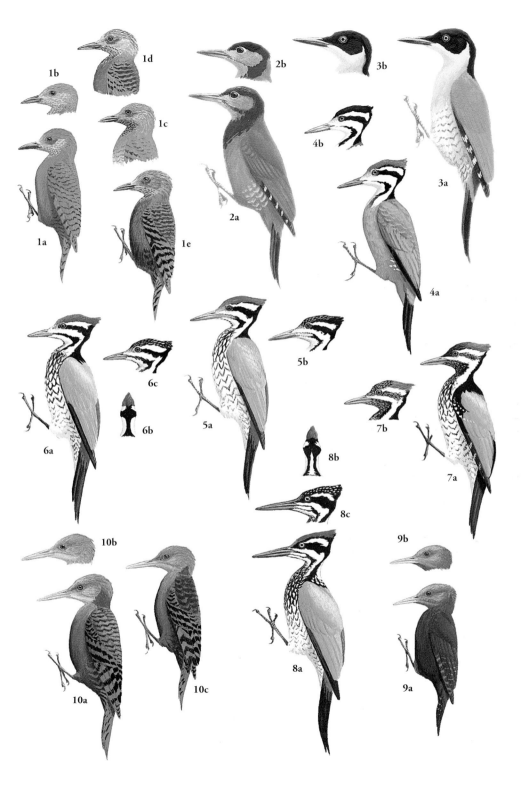

PLATE 15 LARGE WOODPECKERS & BARBETS

1 WHITE-BELLIED WOODPECKER *Dryocopus javensis* 40 cm (**a**) **Male** *feddeni*: Large size, black and white plumage, red crown, crest and submoustachial band. (**b**) **Female**: Red on head restricted to hindcrown. **Juvenile**: Duller with paler throat; male with black-mottled forecrown, smaller red submoustachial. **Other subspecies** *D.j.forresti* (N Myanmar, north W Tonkin): 43.5–47 cm. *D.j.javensis* (S Thailand southwards): Black rump (juvenile may show some white). **VOICE** Staccato *kek-ek-ek-ek-ek* and *kiau-kiau-kiau*. Loud accelerating drums (both sexes). Explosive *keer* or *kyah*. **HABITAT** Broadleaved forests, locally coniferous forest, mangroves. Up to 915 m (to 1,450 m S Annam); above 1,525 m N Myanmar and north W Tonkin. **RANGE** Sc/lfc **R** (except C Thailand, N Laos, E Tonkin, N Annam); rare Singapore.

2 ORANGE-BACKED WOODPECKER *Reinwardtipicus validus* 30 cm (**a**) **Male** *xanthopygius*: Long-neck; red crown/underparts, pale dorsal stripe. (**b**) **Female**: Blackish crown, whitish back/rump, grey-brown below. **Juvenile**: Like female; male sometimes with some red on crown and orange-buff on rump. **VOICE** Trilled *ki-i-i-i-i-ik*. Drums in short, quite weak bursts. Squeaky anxious *kit kit kit kit kit-it* (sharply rising last note). **HABITAT** Broadleaved evergreen forest; up to 730 m. **RANGE** Un **R** S Thailand, Pen Malaysia; formerly Singapore.

3 GREAT SLATY WOODPECKER *Mulleripicus pulverulentus* 48 cm (**a**) **Male** *harterti*: Large, long-necked; grey plumage, red submoustachial patch, buff throat/foreneck. (**b**) **Female**: No red submoustachial. **Juvenile**: Duller, head less speckled, throat/foreneck whitish; males with larger red submoustachial, sometimes red on crown. **Other subspecies** *M.p.pulverulentus* (southern S Thailand southwards): Much more blackish-slate. **VOICE** Loud wavering, whinnying 2–5 note *woi-kwoi-kwoi-kwoik...woi-kwoi-kwoi-kwoik..* (mainly in flight). Single *dwot* and soft *whu-ick*. **HABITAT** Broadleaved forest, mangroves; up to 1,065 m (below 215 m Pen Malaysia). **RANGE** Un/fc **R** (except C Thailand, W,E Tonkin); formerly Singapore.

4 FIRE-TUFTED BARBET *Psilopogon pyrolophus* 28 cm (**a**) **Adult**: Brownish-maroon hindcrown/nape, whitish forecrown-band, pale yellowish-green bill with dark band, grey ear-coverts, yellow and blackish breast-bands. (**b**) **Juvenile**: Olive-brown hindcrown/nape, dull supercilium. **VOICE** Strange cicada-like buzzing, starting with spaced notes, then speeding up and rising toward end. **HABITAT** Broadleaved evergreen forest; 1,070–2,010 m. **RANGE** Un/co **R** extreme S Thailand, Pen Malaysia.

5 GREAT BARBET *Megalaima virens* 32–33 cm (**a**) **Adult** *virens*: Large; pale bill, dark head, brownish mantle, streaked on belly, red undertail-coverts. **Other subspecies** *M.v.magnifica* (SW,W,west S Myanmar); *clamator* (east N Myanmar). **VOICE** Loud *kay-oh* (once a second). Continuous *piou-piou-piou-piou...* (female?), often with former in duet. Grating *keeah*. **HABITAT** Broadleaved evergreen (rarely deciduous) forest; 600–2,800 m (locally 440 m N Myanmar). **RANGE** Co **R** Myanmar (except southern Tenasserim), W,NW,NE (northwest) Thailand, N,C Laos, W,E Tonkin, N Annam.

6 RED-VENTED BARBET *Megalaima lagrandieri* 29.5–34 cm (**a**) **Adult** *lagrandieri*: Large, darkish bill, brownish head with greyish sides/throat, blue eyebrow, red undertail-coverts. (**b**) **Juvenile**: Uniform greyish-brown head, but orange-red forehead-tuft. **Other subspecies** *M.l.rothschildi* (W,E Tonkin, N Annam). **VOICE** Strident, throaty *choa* or *chorwa* (every 1–2 seconds). Descending *uk uk-ukukukukukuk..* (often with former in duet). Grating *grrric..grrric....grrric...* **HABITAT** Broadleaved evergreen/semi-evergreen forest; up to 1,900 m. **RANGE** Un/co **R** north-eastern Cambodia, C,S Laos, Vietnam.

7 LINEATED BARBET *Megalaima lineata* 27–28 cm (**a**) **Adult** *hodgsoni*: Thick yellowish bill, broad whitish head-and breast-streaks, yellow eyering. **VOICE** Male territorial call is loud mellow *poo-poh* (*poh* higher), about once a second. Rapid bubbling *koh-koh-koh-koh-koh...* **HABITAT** Deciduous forest, scattered trees in open areas, plantations; up to 1,220 m (below 800 m Thailand, lowlands Pen Malaysia). **RANGE** Co **R** (except south Pen Malaysia, Singapore, W,E Tonkin, N Annam).

8 GREEN-EARED BARBET *Megalaima faiostricta* 25–27 cm (**a**) **Adult** *faiostricta*: Mostly dark bill, dark around eye, green ear-coverts, all-green mantle, red spot on breast-side. **Other subspecies** *M.f.praetermissa* (E Tonkin). **VOICE** Throaty *took-a-prruk* (more than once a second) from male. Mellow fluty, rising *pooouk*. **HABITAT** Broadleaved forests; up to 1,015 m. **RANGE** Co **R** Thailand (except C,S), Indochina.

9 GOLD-WHISKERED BARBET *Megalaima chrysopogon* 30 cm (**a**) **Adult** *laeta*: Large dark bill, broad eyestripe above large yellow patch on lower head-side, pale throat. **Juvenile**: Duller yellow on lower head-side. **VOICE** Male territorial call is loud, rather deep *tehoop-tehoop-tehoop-tehoop-tehoop...* Also a repeated, long, low-pitched trill on one note, gradually slowing and eventually breaking up into 3–4 note phrases. **HABITAT** Broadleaved evergreen forest; up to 1,065 m, occasionally to 1,525 m. **RANGE** Un/co **R** W(south),S Thailand, Pen Malaysia.

10 RED-CROWNED BARBET *Megalaima rafflesii* 25–27 cm (**a**) **Adult** *malayensis*: Red crown, blue throat and supercilium, black eyestripe bordered yellow and red below. (**b**) **Juvenile**: Much duller with less defined head pattern. **VOICE** Male territorial call is 1–2 *took* notes, followed after a pause by up to 20 rapidly repeated, shorter *tuk* notes. **HABITAT** Broadleaved evergreen forest; up to 200 m. **RANGE** Sc/lfc **R** south Tenasserim, S Thailand, Pen Malaysia, Singapore.

11 RED-THROATED BARBET *M.mystacophanos* 23 cm (**a**) **Male** *mystacophanos*: Yellow forehead, red crown, red throat, blue cheeks. (**b**) **Female**: Mostly greenish head, red patches on lores, hindcrown and upper breast-side. (**c**) **Juvenile**: Green head with yellower forehead and throat. **VOICE** Male utters slow series of 1–2 (or 3) deep notes at uneven intervals: *chok..chok-chok..chok-chok..chok...* Also a repeated high-pitched trill, which gradually shortens. **HABITAT** Broadleaved evergreen forest; up to 760 m. **RANGE** Co **R** south Tenasserim, S Thailand, Pen Malaysia.

PLATE 16 HONEYGUIDES & BARBETS

1 MALAYSIAN HONEYGUIDE *Indicator archipelagicus* 18 cm
(**a**) **Male**: Nondescript, thick-billed and passerine-like, resembling some bulbuls. Upperparts cold dark olive-brown with narrow olive-green streaks, mainly on wings, scapulars and uppertail-coverts; underparts whitish with greyish wash across breast and broad dark streaks on belly/lower flanks. Long lemon-yellow shoulder-patch (often hidden), reddish eyes. **Female**: No shoulder-patch. **Juvenile**: Like female but indistinctly streaked below, eyes brown. **VOICE** Sings with 1–2 mewing notes followed by ascending nasal rattle: *miaw-krrrruuu*. **HABITAT & BEHAVIOUR** Broadleaved evergreen forest; up to 915 m. Sits motionless on exposed perch. **RANGE** Sc/un **R** W,S Thailand, Pen Malaysia.

2 YELLOW-RUMPED HONEYGUIDE *I.xanthonotus* 15 cm
(**a**) **Male**: Bright orange-yellow forecrown, cheeks and band down centre of lower back and rump, white inner tertial fringes. Throat streaked greyish and whitish, rest of underparts largely dusky-whitish with broad dark streaks. (**b**) **Female**: Duller with less yellow on forehead and cheeks. **VOICE** Single *weet* is said to be uttered in flight. **HABITAT & BEHAVIOUR** Cliffs and adjacent evergreen forest; recorded at 2,285 m. Sits motionless; usually near bee nests. **RANGE** Ra **R** N Myanmar.

3 GOLDEN-THROATED BARBET *Megalaima franklinii* 22 cm
(**a**) **Adult** *ramsayi*: Red forehead and hindcrown, yellow midcrown, grey-streaked blackish lower ear-coverts, yellow upper throat, pale greyish lower throat. Broad black band through eye streaked with grey, outer fringes of secondaries and outer wing-coverts distinctly blue-washed. (**b**) **Juvenile**: Duller with less distinct head pattern. (**c**) **Adult** *auricularis* (S Laos, S Annam): All-black band through eye, violet-washed lower ear-coverts, mostly yellow throat with dark border, narrow blue lower border to throat continuing in narrow line to rear of black eyestripe. (**d**) **Adult** *franklinii* (N Myanmar, east NW,NE Thailand, N Indochina): All-black band through eye and deeper yellow on throat. **Other subspecies** *M.f.minor* (Pen Malaysia): All-black band through eye, deeper yellow on throat, some blue behind ear-coverts. *M.f.trangensis* (S Thailand). **VOICE** Male territorial call is a very loud, ringing *pukwowk*, repeated about once a second. **HABITAT** Broadleaved evergreen forest; 800–2,565 m (above 1,280 m in Pen Malaysia, rarely down to 500 m in Laos and 225 m in C Annam). **RANGE** Co **R** (except C,SE Thailand, Singapore, Cambodia, Cochinchina).

4 BLACK-BROWED BARBET *Megalaima oorti* 21.5–23.5 cm
(**a**) **Adult** *oorti*: Head-sides blue, throat yellow with broad blue lower border, red spot on side of upper breast, no side of face to wing feathers; medium-width black eyestripe/supercilium. (**b**) **Juvenile**: Duller, less distinct head pattern. (**c**) **Adult** *annamensis* (S Laos, S Annam): Broader black supercilium, more blue on lower throat. **VOICE** Male territorial call is throaty *toka-r'ut*, about once a second. **HABITAT** Broadleaved evergreen forest; 600–1,450 m, rarely down to 250 m. **RANGE** Fc/co **R** extreme S Thailand, Pen Malaysia, east Cambodia, S Laos, C,S Annam.

5 BLUE-THROATED BARBET *Megalaima asiatica* 23 cm
(**a**) **Adult** *davisoni*: All-blue head-sides and throat. Red crown with blue band across centre, narrow black supercilium.

(**b**) **Juvenile**: Duller; fainter head pattern. (**c**) **Adult** *asiatica* (Myanmar; except Tenasserim): Black and yellow bands across mid-crown. (**d**) **Adult** *chersonesus* (S Thailand): Bluer crown. **VOICE** Loud, quickly repeated *took-arook* from male. **HABITAT** Broadleaved evergreen forest, secondary growth; 400–2,400 m (mainly 600–1,830 m). **RANGE** Co **R** Myanmar, Thailand (except C,SE), N Laos, W,E Tonkin, N Annam.

6 MOUSTACHED BARBET *Megalaima incognita* 23 cm
(**a**) **Adult** *elbeli*: Crown greenish with red at front and rear, black submoustachial, blue throat. (**b**) **Juvenile**: Duller; ill-defined head pattern. **Other subspecies** *M.i.incognita* (Tenasserim, W Thailand); *euroa* (SE Thailand, Indochina). **VOICE** Male territorial call like Blue-throated but notes spaced, deliberate: *u'ik-a-ruk u'ik-a-ruk u'ik-a-ruk...*. **HABITAT** Broadleaved evergreen forest; 600–1,700 m. **RANGE** Fc/co **R** northern Tenasserim, W,NW,NE,SE Thailand, Cambodia, Laos, Vietnam (except Cochinchina).

7 YELLOW-CROWNED BARBET *Megalaima henricii* 22–23 cm
(**a**) **Adult** *henricii*: Smallish size, yellow front/sides of crown, green head-side, blue throat. (**b**) **Juvenile**: Duller; washed-out head pattern. **VOICE** Male territorial call of 4–6 loud *tok* notes introduced by short trill: *trrok....tok-tok-tok-tok...*, with one phrase about every 2 s. **HABITAT** Broadleaved evergreen forest; up to 975 m. **RANGE** Un/fc **R** S Thailand, Pen Malaysia.

8 BLUE-EARED BARBET *Megalaima australis* 17–18 cm
(**a**) **Male** *cyanotis*: Small; black forehead, orange-red cheek-patch, red above and below blue ear-coverts, blue throat with narrow black border. (**b**) **Female**: Duller head pattern. (**c**) **Juvenile**: Very uniform; blue-tinged ear-coverts/throat. (**d**) **Male** *duvaucelii* (Pen Malaysia): Black ear-coverts with larger red patches above/below; red cheek-patch, broad black band on upper breast. **Other subspecies** *M.a.stuarti* (Tenasserim, W,S Thailand). **VOICE** Monotonous, rapidly repeated *ko-tek*. Shrill whistled *pleow* notes (c.1 per s). **HABITAT** Broadleaved forests; up to 1,525 m (below 975 m in Pen Malaysia). **RANGE** Co **R** (except C Thailand); formerly Singapore.

9 COPPERSMITH BARBET *Megalaima haemacephala* 17 cm
(**a**) **Adult** *indica*: Small; yellow head-sides/throat, black eye-stripe/submoustachial, pale greenish below with dark green streaks. Crown red at front, black towards rear; red breast-band. (**b**) **Juvenile**: Dark of head duller, yellow of head-sides and throat paler, no red on crown or breast. **VOICE** Resonant *tonk-tonk-tonk-tonk-tonk..* (<100+ notes). **HABITAT** Deciduous forest, scattered trees, mangroves, parks, gardens, plantations; up to 915 m. **RANGE** Co **R** (except W,E Tonkin).

10 BROWN BARBET *Calorhamphus fuliginosus* 20 cm
(**a**) **Adult** *hayii*: Brown with whiter breast to vent; orangey legs and feet. **VOICE** Thin, forced *pseeoo* notes. **HABITAT & BEHAVIOUR** Broadleaved evergreen forest, secondary growth; up to 1,065 m. Forages in small parties. **RANGE** Fc/co **R** south Tenasserim, S Thailand, Pen Malaysia; formerly Singapore.

1 and 2 to different scale

PLATE 17 LARGER HORNBILLS

1 RHINOCEROS HORNBILL *Buceros rhinoceros* 91–122 cm (**a**) Male *rhinoceros*: Bright red and yellow upward-curved casque with black base. Mostly black with white lower belly and undertail-coverts, and white tail with broad black band across centre. Bill mostly pale yellowish to whitish, eyes reddish, eye-ring blackish. (**b**) Female: Smaller, eyes whitish, eyering reddish. **Juvenile**: Bill yellow with orange base, casque barely developed, eyes pale blue-grey, eyering blue-grey. VOICE Male utters deep, forceful *hok* notes, female a higher *hak*, often in duet: *hok-hak hok-hak hok-hak...* Also a loud throaty *ger-ronk* by both sexes when flying (often simultaneously or antiphonally). HABITAT & BEHAVIOUR Broadleaved evergreen forest; up to 1,220 m. Usually found in pairs or small groups, occasionally larger flocks of up to 25. RANGE Sc/lc **R** extreme S Thailand, Pen Malaysia. **Frc** Singapore.

2 GREAT HORNBILL *Buceros bicornis* 119–122 cm (averages smaller in S Thailand and Pen Malaysia)
(**a**) Male *homrai*: Mostly yellowish bill and casque, mostly blackish plumage with white nape and neck, white vent, white tail with broad black central band. In flight (above and below) shows broad white band across greater coverts and broadly white-tipped flight feathers. Neck and greater covert bar variably stained yellowish, eyes reddish, eyering blackish. (**b**) Female: Smaller, eyes whitish, eyering red. **Juvenile**: Bill much smaller, casque barely developed, eyes pale blue-grey, eyering pinkish. VOICE Very loud, deep *gok* or *kok* notes (given by duetting pairs), leading to loud harsh roaring and barking. Deep coarse *who* by male and *whaa* by female; double *who-whaa* at take-off or in flight is duet. HABITAT & BEHAVIOUR Broadleaved evergreen and mixed deciduous forest, forest on some larger islands; up to 1,525 m. Usually found in pairs or small groups. RANGE Sc/lc **R** (except C Thailand, Singapore).

3 HELMETED HORNBILL *Buceros vigil*
127 cm (central tail <50 more)
(**a,b**) Male: Elongated central tail feathers, bare dark red skin on head-sides, throat and neck. Has short, straight, yellowish bill with reddish base, short and rounded reddish casque with yellow tip and mostly blackish plumage with white rump, vent and tail-coverts. Tail whitish with black central and subterminal bands. In flight, also shows broadly white-tipped secondaries and primaries. Female: Bill speckled black at tip, skin of face and neck tinged pale lilac. **Juvenile**: Bill yellowish-olive, casque poorly developed, head/neck skin pale greenish-blue, central tail shorter. VOICE Loud, resonant, protracted series of notes, starting with spaced *hoop* notes, slowly quickening to *ke-hoop* and ending with manic laughter. Clanking *ka-bank ka-bank..*, usually in flight. HABITAT & BEHAVIOUR Broadleaved evergreen forest; up to 1,400 m. Usually found singly or in pairs. RANGE Sc/un **R** Tenasserim, S Thailand, Pen Malaysia.

4 RUFOUS-NECKED HORNBILL *Aceros nipalensis* 117 cm (**a**) Male: Bright rufous head, neck and underparts. Rest of upperside black with white-tipped outer primaries, tail white with black basal half/third, bill pale yellowish with row of vertical dark ridges on upper mandible and almost no casque, orbital skin blue, gular skin red. (**b,c**) Female: Head, neck and

underparts black, orbital skin a little duller. From Wreathed and Plain-pouched by bill structure/pattern, opposite colour of bare head-skin, less inflated gular pouch, lack of obvious crest, white-tipped outer primaries and black tail-base. **Juvenile**: Like male but bill smaller with no dark ridges, tail feathers may be narrowly dark-tipped. VOICE Barking *kup* notes; less deep than similar calls of Great. HABITAT & BEHAVIOUR Broadleaved evergreen forest; 600–2,900 m. Usually in pairs, sometimes small groups. RANGE Ra/ul Myanmar (except SW), W,NW Thailand, N,C Laos, W Tonkin, N Annam.

5 WRINKLED HORNBILL *Aceros corrugatus* 81–82 cm (**a,b**) Male: Smaller than Wreathed, smaller yellow bill with reddish base, squarer-looking reddish casque, blue orbital skin, unmarked and less bulging gular pouch, blacker crown-centre and nape, black tail-base (hard to see). White of tail usually strongly stained buffish to yellowish. (**c**) Female: Smaller than Wreathed, plain yellowish bill with squarer casque, blue orbital skin, plain, less bulging gular pouch, less pronounced crest, black tail-base. **Juvenile**: Like male, but bill unridged and pale yellow with orange wash at base, casque undeveloped, orbital skin pale yellow; may have blackish base to upper mandible. VOICE Sharp, barking *kak kak-kak* etc. HABITAT & BEHAVIOUR Broadleaved evergreen forest, freshwater swamp forest; up to 800 m. Usually found in pairs or small flocks. RANGE Ra/un **R** S Thailand, Pen Malaysia. **Frc** Singapore.

6 WREATHED HORNBILL *Aceros undulatus* M 100.5–115, F 84–98 cm (smaller S Thailand, Pen Malaysia)
(**a,b**) Male: Brownish-white head-sides, neck and breast, all-white tail, bulging yellow gular pouch with blackish lateral streak. Crown-centre to hindneck shaggy warmish dark brown, bill pale dull yellowish with darker corrugated base (not always obvious), casque small with dark ridges, orbital skin reddish. Tail often lightly stained yellowish/brownish. (**c**) Female: Head, neck and breast black, gular pouch blue. **Juvenile**: Like male but casque undeveloped, bill uncorrugated, gular pouch streak fainter. VOICE Loud, rather breathless *kuk-KWEHK*. HABITAT & BEHAVIOUR Broadleaved evergreen and mixed deciduous forest, forest on islands; up to 1,830 m, rarely 2,500 m N Myanmar. Usually in pairs or small flocks; sometimes very large flocks flying to and from roosts. RANGE Un/lc **R** (except C Myanmar, C Thailand, Singapore, W,E Tonkin).

7 PLAIN-POUCHED HORNBILL *Aceros subruficollis* M 88, f 80 cm
(**a,b**) Male: Somewhat smaller than Wreathed, bill shorter with warm brownish base and no corrugations, casque slightly more peaked with more dark ridges, lacks gular pouch streak. (**c**) Female: From Wreathed as male. **Juvenile**: Like male but casque undeveloped, bill all pale yellowish. May only differ from Wreathed by plain pouch. VOICE Loud *keh-kek-kehk* or *ehk-ehk-ehk* with accentuated end-note; higher and more quacking than Wreathed. HABITAT & BEHAVIOUR Broadleaved evergreen and mixed deciduous forest; up to 915 m. Usually in pairs or small groups, sometimes large flocks during local movements. RANGE Ra/un **R** (local movements) S Myanmar, Tenasserim, W,S(southern) Thailand, north Pen Malaysia.

PLATE 18 SMALLER HORNBILLS, COMMON HOOPOE & ROLLERS

1 ORIENTAL PIED HORNBILL *Anthracoceros albirostris* 69 cm (**a,b**) **Male** *albirostris*: White belly and vent, white facial markings, pale yellowish bill and casque with dark markings; black wings with broad white trailing edge, black tail with broadly white-tipped outer feathers. (**c**) **Female**: Bill and casque smaller, more extensively dark distally. **Juvenile**: Plain bill and very small casque, less white on tail. (**d**) **Male** *convexus* (extreme S Thailand southwards): Mostly white outertail (tail often looks white from below). **VOICE** Loud yelping *kleng-keng kek-kek-kek-kek-kek* and *ayip-yip-yip-yip..* etc. **HABITAT & BEHAVIOUR** Broadleaved evergreen and mixed deciduous forest, island forest, secondary growth, plantations, gardens; up to 1,400 m (below 150 m S Thailand southwards). In flocks, sometimes quite large. **RANGE** Un/lc **R** (except C Thailand); rare Singapore.

2 BLACK HORNBILL *Anthracoceros malayanus* 76 cm (**a,b**) **Male**: Black plumage, white outertail-tips, plain yellowish-white bill and casque, blackish facial skin. (**c**) **Male variant**: Broad white/greyish supercilium. (**d**) **Female**: Bill/casque smaller and blackish, orbital skin and submoustachial patch pinkish. **Juvenile**: Bill pale greenish-yellow (darker when very young), casque undeveloped, facial skin dull yellowish with orange around eye, white tail-tips flecked black. **VOICE** Distinctive loud harsh retching sounds and grating growls. **HABITAT & BEHAVIOUR** Broadleaved evergreen forest; up to 215 m. Usually found in pairs or small flocks, occasionally up to 30 or more. **RANGE** Ra/lfc **R** S Thailand, Peninsular Malaysia.

3 BROWN HORNBILL *Anorrhinus tickelli* 73–74 cm (**a,b**) **Male** *austeni*: Whitish throat/foreneck and upper breast, brownish-rufous belly. Pale yellowish bill with small casque, pale blue orbital skin, white-tipped outertail. Narrowly white-tipped secondaries and outer primaries. (**c**) **Female**: Smaller casque, dark brownish below (foreneck paler). **Juvenile**: Like female but dull greyish-brown below, no white primary tips, smaller bill, pinky orbital skin. (**d**) **Male** *tickelli* (Tenasserim, W Thailand): Bright brownish-rufous below. Female has horn-coloured to blackish bill. **VOICE** Piercing yelps and squeals; upward-inflected *klee-ah*. **HABITAT & BEHAVIOUR** Broadleaved evergreen and sometimes nearby mixed deciduous forest, locally pines in Laos; up to 1,500 m, locally 1,800 m. Usually in flocks. **RANGE** Un/lc **R** W,N Myanmar, Tenasserim, W,NW,NE Thailand, Cambodia, Laos, W,E Tonkin, N,C,north S Annam.

4 BUSHY-CRESTED HORNBILL *Anorrhinus galeritus* 89 cm (**a,b**) **Male**: All dark; thick drooping crest, somewhat paler and greyer vent, paler dirty brownish-grey basal two-thirds of tail. Bill and small casque blackish, bare orbital and gular skin pale bluish. (**c**) **Female**: Casque smaller, bill usually pale yellowish with mostly blackish basal half. **Juvenile**: Browner with whiter belly, bill pale olive, skin of head pale yellowish with pink eyering. **VOICE** Loud rising and falling yelps, *klia-klia-klia kliu-kliu..*; *wah wah wohawaha* etc.; often by all flock members, building to crescendo. High *aak aak aak* in alarm. **HABITAT & BEHAVIOUR** Broadleaved evergreen forest; up to 1,220 m. Usually in flocks of 5–15. **RANGE** Fc/co **R** south Tenasserim, S Thailand, Pen Malaysia.

5 WHITE-CROWNED HORNBILL *Aceros comatus* 90–101 cm (**a**) **Male**: Whitish head, neck, breast and tail, shaggy crest. White-tipped flight feathers, pale blue facial skin. (**b,c**) **Female**: Neck and underparts black. **Juvenile**: Browner than female, blackish bases/shafts to crest feathers, black tail-base, yellowish-brown bill with dark patches; perhaps whitish-tipped greater coverts. Male gradually attains white below. **VOICE** Deep, resonant hooting with lower first note: *hoo hu-hu-hu hu-hu-hu..*, often dying away. **HABITAT & BEHAVIOUR** Broadleaved evergreen forest; up to 1,000 m, rarely to 1,675 m. Usually in small flocks, often low down in forest. Less frugivorous than other hornbills. **RANGE & STATUS** Resident Sumatra, Borneo. **SE Asia** Un/lc **R** south Tenasserim, S Thailand, Pen Malaysia.

6 COMMON HOOPOE *Upupa epops* 27–32.5 cm (**a,b**) **Adult** *longirostris*: Long downcurved bill; dull pale rufous crown, black-tipped crest (often held erect, fan-like), black-and-white/-buff bars on back/rump, broad white bars on black wings and tail, dull dark pinkish throat to upper belly. Mantle pale warm brown (grey-tinged), uppertail-coverts white, flanks streaked black. **Juvenile**: Duller/paler above, browner below. **Other subspecies** *U.e.saturata* (visitor). **VOICE** Soft *hoop-hoop-hoop* (or 2 notes). **HABITAT** Open areas, open woodland, cultivation, gardens; up to 1,525 m, rarely 2,200m. **RANGE** Sc/co **R** (except Pen Malaysia, Singapore). Sc/un **WV** N,S Myanmar, NW,C,S Thailand. **V** Pen Malaysia (formerly **R** in north-west). Also **PM** E Tonkin.

7 INDIAN ROLLER *Coracias benghalensis* 31.5–34.5 cm (**a,b**) **Adult** *affinis*: Turquoise crown (duller centre), uppertail-coverts and vent, greenish-/brownish-olive mantle, scapulars and tertials, dark purplish-blue rump, vinous-brown head-sides/breast, more distinctly light purple throat with narrow pale streaks. Brilliant dark purplish-blue and light turquoise wings and outertail. (**c**) **Juvenile**: Browner-bodied, reduced turquoise on crown, paler, browner head-sides. **VOICE** Harsh, retching *kyak*. **HABITAT & BEHAVIOUR** Open places, cultivation, coastal scrub; up to 1,525 m. Often on telegraph wires, exposed perches; drops down in search of food. **RANGE** Co **R** (except Singapore, E Tonkin); north-east Pen Malaysia only.

8 DOLLARBIRD *Eurystomus orientalis* 27.5–31.5 cm (**a,b**) **Adult** *orientalis*: Dark brown to greenish-brown above, dark bluish-purple to turquoise below, darker/browner breast, light blue throat-streaks; thick red bill. Silvery-turquoise wing-patch. (**c**) **Juvenile**: Browner above, initially all-brown head, some/no turquoise on throat, mostly dark bill. **Other subspecies** *E.o.abundus* (visits Indochina, Pen Malaysia; **BV** E Tonkin at least): Blacker-brown crown/nape/head-sides, mostly green mantle (looks more hooded). *E.o.deignani* (NW,NE Thailand). **VOICE** Hoarse rasping *kreck kreck..*, and repeated *kak* and *kiak* notes. **HABITAT & BEHAVIOUR** Open broadleaved forest, clearings, plantations, mangroves, island forest; up to 1,500 m (mostly 1,220 m). Often on dead treetops; mostly an aerial feeder. **RANGE** Un/co **R** Myanmar, Thailand (except C), Pen Malaysia, Singapore (sc), Cambodia, S Laos, C,S Annam, Cochinchina. Fc **BV** N,C Laos, W,E Tonkin, N Annam. Fc **WV** S Thailand, Pen Malaysia, Singapore. Also **PM** Pen Malaysia.

1c

2b

2c

1a

2d

1d

2a

1b

3a

3d

3c

3b

5a

4c

5b

4a

5c

7a

7c

4b

7b

6–8 to different scale

8a

6a

6b

8b

8c

PLATE 19 TROGONS

1 RED-NAPED TROGON *Harpactes kasumba* 31.5–34.5 cm
(a) **Male** *kasumba*: Like Diard's but crown all black, has broad red nuchal patch meeting broad cobalt-blue facial skin, well-demarcated narrow white breast-band, dull golden-buffish upperparts, usually redder underparts and unmarked white on undertail. (b) **Female**: Brownish-buff lower breast to vent, unmarked white on under tail. **Juvenile**: Similar to female; males soon attain patches of adult plumage. **VOICE** Male territorial call is subdued but rather harsh, evenly pitched, 3–6 note *kau kau kau kau..*, lower/more spaced than Diard's. Female gives quiet whirring rattle. **HABITAT** Broadleaved evergreen and freshwater swamp forest, bamboo; up to 550 m. **RANGE** Sc/lfc **R** S Thailand, Pen Malaysia; formerly Singapore.

2 DIARD'S TROGON *Harpactes diardii* 32.5–35 cm
(a) **Male** *sumatranus*: Black head and upper breast with maroon-washed hindcrown and narrow pink nuchal band; pale pink breast-band, reddish-pink belly/vent. Orbital skin violet/violet-blue, undertail as female. (b) **Female**: Told by combination of rather uniform dull brown head, upper breast and mantle, contrasting reddish-pink to pink belly and dark vermiculations/speckles on white of undertail. Back to uppertail-coverts more rufescent, lower breast more buffish-brown, undertail-coverts buffish-brown mixed with pink. **Juvenile**: Similar to female. Male soon attains patches of adult plumage. **VOICE** Male territorial call is 10–12 *kau* notes, either with the second somewhat higher than first and the rest descending, with the last few slower, or else all evenly spaced. **HABITAT & BEHAVIOUR** Middle storey of broadleaved evergreen forest; up to 600 m, rarely to 915 m in Pen Malaysia. Very unobtrusive. **RANGE** Un/lc **R** S Thailand, Pen Malaysia; formerly Singapore.

3 CINNAMON-RUMPED TROGON *Harpactes orrhophaeus* 25.5–28 cm
(a) **Male** *orrhophaeus*: Larger than Scarlet-rumped, thicker bill, brown rump/uppertail-coverts, pinker below. (b) **Female**: From Scarlet-rumped by lack of pink, darker and richer brown head, with contrasting deep rufous lores/around eye, blackish-brown throat with dull rufous centre; less rufescent above. **Juvenile**: Like female but pale wing-vermiculations much broader, duller/greyer and more uniform above, more deep rufous on lores, head-sides and throat. From Scarlet-rumped by extensive, contrasting deep rufous on head-sides, more uniform above (including rump and uppertail-coverts), darker and less buffish breast. **VOICE** Territorial call of male is weak, descending, 3–4 note *taup taup taup...* or *ta'up ta'up ta'up ta'up* (each note inflected downward). **HABITAT & BEHAVIOUR** Lower to middle storey of broadleaved evergreen forest; up to 200 m. Very shy. **RANGE** Sc/un **R** S Thailand, Pen Malaysia.

4 SCARLET-RUMPED TROGON *Harpactes duvaucelii* 23.5–26.5 cm
(a) **Male**: Black head, blue 'eye-brow', bill and gape, bright red rump/uppertail-coverts and underparts. (b) **Female**: Dark brown head, paler, slightly warmer face/throat, mostly buffy-brown rump/uppertail-coverts (mixed pink), deep buffy-brown breast, pinkish/reddish-pink belly/vent. (c) **Juvenile female**: No obvious pink; rufescent rump and uppertail-coverts, rufous-buff below with pale buff centrally (males show some pink below

and soon attain patches of adult plumage). **VOICE** Male territorial call is accelerating descending *teuk teuk teuk-euk-euk-euk-euk-euk-euk-euk-euk-euk...* Vibrating *chrrrr, charr* and *chowrrr*. **HABITAT** Middle storey of broadleaved evergreen forest; up to 400 m, 1,065 m Pen Malaysia. **RANGE** Un/lc **R** south Tenasserim, W(south),S Thailand, Pen Malaysia.

5 ORANGE-BREASTED TROGON *Harpactes oreskios* 26.5–31.5 cm
(a) **Male** *stellae*: Head and upper breast greenish-olive (throat and central breast more yellowish-tinged), upperparts chestnut-maroon, underparts yellowish-orange with paler, yellower vent. (b) **Female**: Head to back uniform drab olive-brownish, rump and uppertail-coverts duller/paler, throat and upper breast distinctly grey-washed, rest of underparts paler and yellower, broader pale bars on wings. **Juvenile**: Head, upperparts and breast tinged rufous-chestnut, pale wing-barring broader, belly/vent paler/whitish; males have chestnut mantle, scapulars and back. **Other subspecies** *H.o.uniformis* (south Tenasserim/S Thailand southward). **VOICE** Territorial call is subdued, even, rather rapidly delivered 3–5 note *teu-teu-teu...* or *tu-tau-tau-tau...* Female may utter a slower, lower-pitched version. **HABITAT** Middle to upper storey of broadleaf forests, bamboo; up to 1,220 m. **RANGE** Co **R** (except W,N,C Myanmar, C Thailand, Singapore, W,E Tonkin, N Annam).

6 RED-HEADED TROGON *H.erythrocephalus* 31–35.5 cm
(a) **Male** *erythrocephalus*: Dark red head/breast, white breast-band, pinkish-red belly, whitish wing-barring. (b) **Female**: Head and upper breast brown, concolorous with mantle, vermiculations on wings pale warmish brown. **Juvenile**: Like female but head, breast and upperparts rufescent; has less red on underparts. Male has broad buff bars on wings and soon attains red on head and upper breast. **Other subspecies** *H.e.belenae* (N Myanmar): Largest. *H.e.chaseni* (S Thailand, Pen Malaysia): Smallest. *H.e.klossi* (SE Thailand, Cambodia); *annamensis* (NE Thailand, N[south-east],C,S Laos, N,C,S Annam, Cochinchina); *intermedius* (north-east N Laos, W,E Tonkin). **VOICE** Deep, well-spaced, descending 4–5 note *taup taup taup taup taup...* Coarse rattling *tewirr*. **HABITAT & BEHAVIOUR** Middle to upper storey of broadleaved evergreen forest, 305–2,590 m; 700–1,680 m Pen Malaysia, locally 50 m Indochina. Unobtrusive, spends long periods motionless. **RANGE** Co **R** (except C Thailand, Singapore); local S Thailand.

7 WARD'S TROGON *Harpactes wardi* 38 cm
(a) **Male**: Slaty head, upperparts and breast with pinkish-maroon wash, pinkish-red forehead, red bill (purplish gape), pale blue orbital skin, reddish-pink below, blackish uppertail. (b) **Female**: Head, upperparts and breast mostly olive-brownish, bright yellow forehead, pale yellow belly/vent, pale yellow on undertail (pink on male). **Juvenile female**: Warmer mantle/back, much broader warmish brown wing-vermiculations, less yellow on forecrown. **VOICE** Male territorial call is rapid series of loud, mellow *klew* notes, often accelerating and dropping in pitch towards end. Harsh *whirrur*. **HABITAT** Broadleaved evergreen forest; 1,830–2,620 m, sometimes down to 1,220 m in winter. **RANGE** Sc/un **R** N Myanmar, W Tonkin.

PLATE 20 KINGFISHERS

1 BLYTH'S KINGFISHER *Alcedo hercules* 22–23 cm
(**a**) **Male**: Like Blue-eared but much larger with longer, heavier, all-black bill, darker and duller crown and wings, with light blue speckles on crown, nape and wing-coverts, darker lores. **Female**: Base of lower mandible reddish. **VOICE** Call is hoarser than that of Common, closer to Blue-eared but much louder. **HABITAT** Larger streams or smaller rivers in broadleaved evergreen forest, secondary growth; 50–1,220 m. **RANGE** Sc/lc **R** W,N,S Myanmar, Laos, W Tonkin, N,C,S Annam. **Rc** (status?) NW Thailand.

2 COMMON KINGFISHER *Alcedo atthis* 16–18 cm
(**a**) **Male**: *bengalensis*: Rufous ear-coverts, strong turquoise tinge to blue of upperparts, relatively pale rufous underparts. In flight, turquoise strip down upperparts very conspicuous. Bill mostly blackish. **Female**: Base or most of lower mandible orange-reddish. (**b**) **Juvenile**: Underparts paler with dusky wash across breast, base of lower mandible orange-reddish. **VOICE** Usually 2–3 shrill, high-pitched piping notes, particularly in flight. **HABITAT** Streams in open and wooded areas, various inland and coastal wetlands (tends to avoid denser forest); up to 1,830 m. **RANGE** Un **R** Myanmar, W,NW,NE Thailand, Pen Malaysia, N Laos, E Tonkin, N Annam. Co **WV** throughout. Also **PM** Pen Malaysia.

3 BLUE-EARED KINGFISHER *Alcedo meninting* 15.5–16.5 cm
(**a**) **Female** *verreauxii*: Like Common but slightly smaller, with blue ear-coverts, deeper blue crown, upperparts and wings (without turquoise), deeper orange-rufous below. Male bill mostly blackish. (**b**) **Juvenile**: Rufous on cheeks and ear-coverts, dark scales on duller breast, initially mostly reddish bill. (**c**) **Female** *coltarti* (W,N,C,S Myanmar, NW,NE[north-west] Thailand, Indochina): Pale turquoise crown-bars, wing-covert spots and strip down upperparts. **Other subspecies** *A.m.scintillans* (S[east] Myanmar, Tenasserim, W,SE,NE [south-west] Thailand): Roughly intermediate between *verreauxii* and *coltarti*. **VOICE** Typical call is higher-pitched and shorter than in Common, and often given singly. **HABITAT** Streams, smaller rivers and pools in broadleaved evergreen and mixed deciduous forest, mangroves; up to 915 m. **RANGE** Fc **R** (except SW,E Myanmar, C Thailand, W,E Tonkin); sc Singapore.

4 BLUE-BANDED KINGFISHER *Alcedo euryzona* 20–20.5 cm
(**a**) **Male** *peninsulae*: Mostly dull dark brownish wings, blue breast-band. Bill largely blackish. (**b**) **Female**: Similar to Common but larger and bulkier, crown, scapulars and wings much duller and browner, blue stripe down centre of upperparts whiter, no rufous-chestnut on ear-coverts behind eye. Bill has mostly dull reddish lower mandible. **Juvenile male**: More rufous on belly than adult. **VOICE** Similar to Common but less shrill. **HABITAT** Medium-sized and larger streams in broadleaved evergreen forest, sometimes smaller streams; up to 825 m. **RANGE** Sc/un **R** Tenasserim, W,S Thailand, Pen Malaysia.

5 BLACK-BACKED KINGFISHER *Ceyx erithacus* 12.5–14 cm
(**a**) **Adult** *erithacus*: Very small size, bright red bill, rufous, lilac and yellowish plumage with blackish-blue mantle and scapulars, and dark wings. Has blue patches on forehead and

to rear of ear-coverts. **Juvenile**: Underparts duller, more whitish, often with brownish wash across breast; bill duller. **VOICE** Sharp metallic piping, weaker and higher-pitched than Blue-eared; usually given in flight. Contact calls include weak, shrill *tit-sreet* and *tit-tit*. **HABITAT & BEHAVIOUR** Vicinity of small streams and pools in broadleaved evergreen forest, sometimes gardens and mangroves on migration; up to 915 m. Flashes through forest at remarkable speed. **RANGE** Un **R** Myanmar (except W,E), Thailand (except C and southern S), Laos, E Tonkin, N,C Annam, Cochinchina (likely to be **BV** only to some northern areas). Un/fc **WV** S Thailand, Pen Malaysia, Singapore. Un **PM** S Myanmar, C Thailand, Pen Malaysia, Singapore. **Rc** (status?) Cambodia.

6 RUFOUS-BACKED KINGFISHER *Ceyx rufidorsa* 12.5–14.5 cm
(**a**) **Adult** *rufidorsa*: Like Black-backed but mantle and scapulars all rufous, no blackish-blue on forehead and ear-coverts. **Juvenile**: Underparts duller, more whitish, often with brownish wash across breast; bill duller. **VOICE** Similar to Black-backed. Soft high insect-like *tjie-tjie-tjie*, usually in flight, and shrill *tsriet-siet*. **HABITAT** Vicinity of small streams and pools in broadleaved evergreen forest, sometimes mangroves; up to 455 m. **RANGE** Un **R** W,S Thailand, Pen Malaysia. Un **NBV** Singapore.

7 CRESTED KINGFISHER *Megaceryle lugubris* 38–41.5 cm
(**a**) **Male** *guttulata*: Relatively very large, upperside densely speckled and barred blackish and white, underparts white with dark grey and blackish streaks and speckles along malar line and across breast, and blackish bars on flanks. Has uneven tufted crest, often with some pale, washed-out chestnut markings on malar area and breast. In flight, wings appear rather uniform with white underwing-coverts. (**b**) **Female**: Underwing-coverts pale rufous; tends to lack pale chestnut markings on underparts. **Juvenile**: Similar to female but sides of neck, breast, flanks and undertail-coverts washed with pale rufous. **VOICE** Loud squeaky *aick* or indignant *kek*, particularly in flight; rapidly repeated raucous grating notes. **HABITAT** Large streams, medium-sized rivers, lakes, in or near forested areas; up to 1,830 m. **RANGE** Sc/un **R** Myanmar, W,NW Thailand, Laos, Vietnam (except Cochinchina).

8 PIED KINGFISHER *Ceryle rudis* 27–30.5 cm
(**a,b**) **Male** *leucomelanura*: Complex black-and-white plumage, pronounced flattened crest, long white supercilium, white underparts with two black bands on side of breast. Upperwing shows large white patches on flight feathers and coverts, underwing mostly whitish, tail black with white tips and bases of outer feathers. (**c**) **Female**: Only one black breast-band. **Juvenile**: Like female but feathers of lores, throat and breast fringed brownish, breast-band greyish-black, bill shorter. **VOICE** High-pitched, chattering, rather squeaky *kwik* or *kik*, repeated at irregular intervals, loud shrill *chirruk chirruk..* and high *TREEtiti TREEtiti..*; particularly in flight. **HABITAT & BEHAVIOUR** Rivers, canals and lakes in open country, flooded fields; up to 915 m. Often hovers above water. **RANGE** Fc **R** (except NE,S Thailand, Pen Malaysia, Singapore).

PLATE 21 KINGFISHERS

1 BANDED KINGFISHER *Lacedo pulchella* 21.5–24.5 cm
(**a**) **Male** *amabilis*: Chestnut forehead/mask, blue hindcrown and nape, and bars above. (**b**) **Female**: Rufous-and-black bars above; white below with dark-scaled breast/flanks. **Juvenile male**: Dusky scales/bars on ear-coverts/breast, brown bill with orange lower mandible and pale tip. **Juvenile female**: Heavy blackish scales/bars above; bill as juvenile male. **Other subspecies** *L.p.deignani* (S Thailand); *pulchella* (extreme S Thailand, Pen Malaysia). **VOICE** Long whistle, then <15 slow couplets: *wheeeoo chi-wiu chi-wiu chi-wiu chi-wiu...* Sharp *wiak wiak...* **HABITAT & BEHAVIOUR** Broadleaved evergreen and mixed deciduous forest, bamboo, often away from water; up to 1,100 m. Slowly raises/lowers crown. **RANGE** Fc **R** S,E(south) Myanmar, Tenasserim, Thailand (except C), Pen Malaysia, Cambodia, Laos, C,S Annam, Cochinchina.

2 BROWN-WINGED KINGFISHER *Halcyon amauroptera* 37 cm
(**a**) **Adult**: Orange-buff head/underparts, brown mantle, wings and tail. **Juvenile**: Brownish vermiculations on nape/neck, breast and flanks, narrow pale wing-covert fringes. **VOICE** Loud, tremulous, descending *tree treew-treew*. Deep *cha-cha-cha-cha...* Cackles like Stork-billed. **HABITAT** Mangroves, mainly old growth. **RANGE** Fc/lc coastal **R** SW,S Myanmar, Tenasserim, west S Thailand, north-west Pen Malaysia (islands only).

3 STORK-BILLED KINGFISHER *H.capensis* 37.5–41 cm
(**a**) **Male** *burmanica*: Huge red bill, pale brown crown/head-sides, greenish-blue above, buffy below. **Female**: Duller above. **Juvenile**: Brownish-vermiculated nape/neck/breast and flanks. (**b**) **Male** *malaccensis* (S Thailand southward): Darker crown and head-sides, bluer (less turquoise) upperparts, wings and tail. **VOICE** Territorial call is melancholy whistled *iuu-iuu iuu-iuu iuu-iuu iuu-iuu..* (*i* higher); often in duet with rasping calls. Loud *tree-trew* (*trew* lower) and explosive cackling *kek-ek-ek-ek...* **HABITAT** Rivers and large waterbodies in/near broadleaved evergreen and mixed deciduous forest, mangroves (particularly outside range of Brown-winged); up to 800 m. **RANGE** Un/lc **R** (except W,E Tonkin, N Annam).

4 RUDDY KINGFISHER *Halcyon coromanda* 26.5–27 cm
(**a**) **Adult** *coromanda*: Bright rufous; violet-tinged above, bluish-white lower back/rump-patch, red bill. (**b**) **Juvenile**: Much browner above, narrow dark bars below, browner bill; back/rump brilliant blue (less whitish). **Other subspecies** *H.c.minor* (**R** S Thailand southwards): Darker above, much darker below, breast violet-tinged, rump-patch larger. **VOICE** Territorial call is hoarse tremulous *tyuurrrrr* or *quirrr-r-r-r-r*. **HABITAT** Mangroves, island forests, broadleaved evergreen forest near water; up to 900 m. **RANGE** Un **R** W,SE,S Thailand, Pen Malaysia, Singapore. Un **BV** N,C Annam. Un **WV** and **PM** S Thailand, Pen Malaysia, Singapore (ra). Un **PM** NW,NE,C Thailand, N,C Laos, E Tonkin (breeds?). **Rc** (status?) C,S,E Myanmar, Tenasserim, Cambodia (**R** in some coastal areas?).

5 WHITE-THROATED KINGFISHER *H.smyrnensis* 28.5 cm
(**a,b**) **Adult** *perpulchra*: Dark chestnut head/belly, white throat and breast, turquoise above, chestnut and black coverts; whitish wing-patch. **Juvenile**: Duller above, dark-vermiculated throat and breast, browner bill. **VOICE** Whinnying *klilililililili* territorial call. Shrill staccato, descending laughter: *chake ake ake-ake-ake-ake...* **HABITAT** Open habitats, cultivation; up to 1,525 m. **RANGE** Co **R** (some dispersive movements) throughout.

6 BLACK-CAPPED KINGFISHER *H.pileata* 29–31.5 cm
(**a,b**) **Adult**: Black crown/head-sides, white collar, throat and breast, deep blue above with mostly black wing-coverts, red bill; whitish wing-patch. **Juvenile**: Blue parts duller, small rufous-buff loral spot, collar buff-tinged, dark vermiculations on throat-/breast-sides (former sometimes streaked), brownish-orange bill. **VOICE** Ringing, cackling *kikikikikiki..*, higher than similar call of White-throated. **HABITAT** Mangroves, sea coasts, various inland and coastal wetlands, gardens; up to 1,525 m (mostly lowlands). **RANGE** Fc/co **WV** throughout. Also **PM** E Tonkin, Pen Malaysia. **Rc** in summer Pen Malaysia, Singapore. Said to breed (but doubtful) SW,N Myanmar, N Laos.

7 COLLARED KINGFISHER *Todiramphus chloris* 24–26 cm
(**a**) **Adult** *armstrongi*: Blue above with turquoise wash, whitish collar/underparts/loral supercilium, faint creamy-buffish flank-wash. **Juvenile**: Duller/greener above, buff wing-covert fringes, dark-vermiculated collar/breast, often a buffy-brown tinge on collar, breast-sides and flanks. **Other subspecies** *T.c.humii* (Myanmar and S Thailand southwards): Bluer above. *T.c.davisoni* (Coco Is): Smaller; blackish-green head-sides, dusky-olive upper mantle, buff-tinged below. **VOICE** Loud shrieking *kick kyew, kick kyew..* (*kick* rising, *kyew* falling). Loud shrill *krerk krerk krerk krerk..* or *kek-kek-kek-kek..*, often ending with *jee-jaw* notes. **HABITAT** Mangroves, coastal wetland habitats, cultivation, gardens, parks, sometimes large rivers, marshes; lowlands (to 1,300 m on migration). **RANGE** Co coastal **R** (except E Tonkin, N Annam). Locally inland NE Thailand, Pen Malaysia and along Mekong R in Cambodia, Cochinchina; formerly C,S Laos. Also **PM** Pen Malaysia. **Rc** (status?) E Tonkin.

8 SACRED KINGFISHER *Todiramphus sanctus* 18–23 cm
(**a**) **Adult** *sanctus*: Smaller than Collared, blackish-green head-sides (but see *T.c.davisoni*), distinctly buff supercilium, clearly buff-washed nape and flanks. **Juvenile**: From Collared as adult. **VOICE** Rapid short high, usually 4–5 noted *ki-ki-ki-ki* or high squealing, reeling, usually 1–4 noted *schssk-schssk-schssk*, and low squealing *kreee-el kreee-el kreee-el*. **HABITAT** Mangroves, more open coastal habitats, cultivation, gardens; lowlands. **RANGE** **V** Singapore (sight record).

9 RUFOUS-COLLARED KINGFISHER *Actenoides concretus* 25 cm
(**a**) **Male** *concretus*: Green crown, black and blue head-stripes, rufous collar and breast. (**b**) **Female**: Dull green above, buffy-speckled coverts. **Juvenile**: Brownish bill with yellowish tip/base; male has bold mantle-spots. **Other subspecies** *A.c.peristephes* (Tenasserim, S Thailand to Trang). **VOICE** Rising whistles: *kwi-i kwi-i kw-i kw-i kw-i..* (c.1 per s). Series of softer *kwi-irr* notes. **HABITAT** Broadleaved evergreen forest, near water; up to 1,200 m. **RANGE** Sc/un **R** south Tenasserim, W(south),S Thailand, Pen Malaysia. **Frc** Singapore.

PLATE 22 *CLAMATOR* & HAWK CUCKOOS & CORAL-BILLED GROUND CUCKOO

1 PIED CUCKOO *Clamator jacobinus* 31.5–33 cm
(**a**) **Adult** *jacobinus*: Black hindneck/wings, all-white below, white wing marking and broad outertail-tips. (**b**) **Juvenile**: Browner above, throat/breast initially dull greyish, rest of underparts tinged buff, crest shorter, bill browner with yellow-based lower mandible; narrow whitish wing feather tips. VOICE Frequently repeated loud ringing **kleeuw kleeuw kleeuw kleeuw..**; sometimes preceded by shrill **kiu-kewkew..kiu-kewkewkew..kiu-kewkew...** Male often adds fast short rising notes: **kwik-kwik-kwek**. Also, abrupt **kweek**. HABITAT Open deciduous woodland, scrub, cultivation; lowlands. RANGE Fc **BV** C,S Myanmar. Ra **PM** SW Myanmar. **V** NW,C,S Thailand.

2 CHESTNUT-WINGED CUCKOO *Clamator coromandus* 38–41.5 cm
(**a**) **Adult**: Blackish above, white collar, chestnut wings, buffy-rufous throat, dark vent, thin white outertail-tips. (**b**) **Juvenile**: Dark greenish-brown above, buffish tips on upperparts/wings, buffy collar, whitish throat, short crest, paler bill. VOICE Metallic whistled **thu-thu...thu-thu...thu-thu..** territorial call (notes less spaced than Moustached Hawk Cuckoo). Grating **critititi-tit**. HABITAT Second growth, scrub, thickets when breeding, also broadleaved evergreen forest and mangroves when not; up to 1,525 m. RANGE Un **BV** Myanmar (except S,Tenasserim), W,NW,NE,C(some winter?) Thailand, Laos, E Tonkin, N,C Annam. Un **BV/R** S Myanmar, Cambodia, Cochinchina. Sc/un **WV** and **PM** S Thailand, Pen Malaysia, Singapore. Also **PM** C Thailand. **Rc** (status?) Tenasserim, SE Thailand, S Annam.

3 LARGE HAWK CUCKOO *Hierococcyx sparverioides* 40 cm
(**a**) **Adult** *sparverioides*: Slaty-grey on head, brownish-grey on upperparts, extensively dark chin, dark rufous breast-patch, obvious dark streaks on lower throat/breast, dark-barred lower breast/belly/flanks, broad dark tail-bands. Underwing-coverts white with dark brown bars. (**b**) **Juvenile**: Dark brown above with rufous bars, pale rufous nape with dark brown streaks, white below with buffish wash and bold drop-like breast-streaks, then bars on belly/flanks. (**c**) **Immature/subadult**: Greyish-brown crown, dull pale rufous bars above, more like juvenile below but pale rufous breast-patch. Larger than adult Hodgson's (*C.f.fugax*), narrower penultimate dark tail-band, narrow greyish band between that and last dark tail-band, buffier tail-tip (very tip narrowly whitish), more dark on chin, heavier throat-streaks; flanks tend to be barred. **Other subspecies** *H.s.bocki* (resident Pen Malaysia): c.33 cm; dark streaks below restricted to breast, broad orange-rufous breast-band. VOICE Very loud, shrill, spaced, stressed **pwi pwee-wru** (*sparverioides*) or **pi-phu** (*bocki*), repeated on rising pitch to screaming crescendo (territorial). Secondary call (*bocki*) is rapid, more hurried **pipi-pipi-pipi-pipi..** or **phuphu-phuphu..**, rising to fever-pitch, then fading. HABITAT Broadleaved evergreen and deciduous forest, more open habitats, gardens, mangroves etc. on migration; up to 2,565 m (mainly breeds above 650 m). RANGE Fc **R** (some movements) Myanmar (except S and southern Tenasserim), W,NW,NE Thailand, Cambodia, Laos, W,E Tonkin. Sc/un **WV** W,C,NE,SE,S Thailand, Pen Malaysia, Cochinchina; ?Cambodia. Also **PM** S Thailand, **Rc** (status?) S Myanmar, N,C,S Annam. **V** Singapore.

4 COMMON HAWK CUCKOO *Hierococcyx varius* 33–37 cm
(**a**) **Adult**: Ashier-grey above than Large, less blackish chin, rufous below paler/more extensive, less markings below, narrower dark tail-bands. (**b**) **Juvenile**: Fainter markings below than Large, narrower tail-bands. (**c**) **Immature/subadult**: Differs from Large as juvenile. VOICE 4–6 loud shrieking **wee-piwhit** (**piw** stressed) phrases, progressing to frantic shrillness, and ending abruptly. Female utters a strident trilling scream. HABITAT Open deciduous forest, secondary growth; up to 915 m. RANGE Fc **R** SW Myanmar; **V** south W Thailand.

5 MOUSTACHED HAWK CUCKOO *H.vagans* 28–30 cm
(**a**) **Adult**: Dark moustachial/cheek-stripe, whitish upper throat and centre of ear-coverts. Slaty crown/nape, creamy-whitish below with dark streaks; white-tipped tail. **Juvenile**: Probably like adult, but brownish crown/nape. VOICE Loud, well-spaced, monotonously repeated **chu-chu** (territorial). Secondary call is ascending mellow notes, singly after short intervals, then paired and accelerating to fever-pitch. HABITAT Broadleaved evergreen forest, secondary growth; up to 915 m. RANGE Un **R** Tenasserim, W(south),SE,S Thailand, Pen Malaysia, S Laos.

6 MALAYSIAN HAWK CUCKOO *Hierococcyx fugax* 29 cm
(**a**) **Adult**: All-dark head-side, dark chin, mostly pale chestnut tail-tip (very tip narrowly whitish); even tail-bars. (**b**) **Juvenile**: Dark brown above with faint pale fringing, white on nape-side, spot-streaks below. VOICE Shrill high **pi-pwik** or **pi-pwit** phrases, then rapid **ti-tu-tu** phrases, accelerating/ascending to shrill crescendo climax/es; followed by slower **tu-tu-tu-tu..**, before tailing off. HABITAT Broadleaved evergreen forest; to 250 m. RANGE Un **R** (some movements) Tenasserim, S Thailand, Pen Malaysia.

7 HODGSON'S HAWK CUCKOO *H.nisicolor* 27–29.5 cm
(**a**) **Adult**: Greyer above than Malaysian, no rufous bars on wing, inner tertial usually whiter, pinkish-rufous on breast (quite uniform if fine-streaked), penultimate dark tail-band is narrowest. (**b**) **Juvenile**: Warmer/buffier fringes above than Malaysian, usually paler innermost tertial. VOICE Like Malaysian, but followed by rapid **trrrrr-titititititrrrrtrrr...** HABITAT Broadleaved forest; up to 1,550 m (**B** above 500 m). RANGE Un **R/BV** S,E Myanmar, Thailand (except C,S), N,C Laos, W Tonkin, C Annam. Un **WV** and **PM** S Thailand, Pen Malaysia, Singapore. Sc/un **PM** W,C Thailand, Cochinchina. **Rc** (status?) Cambodia, S Laos, E Tonkin, `N,S Annam. NOTE Recently split from *fugax* (see King 2002).

8 CORAL-BILLED GROUND CUCKOO *Carpococcyx renauldi* 69 cm
(**a**) **Adult**: Greyish, with blackish hood/primaries/tail. Fine dark vermiculations on pale underside, red bill and legs, violet and red facial skin. (**b**) **Juvenile**: Browner hood, greenish- and purple-tinged dull brown above, rufescent-tipped scapulars/wing feathers, drab rufous-chestnut throat/breast. Facial skin greyish, legs dark brownish. VOICE Loud moaning **woaaaah** or **wohaaau** (territorial male). Loud rolling **wh ohh-whaaaaohu**. Grumbling **grrrro grrrro..** and **grrroah grrroah...** HABITAT Broadleaved evergreen forest; up to 1,000 m (rarely 1,500 m). RANGE Sc/lfc **R** NW,NE,SE Thailand, Cambodia, N(south),C,S Laos, E(south) Tonkin, N,C Annam.

3–7 to different scale

PLATE 23 *CUCULUS* CUCKOOS, DRONGO CUCKOO & ASIAN KOEL

1 INDIAN CUCKOO *Cuculus micropterus* 31–33 cm
(**a**) **Male** *micropterus*: Brownish tinge to mantle, wings and tail, prominent broad dark subterminal tail-band, dull yellowish to greyish-green eyering. (**b**) **Female**: Rufescent wash across breast. (**c**) **Juvenile**: Crown and head-sides browner than adult, with very broad buffish-white feather-tips, prominent rufous/buffish to whitish feather-tips above, buffish below with broken dark bars; may have rufous-washed throat/breast. **Other subspecies** *C.m.concretus* (resident extreme S Thailand southwards): Smaller and darker-toned. **VOICE** Male territorial call is loud *whi-whi-whi-wu* or *wa-wa-wa-wu*, with lower last note or alternating high and low (may omit last note). Loud hurried bubbling (female only?). **HABITAT** Broadleaved evergreen and deciduous forest; up to 1,830 m (below 760 m Pen Malaysia). **RANGE** Fc/co **R** (except C,SE Thailand, Singapore). Fc **WV** and **PM** W,C,S Thailand, Pen Malaysia, Singapore.

2 EURASIAN CUCKOO *Cuculus canorus* 32.5–34.5 cm
(**a**) **Male** *bakeri*: Hard to tell from Oriental but usually slightly larger, with cleaner white underparts, often with somewhat fainter (less blackish) and sometimes narrower bars, has grey bars on white leading edge of wing (difficult to see in field); typically shows whitish undertail-coverts with prominent blackish bars. **Female:** If present, rufous-buff wash across grey of upper breast usually less extensive than on Oriental. (**b**) **Female hepatic morph**: Rufescent-brown head/upperparts, buffy-rufous throat/breast, white lower underparts, strong blackish-brown bars overall; narrower than on Oriental (particularly back to uppertail and breast). (**c**) **Juvenile**: Dark head and upperside with whitish fringing, white nuchal patch (fresh plumage). Usually more narrowly barred below than Oriental. (**d**) **Juvenile female hepatic morph**: Whitish fringing on upperside, white nuchal patch (fresh plumage). More narrowly barred above than Oriental, and less warm buffish below with less prominent dark bars. **VOICE** Territorial call is loud mellow *cuc-coo* (*coo* lower-pitched). Loud bubbling trill. **HABITAT** Open broadleaved evergreen forest, secondary growth; more open habitats on migration; up to 2,195 m (probably only breeds above 600 m). **RANGE** Un **BV** W,N,C,E Myanmar, N Laos, W,E Tonkin. Sc/un **PM** SW Myanmar. **Rc** (status?) S Myanmar, Tenasserim, NW Thailand (breeds?), C Annam (breeds?).

3 ORIENTAL CUCKOO *Cuculus saturatus* 29.5–32.5 cm
(**a**) **Male** *saturatus*: Like Eurasian but typically buff-tinged below, often somewhat blacker and sometimes slightly broader bars; plain buffish-white/whitish leading edge of wing (hard to see in field), typically less obvious/no blackish bars on undertail-coverts. **Female**: Like male but usually has rufous-buff wash across grey of upper breast, typically more extensive than on female Eurasian. (**b**) **Female hepatic morph**: Similar to Eurasian (see that species). (**c**) **Juvenile**: Like Eurasian but usually broader dark bars below. (**d**) **Juvenile female hepatic morph**: Warmer buffish below than Eurasian, broader dark barring overall. **Other subspecies** *C.s.lepidus* (resident Pen Malaysia): 26 cm; darker, tends to have buffier undertail-coverts. **VOICE** Male territorial call is loud mellow 2–4 note *kuk..PUP-PUP-PUP* or *kuk..HU-HU-HU* (*kuk* softer, shorter). Rapid

uneven *wuk-wuk-wuk-wuk-wuk-wuk-uk...* (female only?). **HABITAT** Broadleaved evergreen forest, open wooded country; up to 2,030 m (breeds above 800 m). **RANGE** Fc **R** Pen Malaysia. Un/fc **BV** W,N Myanmar, N,C Laos, W Tonkin. Sc/un **PM** C,S Myanmar, Tenasserim, Thailand, Pen Malaysia. Cambodia, E Tonkin, S Annam. **V** Singapore.

4 LESSER CUCKOO *Cuculus poliocephalus* 26–26.5 cm
(**a**) **Male**: Smaller than Oriental, darker rump and uppertail-coverts (less contrast), usually buffier below, with wider-spaced and bolder black bars. (**b**) **Female hepatic morph**: Typically hepatic but can resemble male. Usually more rufous than Oriental, can have almost plain crown/nape and rump/uppertail-coverts. (**c**) **Juvenile**: Dark grey-brown above with narrow whitish/rufous bars and whitish nape-spots. Crown/head-sides and mantle darker/more uniform than Oriental, whiter below with bolder bars. (**d**) **Juvenile female hepatic morph**: More prominent bars on crown and mantle, white on nape. **VOICE** Territorial males call with 5–6 loud shrill whistled notes: even *wit-wit-witi-wit wit-wit-witi-wit wit-wit-witi-wit..* (*witi* prolonged and stressed) or rising and falling *wit,it-iti-witu wit,it-iti-witu wit,it-iti-witu...* Starts higher, then gets slower and deeper or lower-pitched. **HABITAT** Broadleaved evergreen forest, deciduous forest on migration; 915–2,285 m (can be lower on migration). **RANGE** Sc/un **BV** W,N Myanmar, NW Thailand, N Laos, W,E Tonkin. Sc/un **PM** C Myanmar. **Rc** (status?) S(east) Myanmar, C Annam, Cochinchina.

Thailand + Laos RNW

5 DRONGO CUCKOO *Surniculus lugubris* 24.5 cm
(**a**) **Adult** *dicruroides*: Glossy black, forked tail, typical cuckoo bill, white-barred undertail/undertail-coverts; some white on nape (often hidden). (**b**) **Juvenile**: Browner; white spots on body and coverts. **Other subspecies** *S.l.brachyurus* (southern S Thailand southwards). **VOICE** Fairly quick, steadily rising, 5–7 note *pi pi pi pi pi..* (territorial). Secondary call is shrill *phew phew phewphewphewphewphew phew phew...*, speeding up/rising, then falling. **HABITAT** Broadleaved forest, secondary growth, occasionally parks, gardens, mangroves etc. (mainly on migration); up to 1,300 m. **RANGE** Fc **R** throughout. **BV** to some northern areas? Un **WV** C(south),S Thailand, Pen Malaysia, Singapore; probably Cochinchina. Un **PM** S Thailand, Pen Malaysia, Singapore, E Tonkin.

6 ASIAN KOEL *Eudynamys scolopacea* 40–44 cm
(**a**) **Male** *chinensis*: Glossy black, greenish bill, red eye. (**b**) **Female**: Mostly streaked/spotted/barred whitish. (**c**) **Juvenile**: White/buff tips on brownish-black upperside, warm brown tail-bars, white/buff belly/vent-bars. (**d**) **Female** *malayana* (**R** W,C Myanmar and W[south],C,SE Thailand southwards): Usually rufous/buff markings. **VOICE** Territorial call is very loud *ko-EL*, repeated with increasing emphasis. Secondary call is descending, bubbling *wreep-wreep-wreep-wreep-wreepwreep-wreep...* **HABITAT** Open woodland, secondary growth, cultivated areas, parks, gardens; up to 1,220 m. **RANGE** Fc/co **R**, subject to some movements (except W,E Tonkin). **BV** to some northern areas? Un/fc **WV** and **PM** S Thailand, Pen Malaysia, Singapore. Fc **PM** E Tonkin. **Rc** (status?) W Tonkin.

1a

1b

1c

2b

2d

2c

2a

3a

4d

4a

4c

4b

3b

3c

3d

6b

6d

5 to different scale

5a

5b

6a

6c

PLATE 24 SMALLER CUCKOOS

1 BANDED BAY CUCKOO *Cacomantis sonneratii* 23–24 cm
(**a**) **Adult** *sonneratii*: Like hepatic female Plaintive but dark mask isolated by broad supercilium; whiter below with narrower bars. (**b**) **Juvenile**: Whitish to pale buff bars on head-sides/upperparts, weaker mask, coarser and more spaced dark barring. **Other subspecies** *C.s.malayanus* (Tenasserim and S Thailand southwards): Smaller, more rufescent. **VOICE** Male utters repeated loud *pi,bi-bi-bi* or *pibu-bibu* on descending scale. Secondary calls include rapid *pi pi pibibi-pi pibibi-pi* on rising scale. **HABITAT** Broadleaved forests; up to 1,500 m. **RANGE** Un/fc **R** (except C Thailand, W Tonkin).

2 GREY-BELLIED CUCKOO *Cacomantis passerinus* 22–23 cm
(**a**) **Male**: Grey with white vent. (**b**) **Female hepatic morph**: Mostly plain rufescent crown, mantle, rump to uppertail, throat and upper breast. **Female grey morph**: Slightly paler than male. (**c**) **Juvenile male**: Darker/browner above and on throat/breast, with fine pale fringing. (**d**) **Juvenile female hepatic morph**: No distinct tail-bars, mostly plain rump and uppertail-coverts, dark breast. **VOICE** Loud clear *phi phi phi wi-wibi* or *phi phi phi wi-hi*, (*phi*'s stressed) from males. Clear *peee peee peee-tcho-cho....peee-tcho-cho..* and *pi-pipee pi-pipee pi-pipee* secondary calls. **HABITAT** Secondary growth, open woodland, scrub and grass, cultivation; up to 1,800 m. **RANGE** Rc N Myanmar (probably in error).

3 PLAINTIVE CUCKOO *Cacomantis merulinus* 21.5–23.5 cm
(**a**) **Male** *querulus*: Grey hood, peachy-rufous below. (**b**) **Female hepatic morph**: Usually in this plumage but can resemble male. Rufescent with even blackish barring, paler with duller barring below, faint supercilium, barred tail. (**c**) **Female hepatic morph variant**: Whiter below, more evenly barred. (**d**) **Juvenile**: Paler/buffier than hepatic female, whiter below, prominent blackish streaks on crown to upper mantle, throat and upper breast. **Other subspecies** *C.m.threnodes* (Pen Malaysia, Singapore): Smaller/paler; male with more contrasting head. **VOICE** Male territorial call is clear high whistled *phi phi phi phi phi phi-pipipi*, hurried/fading at end. Secondary call is ascending *pii-pi-pui....pii-pi-pui..pii-pi-pui..* (accelerates and sounds more agitated). **HABITAT** Secondary growth, open woodlands, scrub, grassland, cultivation, parks, gardens; up to 1,830 m. **RANGE** Co **R** throughout (sc Singapore).

4 RUSTY-BREASTED CUCKOO *Cacomantis sepulcralis* 21–24 cm
(**a**) **Adult** *sepulcralis*: Slightly slatier-grey than male Plaintive, entirely peachy-rufous underparts, yellow eyering. (**b**) **Adult hepatic morph**: Rare (only females?). Slightly larger/longer-tailed than hepatic female Plaintive, much broader blackish bars on upperside, throat and breast, rufous bars limited to notches along outertail feather-fringes. (**c**) **Juvenile**: More uniformly dark above than hepatic adult, with narrow/rather broken buffish/rufous barring. **VOICE** Male utters even, melancholy, gradually descending 6–15 note *whi whi whi whi whi...* Secondary call is accelerating series of *whi-wibu* or *whi-w'bu* phrases. **HABITAT** Broadleaved evergreen forest, secondary growth, mangroves, sometimes gardens; up to 600 m. **RANGE** Un **R** W(south),S Thailand, Pen Malaysia, Singapore.

5 LITTLE BRONZE CUCKOO *Chrysococcyx minutillus* 16 cm
(**a**) **Male** *peninsularis*: Black bill, red eyering, pale forehead, dark ear-patch, quite plain above, glossy bottle-green crown, bronzy-green mantle. (**b**) **Female**: Duller crown, less bronzy mantle, less pale on forehead, dull eyering. (**c**) **Juvenile**: Like female but duller/browner above, almost uniform greyish- to brownish-white below. **VOICE** Descending thin, tremulous 3–5 note *eug eug eug eug..* (territorial); rising, screeching *wireeg-reeg-reeg* sometimes admixed. Secondary call is high, drawn, descending trill. **HABITAT** Mangroves, secondary growth; locally parks, gardens; up to 250 m. **RANGE** Sc/fc **R** W(south),S Thailand, Pen Malaysia, Singapore, Cambodia, Cochinchina.

6 HORSFIELD'S BRONZE CUCKOO *Chrysococcyx basalis* 16 cm
(**a**) **Adult**: Like Little Bronze but browner above, dark forehead, plainer supercilium, brownish-white fringing on scapulars/coverts, brownish throat-streaks, plain belly-centre, more rufous-chestnut on outertail. **Juvenile**: Unlikely to occur. Like Little but crown/mantle usually greyer-brown, forehead dark, bolder brownish-white/buffish fringing above, plain rufous-chestnut on basal half of outertail. **VOICE** Incessantly repeated, descending *tseeeuw* from male. **HABITAT** Secondary growth, open woodland, mangroves. **RANGE** Late summer **V** Singapore.

7 ASIAN EMERALD CUCKOO *Chrysococcyx maculatus* 17 cm
(**a**) **Male**: Glossy gold-tinged emerald-green; white-barred from lower breast to vent, dark-tipped yellowish bill. (**b**) **Female**: Plain rufous crown/nape, coppery-green above, all-barred below. (**c**) **Juvenile**: Less green above than female, with rufous feather-tips and dark and buff bars on crown to mantle, dark tail with more rufous/no white on outer feathers and less white at tip; darker bill, rufous throat/breast-wash. **VOICE** Loud, descending 3–4 note *kee-kee-kee..* (male). Sharp *chweek* or *chut-week* in flight. **HABITAT** Broadleaved evergreen forest, plantations and gardens on passage/in winter; up to 2,440 m (breeds above 600 m?). **RANGE** Un **R** Myanmar, W,NW Thailand, N,C Annam. Un **WV** Thailand, Cambodia, C,S Laos, S Annam, Cochinchina; parts of Myanmar? Rc (status?) N Laos, W,E Tonkin. **V** Pen Malaysia, Singapore.

8 VIOLET CUCKOO *Chrysococcyx xanthorhynchus* 16–17 cm
(**a**) **Male** *xanthorhynchus*: Glossy violet-purple, white-barred lower breast to vent, red-based orange bill. (**b**) **Female**: Browner above than Asian Emerald, mostly bronzy-brown crown/nape, red-based yellowish bill. (**c**) **Juvenile**: Darker than Asian Emerald, more rufous-chestnut base colour to crown/nape, bold rufous-chestnut and dark greenish bars above, rufous-chestnut fringes to flight feathers, no rufous wash on throat/breast. **VOICE** Loud, sharp, spaced *tee-wit* during undulating flight. Secondary call is shrill accelerating, descending trill preceded by triple note: *seer-se-seer, seeseeseesee*. **HABITAT** Broadleaved forests, sometimes parks and gardens during movements; up to 1,100 m (mainly breeds below 600 m). Often in canopy of tall trees. **RANGE** Sc/fc **R** (some movements) W,S,E Myanmar, Tenasserim, W,NW,NE(south-west),SE,S Thailand, Pen Malaysia, Singapore, Cambodia, S Laos, Cochinchina. Sc **WV** C Thailand. Rc (status?) south N Laos.

PLATE 25 MALKOHAS & COUCALS

1 BLACK-BELLIED MALKOHA *Phaenicophaeus diardi* 37 cm
(**a**) **Adult** *diardi*: Smaller and shorter-tailed than Green-billed, darker throat/breast, no whitish facial skin border, narrower white tail-tips. **Juvenile**: Browner crown/mantle, whiter unstreaked throat, smaller/darker bill, brown eyes. VOICE Gruff *gwaup*, quicker *gwagaup*, emphatic *pauk*. HABITAT Broadleaved evergreen forest, secondary growth, plantations; up to 1,220 m. RANGE Fc/co **R** south Tenasserim, W(south),S Thailand, Pen Malaysia; formerly Singapore.

2 CHESTNUT-BELLIED MALKOHA *Phaenicophaeus sumatranus* 40–41 cm
(**a**) **Adult** *sumatranus*: Chestnut belly and vent, orangey facial skin. **Juvenile**: Less white on tail-tip. VOICE Low *tok..tok...* Thin mewing. HABITAT Mangroves, broadleaved evergreen forest, locally old plantations; up to 1,005 m. RANGE Un **R** south Tenasserim, W(local),S Thailand, Pen Malaysia, Singapore.

3 GREEN-BILLED MALKOHA *Phaenicophaeus tristis* 52–59.5 cm
(**a**) **Adult** *longicaudatus*: Large, long-tailed; greyish head and underparts with dark shaft-streaks, dark vent, white-edged red facial skin, green bill. Greyish-green above, tail feathers broadly tipped white. (**b**) **Juvenile**: Browner-tinged above, browner vent, blacker bill, duller face skin with less defined border. **Other subspecies** *P.t.tristis* (W Myanmar); *saliens* (N, north E Myanmar, east NW Thailand, north Indochina). VOICE Mellow, slightly nasal, spaced *oh...oh...oh...oh..* (territorial). Typically a clucking, croaking *ko..ko..ko..*, sometimes with added gruff flurry: *co-co-co-co...* Harsh chuckles in alarm. HABITAT & BEHAVIOUR Broadleaved forests, secondary growth, bamboo, plantations; up to 1,600 m. Forages slowly amongst dense foliage. RANGE Co **R** (except south Pen Malaysia, Singapore).

4 RAFFLES'S MALKOHA *Phaenicophaeus chlorophaeus* 35 cm
(**a**) **Male** *chlorophaeus*: Rufous head/breast, rufous-chestnut above, black tail with bronzey bars and white tip. Blackish back, rump and tail-coverts, greyish belly. (**b**) **Female**: Grey hood, rufous-chestnut tail with black subterminal band and white tip, buffy belly. VOICE Strained descending *kiau...kiau...kiau..* (3–6 notes). 1–2 hoarse strained *beeah* or *baaeew* notes. Strained croaking. HABITAT Broadleaved evergreen forest, forest edge, sometimes plantations; up to 975 m. RANGE Fc/co **R** south Tenasserim, W,S Thailand, Pen Malaysia; formerly Singapore.

5 RED-BILLED MALKOHA *Phaenicophaeus javanicus* 45–45.5 cm
(**a**) **Adult** *pallidus*: Red bill, blue orbital skin, rufous throat and upper breast, chestnut vent, otherwise pale greyish below. **Juvenile**: Tail feathers with less white at tip, primary coverts washed rufous, with pale fringes. VOICE Hard, frog-like *uc...uc...uc... uc..* (may quicken to flurry). HABITAT Broadleaf evergreen forest, secondary growth; up to 1,200 m. RANGE Fc/co **R** south Tenasserim, south W,S Thailand, Pen Malaysia.

6 CHESTNUT-BREASTED MALKOHA *P.curvirostris* 45–46 cm
(**a**) **Male** *singularis*: Chestnut throat/breast and tail-tip, pale yellowish/greenish and red bill, blue eyes. **Female**: Yellow to whitish eyes. **Juvenile**: Less facial skin, darker bill, brown/grey eyes, less chestnut on tail. VOICE Clucking *kuk...kuk...kuk..*, faster *kok-kok-kok..* in alarm, harsh, cat-like *miaou*. HABITAT Broadleaved evergreen forest, sometimes mangroves, mature plantations and gardens; up to 975 m. RANGE Fc/co **R** south Tenasserim, W,S Thailand, Pen Malaysia.

7 SHORT-TOED COUCAL *Centropus rectunguis* 37 cm
(**a**) **Adult**: Smaller/shorter-tailed than Greater, black underwing-coverts. (**b**) **Juvenile**: Black-barred chestnut-brown crown/mantle, thin blackish bars on tertials/coverts, dark brown below with whitish/buff bars and streaks, browner bill. VOICE Slow deep, melancholy, somewhat descending 4–5 note *whu huup-huup-huup-huup*. Sometimes more rapid series on rising scale. HABITAT Broadleaved evergreen forest; up to 600 m. RANGE Sc/un **R** extreme S Thailand, Pen Malaysia.

8 GREATER COUCAL *Centropus sinensis* 48–52 cm
(**a**) **Adult** *intermedius*: Large; glossy black, plain chestnut back/wings. (**b**) **Juvenile**: Duller above with blackish bars; otherwise blackish with whitish streaks/flecks, buffish-barred lower body, brownish-/greyish-white tail-bars, paler bill. **Other subspecies** *C.s.bubutus* (south Pen Malaysia, Singapore). VOICE Territorial call is loud deep, mournful *puup puup puup puup..* or *wuup-uup-uup-uup-uupuupuupuupuup* (latter speeding-up/ascending, then lower and more even; or ascending scale again). Scolding, hissing *shaeoooo*. HABITAT Open forest, secondary growth, scrub, mangroves; up to 1,525 m. RANGE Co **R** throughout (un Singapore).

9 BROWN COUCAL *Centropus andamanensis* 45.5–48.5 cm
(**a**) **Adult**: Buffy greyish-brown head/mantle/underparts, duller vent, dark reddish-chestnut back/wings, dark brownish tail (often shading paler basally). **Juvenile**: Faintly barred paler and darker on supercilium, head-sides and underparts. May differ more during early stages. VOICE Very deep, resonant *boop* notes, running down and up scale, often followed by more *boop* notes (territorial). Single *tok*, scolding cat-like *skaaah*. HABITAT Forest edge, mangroves, plantations, gardens, cultivation. RANGE **R** Great and Little Coco Is and Table I (S Myanmar).

10 LESSER COUCAL *Centropus bengalensis* 38 cm
(**a**) **Adult breeding** *bengalensis*: Relatively dull; pale streaks on head, neck and upperparts. (**b**) **Adult non-breeding**: Dark brown head/upperparts, with whitish-buff streaks, dull buff below with dark bars and whitish-buff shaft-streaks; pale bill. (**c**) **Juvenile**: More rufous above than adult non-breeding, blackish bars on upperside, warmer below with broader dark bars; long uppertail-coverts (also adult non-breeding). **Other subspecies** *C.b.javanensis* (S Thailand southwards). VOICE Territorial call is 3–5 jolly, hollow notes, then 2–5 staccato phrases: *huup huup huup-uup tokalok-tokalok* etc. Metallic clucking, repeated quickly, then slowing and falling slightly before speeding up again and tailing off: *thicthicthicthicthicthicthic-thuc-thuc-thuc-thuc-thuc-thuc-thuc-thuc-thuc-thuc-thuc-thuc-thuc-thucthucucucucuc...* HABITAT & BEHAVIOUR Grassland, including marshy areas, scrub; up to 1,830 m. Secretive but often ascends grass stems or bushes. RANGE Fc/co **R** throughout. Un **WV** northern Thailand? Un **PM** E Tonkin, N Annam.

PLATE 26 BEE-EATERS & SMALL PARROTS

1 RED-BEARDED BEE-EATER *Nyctyornis amictus* 32–35 cm
(a) **Male**: Shaggy red beard, purplish-pink forecrown, broad black undertail-tip. (b) **Female**: Like male but forehead usually red. (c) **Juvenile**: Mostly green head and breast. pale bluish on lores/forehead, whiter belly/vent, duller tail with narrower terminal band. **VOICE** Loud gruff *chachachacha.., quo-qua-qua-qua* and slightly descending, chattering *kak kak-ka-ka-ka-ka...* Guttural croaking *aark, kwok* and *kwakwakoo-googoo*. **HABITAT** Broadleaved evergreen forest, rarely wooded gardens; up to 1,525 m (<1,220 m Pen Malaysia). **RANGE** Un/lc R Tenasserim, W,S Thailand, Pen Malaysia.

2 BLUE-BEARDED BEE-EATER *N.athertoni* 33–37 cm
(a) **Adult** *athertoni*: Blue forecrown and shaggy beard, green-streaked yellowish belly, golden-yellowish undertail with darker tip. **Juvenile**: Apparently some brown on crown and throat-centre, more golden-brown undertail. **VOICE** Loud, guttural croaking and harsh cackling. Purring *grrew-grrew-grrew..*, harsh *kow kow-kow kowkowkow..*, repeated *gikhu* and *gikh* etc. **HABITAT** Broadleaved evergreen, semi-evergreen and mixed deciduous forest, rarely wooded gardens; up to 2,200 m. **RANGE** Fc/co R Myanmar, Thailand (except C,S), Indochina.

3 GREEN BEE-EATER *Merops orientalis* 20 cm (prongs <6)
(a) **Adult** *ferrugeiceps*: Coppery-rufous crown/mantle, green throat, light blue chin/cheek, black gorget, mostly green tail. (b) **Juvenile**: Mostly green crown/mantle, mostly yellowish to buffish throat, no gorget, creamier belly/vent, no tail-prongs. **VOICE** Pleasant trilling *tree-tree-tree-tree..* and staccato *ti-ic* or *ti-ti-ti* in alarm. **HABITAT** Drier open country and cultivation, semi-desert, beach slacks, dunes; up to 1,600 m. **RANGE** Co R (except south Tenasserim, S Thailand, Pen Malaysia, Singapore, W,E Tonkin); some minor movements.

4 BLUE-THROATED BEE-EATER *Merops viridis* 23 cm
(prongs <9 cm more)
(a,b) **Adult** *viridis*: Dark chestnut crown/mantle, blue throat, pale blue rump/uppertail-coverts. (c) **Juvenile**: Green crown and mantle, pale chin, no tail-prongs. **VOICE** Liquid *terrip-terrip-terrip..*, faster *terrip-rrip-rrip*, deeper *trrurrip*; sharp *chip* in alarm. **HABITAT** Open country, banks of large rivers, cultivation; also forest edge and mangroves (mainly non-breeders); up to 800 m. **RANGE** Un R SE Thailand, Cambodia, S Annam, Cochinchina. Un/lc R and BV S Thailand, Pen Malaysia, Singapore. Un/lc R or BV N,C Annam. Fc/co WV and PM SE,S Thailand, Pen Malaysia, Singapore, Cambodia. Un/fc PM W,C,NE Thailand, C Laos, E Tonkin, C Annam, Cochinchina.

5 BLUE-TAILED BEE-EATER *Merops philippinus* 24 cm
(prongs <7 cm more)
(a,b) **Adult**: Bronze-green crown to back, mid-blue rump and uppertail-coverts, pale yellowish upper throat, dull chestnut wash on lower throat and upper breast. (c) **Juvenile**: Washed-out chestnut on lower throat and upper breast, more bluish-green crown and mantle, no tail-prongs. **VOICE** Loud *rillip rillip rillip..*, shorter *trrrit trrrit trrrit..*, rapid *tri-tri-trip*. Stressed *chip* and sharp *pit* notes. **HABITAT** Similar to Blue-throated; to 1,525 m (lowland breeder). **RANGE** Un/lc R (some movements) SW,S Myan-

mar, Tenasserim, W,C,SE Thailand, Pen Malaysia (Penang I only), Cambodia, S Laos, S Annam, Cochinchina. Fc **BV** W,C,N,E Myanmar, NW Thailand. Un/lc R or **BV** N,C Annam. Fc/co **WV** and **PM** Tenasserim, NE(south),S Thailand, Pen Malaysia, Singapore, Cambodia. Fc/co **PM** SW,S Myanmar, C Thailand, N Laos, E Tonkin. Rc (status?) C Laos.

6 CHESTNUT-HEADED BEE-EATER *M.leschenaulti* 21.5 cm
(a) **Adult** *leschenaulti*: Chestnut crown/mantle, blue rump and uppertail-coverts, square tail, yellow throat, chestnut and black gorget. (b) **Juvenile**: Mostly green crown/mantle, some chestnut on hindcrown/nape, faint gorget, paler below. **Other subspecies** *M.l.andamanensis* (Coco Is): Rear mask dull chestnut, some chestnut on upper breast-side. **VOICE** Bubbling *prruuip* or *djewy* etc., airy *chewy-chewy-chewy*. **HABITAT** Open broadleaved forests (often along rivers), forest edge and clearings, coastal scrub, mangroves, sometimes plantations; up to 1,830 m. **RANGE** Fc/co R (some movements) south to northern Pen Malaysia (except C[southern] Thailand, E Tonkin, N Annam). Un **BV** C(southern) Thailand, southern Pen Malaysia.

7 BLUE-RUMPED PARROT *Psittinus cyanurus* 18.5–19.5 cm
(a,b) **Male** *cyanurus*: Small, stocky; greyish-blue head, blackish mantle, yellowish-green covert-fringes; blackish underwing with largely red coverts, red and dark bill. (c) **Female**: Brown head (yellower throat), dark brown bill, green above (blue limited to back), mostly green below, smaller dark red shoulder-patch. (d) **Juvenile female**: Green crown and head-sides, little or no red shoulder-patch. Male may show blue on forehead and head-sides. **VOICE** Sharp, high *chi chi chi..* and *chew-ee* (mostly in flight). Melodious trilling. **HABITAT** Open broadleaved evergreen forest, rarely plantations, mangroves; up to 700 m, rarely 1,300 m. **RANGE** Sc/lfc R (some movements) south Tenasserim, W(south),S Thailand, Pen Malaysia, Singapore.

8 VERNAL HANGING PARROT *Loriculus vernalis* 13–15 cm
(a,b) **Male**: Very small; bright green, red back to uppertail-coverts, light blue on throat/upper breast, red bill, orangey legs; turquoise underwing with green coverts. (c) **Female**: Little/no blue on throat/breast, duller head/underparts, duller red on upperparts (some green on back/rump). **Juvenile**: Like female but back to uppertail-coverts mixed green, duller eyes and legs. **VOICE** High shrill squeaky *tsee-sip* or *pi-zeez-eet* flight-call. **HABITAT & BEHAVIOUR** Broadleaved forests, clearings; up to 1,525 m. Fast direct flight; hangs upside down. **RANGE** Co R Myanmar (except W,N), Thailand (except C), north Pen Malaysia, Indochina (except W,E Tonkin, N Annam).

9 BLUE-CROWNED HANGING PARROT *L.galgulus* 12–14.5 cm
(a) **Male**: Dark blue crown-patch, golden 'saddle', golden-yellow back-band, red on lower throat/upper breast, black bill, dark eyes, greyish-brown/yellowish legs. (b) **Female**: Duller, no red on throat, breast, less distinct colours throughout. (c) **Juvenile**: Duller than female but mantle all green; dusky bill. **VOICE** High shrill *tsi* or *tsrri*, sometimes *tsi-tsi-tsi...* **HABITAT** Broadleaved forests, clearings, wooded gardens and plantations, mangroves; up to 1,280 m. **RANGE** Fc/co R (some movements) extreme S Thailand, Pen Malaysia, Singapore (sc).

PLATE 27 COCKATOOS & PARAKEETS

1 YELLOW-CRESTED COCKATOO *Cacatua sulphurea* 34 cm (**a,b**) **Male** *sulphurea*: White; upcurved yellow crest, black bill; ear-coverts, underwing/-tail suffused yellow. **Female**: Bill slightly smaller, eyes reddish. **Juvenile**: Eyes brownish-grey, bill and legs paler. **Sulphur-crested Cockatoo** *C.galerita* (has also escaped, but not established Singapore): 50 cm; blue eyering. **VOICE** Longer/louder than Tanimbar Corella. Loud raucous screeching, various less harsh whistles/squeaks, 2–6 quite high quavering, nasal screeches. **HABITAT** Open forest, plantations, cultivation, parks, gardens. **RANGE** Sc/un **FER** Singapore.

2 TANIMBAR CORELLA *Cacatua goffini* 32 cm (**a,b**) **Male**: White; salmon-pinkish lores, deep pale bill, short crest; underwing/-tail washed yellow. **Female**: Eyes reddish-brown. **Juvenile**: Eyes dark grey. **VOICE** Loud harsh nasal screeches (varied volume/length) in alarm. Single longer, quavering screech and sweeter squabbling/screeching in flight. **HABITAT** Open forest, cultivation. **RANGE** Fc/co **FER** Singapore.

Cambodia   Angkar 2/13

3 ALEXANDRINE PARAKEET *Psittacula eupatria* 50–58 cm (**a**) **Male** *siamensis*: Large; big red bill, green/yellowish-green head, pale blue-washed hindcrown/nape to upper ear-coverts, maroon-red shoulder-patch. Narrow collar (black at front, pink at rear), otherwise mostly green (duller mantle); blue-washed uppertail, yellowish undertail, green underwing-coverts. (**b**) **Female**: No collar or obvious blue on head, smaller/paler shoulder-patch, shorter tail-streamers. **Juvenile**: Duller than female, smaller shoulder-patch, shorter tail, duller bill. (**c**) **Male** *P.e.avensis* (Myanmar): More uniform green head, with blue only in band bordering collar. **Other subspecies** *P.e.magnirostris* (Coco Is). **VOICE** Loud, ringing *trrrieuw*, loud *kee-ah* and *keeak*, resonant *g'raaak..g'raaak...* **HABITAT** Mixed deciduous forest, temple groves; up to 915 m. **RANGE** Sc/lc **R** Myanmar (except south Tenasserim), C Thailand (?**FER**), Cambodia, S Laos, S Annam, north-west Cochinchina. **FR** (currently?) W,NW,NE Thailand, C Laos, C Annam. **Frc** south N Laos.

4 ROSE-RINGED PARAKEET *Psittacula krameri* 40–42 cm (**a**) **Male** *borealis*: Like Alexandrine but smaller, smaller bill, no shoulder-patch, blackish lower mandible, thin black loral line. (**b**) **Female**: Indistinct dark green collar, no loral line, shorter tail-streamers. **Juvenile**: Slightly paler than female, eyes greyish, tail shorter. Male attains collar in third year. **VOICE** Variable loud, shrill, rather harsh *kee-ak kee-ak kee-ak..*, higher/less guttural than Alexandrine. Rasping *kreh kreh kreh kreh..* by flocks, chattering *chee chee..* in flight. **HABITAT** Open deciduous forest, cultivation, plantations, parks, gardens; up to 915 m. **RANGE** Lc **R** Myanmar (except Tenasserim). Un/lo **FER** C Thailand (Bangkok area), Singapore.

5 GREY-HEADED PARAKEET *Psittacula finschi* 36–40 cm (**a**) **Male**: Slaty head, red and yellow bill, black from throat to behind ear-coverts and narrowly bordering hindcrown, pale blue nuchal collar, small maroon shoulder-patch, purplish-blue (basally) and pale yellowish (distally) tail-streamers (undertail yellow); turquoise-green underwing-coverts, whitish eyes. **Female**: No shoulder-patch or black on throat-centre, shorter

tail-streamers. (**b**) **Juvenile**: Green head (darker crown), bluish-tinged head-sides), dark eyes. Upper mandible usually ruddy. (**c**) **First-summer**: Mostly pale slaty head, no black throat/collar. **VOICE** Short high, shrill, upward-inflected whistles: *dreet..dreet.., sweet..sweet.., swit* etc. **HABITAT** Broadleaf and pine forest; up to 1,910 m. **RANGE** Un/lc **R** Myanmar, W,NW,NE Thailand, Indochina (north only in Cochinchina).

6 BLOSSOM-HEADED PARAKEET *Psittacula roseata* 30–36 cm (**a**) **Male** *juneae*: Pink forehead/head-sides, black throat and collar, yellow and black bill, maroon shoulder-patch, deep turquoise tail-streamers with pale yellow tips; green underwing-coverts. (**b**) **Female**: Violet-grey head, blackish malar patch (no collar), shorter tail-streamers. (**c**) **Juvenile**: Green hindcrown, no shoulder-patch. From Grey-headed by all-yellowish bill, vinous-greyish wash on forehead/ear-coverts, dark on malar, more turquoise uppertail, green underwing-coverts. **Other subspecies** *P.r.roseata* (N Myanmar?): Male greener with smaller shoulder-patch. **VOICE** A rather soft *pwi* and watery *driii*. **HABITAT** Mixed deciduous and open broadleaved evergreen forest; cultivation, temple groves; up to 915 m. **RANGE** Un/fc **R** Myanmar (except N), W,NW,NE,C,S(extreme north) Thailand, Indochina (except W,E Tonkin).

7 RED-BREASTED PARAKEET *Psittacula alexandri* 33–37 cm (**a**) **Male** *fasciata*: Stocky and relatively short-tailed; red and blackish bill, lilac-grey/-blue crown/head-sides, black loral line and broad malar band, yellowish-washed wing-coverts, deep pink breast, largely turquoise tail. (**b**) **Female**: Back bill, richer pink breast (without male's violet tinge), blue-washed head, shorter tail-streamers. (**c**) **Juvenile**: Dull vinous-grey forehead/head-sides, duller dark head markings, green nape, breast/upper belly. **VOICE** Shrill *ek ek..*, repeated sharp nasal *kaink* (rapidly in alarm), nasal honking *cheent cheent..* and more grating notes, raucous *kak-kak-kak-kak...* **HABITAT** Broadleaved forest, temple groves, cultivation; up to 1,220 m. **RANGE** Co **R** Myanmar, Thailand (except southern S), Indochina. **Frc** (status?) north Pen Malaysia. Co **FER** Singapore.

8 LONG-TAILED PARAKEET *Psittacula longicauda* 40–42 cm (**a**) **Male** *longicauda*: Red and dark bill, reddish-pink head-sides/nape, deep green crown, broad black malar band, very pale blue-green mantle, pale turquoise back; long purplish-blue tail-streamers (undertail dull olive). Blackish underwing with yellow coverts. (**b**) **Female**: Darker green above, green nape, dull brown bill, dark green malar band, shorter tail-streamers; reddish-pink on supercilium. (**c**) **Juvenile**: Plainer/greener; pinkish face, dull malar band. (**d**) **Male** *tytleri* (Coco Is): <49 cm, brighter crown, flame-red head-sides, nape as mantle, darker green below. Turquoise and green tail, turquoise-green underwing-coverts. (**e**) **Female**: Brighter crown than *longicauda*, paler head-sides, green supercilium. **VOICE** High, rather melodious *pee-yo pee-yo pee-yo..*, nasal quavering *graak graak graak*, scolding *cheet* notes. **HABITAT** More open lowland broadleaved evergreen forest, clearings, plantations, mangroves. **RANGE** Fc/co **R** (local movements), Coco Is (S Myanmar), Pen Malaysia, Singapore.

PLATE 28 SWIFTLETS & TREESWIFTS

1 WATERFALL SWIFT *Hydrochous gigas* 16–16.5 cm (**a,b**) **Adult**: Wing 156–168 mm, tail 58–66 (outer), 51–52 (inner). Larger and longer-winged than House Swift, darker than other swiftlets (including rump), tail more forked. **Juvenile**: In hand, less obvious greyish-white undertail-covert fringes, pointed central tail feathers. **VOICE** Sharp *wicker* notes and loud twittering. **HABITAT** Waterfalls, nearby broadleaved evergreen forest; 800–1,500 m. **RANGE** Found (status?) Pen Malaysia.

2 GLOSSY SWIFTLET *Collocalia esculenta* 10 cm (**a,b**) **Adult** *cyanoptila*: Blackish above with dark blue-/greenish gloss, whitish vent. Throat/breast dark greyish (sometimes paler fringing). **Juvenile**: Said to have stronger greenish gloss above, pale grey/buff wing-fringing. **Other subspecies** *C.e.elachyptera* (Mergui Archipelago): Supposed to have greener gloss above, paler throat, narrow pale fringes on rump; extensive white rami above (mainly nape/rump). **VOICE** Short grating twittering. **HABITAT & BEHAVIOUR** Forested and open areas; up to 1,900 m. Rapid bat-like flight. **RANGE** Sc/un **R** south Tenasserim, S Thailand, Pen Malaysia. Sc **NBV** (**FR**) Singapore.

3 HIMALAYAN SWIFTLET *Collocalia brevirostris* 13–14 cm (**a,b**) **Adult** *brevirostris* (N Myanmar): Wing 128–137 mm, tail 56–62 (outer), 46–52 (inner). Blackish-brown above (faint gloss), greyish rump-band, quite uniform throat/breast, darker chin, slightly darker ear-coverts; brownish-grey belly/vent. In hand, darker shaft-streaks below (not throat), viariable leg-feathering and rami (can be lacking?). Darker than Germain's; from Germain's and Black-nest by deeper tail-notch. **Juvenile**: Rump-band less defined, fewer leg feathers. (**c**) **Adult** *inopina* (**WV** N Myanmar?, W Tonkin): Slightly longer wings, rump almost as upperparts. (**d**) **Adult** *rogersi* (**B** E Myanmar, NW,W Thailand; **VS** S Thailand; **RC** C Laos; has been split as species): Smaller/shorter-winged than *innominata*; in hand, no white rami, no/slight leg-feathering. **Other subspecies** *C.b.innominata* (**VS**): *brevirostris* and *inopina* (?valid). **VOICE** Low rattling twitter. **HABITAT** Forests, open areas; up to 3,100 m. **RANGE** Un **R** W,E Myanmar, W,NW Thailand. Un **WV** Thailand (except SE), Pen Malaysia, Singapore, E Tonkin, N,C,S Annam, Cochinchina. Also **PM** Pen Malaysia, Singapore. Rc (status?) N,C Myanmar, N Laos, W Tonkin.

4 BLACK-NEST SWIFTLET *Collocalia maxima* 12–13.5 cm (**a,b**) **Adult** *maxima*: Wing 126–133 mm, tail 47–52.5 (outer), 43.5–48 (inner). Throat and breast quite uniform, or grading to darker chin (all paler than ear-coverts). Lacks obvious tail-notch. In hand, faint darker shaft-streaks on throat, dense leg-feathering. Bulkier, bigger-headed and longer-winged than Germain's. Rump band usually narrower/duller than Germain's, more defined than paler-rumped races of Himalayan. (**c**) **Adult** *lowi* (**RC** Gunung Benom, Pen Malaysia): Rump as upperparts. **VOICE** Like Himalayan. **HABITAT** Open areas, sometimes over forest, offshore islets, urban areas; up to 1,830 m. **RANGE** Un/lc **R** Tenasserim, S Thailand, Pen Malaysia, Singapore.

5 EDIBLE-NEST SWIFTLET *Collocalia fuciphaga* 11–12 cm (**a,b**) **Adult** *inexpectata*: Wing 113–121 mm, tail 47–53 (outer), 41–46 (inner). Like Germain's but rump-band nar-

rower and darker (but see *C.g.amechana*), lower breast to undertail-coverts slightly darker. Legs unfeathered. **HABITAT** Open areas, sometimes over forest and mangroves, offshore islets; lowlands. **RANGE** **RC** Tenasserim (**V** or offshore breeder).

6 GERMAIN'S SWIFTLET *Collocalia germani* 11.5–12.5 cm (**a,b**) **Adult** *germani*: Wing 113–123.5 mm, tail 50–53 (outer), 43–46 (inner). Paler on rump (whitish-grey with blackish shaft-streaks) and below than other swiftlets. Throat/upper breast paler than chin, obviously paler than ear-coverts. In hand, legs unfeathered, similar (fainter) dark shaft-streaks on throat to Black-nest. **Other subspecies** *C.g.amechana* (extreme S Thailand, Pen Malaysia [except NW], Singapore): Slightly duller rump-band. **HABITAT** Open areas, sometimes over forest, islets; up to 1,300 m. **RANGE** Lc/co **R** (mostly coastal) S Myanmar, Tenasserim, W(south),C,S Thailand, Pen Malaysia, Singapore, Cambodia, Vietnam (except W Tonkin). **Rc** (status?) N,C Laos.

Angkor Camb 1/13

7 CRESTED TREESWIFT *Hemiprocne coronata* 21–23 cm (**a**) **Male**: Slim, with long and slender dark wings and (very deeply forked) tail; grey above (slightly bluish) with dark erectile crest, pale rufous ear-coverts to upper throat, paler below with whitish belly/vent. (**b,c**) **Female**: No rufous on head, ear-coverts blackish-slate, has dusky-whitish line above eye and along edge of all-grey throat; plain underwing. **Juvenile**: Extensive white feather-fringing above, paler lower back/rump, dusky-whitish below with grey-brown subterminal bands and white tips, broad white tips to tertials and flight feathers. **VOICE** Harsh, rather explosive *kee-kyew* (*kyew* lower); *kip-KEE-kep* when perched. **HABITAT & BEHAVIOUR** Open deciduous forest, forested and open areas; up to 1,400 m. Regularly perches upright on exposed branches. **RANGE** Un/co **R** Myanmar, NW,W,NE Thailand, Cambodia, Laos, C,S Annam, Cochinchina.

8 GREY-RUMPED TREESWIFT *Hemiprocne longipennis* 18–21.5 cm (**a**) **Male** *harterti*: As Crested but dark glossy green crown and mantle, all-grey throat, dull dark chestnut ear-coverts, tail-tip falls short of primary tips, mostly whitish-grey tertials. (**b,c**) **Female**: Blackish ear-coverts. Grey back/rump contrasts with dark mantle; contrasting blackish underwing-coverts (male same). **Juvenile**: Extensive rusty-brown fringing above, off-white below with irregular brown subterminal bands and white tips; scapulars, flight feathers and tail broadly tipped whitish. **VOICE** Harsh, piercing *ki, ki-ki-ki-kew*, staccato *chi-chi-chi-chew*, disyllabic *too-eit* (*eit* more metallic). **HABITAT** Forested and open areas; up to 1,220 m. **RANGE** Fc/co **R** south Tenasserim, W(south),S Thailand, Pen Malaysia, Singapore.

9 WHISKERED TREESWIFT *Hemiprocne comata* 15–16.5 cm (**a**) **Male** *comata*: Olive-bronze, blue-black crown and wings, white head-bands/tertials/vent, chestnut ear-coverts, no crest. (**b,c**) **Female**: Blackish ear-coverts. Dark underwing/belly. **VOICE** Shrill chattering *she-she-she-she-shoo-shee* (*shoo* higher), plaintive *chew*. **HABITAT** Clearings in broadleaved evergreen forest; up to 1,200 m. **RANGE** Un/co **R** south Tenasserim, W(south),S Thailand, Pen Malaysia. Ra **NBV** (**FR**) Singapore.

PLATE 29 NEEDLETAILS & TYPICAL SWIFTS

1 SILVER-RUMPED NEEDLETAIL *Rhaphidura leucopygialis* 11 cm
(a,b) Adult: Robust, blackish; silvery-white lower back to uppertail-coverts, short square tail, broad paddle-shaped wings. Glossed dark bluish above, bare shafts (spines) extend from tail-tip (hard to see in field). **Juvenile**: Less glossy. **VOICE** High-pitched *tirrr-tirrr* and rapid chattering, recalling House Swift. **HABITAT** Broadleaved evergreen forest, clearings; up to 1,250 m. **RANGE** Un/co **R** south Tenasserim, S Thailand, Pen Malaysia; formerly Singapore.

2 WHITE-THROATED NEEDLETAIL *Hirundapus caudacutus* 22 cm
(a,b) Adult *caudacutus*: Like Silver-backed but with clearly defined white throat and short white band from extreme forehead to upper lores; pale saddle tends to be whiter and more extensive; has white tertial markings (difficult to see in field). **Juvenile**: Greyish-brown forehead and lores, less glossy above, white V on underparts marked blackish. **(c) Adult** *nudipes* (**RC** NW Thailand, Cambodia): All-blackish forehead and lores, whitish of saddle tends to be restricted to lower mantle/upper back. **VOICE** Rapid insect-like chattering: *trp-trp-trp-trp-trp-trp...* **HABITAT** Forested and open areas; up to 2,300 m. **RANGE** Sc **PM** NW,NE,SE Thailand, Pen Malaysia, Cambodia, N,C Laos, E Tonkin, S Annam. **V** Singapore. **Rc** (status?) W Myanmar.

3 SILVER-BACKED NEEDLETAIL *Hirundapus cochinchinensis* 22 cm
(a,b) Adult *cochinchinensis*: Like Brown-backed but saddle-centre brownish-white, throat brownish-grey (sometimes looks whitish), no loral spot. When bleached/worn, can show whitish inner webs to tertials and whiter saddle. **Juvenile**: Dark brown markings on white underpart V. **VOICE** Soft, rippling trill. **HABITAT** Forested and open areas, vicinity of large rivers; up to 3,355 m. **RANGE** Un **R** S Annam, Cochinchina. Sc/un (status?) N Myanmar, Thailand (except W,S), Cambodia, Laos, E Tonkin, N,C Annam. Un **WV** and **PM** Pen Malaysia. Sc **PM** Singapore, W Tonkin.

4 BROWN-BACKED NEEDLETAIL *Hirundapus giganteus* 21–24.5 cm
(a,b) Adult *indicus*: Large and bulky; blackish above and dark brown below, brown saddle (lower mantle/back), bold white V on lower flanks/vent. White loral spot (visible at close range), often slightly paler chin/upper throat-centre. **Juvenile**: White loral spot less obvious, white underpart V faintly marked darker. **Other subspecies** *H.g.giganteus* (**R** south Tenasserim, S Thailand, Pen Malaysia): 24.5–26.5 cm; no white loral spot. **VOICE** Rippling trill, slower than White-throated; 2–3 squeaky *cirrwiet* notes, thin squeaky *chiek*. **HABITAT & BEHAVIOUR** Forested and open areas; up to 2,000 m. Has fast gliding flight; wings make loud whooshing sound when zooming overhead. **RANGE** Un/co **R** throughout. Only **BV** to some more northerly areas? Also un **WV** and **PM** Pen Malaysia, Singapore.

Mekong, Laos Jan '13

5 ASIAN PALM SWIFT *Cypsiurus balasiensis* 11–12 cm
(a,b) Adult *infumatus*: Small; rather uniform greyish-brown, long slender wings, long, deeply forked tail. Tail appears long, narrow and pointed when closed; rump, head-sides, breast and belly somewhat paler, throat paler still. Resembles some swiftlets when viewed distantly and tail closed, but wings and tail much more slender, never glides with wings held stiffly below horizontal. **Juvenile**: Tail somewhat less sharply and deeply forked. **VOICE** Frequently uttered, high trilled *sisisi-soo-soo* or *dee-dle-ee-dee*. **HABITAT & BEHAVIOUR** Open country, urban areas, often near palm trees; up to 1,525 m. Often found in small, highly active groups. **RANGE** Un/co **R** throughout.

6 ALPINE SWIFT *Tachymarptis melba* 20–23 cm
(a,b) Adult *nubifuga*: Large, long-winged; dark brown, with white throat (often hard to see at distance) and breast/belly patch. **Juvenile**: Slightly darker above; extensive white fringing, particularly on wing-coverts (also shown by fresh adults in winter/spring). **VOICE** Twittering *ti ti tititititititititititi-ti-ti-ti-ti tu tu*, accelerating, then decelerating/dropping slightly in pitch. Single *zri* and *ziiu*. **HABITAT & BEHAVIOUR** Forested and open areas; found in plains. Rather slow, deep wingbeats compared to *Apus* swifts. **RANGE** **V** N Myanmar.

7 FORK-TAILED SWIFT *Apus pacificus* 18–19.5 cm
(a,b) Adult *cooki*: Relatively large, with long sickle-shaped wings, and sharply forked tail (may be closed); blackish with clear-cut narrow white rump-band (hard to see at distance). Has slightly paler throat, indistinct whitish scales on rest of underparts, and darker shaft-streaks on rump-band and throat (all hard to see in field). **Juvenile**: Secondaries and inner primaries narrowly tipped whitish. **(c) Adult** *pacificus* (widespread **PM**): Browner and almost glossless above, head and nape slightly paler than mantle with narrow greyish-white feather margins, white rump-band broader, dark shaft-streaks on rump-band and throat narrower and less obvious, throat whiter. **Other subspecies** *A.p.kanoi* (**VS** Indochina, Pen Malaysia): Said to be intermediate between *cooki* and *pacificus*. **VOICE** Shrill *sreee*. **HABITAT** Forested and open areas; up to 2,600 m. **RANGE** Un **R** (some movements) E Myanmar, NW Thailand, N,C Laos, W Tonkin, C Annam. Un/lc **WV** Thailand (except C), Pen Malaysia, Cambodia. Un/lc **PM** C,S Thailand, Pen Malaysia, Singapore, Cambodia, W,E Tonkin, N,S Annam, Cochinchina. **Rc** (status?) Myanmar (except E), S Laos.

8 DARK-RUMPED SWIFT *Apus acuticauda* 17–18 cm
(a,b) Adult: Like Fork-tailed but no white rump-band, tends to have darker, more heavily marked throat, sharper tail-fork with narrower and more pointed outer feathers. **Juvenile**: Probably differs as Fork-tailed. **VOICE** Very high-pitched, rapid, sibilant, quavering *tsrr'i'i'i'i* and *tsrr'i'i'i'is'it* etc. at nest sites. **HABITAT** Forested areas, cliffs; 1,000–2,300 m. **RANGE** Rc in winter (status?) N Myanmar, NW Thailand.

9 HOUSE SWIFT *Apus affinis* 14–15 cm *All over Laos Camb*
(a,b) Adult *subfurcatus*: Blackish, with whitish throat, broad clear white rump-band, only slightly notched, squarish tail-tip. Narrow dark shaft-streaks on rump-band (not visible in field). **Juvenile**: Tends to have paler-fringed wing feathers. **VOICE** Harsh rippling trilled *der-der-der-dit-derdiddidoo*, rapid shrill *siksiksiksik-sik-sik-siksiksiksik...*, and staccato screaming. **HABITAT** Urban and open areas, sometimes over forest; up to 2,300 m. **RANGE** Co **R**, subject to some local movements (except SW,W Myanmar). **Rc** (status?) SW,W Myanmar.

PLATE 30 SMALLER OWLS

1 WHITE-FRONTED SCOPS OWL *Otus sagittatus* 27–29 cm (**a**) **Adult**: Relatively large and long-tailed, recalls Reddish but brighter rufous/rufous-chestnut above (sometimes also breast), broad whitish forehead-patch, plain primaries. VOICE Vibrating hollow tremolo, lasting 13–14 s: *wuwuwuwuwuwu...* or *w'w'w'w'w'w'w'w'...* (rising somewhat in volume and ending quite abruptly). HABITAT Broadleaved evergreen forest; up to 610 m. RANGE Ra **R** Tenasserim, W,S Thailand, Pen Malaysia.

2 REDDISH SCOPS OWL *Otus rufescens* 19 cm (**a**) **Adult** *malayensis*: Rufescent-tinged plumage, brown eyes. Plainer above than Mountain, less distinct scapular markings, plain rufous-buff below with blackish spots (highlit above with pale buff); primariesbroadly pale dark-and-buff. VOICE Territorial call is hollow whistled *hoooo*, fading at the end, repeated every 7–11 s. HABITAT Broadleaved evergreen forest; up to 200 m. RANGE Sc/un **R** southern S Thailand, Pen Malaysia.

3 MOUNTAIN SCOPS OWL *Otus spilocephalus* 20 cm (**a**) **Adult** *siamensis*: Short ear-tufts, rufescent above, large white scapular markings, unstreaked buffish/rufous below with white markings and dark vermiculations, yellow eyes. (**b**) **Adult** *spilocephalus* (SW,W,N Myanmar): More greyish-brown variant. Ranges from less to more rufescent. (**c**) **Adult** *vulpes* (Pen Malaysia): Deeper rufous (particularly below), coarser blackish markings above. **Other subspecies** *O.s.latouchei* (northern Indochina): Quite plain and very rufous above (rufous to buffy-brown), dark crown-streaks. **Juvenile**: Head/body paler/buffier with dark bars, scapulars unmarked. VOICE Clear spaced *phu-phu* or *toot-too*, every 5–7 s (territorial). HABITAT Broadleaved evergreen forest; up to 2,200 m, mainly mountains (above 800 m Pen Malaysia). RANGE Fc/co **R** (except C Thailand, Singapore).

4 ORIENTAL SCOPS OWL *Otus sunia* 19 cm (**a**) **Adult** greyish morph *distans*: Yellow eyes, no nuchal collar, bold white scapular marks, dark streaks below. (**b**) **Adult** rufous morph: Black crown-streaks, obvious ear-tufts, whitish belly with blackish to rufous markings. (**c**) **Adult** rufous morph *stictonotus* (VS Thailand, Cambodia, Cochinchina): Paler, more rufous, less rufous-chestnut. **Juvenile**: Head/body paler with more dark bars, fewer streaks, no scapular markings. **Other subspecies** Unclear/unresolved. *O.s.malayanus* (VS Tenasserim, Pen Malaysia, Singapore) at least. VOICE Loud clear, measured *toik..toik'to-toik* or *toik'to-toik* from *stictono-tus*. HABITAT Broadleaved forests; also (migrants) mangroves, plantations; up to 2,000 m (breeds below 1,000 m?). RANGE Un/fc **R** SW,W,N,E Myanmar, north Tenasserim, W,NW,NE Thailand, Cambodia, S Laos, N,S Annam. Un **WV** S Myanmar, Thailand, Pen Malaysia, Cambodia. **PM** Pen Malaysia. **V** Singapore. Rc (status?) N,C Laos, W,E Tonkin, C Annam.

5 COLLARED SCOPS OWL *Otus bakkamoena* 23 cm (**a,b**) **Adult** *lettia*: Greyish variant. Broad whitish eyebrows/nuchal collar, obvious ear-tufts, dark eyes, greyish-brown above with buff markings, whitish below with fine vermiculations and sparse streaks. (**c**) **Adult**: Buff variant. Buffish eyebrows and nuchal collar, deep buff below. (**d**) **Juvenile**: Paler (often warmer) head/body, darker bars overall. **Other subspecies** *O.b.erythro-*

campe (E Tonkin): Larger, typically darker above, much bolder streaks below. **Other subspecies** Uncertain/unresolved. VOICE Quite soft, clear, slightly falling *bouu* (every c.12 s); pitch varies (also between sexes?). Rarely, strident *kuuk-kuuk-kuuk*. HABITAT Broadleaved forests, wooded cultivation, gardens, plantations; up to 2,200 m. RANGE Fc/co **R** throughout. WV Pen Malaysia?

6 COLLARED OWLET *Glaucidium brodiei* 16–16.5 cm (**a,b**) **Adult** *brodiei*: Very small; buff and blackish imitation face on nape, speckled crown, streaked belly, no obvious white on coverts. **Adult** rufous morph (rc northern Vietnam at least): Very rufous, except for white of eyebrows/underparts. **Juvenile**: Crown no mantle unmarked, but whitish streaks on forecrown. VOICE Loud, rhythmic, hollow, piping *pho pho-pho pho* (often in daytime). HABITAT Broadleaved evergreen forest; up to 3,100 m (mostly above 400 m). RANGE Fc/co **R** (except SW Myanmar, C Thailand, Singapore, Cochinchina).

7 ASIAN BARRED OWLET *Glaucidium cuculoides* 20.5–23 cm (**a**) **Adult** *bruegeli*: Broad rounded head, no ear-tufts, dull brown with pale buffish bars, narrow whitish eyebrows, white ventral line, whitish belly and lower flanks with broad brown streaks. (**b**) **Juvenile**: Diffuse pale bars above, diffuse dark bars below, streaking more diffuse, crown more speckled. (**c**) **Adult** *deignani* (south-eastern Thailand, southern Indochina): Rustier belly-streaks, grey head with whiter bars. **Other subspecies** *G.c.rufescens* (Myanmar except northern N and Tenasserim) and *austerum* (west N Myanmar): Larger, darker and more rufescent. *G.c.delacouri* (N Laos, W Tonkin), *whitelyi* (east N Myanmar, E Tonkin). VOICE Descending, eerie quavering trill: *wu'u'u'u'u'u'u'u'u..* (c. 10 s long), gradually increasing in volume. Mellow *hoop* notes, then long series of raucous double-notes, increasing in pitch/volume. HABITAT & BEHAVIOUR Relatively open broadleaved forests, clumps of trees; up to 1,980 m. Often perched in open during day. RANGE Co **R** Myanmar, W,NW,NE,SE,C,north S Thailand, Indochina.

8 JUNGLE OWLET *Glaucidium radiatum* 20.5 cm (**a**) **Adult** *radiatum*: More densely barred than Asian Barred, prominent dull rufous bars on flight feathers, smaller white scapular markings, all-barred below. VOICE Slightly raucous *PRAA-PRAA-PRAA-praa-pruu* or *prr-prr-prr-praa-praa-praa-praa-praa-praa-praa'praa'praa*. HABITAT Deciduous forest; up to 1,220 m. RANGE Un/fc **R** SW,W Myanmar.

9 SPOTTED OWLET *Athene brama* 20–20.5 cm (**a**) **Adult** *mayri*: White spots above, white eyebrows, broken dark foreneck collar, broken bars below. **Juvenile**: More washed-out/less spotted above, more diffuse bars below (belly may have light streaks). **Other subspecies** *A.b.pulchra* (Myanmar). VOICE Screeching *chirurr-chirurr-chirurr..* etc., followed by or mixed with *cheevak cheevak cheevak...* High-pitched screeching and chuckling. HABITAT Open woodland, semi-desert, cultivation, urban areas; up to 1,220 m (mostly lowlands). RANGE Co **R** SW,W,C,S,E Myanmar, Thailand (except S), Cambodia, C,S Laos, C Annam, Cochinchina.

1a

2a

3a

3c

3b

4a

4b

4c

5b

5d

5c

6a

6b

7a

7b

7c

5a

8a

9a

PLATE 31 LARGER OWLS

1 EURASIAN EAGLE OWL *Bubo bubo* 54.5–56 cm
(a) **Adult** *bengalensis*: Orange eyes, dark bill, black facial disc border, thick breast-streaks. **Juvenile**: Head and body creamy-buffish, striated and vermiculated slightly darker. **VOICE** Loud, resonant ***tu-whooh***, with second note rising in tone. **HABITAT** Bush-covered rocky country, ravines, wooded semi-desert and cultivation; lowlands. **RANGE** RC (status?) SW Myanmar.

2 SPOT-BELLIED EAGLE OWL *Bubo nipalensis* 61 cm
(a) **Adult** *nipalensis*: Long ear-tufts, whitish below with black-ish heart-shapes/bars, dark eyes, pale yellow bill. (b) **Juvenile:** Head/body whitish to buffy-white, barred blackish-brown (particularly above). **VOICE** Deep ***HU   HUU*** (gap c.2 s), every 1–2 mins. Eerie moaning, screaming ***waayaoaah***, quieter ***aayao*** at roost-site. **HABITAT** Broadleaved forests; up to 1,200 m. **RANGE** Sc/un R S,E Myanmar, north Tenasserim, Thailand (except C,S), Cambodia, N,S Laos, W,E Tonkin, C,S Annam, Cochinchina.

3 BARRED EAGLE OWL *Bubo sumatranus* 45.5–46.5 cm
(a) **Adult** *sumatranus*: Brown-and-buff bars above, blackish-and-whitish bars below (denser on breast). **Juvenile** Bars narrower/denser than Spot-bellied. **VOICE** Loud deep ***uk OOO OO*** (***uk*** quiet); c.2 s between main notes. Quacking ***gagaga-gogogo***. **HABITAT** Broadleaved evergreen forest, plantations; up to 610 m, locally 1,400 m. **RANGE** Sc/un R south Tenasserim, W(south), S Thailand, Pen Malaysia, Singapore (now V?).

4 DUSKY EAGLE OWL *Bubo coromandus* 54–58 cm
(a) **Adult** *klossii*: Rather plain drab greyish-brown, unbarred primaries, quite erect ear-tufts. (b) **Juvenile**: Creamy-whitish, faint markings; wings/tail as adult. **VOICE** Loud hollow ***kok kok kok-kok-kokaloo***. **HABITAT** Open woodland near water; lowlands. **RANGE** Ra/lc R SW,C Myanmar, Tenasserim, Pen Malaysia; formerly W(coastal),S(north) Thailand.

5 BROWN FISH OWL *Ketupa zeylonensis* 49–54 cm
(a) **Adult** *leschenault*: Buffy-brown, floppy ear-tufts, blackish-brown and whitish/buff wing markings, whitish scapular markings and gorget, dark streaks and narrow cross-bars below. (b) **Juvenile**: More creamy-buffish, paler wings than adult. **Other subspecies** *K.z.orientalis* (Indochina). **VOICE** Deep hollow moaning ***hu OOO-hu*** (last note barely audible). Deep mutterings, rising to crazy laughter (before end): ***hu-hu-hu-hu-hu hu ha*** or ***oof uh-oof uh-oof uh-oof uh-oof uh-oof u-uh-h-HA-oo-oo-oof***. Rather hoarse mournful scream. **HABITAT** Broadleaved forests near water; up to 915 m. **RANGE** Un/fc R Myanmar, Thailand (except C,SE), north-west Pen Malaysia, Indochina (except W Tonkin).

6 TAWNY FISH OWL *Ketupa flavipes* 58.5–61 cm
(a) **Adult**: More unmarked buff on coverts than smaller Buffy, warmer wing-/tail-bars, broader streaks below (mainly breast). **Juvenile**: Only from Buffy by size? **VOICE** Deep ***whoo-hoo*** and cat-like mewing. At roost, hissing ***fshhht***, weak falling whistled ***pheeeeoo***. **HABITAT** Broadleaved evergreen, semi-evergreen and swamp forest along rivers/near fresh water; up to 600 m. **RANGE** Ra/lo R W,N Myanmar, N,C Laos, W Tonkin, Cochinchina.

7 BUFFY FISH OWL *Ketupa ketupu* 45.5–47 cm
(a) **Adult** *aagaardi*: Rich buff. Broadly blackish-marked upper-parts contrast with bar-free underparts, white forehead/eye-brows, broadly streaked ear-tufts. **Juvenile**: Like Brown but richer buff. (b) **Adult** *ketupu* (Pen Malaysia, Singapore): Warmer, richer buff overall. **VOICE** Monotonous ***bup-bup-bup-bup-bup..***, high screeching/yelping ***yiark, yark, yark, yeek***. Subdued hoarse, rather hissing ***hyiiii*** or ***hyiiii-ih*** at roost. **HABITAT** Broadleaved evergreen forest near water, mangroves, plantations, gardens; up to 800 m. **RANGE** Sc/fc R SW,S Myanmar, Tenasserim, W,NE(south),SE,S Thailand, Pen Malaysia, Singapore, Cambodia, C Annam, Cochinchina.

8 SPOTTED WOOD OWL *Strix seloputo* 44.5–48 cm
(a) **Adult** *seloputo*: Plain rufous-buff facial discs, white speckles and spots above, white to buffy-white below (mixed rich buff) with well-spaced bars. **Juvenile**: Initially like Brown but no dark around eyes, contrasting even bars on wings/tail. **VOICE** Abrupt booming ***WHO*** or ***UUH***, every 8–11 s. Deep quavering ***WRRRROOH WRRRROOH WRRRROOH...*** **HABITAT** More open broadleaved evergreen forest, plantations, wooded parks, sometimes mangroves; below 305 m. **RANGE** Un/lc R S,E Myanmar, Tenasserim, NE,C,S Thailand, Pen Malaysia, Singapore, Cambodia, S Laos, Cochinchina.

9 MOTTLED WOOD OWL *Strix ocellata* 44–48.5 cm
(a) **Adult** *grisescens*?: Less distinct facial discs than Spotted, narrower bars below, overall less contrastingly patterned, with greyish vermiculations and rufous patches. **VOICE** Loud eerie, quavering ***UUWAHRRRR***, shorter ***W'RROH W'RROH W'R-ROH...*** by different sexes of pair. **HABITAT** Open lowland woodland, wooded gardens/cultivation **RANGE** Sc/un R SW Myanmar.

10 BROWN WOOD OWL *Strix leptogrammica* 47–53 cm
(a) **Adult** *laotiana*: No ear-tufts; buffy-brown facial discs with dark border, dark eyes and their surrounds dark brown above, whitish/buff scapular/mantle markings, dark brown bars on buff belly (breast often dark brown). (b) **Juvenile**: Whitish-buff with narrow dark bars, contrasting dark and rufous bars on wings. **Other subspecies** *S.l.newarensis* (N,C Myanmar); *rileyi* (Tenasserim); *ticehursti* (S,E Myanmar); *maingayi* (S Thailand southwards). **VOICE** Deep vibrating ***HU-HU-HU'HUHRRROO*** or ***HOO HOO-HOO-HOO-(HOO)***. Eerie screaming ***eeeeoooow***, or more subdued ***ayaarrrh***. **HABITAT** Broadleaved forest; up to 2,590 m. **RANGE** Un/fc R (except SW Myanmar, C Thailand, Singapore, W Tonkin, Cochinchina).

11 TAWNY OWL *Strix aluco* 43 cm
(a) **Adult pale morph** *nivicola*: Cryptic blackish-brown, buff and greyish markings above, buffy-white scapular/covert markings, greyish facial discs, buffy-white below with heavy dark streaks and bars. (b) **Adult dark morph**: Blacker-brown and richer rufous above, rufescent discs, rufous and white mixed below. (c) **Juvenile pale morph**: Paler/more uniform with even dark bars. Juvenile dark morph differs likewise. **VOICE** Loud ***HU-HU***. **HABITAT** Broadleaved evergreen and coniferous forest; 2,450–3,080 m. **RANGE** Un R W,N,E Myanmar, W Tonkin.

4b

4a

1a

2b

2a

7b

7a

3a

6a

5a

5b

10a

10b

8a

11c

11a

11b

9a

PLATE 32 OWLS & FROGMOUTHS

1 BARN OWL *Tyto alba* 34–36 cm
(**a,b**) **Adult** *stertens*: Pale buffy-grey above with golden-buff markings, pale facial discs, buffy-white below with sparse blackish speckles; relatively pale, uniform upperside. **Other subspecies** *T.a.javanica* (S Thailand southwards). **VOICE** Eerie screeching, rasping and hissing. **HABITAT** Cultivation, open country, marsh and swamp borders, urban areas; up to 1,220 m. **RANGE** Un/lc **R** (except SW,W,N Myanmar, W Tonkin, N Annam).

2 GRASS OWL *Tyto capensis* 35.5 cm
(**a,b**) **Adult** *pithecops*: Mostly dark brown above with deep golden-buff markings, rufous-washed discs/neck/breast; more contrast between upper- and underside than Barn, golden-buff primary-patch, broadly dark-tipped primary coverts. **Other subspecies** *T.c.chinensis* (Indochina). **VOICE** Similar to Barn Owl. **HABITAT** Grassland; up to 1,450 m. **RANGE** Ra/sc **R** C,S,E Myanmar, E Tonkin, C,S Annam, Cochinchina.

3 ORIENTAL BAY OWL *Phodilus badius* 29 cm
(**a**) **Adult** *badius*: Dark-framed buffy discs, rudimentary ear-tufts, rufescent above with sparse black and white marks, pinkish-buff below with sparse spots, mainly golden-buff nape and scapulars. **Other subspecies** *P.b.saturatus* (W,N Myanmar?): Brown parts darker. **VOICE** Eerie upward-inflected whistles, rising then fading: *oo hlii hoo hu-i-li hu-i-li hu-i-li hu-i-li*. **HABITAT & BEHAVIOUR** Broadleaved evergreen forest, plantations, edge of mangroves; up to 1,220 m, rarely 2,200 m. Often low down on vertical stems. **RANGE** Un **R** (except W,C Myanmar, C Thailand, Singapore, W Tonkin, S Annam). **Frc** Singapore.

4 BROWN HAWK OWL *Ninox scutulata* 30–31 cm
(**a**) **Adult** *burmanica*: Mostly dark slaty-brown above, whitish between eyes, broad drab chestnut-brown spots/streaks below, longish barred tail, golden-yellow eyes. **Juvenile**: Paler/warmer above, more diffuse markings below. **Other subspecies** *N.s.scutulata* (resident Pen Malaysia, Singapore): Darker head-sides/upperparts (vaguely warm), darker/denser belly and vent markings (slightly more chestnut-tinged). *N.s.japonica* (**VS**): A little darker above, colder/darker markings below. **VOICE** Haunting deep, rising *whu-up*, just over once per s (territorial). **HABITAT** Open forest, mangroves; migrants also parks/gardens; up to 1,200 m. **RANGE** Fc/co **R** (except C Thailand, W Tonkin, S Annam). Un **WV** C,S,?W(south) Thailand, Pen Malaysia (also **PM**), Singapore, Cambodia.

5 LONG-EARED OWL *Asio otus* 35–37 cm
(**a,b**) **Female** *otus*: Long ear-tufts, dark bars below, rufescent facial discs, orange eyes, less boldly barred wings/tail, rufous-buff primary-patch. **Male**: Discs/underparts/underwing-coverts usually less richly coloured, less boldly streaked above. **First winter**: 4–6 (not 3–5) dark bars on outer primaries, 5–6 (not 4) on tail (beyond uppertail-coverts). **VOICE** Territorial males give soft, muffled, quite far-carrying *ooh* notes, recalling sound of air being blown into bottle. Female utters weak, nasal *paah*. Sharp barking *kvik kvik kvik..* and yelping or squealing sounds when alarmed. **HABITAT** Woodland, plantations; recorded at 1,065–1,385 m. **RANGE** V N Myanmar, N Laos.

6 SHORT-EARED OWL *Asio flammeus* 37–39 cm
(**a**) **Female** *flammeus*: No obvious ear-tufts, facial discs form rough circle, pale cross between eyes, boldly streaked below, yellow eyes. Longer-winged than Barn/Grass, bolder dark wing/tail bars, buff primary-patch, dark primary coverts; underwing with black bar at primary-covert tips. (**b**) **Male**: Overall less dark buff, less boldly marked, less uniformly buff below. **VOICE** Hollow muffled *boo-boo-boo-boo-boo..* (male, mainly in display). Rasping *cheeee-op*. Barking *chef-chef-chef*. **HABITAT & BEHAVIOUR** Grassland, marshes, open areas; up to 1,830 m. Only flies in daylight. **RANGE** Ra/sc **WV** W,N,C,S Myanmar, NW Thailand, N Laos, E Tonkin, C Annam. **V** C Thailand, Pen Malaysia, Singapore.

7 LARGE FROGMOUTH *Batrachostomus auritus* 39–42 cm
(**a**) **Adult**: Large; big white covert tips, warm brown throat and breast with few white marks. Female duller/plainer? **Juvenile**: Paler/plainer, no nuchal collar or spots above. **VOICE** 4–8 loud bubbling trills: *prrrrrooh prrrrrooh prrrrrooh prrrrrooh..* (rising or even). **HABITAT** Broadleaved evergreen forest; up to 200 m. **RANGE** Ra/sc **R** S Thailand, Pen Malaysia.

8 GOULD'S FROGMOUTH *Batrachostomus stellatus* 23–26.5 cm
(**a**) **Adult**: White covert-spots, warm scales below, protruding bill. (**b**) **Adult**: Colder/browner bird (female?). (**c**) **Juvenile**: More uniform; dark bars above. **VOICE** Males give eerie, weakish, whistled *woah-weeo* (*weeo* falling). Female utters growling and rapid yapping *wow* notes, 3–5 higher *wek* notes and descending whistled *weeeoh*. **HABITAT** Broadleaved evergreen forest; up to 185 m. **RANGE** Sc/fc **R** S Thailand, Pen Malaysia.

9 HODGSON'S FROGMOUTH *B.hodgsoni* 24.5–27.5 cm
(**a**) **Male** *indochinae*: Like Javan (*affinis*) but heavier black markings above/on breast, no rufous on breast. (**b**) **Female**: Paler, with more bolder white markings below than Javan. (**c**) **Juvenile**: Warm-tinged above with blackish and pale brown bars, no nuchal collar, similar below, grading to plainer/whiter vent. **Other subspecies** *B.h.hodgsoni* (W,N Myanmar). **VOICE** <10 soft, slightly trilled rising whistles: *whaaee, whaaow,* or *wheeow-a* (1–7 s apart). Soft chuckling *whoo* notes. **HABITAT** Broadleaved evergreen and mixed broadleaved/coniferous forest, secondary growth; 900–1,900 m, locally 305 m. **RANGE** Un W,N,E Myanmar, NW Thailand, Laos, C Annam.

10 JAVAN FROGMOUTH *Batrachostomus javensis* 23–24 cm
(**a**) **Male** *continentalis*: Warm brown above, finely marked buff/white/blackish, white nuchal collar/scapular spots; buffy-white below (more rufous throat/breast), with fine dark and large white marks. (**b**) **Female**: Plain rufous-chestnut, white nuchal band, large scapulars spots, and smallish breast markings. (**c**) **Male** *affinis* (extreme S Thailand southward): Less rufous, usually more black markings, more whitish marks on crown, more contrasting tail bars. **VOICE** Wavering whistled *tee-loo-eee* (*loo* falling, *eee* rising) etc., *KWAH-a* or *e-ah*, and falling *whah* or *gwaa* notes (male). Descending laughing *grra-ga-ga-ga* etc. (female). **HABITAT** Broadleaved forest, secondary growth; up to 800 m. **RANGE** Un **R** Tenasserim, Thailand (except C), Pen Malaysia, Cambodia, N,S Laos, Cochinchina.

7–10 to different scale

PLATE 33 NIGHTJARS

1 MALAYSIAN EARED NIGHTJAR *Eurostopodus temminckii* 27 cm (**a,b**) **Adult**: Darkest nightjar in region. Much smaller than Great, crown darker, ear-tufts less pronounced, tail darker and less contrastingly barred. Females are possibly more rufescent than males. **Juvenile**: Upperparts somewhat paler, warmer and less heavily vermiculated, pale bars on underparts duller. **VOICE** Similar to Great but introductory note louder and always audible, second note shorter: *tut wee-ow*, repeated 5–7 times after shortish intervals. **HABITAT** Open areas and clearings in or near broadleaved evergreen forest; up to 1,000 m. **RANGE** Sc/un **R** extreme S Thailand, Pen Malaysia, Singapore.

2 GREAT EARED NIGHTJAR *Eurostopodus macrotis* 41 cm (**a,b**) **Adult** *cerviniceps*: Much larger, longer-winged and longer-tailed than other nightjars, lacking whitish or pale markings on wings/tail. Buffish-grey crown with a few dark central markings, contrasting dark head-sides, narrow collar (white on throat, pale buff on nape), relatively dark/uniform upperparts with paler scapulars and distinctly chestnut-tinged shoulders; uppertail distinctly and broadly barred blackish and buffish-brown, throat and upper breast blackish-brown, rest of underparts barred blackish and pale buff. Pronounced ear-tufts (sometimes visible when perched). **Juvenile:** Paler, plainer and buffier above with fewer, more contrasting markings, paler/plainer and more pale chestnut-tinged wing-coverts, diffuse barring below. **VOICE** Long double whistle, introduced by a short, well-separated note (audible at close range): *put PEE-OUW*. **HABITAT & BEHAVIOUR** Open areas and clearings in or near broadleaved evergreen and deciduous forest, freshwater swamp forest; up to 1,220 m. Flies with slow leisurely wingbeats, resembling smaller harriers *Circus*; often feeds high in air. **RANGE** Fc **R** Myanmar, Thailand (except C), north Pen Malaysia, Cambodia, Laos, E Tonkin (lo), C Annam, Cochinchina.

3 GREY NIGHTJAR *Caprimulgus indicus* 28–32 cm (**a–c**) **Male** *bazarae*: Similar to Large-tailed but somewhat smaller, crown darker; lacks rufescent tinge on nape, has somewhat heavier black vermiculations above, duller and darker ear-coverts and throat, usually less whitish on lower throat (may appear as two patches or 'headlights'), breast somewhat darker, scapulars less contrasting, with black, buff and whitish bars and vermiculations overall; shows less obvious whitish to buff bars across wing-coverts. In flight, smaller white wing-/tail-patches. (**d**) **Female**: Wing-patches smaller and buff (may be very indistinct), no obvious pale tail-patches (outer feathers narrowly tipped brownish-white to brownish-buff). **Juvenile**: Paler than female; flight feathers narrowly tipped pale warm buff. **Other subspecies** *C.i.jotaka* (wintering race). **VOICE** Male territorial call is rapid *tuctuctuctuctuctuc..* (up to 16 notes at rate of 3–4 per s), repeated monotonously after short pauses. Also, fast deep *quor-quor-quor* (females only?). **HABITAT** Open broadleaved evergreen and coniferous forest, secondary growth; non-breeders also in open areas, gardens; up to 2,565 m (breeds above 600 m). **RANGE** Un/fc **R** W,N,E,S(east) Myanmar, NW,W Thailand, probably W,E Tonkin; ? **BV** to some northern areas. Un **WV** (except SW,C,S Myanmar, SE Thailand). Sc **PM** Singapore (may winter).

4 LARGE-TAILED NIGHTJAR *Caprimulgus macrurus* 31.5–33 cm (**a–c**) **Male** *bimaculatus*: Told by combination of size, relatively pale crown with dark median stripe, prominent row of black scapulars with pronounced broad buff to whitish-buff outer fringes, and prominent large white patches on primaries and distal part of outertail feathers (obvious in flight). Has rather prominent whitish to buff bars across wing-coverts, large area of white to buffish-white across lower throat, brownish-grey tail with rather uneven dark bars, and pale buffish-brown remainder of underparts with blackish bars; often shows strong rufescent tinge to nape. (**d**) **Female**: Tends to be paler and greyer on upperparts and breast, wing-patches smaller and buff, tail-patches much duller, buffish to buffish-white. **Juvenile**: Paler and buffier than female, with duller tail-patches. **VOICE** Territorial males utter monotonous loud, resonant *chaunk* notes, roughly one per second (variable); sometimes preceded by low grunting or croaking. May give deep harsh *chuck* when flushed. **HABITAT** Open forest, secondary growth, cultivation; up to 2,135 m. **RANGE** Co **R** throughout.

5 INDIAN NIGHTJAR *Caprimulgus asiaticus* 23–24 cm (**a–c**) **Male** *asiaticus*: Smallest and palest nightjar in region. Like Large-tailed but smaller, shorter-tailed and paler, distinct buff nuchal collar with darker markings, broader whitish-buff scapular fringes, typically has two large round white patches on throat ('headlights'); slightly smaller white/buffy-white wing-/tail-patches (tend to slightly smaller still on females). **Juvenile**: Somewhat paler and plainer; upperpart streaking restricted to hindcrown and nape, scapular fringes more rufous. **VOICE** Territorial call of male is knocking *chuk-chuk-chuk-chuk-k'k'k'roo* (2–4 *chuk* notes), like ping-pong ball bouncing to rest on hard surface. Short sharp *quit-quit* or *chuk-chuk* sometimes given in flight. **HABITAT** Open dry forest, semi-desert, dry scrub and cultivation; up to 915 m. **RANGE** Un/co **R** SW,W,C,E,S Myanmar, north Tenasserim, Thailand (except S), Cambodia, N,S Laos, C,S Annam.

6 SAVANNA NIGHTJAR *Caprimulgus affinis* 25–25.5 cm (**a–c**) **Male** *monticolus*: Told from other nightjars by rather uniform, heavily vermiculated brownish-grey upperparts, lack of defined dark median crown-stripe, ill-defined scapular pattern (though often with some contrasting warm buff feather fringes) and white outertail feathers (often dusky-tipped). Has indistinct, broken buffish nuchal band, little or no pale moustachial line, typically a distinct roundish white to buffish-white patch on each side of throat, and large white wing-patches. (**d**) **Female**: Wing-patches slightly smaller and buff, no obvious pale or whitish tail markings. **Juvenile**: Somewhat paler. **Other subspecies** *C.a.affinis* (Pen Malaysia, Singapore): Smaller and more heavily marked; smaller wing-patches. **VOICE** Male territorial call is constantly repeated, loud rasping *chaweez* or *chweep*. **HABITAT** Open dry dipterocarp, pine and broadleaved evergreen forest, grassland, scrub; up to 915 m. **RANGE** Sc/un **R** Myanmar (except SW,E), Thailand (except S), south Pen Malaysia, Singapore, Cambodia, Laos, C,S Annam, Cochinchina.

PLATE 34 COLUMBA & IMPERIAL PIGEONS

1 ROCK PIGEON *Columba livia* 33 cm
(**a,b**) **Adult** *intermedia*: Pure stock are predominantly grey with noticeably darker hood and breast, blackish tail-tip and paler wing-coverts with two broad blackish bars. Neck glossed green and purple. Shows silvery-whitish underwing-coverts in flight. (**c–e**) **Adult feral variants**: Highly variable, with patches of white and brown in plumage; some are all blackish. (**f**) **Juvenile**: Pure stock are duller/browner than adult, head, neck and breast greyish-brown with little or no gloss, wing-coverts mostly pale greyish-brown. **VOICE** Song is a soft, guttural **oo-roo-coo**. **HABITAT** Cliffs, ruins, groves in open and cultivated places, urban areas; up to 1,450 m. **RANGE** Co **R** throughout. Possibly pure stock in SW,C and perhaps elsewhere in Myanmar.

2 SNOW PIGEON *Columba leuconota* 34.5 cm
(**a,b**) **Adult** *gradaria*: Slaty-grey head, sharply contrasting white collar and underparts. Blackish tail with broad whitish central band (conspicuous in flight), white patch on lower back, blackish rump and uppertail-coverts, greyish upperwing-coverts with three dark bands. **Juvenile**: Head duller, collar and breast dull pinkish-grey, has paler tips to scapulars and wing-coverts. **VOICE** Double hiccup-like note followed by **kuck-kuck** and ending with another hiccup. **HABITAT** Open alpine areas, cultivation, cliffs, rocky screes; 3,355–4,570 m. **RANGE** Rc (R?) N Myanmar.

3 SPECKLED WOOD PIGEON *Columba hodgsonii* 38 cm
(**a,b**) **Male**: Told by combination of pale grey head, neck and upper breast, dark maroon mantle, dark maroon scapulars and lesser coverts with bold whitish speckles, and dark belly and vent. Has maroon and pale grey streaks and scales on lower hindneck, upper mantle, lower breast and belly, and dark greenish to greyish legs and feet. (**c**) **Female**: Head and breast darker grey than male, mantle cold and rather slaty dark brown (no maroon), lacks maroon on scapulars and lesser coverts, base colour of underparts dark brownish-grey without maroon. **Juvenile**: Like female but dark parts of body and wings browner with indistinct speckles on scapulars and wing-coverts. **VOICE** Deep, throaty **whock-whrooooo..whrrrrooo**. **HABITAT** Broadleaved evergreen forest; 1,675–2,565 m, down to 1,350 m in winter. **RANGE** Un **R** W,N,C,E Myanmar. Sc/un **WV** (lc **R**?) NW Thailand, west N Laos.

4 ASHY WOOD PIGEON *Columba pulchricollis* c.36 cm
(**a,b**) **Adult**: Dark slaty upperside and breast, contrasting grey head with broad buffish neck-collar and whitish throat. Upper mantle and upper breast glossed green, legs and feet red. In flight, told from Speckled and Mountain Imperial by relatively small size, dark breast, pale belly and vent, and all-dark tail. (**c**) **Juvenile**: Buffish neck-collar little developed and largely pale grey, no green gloss on upper mantle and upper breast, crown darker grey, wings and breast browner (breast obscurely barred dull rufous), lower breast and central abdomen tinged rufous. **VOICE** Song is deep resonant **whoo**, given singly or repeated up to 5 times. **HABITAT** Broadleaved evergreen forest; 1,400–2,745 m. **RANGE** Un/lfc **R** SW,W,N,E Myanmar, NW Thailand, N Laos, W Tonkin.

5 PALE-CAPPED PIGEON *Columba punicea* 36–40.5 cm
(**a,b**) **Male**: Overall dark plumage with contrasting whitish-grey crown. Upperparts purplish-maroon with faint green gloss on sides and back of neck, more strongly iridescent mantle and back and dark slate-coloured rump and uppertail-coverts. Ear-coverts, throat and underparts vinous-brown, undertail-coverts slaty-grey, tail and flight feathers blackish, orbital skin and base of pale bill red. (**c**) **Female**: Like male but crown generally greyish. (**d**) **Juvenile**: Wing-coverts and scapulars duller than adult with rufous fringes, crown initially concolorous with mantle, gloss on upperparts much reduced, underparts greyer. **HABITAT** Broadleaved evergreen forest, secondary growth, sometimes mangroves, island forest and more open areas (mainly during migratory movements); up to 1,400 m. **RANGE** (local, nomadic movements) Myanmar (except W,N), east Cambodia, C,S Laos, C,S Annam, Cochinchina. **Rc** (status?) W,NE,SE,S Thailand (probably breeds locally, perhaps on offshore islands in S).

6 GREEN IMPERIAL PIGEON *Ducula aenea* 42–47 cm
(**a,b**) **Adult** *sylvatica*: Similar to Mountain but upperparts mostly dark metallic green (may be hard to discern) with variable rufous-chestnut gloss; head, neck and underparts rather uniform vinous-tinged pale grey, undertail-coverts dark chestnut, tail all dark. **Juvenile**: Duller above than adult; head, neck and underparts paler, with almost no vinous tones. **Other subspecies** *D.a.polia* (southern S Thailand southwards). **VOICE** Song is very deep, repeated **wah-whhoo**; **wah-whhrrooo** or **wah-wahrroo** etc. Also gives a deep **hoooo** or **huuooo** and rhythmic purring **crrhhoo**. **HABITAT** Broadleaved evergreen, semi-evergreen, mixed deciduous and island forest, mangroves; up to 915 m. **RANGE** Sc/lfc **R** (except C Thailand); mostly coastal in Pen Malaysia. Sc **NBV** (**FR** and may still be locally) Singapore.

7 MOUNTAIN IMPERIAL PIGEON *Ducula badia* 43–51 cm
(**a,b**) **Adult** *griseicapilla*: The largest pigeon in the region. Distinguished by mostly purplish-maroon mantle and wing-coverts, bluish-grey crown and face, white throat, vinous-tinged pale grey neck (more vinous at rear) and underparts, whitish-buff undertail-coverts and dark tail with contrasting broad greyish terminal band. Red eyering and red bill with pale tip. (**c**) **Juvenile**: Like adult but less pink on hindneck, rusty-brown fringes to mantle, wing-coverts and flight feathers. (**d**) **Adult** *badia* (south Tenasserim and S Thailand southward): Upperparts more extensively and intensely purplish-maroon (including rump), crown and face duller and more vinous-grey (contrasting less with hindneck), underparts have darker, stronger vinous-pink tinge, contrasting more with (buffish) undertail-coverts. **VOICE** Song is loud, very deep **uh**, **WROO-WROO** or **uhOOH-WROO-WROO** (**uh** only audible at close range) or just **uOOH-WROO**. Repeated after rather long intervals. **HABITAT** Broadleaved evergreen forest; up to 2,565 m (mostly in mountains). **RANGE** Fc/co **R** Myanmar, W,NW,NE,SE,extreme S Thailand, Pen Malaysia, Indochina (except Cochinchina). **Rc** (status?) Cochinchina.

PLATE 35 DOVES & CUCKOO DOVES

1 ORIENTAL TURTLE DOVE *Streptopelia orientalis* 31–33 cm
(**a,b**) **Adult** *agricola*: Larger, bulkier, shorter-tailed and darker than Spotted, rufous fringing on lower mantle and coverts, barred rather than spotted neck-patch, bluish-slate rump and uppertail-coverts. Crown bluish-grey (forehead more buffish), head-sides, neck, upper mantle and throat to belly rather uniform pale vinous-brownish, undertail-coverts grey. Greyish tail-tips, no obvious pale bar on upperwing. (**c**) **Juvenile**: Paler with narrower, paler rufous fringes to lower mantle, scapulars and wing-coverts, paler fringes to breast, much smaller or absent neck-patch. (**d**) **Adult** *orientalis* (**WV**): Larger and greyer, less vinous hood and underparts, rather more distinct breast-band/collar, contrasting with the paler creamy throat and paler buffish belly. **VOICE** Song is husky *wu,whrroo-whru ru* (sometimes without *ru*) or faster *er-her-herber*. **HABITAT** Open forest, secondary growth, cultivation; up to 2,135 m. **RANGE** Lc **R** Myanmar, W,NW,NE Thailand. Un **WV** N Myanmar, NW,NE Thailand, Indochina (resident in north?).

2 SPOTTED DOVE *Streptopelia chinensis* 30–31 cm
(**a,b**) **Adult** *tigrina*: Broad, white-spotted black neck-patch, long graduated tail with broadly white-tipped outer feathers, pale greyish bar across greater coverts (prominent in flight). Otherwise greyish-brown above, with indistinct dark streaks and narrow light edging, pale grey crown and ear-coverts, pale vinous-brownish neck/underparts, whitish throat and vent. (**c**) **Juvenile**: Much browner; warmer and less vinous-pink below, distinct buff fringes above and on breast, little grey on crown and wing-coverts, faint dark brown neck-patch with buffish-brown bars. (**d**) **Adult** *chinensis* (north E Tonkin): Bluer-grey crown, unstreaked brown upperparts, deeper pinkish neck and breast, greyer undertail-coverts and darker slaty-grey on wing-coverts. **VOICE** Song is soft *wu hu'crrroo*; *wu-crrroo* or *wu huuu-croo*, or more hurried *wu-hwrrroo..wu-hwrrroo..* etc. **HABITAT** Open areas, open woodland, scrub, cultivation, parks and gardens; up to 2,040 m. **RANGE** Co **R** throughout.

3 RED COLLARED DOVE *Streptopelia tranquebarica* 23–24.5 cm
(**a**) **Male** *humilis*: Largely brownish vinous-red; pale bluish-grey on head , black neck-bar, grey rump and uppertail-coverts, rather short square tail with broadly white-tipped outer feathers, whitish undertail-coverts. (**b,c**) **Female**: Similar pattern to male but body and wing-coverts mostly brownish, less grey on head; vent whitish. (**d**) **Juvenile**: Like female but no neck-bar, upperparts, wing-coverts and breast fringed buffish, primaries, primary coverts and alula tipped dull rufous, crown rufescent-tinged. **VOICE** Song is soft, throaty, rhythmically repeated *croodle-oo-croo*. **HABITAT** Drier open country, scrub, cultivation; up to 1,200 m. **RANGE** Co **R**, subject to local movements (except S Thailand, Pen Malaysia, Singapore). **FER** (expanding range) west and south Pen Malaysia (ra), Singapore. **V** S Thailand.

4 EURASIAN COLLARED DOVE *Streptopelia decaocto* 33 cm
(**a,b**) **Adult** *xanthocyclus*: Like smaller, shorter-tailed female Red but has paler mantle, no slaty-grey on rump and uppertail-coverts, paler and more pinkish-grey breast, grey vent, much

pale grey on wing-coverts. (**c**) **Juvenile**: Crown, mantle and underparts browner, no neck-bar, narrow buff fringes above and on breast. From Red as adult, plus less distinct buff fringing, no dull rufous tips to primaries etc. **VOICE** Song is soft *coo-cooo cu* or *wu-hooo hu*. Calls with husky *vrrrrr* or *vvrrrroo*. **HABITAT** Dry open country, scrub, cultivation; lowlands. **RANGE** Co **R** SW,N(south-east),C,S(north-west) Myanmar.

5 BARRED CUCKOO DOVE *Macropygia unchall* 38–41 cm
(**a,b**) **Male** *tusalia*: Slender, long tail, dark-looking wings/tail, dark rufescent above with blackish bars. Unbarred paler head, buffish-brown below, vinous-tinged and finely blackish-barred breast, violet-/green-glossed nape, upper mantle and (less so) breast. (**c**) **Female**: Paler above with dense blackish bars (throat/vent plainer). (**d**) **Juvenile**: Darker than female, all-barred head and neck. **Other subspecies** *M.u.minor* (N Indochina), *unchall* (Pen Malaysia). **VOICE** Song is deep *who-OO* or *wu-OO*, every 1–2 s; sometimes quicker *wuOO* or longer *wuOOO*. **HABITAT** Broadleaved evergreen and semi-evergreen forest; 140–1,800 m. **RANGE** Lc **R**, subject to some movements (except SW Myanmar, C,S Thailand, Singapore).

6 LITTLE CUCKOO DOVE *Macropygia ruficeps* 28–33 cm
(**a,b**) **Male** *assimilis*: Smaller than Barred, unbarred above, crown distinctly rufous-chestnut, more uniform below, breast rufous-buff with heavy whitish scales, underwing-coverts rufous-buff. (**c**) **Female**: Breast heavily mottled blackish, wing-coverts more distinctly fringed chestnut. **Juvenile**: Similar to female but mantle and belly a little more barred, lower throat/breast more boldly marked. (**d**) **Male** *malayana* (Pen Malaysia; presumably S Thailand): Darker overall, blackish mottling on breast, broader chestnut fringes to wing-coverts. (**e**) **Female**: Heavier black mottling on lower throat and upper breast; otherwise differs as male. **Other subspecies** *M.r.engelbachi* (N Indochina). **VOICE** Song is soft monotonous *wup-wup-wup-wup-wup...* (c.2 notes per s). Each bout consists of up to 40 notes. **HABITAT** Broadleaved evergreen forest, sometimes adjacent deciduous forest, forest edge; 500–1,830 m. **RANGE** Sc/lc **R** S(east),E Myanmar, Tenasserim, W,NW,NE,extreme S Thailand, Pen Malaysia, N Laos, W Tonkin, N Annam.

7 PEACEFUL DOVE *Geopelia striata* 21–21.5 cm
(**a,b**) **Male**: Like a miniature Spotted but greyer above, with dark bars and no streaks, neck and flanks barred black and white, centre of breast unbarred vinous-pink, forehead and face distinctly pale bluish-grey, orbital skin pale grey-blue. **Female**: Like male but bars extend further onto breast, possibly has less distinctly blue-grey forecrown. (**c**) **Juvenile**: Duller, less contrasting bars on hindneck, rather uniform dark brownish and buffish-brown bars on crown, upperparts and wing-coverts, less distinct bars on underparts, but extending further across breast (which almost lacks vinous-pink), warm buffish fringes to tail and flight feathers. **VOICE** Song is high soft trilling, leading to rapidly delivered *coo* notes. **HABITAT** Scrub in open country and along coasts, parks, gardens, cultivation; up to 2,030 m (usually lowlands). **RANGE** Co **R** south Tenasserim, S Thailand, Pen Malaysia, Singapore. Un/co **FER** (expanding range) rest of Thailand, north-west Cambodia, N Laos (Vientiane).

PLATE 36 GREEN PIGEONS

1 CINNAMON-HEADED GREEN PIGEON *Treron fulvicollis* 26 cm
(a) **Male** *fulvicollis*: Rufous-chestnut hood. (b) **Female**: Like Thick-billed but bill distinctly narrower, eyering much narrower, crown greener, thighs yellowish, undertail-coverts streaked (not barred). **Juvenile**: Initially like female. **VOICE** Sings like Little but less whining, more syllabic. **HABITAT** Freshwater swamp forest, mangroves, coastal forest; lowlands (rarely to 1,250 m Pen Malaysia). **RANGE** Ra/un **R** (some movements) south Tenasserim, S Thailand, Pen Malaysia. Ra **NBV** (**FR**) Singapore.

2 LITTLE GREEN PIGEON *Treron olax* 20–20.5 cm
(a) **Male**: Bluish-grey hood, maroon above, orange breast-patch, dark slaty tail with paler terminal band. (b) **Female**: Dark grey crown, dark green above, dull green below, buffish green-streaked undertail-coverts, blackish-slate outertail, no red on bill. **Juvenile**: Initially like female but a little darker above, crown less distinctly grey, scapulars, tertials and lesser coverts tipped chestnut (obscurely on mantle). **VOICE** Song is high, rather nasal and well structured: roughly *wiiiiii-iiu-iiu iiu-iiui iiui-iiuwu*. **HABITAT** Broadleaved evergreen forest, freshwater swamp forest; up to 1,220 m. **RANGE** Sc/fc **R** (local movements) S Thailand, Pen Malaysia. Sc **NBV** (**FR**) Singapore.

3 PINK-NECKED GREEN PIGEON *Treron vernans* 26.5–32 cm
(a) **Male** *griseicapilla*: Grey head, pinkish nape/neck, blackish tail-band. (b) **Female**: Plainer/greyer above than Orange-breasted, blackish tail-band. **Juvenile**: Initially as female but tertials browner, scapulars/tertials fringed whitish to buffish, primary tips browner. **VOICE** Bubbling/gargling, then harsh grating. Hoarse rasping *krrak, krrak...* **HABITAT** Lowland scrub, mangroves, swamp and island forest. **RANGE** Co, mostly coastal **R** (local movements) south Tenasserim, Thailand (except NE), Pen Malaysia, Singapore, Cambodia, S Annam, Cochinchina.

4 ORANGE-BREASTED GREEN PIGEON *T.bicincta* 29 cm
(a) **Male** *bicincta*: Green head, grey nape, green above with brownish tinge, vinous-pink and orange breast, grey central tail. Rufescent undertail-coverts, broad grey terminal band on blackish undertail. (b) **Female**: Green breast. **Juvenile**: Initially as female but greener nape, dull buffish scapular/tertial fringes (vaguely mantle), rufescent fringes on lesser coverts, pale primary tips. **VOICE** Song is mellow wandering whistle and low gurgles. Calls with *ko-WRRROOOK, ko-WRRROOOK..* and *kreeeew-kreeeew-kreeeew*. **HABITAT** More open broadleaved forests, sometimes mangroves; up to 800 m. **RANGE** Un/lfc **R** (except C Thailand, Singapore, N,C Laos, W,E Tonkin).

5 POMPADOUR GREEN PIGEON *T.pompadora* 25.5–26 cm
(a) **Male** *phayrei*: Like Thick-billed but lacks broad eyering, bill thinner and greyish, orange breast-wash, yellower-tinged throat. Undertail-coverts brick-red. (b) **Female**: From Thick-billed as male (except breast-wash), plus short-streaked (not scaled) undertail-coverts. **Juvenile**: Initially like female but darker above, less grey on crown, pale primary tips, vague paler tips above. **Other subspecies** *T.p.chloroptera* (Coco Is): Much larger/thicker-billed. Male has green lesser coverts, bright lime-

green rump, grey-green undertail-coverts with pale yellow tips; female has bright lime-green rump/undertail-coverts. **VOICE** Sings with ascending and descending, pleasant wandering whistles. **HABITAT** Broadleaved evergreen/semi-evergreen forest; up to 800 m. **RANGE** Sc/lc **R** (minor movements) Myanmar, Thailand (except S), Cambodia, Laos, Cochinchina.

6 THICK-BILLED GREEN PIGEON *Treron curvirostra* 25.5–27 cm
(a) **Male** *nipalensis*: Thick, red-based, pale greenish bill, broad greenish-blue eyering, grey crown, maroon above, green below. Undertail-coverts dull chestnut. (b,c) **Female**: No maroon above, undertail-coverts creamy-buff with dark green scales, thighs dark green with whitish scales. **Juvenile**: Initially as female but rusty fringes on scapular/tertial/primary tips. **Other subspecies** *T.c.curvirostra* (S Thailand southwards). **VOICE** Song similar to Little Green but fuller, lower-pitched and more phrased. Guttural hissing and growling when foraging. **HABITAT** Broadleaved forests; up to 1,280 m. **RANGE** Co **R** (except C Thailand, Singapore, W Tonkin); local movements. Ra/un **NBV** C Thailand, Singapore (**FR**).

7 LARGE GREEN PIGEON *Treron capellei* 35.5–36 cm
(a) **Male**: Large; yellowish eyering/legs, greyish face, yellow-orange breast-patch. (b) **Female**: Yellowish breast-patch, no chestnut on undertail-coverts. **Juvenile**: As female, but male has more orange breast-patch, pale rufous undertail-coverts. **VOICE** Sings with deep nasal creaking *oo-oo-aah oo-oo-aah aa-aa-aah* and *ooo0Oah oo-aah* etc. Deep grumbles and growls. **HABITAT** Broadleaved evergreen and freshwater swamp forest; up to 200 m, rarely 1,220 m. **RANGE** Ra/un **R** (some movements) south Tenasserim, S Thailand, Pen Malaysia.

8 WEDGE-TAILED GREEN PIGEON *Treron sphenura* 33 cm
(a) **Male** *sphenura*: Maroon upper mantle/lesser coverts, yellow forehead, apricot crown-/breast-wash, wedge-shaped tail, blue bill-base. (b,c) **Female**: No apricot or maroon. **Juvenile**: Initially as female. (d) **Male** *robinsoni* (Pen Malaysia): 28–29 cm. Darker; little/no apricot on crown/breast, maroon only on shoulder, undertail-coverts like female. Female is darker than *sphenura*, less contrasting forehead. **Other subspecies** *T.s.delacouri* (S Laos, C,S Annam): Like *robinsoni* but male undertail-coverts typical. *T.s.yunnanensis* (W Tonkin). **VOICE** Song long and quite high, with rolling introduction: *phruuu-uah-po phuu phuuuu phuu-phu phuo-oh po-oh-oh-po-po-ohpopopo puuuuuuuah puuooaha wo-pi-ohaauah* etc. (may be no introduction). **HABITAT** Broadleaved evergreen forest; 600–2,565 m, non-breeders rarely in plains (Indochina). **RANGE** Lc **R**, subject to local movements (except C,S Thailand, Singapore, E Tonkin, Cochinchina).

9 WHITE-BELLIED GREEN PIGEON *Treron sieboldii* 33 cm
(a) **Male** *murielae*: Like Wedge-tailed but mostly whitish belly, whiter on undertail-coverts, no maroon on mantle, undertail blackish, narrowly tipped grey. (b) **Female**: From Wedge-tailed as male. **VOICE** Repeated mournful *o-aooh* or *oo-whooo*, (o-/oo-* higher). Short *pyu* in alarm. **HABITAT** Broadleaved evergreen forest; 200–900 m (to 2,000 m Thailand). **RANGE** Sc/lo **R** W,NW,NE Thailand, C Laos, E Tonkin, N,C Annam.

PLATE 37 MISCELLANEOUS DOVES & PIGEONS

1 EMERALD DOVE *Chalcophaps indica* 23–27 cm
(**a,b**) **Male** *indica*: Metallic green mantle/wings, blue-grey crown/nape, white forehead/eyebrow, dark vinous-pinkish below; whitish/pale grey back-bands, white shoulder-patch, red bill. (**c**) **Female**: Head, mantle and breast much browner, belly paler and more buffish, grey restricted to forehead/eyebrow, no white on shoulder. (**d**) **Juvenile**: Crown, mantle and breast darker brown than female, plumage mostly barred rufous-buff (less on crown-/mantle-centre, boldest on breast), almost lacks green above. **Other subspecies** *C.i.maxima* (Cocos Is, S Myanmar). **VOICE** Song is deep soft *tit-whoooo* or *tik-whooOO* (clicking *tit/tik* barely audible), repeated after c.1 s intervals. **HABITAT & BEHAVIOUR** Broadleaved forest; up to 1,500 m. Often flushed from forest trails and stream-beds. **RANGE** Un/co **R**, subject to some movements (except C Thailand).

2 NICOBAR PIGEON *Caloenas nicobarica* 40.5–41 cm
(**a,b**) **Adult** *nicobarica*: All dark with white uppertail-coverts and short white tail. Head, neck (including long hackles) and breast blackish-slate with golden-green/blue gloss, otherwise mostly blue and green with copper highlights above, bill blackish with short 'horn' near base. (**c**) **Juvenile**: Duller/browner; rather uniform dark greenish-brown head, mantle and under-parts, no neck-hackles, dark brownish-green tail with blue tinge (kept for several years). **VOICE** Harsh guttural croaking or barking *ku-RRAU* and low reverberating *rrr-rrr-rrr-rrr...*. **HABITAT & BEHAVIOUR** Small wooded islands, dispersing to but rarely seen in mainland coastal forest. Mostly terrestrial, runs from danger or flies up to hide in trees. **RANGE** Sc/lo **R** (local movements) on islands off S Myanmar (Coco Is), Tenasserim, west S Thailand, Pen Malaysia, Cochinchina. Visits mainland coasts.

3 YELLOW-FOOTED GREEN PIGEON *Treron phoenicoptera* 33 cm
(**a**) **Male** *annamensis*: Grey crown/nape, pale green throat, yellowish-green neck and upper breast, pale grey-green above, grey lower breast/belly, yellow legs/feet. Has small pinkish-maroon shoulder-patch, bright yellowish-olive tail with grey terminal half and dark maroon undertail-coverts with creamy-buff bars. **Female**: Typically has fainter shoulder-patch. **Juvenile**: Paler/duller than female, little/no shoulder-patch. (**b**) **Male** *viridifrons* (Myanmar): Paler, yellower-green throat and breast (washed golden on latter), greenish-golden hindneck (collar), green forecrown, paler/greener (less greyish) above, slightly paler grey below. **VOICE** c.10 modulated mellow musical whistles, recalling Orange-breasted but louder and lower-pitched. **HABITAT** Mixed deciduous forest, secondary growth; lowlands, sometimes up to 1,220 m. **RANGE** Sc/lc **R** Myanmar, W,NW,NE Thailand, Cambodia, C,S Laos, C,S Annam, north Cochinchina.

4 PIN-TAILED GREEN PIGEON *Treron apicauda* 30.5–40.5 cm
(**a**) **Male** *apicauda*: Wedge-shaped grey tail (outer feathers blackish near base) with long and pointed central feathers (prongs). Has bright blue naked lores and base of rather slender bill, mostly brightish green body, apricot breast-flush, green belly (any white restricted to vent), chestnut undertail-coverts with outer webs fringed buffish-white. In hand, distinctive lobe on inner fringe of third and fourth primaries. (**b,c**) **Female**: Breast all green, sometimes less chestnut on undertail-coverts (and more whitish), tail-prongs shorter (still long and pointed). **Juvenile male**: Tail-prongs shorter/blunter, wing-coverts rounder, creating different pattern of yellow fringes; primary tips faintly tinged pale grey-green. (**d**) **Male** *lowei* (southern Indochina): Duller green head with feathered lores, light brownish-grey wash on neck/coverts, contrasting greenish-yellow rump/uppertail-coverts, all green below. In hand, distinctive indentation on inner web of third primary. (**e**) **Female**: Differs as male; also lacks chestnut on undertail-coverts. **Other subspecies** *T.a.laotinus* (northern Indochina). **VOICE** Sings with musical, wandering whistles: *ko-kla-oi-oi-oi-oilli-illio-kla* (by duetting pair?). Said to be more tuneful and less meandering than that of Wedge-tailed. **HABITAT** Broadleaved evergreen forest; 600–1,830 m, sometimes 300 m or lower. **RANGE** Un **R** (local movements) Myanmar, north Tenasserim, W,NW,NE Thailand, east Cambodia, Laos, W,E Tonkin, N,C,S(north and west) Annam. **Rc** (status?) Cochinchina.

5 YELLOW-VENTED GREEN PIGEON *Treron seimundi* 26–33 cm
(**a,b**) **Male** *seimundi*: Like Pin-tailed but much shorter tail-prongs, generally darker green, maroon shoulder-patch, whitish belly-centre, mostly yellow undertail-coverts with narrow green centres. Has golden-tinged forecrown, pinkish-orange breast-wash, blue bill with horn-grey tip, blue naked lores/eyering. (**c**) **Female**: Broader green undertail-covert centres, no maroon on shoulder, greener breast. **Other subspecies** *T.s.modestus* (Indochina): All-green crown/breast. **VOICE** Song is high *pooaah po-yo-yo-pooaah*. **HABITAT** Broadleaved evergreen forest, forest edge; 250–1,525 m. **RANGE** Ra/lfc **R** (local movements) W,NW,SE Thailand, Pen Malaysia, C,S Laos, Vietnam (except W Tonkin). **Rc** (status?) C Thailand.

6 JAMBU FRUIT DOVE *Ptilinopus jambu* 26.5–27 cm
(**a**) **Male**: Greenish above, crimson face, white eyering, white below with pink flush on foreneck/upper breast. Bill orange-yellow, undertail-coverts chestnut. (**b**) **Female**: Mostly green with greyish-purple face, white eyering, maroon gular stripe, paler vent, buffish undertail-coverts. (**c**) **Juvenile**: As female but face brownish, throat-centre whitish (washed dull rufous). Initially has warm brown fringing above. **VOICE** Repeated soft *booo*. **HABITAT** Broadleaved evergreen forest, rarely mangroves; up to 1,280 m. **RANGE** Sc/un **R** (local movements) southern S Thailand, Pen Malaysia. Sc **NBV** Singapore.

7 PIED IMPERIAL PIGEON *Ducula bicolor* 38–41 cm
(**a,b**) **Adult**: White with black flight feathers and black tail with white on outer feathers. **Juvenile**: White feathers tipped buffish, particularly above. **VOICE** Deep, rather quiet *cru-croo* or *croo croo-oo*. Deep resonant *rruuu* or *wrrooom*, every 1–3 s. Also *whoo whoo whoo boo boo* (notes descending in pitch and gradually getting shorter). **HABITAT** Island forest, sometimes mangroves and mainland forest; lowlands. **RANGE** Lc coastal **R** (local movements) SW Myanmar, Tenasserim, SE,S Thailand, Pen Malaysia, Cambodia, Cochinchina (Con Dao I only?). Mostly on offshore islands. Sc **NBV** (mainly coastal) W Thailand, Singapore. **Rc** (status?) Coco Is, S Myanmar.

82

PLATE 38 BUSTARDS, CRANES & MASKED FINFOOT

1 GREAT BUSTARD *Otis tarda* 75–105 cm
(**a,b**) **Male non-breeding** *dybowskii*: Very large, robust; bluish-grey head/neck, warm buffish above with blackish vermiculations, mostly white below, rufous-chestnut on lower hindneck. Extensively white/pale grey upperwing with broad blackish band across flight feathers (lesser coverts as upperparts), whitish underwing with blackish trailing edge. (**c**) **Male breeding**: Long white whiskers, thicker neck, rufous-chestnut collar/breast-band. (**d**) **Female**: As male non-breeding but up to 50% smaller, bill and neck relatively thinner, has less white on upperwing (coverts more extensively as upperparts). **First winter**: Like female. Males reach adulthood between 3rd and 5th summers. **VOICE** Nasal *ock* in alarm. **HABITAT & BEHAVIOUR** Open country, grassland, cultivation; recorded at 455 m. Hides in long grass, crops; strong direct flight. **RANGE** V N Myanmar.

2 BENGAL FLORICAN *Houbaropsis bengalensis* 66–68.5 cm
(**a,b**) **Male** *blandini*: Largely black with mostly white wings; buff markings on mantle to uppertail and tertials. (**c,d**) **Female**: Buffish-brown with blackish markings above, blackish crown-sides, warm buff supercilium and median crown-stripe, pale buff neck/upper breast with fine dark brown vermiculations, otherwise rather plain buff below (whiter in centre) with sparse dark flank markings; more plain buff on wing-coverts than male, outer primaries mostly blackish. **Juvenile**: Like female but buff plumage noticeably richer/warmer. **First-summer male**: Resembles adult male but reverts to female-like plumage in second winter; fully adult by second summer. **VOICE** Croaks and strange deep humming during display. Shrill metallic *chik-chik-chik* in alarm. **HABITAT & BEHAVIOUR** Grassland, nearby cultivation; lowlands. Displaying male leaps 8–10 m in air, hovers on quivering wings, then floats down. Approaches female with raised, spread tail and trailing wings. **RANGE** Ra **R** (local movements) north-west, central and south-east Cambodia, western and north-west Cochinchina.

3 SARUS CRANE *Grus antigone* 152–156 cm
(**a,b**) **Adult**: *sharpii*: Huge; rather uniform grey, mostly naked red head/upper neck. Primaries and primary coverts blackish, secondaries mostly grey, bill longish and pale greenish-brown, legs pale reddish. Red of head/neck brighter when breeding. (**c**) **Juvenile**: Head/upper neck buffish and feathered, duller overall with brownish-grey fringing (more cinnamon-brown above). **Other subspecies** *G.a.antigone* (reported SW Myanmar): Paler (particularly below), whiter midneck and tertials. **VOICE** Very loud trumpeting, usually by duetting pairs. **HABITAT & BEHAVIOUR** Marshy grassland, open country, rice paddies; up to 1,000 m. Display by pairs includes wing-spreading, bowing, head-lowering and leaps into air. **RANGE** Ra/lo **R** (local movements) N,C,E,S Myanmar, Cambodia, S Laos, S Annam. **FR** SW,W Myanmar, Tenasserim, NW,C,NE,S Thailand, north-west Pen Malaysia, C Laos, Cochinchina. Sc/lo **NBV** Cochinchina.

4 DEMOISELLE CRANE *Grus virgo* 90–100 cm
(**a,b**) **Adult**: Smaller and smaller-billed than Common, shorter neck, longer, more pointed tertials; mostly blackish head/neck-sides, long black feathers on lower foreneck/upper breast, grey

crown and hindneck-centre, long white postocular tufts. (**c**) **First winter** Black of head/neck duller, pale plumage brownish-grey, lower foreneck feathers and inner secondaries shorter, postocular tufts shorter and greyer. **VOICE** Loud *garroo* in flight, higher than in Common. Rasping *krruorr* courtship call (more guttural than in Common). **HABITAT** Marshes, open areas, cultivation; up to 800 m. **RANGE** V SW,W,E Myanmar.

5 COMMON CRANE *Grus grus* 110–120 cm
(**a,b**) **Adult** *lilfordi*: Blackish head/upper neck, with red patch on crown and broad white band from ear-coverts down upper neck-side. Long drooping tertials mixed with black. In flight, blackish flight feathers contrast with grey wing-coverts. (**c**) **First winter**: Head/upper neck warm buffish to grey, rest of plumage (particularly above) often mixed with brown; may show whitish to buffy-whitish patch behind eye. Smaller and much shorter-billed than Sarus, dark markings on wings, dark legs. More like adult by first spring, fully adult by third winter/spring. **VOICE** Loud bugling *krooh*, *krrooah* and *kurr* etc., higher-pitched *klay*, croaking *rrrrrrer* and various honking sounds; mainly in flight. Duets by bonded pairs include: *kroo-krii-kroo-krii…* **HABITAT** Marshes, open areas, cultivation; up to 3,100 m. **RANGE** Ra/un **WV** N(lc),E Myanmar, E Tonkin; formerly N,C Annam. **V** NW Thailand, **Rc** (status?) SW Myanmar.

6 BLACK-NECKED CRANE *Grus nigricollis* 139 cm
(**a,b**) **Adult**: Head/upper neck all black, with white spot behind eye and mostly dull red naked crown; paler and whiter than Common with all-blackish tertials. In flight, shows more contrasting upperwing. (**c**) **Juvenile/immature**: Juvenile buff-washed/-scaled. At three months crown feathered and buffish, black of neck mixed with whitish. At eight months, like adult but shows some buff scales above, neck greyish-black. As adult after one year. **VOICE** Somewhat higher than Common. **HABITAT** Marshy areas, cultivation; lowlands. **RANGE** Formerly ra/sc **WV** E Tonkin.

7 MASKED FINFOOT *Heliopais personata* 52–54.5 cm
(**a**) **Male**: Black throat/upper foreneck with white border, black forecrown/line along crown-side, thick yellow bill with small horn at base (spring only?). Brown above, greyer nape to mantle, mostly whitish below, brown flanks/undertail-coverts with some whitish bars, eyes dark brown, legs/feet bright green. (**b**) **Female**: Throat/upper foreneck and forelores whitish, no horn, yellow eyes. **Juvenile**: Browner above than female, no black on forecrown, more mottled black on neck, paler bill. **Male first winter**: Like adult but has white centre to throat and upper foreneck and small amount of white on lores. **VOICE** Series of rather high-pitched bubbling sounds (like air being blown through tube into water), possibly followed by series of clucks which increase in tempo. **HABITAT & BEHAVIOUR** Rivers in broadleaved evergreen forest, mangroves, swamp forest, sometimes pools and lakes away from forest; up to 700 m but recorded up to 1,220 m on migration. Usually very secretive. **RANGE** Sc **R** S Myanmar, Cambodia. Sc **WV** and **PM** (probably also lo **R**) S Thailand, Pen Malaysia. **V** Singapore. **Rc** (status?) SW,N,C,E Myanmar, Tenasserim, W,NW,NE,SE Thailand, S Laos, C,S Annam.

7 to different scale

PLATE 39 CRAKES, GALLINULES & JACANAS

1 CORN CRAKE *Crex crex* 24.5–28.5 cm
(**a,b**) **Male non-breeding**: Smaller than female Watercock, greyish supercilium, plain breast, rufous-and-whitish barred flanks; rufescent upperwing. (**c**) **Male breeding**: More defined blue-grey supercilium/foreneck, and tinge to breast. **Female non-breeding**: Less grey supercilium than male; often no grey on cheeks/neck/breast. **Female breeding**: Buffier/less greyish above than male, supercilium thinner/greyer, often less grey on cheeks/neck/breast. **First winter**: Similar to female non-breeding. **VOICE** Short, loud *tsuck* in alarm. **HABITAT** Lowland grassland, rice fields and other cultivation. **RANGE** V Cochinchina.

2 WHITE-BREASTED WATERHEN *Amaurornis phoenicurus* 32 cm
(**a**) **Adult** *phoenicurus*: White face to belly, rufous-chestnut vent. Yellowish bill (red at base) and legs. (**b**) **Juvenile**: Browner; darker lores, forehead and ear-coverts, broken bars below, dull bill. **Other subspecies** *A.p.insularis* (Coco Is, S Myanmar): Often more white on forecrown, abdomen has less white (bordered black), vent richer chestnut. **VOICE** Weird bubbling, roaring, quacking and croaking: *kru-ak kru-ak kru-ak-a-wak-wak* etc *kwaak* and *kuk* notes. Quick *pwik* notes. **HABITAT** Wide variety of wetlands, tracks, roadsides; up to 1,525 m. **RANGE** Co R throughout. Fc **WV** S Thailand, Pen Malaysia, Singapore, N Laos. Also **PM** S Thailand, Pen Malaysia.

3 WATERCOCK *Gallicrex cinerea* M 41–43 cm; f 31–36 cm
(**a**) **Male breeding**: Blackish; grey/buff fringing above, mostly yellow bill, red frontal shield/legs. (**b**) **Male non-breeding**: As female non-breeding; possibly broader/bolder bars below. (**c,d**) **Female breeding**: Dark brown above with buff fringing, buff below with greyish-brown bars, greenish bill/legs. Non-breeders have heavier bars below. (**e**) **Juvenile**: As female non-breeding, but warmer, broader streaks above and less distinct bars below. **VOICE** Territorial call is 10–12 *ogh* notes, then 10–12 metallic booming *ootoomb* notes, then 5–6 *kluck* notes. Nasal *krey* in alarm. **HABITAT** Freshwater marshes/grassland, rice paddies; up to 1,220 m. **RANGE** Un/fc R C Myanmar, W,C,NE(south-west),SE,S Thailand, Pen Malaysia, Cambodia, S Laos, C,S Annam, Cochinchina. Un/lc **BV** N Myanmar, NW,C(north),NE Thailand. Fc **WV** S Thailand, Pen Malaysia, Singapore, Cambodia, Cochinchina. Un/fc **PM** Pen Malaysia, N Laos, E Tonkin. **Rc** (status?) SW,S Myanmar, Tenasserim, C Laos.

4 PURPLE SWAMPHEN *Porphyrio porphyrio* 28.5–42 cm   Ga y pr 10 14
(**a**) **Adult** *poliocephalus*: Purple-blue; big red bill and frontal shield, red legs, silvery-washed face, dark turquoise throat to upper breast and wings, white undertail-coverts. (**b**) **Juvenile**: Browner hindneck to rump, smaller, blackish bill/shield. (**c**) **Adult** *viridis* (southern Myanmar, southern C Thailand and southern Indochina southward): Mostly blackish-brown above, turquoise on shoulder. **Other subspecies** *P.p.indicus* (Singapore?): As *viridis* but hindcrown, head-sides and upper throat blacker, no silvery wash on head/neck. **VOICE** Powerful, rattling nasal *quinquinkrrkrrquinquinkrrkrr...* Chuckling and cackling. Soft *puk-puk..*, and rising nasal *cooah* in alarm. **HABITAT** Freshwater marshes, well-vegetated lakes; up to 1,000 m. **RANGE** Sc/lc **R**, subject to minor movements (except W Myanmar, SE Thailand, W Tonkin).

5 COMMON MOORHEN *Gallinula chloropus* 30–35 cm
(**a**) **Adult** *chloropus*: Dark slaty-brown (greyer below), white lateral undertail-coverts and flank-line, yellow-tipped red bill, red frontal shield, yellow-green legs. (**b**) **Juvenile**: Browner; pale head-sides/underparts, whitish throat/centre of abdomen, greenish-brown bill. **First winter/summer**: Browner head, neck and underparts than adult. **Other subspecies** *G.c.orientalis* (south of c.9°N): Smaller/darker, relatively large shield. **VOICE** Loud *krrrruk* or *kark* (territorial). Muttering *kook*, loud *kekuk* or *kittick*; loud *keh-keh* in alarm. **HABITAT** Freshwater lakes, pools, marshes, rice paddies; up to 1,000 m. **RANGE** Some movements (except W,N Myanmar, N Laos, W Tonkin, N Annam). Lc **WV** N,C,E Myanmar, Cambodia, N Laos, N Annam, Cochinchina, ? S Thailand.

Two groups Cambodia paddic

6 COMMON COOT *Fulica atra* 40.5–42.5 cm
(**a**) **Adult** *atra*: Slaty-black; white bill and frontal shield. (**b**) **Juvenile**: Browner-tinged; whitish throat and foreneck-centre, paler belly, smaller frontal shield. **VOICE** Combat call is explosive *pssi* or *pyee* (male); croaking *ai* or *u*, becoming *ai-oeu-ai-ai-oeu...* etc. in alarm (female). Short *kow*, *kut* or sharper *kick* (two notes may be combined) contact calls. Also hard, smacking *ta* or *p* notes from male. **HABITAT** Freshwater lakes, marshes; up to 800 m. **RANGE** Ra/un **WV** Myanmar (lc in N), NW,NE,C Thailand, Cambodia, N,S Laos, E Tonkin, N,C Annam, Cochinchina. **V** S Thailand, Pen Malaysia, Singapore.

7 PHEASANT-TAILED JACANA *Hydrophasianus chirurgus* 29–31.5 cm (breeding adult tail up to 25 cm more)
(**a**) **Adult breeding**: Blackish-brown; white head/foreneck, yellow-buff hindneck, long blackish tail, mostly white wings. (**b,c**) **Adult non-breeding**: Drab brown above, pale buff supercilium/neck-side bordered by black eyestripe that leads to breast-band, white below, shorter tail. (**d**) **Juvenile**: As adult non-breeding but rufous-chestnut crown, rufous-buff fringing above, weaker breast-band. **VOICE** Deep rhythmic *t'you* or *me-onp* notes, and nasal mewing *jaew* or *tewn* notes (territorial). Sharp *tic-tic-tic..* and nasal *brrr-brrp*; high whining *eeeaaar* in alarm. **HABITAT** Well-vegetated freshwater marshes, lakes and pools, also mangroves, large rivers on passage; up to 1,000 m. **RANGE** Un/lc **R** (some movements) Myanmar (except W), C,NE Thailand, Cambodia. Sc/lfc **WV** Thailand, Pen Malaysia, Cambodia, N,S Annam, Cochinchina. Sc/un **PM** C Thailand, Pen Malaysia, N Laos, E Tonkin (formerly bred), C Annam. **V** Singapore. **Rc** (status?) C,S Laos.

8 BRONZE-WINGED JACANA *Metopidius indicus* 27–30 cm
(**a**) **Adult**: Green-glossed black head/neck/underparts, white supercilium, purplish-glossed lower hindneck, bronze-olive lower mantle to wing-coverts, chestnut-maroon back to upper-tail. (**b**) **Juvenile**: Dull chestnut crown, blacker on hindneck, whitish face and underparts with rufous-buff on neck, black and white tail. **VOICE** Short low harsh guttural grunts and wheezy piping *seek-seek-seek...* **HABITAT** Well-vegetated freshwater marshes, lakes, pools; up to 1,000 m. **RANGE** Un/lc **R** Myanmar (except W), Thailand (except SE), Indochina (except W,E Tonkin, N,C Annam); formerly north-west Pen Malaysia.

4–8 to different scale

PLATE 40 CRAKES & RAILS

1 RED-LEGGED CRAKE *Rallina fasciata* 22–25 cm
(a) **Adult**: Blackish-and-whitish wing markings, and vent bars, red legs. (b) **Juvenile**: Duller; brownish-yellow legs. **VOICE** Territorial call (often at night) is loud rapid hard *UH-UH-UH-UH-UH-UH..*, every 1.5–3 s. Also, quacking nasal *brrr*, *brr'ay* or *grr'erb*. **HABITAT** Wet areas in broadleaved forest, clearings, nearby cultivation; up to 200 m (migrants to 1,220 m). **RANGE** Un **R** W(south),S Thailand, Singapore. Un **BV** W,NW Thailand. Un **R/BV** S Thailand, S Laos, Cochinchina. Un **WV** Pen Malaysia (breeds?), Singapore. Also un **PM** C Myanmar, S Thailand, Pen Malaysia. **Rc** (status?) W,E(south),S Myanmar, Tenasserim.

2 SLATY-LEGGED CRAKE *Rallina eurizonoides* 26–28 cm
(a) **Adult** *telmatophila*: Plain wings, grey/blackish legs. (b) **Juvenile/first winter**: Plain coverts, pale face. **VOICE** Persistent *kek-kek kek-kek kek-kek..* (territorial). Low *krrrr* alarm. Drummed *krrrrrrrr-ar-kraa-kraa-kraa-kraa*. **HABITAT** Wet areas in broadleaved forest, plantations (migrants also gardens, marshes); to 1,830 m. **RANGE** Sc **BV** E Tonkin. Sc **WV** S Thailand, Pen Malaysia, S Annam. Sc **PM** W,NE,C,S Thailand, Pen Malaysia, E Tonkin. V Singapore. **Rc** (status?) E,S Myanmar, NW Thailand, S Laos, C Annam, Cambodia, Cochinchina.

3 SLATY-BREASTED RAIL *Gallirallus striatus* 26–31 cm
(a) **Adult** *albiventer*: Chestnut crown, grey breast, black-and-white spots/bars above, dark legs. (b) **Juvenile**: Browner; blackish streaks above, duller vent-bars. **Other subspecies** *G.s.gularis* (Pen Malaysia, Singapore, Indochina). **VOICE** Stony *kerrek* or *trrrik* notes (territorial), which may run to kind of song lasting <30 s. Low *kuk* and *ka-ka-kaa-kaa* (courting male). **HABITAT** Marshes, mangroves, rice fields; up to 1,300 m. **RANGE** Co **R**, subject to some movements (except W Myanmar, NE,SE Thailand, S Annam). Also **PM** E Tonkin, N Annam.

4 WATER RAIL *Rallus aquaticus* 27–30 cm
(a) **Adult** *indicus*: Brownish crown and eyestripe, grey supercilium, broad blackish streaks above, fleshy-brown legs. **First winter**: Browner; some pale scales on breast. **VOICE** Drawn-out, squealing, grunting *grui* or *krueeb* notes, crescendoing to longer high whistles (like squealing piglets). Sharp *tic* notes, then wheezy screaming *wheee-ooo*; sharp *krribk*. **HABITAT** Freshwater marshes, reedbeds; up to 700 m. **RANGE** Ra **WV** SW,N,E Myanmar, NW,C,W(coastal) Thailand, N Laos, E Tonkin.

5 BROWN CRAKE *Porzana akool* 23.5–29 cm
(a) **Male** *akool*: Dark olive-brown above, grey below, greenish bill, dull legs. **Female**: Darker upper mandible and bill-tip. **Juvenile**: Darker above, browner below, bill as female. **Other subspecies** *P.a.coccineipes* (E Tonkin). **VOICE** Trills like Black-tailed. Stressed high *tuc* notes. **HABITAT** Overgrown waterways, swamps; to 800 m. **RANGE** Sc/un **R** SW Myanmar, E Tonkin.

6 BLACK-TAILED CRAKE *Porzana bicolor* 21–24 cm
(a) **Adult**: Rufescent above, black tail, slaty head/underparts, reddish legs. (b) **Juvenile**: Blacker above, browner below. **VOICE** Trill as Ruddy-breasted but more descending; often preceded by subdued *waak-waak*. High *kek* or *kik* notes. **HABITAT**

Swamps/streams near broadleaved evergreen forest, nearby cultivation; 1,000–1,830 m (locally c.200 m N Myanmar). **RANGE** Sc **R** W,N,E,S(east) Myanmar, NW Thailand, N Laos, W Tonkin.

7 BAILLON'S CRAKE *Porzana pusilla* 19–20.5 cm
(a) **Adult** *pusilla*: Greenish bill/legs, blackish-and-white streaks and speckles above, grey supercilium/below, black-and-white vent-bars; greenish legs. (b) **Juvenile**: No grey; whitish throat to belly-centre. **VOICE** Short *tac* or *tyiuk* alarm. Territorial call is creaky rasping *trrrrr-trrrrr*, every 1–2 s (may be preceded by dry *t* sounds). **HABITAT** Well vegetated freshwater wetlands; up to 1,400 m. **RANGE** Sc/un **WV** (except W,N Myanmar, SE Thailand, C,S Laos, W,E Tonkin, N Annam). Un/fc **PM** NW Thailand, Pen Malaysia, E Tonkin, C,S Annam, Cochinchina.

8 SPOTTED CRAKE *Porzana porzana* 21–24 cm
(a) **Male non-breeding**: More white above than Baillon's, brown below with white spots/bars, buff undertail-coverts. (b) **Male breeding**: Distinctly blue-grey supercilium, throat and breast, redder bill-base. **Female**: Less grey and more white on head than male non-breeding. (c) **First winter**: Throat white, head/neck-sides densely speckled whitish, dull bill. **VOICE** Sharp *tck* alarm notes. Territorial call is loud, rather high ascending *kwit* or *whitt*, about once per s. **HABITAT** Marshes, reedbeds; lowlands. **RANGE** V SW Myanmar, W(coastal),C Thailand.

9 RUDDY-BREASTED CRAKE *Porzana fusca* 21–26.5 cm
(a) **Adult** *fusca*: Plain wings, reddish-chestnut below, vague whitish-and-blackish vent-bars, green-based dark bill, red legs. (b) **Juvenile**: Whitish below with brownish-grey bars/mottling, dull legs. **Other subspecies** *P.f.erythrothorax* (visitor): Paler; less reddish below. **VOICE** Hard *tewk* or *kyot* notes (often speeding up), usually followed by high, slightly descending trill (territorial). Low *chuck* notes. **HABITAT** Freshwater wetlands, also drier areas, mangroves (mainly migrants); up to 1,450 m. **RANGE** Co **R**, subject to movements (except W Myanmar, Tenasserim, C Laos, E Tonkin, N,S Annam); **BV** in some northern areas. Co **WV** E Myanmar, Thailand (except S), E Tonkin, Cochinchina. Also co **PM** C Thailand, E Tonkin, C,S Annam.

10 BAND-BELLIED CRAKE *Porzana paykulli* 27 cm
(a) **Adult**: Cold brown crown/nape, extensive chestnut below, whitish and dark wing markings, red legs. (b) **First winter**: Paler head-sides/breast (vaguely barred) to upper belly, browner legs. **VOICE** Territorial call is loud metallic clangour running to brief trills (like wooden rattle). **HABITAT** Vegetated freshwater wetlands; up to 1,220 m (mostly lowlands). **RANGE** Ra/sc **PM** C Thailand, Pen Malaysia (also winters), E Tonkin, Cochinchina.

11 WHITE-BROWED CRAKE *Porzana cinerea* 19–21.5 cm
(a) **Adult**: Streaked above, black-and-white face-lines, greenish bare parts. **Juvenile**: More washed out, no red at bill-base, greyer. **VOICE** 10–12 loud nasal, rapidly repeated *chika*, notes. Loud *kek-kro*, nasal *bee* notes and quiet *charr-r* in alarm. **HABITAT** Well-vegetated lowland freshwater wetlands. **RANGE** Un/lc **R** C,W(coastal),S Thailand, Pen Malaysia, Singapore, Cambodia, N(south) Laos, Cochinchina.

PLATE 41 EURASIAN WOODCOCK & SNIPES

1 EURASIAN WOODCOCK *Scolopax rusticola* 33–35 cm
(**a,b**) **Adult**: Heavy, robust; black-barred hindcrown, soft rufescent-brown and buff pattern above (no long pale stripes), all-barred brown-and-buff below. VOICE When flushed, may give snipe-like *scaap* notes. Weak high *pissipp* and guttural *aurk-aurk-aurk* during display. HABITAT & BEHAVIOUR Damp areas in forest, cover along streams; up to 2,565 m (breeds above 1,830 m in Himalayas). Often flushed in daytime. Males perform roding display at dawn/dusk when breeding, flying circuits over trees, with deliberate wingbeats. RANGE Un **R** N Myanmar. Un/fc **WV** Myanmar, Thailand (except S), Indochina (except Cochinchina). **V** S Thailand, Pen Malaysia, Singapore.

2 SOLITARY SNIPE *Gallinago solitaria* 29–31 cm
(**a–c**) **Adult** *solitaria*: Relatively large; whitish face and mantle-lines, extensive rufous vermiculations above, gingery breast-patch, white-edged median coverts (forming pale panel), bright rufous-chestnut on tail. Legs pale yellowish-green to yellowish-brown. In flight, toes do not project beyond tail. VOICE May give harsh *kensh* when flushed, somewhat deeper than Common. HABITAT & BEHAVIOUR Streams, swampy pools, sometimes rice paddies and marshes; 1,000–1,675 m. Flies like Common but somewhat slower and heavier. RANGE Ra **WV** W,N,E Myanmar.

3 WOOD SNIPE *Gallinago nemoricola* 28–32 cm
(**a–c**) **Adult**: Relatively large/bulky/short-billed; dark above with bold buff stripes/scaling, all-barred lower breast to vent. In flight, wings relatively broad/rounded, with densely dark-barred underwing-coverts. (**d**) **Juvenile**: Finer, whiter edges to mantle/scapulars, paler buff median covert fringes. VOICE May give guttural croak or *che-dep che-dep..* when flushed. HABITAT & BEHAVIOUR Streams and other wet areas in or near broadleaved evergreen forest, marshes and swamps with thick cover; 520–1,830 m. Rarely flies far when flushed. Flight slower/more laboured than Solitary. RANGE Ra **WV** W,N,C,E,S Myanmar, north Tenasserim, W,NW Thailand, N,C Laos, W Tonkin.

4 PINTAIL SNIPE *Gallinago stenura* 25–27 cm
(**a–c**) **Adult** Shorter-billed than Common, supercilium broader than eyestripe at bill-base, narrower pale brown/whitish scapular edges, tail only projects slightly beyond wing-tips, primaries only project slightly beyond tertials. Legs greyish-/brownish-green. In flight, tail looks shorter, most of toes extend beyond tail, contrasting buffy lesser/median coverts, almost no pale trailing edge to secondaries, heavier bars on underwing-coverts, almost no white on tail-corners. (**d**) **Juvenile**: Narrower whitish edges to mantle/scapulars, narrower/duller whitish-buff wing-covert fringes. VOICE Short, rasping *squok*, *squack* or *squick* when flushed, weaker/lower than Common. HABITAT & BEHAVIOUR Open marshy areas, rice paddies; up to 2,135 m. Often in drier areas than Common; tends to feed more by picking; flight typically shorter, more direct. RANGE Fc/co **WV** (except N Annam). Also **PM** S Myanmar, Pen Malaysia, Cambodia.

5 SWINHOE'S SNIPE *Gallinago megala* 27–29 cm
(**a–c**) **Adult**: Very similar to Pintail. Bill longer (relatively as Common), tail projects more beyond wing-tips, primaries may project clearly beyond tertials; wings slightly longer and more pointed, toes project less, more white on tail (less than Common). Slightly larger, and larger- and squarer-headed than Pintail/Common, crown-peak more behind eye (eye also further back), heavier-chested. Legs thicker than Common, usually thicker than Pintail, often rather yellow (greenish/greenish-yellow). In spring, face/neck-sides/flanks (sometimes breast) may look quite dusky/heavy-barred (distinctly darker than Pintail/Common). (**d**) **Juvenile**: Narrower whitish edges to mantle/scapulars, clear whitish-buff wing-covert/tertial fringes. VOICE Quieter than Pintail/Common. May call similarly to Pintail, but perhaps slightly less hoarse, rather thinner and quite nasal, with a slight rattling quality. HABITAT & BEHAVIOUR Marshy areas, rice paddies and their margins. Prefers drier areas and possibly less open, more wooded areas than Pintail/Common. Take-off rather slow/laboured compared to Pintail/Common. Flight rather direct, usually for short distance. RANGE Ra/sc **WV** N,C,S Myanmar, C Thailand, Pen Malaysia, Singapore, S Laos.

6 GREAT SNIPE *Gallinago media* 27–29 cm
(**a–c**) **Adult**: Quite large/bulky/short-billed; bold white wing-covert tips, relatively indistinct pale lines above, lower breast to vent mostly heavily dark-barred. In flight, greater coverts distinctly dark with thin white border at front and rear, narrow white trailing edge to secondaries, more extensive dark bars on underwing-coverts than Common, much unmarked white on tail-corners. (**d**) **Juvenile**: Narrow streaks above, less white on coverts, white of tail has some brown barring. VOICE May give weak croaking *etch* or *aitch* notes when flushed. HABITAT & BEHAVIOUR Open marshy areas, also drier ground, short grassy areas; recorded at sea level. Flight relatively short, direct and level. RANGE **V** north Tenasserim.

7 COMMON SNIPE *Gallinago gallinago* 25–27 cm
(**a–c**) **Adult** *gallinago*: Relatively long bill, eyestripe broader than supercilium at bill-base, bold pale buff/white lengthwise stripes above, largely white belly/vent, no obvious white wing-covert tips, tail clearly projects beyond closed wings. In flight, prominent white trailing edge to secondaries, panel of unbarred white on underwing-coverts, toes project only slightly beyond tail, little white on outertail (more than Pintail/Swinhoe's). (**d**) **Juvenile**: Fine whitish mantle/scapular lines, narrower buffish-white covert-fringes. VOICE Rasping, often slightly rising *scaaap* when flushed, more drawn-out than Pintail/Swinhoe's. HABITAT & BEHAVIOUR Open marshy areas, rice paddies; up to 1,220 m. Flight-style fast and erratic, often zig-zagging. RANGE Un/co **WV** (except W Tonkin, N,S Annam). Also **PM** Cambodia.

8 JACK SNIPE *Lymnocryptes minimus* 17–19 cm
(**a–c**) **Adult**: Small; dark crown-centre, 'split supercilium', dark above with purple/green gloss and bold buff lines, dark-streaks below; all-brown tail, white panel on underwing. VOICE May utter barely audible *gah* when flushed. HABITAT & BEHAVIOUR Marshy areas, ditches; up to 1,500 m. Feeds with nervous rocking action. Flight often looks relatively weak and fluttery, usually for short distance. RANGE Sc **WV/V** SW,N,C,E,S Myanmar, N Tenasserim, W,NW,C Thailand, W Tonkin, Cochinchina.

PLATE 42 GODWITS, CURLEWS & RUFF

1 BLACK-TAILED GODWIT *Limosa limosa* 36–40 cm (**a,b**) **Adult non-breeding** *melanuroides*: Fairly large, greyish; long black legs and bicoloured bill, long neck; white upperwing-bar and rump-band, and mostly black tail in flight. (**c**) **Male breeding**: Head-sides to breast reddish-rufous, otherwise dark-barred below, bold blackish and chestnut markings above. (**d**) **Female breeding**: Larger/longer-billed than male breeding; differs less from non-breeding. (**e**) **Juvenile**: Like breeding female but more heavily marked above, wing-coverts fringed cinnamon-buff. **VOICE** Single or repeated yelping *kip* notes in flight. Chattering *kett* and *chuk* notes from feeding flocks. **HABITAT & BEHAVIOUR** Mud-/sandflats, coastal pools, marshes, wet rice paddies; lowlands. Feeds by picking/forward-probing, often in deeper water than Bar-tailed. **RANGE** Un/fc coastal **WV** and **PM** (except N Annam). Sc/un inland **PM** N(also winters),C,S Myanmar, C(also winters),NE Thailand. **Rc** in summer Pen Malaysia.

2 BAR-TAILED GODWIT *Limosa lapponica* 37–41 cm (**a,b**) **Adult non-breeding** *lapponica*: More streaked than Black-tailed, buffier, slightly upturned bill. In flight, no wing-bar, white base to uppertail-coverts, dark-barred white tail, whitish underwing. (**c**) **Male breeding**: Mostly reddish-chestnut with dark-marked upperparts. (**d**) **Female breeding**: Larger/longer-billed than male. Differs relatively little from non-breeding, but darker-marked above, deep apricot flush on head-sides/neck/breast. (**e**) **Juvenile**: From non-breeding adult by brown centres and broad buff edges to upperpart feathers, fine dark streaks on neck/breast. (**f**) **Adult non-breeding** *baueri* (**rc** C Thailand southward): Dark back/rump, dark-barred uppertail-/underwing-coverts. **VOICE** Abrupt *kik* or *kiv-ik* (often repeated) flight calls, barking *kak-kak*, nasal *ke-wuh* or *kirruc*. **HABITAT & BEHAVIOUR** Mud-/sandflats, beaches, coastal pools. Often on open mud/sand and in shallower water than Black-tailed. **RANGE** Sc/fc coastal **WV** and **PM** S Myanmar, Thailand, Pen Malaysia, Singapore, Cambodia, E Tonkin, C,S Annam, Cochinchina. **Rc** in summer S Thailand, Pen Malaysia.

3 LITTLE CURLEW *Numenius minutus* 29–32 cm (**a,b**) **Adult**: Like small Whimbrel, but finer bill, sharper head pattern, buffier below, legs yellowish to bluish-grey, underwing-coverts mostly buffish-brown. **VOICE** In flight, excited 3–4 note *weep-weep-weep..* or *qwee-qwee-qwee..*, sharper than Whimbrel. Rougher *tchew-tchew-tchew* and harsh *kweek-ek* in alarm. **HABITAT** Short grassland, barren cultivation, wetland margins; lowlands. **RANGE** V C Thailand, Singapore.

4 WHIMBREL *Numenius phaeopus* 40–46 cm (**a,b**) **Adult** *phaeopus*: Markedly down-kinked bill, cold greyish-brown above with whitish to pale buff mottling, blackish lateral crown-stripes and eyestripe, broad whitish supercilium, buffy-white below with heavy dark streaks. Female slightly larger/longer-billed than male. In flight, dark above with clean white back/rump, mostly whitish underwing-coverts. (**c**) **Juvenile**: Clear buff on scapulars/tertials, buffish breast. (**d**) **Adult** *variegatus* (widespread): Back/rump as mantle, dark-barred underwing-coverts. Intergrades occur. **VOICE** Clear whinny/titter: *didi-didididi..* or *puhuhuhuhu..* (intensity varies) in flight.

Plaintive *curlee* notes. **HABITAT & BEHAVIOUR** Coastal wetlands, large rivers; lowlands. Feeds mostly by picking rather than probing. **RANGE** Fc/co coastal **WV** and **PM** throughout. Sc/un inland **PM** N,C,E Myanmar, Cambodia. **Rc** in summer C,S Thailand, Pen Malaysia, Singapore.

5 EURASIAN CURLEW *Numenius arquata* 50–60 cm (**a,b**) **Adult non-breeding** *orientalis*: Larger than Whimbrel, longer and more downcurved bill, more uniform head, coarsely marked above, bolder streaks below. Female larger/longer-billed. In flight, contrast between outer and inner wing, white back/rump, largely white underwing-coverts. **Adult breeding**: Buffier fringing above, buffier head-sides to breast. (**c**) **Juvenile**: Buffier than adult breeding, shorter bill. **VOICE** Loud rising, ringing *cour-lee* or *cour-loo*, low *whaup* or *were-up*. Loud, rapid *tyuyuyuyu..* or *tututu..* in alarm. **HABITAT & BEHAVIOUR** Mud-/sandflats, coastal wetlands, large rivers; lowlands. Feeds mostly by probing. **RANGE** Un/fc coastal **WV** and **PM** (except N,C Annam). Sc inland **PM** N(also winters),C,E Myanmar, NE Thailand. **V** SE Thailand (inland), N Laos.

6 EASTERN CURLEW *N.madagascariensis* 60–66 cm (**a,b**) **Adult non-breeding**: Larger/longer bill than Eurasian, more uniform and browner/buffier below. In flight, rufescent-tinged greyish-brown back/rump, densely barred underwing. Female larger/longer-billed than male. (**c**) **Adult breeding**: Distinctly rufous-washed above, warmer below. **Juvenile**: As adult non-breeding but extensive neat buffish-white markings above/on wing-coverts, finer dark streaks below, shorter bill. **VOICE** *coor-ee*, flatter/less fluty than Eurasian. Strident *ker-ee ker-ee..* (or *carr-eeir*) in alarm, occasional bubbling trills. **HABITAT** Mud-/sandflats. **RANGE** Ra coastal **PM** W,C,S Thailand, Pen Malaysia, Singapore, E Tonkin, S Annam, Cochinchina. Rarely winters Pen Malaysia, E Tonkin, ? Cochinchina.

7 RUFF *Philomachus pugnax* M 29–32, f 22–26 cm (**a**) **Male non-breeding**: Longish neck, small head, drooping bill. Greyish-brown above with pale buff/whitish fringing, mainly whitish below with greyish wash and mottling on foreneck/breast. Longish, usually orange/yellowish legs. (**b**) **Male breeding**: Black or white to rufous-chestnut broad, loose 'ruff', bare face, pinkish bill. (**c**) **Male breeding/non-breeding (transitional)**: Face feathered, bill bicoloured, patchy plumage. (**d**) **Female non-breeding**: Notably smaller than male. Both sexes show broad-based wings, white rump-sides, narrowish white wing-bar, toes projecting beyond tail. (**e**) **Female breeding**: Greyish-brown with blackish markings above, variable bold blackish markings on neck/breast. **Juvenile male**: As breeding female above, but simpler warm buff/whitish fringing; head-sides to breast rather uniform buff. (**g**) **Juvenile female**: Usually darker buff neck/breast than juvenile male, smaller. **VOICE** Occasional low *kuk* or *wek* in flight. **HABITAT & BEHAVIOUR** Marshes, grassy areas, rice paddies, coastal pools, rarely mudflats; lowlands. Surface-pecks and also wades in deepish water. **RANGE** Ra/sc **WV** SW,S Myanmar, Tenasserim, Thailand (except SE), Pen Malaysia, Cambodia, Cochinchina. **V** S Laos, E Tonkin.

PLATE 43 SANDPIPERS, TATTLERS, TURNSTONES & DOWITCHERS

1 GREEN SANDPIPER *Tringa ochropus* 21–24 cm
(a,b) Adult non-breeding: Blackish olive-brown above/on breast-sides with buff speckling, white rump/uppertail-coverts and underparts. Plainer/darker than Wood, greener legs, short supercilium, bold tail-bars. Larger/darker than Common, more extensively dark breast, different pattern to upperside in flight. **(c) Adult breeding**: Bold streaks on crown/neck/breast, more distinct white speckles above. **Juvenile**: As adult non-breeding but browner above/on breast, less distinct small deep buff spots on scapulars/tertials. VOICE Loud, sharp *klU-Uweet-wit-wit* and *tluee-tueet* in flight. Sharp *wit-wit-wit* in alarm. HABITAT & BEHAVIOUR Various lowland wetlands, rarely mudflats; up to 800 m. Occasionally bobs rear end. RANGE Sc/fc WV throughout; rare S Thailand southwards. Also PM Cambodia.

2 WOOD SANDPIPER *Tringa glareola* 18.5–21 cm
(a,b) Adult non-breeding: Dark brown above with buffish speckles, whitish supercilium, light breast-streaks, yellowish legs. In flight, quite uniform above, darker flight feathers, white rump, weakly tail-bars. **(c) Adult breeding**: Blacker above with bolder whitish speckles/fringes, more clearly streaked head/neck/breast. **Juvenile**: As adult non-breeding but browner upperparts/coverts with finer/denser buff speckles, more defined streaks on foreneck/breast. VOICE Nervous *chiff-if* or *chiff-iff-iff*, mainly in flight. Sharp *chip* (often rapidly repeated) in alarm. HABITAT & BEHAVIOUR Marshes, flooded rice paddies, lake margins, large rivers, rarely mudflats; up to 800 m. Gregarious. RANGE Un/co WV and PM (except W Tonkin).

3 TEREK SANDPIPER *Xenus cinereus* 22–25 cm
(a,b) Adult non-breeding: Upturned yellow-based bill, orange-yellow legs. In flight, white trailing edge to secondaries. **(c) Adult breeding**: Clearer grey above with black scapular lines, dark bill. **(d) Juvenile**: Browner above than non-breeding adult, with buffish fringes, short blackish scapular lines. VOICE Rippling *du-du-du-du-du..* and mellow *chu-du-du* in flight. Sharp *tu-li* in alarm. HABITAT Mud-/sandflats, saltpans and other coastal wetlands, rarely wet rice paddies on passage; up to 1,150 m. RANGE Un/fc WV and PM throughout. V N Laos. Rc in summer Pen Malaysia, Singapore.

4 COMMON SANDPIPER *Actitis hypoleucos* 19–21 cm
(a,b) Adult non-breeding: Plain upperside/lateral breast-patches. Tail extends beyond wings, legs greyish/yellowish. In flight, white wing-bar. **(c) Adult breeding**: Dark streaks/bars above, browner, dark-streaked breast-patches. **(d) Juvenile**: As non-breeding adult but narrowly fringed buff above, with some darker subterminal markings, coverts with prominent buff tips and subdued dark bars. VOICE High ringing *tsee-wee-wee.. or swee-swee-swee..*, mainly in flight. Single *sweet* or *sweeee-eet* in alarm. Song is repeated excited, rising *kittie-needie*. HABITAT & BEHAVIOUR Various wetlands, tidal creeks, coastal rocks, lakes, rivers; up to 2,100 m. Often 'bobs' rear end. Flies with flicking wingbeats. RANGE Co WV and PM throughout. Rc in summer Pen Malaysia, Singapore.

5 GREY-TAILED TATTLER *Heteroscelus brevipes* 24–27 cm
(a,b) Adult non-breeding: Plain grey above/on upper breast, white supercilium, straight yellowish-based bill, shortish yellow legs. In flight, grey above with darker outer wing. **(c) Adult breeding**: Neck streaked grey, breast/flanks scaled grey, bill-base duller. **Juvenile**: As adult non-breeding but neat whitish spots/fringes above/on coverts; outertail-fringes notched white. VOICE Plaintive *tu-weet* or *tu-whip* (may be repeated) in flight. Quick *tu-wiwi, twi-wi* and *twiwiwi* in alarm. HABITAT & BEHAVIOUR Reefs, rocky shores, mud-/sandflats, sometimes saltpans/prawn ponds. Gait recalls Common Sandpiper. RANGE Ra/un coastal PM C,SE,S Thailand, Pen Malaysia, Singapore, E Tonkin, C,S Annam, Cochinchina. Has wintered S Thailand, Pen Malaysia, Singapore. V NE Thailand & C Laos (same record).

6 RUDDY TURNSTONE *Arenaria interpres* 21–24 cm
(a,b) Adult non-breeding *interpres*: Brown above, orange-red legs, blackish pattern on neck/breast. In flight, bold white markings above. **(c) Male breeding**: Black-and-white head pattern, blackish and orange-chestnut above. **(d) Female breeding**: Browner crown/nape. **(e) Juvenile**: Dull; buffish-fringed above, legs duller. VOICE Rattling *tuk tuk-i-tuk-tuk, trik-tuk-tuk-tuk* or *tuk-e-tuk*. Low *tuk* when foraging, sharp *chik-ik* and *kuu* or *teu* in alarm. HABITAT Mud-/sandflats, beaches, saltpans and other coastal wetlands. RANGE Sc/fc WV and PM (except E Tonkin, N Annam). Rc in summer Pen Malaysia, Singapore.

7 LONG-BILLED DOWITCHER *Limnodromus scolopaceus* 29 cm
(a,b) Adult non-breeding: Plainer than Asian, quite plain brownish-grey neck/breast, greenish bill-base, shorter and paler legs. In flight, clean white back, darker inner primaries and secondaries with thin white trailing edge, dark-barred underwing-coverts. **(c) Adult breeding**: Bold mottling (not streaks) above, paler supercilium/head-sides than Asian, dark speckles/bars below. Bill/legs like non-breeding. **(d) Juvenile**: Darker than adult non-breeding with fine chestnut fringes, buff-washed head-sides/breast. VOICE Single or repeated sharp *kik* or *keek*; also shriller *keeek* notes in alarm. HABITAT & BEHAVIOUR Coastal marshes, pools, sometimes mudflats. Feeds like Asian. RANGE Coastal V C,W Thailand, Singapore, E Tonkin.

8 ASIAN DOWITCHER *L.semipalmatus* 34–36 cm
(a,b) Adult non-breeding: Smaller than Bar-tailed Godwit (*baueri*), shorter-necked/-legged, flattish forehead, straight all-black bill (tip slightly swollen). In flight, secondaries, greater coverts and inner primaries somewhat paler than rest of wing, underwing-coverts white. **(c) Male breeding**: From Bar-tailed Godwit by size/shape/bill; usually has mostly white vent. **(d) Female breeding**: Duller than male. **(e) Juvenile**: Like non-breeding adult but blacker above with neat pale buff fringes, buff-washed and lightly streaked neck/breast. VOICE Airy *chaow* or *chowp*, yelping *chep-chep*, soft *kiaow* (in flight). HABITAT & BEHAVIOUR Mudflats, coastal marshes, pools. Feeds by continuous vertical probing, usually knee-deep in water. Gregarious, often with godwits. RANGE Ra/sc coastal PM (except Myanmar). Has wintered C Thailand, west Pen Malaysia, ? Cochinchina. Rc in summer Pen Malaysia. Rc (status?) S Myanmar.

1c

1a

1b

2b

2a

2c

3b

3a

3d

3c

4d

4b

4c

4a

5a

5b

6d

5c

6c

6b

6e

6a

7 and 8 to different scale

8d

7b

8a

8b

7a

7c

8c

8e

7d

PLATE 44 LARGER SANDPIPERS

1 SPOTTED REDSHANK *Tringa erythropus* 29–32 cm
(**a,b**) **Adult non-breeding**: Paler than Common, bill longer, slenderer and finer-tipped; bold white supercilium, unstreaked above, longer legs. Rather uniform above with clean white back in flight. (**c**) **Adult breeding**: Blacker above, otherwise almost uniform blackish. Some (mainly females) have faint pale scales on head/neck/underparts. (**d**) **Juvenile**: Recalls adult non-breeding but brownish-grey with finely white-speckled upper-parts/wing-coverts, dark-streaked neck and closely dark-barred breast to undertail-coverts. **VOICE** Loud, rising *chu-it* in flight. Conversational *uck* when feeding, and short *chip* in alarm. **HABITAT & BEHAVIOUR** Freshwater marshes, flooded rice paddies, coastal pools, large rivers; up to 450 m. Gregarious. Often feeds in quite deep water. **RANGE** Sc/lc **WV** (except W Myanmar, SE,S Thailand, W Tonkin, S Annam). **V** S Thailand.

2 COMMON REDSHANK *Tringa totanus* 27–29 cm
(**a,b**) **Adult non-breeding** *eurhinus*: Plain-looking brownish-grey above, fine dark breast-streaks, straight red bill with dark distal half, bright red legs. Head-sides greyish with whitish eyering but no clear supercilium. Big white wing-patch in flight. (**c**) **Adult breeding**: Browner above with small blackish markings, heavier streaks elsewhere. (**d**) **Juvenile**: As adult breeding but neat buffy spots/spangles above, weaker breast-streaks, often more yellowish-orange legs. **Other subspecies** *T.t.craggi, terrignotae, ussuriensis* (ranges unclear but all recorded Pen Malaysia): Told by minor detail in breeding plumage. **VOICE** Plaintive *teu-hu-hu* in flight. Mournful *tyuuuu* and rapid repetition of call in alarm. **HABITAT** Coastal wetlands, lowland marshes, large rivers. **RANGE** Co coastal **WV** and **PM** throughout. Sc/un inland **PM** N,E,C,S Myanmar, C,NE Thailand, N,C Laos. **Rc** in summer C,S Thailand, Pen Malaysia, Singapore.

3 MARSH SANDPIPER *Tringa stagnatilis* 22–25 cm
(**a,b**) **Adult non-breeding**: Smaller/slimmer/longer-legged than Common Greenshank, thin straight blackish bill, white supercilium, fainter streaks on head/neck/mantle, paler lores. Legs greenish. (**c**) **Adult breeding**: Bold black markings above and dark speckles/streaks on crown, neck and breast; legs often yellowish-tinged. **Juvenile**: Browner mantle/coverts than adult non-breeding, with thin dark subterminal bars and pale buff fringes. **VOICE** Mellow *keeuw* or *plew* notes, higher/thinner than Common Greenshank. Loud *yip* or *chip* (often rapidly repeated) in alarm. **HABITAT** Mudflats, marshes, large rivers, various wetlands; lowlands. **RANGE** Co (mostly coastal) **WV** and **PM** (except W Myanmar, NW Thailand, S Laos, W Tonkin, C Annam). **Rc** in summer Pen Malaysia, Cochinchina.

4 COMMON GREENSHANK *Tringa nebularia* 30–34 cm
(**a,b**) **Adult non-breeding**: Longish neck, stout-based and slightly upturned greenish-grey bill with darker tip, long greenish legs. Prominently streaked crown, ear-coverts, hindneck, mantle and breast-sides, greyish above with somewhat darker lesser coverts, distinctly dark loral stripe, lacks white supercilium behind eye. In flight, quite uniform above with contrasting white back to uppertail (longer uppertail-coverts and tail with dark bars), toes extending beyond tail-tip. (**c**) **Adult breeding**:

Some prominent blackish scapular centres, heavy blackish streak/spots on crown/neck/breast. **Juvenile**: Slightly browner above than adult non-breeding, with clear pale buff fringes, darker median/lesser coverts, somewhat bolder neck/breast streaks. **VOICE** Loud clear ringing *teu-teu-teu* or *chew-chew-chew* in flight. In alarm, throaty *kiu kiu kiu* or *kyoup-kyoup-kyoup*, recalling Common Redshank, and a sharp *tchuk* or *chip*. **HABITAT** Various wetlands, mudflats, large rivers; up to 450 m. **RANGE** Fc/co **WV** and **PM** throughout. **Rc** in summer C Thailand, Pen Malaysia, Singapore.

5 NORDMANN'S GREENSHANK *Tringa guttifer* 29–32 cm
(**a,b**) **Adult non-breeding**: From Common by shorter (particularly above joint), yellower legs, shorter neck, distinctly bicoloured bill, more uniform (only faintly) darker crown, nape and breast-sides, much plainer above, without obvious dark markings, more white above eye, paler lores. In flight, all-white uppertail-coverts and rather uniform greyish tail, toes do not extend beyond tail-tip. (**c**) **Adult breeding**: Largely blackish above with whitish spots/spangles, heavily dark-streaked head/upper neck, broad blackish crescentic spots on lower neck/breast, darker lores. (**d**) **Juvenile**: Like adult non-breeding but browner above, whitish notching on scapular and tertial fringes, pale buff wing-covert fringes; breast has slight brown wash and faint dark streaks at sides. **VOICE** Flight call is distinctive *kwork* or *gwaak*. **HABITAT** Mud-/sandflats, rarely other coastal wetlands. **RANGE** Ra coastal **WV** west S Thailand, west Pen Malaysia, E Tonkin. Ra coastal **PM** C,W,S Thailand, Cambodia, E Tonkin, Cochinchina (winters?). **V** Singapore (formerly wintered). **Rc** (status?) S Myanmar, Tenasserim.

6 PECTORAL SANDPIPER *Calidris melanotos* 19–23 cm
(**a,b**) **Adult non-breeding**: From Sharp-tailed by less striking head pattern, dark-streaked breast sharply demarcated from belly. (**c**) **Male breeding**: Foreneck/breast may be blackish with whitish mottling. (**d**) **Female breeding**: Blackish-brown above with rufous-buff fringes, buffish-washed foreneck/breast. (**e**) **Juvenile**: Like breeding female but usually white lengthwise mantle-lines, neat buffish/whitish-buff wing-covert fringes. **VOICE** Reedy *kirrp* or *chyrrk* in flight, harsher but similar to Curlew Sandpiper. **HABITAT & BEHAVIOUR** Marshes, saltpans, coastal wetlands. Feeds by pecking and shallow probing, often on drier wetland margins. **RANGE** **V** Pen Malaysia, Singapore.

7 SHARP-TAILED SANDPIPER *Calidris acuminata* 17–21 cm
(**a,b**) **Adult non-breeding**: Slightly down-tapering dark bill, rich brown crown, whitish supercilium, diffuse neck/breast-streaking. Recalls smaller Long-toed Stint. (**c**) **Adult breeding**: Dark-streaked rufous crown, blackish-brown above with bright rufous fringing, boldly streaked neck/breast, then arrow-head markings below. (**d**) **Juvenile**: As breeding adult but supercilium/throat plainer/whiter, breast lightly streaked rich buff, otherwise white below. **VOICE** Soft *ueep* or *wheep* (often repeated) in flight. Twittering *teet-teet-trrt-trrt* or *prtt-wheet-wheet*. **HABITAT & BEHAVIOUR** Marshes, fish ponds, mudflats. Often on drier wetland margins. **RANGE** **V** S Myanmar, C,S Thailand, Pen Malaysia, Singapore, E Tonkin, S Annam.

PLATE 45 SMALL SANDPIPERS

1 SANDERLING *Calidris alba* 18–21 cm
(**a,b**) **Adult non-breeding**: Pale grey ear-coverts and upperside, snowy-white underside. Often contrastingly darker at wing-bend, legs blackish, no hind toe. In flight, broad white wing-bar. (**c**) **Adult breeding**: Brighter individuals very similar to Red-necked Stint but larger, dark streaks on somewhat duller, more chestnut head-sides, throat and breast (including lower breast-sides), mostly chestnut scapular centres. In flight, much broader white wing-bar. (**d**) **Adult breeding variant**: Duller (fresh) bird, with faint rufous/chestnut on head/breast, more contrasting breast markings. (**e**) **Juvenile**: Similar to adult non-breeding but darker streaks on crown/hindneck, blackish mantle/scapulars, boldly patterned with buffishwhite, buff-washed breast with dark streaks at sides. **VOICE** Typical flight call is quiet liquid *klit* or *twik* (often repeated), sometimes extending to short trill. **HABITAT & BEHAVIOUR** Sand-/mudflats, beaches, sometimes saltpans, large rivers. Feeds by rapid probing and pecking, runs very fast. **RANGE** Sc/un coastal **WV** and **PM** (except SW Myanmar, Tenasserim, SE Thailand, Cambodia, N,C Annam). Ra inland **PM** C Myanmar, S Laos.

2 SPOON-BILLED SANDPIPER *Calidris pygmeus* 14–16 cm
(**a,b**) **Adult non-breeding**: Like Red-necked Stint but has spatulate-shaped bill (less obvious in profile), somewhat bigger head, whiter forehead and breast, broader white supercilium. (**c**) **Adult breeding**: Apart from bill, very like Red-necked Stint but more uniform rufous-buff scapular fringes. (**d**) **Juvenile**: Like Red-necked and Little Stints (apart from bill) but whiter forehead/face, somewhat darker and more contrasting lores and ear-coverts, more uniform buff/buffish-white mantle and scapular fringes. **VOICE** Quiet rolling *preep* and shrill *wheet* in flight. **HABITAT & BEHAVIOUR** Mud-/sandflats, sometimes sandy beaches, saltpans, prawn ponds. Feeds in shallow water and on soft, wet mud, sweeping bill from side to side or patting surface of wet mud with bill. **RANGE** Sc and lo **WV** C Thailand, E Tonkin. Ra coastal **PM** SW,S Myanmar (may winter). Coastal **V** Tenasserim, W,S Thailand, Pen Malaysia, Singapore, S Annam. **Rc** (status?) Cochinchina.

3 LITTLE STINT *Calidris minuta* 14–15.5 cm
(**a,b**) **Adult non-breeding**: Very like Red-necked but slightly slimmer/longer-legged, finer, often slightly drooping bill, broader dark feather-centres above, grey of head/breast usually more streaked. (**c**) **Adult breeding**: From Red-necked by whitish throat, more orange-rufous breast (usually all dark-streaked/speckled), usually rufous on lower breast-sides, mostly blackish coverts/tertials with bright rufous edges; often narrow pale buffish lateral crown-/mantle-stripes. (**d**) **Juvenile**: Usually more contrasting head pattern than Red-necked, darker centres and more rufous feather-fringes above (especially lower scapulars/tertials/coverts), coarser streaks on breast-sides. Head pattern less contrasting than Long-toed, neck/breast less boldly streaked, shorter neck, dark legs. **VOICE** Sharp *kip* or *tit* notes in flight (can run to short trill). **HABITAT** Saltpans, prawn ponds, mudflats, large lowland rivers. **RANGE** Sc/un coastal **WV** and **PM** SW,S Myanmar, Tenasserim. Sc/un **PM** N,C Myanmar. Coastal **V** W,C Thailand, Pen Malaysia, E Tonkin.

4 RED-NECKED STINT *Calidris ruficollis* 14–16 cm
(**a,b**) **Adult non-breeding**: Plain greyish above with dark shaft-streaks, greyish lateral breast-patches with slight streaks. (**c**) **Adult breeding**: Plain rufous/brick-red head-sides to upper breast, whitish/brick-red supercilium, blackish central markings and rufous/brick-red fringes on mantle/scapulars, mostly greyish-white tertial/covert-fringes, usually dark-streaked whitish lower breast-sides. (**d**) **Adult pre-breeding**: In fresh plumage, little rufous/chestnut on head and breast, greyer mantle/scapular fringes. (**e**) **Juvenile**: Darker above than adult non-breeding, mantle/upper scapulars blackish with pale warm fringes, lower scapulars grey with dark subterminal markings and whitish fringes, tertials grey with whitish/buffish fringes, coverts edged whitish, breast-sides washed pinkish-grey and faintly streaked; sometimes faint whitish mantle-lines, rarely obvious 'split supercilium'. **VOICE** Thin *kreep* or *creek* in flight. Also, shorter *krep* or *klyt*. May give short trill in alarm. **HABITAT & BEHAVIOUR** Saltpans, coastal pools, mud-/sandflats, sometimes large rivers and other inland wetlands; up to 450 m. Feeds by rapid pecking, also probes. **RANGE** Un/co coastal **WV** and **PM** throughout. Ra/sc inland **PM** N,C Myanmar, NW,C Thailand, Laos, Cambodia. **Rc** in summer S Thailand, Pen Malaysia, Singapore.

5 TEMMINCK'S STINT *Calidris temminckii* 13.5–15 cm
(**a,b**) **Adult non-breeding**: Attenuated shape, tail often projects slightly beyond wing-tips, relatively uniform cold greyish-brown above, plain-looking, drab brownish-grey ear-coverts and breast (centre can be slightly paler), greenish-yellowish legs. Recalls miniature Common Sandpiper. In flight, white tail-sides. (**c**) **Adult breeding**: More dull olive-brown above, with irregular blackish feather-centres and rufous fringes, head-sides/breast washed brown, indistinct darker streaks on head-sides and neck/breast. (**d**) **Juvenile**: Like adult non-breeding but mantle/scapulars/coverts browner with narrow buff fringes and blackish subterminal markings, head-sides/breast washed buffish. **VOICE** Rapid stuttering *tirrr* (often repeated) or longer *tirrr'r'r* or *trrrrrit* in flight. **HABITAT** Muddy freshwater wetlands, rice paddies, large rivers, saltpans, prawn ponds, rarely mudflats; up to 450 m. **RANGE** Sc/lc **WV** (except W Myanmar, W Tonkin, N,S Annam). Also **PM** C Myanmar, E Tonkin.

6 LONG-TOED STINT *Calidris subminuta* 14–16 cm
(**a,b**) **Adult non-breeding**: Longer-necked than Red-necked, finer bill with pale-based lower mandible, browner above with larger dark feather-centres, brown-washed and distinctly darker-streaked neck-sides/breast, yellowish-brown/greenish legs, longer toes. (**c**) **Adult breeding**: Dark-streaked rufous crown, broad rufous fringing above, creamy-buff wash on boldly dark-streaked neck-sides/breast (breast-centre may be paler). (**d**) **Juvenile**: As adult breeding but obvious white mantle-lines, greyer lower scapulars. **VOICE** Liquid *kurrrip* or *chirrup* and shorter *prit* in flight. **HABITAT & BEHAVIOUR** Freshwater marshes, wet rice paddies, saltpans, coastal pools, rarely mudflats; lowlands. Often feeds amongst vegetation. May stand erect with neck stretched up when alarmed. **RANGE** Un/co **WV** (except W,N Myanmar, C Laos, W Tonkin, N Annam). Also **PM** Pen Malaysia, Singapore, Cambodia, Cochinchina. **Rc** in summer Singapore.

PLATE 46 SMALLER SANDPIPERS & RED-NECKED PHALAROPE

1 GREAT KNOT *Calidris tenuirostris* 28–29.5 cm
(a,b) **Adult non-breeding**: Attenuated shape, broad-based, slightly down-tapering blackish bill, grey above, streaked greyish head to upper breast, blackish spots on breast-sides and upper flanks. In flight, blackish primary coverts, white uppertail-coverts, dark tail. (c) **Adult breeding**: Scapulars bright chestnut and black, head/neck bold streaked black, breast and flanks densely spotted black. (d) **Juvenile**: Like non-breeding adult but bolder blackish streaks above, blackish-brown scapulars with whitish/buffish fringes, buffish washed and more distinctly dark-spotted/streaked breast. VOICE Muffled *knut* or *nyut* notes in flight, harsher *chak-chuka-chak* and *chaka-ruk-chak* in alarm. HABITAT & BEHAVIOUR Mud-/sandflats, sometimes coastal pools, saltpans. Feeds mostly by probing. RANGE Ra/un coastal **PM** (except Cambodia, N,C,S Annam). Lc **WV** C(annual?),S(west) Thailand, west Pen Malaysia, E Tonkin, probably Cochinchina. Also **rc** in summer Pen Malaysia.

2 RED KNOT *Calidris canutus* 23–25 cm
(a,b) **Adult non-breeding** *canutus*: Smaller/more compact than Great, shorter bill, no black breast-spots; uniform dark bars on rump, greyer tail. (c) **Adult breeding**: Blackish and chestnut above, deep reddish-chestnut face and underparts. (d) **Adult post-breeding**: Mostly blackish scapulars; moults head first. (e) **Juvenile**: Like non-breeding adult but slightly buffier with scaly pattern above, finely dark-streaked below. **Other subspecies** *C.c.rogersi* (**rc** Pen Malaysia, Vietnam). VOICE Soft nasal *knut* or *wutt* notes; *kikkik* in alarm. HABITAT & BEHAVIOUR Mostly mud-/sandflats. Probes and picks for food. RANGE Sc/un coastal **PM** S Myanmar, C,W,S Thailand, Pen Malaysia, Singapore, E Tonkin, C Annam, Cochinchina. Occasionally winters C,W Thailand, E Tonkin, Cochinchina?

3 DUNLIN *Calidris alpina* 17–21 cm
(a,b) **Adult non-breeding** *sakhalina*: Shorter bill/neck/legs than Curlew Sandpiper, bill less curved, supercilium less distinct, foreneck/upper breast duller with fine streaks; dark centre to rump/uppertail-coverts. From Broad-billed by larger size, longer legs, no distinct kink in bill or 'split supercilium'. (c) **Adult breeding**: Black belly-patch, mostly bright rufous-chestnut mantle/scapulars. (d) **Juvenile**: Blackish mantle/scapulars with rufous, buff and whitish fringing, extensive blackish streaks on hindneck, breast and belly. VOICE Harsh *treeep* or *kreee* in flight. Soft twittering notes when foraging. HABITAT & BEHAVIOUR Mudflats, saltpans, prawn ponds, large rivers. Feeds like Curlew Sandpiper. RANGE Ra/sc **WV** NW,NE Thailand, N Laos, coastal E Tonkin (lc). **V** C,S Thailand, Pen Malaysia, Singapore. **Rc** (status?) coastal C Annam, Cochinchina.

4 CURLEW SANDPIPER *Calidris ferruginea* 19–21.5 cm
(a,b) **Adult non-breeding**: Rather long downcurved blackish bill, fairly long blackish legs, rather plain greyish above, white supercilium/underparts (greyish breast-wash), thin white wing-bar, white lower rump/uppertail-coverts. (c) **Female breeding**: Deep reddish-chestnut head/underparts, with dark crown-streaks, whitish facial markings, scaled breast/belly and mostly white vent; bold chestnut, black and whitish on mantle/

scapulars. **Male breeding**: Slightly deeper reddish-chestnut below than female, with fewer whitish scales. (d) **Juvenile**: Like non-breeding adult but upperparts browner with buff-and-dark scaly pattern, head and breast washed peachy-buff and faintly dark-streaked. VOICE Rippling *kirrip* or *prrriit* in flight. HABITAT & BEHAVIOUR Mud-/sandflats, coastal pools, large rivers; lowlands. Feeds by pecking and vigorous probing, often in deeper water than Dunlin. RANGE Fc/co coastal **WV** and **PM** (except N,S Annam). Ra/sc inland **PM** C,S Myanmar, C,NE Thailand, N,S Laos. **Rc** in summer C,S Thailand, Pen Malaysia.

5 STILT SANDPIPER *Micropalama himantopus* 18–23 cm
(a,b) **Adult non-breeding**: From Curlew Sandpiper by longer, straighter, less curved bill (slightly down-turned at tip), longer dull yellowish/greenish legs, greyish-streaked foreneck, breast and flanks. In flight, white lower rump/uppertail-coverts but almost no wing-bar, feet project prominently beyond tail-tip. (c) **Adult breeding**: Bright chestnut on crown/head-sides, bold blackish streaks/spots on neck/upper breast, blackish- barred lower breast to vent, variable buffish-pink wash below, blackish mantle/scapulars with bold rufous/pinkish/white fringes; white of rump/uppertail-coverts may be part-obscured by dark markings. (d) **Juvenile**: From Curlew by structure, darker feather-centres above, rufescent upper scapular fringes, lightly streaked flanks, more contrasting head pattern. VOICE Soft rattled *kirr* and *drr* and hoarser whistled *djew* in flight. HABITAT & BEHAVIOUR Coastal wetlands. Feeds in similar way to dowitchers, often belly-deep in water. RANGE **V** Singapore.

6 BROAD-BILLED SANDPIPER *Limicola falcinellus* 16–18 cm
(a,b) **Adult non-breeding** *sibirica*: Stint-like but larger, bill longer, tip kinked down. White 'split supercilium', white below with lateral breast-streaks; dark leading edge to upperwing-coverts. (c) **Adult breeding**: Fresh plumage (May). Blackish crown, white 'split supercilium', blackish above with rufous and whitish fringing, white mantle/scapular lines, bold neck/breast-streaking. (d) **Juvenile**: As breeding adult but more prominent mantle-lines, broadly buff-fringed wing-coverts. VOICE Dry trilled *trrreet* or *chrrreeit* and shorter *trett* in flight. HABITAT & BEHAVIOUR Mud-/sandflats, saltpans, coastal pools. Feeding action similar to Dunlin and Curlew Sandpiper; slower than stints. RANGE Un/fc coastal **WV** and **PM** (except SE Thailand, N Annam).

7 RED-NECKED PHALAROPE *Phalaropus lobatus* 17–19 cm
(a,b) **Adult non-breeding**: Needle-like bill, blackish mask, grey above, white below; blackish upperwing with narrow white wing-bar. (c) **Female breeding**: Slaty head/breast with rufous-chestnut band from ear-coverts to foreneck. (d) **Male breeding**: Duller/more washed out. (e) **Juvenile**: Like non-breeding adult but blacker mask/upperside, latter with rufous-buff markings. **First winter**: Blacker crown than non-breeding, few grey feathers above. VOICE Sharp *kip* or *twick*, harsher *cherp* or squeaky *kirrik* in flight. HABITAT & BEHAVIOUR Open sea, coastal pools, mudflats; rarely lowland rivers/pools inland. Swims, often spins around, also wades to feed. RANGE Ra/sc coastal **PM** W,C,SE Thailand, Pen Malaysia, Singapore, Cambodia, C,S Annam. **V** NW,S Thailand, N,S Laos, inland C Annam & Cochinchina.

PLATE 47 PAINTED-SNIPES, PRATINCOLES & VARIOUS LARGE WADERS

1 GREATER PAINTED-SNIPE *Rostratula benghalensis* 24 cm (a–c) **Female** *benghalensis*: Drooping bill, mostly plain and dark, whitish spectacles, buffy median crown-stripe and mantle-lines, white below. Barred tail/flight feathers, largely clear white underwing-coverts. (d,e) **Male**: Greyish-brown head to breast and upperside, buffish spectacles. Large rich buff markings on wing-coverts. **Juvenile**: Like male but coverts greyer with smaller buff markings. **VOICE** Female territorial call is 20–80 or so short *kook* or *koh* notes (like blowing into empty bottle), usually at dusk/night. Single *kook* during roding display. May give explosive *kek* when flushed. **HABITAT & BEHAVIOUR** Marshy areas, wet rice paddies; up to 1,525 m. Quite secretive, mainly crepuscular. Legs trail in flight. Female has 'roding' display, low over ground. **RANGE** Un **R** (except N,S Annam).

2 EURASIAN THICK-KNEE *Burhinus oedicnemus* 40–44 cm (a,b) **Adult** *indicus*: Smaller/smaller-billed than other thick-knees, streaked. Pale sandy-brown above with blackish and white bands along folded wing. Flight feathers blackish, primaries with relatively small white patches. (c) **Juvenile**: Scapulars, inner coverts and tertials fringed rufous-buff, indistinct bars on closed wings, whiter-tipped greater coverts. **VOICE** Territorial call of slurred whistles: *kikiweek* and *kiweek* etc., building in pitch/volume to loud clear *kur-lee* phrases before dying away again. Loud, haunting rising *kur-lee* and more churring *churrrrreee*. Normally calls at dusk/night. **HABITAT & BEHAVIOUR** Dry barren areas, semi-desert, sand-dunes, scrub, riverine sandbanks; lowlands. Mostly crepuscular and nocturnal; rests in shade during daytime. **RANGE** Sc/un **R** Myanmar (except W,E), C,SE Thailand, Cambodia. **V** S Thailand. Sc (status?) W(probably R),NW Thailand, S Laos, C,S Annam.

3 GREAT THICK-KNEE *Esacus recurvirostris* 49–54 cm (a,b) **Adult**: Very thick, slightly upturned black bill with yellow base. Black/white/sandy-greyish head pattern, sandy-grey above with narrow blackish and whitish bands along lesser coverts, whitish below with brownish-washed foreneck/breast. In flight, mostly grey greater coverts, mostly black flight feathers, large white primary patches. **Juvenile**: Initially buffish fringes/spots above. **VOICE** Territorial call of wailing rising whistles: *kree-kree-kree kre-kre-kre-kre-kre...* etc. Loud harsh *see-eek* in alarm. **HABITAT & BEHAVIOUR** Shingle/sandbanks along large rivers, sand-dunes, dry lake shores, sometimes coastal mud-/sandflats, saltpans; lowlands. Mainly crepuscular and nocturnal. **RANGE** Sc/un **R** SW,N,C,E,S Myanmar, north Tenasserim. Ra/sc **R** NW,NE Thailand (now along Mekong R only), eastern Cambodia, Laos, C,S Annam (mainly coastal). Rc (status?) coastal E Tonkin. Coastal **V** C Thailand (**FR**).

4 BEACH THICK-KNEE *Esacus neglectus* 53–57 cm (a,b) **Adult**: Bill bulkier than Great, head largely blackish with white supercilium. In flight, mostly grey secondaries, mostly white inner primaries. **Juvenile**: Slightly paler above with buffy fringes, duller bands along upper lesser coverts, grey-brown median/greater coverts with narrow buffish-white fringes and faint dark subterminal markings. **VOICE** Repeated harsh wailing *wee-loo* (territorial). Rising *quip-ip-ip* and weak *quip* or

peep in alarm. **HABITAT** Undisturbed sandy beaches and sand-flats, often near mangroves. **RANGE** Ra/sc and lo **R** S Myanmar (Coco Is), southern Tenasserim, west S Thailand (islands only), Singapore; formerly west Pen Malaysia.

5 EURASIAN OYSTERCATCHER *Haematopus ostralegus* 43 cm (a) **Adult non-breeding** *osculans*: Black/blackish-brown with white back to uppertail-coverts and lower breast to vent, may show a little white on lower throat, long orange-red bill with duller tip, pink legs. (b) **Adult breeding**: Throat all black, bill all orange-red; broad white wing-band (all seasons). (c) **First winter**: Browner than adult non-breeding, bill duller/narrower. **VOICE** Loud shrill piping *kleep* or *ke-beep* (often repeated). Soft *weep* and repeated sharp *pik* in alarm. **HABITAT** Mud-/sandflats, rocky coasts. **RANGE** V SW,S Myanmar, Pen Malaysia, E Tonkin.

6 IBISBILL *Ibidorhyncha struthersii* 38–41 cm (a,b) **Adult non-breeding**: Greyish neck/upperparts, blackish face with white mottling, black crown, white and black breast-bands, downcurved reddish bill. In flight, dark flight feathers with slight white bar. **Adult breeding**: Face all black, bill all orange-red. (c) **Juvenile**: Browner above with buff fringes, whitish to dark brown face with white feather-tips, no white breast-band, browner lower breast-band. **VOICE** Repeated ringing *klew-klew* and loud rapid *tee-tee-tee-tee*. **HABITAT & BEHAVIOUR** Rocky rivers, stony riverbeds; 800–3,355 m. Often well hidden amongst stones/boulders. **RANGE** Sc/un **WV** N Myanmar.

7 ORIENTAL PRATINCOLE *Glareola maldivarum* 23–24 cm (a–c) **Adult breeding**: Short bill/legs, long pointed wings, short forked tail. Warmish grey-brown, buff throat/upper foreneck with black 'necklace', red bill-base. In flight, white rump and uppertail-coverts, chestnut underwing-coverts. (d) **Adult non-breeding**: Duller, necklace frayed. (e) **Juvenile**: Whitish to buff and blackish fringing above, greyish-brown streaks and mottling on breast. **VOICE** Sharp tern-like *kyik* or *kyeck*, *chik-chik* and *chet* etc., mainly in flight. Loud *cherr* and rising *trooeet*. **HABITAT** Marshes, large rivers, lakes, dry rice paddies and open country, coastal pools; up to 1,200 m. **RANGE** Sc/lc **BV** (some overwinter) Myanmar, Thailand, Pen Malaysia, Cambodia, C,S Annam, Cochinchina. Mostly **R** in parts of Myanmar, Cochinchina? Sc/fc **PM** S Myanmar, S Thailand, Pen Malaysia, Singapore, Cambodia, Laos, E Tonkin, C Annam.

8 SMALL PRATINCOLE *Glareola lactea* 16–19 cm (a–c) **Adult breeding**: Small and pale, no necklace. In flight, broad white wing-band and black trailing edge, black band on squarish tail. (d) **Adult non-breeding**: Paler lores, faint throat-streaks. (e) **Juvenile**: Lower throat bordered by brownish spots/streaks, buffish-and-brownish fringing above. **VOICE** High *prrip* or *tiririt* in flight. Short *tuck-tuck-tuck...* **HABITAT & BEHAVIOUR** Large rivers, dry lake/marsh margins, rarely coastal pools, sandy areas; up to 450 m. Highly gregarious. **RANGE** Un/lc **R** (some movements) Myanmar, NW,NE,C(north) Thailand, Cambodia, Laos. **V** C(south),W(coastal) Thailand, Singapore, Cochinchina.

PLATE 48 STILTS, PIED AVOCET, RINGED PLOVERS & CRAB-PLOVER

1 BLACK-WINGED STILT *Himantopus himantopus* 37.5 cm
(**a,b**) **Adult non-breeding** *himantopus*: Black and white, slim build, needle-like blackish bill, very long pinkish-red legs. Grey cap and hindneck, black ear-coverts, black upper mantle, scapulars and wings. Female browner above. (**c**) **Male breeding**: Head/neck typically all white. Can have some variable grey or black on head/hindneck. (**d**) **Female breeding**: Browner above, may show grey and black on head/hindneck. (**e**) **Juvenile**: Brownish-grey crown/hindneck, greyish-brown above with buffy fringes. **VOICE** Sharp nasal *kek* and yelping *ke-yak*. Monotonous high *kik-kik-kik-kik..* in alarm. **HABITAT** Borders of open wetlands, saltpans, coastal pools, large rivers; lowlands. **RANGE** Sc/lo **R** (some movements) C,S Myanmar, C,S(east) Thailand (coastal), Cambodia, N,C Laos, Cochinchina. Sc/fc **WV** Thailand, Pen Malaysia, Singapore. **Rc** (status?) SW,W,N,E Myanmar, E Tonkin, N,C,S Annam.

2 WHITE-HEADED STILT *Himantopus leucocephalus* 35 cm
(**a**) **Adult**: Like breeding male Black-winged, but long black 'mane'. Slightly smaller, but wing and bill longer relative to body size. (**b**) **First immature**: On current knowledge, possibly not distinguishable from non-breeding adult Black-winged. **VOICE** Feeble puppy-like *yap-yap-yap..* (incessant when agitated); plaintive mournful piping. **HABITAT** Similar to Black-winged. **RANGE** **V** Cochinchina (sight record).

3 PIED AVOCET *Recurvirostra avosetta* 42–45 cm
(**a,b**) **Male**: Black and white, narrow, strongly upturned blackish bill, long bluish-grey legs. Mainly white with black face, crown and upper hindneck and mostly black scapulars, median and lesser coverts and primaries. **Female**: Bill shorter, more strongly upturned. (**c**) **Juvenile**: Dark of plumage obscured with dull brown, white of mantle/scapulars mottled pale greyish-brown. **VOICE** Clear melodious liquid *kluit*, often repeated. More emphatic *kloo-eet* and shrill *krrree-yu* in alarm. **HABITAT** Coastal pools, mud-/sandflats, lakes, large rivers; lowlands. **RANGE** Former lo **WV** (currently?) C Myanmar. **V** N,S Myanmar, NW,C,W(coastal) Thailand, E Tonkin, Cochinchina.

4 COMMON RINGED PLOVER *Charadrius hiaticula* 19 cm
(**a,b**) **Adult non-breeding** *tundrae*: Larger/more robust than Little Ringed, broader breast-band, dull orange lower mandible-base, orange legs. In flight, white wing-bar. (**c**) **Male breeding**: From Little Ringed by orange bill with black tip, orange legs, broader, less even breast-band, no obvious yellow eyering or white band across midcrown. **Female breeding**: Ear-coverts and breast-band brownish-black. (**d**) **Juvenile**: Narrower breast-band than adult non-breeding, buffish fringes and narrow dark subterminal markings above, all-dark bill, duller/more yellowish leg. Best separated from Little Ringed by size, proportions, colder-toned upperside, whiter forehead and supercilium, lack of obvious eyering, often more orange-tinged legs, white wing-bar. **VOICE** Mellow rising *too-lee*, usually in flight. Short *wip*. Soft low *too-weep* in alarm. **HABITAT & BEHAVIOUR** Mud-/sandflats, saltpans, coastal pools, large rivers; up to 450 m. Feeding action and wingbeats slightly slower than Little Ringed. **RANGE** **V** SW Myanmar, NW,C Thailand, Pen Malaysia, Singapore.

5 LONG-BILLED PLOVER *Charadrius placidus* 19–21 cm
(**a,b**) **Adult non-breeding**: Larger and even more slender and attenuated than Little Ringed, longer bill, broader dark forecrown-band, broader buff supercilium, narrower, more even breast-band. Bill blackish with dull yellow at base of lower mandible, pinkish-yellow legs. In flight, narrow white wing-bar, thin white trailing edge to secondaries, faint greyish panel on flight feathers, more contrasting blackish primary coverts. (**c**) **Adult breeding**: White forehead/supercilium, broad black forecrown-band, narrow, even black breast-band. Lacks black lores/ear-coverts of Little Ringed, duller eyering. (**d**) **Juvenile**: Initially neat warm buff fringes above, no dark forecrown-band, buffier supercilium, greyish-brown breast-band. **VOICE** Clear rising *piwee* or *piwii-piwii-piwii..*, musical *tudulu*. **HABITAT** Larger rivers, dry fields, sometimes mud-/sandflats, beaches; up to 1,830 m. **RANGE** Ra **WV** N(un),C Myanmar, NW,C Thailand, N,C Laos, E Tonkin, C Annam. **V** Pen Malaysia, Singapore.

6 LITTLE RINGED PLOVER *Charadrius dubius* 14–17 cm
(**a,b**) **Adult non-breeding** *jerdoni*: Rather dainty and small-headed, quite attenuated rear end, slender dark bill, pinkish to yellowish legs, white collar, complete greyish-brown breast-band (or slightly broken in centre). No wing-bar in flight. Otherwise greyish-brown above, apart from buffish-white forehead and indistinct supercilium. Narrow pale yellowish eyering. (**c**) **Male breeding**: Black lores/ear-coverts/breast-band, white forehead/supercilium, prominent black forecrown-band, backed by narrow white band, broad yellow eyering. **Female breeding**: Eyering slightly narrower, ear-coverts/breast-band tinged brownish. (**d**) **Juvenile**: Sandier-brown above than adult non-breeding, with warm buff fringes and indistinct darker subterminal markings, breast-band browner and more like lateral patches, supercilium buffier. **Other subspecies** *C.d.curonicus* (wintering race). **VOICE** Harsh territorial *cree-ah*, often during display flight. Plaintive *pee-oo* (*pee* stressed), mainly in flight. Shorter *peeu* and rapid *pip-pip-pip-pip..* in alarm. **HABITAT & BEHAVIOUR** Large rivers, lakes, marshes, rice paddies, coastal pools; up to 1,450 m. Courtship display involves puffing-out breast, tail-fanning and prancing. Gliding display flight with wings raised in shallow V. **RANGE** Sc/lfc **R** Myanmar, NW,NE Thailand, Cambodia, Laos, N Annam, Cochinchina. Co **WV** (except SW,E Myanmar).

7 CRAB-PLOVER *Dromas ardeola* 38–41 cm
(**a,b**) **Adult**: Very thick, pointed blackish bill, long bluish-grey legs, mainly white with black mantle/scapulars and mostly black upperside of flight feathers, primary coverts and outer greater coverts. Sometimes blackish speckles on hindcrown/nape. (**c**) **Juvenile**: Hindcrown/nape more heavily speckled blackish, mostly greyish above with paler brownish-grey scapulars and coverts, dark of upperwing greyer. **VOICE** Yappy *kirruc* in flight. Repeated barking *ka* or *ka-how* and *kwerk-kwerk-kwerk-kwerk...* Sharp *kew-ki-ki* and *ki-tewk* recorded from breeding grounds. **HABITAT & BEHAVIOUR** Undisturbed sandy beaches, dunes, mud-/sandflats. Mainly a crepuscular and nocturnal feeder. Likely to be found in family parties or small flocks. **RANGE** Ra **NBV** S Thailand. **V** west Pen Malaysia.

PLATE 49 *CHARADRIUS* PLOVERS

1 KENTISH PLOVER *Charadrius alexandrinus* 15–17.5 cm (a,b) **Adult non-breeding** *dealbatus*: From other small plovers by plain upperside, white nuchal collar, well-defined and rather narrow dark lateral breast-patches, blackish bill, rather long bluish-grey to greyish (sometimes distinctly olive or pinkish) legs. In flight, obvious white wing-bar and white outertail feathers. (c,d) **Adult non-breeding**: Worn, faded individuals can be very pale and greyish above ('bleached'). (e) **Male breeding**: White forehead and short supercilium, black patch on midcrown, strongly rufous-washed remainder of crown and nape, broad blackish eyestripe, well-defined narrow black lateral breast-patches. (f) **Male breeding variant**: Less well marked. (g) **Female breeding**: Usually has little or no rufous on crown and nape, may lack black on head and breast markings shown by male (more like adult non-breeding). (h) **Juvenile**: Like adult non-breeding but somewhat paler-headed, forehead and supercilium washed buff, upperparts and wing-coverts neatly fringed buff, lateral breast-patches somewhat paler and more diffuse. **Other subspecies** *C.a.alexandrinus* (R S Myanmar; VS southern Myanmar, NW Thailand). **VOICE** Soft *pit* or *pi* notes and hard trilled *prrr* or *prrrtut* in flight, harsher than similar call of Lesser Sand. Plaintive *too-eet* or *pweep* in alarm. Sharp rattling *tjekke-tjekke-tjekke..* during display flight. **HABITAT & BEHAVIOUR** Beaches, sand-/mudflats, coastal pools, large rivers, dry lake margins; up to 450 m. Male performs stiff-winged territorial display flights with body tilting from side to side. Pair displays include wing-/tail-spreading. **RANGE** Lo coastal R S Myanmar, S Annam, probably N Annam. Un/co (mainly coastal) **WV** (except W,E Myanmar, W Tonkin). Also **PM** S Myanmar, S Thailand, Pen Malaysia, Singapore, Cambodia, E Tonkin.

2 MALAYSIAN PLOVER *Charadrius peronii* 14–16 cm (a) **Male**: Slightly smaller/shorter-billed than breeding male Kentish, upperparts/wing-coverts with prominent pale fringes (appear scaly or mottled), narrower black lateral breast-patches which extend in complete band below white nuchal collar; legs often tinged yellowish or pinkish. (b,c) **Female**: Lacks black markings. From Kentish by rufous-washed ear-coverts and lateral breast-patches, scaly upperparts; crown always washed rufous. (d) **Juvenile**: Slightly duller than female. **VOICE** Soft *whit* or *twik*, recalling Kentish. **HABITAT & BEHAVIOUR** Undisturbed sandy, coralline and shelly beaches, sometimes nearby mudflats. Usually in pairs. **RANGE** Ra/lfc coastal **R** Thailand, Pen Malaysia, Singapore, Cambodia, Cochinchina.

3 LESSER SAND PLOVER *Charadrius mongolus* 19–21 cm (a,b) **Adult non-breeding** *schaeferi* (Thailand, Pen Malaysia, ? parts of Myanmar and Indochina): From other small plovers (except Greater Sand) by broad lateral breast-patches and lack of white nuchal collar. Sandy greyish-brown above with whitish forehead and supercilium. Best separated from Greater by combination of following subtle features: smaller size, neater proportions, rounder head, shorter and blunter-tipped bill (length roughly equal to distance from bill-base to rear of eye), tibia obviously shorter than tarsus, dark grey to greenish-grey legs, toes only project slightly beyond tail-tip in flight. Bill length varies from longest in this race to shortest in *mongolus*. (c) **Male breeding**: Black

forehead, lores and ear-coverts, deep orange-rufous sides of neck and broad breast-band. May show very small whitish markings on sides of forehead. (d) **Female breeding**: Much duller; less orange-rufous on neck and breast, browner forehead and mask. (e) **Juvenile**: Like adult non-breeding but buffish-fringed above, buff-washed and often less pronounced supercilium, buffish mixed-in on lateral breast-patches. (f) **Adult non-breeding** *mongolus* (rc Indochina, Thailand?): Smaller bill. (g) **Male breeding**: White forehead, bisected by vertical black line, narrow blackish upper border to breast-band. **Other subspecies** *C.m.atrifrons* (rc Myanmar, Pen Malaysia): Often a small white patch on side of forehead. **VOICE** Rather short sharp hard *kruit* or *drrit* notes in flight; also hard *chitik* and *chi-chi-chi*. **HABITAT** Mud/sandflats, coastal pools, rarely large rivers, other inland wetlands; up to 1,065 m. **RANGE** Co coastal **WV** and **PM** throughout. Sc inland **PM** NE,C Thailand, N,C Laos. Rc in summer C,S Thailand, Pen Malaysia, Singapore.

4 GREATER SAND PLOVER *Charadrius leschenaultii* 22–25 cm (a,b) **Adult non-breeding** *leschenaultii*: Very similar to Lesser Sand but differs by combination of following subtle features: larger size, longer appearance, squarer head, longer bill with more tapered tip (length greater than distance from bill-base to rear of eye), longer tibia (may look almost as long as tarsus), typically somewhat paler legs (usually tinged greenish or yellowish), toes project distinctly beyond tail-tip in flight. (c) **Male breeding**: Like Lesser (race *mongolus*) but narrower orange-rufous breast-band, with no black upper border. (d) **Female breeding**: Like adult non-breeding but narrow orange-brown breast-band. (e) **Juvenile**: Differs from adult as Lesser. **VOICE** Trilled *prrrirt*, *kyrrrr trr* and *trrri* etc., softer and longer than similar calls of Lesser (recalls Ruddy Turnstone). **HABITAT & BEHAVIOUR** Mud/sandflats, beaches, saltpans, coastal pools, rarely large rivers on passage. Often associates with Lesser, but generally less common. **RANGE** Un/lc coastal **WV** and **PM** throughout. Sc **PM** inland Cambodia, N,C Laos. Rc in summer C Thailand, Pen Malaysia, Singapore.

5 ORIENTAL PLOVER *Charadrius veredus* 22–25 cm (a–c) **Adult non-breeding**: Larger/slimmer-looking than sand plovers, longer neck/legs/wings, slenderer bill, typically longer and more prominent supercilium, buffish-brown upper breast. When fresh, narrow rufous/warm buff fringes above. Legs yellow to orange (tinged pinkish to greenish). In flight, very long, all-dark wings with paler upperwing-coverts. (d) **Male breeding**: Head and neck largely whitish with greyish-brown cap, rufous-chestnut breast-band with broad black lower border. (e) **Female breeding**: Like adult non-breeding but upper breast with rufescent wash. (f) **Juvenile**: Like fresh adult non-breeding but more pronounced and paler buff fringing above. **VOICE** Sharp whistled *chip-chip-chip*, short piping *klink* and various trilled notes in flight. **HABITAT & BEHAVIOUR** Dry mud near fresh or brackish water, short grassy areas, sometimes saltpans, mud-/sandflats; lowlands. Runs very fast, flight fast, high and rather erratic. **RANGE** V/ra **PM** W(coastal),C,SE,S Thailand, Pen Malaysia, Singapore, Cambodia, C,S Annam.

PLATE 50 *PLUVIALIS* PLOVERS & LAPWINGS

1 PACIFIC GOLDEN PLOVER *Pluvialis fulva* 23–26 cm
(a,b) **Adult non-breeding**: Medium-sized, short-billed; quite nondescript with golden spangling above, pale buffish-grey head-sides, dusky-grey streaks/mottling on neck/breast. Dark patch on rear ear-coverts. In flight, quite uniform above with indistinct whitish wing-bar and dull underwing with dusky-grey coverts. (c) **Male breeding**: Black from ear-coverts/throat to belly, broad white band from lores over/behind ear-coverts to breast-side, white flanks; vent marked black. **Female breeding**: Usually less black below. (d) **Juvenile**: As adult non-breeding but bolder yellowish-buff pattern above, strongly golden-washed head-sides/neck/breast, the latter finely spotted and streaked darker. **VOICE** Clear rapid *chu-it* (recalling Spotted Redshank) in flight. More drawn-out *klu-ee* and extended *chu-EE*. **HABITAT** Cultivated lowlands, dry areas, coastal habitats. **RANGE** Un/fc **WV** throughout. Also **PM** Cambodia, Laos, W,E Tonkin. **Rc** in summer Pen Malaysia, Singapore.

2 GREY PLOVER *Pluvialis squatarola* 27–30 cm
(a,b) **Adult non-breeding**: Larger/stockier/bigger-headed than Pacific Golden, stouter bill, more uniform above and distinctly greyish with whitish speckling and spangling, whitish (not buffish) supercilium, mostly greyish head-sides, whiter base colour to neck/breast. In flight, prominent white wing-bar, white uppertail-coverts, boldly barred tail, largely whitish underwing with obvious black axillaries. (c) **Male breeding**: Black ear-coverts and throat to belly, very broad white band from lores over/behind ear-coverts to breast-sides. Black mid-flanks, white vent; bold silvery-white spangling above. **Female breeding**: Typically somewhat browner above, with less black on head-sides, variable amounts of white admixed below. (d) **Juvenile**: Like adult non-breeding but blacker above with more defined yellowish-white/-buff speckles and spangling, yellowish-buff washed and more distinctly dark-streaked neck/breast. **VOICE** Loud melancholy *tlee-oo-ee* in flight. **HABITAT** Mud-/sandflats, beaches, coastal pools. **RANGE** Un/fc coastal **WV** and **PM** throughout. Inland **V**/ra **PM** C Thailand, Cambodia, N Laos. **Rc** in summer S Thailand, Pen Malaysia, Singapore.

3 NORTHERN LAPWING *Vanellus vanellus* 28–31 cm
(a,b) **Adult non-breeding**: Looks black and white at distance with long swept-back crest. Crown/crest black, head-sides buffish/whitish with black patch, mostly dark glossy green above with some buffish fringes, white below with broad blackish breast-band, orange-rufous undertail-coverts. In flight, very broad wings, black flight feathers, pale band across primary tips, white underwing-coverts. (c) **Male breeding**: Whiter head-sides, black lores and throat. (d) **Female breeding**: Like breeding male but lores and throat marked with white. (e) **Juvenile**: More obvious warm buff fringing above than adult non-breeding, shorter crest. **VOICE** Loud shrill *cheew* and more plaintive *cheew-ip* or *wee-ip*. **HABITAT** Open country, cultivation, marshes; up to 500 m. **RANGE** Ra/lfc **WV** N,C Myanmar, NW,NE,C,SE Thailand, N Laos, E Tonkin, N Annam.

4 YELLOW-WATTLED LAPWING *Vanellus malabaricus* 26–28 cm
(a,b) **Adult non-breeding**: Blackish crown (mixed brown), yellow face-wattle, white postocular band, thin blackish breast-band, yellow legs. In flight, more prominent wing-bar than Red-wattled, more white on underwing. **Adult breeding**: Crown all black. (c) **Juvenile**: Buffish-speckled brown crown, buff fringes and dark subterminal bars above, mostly whitish chin/throat, smaller/duller wattles, no breast-band. **VOICE** Strident shrill *tchee-it* or *tiii-ic* and *tii'i*, and hard sharp *tit-tit-tit..* and *whit-it'it'it'it'it..* in alarm. **HABITAT** Dry lowland grassland and open areas, agriculture, wetland margins. **RANGE** V S Myanmar, Pen Malaysia.

5 RIVER LAPWING *Vanellus duvaucelii* 29–32 cm
(a,b) **Adult**: Black crown, face to upper breast, bill and legs, long crest, otherwise whitish head/neck. White below, sandy greyish-brown breast-band, small black belly-patch; black spur on wing-bend (often hidden). In flight, broad white wing-bar, black strip on outer coverts, black tail-tip. (c) **Juvenile**: Black of head partly obscured by brownish tips, sandy-brown above with buff fringes and slightly darker subterminal markings. **VOICE** Sharp high *tip-tip* or *did did did..*, sometimes ending with *to-weet* or *do-weet*. **HABITAT & BEHAVIOUR** Large rivers and surrounds; up to 600 m. Breeding display includes stooping, spinning and upstretching. **RANGE** Sc/lc **R** Myanmar, Thailand (except SE), Indochina (except N,S Annam). **FR** (currently?) Cochinchina.

6 GREY-HEADED LAPWING *Vanellus cinereus* 34–37 cm
(a,b) **Adult non-breeding**: Mostly plain brownish-grey head, neck and upper breast, rather long yellowish bill with black tip, yellowish legs. Chin and centre of throat whitish, broad, partly obscured, blackish breast-band. In flight, white greater coverts and secondaries (above and below). **Adult breeding**: Head, neck and upper breast grey, neat broad blackish breast-band. (c) **Juvenile**: Head, neck and breast brownish, breast-band vague or absent, neatly fringed buffish above. **VOICE** Plaintive *chee-it*, often repeated. Rasping *cha-ha-eet* and sharp *pink* in alarm. **HABITAT** Marshes, wet rice paddies, cultivation; up to 1,250 m. **RANGE** Sc/lc **WV** (except SE Thailand, Singapore, W Tonkin, S Annam). Also **PM** Cambodia. **V** Singapore.

7 RED-WATTLED LAPWING *Vanellus indicus* 31.5–35 cm
(a,b) **Adult** *atronuchalis*: Black hood and upper breast, white patch on ear-coverts, red facial skin, black-tipped red bill. Cold sandy greyish-brown above with narrow white band across upper mantle, whitish remainder of underparts, long yellow legs. In flight, prominent white wing-bar, blackish flight feathers, white band across rump and uppertail-coverts, mostly black tail with white corners. (c) **Juvenile**: Duller hood, whitish throat, duller and reduced facial skin, duller bill and legs. **VOICE** Loud rapid *did-ee-doo-it* (*did* often repeated). During display flight utters frenzied series of typical calls, mixed with *did-did-did..* or *kab-kab-kab...* Sharp incessant *trint* and high-pitched *pit* notes in alarm. **HABITAT & BEHAVIOUR** Margins of lakes and large rivers, marshes, agriculture, wasteland; up to 1,525 m. Display flight involves short, dipping wingbeats, downward swoops and acrobatic tumbling dives. **RANGE** Un/co **R** throughout (no longer **B** Singapore?).

PLATE 51 LARGER GULLS & BLACK-LEGGED KITTIWAKE

1 BLACK-TAILED GULL *Larus crassirostris* 45–48 cm (**a,b**) **Adult non-breeding**: Dark grey upperside, broad black tail-band. Greyish streaked/smudged hindcrown and nape, longish yellow bill with black and red at tip, greenish-yellow legs, pale yellowish eyes, red eyering. In flight (from above), mostly blackish outer primaries and broad white trailing edge to secondaries. (**c**) **Adult breeding**: All-white head and neck. (**d,e**) **First winter**: From other medium-sized gulls by dark-tipped pinkish bill, rather uniform greyish-brown body with contrasting whitish forehead, throat, rump, uppertail-coverts and vent; blackish tail with fine white terminal band. (**f**) **Second winter**: Like adult non-breeding but mantle/scapulars mixed brown, upperwing paler/browner. HABITAT Mud- and sandflats, coasts. RANGE Ra coastal **WV** C Thailand, E Tonkin.

2 MEW GULL *Larus canus* 43–46 cm (**a,b**) **Adult non-breeding**: *kamtschatschensis*: Smaller than Heuglin's, smaller bill, rounder head with heavier streaks, paler above, larger white wing-tip 'mirrors'. (**c**) **Adult breeding**: Bill uniform yellow, head/neck all white. (**d,e**) **First winter**: From similar medium-sized gulls by black-tipped pinkish bill, pinkish legs, heavy dark markings on head, neck, breast-sides and flanks, mostly plain grey mantle, back and scapulars, mostly plain brownish-grey greater coverts, which contrast with dark brown pale-fringed wing-coverts. In flight, clear-cut broad blackish subterminal band. (**f**) **Second winter**: Like non-breeding adult but upper primary coverts marked black, 'mirrors' smaller. VOICE Shrill high nasal *glieeoo*, nasal *keow*; *gleeu-gleeu-gleeu..* in alarm. HABITAT Coastal pools, sand- and mudflats. RANGE V/ra **WV** N Myanmar. Coastal **V** C Thailand, E Tonkin.

3 MONGOLIAN GULL *Larus mongolicus* 60–67 cm (**a,b**) **Adult non-breeding**: Averages larger than Heuglin's, distinctly paler grey above (similar to north European Herring Gull *L.a.argentatus*, but perhaps slightly bluer-tinged); typically whiter-headed. Eyes usually look yellowish in field, legs yellowish-flesh to flesh/pink (rarely yellow). In February/March, already has white head of breeding plumage (while Heuglin's still shows head-streaking). (**c**) **Adult breeding**: Head and neck all white. (**d,e**) **First winter**: Best separated from Heuglin's by paler greater upperwing-coverts and somewhat paler inner primaries. (**f**) **Second winter**: From Heuglin's by same features as first winter; additionally shows paler grey on upperparts. HABITAT Coasts, sand- and mudflats, coastal pools. RANGE Not definitely recorded in the region but unconfirmed recent winter sight records C Thailand, E Tonkin. NOTE On current knowledge, best treated as a distinct species; otherwise as a race of extralimital Vega Gull *L.vegae* (see Yésou 2001, 2002).

4 HEUGLIN'S GULL *Larus heuglini* 58–65 cm (**a,b**) **Adult non-breeding** '*taimyrensis*': From Mongolian by distinctly darker grey upperparts; typically heavy-streaked head and hindneck. Legs usually yellowish, eyes usually pale. Moult starts later than Mongolian; large gulls with white head and retained, faded and worn primaries in September and October should be this species. By February/March, still has head-streaks

of non-breeding plumage and may have outermost primaries growing, while most/all Mongolian will have white heads. (**c**) **Adult breeding**: Head and neck all white. **Juvenile**: Heavy dull brownish streaks and mottling on white of head, underside, rump and uppertail-coverts, dark brownish above with whitish to brownish-white fringing and notching, mostly blackish tail with dark-speckled white base and narrow white terminal band, blackish bill, dull pinkish legs. In flight, quite blackish upperwing with contrasting paler median coverts and slightly paler, dark-tipped inner primaries (paler when worn). (**d,e**) **First winter**: Moults in new scapulars and tertials, which are greyer with more diffuse darker central markings and less defined pale borders; head and underside somewhat whiter, particularly face, head and neck. (**f**) **Second winter**: Like first winter, but mantle, back and scapulars mostly grey. HABITAT Coasts, sand- and mudflats, lakes, large rivers; lowlands. RANGE Ra/lo (mostly coastal) **WV** N Myanmar, C,W Thailand, E Tonkin. **V** Singapore? NOTE Currently, '*taimyrensis*' is thought to be an invalid taxon, comprising hybrids between *L.(b.) heuglini* and Vega Gull *L. vegae* (Yésou 2002). It is unclear at present whether true *heuglini* occurs in the region.

5 PALLAS'S GULL *Larus ichthyaetus* 58–67 cm (**a,b**) **Adult non-breeding**: Yellowish bill with blackish subterminal band, mask of streaks, pale grey above, little black on outer primaries. (**c**) **Adult breeding**: Head black with broken white eyering, bill with yellower base and more red near tip. (**d,e**) **First winter**: Similar to second-winter Heuglin's and Mongolian but dark mask and hindcrown- streaking (as adult non-breeding), densely dark-marked lower hindneck and breast-sides, paler grey on mantle, back and scapulars, mostly grey, unbarred greater coverts, white rump, uppertail-coverts and tail-base, contrasting sharply with broad blackish subterminal tail-band. (**f**) **Second winter**: Like non-breeding adult, but with remnants of dark markings on upperwing-coverts, mostly black outer primaries, narrow subterminal tail-band. VOICE Deep low *kyow-kyow* and nasal crow-like *kraagh* or *kra-ah*. HABITAT Coasts, sand- and mudflats, large rivers. RANGE Ra/sc **WV** N,C,S Myanmar (un/lc), coastal C,W Thailand, coastal E Tonkin. **V** NW Thailand, N Laos. **Rc** (status?) SW,E Myanmar, north Tenasserim.

6 BLACK-LEGGED KITTIWAKE *Rissa tridactyla* 37–42 cm (**a,b**) **Adult non-breeding** *pollicaris*: Relatively dark grey upperparts and upperwing, grey nape, vertical blackish bar behind eye, yellowish bill, shortish dark brown to blackish legs (rarely tinged pinkish to reddish). Tail slightly notched. Rather narrow outer wing turns whitish before neat black tip. (**c**) **Adult breeding**: Head all white. (**d,e**) **First winter**: Differs from non-breeding adult by upperwing pattern, with broadly black outer primaries and black diagonal band across coverts, contrasting sharply with largely whitish secondaries and inner primaries. Black-tipped tail, black bill (may be slightly paler at base); head as non-breeding adult but may show black band across hindneck. VOICE May give short nasal *kya* in flight, or short knocking *kt kt kt..* in alarm. HABITAT Open seas, rarely inshore. RANGE **V** C Thailand.

PLATE 52 SMALLER GULLS

1 BROWN-HEADED GULL *Larus brunnicephalus* 42–46 cm
(**a,b**) **Adult non-breeding**: Like Black-headed but a little larger, bulkier, thicker-billed and thicker-necked, with pale eyes. In flight, broader and more rounded wings with distinctive broadly black-tipped outer primaries, enclosing up to three white 'mirrors', and more extensively blackish underside of primaries with white 'mirrors' near wing-tip. (**c**) **Adult breeding**: Dark brown hood with broken white eyering and paler face, uniform dark red bill. (**d,e**) **First winter**: From Black-headed, on plumage, by black outer primaries, broader black tips to inner primaries (above and below) and whitish patch extending over primary coverts and inner primaries on upperwing. VOICE Like Black-headed but deeper and gruffer. HABITAT Large rivers, lakes, coasts, coastal pools; up to 1,830 m. RANGE Un/c **WV** SW,N,C,E,S Myanmar, Tenasserim, Thailand, Pen Malaysia, Indochina (except W Tonkin, N,C,S Annam). Also **PM** S Myanmar, Cambodia, N Laos. **V** W Myanmar, Singapore. Also **rc** in summer C Thailand.

2 BLACK-HEADED GULL *Larus ridibundus* 35–39 cm
(**a,b**) **Adult non-breeding**: Relatively small and slim with rather narrow black-tipped red bill, dark red legs and pale grey upperside. Head mainly white, with prominent dark ear-spot and dark smudges on side of crown. Eyes dark. In flight, upperwing appears very pale with prominent white leading edge to outer wing and smallish black tips to outer primaries; underwing pattern mirrors this but coverts all greyish, outer primaries having more black and less white. (**c**) **Adult breeding**: Dark brown hood with broken white eyering, uniform darker red bill. (**d,e**) **First winter**: At rest resembles non-breeding adult but bill paler and duller with more contrasting dark tip, legs duller and more pinkish, greyish-brown centres to median and lesser coverts, inner greater coverts and tertials. In flight, upperwing shows broad greyish-brown band across coverts and broad blackish band along secondaries and tips of primaries; blackish subterminal tail-band. VOICE High-pitched screaming *kyaaar* and *karrr*. Short *kek* and deeper *kuk* notes. HABITAT Large rivers, lakes, coasts, coastal pools; up to 800 m. RANGE Sc/lc **WV** N,C,E,S Myanmar, north Tenasserim, coastal W,C,SE Thailand, Pen Malaysia, Singapore, Cambodia, N Laos, Vietnam (except W Tonkin). Also **PM** Cambodia. **V** NW,NE,C(inland),S Thailand.

3 SLENDER-BILLED GULL *Larus genei* 37–42 cm
(**a,b**) **Adult non-breeding**: Like Black-headed but longer-necked and longer-billed, has longer, more sloping forehead, all-white head (sometimes with faint ear-spot) and pale eyes. (**c**) **Adult breeding**: Head white, bill dark, sometimes appearing almost blackish (particularly at distance), underparts may be washed pink. (**d,e**) **First winter**: Apart from shape, differs from Black-headed by paler, more orange bill with less obvious dark tip, much fainter head markings, pale eyes and longer, paler legs. In flight, less contrasting band across upperwing-coverts (feather-centres paler) and a little more white on outer primaries. VOICE Like Black-headed but slightly deeper, lower-pitched and more nasal. HABITAT Coastal pools, large lowland rivers. RANGE **V** N Myanmar, coastal C Thailand.

4 SAUNDERS'S GULL *Larus saundersi* 33 cm
(**a,b**) **Adult non-breeding**: At rest, similar to Black-headed but smaller and more compact with shorter, thicker, blackish bill, white tips to primaries. In flight has similar wing pattern but upperside of outer primaries have white tips and small black subterminal markings. (**c**) **Adult breeding**: Black hood (including nape) with broad, broken white eyering. (**d,e**) **First winter**: Apart from size and bill, best separated from Black-headed in flight, by different upperwing pattern, with smaller isolated black tips to inner primaries, narrower and more broken dark band along secondaries, and lack of white leading edge to outer wing; narrower black tail-band. HABITAT Estuaries, mud-/sandflats. RANGE Lo **WV** E Tonkin.

5 RELICT GULL *Larus relictus* 44–45 cm
(**a,b**) **Adult non-breeding**: Recalls Brown-headed and Black-headed but larger, stockier, thicker-billed and longer-legged, with more uniformly dark-smudged ear-coverts and hindcrown (no obvious dark ear-spot), white tips to primaries. Bill dark red. In flight, upperwing shows white-tipped primaries, prominent, separated black subterminal markings on outer primaries and no white leading edge to outer wing. (**c**) **Adult breeding**: Blackish hood (including nape) with broad broken white eyering. (**d,e**) **First winter**: Told by size, blackish bill and legs, mostly rather pale grey upperside, and sharply contrasting dark markings on wing-coverts and tertials. Dark speckles and markings on nape/neck/breast-sides, paler, greyish basal half of lower mandible. In flight, solid black outer primaries, only small dark markings on inner primary tips and secondaries, no obvious white on outer wing; narrow black subterminal tail-band. (**f**) **Second winter**: Poorly documented. Similar to adult non-breeding but bill black with dark red base, tertials blackish-brown with white edges, primaries with slightly broader white tips. VOICE Nasal downward-inflected *kyeu* and low-pitched, drawn-out *ke'arr*. HABITAT & BEHAVIOUR Estuaries, mud-/sandflats. Often walks with a very upright gait, neck upstretched. RANGE Coastal **V** E Tonkin.

6 LAUGHING GULL *Larus atricilla* 36–41 cm
(**a,b**) **Adult non-breeding**: Told by size, relatively dark grey upperside, longish dark bill (tip often reddish), reddish-black legs, dark greyish-smudged ear-coverts/hindcrown (no defined ear-spot). In flight, uniform grey upperwing with black tips and bold white trailing edge to secondaries and inner primaries. (**c**) **Adult breeding**: Black hood (including nape) with broken white eyering, dark red bill and legs (former usually with black subterminal band). (**d,e**) **First winter**: Head, mantle, scapulars and underparts similar to adult non-breeding, but dusky nape/breast-band/flanks; blackish bill/legs. Mostly dark greyish-brown wing-covert/tertial centres. In flight, mostly blackish flight feathers, with similar trailing edge to adult, dark markings across mid-part of underwing; tail with broad black subterminal band and dark greyish sides. (**f**) **Second winter**: Like adult non-breeding but greyer nape to breast-sides/flanks, some dark markings on primary coverts, may show faint suggestion of tail-band. VOICE Yelping *kee-agh*, recalling Mew. HABITAT Coasts, mud-/sandflats. RANGE **V** west Pen Malaysia (sight record).

PLATE 53 JAEGERS, INDIAN SKIMMER, PELAGIC TERNS & NODDIES

1 POMARINE JAEGER *Stercorarius pomarinus* 47–61.5 cm
(**a**) **Adult pale morph non-breeding**: Heavy build; throat and neck dark-mottled, tail-coverts barred whitish. (**b**) **Adult pale morph breeding**: Broad whitish collar, neck washed yellowish, large whitish belly-patch, long broad twisted central tail feathers; whitish shaft-streaks at base of primaries, underwing with white crescent at base of primaries. **Adult dark morph**: Blackish-brown with primary pattern like pale morph. (**c**) **Juvenile pale morph**: Dark face, boldly pale-barred uppertail-coverts, double pale patch on underside of primaries. **First-winter pale morph**: As juvenile but pale hindcollar, no pale tips above. (**d**) **Second-winter pale morph**: Similar to non-breeding adult but underwing-coverts like juvenile. **Third-winter pale morph**: Lower breast/belly whiter than adult, may lack bars on greater underwing-coverts. (**e**) **Juvenile dark morph**: Blackish-brown, pale-barred tail-coverts; double patch on underside of primaries. HABITAT & BEHAVIOUR Open seas, sometimes inshore. Flight quite slow, gull-like; piratical flight relatively laboured. RANGE Ra/sc offshore **NBV** Tenasserim, C,SE,S Thailand, Pen Malaysia, Singapore, Cambodia.

2 PARASITIC JAEGER *Stercorarius parasiticus* 42–54.5 cm
(**a**) **Adult pale morph non-breeding**: Mottled breast-band, barred tail-coverts, duller cap than breeding, smaller/slimmer than Pomarine. (**b**) **Adult pale morph breeding**: Pointed tail-streamers. **Adult dark morph**: From Pomarine by size, shape and tail. Intermediates with pale morph occur. (**c**) **Juvenile pale morph**: Warmer than Pomarine, rarely has double patch on underside of primaries. **First-winter pale morph**: As juvenile but develops pale areas on head/body; warmer individuals become colder. (**d**) **Second-winter pale morph**: From non-breeding adult as Pomarine but no double patch on underwing. **Third-winter pale morph**: Gradually resembles non-breeding adult. (**e**) **Juvenile dark morph**: From Pomarine by all-dark underwing-coverts (including primary coverts). HABITAT & BEHAVIOUR Like Pomarine but flight typically faster and more falcon-like, with occasional shearwater-like glides; piratical flight faster and more acrobatic. RANGE Offshore **V/sc NBV** W,C,SE Thailand, Pen Malaysia, Singapore, Cambodia.

3 LONG-TAILED JAEGER *Stercorarius longicaudus* 47–67.5 cm
(**a**) **Adult non-breeding** *pallescens*: Slight build; dark underwing, little white on upperside of primaries. (**b**) **Adult breeding**: Very long tail, wing pattern like non-breeding, two-tone upperwing; underparts greyer towards vent. (**c**) **Juvenile pale morph**: Greyer and more contrasting pattern on underparts and underwing than Parasitic, darker primaries. (**d**) **Juvenile dark morph**: From Parasitic by boldly barred tail-coverts/axillaries, darker primaries. **First winter**: Like juvenile but plain greyish-brown upperparts/coverts, cleaner/whiter belly, more pointed, usually longer central tail feathers. (**e**) **Second winter**: Like non-breeding adult but underwing somewhat barred. **Third winter**: As adult non-breeding but may show pale bars on underwing-coverts. HABITAT & BEHAVIOUR As Parasitic but flight lighter, can recall smallish gull or tern; piratical attacks less confident/briefer. RANGE Offshore **V** S Thailand (also once inland), Pen Malaysia. Sc/un offshore **PM** Cambodia.

4 INDIAN SKIMMER *Rynchops albicollis* 40–43 cm
(**a,b**) **Adult breeding**: Black above, white face/collar/underparts, yellow-tipped orange bill with longer lower mandible; white trailing edge to upperwing. **Adult non-breeding**: Duller and browner-tinged above. (**c**) **Juvenile**: Mostly greyish-brown above, with whitish/pale buff fringing. VOICE Rather high, nasal *kap* or *kip* notes, mainly in flight. HABITAT & BEHAVIOUR Large rivers, lakes, rarely coasts; lowlands. Skims lower mandible through water to feed. RANGE Ra/sc **R** W,N,E,C,S Myanmar, formerly SW Myanmar, C,S Laos, Cambodia (bred?). **V** C Thailand.

5 BRIDLED TERN *Sterna anaethetus* 37–42 cm
(**a**) **Adult non-breeding** *anaethetus*: Brownish-grey above; uneven paler feather-tips, whitish forehead, blackish crown, nape and mask. (**b–d**) **Adult breeding**: White forehead/eyebrow, black eyestripe/crown/nape, brownish-grey above; darker trailing edge to whitish underwing. (**e**) **Juvenile**: Whitish tips and dark bars above, head as non-breeding adult. VOICE Yapping *wep-wep...* HABITAT Open seas, islets. RANGE Sc/lc offshore **R** (some movements) SE,S Thailand, Pen Malaysia, Cochinchina. Ra/un offshore/coastal **NBV** Thailand, Pen Malaysia, Singapore, Cambodia, C,S Annam. **V** inland N Annam.

6 SOOTY TERN *Sterna fuscata* 42–45 cm
(**a**) **Adult non-breeding** *nubilosa*: Blacker above than Bridled, no eyebrow. (**b–d**) **Adult breeding**: All-blackish crown/hindneck/upperside, square forehead-patch, blackish trailing edge to underwing. (**e**) **Juvenile/first winter**: Mostly sooty-blackish; whitish vent and feather-tips above. **First summer**: Plumage between juvenile/adult non-breeding; variably dark-marked below (mainly breast/flanks). VOICE High *ker-wacki-wah*, shorter *kraark*. HABITAT Open seas, islets. RANGE Offshore/coastal **V** S Myanmar, C,S Thailand, Pen Malaysia.

7 BROWN NODDY *Anous stolidus* 40–45 cm
(**a,b**) **Adult** *pileatus*: Dark brown; whitish forehead, grey crown, long wedge-shaped tail; paler wing-band. (**c**) **Juvenile**: Mostly with pale buffish fringing above (also crown), browner forecrown. VOICE Harsh *kaark* and *kwok kuok...* HABITAT Open seas, islets. RANGE Ra/un offshore **NBV** Pen Malaysia, Cambodia (may still breed). **FB** SE Thailand, west Pen Malaysia. Coastal/offshore **V** Tenasserim, west S Thailand, Cochinchina.

8 BLACK NODDY *Anous minutus* 34–39 cm
(**a,b**) **Adult** *worcesteri*: Smaller and slimmer than Brown; longer/thinner bill (longer than head), blacker plumage with whiter crown, shorter tail; all-dark upperwing. (**c**) **Juvenile**: From Brown by size/structure, narrower brownish-buff fringing above, whiter forehead/crown. VOICE Querulous *krrrk* and rapid laughing *k'k'k'k'...* HABITAT Sea coasts, open ocean, islets. RANGE Offshore **V** south-west Pen Malaysia ('Malacca').

9 WHITE TERN *Gygis alba* 28–33 cm
(**a,b**) **Adult** *monte*: Small, white; blackish bill/eyering/legs. (**c**) **Juvenile**: Dark flecks on crown and nape, brown and buff bars/scales above. VOICE Guttural *heech heech...* HABITAT Open seas, islets. RANGE Coastal **V** Cochinchina.

4–9 to different scale

PLATE 54 CRESTED & TYPICAL TERNS

1 LESSER CRESTED TERN *Sterna bengalensis* 35–40 cm
(a–c) Adult non-breeding *bengalensis*: Smaller than Great, thinner yellowish-orange bill, more solid black hindcrown and nape 'mane', paler grey above; when worn, darker outer primaries and bar on secondaries. **(d) Adult breeding**: Black crown/nape (including extreme forehead), more orange bill. **(e) Juvenile**: From Great by size/bill, upperside of inner primaries darker. **(f) First winter**: Greater/median upperwing-coverts plainer grey than Great (not illustrated), head as adult non-breeding. **VOICE** Harsh *krrrik-krrrik* in flight. **HABITAT** Open seas, coasts. **RANGE** Sc/un coastal NBV (mostly winter) SW,S Myanmar, Tenasserim, west S Thailand, west Pen Malaysia, Singapore; rarely W,C Thailand, Cambodia, Cochinchina.

2 GREAT CRESTED TERN *Sterna bergii* 45–49 cm
(a–c) Adult non-breeding *velox* (Myanmar; ? to west Pen Malaysia). Largish; cold yellowish bill, white forecrown, white-streaked black hindcrown/nape; plain wings with darker outer primary tips (patchier if worn). **(d) Adult breeding**: Brighter bill, white extreme forehead, black crown/nape. **(e) Juvenile**: Dull bill, brownish-grey above with whitish fringing, darker tail; dark bands across upperwing. **First winter**: As juvenile but uniform grey mantle and scapulars. Juvenile coverts gradually lost, often resulting in patchy appearance. **(f) Second winter**: As non-breeding adult but retains juvenile outer primaries/primary coverts/secondaries. **Other subspecies** *S.b.cristata* (east of range, western limit unclear): Paler grey above. **VOICE** Harsh grating *krrrik*, *kerrer* and *kerrak*, mainly in flight. **HABITAT** Open seas, coasts, mud-/sandflats, islets. **RANGE** Ra/lo coastal (mostly offshore) R (some movements) SW Myanmar, Tenasserim, Cambodia, Cochinchina, formerly SE Thailand. Un/lc coastal NBV (except N,C Annam).

3 CHINESE CRESTED TERN *Sterna bernsteini* 43 cm
(a–c) Adult non-breeding: Like Great Crested but smaller with blackish-tipped yellow bill, paler grey above with blackish outer primaries. **(d) Adult breeding**: Black-tipped yellow bill. **HABITAT** Open seas, coasts. **RANGE** Rc in winter east S Thailand.

4 ROSEATE TERN *Sterna dougallii* 33–39 cm
(a,b) Adult non-breeding *bangsi*: Slimmer than Common, paler above, longer/thinner bill, white line along inner edge of wing. In flight, whiter secondaries, less dark primaries, faintly dark on underside of primary tips. **(c,d) Adult breeding**: Only bill-base red, often pinkish below, very long tail; upperwing paler/plainer than Common, no dark on mid-primaries. **(e) Juvenile**: From Common by all-dark bill, darker forecrown, bolder subterminal markings above. **(f) First winter/summer**: From non-breeding adult by dark bands on coverts/secondaries, darker leading edge of outer wing. **(g) Adult breeding** *korustes* (Myanmar, ? to west Pen Malaysia): Less black on bill. **VOICE** Incisive, clicky *dju-dik* in flight. Low rasping *kraak*, *zraaach* or *aaabrk* in alarm. **HABITAT & BEHAVIOUR** Open seas, coasts, islets. Usually shallower, stiffer and faster wingbeats than Common. **RANGE** Vl coastal/offshore R (some movements) SE,S Thailand, Pen Malaysia, Cochinchina (Con Dao Is); probably Tenasserim. Sc/un offshore NBV (except SW Myanmar, Cambodia, E Tonkin, N,S Annam). V Singapore.

5 BLACK-NAPED TERN *Sterna sumatrana* 30–35 cm
(a) Adult breeding *sumatrana*: Crown white, neat nape-band; blackish bill/legs. **(b) Adult non-breeding**: Dark streaks on hindcrown; very pale above with blackish edge of outermost primary. **(c) Juvenile**: Dark crown-streaks, blackish subterminal markings above, dark-centred tail feathers, darker flight feathers. **First winter**: As adult non-breeding but narrow dark band across lesser coverts, juvenile primaries, darker greyish markings on tertials/tail. **VOICE** Sharp *kick*, *tsii-chee-ch-chip* and *chit-chit-chit-er* in flight. **HABITAT** Open seas, coasts, islets. **RANGE** Lo coastal/offshore R (some movements) SE,S Thailand, Pen Malaysia, Singapore, Cambodia, Cochinchina. Sc/lfc offshore NBV elsewhere (except SW Myanmar, C Thailand, E Tonkin).

6 COMMON TERN *Sterna hirundo* 33–37 cm
(a,b) Adult non-breeding *tibetana*: Thin blackish bill, dark red legs, white forehead, blackish mask/nape; medium grey above, white rump/uppertail-coverts, dark-tipped underside of outer primaries. **(c,d) Adult breeding**: Black-tipped orange-red bill, black forehead to nape, longer tail; dark wedge on mid-primaries. **(e) Juvenile (late)**: Head as non-breeding adult, dark brown subterminal markings above (also buffish fringes initially); blackish leading edge to upperwing. **(f) First winter/summer**: Bolder bands across upperwing than non-breeding adult. **(g) Adult breeding**: *S.b.longipennis* (rc C Thailand to C Annam): Mostly black bill, greyer overall, bolder white cheek-stripe, dark reddish-brown legs. **VOICE** Harsh *kreeeah*, short *kik* and rapidly repeated *kye* and *kirri* notes. **HABITAT** Coastal habitats, open ocean, large rivers/lakes. **RANGE** Sc/fc coastal NBV (except Myanmar, N Annam).

7 ARCTIC TERN *Sterna paradisaea* 33–39 cm
(a) Adult breeding: Shortish dark red bill, shorter neck than Common, very short legs. flight feathers near-white (apart from black-tipped outer primaries), translucent from below; tail-streamers longer than Common (extend a little beyond wing-tips at rest, rather than roughly equal). **Adult non-breeding**: As breeding but white forehead, blackish bill, shorter tail. Unlikely to occur in this plumage. **(b,c) Juvenile/first winter**: From Common by less patterned upperwing, whitish secondaries/inner primaries; bill all black from Aug/Sep. **(d) First summer**: Darker leading edge to upperwing than non-breeding adult. **VOICE** Piping *pi* and *pyu* notes, ringing *prree-eh*, hard rattled *kt-kt-kt-krrr-kt..*; *krri-errrrr* alarm. **HABITAT** Coasts. **RANGE** V Cochinchina (sight record).

8 ALEUTIAN TERN *Sterna aleutica* 32–34 cm
(a,b) Adult non-breeding: Whitish crown, dark band along underside of secondaries. **(c,d) Adult breeding**: Blackish bill/legs, white forehead/cheeks, grey below; broad white edge to inner wing, pale inner primaries, dark secondary band on underwing. **(e) Juvenile**: More uniform warm brown forehead than Common, mostly dark brown above with buff tips. **First winter**: As non-breeding adult but gingery lower nape; may show juvenile tertials/secondaries/lesser coverts (early winter). **Second winter**: Darker upperwing markings than non-breeding adult. **VOICE** Soft *twee-ee-ee*. **HABITAT** Open sea. **RANGE** Sc offshore WV east Pen Malaysia, Singapore. Sc WV/PM Cambodia.

PLATE 55 COASTAL, RIVERINE & MARSH TERNS

1 GULL-BILLED TERN *Gelochelidon nilotica* 34.5–37.5 cm
(**a–c**) **Adult non-breeding** *affinis*: Largish; white head with dark mask, heavy dark bill, slender wings, silver-grey rump and uppertail, shallow tail-fork. (**d**) **Adult breeding**: Forehead to nape black. (**e,f**) **First winter**: Secondaries/primary coverts darker than non-breeding adult, tail dark-tipped. **Other subspecies** *G.n.nilotica* (SW,C,E,S Myanmar; Thailand?). **VOICE** Low nasal *ger-erk* and *kay-vek* and loud metallic *kak-kak* in flight. Nasal *kvay-kvay-kvay..* in alarm. **HABITAT** Coasts, mud-/sandflats, lakes, large rivers; lowlands. **RANGE** Un/fc **WV** (mostly coastal) SW,C,E,S Myanmar, Tenasserim, W,C,S,E S Thailand, Pen Malaysia, Singapore, Cambodia, E Tonkin, Cochinchina. Rc in summer C Thailand, Pen Malaysia, Singapore.

2 CASPIAN TERN *Sterna caspia* 48–55 cm
(**a–c**) **Adult non-breeding**: Huge; thick red bill. (**d**) **Adult breeding**: Forehead to nape and mask all black. (**e**) **First winter**: Like non-breeding adult but somewhat darker secondaries/primary coverts/tail. **VOICE** Loud croaking *kraah* and *krakrah*, hoarse *kretch*. **HABITAT** Coastal pools, mud-/sandflats, large rivers, lakes; lowlands. **RANGE** Ra/sc coastal **WV** S Myanmar, C,W,S Thailand, Pen Malaysia, Singapore, Cambodia, E Tonkin, Cochinchina. Also **PM** Cambodia. Rc in summer Pen Malaysia. Rc inland Cambodia, Cochinchina (June).

3 RIVER TERN *Sterna aurantia* 38–46 cm (outertail < 23 cm)
(**a**) **Adult non-breeding**: Dark-tipped yellow bill, greyish dark-streaked crown, black mask/nape, reddish legs; greyish-white below. (**b**) **Adult breeding**: Bill orange-yellow, forehead to nape and mask black. Upperwing all grey, streamer-like outertail. May remain in this plumage outside breeding season. (**c**) **Juvenile**: Dark-tipped yellow bill, blackish mask/head-streaks, whitish supercilium, blackish-brown fringing above, blackish primary tips. **First winter**: As non-breeding adult but juvenile tertials/primaries/tail. **VOICE** High nasal *kiaah*. Rapid *kierr-wick kierrwick-kierr-wick..* when displaying, often accelerating to crescendo. **HABITAT** Large rivers, also lakes; up to 1,200 m (mostly breeds below 450 m). **RANGE** Sc/lfc **R** (some movements) Myanmar, Cambodia, S Laos; ra (still **B**?) Mekong R in NW,NE Thailand, N,C Laos. **V** C Thailand.

4 LITTLE TERN *Sterna albifrons* 22–25 cm
(**a,b**) **Adult non-breeding/first winter/summer** *sinensis*: Small; dark bill/legs, blackish hindcrown/nape and eye-patch, dark leading edge to inner wing, blackish outermost primaries. (**c,d**) **Adult breeding**: Black-tipped yellow bill, orange/yellow legs, neat white forehead. (**e**) **Juvenile**: Dark subterminal markings above; dark leading edge to upperwing. **Other subspecies** *S.a.albifrons* (rc in winter west S Thailand, west Pen Malaysia): Slightly darker grey above, longer tail-streamers, dark shafts on outer primaries. **VOICE** Sharp *kik* or *ket* notes in flight, rasping *kyik* in alarm. Rapid *kirrikikki kirrikikki...* **HABITAT** Coasts, beaches, saltpans, mud-/sandflats, large rivers; lowlands. **RANGE** Sc/un coastal **R** Myanmar, SE,C,W,S(east) Thailand, east Pen Malaysia, Singapore, Cambodia, C,S Annam; inland C,S,E Myanmar, Cambodia (now ra), S Laos (now ra). Un/fc coastal **WV** (except Myanmar?, N Annam?).

5 BLACK-BELLIED TERN *Sterna acuticauda* 30–33 cm
(**a**) **Adult non-breeding**: Same habitat as River, but smaller, dark-tipped orange bill, sometimes mottled blackish towards vent. (**b**) **Adult breeding**: Black crown/nape, orange bill, grey breast, blackish belly/vent, whitish head-sides/throat, deeply forked tail. (**c**) **Juvenile**: From River by size, bill (similar to non-breeding adult), lack of whitish supercilium, whiter head-/neck-sides. **VOICE** Clear piping *peuo*. **HABITAT** Large rivers, sometimes lakes, marshes; up to 450 m. **RANGE** Sc/un **R** Myanmar. **FR** (now rare; still breeds?) NW Thailand, north-east Cambodia(ra), Laos. **Frc** (status?) Cochinchina. **V** C Annam.

6 WHISKERED TERN *Chlidonias hybridus* 24–28 cm
(**a,b**) **Adult non-breeding/first winter** *javanicus*: Quite small /compact; blackish bill/mask/nape, white crown with dark streaks at rear, dark reddish legs, shortish shallow-forked tail; darker secondaries/outer primaries. (**c**) **Adult breeding**: Dark red bill/legs, black crown/nape, white throat/lower head-sides, dark grey below with white vent. (**d**) **Juvenile**: Like non-breeding adult but 'saddle' fawn-brown, barred/scaled blackish-and-buff, forecrown/face washed brownish-buff. **VOICE** Short rasping *kersch* and short *kek* notes in flight. **HABITAT** Coastal pools, mud-/sandflats, marshes, lakes, large rivers, wet rice paddies; up to 800 m. **RANGE** Un/co **WV** (except W,N Myanmar, SE Thailand, Laos, W Tonkin); sc Singapore. Ra/un **PM** S Myanmar, Pen Malaysia, Laos. Rc in summer S Thailand.

7 WHITE-WINGED TERN *Chlidonias leucopterus* 20–24 cm
(**a,b**) **Adult non-breeding/first winter**: Smaller/finer-billed than Whiskered; roundish ear-patch ('headphones'). In flight, white rump and uppertail-coverts, darker outer primaries, dark bands across lesser coverts/secondaries. (**c**) **Adult breeding**: Black head/body/underwing-coverts, white upperwing-coverts, rump and tail-coverts. (**d**) **Adult non-breeding/breeding (transitional)**: Patchy plumage. (**e**) **Juvenile**: Like Whiskered but white rump/uppertail-coverts, darker/more uniform 'saddle', darker lesser coverts/secondaries. **VOICE** Harsh high *kreek* and harsh creaking *kesch* in flight. **HABITAT** Coasts, coastal pools, marshes, wet rice paddies, lakes, large rivers; up to 450 m. **RANGE** Sc/lc **PM** S,E Myanmar, NW,W(coastal),C,S Thailand, Pen Malaysia, Singapore, Cambodia, Laos, C,S Annam, Cochinchina. Lo **WV** S Myanmar, C,S Thailand, Pen Malaysia, Singapore. Rc in summer S Thailand, Pen Malaysia, Singapore.

8 BLACK TERN *Chlidonias niger* 22–26 cm
(**a,b**) **Adult non-breeding/first winter** *niger*: Like White-winged but more solidly black hindcrown, larger ear-patch, dark smudge on breast-side, darker grey above, including rump/uppertail-coverts. (**c**) **Adult breeding**: Rather uniform greyish; darker grey body, blackish hood, white vent. Legs blackish. In flight, pale grey underwing-coverts. (**d**) **Juvenile**: Differs from White-winged by greyer, more clearly barred/scaled 'saddle' (contrasts less with darker grey upperwing), grey rump and uppertail-coverts, prominent dark smudge on breast-side. **VOICE** Weak sharp *kik* notes, and a short shrill nasal *kyeh* or *kja* in flight. **HABITAT** Marshes, coastal pools. **RANGE** **V** Singapore.

PLATE 56 BAZAS, ORIENTAL HONEY-BUZZARD, BAT HAWK & KITES

1 JERDON'S BAZA *Aviceda jerdoni* 46 cm
(**a–c**) **Adult** *jerdoni*: Long white-tipped blackish crest, warm brown head-sides/nape, paler area on coverts, dark mesial streak, indistinct rufous breast-streaks, broad rufous bars on belly/vent; cinnamon-rufous and white bars on underwing-coverts, few dark bars on flight feathers, three unevenly spaced blackish tail-bands. (**d,e**) **Juvenile**: Head mostly buffish-white with blackish streaks, four evenly spaced dark tail-bands. VOICE High airy *pee-weeeow* or *fiweeoo* and repeated shorter *ti-wuet*. When agitated, very high *chi chichitchit chit-chit* and *chu chit-chit chu-chit chu-chit* etc., mixed with *he-he-hew* or descending *he-he-wi-wiwi*. HABITAT & BEHAVIOUR Broadleaved evergreen forest, freshwater swamp forest; up to 1,900 m. Rarely soars high over forest; often travels/hunts below canopy. RANGE Sc/un R Tenasserim, W,NE,SE,S Thailand, Pen Malaysia (ra), E Tonkin, N,S Annam, Cochinchina, Cambodia. Rc (status?) S Myanmar, NW Thailand, Laos.

2 BLACK BAZA *Aviceda leuphotes* 31.5–33 cm
(**a–c**) **Adult** *syama*: Relatively small, head black with long crest, mostly black above, bold white on scapulars, white and chestnut on greater coverts and secondaries, whitish underparts with black and chestnut bars, black vent; underwing shows black coverts and primary tips, white remainder of primaries, grey secondaries. (**d**) **Juvenile**: More white markings above; small streaks below. **Other subspecies** *A.l.leuphotes* (breeds SW,S,E Myanmar, W,NW Thailand): Apparently tends to have more chestnut and white above, mostly chestnut breast-band, less barring on more rufous-buff lower breast and belly. VOICE High, rather shrill *chi-aah*, *tchi'euuah* or *tcheeoua* (first syllable stressed). HABITAT & BEHAVIOUR Broadleaved forests, other habitats on migration; up to 1,500 m. Often in flocks, particularly when migrating. RANGE Un/co R Myanmar (except Tenasserim), W,NW,SE Thailand, Cambodia, Laos, N,C,S Annam, Cochinchina. Un/fc WV and PM Tenasserim, Thailand, Pen Malaysia, Singapore. Un/fc PM Cambodia, C Laos, E Tonkin, N Annam. Rc (status?) Tenasserim.

3 ORIENTAL HONEY-BUZZARD *Pernis ptilorhyncus* 55–65 cm
(**a–c**) **Male pale morph** *ruficollis*: Relatively small head and longish neck, short crest. Typically has greyish head-sides, pale below with dark throat-border and mesial streak, gorget of dark streaks on lower throat/upper breast, warm bars on lower breast to vent. Eyes brown, cere grey. May have mostly cinnamon-rufous or whitish head/underparts (latter streaked and/or barred or unmarked). In flight, relatively long broadish wings and long narrow tail with two well-spaced blackish bands (can look blackish with pale central band); underwing typically whitish with blackish trailing edge, narrow dark bars on coverts and (usually) three blackish bands across primaries/outer secondaries. Dark markings on flight feathers visible from above. (**d**) **Female pale morph**: Narrower tail-bands, narrower trailing edge to underwing, which has three bands across secondaries/inner primaries. (**e,f**) **Adult dark morph**: Mostly dark brown head, body and coverts. (**g**) **Adult dark morph variant**: Whitish bars and scales below/on underwing-coverts (probably only in *torqua-*

tus). (**h,i**) **Juvenile pale morph**: Typically paler head, neck, underparts and underwing-coverts; less distinct dark bands on underside of flight feathers, 3+ dark tail-bands. May have dark mask and/or streaks below. Eyes yellow. **Other subspecies** *P.p.torquatus* (R S Tenasserim/south W Thailand southwards): Clear crest (6–7 cm). *P.p.orientalis* (VS race): Large, long-winged; little/no crest. VOICE Screaming whistled *wheeew*. HABITAT & BEHAVIOUR Broadleaved forest/open woodland; up to 2,000 m (B mostly below 1,220 m). Level wings when soaring, often slightly arched when gliding. Flight display of shallow upward swoop and almost vertical upstretching of wings, which are briefly winnowed. RANGE Fc R (except C,SE Thailand, Singapore, W,E Tonkin). Un/fc PM and WV W,NE,SE,S Thailand, Pen Malaysia, Singapore. Un/fc PM C Thailand, N Laos, W,E Tonkin.

4 BAT HAWK *Macheiramphus alcinus* 46 cm
(**a,b**) **Adult** *alcinus*: Falcon-like; blackish-brown, whitish throat and upper breast-centre, dark mesial streak. (**c**) **Juvenile**: Browner; paler base to uppertail, more extensive whitish areas below. VOICE High yelping *kwik kwik kwik kwik...* HABITAT & BEHAVIOUR Open areas in/near broadleaved evergreen forest, vicinity of bat caves; up to 1,220 m. Mostly hunts at night, on shallow stiff wingbeats. RANGE Sc/un R south Tenasserim, S Thailand, Pen Malaysia. V Singapore.

5 BLACK KITE *Milvus migrans* 55–60 cm
(**a–c**) **Adult** *govinda*: Dull brownish; shallow-forked tail; outer wing fingered and angled back, pale covert-band, whitish patch at base of primaries on underwing. (**d,e**) **Juvenile**: Head to mantle and belly streaked whitish-buff, rest of upperside and underwing-coverts tipped whitish-buff. (**f,g**) **Adult** *lineatus* (visitor throughout): Larger; warmer, typically whiter face/throat, more whitish on underside of primaries. (**h,i**) **Juvenile**: Broader, whiter streaks/feather-tips than *govinda*, more obvious mask. VOICE High whinnying *pee-errrr* or *ewe-wirrrrr*. HABITAT & BEHAVIOUR Open areas, coastal habitats, large rivers, cities; up to 800 m. Soars/glides with wings slightly arched; twists tail. RANGE Sc/lc R (some movements) Myanmar, C Thailand, Cambodia, E Tonkin. FR (currently?) Cochinchina. Ra/un WV Myanmar, Thailand, Pen Malaysia, Singapore, Cambodia, E Tonkin, N,S Annam, Cochinchina. FWV (currently?) Laos, C Annam. Sc/un PM N,C Myanmar, Tenasserim, NW,W,S Thailand, Pen Malaysia, Singapore, N,C Laos, W Tonkin.

6 BRAHMINY KITE *Haliastur indus* 44–52 cm
(**a,b**) **Adult** *indus*: Bright cinnamon-rufous, narrowly streaked whitish hood/breast; black wing-tips. (**c,d**) **Juvenile**: Smaller than Black, warmer; shorter rounded tail, less streaked; shorter, broader wings, plain buffish-white on underside of primaries. **Other subspecies** *H.i.intermedius* (south Tenasserim and south Thailand southwards): Tends to have narrower streaks on hood/breast. VOICE Stressed thin note, then hoarse gasping: *tsss*, *herhehhehhehhehheh...* Drawn-out mewing *kyeeeer* or *kyerrh*. HABITAT & BEHAVIOUR Coastal areas, large lakes, rivers; mostly lowlands. Scavenges around harbours. RANGE Lc (mostly coastal) R (except NW Thailand, W Tonkin, N,C Laos). FR (currently?) C Laos. Rc (status?) N Laos.

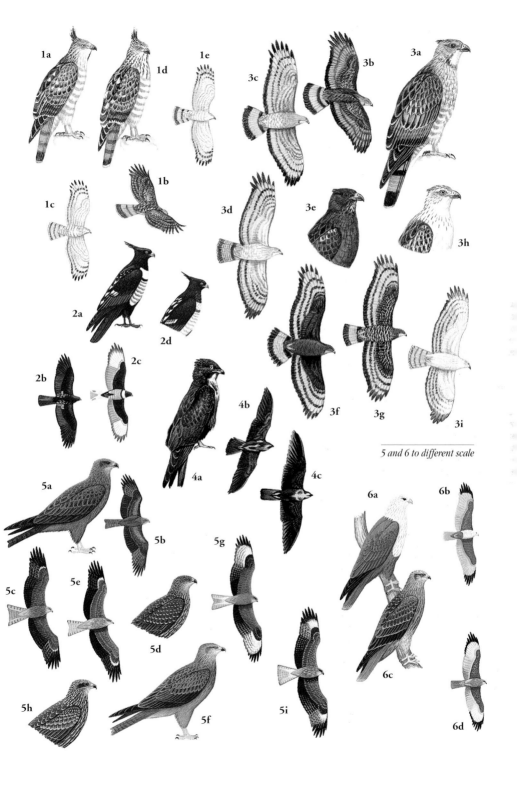

5 and 6 to different scale

PLATE 57 OSPREY, SEA EAGLES & FISH EAGLES

1 OSPREY *Pandion haliaetus* 55–63 cm
(**a**) **Male** *haliaetus*: Fairly large, uniform dark brown above, white head and underparts, dark line through eye, dark breast-streaks (often forming complete band). (**b**) **Female**: Breast-band broader. In flight, adults show long, rather slender wings (typically angled back from carpal and bowed), relatively shortish tail, white underwing-coverts with blackish primary coverts and greater covert tips, evenly barred tail. (**c**) **Juvenile**: Broadly fringed white/buffish above, less defined breast markings. VOICE Hoarse falling whistles: ***piu-piu-piu-piu…***. HABITAT & BEHAVIOUR Lakes, large rivers, sea coasts; up to 1,400 m. Catches fish in feet in plunge-dive onto water; often hovers over water. RANGE Sc/fc **WV** (except W Tonkin). Also **PM** S Thailand, Pen Malaysia, Cambodia. **Rc** in summer N,C,S Myanmar, C,S Thailand, Pen Malaysia, Singapore, Cochinchina.

2 WHITE-BELLIED SEA EAGLE *Haliaeetus leucogaster*
(**a,b**) **Adult**: 70–85 cm. Very large, grey above, white head, neck and underparts, diamond-shaped white tail with blackish base. In flight, bulging secondaries, relatively narrow outer wing, white coverts contrast with rest of underwing. (**c,d**) **Juvenile**: Mostly dark brownish above, dull cream/buffish head, neck and underparts with dingy brownish breast-wash, off-white tail with broad dark brownish subterminal band. In flight, paler band across median coverts and paler area on inner primaries; underwing has warm buffish coverts and large whitish patch on primaries (contrasts with blackish secondaries and primary tips). (**e**) **Third year**: Duller breast than adult, underwing with duller coverts, paler secondaries and black-tipped whitish primaries. VOICE Loud, honking ***kank kank kank..*** or ***blank blank blank blank..***, shorter ***ken-ken-ken..*** and ***ka ka kaa…*** HABITAT & BEHAVIOUR Rocky coasts, islets, sometimes larger inland waterbodies up to 1,400 m. Glides/soars with wings in V. Courtship display includes somersaults, side-slipping and stoops. RANGE Sc/un coastal **R** (except C Thailand, N,C Annam). May travel some distance inland to feed, formerly as far as S Laos.

3 PALLAS'S FISH EAGLE *Haliaeetus leucoryphus* 76–84 cm
(**a,b**) **Adult**: Recalls Grey-headed but larger, warm buffish to whitish hood, darker brown above, dark brown thighs and vent, blackish tail-base. In flight, longer, straighter wings, longer blackish tail with broad white central band. (**c,d**) **Juvenile**: Similar to White-bellied Sea Eagle but more uniformly dark below, thin pale supercilium, blackish mask, blackish-brown tail. In flight, similar underwing pattern but coverts mostly dark brown with whitish band across median coverts to axillaries, outer primaries all dark. (**e**) **Second/third year**: Similar to juvenile but paler and more uniform below. In flight, underwing shows broader whitish band across median coverts, almost all-dark flight feathers. VOICE Loud, guttural notes: ***kha-kha-kha-kha..***; ***gho-gho-gho-gho..***; ***gao-gao-gao-gao..*** etc. Calling may run to higher-pitched excited yelping. HABITAT Large lakes/rivers, marshes; lowlands. RANGE Ra/sc **R** (some movements) S Myanmar. **FR** (currently?) SW,N,C Myanmar, north Tenasserim. **V** NW Thailand, Cambodia, Cochinchina.

4 WHITE-TAILED EAGLE *Haliaeetus albicilla* 70–90 cm
(**a,b**) **Adult** *albicilla*: Very large, big yellow bill, short white diamond-shaped tail. Pale brown/creamy-whitish hood, mostly blackish flight feathers, indistinct darker streaks on head/body, mottled wing-coverts. (**c–e**) **Juvenile**: Mostly darker, warmish brown above with blackish tips, head and underparts blackish-brown with pale streaks on neck/breast, bill dusky-greyish, tail feathers broadly bordered blackish. In flight, very broad, parallel-edged wings, dark underwing with whitish axillaries and thin whitish bands across coverts, whitish spikes on tail feathers. (**f**) **Second/third year**: Broad buffish-white line on underwing-coverts, brown-buff belly/vent. **Third/fourth year**: Darker body than juvenile. In flight, less prominent whitish bands across underwing-coverts, white tail with narrow blackish terminal band. VOICE Loud rapid yelping ***klee-klee-klee-klee-klee…*** HABITAT & BEHAVIOUR Large lakes/rivers, open country; lowlands. Soars with wings held level or only slightly raised; glides on level wings or with outer wing slightly depressed. RANGE Sc/lo **WV** N Myanmar. **V** C Thailand.

5 LESSER FISH EAGLE *Ichthyophaga humilis* 51–68 cm
(**a–c**) **Adult** *humilis*: Smaller than Grey-headed, somewhat paler, dull greyish tail with darker terminal band (can look uniform). In flight, underwing may show whitish bases to outer primaries, undertail dark brownish with darker terminal band. (**d,e**) **Juvenile**: Plainer than Grey-headed, only vague paler streaks, more contrasting white vent, darker tail. **Other subspecies** *I.h.plumbea* (N,E,S Myanmar, W,NW Thailand, Indochina): Averages 20% larger (within range given). VOICE Deep yelping/whining gull-like sounds: ***yow***; ***ow-ow-ow-ow***; ***yaa'aaah***; ***eeyaauuah***; ***yow-eee-aaa…yow-aaa*** etc. HABITAT & BEHAVIOUR Larger rivers in forest; up to 900 m. Loafs in waterside trees. Glides/soars on level wings. RANGE Sc/lfc **R** N,E,S Myanmar, Tenasserim, W,NW,S Thailand, Pen Malaysia, Indochina (except E Tonkin, N Annam).

6 GREY-HEADED FISH EAGLE *I.ichthyaetus* 69–74 cm
(**a–c**) **Adult** *ichthyaetus*: Plain greyish hood, sharply contrasting white thighs and vent, rounded white tail with broad black terminal band. Greyish-brown above, mostly warm brown to brownish-grey breast. In flight, wings rather broad/rounded, white tail-base and vent contrast with all-dark wings. (**d,e**) **Juvenile**: Mostly warm brownish head/neck/breast/upper belly with narrow white supercilium and whitish streaks on crown, head-sides and foreneck/breast; browner-tinged above than adult, dark tail with whitish mottling showing as faint pale bands. In flight, underwing-coverts mostly whitish, flight feathers mostly whitish with darker tips and some faint narrow darker bars towards their tips. Immature plumages poorly documented. (**f**) **Second/third year**: Whitish patches on primaries, white thighs and vent, dark end to tail. VOICE During courtship display utters powerful barking ***kroi-ork*** and repeated loud eerie ***tiu-weeeu***. HABITAT & BEHAVIOUR Lakes, swamps, large rivers; up to 1,525 m. Soars with wings held level or in shallow V. RANGE Ra/sc **R** Myanmar, W(south),NE(south-west),S Thailand, Pen Malaysia, Singapore, Cambodia (still widespread), N,S Laos, Vietnam (except E Tonkin). **FR** (currently?) NW,C Thailand, E Tonkin. **Rc** (escapee?) SE Thailand.

1a
2a
2b
2d
2e
1b
1c
2c
4e
4f
4b
3b
3d
3e
3a
4d
5b
5c
5e
4a
3c
5a
4c
5d
6a
6d
6b
6c
6e
6f

PLATE 58 VULTURES

1 WHITE-RUMPED VULTURE *Gyps bengalensis* 75–85 cm (**a–c**) **Adult**: Blackish plumage with contrasting white neck-ruff, lower back and rump. Has mostly greyish-brown naked head and longish neck and rather short, thick dark bill with pale bluish-grey upper mandible. In flight, very broad wings with well-spaced fingers, short tail, white patch on back and rump, mostly greyish secondaries and inner primaries (above and below) and white underwing-coverts with black leading edge. (**d,e**) **Juvenile**: Browner overall, neck-ruff dark brownish, back and rump dark brownish, head and neck mostly covered with whitish down, bill blackish, lesser and median wing-coverts vaguely streaked paler, underparts narrowly streaked whitish. In flight, rather uniform dark plumage with short narrow whitish bands across underwing-coverts; leading edge of underwing-coverts darker than greater underwing-coverts. **Second/third year**: Like juvenile but primary and greater underwing-coverts mostly whitish (shows some whitish feathers on lower back and beginnings of short buffy neck-ruff). **VOICE** Occasional grunts, croaks, hisses and squeals at nest sites, roosts and when feeding. **HABITAT** Open country, vicinity of abattoirs, cliffs; mostly lowlands but up to 2,600 m. **RANGE** Ra/sc **R** (some movements) N,W Myanmar, southern S Thailand, Cambodia, S Laos, S Annam; formerly W,C Thailand, northern Pen Malaysia, N,C Laos, Cochinchina. **FR** (currently?) Myanmar (except N,W). Ra **WV** W,NW,NE Thailand. **Rc** (escapee?) SE Thailand.

2 SLENDER-BILLED VULTURE *Gyps tenuirostris* 80–95 cm (**a–c**) **Adult**: Told by mostly rather pale sandy-brown body and wing-coverts and contrasting naked blackish head and longish neck. Narrow head profile, relatively long, slender dark bill, relatively small whitish neck-ruff, whitish lower back and rump, dark-centred greater coverts (above and below), dark greyish legs. In flight, relatively uniform pale upper- and underwing-coverts and underbody contrast with dark head and neck and blackish secondaries and primaries. (**d,e**) **Juvenile**: Neck-ruff browner, upperwing-coverts duller and browner and vaguely streaked, underwing-coverts and underparts duller and browner. Gradually becomes paler with age. **VOICE** Occasional hissing and cackling sounds. **HABITAT** Open country; lowlands. **RANGE** Ra/sc **R** (local movements) N Myanmar, S Laos, Cambodia; formerly NW,NE,C,SE Thailand, N,C Laos, Cochinchina. **FR** (currently?) Myanmar (except N), S Annam. Former ra **NBV** S Thailand, Pen Malaysia. **NOTE** Formerly united with Indian Vulture *G. indicus*, as Long-billed Vulture *G. indicus* (see Rasmussen and Parry 2001).

3 HIMALAYAN GRIFFON *Gyps himalayensis* 115–125 cm (**a–c**) **Adult**: Huge and bulky with shortish, thick pale bill, pale head, thickish neck and mostly sandy-buffy body and wing-coverts. Neck-ruff brownish-buff, legs and feet pinkish. In flight, plumage resembles Slender-billed but head pale, upper body and wing-coverts much paler and more contrasting, underwing-coverts (including greater coverts) uniformly whitish with narrow dark leading edge. (**d,e**) **Juvenile**: Similar to White-rumped but considerably larger and more heavily built, with whitish streaks on mantle to uppertail-coverts and scapulars, broader, more prominent whitish streaks on upper- and underwing-coverts and underparts, and paler legs and feet. In flight, plumage very similar to White-rumped but underwing-coverts typically have longer, more clearly separated buffish bands, leading edge of underwing-coverts same colour as greater underwing-coverts (not darker). (**f**) **Subadult**: Develops paler underbody and upperwing-coverts, aiding separation from White-rumped. **VOICE** Occasional grunts and hissing sounds. **HABITAT** Open country; recorded in lowlands. **RANGE** **V** NW,C,W(coastal),S Thailand, Pen Malaysia, Singapore.

4 CINEREOUS VULTURE *Aegypius monachus* 100–110 cm (**a,b**) **Adult**: Huge size, uniform blackish-brown plumage. Bill larger than other vultures, pale crown and nape contrast with black face and foreneck, legs and feet greyish-white. In flight, very broad, relatively straight-edged wings, appears all dark except for narrow pale line at base of flight feathers. (**c**) **Juvenile**: Even blacker, head and neck mostly blackish. **HABITAT** Open country; lowlands. **RANGE** V/ra **WV** N,E,S Myanmar, W,NE,SE,S Thailand, Pen Malaysia, Cambodia, E Tonkin.

5 RED-HEADED VULTURE *Sarcogyps calvus* 81–85 cm (**a,b**) **Male**: Blackish plumage and red head, neck, legs and feet. Yellowish eyes, paler dark-tipped tertials and secondaries, white frontal part of neck-ruff and white lateral body-patches. In flight, these white areas and pale band across bases of flight feathers (less pronounced on upperwing) contrast sharply with black remainder of wings and body. **Female**: Eyes dark brown to dark red, lower scapulars white. (**c,d**) **Juvenile**: Somewhat browner, head and neck pinkish with some whitish down, eyes brown, legs pinkish, vent whitish, flight feathers uniform (above and below). In flight, similar underside pattern to adult, apart from all-dark flight feathers and whitish vent. **VOICE** Occasional squeaks, hisses and grunts. **HABITAT** Open country and wooded areas, dry deciduous forest with rivers; up to 1,525 m (mostly lowlands). **RANGE** Ra **R** W Thailand, S Laos, north-east Cambodia, N,S Annam; formerly NW,C,S Thailand, northern Pen Malaysia, N,C Laos, Cochinchina. **FR** (currently) Myanmar, C Annam. **FO** (status?) Singapore.

PLATE 59 MISCELLANEOUS RAPTORS

1 BLACK-SHOULDERED KITE *Elanus caeruleus* 31–35 cm (**a,b**) **Adult** *vociferus*: Quite small, pale grey above with black lesser/median coverts. Whitish below, black eyebrow, shortish white tail with grey central feathers. In flight, wings also show black underside of primaries. (**c**) **Juvenile**: Crown streaked darker, browner-tinged above with whitish-buff tips, tail darker-tipped, ear-coverts and breast initially washed warm buff, breast and flanks sparsely streaked brown. **VOICE** Soft piping *pii-uu* or *pieu* (mainly during display). Sharp *gree-ah* or harsh, screaming *ku-eekk* in alarm. **HABITAT & BEHAVIOUR** Open country, semi-desert, cultivation; up to 1,500 m. Glides/soars with wings raised; often hovers. Male display includes mock dive-attacks at female. **RANGE** Co **R** (except W Tonkin).

2 EGYPTIAN VULTURE *Neophron percnopterus* 60–70 cm (**a–c**) **Adult** *ginginianus*: Rather slim, mostly dirty-whitish, shaggy nape, naked yellowish face, slender yellowish bill, pointed, diamond-shaped whitish tail. In flight, mostly whitish above with black-tipped greater coverts and secondaries, mostly black primaries/primary coverts; underwing black with contrasting whitish coverts. (**d,e**) **Juvenile**: Dark brownish with paler vent, mostly dull greyish tail with darker base; facial skin grey, bill pale (tip often dark). In flight, mostly blackish-brown upperwing with narrow whitish bands across coverts, fairly uniform dark underwing. (**f**) **Second/third year**: Paler body/underwing-coverts, shadowing adult pattern. **Third/fourth year**: Like adult but dark brownish collar, some darker mottling below, duller tail. In flight, dark mottling on underwing-coverts. **VOICE** Mewing, hissing and low grunting sounds in alarm. **HABITAT & BEHAVIOUR** Open country; recorded at c.1,000 m. Soars with wings held level or slightly bowed. **RANGE** V E Myanmar.

3 SHORT-TOED SNAKE EAGLE *Circaetus gallicus* 62–67 cm (**a,b**) **Adult pale individual**: Medium-sized, quite big head (looks top-heavy), yellow/orange-yellow eyes, longish naked legs, relatively long wings (reaching tail-tip at rest). Whitish below with indistinct markings. In flight, long broad wings (distinctly pinched-in at base), narrow dark barring and trailing edge on pale, rather featureless underwing, three bands across undertail (terminal band broadest). (**c**) **Adult dark individual**: Distinctive dark hood, extensive dark bars below, darker bands on underwing. **Juvenile**: Uniform narrow pale tips to wing feathers, paler and more contrasting median and lesser coverts, pale-tipped greater coverts, poorly marked underwing, with no trailing edge. **VOICE** Musical whistled *weeo* or *weeooo*, sometimes followed by gull-like *woh-woh-woh* or *quo-quo-quo*. **HABITAT & BEHAVIOUR** Open and coastal areas; lowlands. Flies with rather slow, heavy wingbeats; soars with wings flat or slightly raised (primaries gently drooping); frequently hovers. **RANGE** V SW,S Myanmar, north Tenasserim, W,NE,C,S Thailand, Pen Malaysia, Singapore, Cambodia, N,S Laos, C Annam.

4 CRESTED SERPENT EAGLE *Spilornis cheela* 56–74 cm (**a,b**) **Adult** *burmanicus*: Large head, mostly dark brownish, yellow cere/face-skin/eyes, full, white-marked blackish nuchal crest; small white spots on median/lesser coverts, paler, warm-tinged head-sides/neck/underparts, with black-edged whitish

speckles turning to short bars on lower breast to vent. Very broad-winged in flight; broad white band, then broad black trailing edge across underwing, black tail with broad white central band. (**c,d**) **Juvenile**: Head scaled black and whitish with blackish ear-coverts; whitish tips/fringes above, whitish below, usually with faint buffish wash and dark streaks on throat-centre, breast and belly; whitish tail with three blackish bands. In flight, mostly whitish underwing, with buff-washed and dark-streaked wing-coverts, many fine dark bars across underside of flight feathers, indistinct broad darker trailing edge. (**e**) **Adult** *malayensis* (south Tenasserim and S Thailand southwards): Distinctly smaller, darker head-sides and underparts, more pronounced markings below. **Other subspecies** *S.c.ricketti* (E Tonkin): Averages larger; somewhat paler above, thin whitish bars on breast, fewer spots/bars on rest of underparts. **VOICE** Loud plaintive, high 2–4 note *hwiii-hwi*; *h'wi-hwi*; *hwi-hwi-hwi*; *h'wee hew-hew*; *hii-hwi-hwi* etc., sometimes preceded by spaced *hu-hu-hu-hu...* 'Song' is sustained crescendo: *ha-ha-ha-ha hu-hu-hu-hu-h'weeooleeoo*. **HABITAT & BEHAVIOUR** Broadleaved forests; up to 2,470 m. Soars with wings in shallow V. Displaying pairs soar with head and tail raised, dive at one another and make short flights with wings winnowed shallowly below horizontal. **RANGE** Fc **R** (minor movements) throughout; ra (still breeds?) Singapore.

5 WESTERN MARSH HARRIER *Circus aeruginosus* 48–56 cm (**a–c**) **Male** *aeruginosus*: Browner-marked head/neck/breast than Eastern, pale ear-coverts, brown/more uniform upperparts /coverts, rufous-chestnut lower underparts/thighs. In flight, dark leading edge to inner wing. (**d–f**) **Female**: Like juvenile Eastern but dark eye-line/neck-side, no neck-streaks. In flight, smaller pale flash on underside of primaries; normally broad creamy-buff leading edge to inner wing, creamy-buff breast-band. (**g,h**) **Juvenile**: Like female but no creamy-buff on wing-coverts and breast. Male gradually acquires grey parts of plumage. **VOICE** Weak *kyik* or cackling *chek-ek-ek-ek...* **HABITAT** Marshes, rice paddies, open areas; mostly lowlands. **RANGE** Un/fc **WV** Myanmar, C Thailand (ra). **V** S Thailand, Pen Malaysia.

6 EASTERN MARSH HARRIER *Circus spilonotus* 48–56 cm (**a–c**) **Male** *spilonotus*: From Pied by black-streaked neck and breast, no large white patches on wing-coverts, pale scaling above. (**d–f**) **Female**: Recalls Pied but dull rufous belly/thighs. In flight, also lacks pale leading edge to inner wing, tail with thinner bars and plain central feathers, largely dull chestnut-brown underwing-coverts, less boldly marked underside of secondaries. (**g,h**) **Juvenile**: (Dark bird illustrated): Rather uniform dark brown (faint paler area across breast) with pale hood (with/without dark crown and band across lower throat); head-sides rather uniform, often variable darker neck-streaking, sometimes prominent creamy-buff mantle-streaks. In flight, blackish-tipped creamy-greyish underside of primaries, contrasting dark remainder of underwing. Male gradually acquires grey plumage parts. **VOICE** May utter kite-like mewing *keeau* particularly at roost sites. **HABITAT** Marshes, rice paddies, open areas. **RANGE** Un/fc **WV** (except SW Myanmar, W Tonkin, S Annam). Also **PM** C Myanmar, S Thailand, Cambodia, N Laos.

126

1, 2–4 and 5–6 to different scales

PLATE 60 HARRIERS

1 HEN HARRIER *Circus cyaneus* 44–52 cm
(**a–c**) **Male** *cyaneus*: Grey plumage with contrasting white lower breast to undertail-coverts. When perched, wing-tips fall well short of tail-tip. In flight, all-black, 'five-fingered' outer primaries (above and below), darker trailing edge to rest of wing (more prominent below), obvious white band across uppertail-coverts. (**d–f**) **Female**: Rather nondescript brownish, with dark-barred wings and tail and dark-streaked pale neck and underparts. Difficult to separate from Pallid and Montagu's. Best told by heavy arrowhead or drop-shaped markings on thighs and undertail-coverts (wide arrowhead shapes on undertail-coverts are diagnostic), and wing-tips at rest (see male). In flight, rounder-winged with clearly defined broad white uppertail-covert band; two well-marked dark bands on upperside of secondaries (terminal one broadest, most obvious); underwing has broadest dark band along trailing edge, other two differing in width and variably spaced, but with pale bands between them reaching body; dark inner primary tips, dark, unpatterned axillaries. (**g,h**) **Juvenile**: Similar to female but generally rustier, with darker underside of secondaries. From Pallid and Montagu's by boldly streaked, duller underparts, less solid and distinct pale band across upperwing-coverts; always has narrow whitish collar. VOICE Rapid, quacking chatter, *quek-ek-ek-ek*, *quik-ik-ak-ik-uk-ik* etc. HABITAT & BEHAVIOUR Open areas; up to 1,500 m. Glides with wings in shallow V. RANGE Ra/un WV N Myanmar, NW Thailand, N Laos. V NE,S Thailand, Pen Malaysia, Singapore, Cambodia, C Laos, E Tonkin, Cochinchina.

2 PALLID HARRIER *Circus macrourus* 40–48 cm
(**a–c**) **Male**: Smaller/slimmer/paler than Hen, less contrast between breast and belly. In flight, wings narrower/more pointed, thinner black wedge on primaries, less white on uppertail-coverts, no darker trailing edge to wing (subadult male has dusky trailing edge to secondaries). (**d–f**) **Female**: Very like Hen and Montagu's. In flight, upperwing usually lacks pale bar through dark secondaries, white uppertail-covert band usually narrower than Hen; on underwing, primaries paler than secondaries with dark bars sometimes absent from bases (may show distinctive pale crescent at base of primaries), inner primary tips relatively pale, broadest/darkest band is along trailing edge of secondaries, pale bands get narrower/darker towards body, underwing-coverts/axillaries lack bold bars. (**g,h**) **Juvenile**: Typically less white above/below eye than Montagu's, more dark brown on head-sides (extending under base of lower mandible), wider, paler, unstreaked collar bordered behind/below by uniform dark brown. No faint narrow streaks on breast-sides/flanks (shown by most juvenile Montagu's). In flight, underwing has outer primaries either evenly barred or pale with narrow dark tips, inner primaries have paler tips (may show pale crescent on primary bases like female); paler buff coverts and axillaries, with no obvious dark bars. First-spring males are often almost unmoulted, though more faded on head and breast (juvenile head pattern still clear); during moult, thin rusty streaks (similar to Montagu's) appear on body. VOICE High plaintive single or repeated *siehrrr*. HABITAT Open country, cultivation; up to 1,320 m (mostly lowlands). RANGE Sc/un WV SW,N,C,S,E Myanmar. V S Thailand, Pen Malaysia, E Tonkin (old sight record).

3 PIED HARRIER *Circus melanoleucos* 43–46 cm
(**a–c**) **Male**: Black head to back, upper breast and median coverts, large whitish patch on lesser coverts. In flight, black outer primaries (above and below), contrasting black band across upperwing-coverts. (**d–f**) **Female**: Told by whitish leading edge to upperwing, grey outer edge to wing-coverts and secondaries, almost plain whitish thighs/vent. In flight, from above, whitish uppertail-covert band, uniformly barred tail, grey primary coverts and flight feathers with dark bars; broadly dark-tipped primaries, darker trailing edge to wing. Underwing pattern most like Montagu's but overall paler with narrower dark bands across secondaries. (**g,h**) **Juvenile**: Similar to Pallid and Montagu's but more uniform dark rufous-brown wing-coverts, dark rufous-brown below. More rufous-brown than Eastern Marsh. In flight, narrow whitish uppertail-covert band, from below, darkish rufous-brown body/coverts, indistinct paler bands across blackish secondaries (tapering towards body), pale greyish primaries with dark bars restricted to tips and inner feathers (leading edge also darker). VOICE Displaying male gives *keee-veeee* calls and female a rapid *kee-kee-kee* or chattering *chak-chak-chak-chak...* Rapid *wek-wek-wek*. HABITAT Marshes, grassland, cultivation; to 800 m. RANGE Un/fc WV (except W Tonkin, N Annam). Also PM S Thailand, W,E Tonkin, Cambodia. Has bred N Myanmar. V Singapore.

4 MONTAGU'S HARRIER *Circus pygargus* 43–47 cm
(**a–c**) **Male**: Similar to Hen and Pallid at rest but belly streaked rufous-chestnut, closed wing-tips extend to tail-tip (all plumages). In flight, blackish bar across upperside of secondaries, two blackish bars on underside of secondaries, dark bands across underwing-coverts and axillaries. (**d–f**) **Female**: Very similar to Hen and Pallid but somewhat smaller and slimmer than former, underparts quite narrowly and evenly marked, with narrow dark streaks on thighs and undertail-coverts. In flight, narrower-winged than Hen, narrower white uppertail-covert band, upperside of flight feathers usually clearly barred; underwing has inner primaries darker-tipped than Pallid, broadest dark band on secondaries at trailing edge but central band darkest, pale intervening bands reaching body; boldly barred axillaries, chequered barring on underwing-coverts. (**g**) **Adult dark morph**: Rare (may not occur in region). Sooty to blackish overall with paler tail and dark-tipped silvery underside of primaries with darker bars on outer feathers. (**h,i**) **Juvenile**: Unstreaked buffish-rufous below. Very like Pallid but typically has narrow dark streaks on breast-sides/flanks, more white above and below eye, less dark brown on head-sides, no clear pale collar, sometimes with darker neck-sides but usually mottled/streaked and not uniform (may have diffuse paler area behind ear-coverts but never forms collar). In flight, underwing has blackish primary tips (broader on outer feathers), usually more rufescent coverts and axillaries with prominent blackish barring. First-spring male usually has head and body similar to adult and some strong rusty streaks on belly. VOICE Occasional *chock-chock*, *chock-ok-ok*; other calls similar to Hen. HABITAT Open areas, cultivation; lowlands. RANGE V Myanmar? Doubtful old records from S,E[south] Myanmar, Tenasserim; no specimens.

PLATE 61 *ACCIPITERS*

1 CRESTED GOSHAWK *Accipiter trivirgatus* 40–46 cm (**a,b**) **Male** *indicus*: Relatively large, short crest, slaty crown and head-sides, brownish-grey above, dark mesial streak, streaked breast, barred belly; uppertail greyish with equal-width bands. In flight, wings broad and rounded. **Female**: Larger; browner-tinged crown and head-sides, browner breast-streaks and bars on belly. (**c**) **Juvenile**: Like adult but browner head/upperparts (latter fringed buff), neck/underparts mostly streaked brown. VOICE Shrill, screaming *he he hehehehe* and squeaky *chiup* in alarm. HABITAT & BEHAVIOUR Broadleaved and mixed broadleaved/coniferous forest; up to 1,950 m (below 245 m in Pen Malaysia). Display-flights with shallow, winnowing, bowed wings and fluffed-out undertail-coverts. RANGE Fc/co R (except SW Myanmar, C Thailand); ra Singapore.

2 SHIKRA *Accipiter badius* 30–36 cm (**a–c**) **Male** *poliopsis*: Pale grey head-sides, upperparts and tail, dark primary tips, white throat with faint grey mesial streak, dense narrow orange-rufous bars on breast and belly; underwing whitish with some dark bars across outer primaries, undertail with four dark bands in centre. Eyes reddish. (**d,e**) **Female**: Larger; yellow eyes, washed brownish above; more dark tail-bands. (**f,g**) **Juvenile**: Crown and upperparts brown with paler fringing, darker mesial streak, tear-drop breast-streaks (bars on flanks and spots on thighs), five dark bands on brown uppertail; even dark bars across whitish underside of flight feathers. VOICE Loud harsh thin *titu-titu* and long, drawn-out screaming *iheeya iheeya...* HABITAT Open forest and other open areas, cultivation; up to 1,600 m. RANGE Co R, subject to some movements (except S Thailand, Pen Malaysia, Singapore, W Tonkin). Ra/sc WV S Thailand, northern Pen Malaysia. V southern Pen Malaysia, Singapore.

3 CHINESE SPARROWHAWK *Accipiter soloensis* 29–35 cm (**a**) **Male**: Darker grey than Shikra, breast indistinctly barred pale pinkish-rufous; whitish underwing with black-tipped primaries, grey trailing edge and unmarked, pinkish-buff-washed coverts. Eyes reddish. (**b**) **Female**: More rufous on underparts, underwing-coverts more rufous-tinged, eyes yellow. (**c,d**) **Juvenile**: Slate-greyish crown and head-sides, dark brown upperparts, chestnut tinge to neck-streaks, upperpart- fringing and underpart markings, four dark bands on uppertail, barred thighs; underwing-coverts unbarred, two dark bands across inner secondaries (apart from trailing edge); undertail has three dark bands, five narrow ones on outertail. VOICE Rapid shrill, nasal, accelerating *kee pe-pe-pe-petu-petu* (descending in pitch) on breeding grounds. HABITAT & BEHAVIOUR Open country, wooded areas; up to 2,135 m. Often seen in migrating flocks. RANGE Sc/un PM Tenasserim, Thailand, Pen Malaysia, Singapore, Indochina (except N,C Annam).

4 JAPANESE SPARROWHAWK *Accipiter gularis* 25–31 cm (**a–c**) **Male** *gularis*: Like Besra but somewhat paler above, underparts diffusely barred pale pinkish-rufous, uppertail with narrow dark bands (usually four visible); wings appear more pointed. (**d,e**) **Female**: Larger and browner than male, more prominent mesial streak, more obviously barred below; darker and plainer above than female Besra, no breast-streaks and narrower tail-bands. (**f**) **Juvenile (female)**: Very like Besra but mesial streak normally much thinner, breast-streaks less pronounced (never black), often less heavily marked belly and flanks and narrower dark bands on uppertail (as adult); show slaty-grey hindcrown contrasting somewhat with mantle. In flight, from above, narrower, less distinct dark bands across flight feathers and tail than Besra; underside very similar. Eyes yellow. HABITAT & BEHAVIOUR Open country, forest edge, lightly wooded areas; up to 2,135 m. Often seen in migrating flocks. RANGE Un/fc PM (except SW,W,N,C,E Myanmar, N Annam). WV S(south) Thailand, Pen Malaysia, Singapore.

5 BESRA *Accipiter virgatus* 26–32 cm (**a,b**) **Male** *affinis*: Very dark slate-greyish upperside, prominent dark mesial streak, blackish and rufous-chestnut breast-streaks, broad rufous-chestnut bars on underparts, broad dark tail-bands; wings short and rounded. Eyes reddish. (**c,d**) **Female**: Larger; yellow eyes, browner-tinged upperside with contrasting blackish crown and nape. (**e**) **Juvenile (female)**: Difficult to separate from Shikra and Japanese Sparrowhawk but more prominent dark mesial streak, blacker breast-streaks, even-width dark and pale tail-bands. In flight, blunter wings. Also differs from Japanese by lack of any contrast between hindcrown and mantle and, in flight, by broader, more pronounced dark bands across underside of flight feathers and tail. VOICE Loud squealing *ki-weeer* and rapid *tchew-tchew-tchew...* HABITAT & BEHAVIOUR Broadleaved evergreen and mixed broadleaved forest; up to 2,000 m, commoner at higher levels. Generally hunts birds inside wooded habitats and less likely to be seen soaring overhead than other accipiters. RANGE Sc/un R (except Tenasserim, S Thailand, Pen Malaysia, Singapore, E Tonkin, N Annam, Cochinchina). V Singapore.

6 EURASIAN SPARROWHAWK *Accipiter nisus* 28–38 cm (**a–c**) **Male** *nisosimilis*: Slaty-grey upperside, orange-rufous wash on cheeks, faint orange-rufous bars on underparts, faint darker bands on uppertail, no mesial streak. Relatively long-winged and long-tailed. (**d,e**) **Female**: Larger, with more prominent whitish supercilium, somewhat browner-tinged upperside, more obvious dark uppertail-bands, darker, more pronounced markings below. Size, prominent supercilium, unstreaked breast and tail pattern rule out Japanese and Besra. (**f**) **Juvenile**: Best separated from other smaller accipiters by size, heavy rufous-chestnut to blackish barring on underparts, and tail pattern (like female). Some can show more streak-like markings or arrowhead shapes on breast. **Other subspecies** *A.n.melaschistos* (Myanmar except SW): Darker grey upperside with almost blackish crown and mantle, stronger rufescent barring on underparts. VOICE Loud shrill *kyi-kyi-kyi..* when alarmed. HABITAT Forested and open areas; up to 3,000 m (mainly in mountains), breeding above 1,400 m in Himalayas. RANGE Sc/un WV Myanmar (except SW), NW Thailand, N,C Laos, W,E Tonkin, N,C Annam. Un PM W Tonkin. V NE,C Thailand. Likely to breed N Myanmar.

PLATE 62 NORTHERN GOSHAWK & BUZZARDS

1 NORTHERN GOSHAWK *Accipiter gentilis* 48–62 cm
(**a**) **Male** *schvedowi*: Most like female Eurasian Sparrowhawk. Usually larger, has bolder white supercilium, crown and head-sides darker than mantle, lower head-sides/throat quite uniform whitish, rest of underparts barred brownish-grey. In flight, proportionately longer-winged, shorter-tailed and heavier-chested, underwing has much bolder dark barring on flight feathers, much less contrasting darker bands across flight feathers. (**b,c**) **Female**: Considerably larger than male, browner-tinged above, eyes orange-yellow (*vs* orange-red), banding on underwing more obvious. (**d,e**) **Juvenile**: Darker and browner above than adult with buffish/whitish fringes, less distinct buffish supercilium, buff neck/underparts with bold dark brown streaks, distinct irregular broad dark bands on uppertail. In flight, more bulging secondaries, heavier markings on underwing, with dark streaks/spots on pale buffish coverts. Eyes yellow. **VOICE** Loud, guttural *kyee-kyee-kyee..* in alarm. **HABITAT** Wooded habitats, sometimes more open areas; up to 2,800 m. **RANGE** Ra **WV** W,N Myanmar, NW Thailand, W,E Tonkin. Sc **PM** W Tonkin, **V** Cambodia, S Annam, Cochinchina.

2 WHITE-EYED BUZZARD *Butastur teesa* 41–43 cm
(**a–c**) **Adult**: Recalls Grey-faced but eyes whitish, head browner, paler lores, broad pale area across coverts, rufescent rump to uppertail, latter with single dark subterminal band (sometimes many indistinct narrower bars). In flight, pale covert-band, darker axillaries and lesser underwing-coverts, rump to uppertail colour, narrower bands across undertail. (**d,e**) **Juvenile**: Creamy to deep rich buff head/neck/underparts, narrow dark streaks on crown/hindneck/breast/belly; very faint mesial streak, prominent pale wing-covert band, rufous-chestnut-tinged uppertail (greyer than adult), rich buff base-colour to underwing-coverts. **VOICE** Clear mewing *pit-weeer pit-weeer pit-weere...* **HABITAT & BEHAVIOUR** Semi-desert, dry open country; lowlands. Loafs in small trees and bushes. **RANGE** Un/co **R** SW,W,C,S Myanmar, north Tenasserim.

3 RUFOUS-WINGED BUZZARD *Butastur liventer* 38–43 cm
(**a–c**) **Adult**: Size/shape recalls Grey-faced but mostly greyish head/underparts contrast with mostly rufous-brown/-chestnut upperside. Indistinct dark streaks on crown/neck/breast, no dark mesial stripe, strongly rufescent uppertail. In flight, mostly uniform rufous-chestnut flight feathers and rump to tail, relatively plain whitish underwing-coverts, indistinctly patterned undertail. (**d**) **Juvenile**: Browner head, narrow white supercilium; duller and brower upperparts/lesser coverts/breast/belly. **VOICE** Shrill *pit-piu* (*pit* higher). **HABITAT** Dry deciduous forest, secondary growth; up to 1,525 m (800 m in Thailand). **RANGE** Sc/un **R** Myanmar (except southern Tenasserim), W,NW,NE Thailand, Cambodia, C,S Laos, S Annam, Cochinchina.

4 GREY-FACED BUZZARD *Butastur indicus* 41–49 cm
(**a–c**) **Male**: Recalls *Accipiter* and *Buteo*. Mostly rather plain greyish-brown above/on breast, white throat, blackish submoustachial/mesial stripes, greyish-brown and white belly-bars, three dark tail-bands; underwing rather pale with darker trailing edge (primary tips blackish). **Female**: Typically more

pronounced supercilium, browner ear-coverts, whiter breast-barring. **Adult dark morph**: Dark brown head, body and wing-coverts (above and below), wings/tail otherwise typical. (**d**) **Juvenile**: Brown crown/neck with thin whitish streaks, broad white supercilium framing blackish-brown 'mask', darker upperparts/coverts, dull whitish below with bold dark streaks. **Juvenile dark morph**: Rare. Mainly differs by dark brown eyes. **VOICE** Clear high *tik HWEEER* or *tik H'WEEER*. **HABITAT & BEHAVIOUR** Open coniferous, broadleaved and mixed forest, other open areas; up to 1,800 m. Flight rather direct interspersed glides. Soars on level wings. **RANGE** Un/co **WV** Tenasserim, W,NW,NE,S Thailand, Pen Malaysia, Singapore (ra), Cambodia, S Laos, C,S Annam, Cochinchina. Fc/co **PM** Tenasserim, Thailand, Pen Malaysia, Singapore, Cambodia, N,C Laos, W,E Tonkin, N Annam. **Rc** (status?) W Myanmar.

5 COMMON BUZZARD *Buteo buteo* 51–57 cm
(**a–c**) **Adult pale morph** *japonicus*: Robust, large-headed, mottled brown above, dark-streaked whitish below with dark brown belly-patch, greyish-brown uppertail with many narrow darker bars and broader subterminal band; broad rounded wings, shortish rounded tail, paler area across upperside of primaries, underwing pale with dark outer primary tips and carpal patches. (**d–f**) **Adult dark morph**: Rather uniform blackish-brown head/body/coverts (above and below), broader terminal tail-band; rest of underwing similar to pale morph. **Juvenile pale morph**: Less heavily streaked below than adult, narrower, paler and more diffuse trailing edge to underwing, evenly barred tail, without broader subterminal band. **VOICE** Clear mewing *peeeoooo* or *peee-oo* (*peee* stressed). **HABITAT & BEHAVIOUR** Open country, open forest, cultivation; up to 3,660 m. Soars with wings in shallow V and tail spread; glides on level wings; often hovers. **RANGE** Sc/un **WV** (except SE Thailand, S Laos, W Tonkin). Sc/un **PM** S Thailand, Pen Malaysia, Singapore, W Tonkin.

6 LONG-LEGGED BUZZARD *Buteo rufinus* 57–65 cm
(**a–c**) **Adult pale morph** *rufinus*: Larger and larger-headed than Common, rufous on upperparts, underparts and tail. Typically has pale cream head, neck and breast, with indistinct darker streaks on crown, hindneck and breast, slight darker eye-stripe/malar line, rufous thighs/belly-patch, rather plain pale rufous/cinnamon tail. Rufous on underparts usually heavier on belly than breast. In flight, longer, more eagle-like wings, underwing-coverts often tinged rufescent. (**d**) **Adult dark morph**: Best told from Common by size and shape, typically has broader dark tail-bars, heavier dark bands on undersides of secondaries. (**e**) **Adult rufous morph**: Deep rufous to rufous-chestnut head, body and wing-coverts (above and below); underwing (including carpal patches) and tail similar to pale morph. (**f,g**) **Juvenile pale morph**: Browner above, less rufous and more brownish below, tail has faint narrow dark bars towards tip. In flight, narrower, paler and more diffuse trailing edge to underwing. **VOICE** Clear, slightly descending *eeeeaaab*, mellower and lower-pitched than Common. **HABITAT & BEHAVIOUR** Open country; recorded at 450 m. Soars with wings in deeper V than Common, recalling Western Marsh Harrier; glides with inner wing slightly raised; often hovers. **RANGE** **V** N Myanmar.

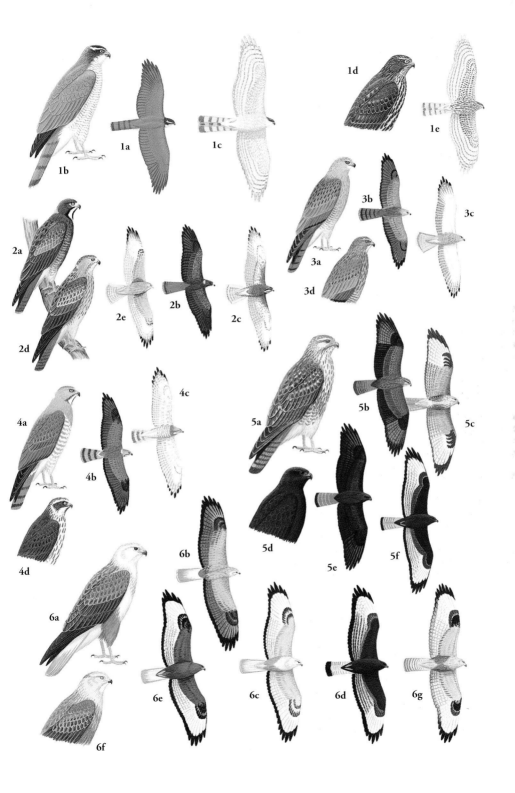

PLATE 63 *AQUILA* EAGLES

1 INDIAN SPOTTED EAGLE *Aquila hastata* 59–65.5 cm
(**a–c**) **Adult** Like Greater Spotted but somewhat smaller; has proportionately smaller bill with larger gape (shows pronounced wide flange or 'thick lips'; extending further under eye than illustrated). Head, upperparts and upperwing-coverts should be darker than illustrated; very dark brown with black shaft-streaks. In flight, has more prominent whitish flash at base of primaries on upperwing than Greater Spotted, double whitish crescent in vicinity of primary underwing-coverts. Underwing-coverts are uniform apart from paler brown lesser coverts (uniform with darker greater coverts in extralimital Lesser Spotted *A.pomarina*). (**d–f**) **Juvenile**: Head, body and wing-coverts paler than Greater; less pronounced white spotting on tertials, median and lesser upperwing-coverts, buffish-brown below with darker streaks (brown with very pale brown breast-streaks in *pomarina*). Nape should lack the warm patch illustrated; uppertail-coverts are very pale brown with white barring (white in *pomarina*). In flight, differs from Greater Spotted in same way as adult. (**g**) **Subadult**: Mixture of adult and juvenile characters. **VOICE** Repeated high-pitched yapping *kyek* in breeding season. **HABITAT & BEHAVIOUR** Wooded areas and open country; lowlands. Glides and soars on level to slightly raised wings with primaries angled downwards. **RANGE** Rc (**FR**?) SW,S Myanmar. **NOTE** Best treated as distinct from *A.pomarina* (see Parry *et al.* 2002).

2 GREATER SPOTTED EAGLE *Aquila clanga* 65–72 cm
(**a–c**) **Adult**: Differs from similar large dark eagles by relatively shorter wings, smallish bill, shortish tail. In flight, wings appear relatively short and broad, upperside rather uniformly dark with paler area on bases of primaries and narrow pale band across uppertail-coverts; underwing rather uniformly dark with distinctive whitish patch or crescent at base of outer primaries. (**d–f**) **Juvenile**: Blackish, with pronounced whitish spots on upperwing-coverts, whitish tips to scapulars, tertials, most other wing feathers and tail; broad pale buffish streaks on belly and thighs (sometimes also or only on breast or lacking altogether). In flight, whitish bands across upperwing-coverts and whitish band across uppertail-coverts contrast sharply with dark upperparts, rest of wing-coverts and secondaries; underwing has darker coverts than flight feathers, paler bases of primaries than adult, faint dark bars across secondaries and inner primaries. (**g**) **Subadult**: Mixture of adult and juvenile characters. **Adult pale ('*fulvescens*') morph**: Rare. Mostly buffish to rufous body, median and lesser upper- and underwing-coverts. (**h,i**) **Juvenile pale morph**: Mostly buffy head, body and wing-coverts, whitish tips to upperwing-coverts, secondaries, inner primaries and tail. (**j**) **Juvenile pale morph**: Younger individual with rufescent-brown body and wing-coverts. **VOICE** Series of short quick high-pitched notes: *hi-hi-hi-hi-hi..*; *hihi hihi-hi..* etc. **HABITAT & BEHAVIOUR** Marshes, lakes, rivers, open country; up to 2,135 m (winters below 800

m). Soars on flattish wings, glides with primaries distinctly angled downwards. **RANGE** Ra/sc **WV** N,S Myanmar, Tenasserim, Thailand, Pen Malaysia, Cambodia(has remained until July), N,C Laos, Cochinchina. **FWV** (currently?) SW,C,E Myanmar. Sc **PM** S Thailand, Cambodia, W,E Tonkin. **V** Singapore.

3 TAWNY EAGLE *Aquila rapax* 64–71 cm
(**a–c**) **Adult pale morph** *vindhiana*: Difficult to separate from pale morph Greater Spotted but has somewhat larger bill, longer neck, fuller and longer 'trousers', yellowish eyes. In flight, underwing has paler inner primaries and bases of outer primaries, without well-defined whitish patch or crescent. **Adult dark morph**: Rare. Difficult to separate from Steppe at rest but somewhat more powerfully built, lacks rufescent nape-patch, has dark throat. At very close range, gape typically ends below centre of eye (extends behind eye in Steppe). In flight, underwing has greyish inner primaries and bases of outer primaries contrasting with uniformly dark secondaries. Best separated from spotted eagles by size, structure, underwing pattern, yellowish eyes. (**f,g**) **Juvenile pale morph**: Similar to adult but with creamy tips to upperwing-coverts, secondaries, inner primaries and tail (juvenile dark morph differs similarly). When fresh, strongly rufescent head, body and wing-coverts (pale morph). **VOICE** Repeated barking *kowk*. **HABITAT & BEHAVIOUR** Open country; recorded in lowlands. Often adopts more upright posture than Steppe at rest. Glides with inner wing slightly raised and primaries slightly angled downwards. **RANGE** V N,C,S Myanmar, NW Thailand, W,E Tonkin.

4 STEPPE EAGLE *Aquila nipalensis* 76–80 cm
(**a–c**) **Adult** *nipalensis*: Larger, and larger-billed, than other large, uniformly dark eagles. Best separated from spotted eagles and dark morph Tawny by size, structure, full 'trousers', rufous-buff nape-patch, somewhat paler throat, distinct dark bars on secondaries. At very close range, gape typically ends behind eye. In flight, wings and tail distinctly longer than spotted eagles. Underwing with mostly blackish primary coverts, and contrasting darker trailing edge and dark bars across flight feathers. (**d–f**) **Juvenile**: Head, body and wing-coverts paler and more grey-brown than adult, with whitish tips to greater and primary upperwing-coverts, secondaries and tail feathers, broader, whiter band across uppertail-coverts. In flight, separated from other large dark eagles by broad whitish trailing edge to underwing-coverts (wide band across underwing). (**g**) **Subadult**: Lacks obvious whitish band on underwing but already developing distinctive adult-like underwing. **VOICE** Slightly hoarse *akh akh akh akh...* Repeated, deep barking *ow* also reported. **HABITAT & BEHAVIOUR** Open country; lowlands (but up to 2,100 m on migration). Soars on flatter wings than spotted eagles. **RANGE** Ra **WV/V** C,S,E Myanmar, Tenasserim, C,W(coastal),S Thailand, Pen Malaysia, Singapore, E Tonkin. Sc/un **PM** N Myanmar.

1a

1d

1b

1e

1c

1f

1g

2a

2c

2b

2h

2j

2f

2e

2i

2g

2d

3a

3d

3c

3g

3b

3e

3f

4b

4e

4c

4a

4d

4f

4g

PLATE 64 BLACK, IMPERIAL & *HIERAAETUS* EAGLES

1 BLACK EAGLE *Ictinaetus malayensis* 69–81 cm
(a,b) **Adult** *malayensis*: Blackish overall with yellow cere and feet. Rather long tail with indistinct narrow pale bands; closed wing-tips fall close to or beyond tail-tip. In flight, long broad wings with pinched-in bases and well-spread 'fingers', longish tail. (c,d) **Juvenile**: Head, neck and underparts pale buffish with heavy blackish streaks; some pale tips on upper-parts and wing-coverts. In flight, also shows pale buffish underwing-coverts with blackish streaks and more obviously pale-barred underside of flight feathers and tail. **Other sub-species** *I.m.perniger* (Myanmar). **VOICE** Shrill yelping *wee-a-kwek* etc., particularly during display flight. **HABITAT & BEHAVIOUR** Broadleaved evergreen forest and nearby open areas; up to 3,170 m. Soars with wings in V, often spiralling gently downwards into forest clearings. Display flight involves steep dives through U-loop, up to near-vertical stall. **RANGE** Un/fc **R** (except SW,C,S,E Myanmar, C Thailand, Singapore).

2 IMPERIAL EAGLE *Aquila heliaca* 72–83 cm
(a–c) **Adult**: Large, with large head and bill, blackish-brown, with golden-buff supercilium, ear-coverts, nape and hindneck, prominent white markings on upper scapulars, pale undertail-coverts, broadly black-tipped greyish tail. In flight, almost uniformly blackish underwing, pale undertail-coverts. (d–f) **Juvenile**: Recalls pale morph Greater Spotted and Tawny but larger, with distinct dark streaks on nape, neck, breast and wing-coverts (above and below). In flight, also shows pale greyish wedge on inner primaries. **VOICE** Repeated deep barking *owk*. **HABITAT & BEHAVIOUR** Open country, cultivation; up to 400 m. In flight, wings held more level than other eagles. **RANGE** V/ra **WV** E,S Myanmar, north Tenasserim, W(coastal),NW,NE,C Thailand, Pen Malaysia, Singapore, Cambodia, N,S Laos, E Tonkin.

3 BONELLI'S EAGLE *Hieraaetus fasciatus* 65–72 cm
(a,b) **Adult** *fasciatus*: Dark brown above, whitish below with dark streaks on foreneck to breast and dark-barred thighs. Recalls some hawk eagles. Differs primarily by com-bination of size, whitish patch on mantle, relatively uniform greyish tail with broad blackish subterminal band, and lack of crest. In flight, faintly barred greyish underwing with whitish leading edge to mostly black coverts, grey tail with pronounced black subterminal band. (c–e) **Juvenile**: Head, upperparts and upperwing-coverts paler and browner than adult, uppertail browner with even, narrow darker bars; throat and underparts warm buffish with dark streaks on lower throat and breast. In fresh plumage, head, underparts and underwing-coverts are rufous; this fades to dull rufous in time, later to buffy and, in some cases, to creamy. In flight, from below, warm buffish wing-coverts usually with distinc-tive dark tips to greater and primary coverts forming narrow dark line across underwing; undertail evenly and finely dark-barred. **VOICE** Repeated shrill melodious *iuh* and longer

whistled *eeeoo* (lower-pitched at end) during display flight. **HABITAT & BEHAVIOUR** Forested areas, often near cliffs; 500–1,900 m. Glides on flat wings. **RANGE** Sc **R** C,E Myanmar, E Tonkin. **V** Cochinchina. **Rc** (probably **R**) NW Thailand, N Laos.

4 BOOTED EAGLE *Hieraaetus pennatus* 50–57 cm
(a–c) **Adult pale morph**: Relatively small with pale crown, dark head-sides, mostly whitish underparts. Pale scapulars, uppertail-coverts, and band across wing-coverts contrast with mostly dark remainder of upperside. In flight, whitish under-wing-coverts and pale wedge on inner primaries contrast sharply with otherwise blackish underwing, undertail greyish with dis-tinct dark terminal band and central feathers. (d,e) **Adult dark morph**: Head and body rather uniform dark brown. In flight, can resemble Black Kite but distinctive tail (as in pale morph), contrasting paler scapulars and uppertail-coverts, sharply con-trasting pale band across upperwing-coverts. (f) **Adult rufous morph**: Shows strongly rufescent head, body and underwing-coverts. Size, narrow wings, longish tail and wing pattern rules out *Aquila* eagles. **Juvenile**: Like adult but shows prominent white trailing edge to wings and tail in fresh plumage. **VOICE** Clear shrill chattering *ki-ki-ki..* or longer *kee-kee-kee...* **HABITAT & BEHAVIOUR** Open and wooded areas, cultivation; lowlands. When gliding and soaring, holds wings slightly forwards and level, or with primaries angled slightly downwards; sometimes twists tail like Black Kite. **RANGE** Ra/sc **PM** Tenasserim, S Thailand. **V** C,S,E Myanmar, W,NW,NE,SE Thailand, Pen Malaysia, Singapore, S Laos (probably regular **PM** in at least some of these areas).

5 RUFOUS-BELLIED EAGLE *Hieraaetus kienerii* 53–61 cm
(a,b) **Adult** *formosae*: Blackish head-sides and upperside, white throat and upper breast, rufous-chestnut remainder of underparts. Slight crest, narrow dark streaks on breast to under-tail-coverts. In flight, from below, mostly rufous-chestnut wing-coverts, dark trailing edge to wings, narrow dark bars across rather pale greyish flight feathers and tail (latter with blackish subterminal band). (c,d) **Juvenile**: Upperside brown, head-sides whitish with blackish eyeline, underparts whitish with black area on flanks. In flight, from below, has whitish wing-coverts with broken dark trailing edge and narrower, less pro-nounced trailing edge to flight feathers and tail. Distinguished from similar hawk eagles by dark upperside with brown pri-maries, blackish eyeline and flank-patch, indistinctly barred tail, underwing-covert pattern and lack of obvious crest. **VOICE** Fairly clear but low-pitched series of notes terminated by very thin breathless note: *WHI-WHI-WHI-WHI yii*. **HABITAT & BEHAVIOUR** Broadleaved evergreen forest; up to 2,000 m. Usually glides and soars with wings held level. **RANGE** Sc/un **R** N,S Myanmar, Thai-land (except C), Pen Malaysia, Cambodia, S,S Laos, Vietnam (except W Tonkin). Sc **NBV** Singapore.

PLATE 65 HAWK EAGLES

1 CHANGEABLE HAWK EAGLE *Spizaetus cirrhatus* 61–75 cm **(a–c) Adult pale morph** *limnaetus*: Rather nondescript brown above, whitish below with dark mesial streak, dark streaks on breast and belly, faint narrow rufous barring on thighs and undertail-coverts; has four dark bands on tail (terminal one broader), crest distinctly short. In flight, broad, rather parallel-edged wings. From other hawk eagles by lack of belly-barring, relatively plain underwing-coverts, undertail pattern with three narrowish dark bands and broader dark terminal band. **(d,e) Adult dark morph**: Blackish with greyer, broadly dark-tipped tail. In flight, underwing has greyer bases to flight feathers. Recalls Black Eagle but wings much more parallel-edged, no bars on underwing and undertail (apart from terminal band). **(f–h) Juvenile pale morph**: Head, neck and underparts almost unmarked whitish (can show darker half-collar and eye-patch); has prominent whitish fringes to upperpart feathers (particularly wing-coverts), narrower, more numerous dark tail-bands (no wide dark terminal band). In flight, underside similar to adult apart from paler body and wing-coverts, tail pattern. **Juvenile dark morph**: Like adult but may show some dark barring on underside of flight feathers and tail. **Other subspecies** *S.c.andamanensis* (Coco Is, off S Myanmar): Smaller and darker. **VOICE** Somewhat ascending series of loud, shrill, high-pitched whistles, terminated by thin stressed high-pitched note: *wi-wiwiwiwi-hii*; *wi-wi-wi-wi-wi-wi-wi-hiii*; *kwi-kwi-kwi-kwiii* etc. Also *k'wi-wi* or *kerWI-WI* recalling Crested Serpent Eagle. Juveniles give shrill *klit-klit* and *klit-kli* with stressed second note. **HABITAT & BEHAVIOUR** Broadleaved evergreen and deciduous forest; up to 2,135 m. Soars and glides with wings held level. During display flight, stretches neck forwards, lifts tail and holds wings in shallow V. **RANGE** Un/fc **R** (except C Thailand, W,E Tonkin, N,C Annam).

2 MOUNTAIN HAWK EAGLE *Spizaetus nipalensis* 66–75 cm **(a–c) Adult** *nipalensis*: Similar to pale morph Changeable but has long erectile white-tipped blackish crest, whitish bars on rump, broader dark mesial streak, broad dark bars on belly, equal-width dark and pale tail-bands. In flight, from below, wings somewhat broader and more rounded (more pinched-in at base of secondaries), tail relatively shorter, wing-coverts with heavy dark markings, dark tail-bands broader. **(d,e) Juvenile**: From Changeable by crest (similar to adult), pale to warm buff head and underparts, darker-streaked crown, hindneck and head-sides, buff barring on rump. In flight, from below, also differs by shape, equal-width pale and dark tail-bands. Underwing-coverts plain creamy-white.

VOICE Shrill *tlueet-weet-weet*. **HABITAT & BEHAVIOUR** Broadleaved evergreen, deciduous and mixed forests; up to 2,565 m. Glides with wings held level; soars with wings in shallow V. **RANGE** Sc/un **R** (some movements) W,N Myanmar, Tenasserim, W,NW,S(northern) Thailand. Sc/un (status unclear, but probably **R** in some of these areas) SW,C,S Myanmar, NE,SE,S(southern) Thailand, Indochina.

3 BLYTH'S HAWK EAGLE *Spizaetus alboniger* 51–58 cm **(a–c) Adult**: Head-sides and crown to mantle distinctly blacker than other hawk eagles, underparts whitish with prominent black mesial streak, bold blackish breast-streaks, bold blackish bars on belly, thighs and vent; tail blackish with pale greyish broad central band and narrow tip. Crest long and erectile, blackish or with fine white tip. In flight, whitish underwing with heavy blackish bars on coverts, blackish bands across flight feathers, distinctive tail pattern. **(d,e) Juvenile**: Crown, hindneck and ear-coverts sandy-rufous, upperside browner than adult with whitish fringes, underparts plain pale buff to whitish with buffish breast and flanks, tail whitish with two or three medium-width dark bands and slightly broader terminal dark band, underwing-coverts plain creamy-whitish; crest similar to adult. From Mountain by smaller size, more rufescent unstreaked head and hindneck, and different tail pattern, with four dark bands on upperside. In flight, also differs by shorter, more parallel-edged wings. Moults directly into adult plumage. **VOICE** Very high-pitched, fast, slightly metallic *wiii-hi*, *eeee'ha*, *wiii'a* or *wee'ah*, and shrill *pik-wuee* slightly rising second note. **HABITAT & BEHAVIOUR** Broadleaved evergreen forest; up to 1,980 m. Soars with wings held level. **RANGE** Un/fc **R** S Thailand, Pen Malaysia. **V** Singapore.

4 WALLACE'S HAWK EAGLE *Spizaetus nanus* 46 cm **(a–c) Adult** *nanus*: Similarly patterned to Blyth's but smaller, browner overall, head-sides and hindneck rufescent-brown with blackish streaks, crest broadly white-tipped, tail greyish with three dark bands (terminal one slightly broader). In flight, underside differs by buffish-white base colour to flight feathers, warm buffish coverts with narrow dark barring, and tail pattern. Best separated from Mountain by much smaller size and tail pattern. **(d,e) Juvenile**: Very similar to Blyth's but has broad white tip to tail pattern. **VOICE** Shrill high-pitched *yik-yee* or *kliit-kleeik*, with upward-inflected second note. Fledged juveniles give up to eight high-pitched breathless whistles: *yii-yii-yii-yii..* and *ee-ee-ee-ee-eeee*. **HABITAT** Broadleaved evergreen forest; up to 580 m. **RANGE** Ra/un **R** south Tenasserim, S Thailand, Pen Malaysia.

PLATE 66 FALCONETS & SMALLER FALCONS

1 WHITE-RUMPED FALCON *Polihierax insignis* 25–26.5 cm (**a,b**) **Male** *cinereiceps*: Smallish, long tail, pale greyish ear-coverts/forehead to upper mantle with blackish streaks, white rump/uppertail-coverts, plain whitish below. Otherwise dark slate-grey above; often a whiter nuchal collar. (**c**) **Female:** Crown to upper mantle deep rufous. (**d**) **Juvenile:** Like male but lower nape/upper mantle broadly rufous, rest of upperparts washed brown. (**e**) **Male** *insignis* (W,C,S Myanmar): Much paler grey mantle/scapulars, blackish streaks on lower throat, breast and flanks. **Female:** Paler grey above than *cinereiceps*, blackish streaking below (mainly lower throat/breast/flanks), often mixed with some dark rufous. **Juvenile:** Differs as *cinereiceps* and also more streaked below than adult male. **Other subspecies** *P.i.harmandi* (Indochina): Whiter crown to upper mantle, with less distinct streaks. **VOICE** Long falling whistle. **HABITAT & BEHAVIOUR** Open deciduous woodland, clearings in deciduous forest; up to 915 m. Often perches (in concealed or exposed position) for long periods. **RANGE** Sc/un **R** SW,W,C,S Myanmar, north Tenasserim, W,NW,NE Thailand, Cambodia, C,S Laos, S Annam, Cochinchina.

2 COLLARED FALCONET *Microhierax caerulescens* 16–18 cm (**a,b**) **Adult** *burmanicus*: Very small; black ear-covert patch and upperside, broad white forehead and supercilium (latter meeting white nuchal collar), chestnut throat. Thighs and vent chestnut, breast-centre and belly variable, white to chestnut. (**c**) **Juvenile:** Pale areas of forehead, head-sides and supercilium washed pale chestnut, throat whitish, chestnut of underparts paler and restricted mainly to undertail-coverts. **VOICE** High *kli-kli-kli* or *killi-killi-killi*. **HABITAT & BEHAVIOUR** Deciduous forest, clearings in broadleaved evergreen and mixed forests; up to 1,830 m, rarely 2,310 m. Perches in exposed places. Flight direct, rapid, shrike-like. **RANGE** Fc **R** Myanmar, Thailand (except S), Cambodia, Laos, S Annam, Cochinchina.

3 BLACK-THIGHED FALCONET *Microhierax fringillarius* 15–17 cm (**a**) **Adult**: No white collar, less white on forehead/supercilium than Collared, more black on ear-coverts, whiter throat, black lower flanks to thighs. **Juvenile:** Pale areas of forehead, head-sides and supercilium washed very pale chestnut, throat white, much paler chestnut below. **VOICE** Shrill squealing *kweer WEEK*. **HABITAT** Clearings in broadleaved evergreen forest, partly wooded cultivation and parkland; up to 1,700 m. **RANGE** Fc/co **R** south Tenasserim, S Thailand, Pen Malaysia, Singapore (sc).

4 PIED FALCONET *Microhierax melanoleucus* 19–20 cm (**a**) **Adult**: Larger than black-thighed, no chestnut below. **VOICE** Shrill whistle, low chattering; prolonged hissing in alarm. **HABITAT** Clearings in broadleaved evergreen forest, forest edge; up to 1,080 m. **RANGE** Sc **R** N,C Laos, W,E Tonkin, N,C Annam.

5 LESSER KESTREL *Falco naumanni* 29–32 cm (**a–c**) **Male:** Like Common, but slightly smaller/slimmer, plain bluish-grey crown/nape/head-sides, plain rufous-chestnut mantle to median coverts, mostly bluish-grey tertials, greater coverts and median covert tips; plainer vinous-tinged warm buff below with fewer, rounder markings. At rest, wing-tips reach tail-band.

In flight, underwing cleaner, with dark tip (and often diffuse trailing edge), tail narrower, usually with more projecting central feathers. (**d–f**) **Female:** Usually finer, more diffuse moustachial-/cheek-stripe than Common, no dark postocular stripe, plainer/whiter cheeks (often to throat), usually finer crown-streaks and more V-shaped markings above; usually neater, sparser and finer streaks below (typically denser on upper breast). In flight, uppertail-coverts more often washed pale greyish; underwing usually cleaner/whiter (relatively dark primary tips contrast more). **Juvenile:** Differs as Common. **First-summer male:** Like adult but no grey on wings, some dark and pale brown bars on upperside of flight/outertail feathers. **VOICE** Weaker and less piercing than Common; rapid, rather rasping *kik-kik-kik-kik-kik...* or *keh-chet-chet-kick*, hoarse *kye-kye* or *kye-kiki*, rasping *kee-chee-chee* and *kihik* or *kichit*. **HABITAT & BEHAVIOUR** Open areas, cultivation; up to 1,065 m. Flight more buoyant than Common's (slower/deeper/softer wingbeats). Likely to be encountered in loose flocks. **RANGE** Ra **WV/PM** N,S Myanmar, N Laos. **V** Singapore.

6 COMMON KESTREL *Falco tinnunculus* 30–34 cm (**a–c**) **Male** *interstinctus* (throughout): Medium-sized, slaty-grey crown, nape and rump to uppertail, otherwise rufous above with blackish markings. Dark moustachial/cheek-stripe, pale buffish below with dark streaks/spots on breast, belly and flanks. Wing-tips fall short of dark subterminal tail-band at rest. In flight, underwing largely whitish with dark markings (mainly on coverts), tail quite strongly graduated. (**d–f**) **Female:** Usually lacks grey (unless some on uppertail-coverts and uppertail), dark-streaked warm brown crown/nape, dark line behind eye, long dark moustachial/cheek-stripe, blackish-barred rufous uppertail, duller/paler rufous above than male with more/more distinct dark bars, more heavily streaked. below. **Juvenile:** Like female but typically more strongly marked above and on flight/tail feathers, rufescent grey-brown uppertail-coverts. **Other subspecies** *F.t.tinnunculus* (rc east to NW,C Thailand): Paler-toned, less heavily marked. **VOICE** Piercing *keee-keee-keee..*; *kik* notes, and trilling *kreeeee* or *wrreeee* in alarm. **HABITAT & BEHAVIOUR** Various open habitats, cultivation, cliffs; up to 2,000 m. Often hovers. Flies with shallow, winnowy wingbeats. **RANGE** Lo **R** E Tonkin. Sc/fc **WV** throughout. Also **PM** SW Myanmar, Cambodia, E Tonkin.

7 MERLIN *Falco columbarius* 25–30 cm (**a–c**) **Male** *insignis*: Fairly small/compact, mostly bluish-grey above, warm buffish below with dark streaks, only faint moustachial/cheek-stripe, buffish-white supercilium, rufous nuchal collar; wings short/broad/pointed, close-barred underwing, broad whitish and blackish undertail-bands. (**d–f**) **Female:** Drab brownish above with pale buffish-brown markings, faint moustachial/cheek-stripe, pale supercilium, similar underparts/underwing to male, but tail broadly barred buff-and-blackish above. **Juvenile:** Like female but tends to be darker above. **VOICE** Shrill chattering *quik-ik-ik-ik* or *kek-kek-kek* in alarm; coarse lower *zek-zek-zek* from females. **HABITAT** Open areas, cultivation; up to 1,065 m. Flight rapid/direct; does not hover. **RANGE** **V** NW Thailand, N Laos, E Tonkin, C Annam.

PLATE 67 FALCONS

1 AMUR FALCON *Falco amurensis* 28–31 cm
(**a,b**) **Male**: Slaty-grey overall with paler grey underparts, rufous-chestnut thighs and vent, red eyering, cere and feet. In flight, white underwing-coverts contrast sharply with blackish remainder of underwing. (**c,d**) **Female**: Similar to adult Eurasian Hobby but with dark-barred upperparts and uppertail, buffy-white thighs and vent, different bare-part colours (similar to male). In flight, differs by whiter base-colour of underwing (particularly coverts), more pronounced dark and pale bars on undertail. Thighs and undertail-coverts are buffy. (**e,f**) **Juvenile**: Similar to Eurasian Hobby but upperparts and wing-coverts more broadly and prominently tipped/fringed buff, has dark-barred upperparts and uppertail, pale parts of head, underparts and underwing somewhat whiter, feet reddish, eyering and cere pale yellow. (**g**) **First-summer male**: Variable, showing mixed characters of adult and juvenile. VOICE Shrill screaming *kew-kew-kew..* at roost sites. HABITAT & BEHAVIOUR Various open habitats, wooded areas; up to 1,900 m. Likely to be encountered in flocks. Often hovers. RANGE Sc/un (erratic) **PM** W,C,S,E Myanmar, W,NW Thailand, N Laos, W Tonkin(lc). **V** SE Thailand, Pen Malaysia.

2 EURASIAN HOBBY *Falco subbuteo* 30–36 cm
(**a–c**) **Adult** *streichi*: Similar to Peregrine Falcon but smaller, moustachial stripe narrower, upperparts more uniform, uppertail unbarred, breast and belly heavily streaked blackish, thighs and vent reddish-rufous. In flight, has more slender wings. (**d,e**) **Juvenile**: Crown, upperparts and wing-coverts duller with narrow pale buffish feather-fringes, darkly streaked underparts, buffish vent. From Peregrine Falcon by size, shape, lack of obvious pale supercilium, plainer, deeper buff or rufous vent. VOICE Rapid sharp scolding *kew-kew-kew-kew...* HABITAT & BEHAVIOUR Wooded and open areas; up to 2,000 m. Flight swift, direct and dashing. Does not hover. RANGE Ra/lo **PM** NW Thailand (also **WV**?), N Laos, W,E Tonkin. Ra **WV** N Myanmar (also **PM**?). Ra **WV** or **PM** W,E Myanmar, NE Thailand. **V** W(coastal),C Thailand, Pen Malaysia, Singapore.

3 ORIENTAL HOBBY *Falco severus* 27–30 cm
(**a,b**) **Adult** *severus*: All-blackish head-sides, buffish-white throat and forecollar, reddish-rufous remainder of underparts. Upperside slate-grey with darker flight feathers. In flight, also shows distinctive reddish-rufous underwing-coverts. Size and shape recalls Eurasian. (**c,d**) **Juvenile**: Resembles adult but upperparts and wing-coverts darker and browner with narrow pale feather-fringes, breast to vent rufous with blackish drop-like streaks on breast and belly, outertail feathers barred. In flight shows rufous underwing-coverts with indistinct darker markings. VOICE High-pitched rapid *ki-ki-ki-ki-ki-ki..* or *hiu-hiu-hiu-hiu-hiu-hiu..*, repeated at intervals. HABITAT & BEHAVIOUR Open areas in broadleaved evergreen and deciduous forest, secondary growth, cultivation, mangroves, vicinity of limestone cliffs; up to 1,915 m. Flight swift and dashing; does not hover. RANGE Sc/un **R** (except SE Thailand, Pen Malaysia, Singapore, W Tonkin). Ra (status?) Pen Malaysia.

4 LAGGAR FALCON *Falco jugger* 41–46 cm
(**a–c**) **Adult**: Similar to Peregrine but rufous crown with dark streaks, whitish forehead and supercilium, much narrower moustachial streak, unbarred uppertail, unmarked whitish breast, broad dark greyish-brown patch on lower flanks and thighs, narrow dark streaks on lower belly. In flight, wings less broad-based and pointed; from below, shows dark area on axillaries and flanks/thighs and mostly solid dark brownish-grey greater and primary coverts. (**d,e**) **Juvenile**: More uniformly dark brown underparts and underwing-coverts, with a few whitish streaks; upperside similar to Peregrine. VOICE Occasionally utters shrill *whi-ee-ee*, particularly on breeding grounds. HABITAT & BEHAVIOUR Semi-desert, dry cultivation; lowlands. Flight direct, not as heavy as that of Peregrine, with relatively shallow but strong wingbeats. RANGE Un **R** C,S(north),E Myanmar.

5 PEREGRINE FALCON *Falco peregrinus* 38–48 cm
(**a–c**) **Adult** *japonensis* (*calidus*?): Told by large size, slate-grey upperside, broad blackish moustachial streak, whitish lower head-sides and underparts with dark bars on flanks and belly to undertail-coverts. Has somewhat paler back and rump, indistinct bands on uppertail (terminal one broader). In flight, wings broad-based and pointed, tail shortish, underwing uniformly darkish (due to dense dark barring), with darker-tipped primaries and darker trailing edge. (**d,e**) **Juvenile**: Upperparts and wing-coverts duller with narrow warm brown to buffish fringes, forehead and supercilium whitish with indistinct dark streaks, lower head-sides and underparts buffy with dark streaks (turning to chevrons on vent), has some broken buffish bars on uppertail. In flight, underwing similar to adult but coverts more boldly marked. (**f,g**) **Adult** *peregrinator* (**R** Myanmar, **rc** C Thailand): Strongly rufous-washed below (usually barred) with whiter throat and neck-sides, buffish tail-tip, rufous-washed underwing-coverts. (**h**) **Juvenile**: Darker, browner upperside than *japonensis*, no obvious whitish forehead-patch or supercilium, strongly rufous-washed underparts and underwing-coverts. (**i,j**) **Adult** *ernesti* (**R** E Tonkin at least): Smaller; darker upperside (can appear blackish), solid blackish head-sides, duller breast to vent with denser dark barring. **R** birds further south in region (S Thailand, Pen Malaysia; ? W,NE Thailand) have plainer breast than illustrated, varying from whitish to strongly reddish, lower underparts more densely barred and grey-washed, appearing blackish in field. Perhaps an undescribed taxon? VOICE Shrill *kek-kek-kek..* when alarmed. HABITAT & BEHAVIOUR Various open habitats including wetlands, coastal habitats, offshore islets, cliffs; up to 2,900 m. Large, powerful falcon that captures birds in mid-air, usually after a spectacular stoop. RANGE Un **R** S,E Myanmar, north Tenasserim, W,NE,S Thailand, Pen Malaysia, E Tonkin. Sc/un **WV** throughout. Also **PM** C Myanmar, S Thailand.

PLATE 68 DARTER, CORMORANTS & FRIGATEBIRDS

1 DARTER *Anhinga melanogaster* 85–97 cm
(**a,b**) **Adult non-breeding** *melanogaster*: Longish slender pointed bill, long thin neck, relatively long tail. Head, neck and mantle mostly dark brown with pale throat and long whitish stripe extending from eye down neck-side, bold white streaks on upper mantle/scapulars/coverts. **Adult breeding**: Crown, hindneck and base-colour of upper mantle blackish, foreneck more chestnut. **Juvenile**: Paler/browner, buffish-white below with dark flanks/vent, buff-fringed coverts, narrow pale tail-tip. VOICE Gruff, slightly nasal *uk ukukukuk-errr uk-uk* or *ok ok ok ok ukukukukuk-err rerr-rerr-rer-ruh* when breeding. HABITAT & BEHAVIOUR Lakes, marshes, large rivers; up to 1,200 m. Often submerges, with only snake-like neck visible. Sometimes soars. RANGE Sc/lfc **R** (local movements) S Myanmar, Cambodia, Cochinchina; formerly NW,S Thailand. **FR** (currently?) Myanmar (except S), C Annam. Ra/sc (still breeds?) W,C,NE Thailand, Laos (**FB** throughout), S Annam (**FB**), E Tonkin. **V** western Pen Malaysia (**FR**?).

2 LITTLE CORMORANT *Phalacrocorax niger* 51–54.5 cm
(**a,b**) **Adult non-breeding**: Relatively small/short-necked, stubby bill. Mostly blackish-brown, greyer scapulars and wings with black feather-edges, whitish chin, mostly dull greyish-flesh bill. In flight, relatively short-necked, small-winged and long-tailed. (**c**) **Adult breeding**: Head/neck/underparts black with bluish to greenish gloss and dense silvery-white streaks on crown, ear-coverts and nape, bill blackish. (**d**) **Juvenile**: Similar to adult non-breeding but browner overall, head and neck paler and browner, throat whitish, underparts streaked/scaled pale brownish. Has paler crown and hindneck and darker belly than other cormorants. HABITAT Various freshwater wetlands, also estuaries, mangroves; up to 1,450 m (lowland breeder). RANGE Sc/lfc **R** (local movements) N(still **R**?),S,E Myanmar, C,W(coastal),SE Thailand, Cambodia, Cochinchina. **FR** (currently?) Myanmar (except N,S,E), N,C Laos, E Tonkin, C,S Annam. Sc/lc **NBV** W,NW,S Thailand, S Laos (**FB**). **V** west Pen Malaysia, Singapore. **Rc** (status?) N Annam.

3 INDIAN CORMORANT *Phalacrocorax fuscicollis* 61–68 cm
(**a,b**) **Adult non-breeding**: Similar to Little but larger, bill relatively long and slender, head, neck and underparts blacker with whitish lower head-sides/throat, and uneven whitish/pale brown streak-like markings on foreneck/breast, base colour of scapulars and wings browner. In flight, longer-necked, larger-winged and shorter-tailed; more closely resembles Great but smaller, slimmer and thinner-necked with smaller, more oval-shaped head, relatively longer tail. (**c**) **Adult breeding**: Apart from size/shape, similar to Little but silvery peppering over eye, white tuft on rear head-side, browner base-colour of scapulars and wings. (**d**) **Juvenile**: Browner above than adult non-breeding, mostly whitish below with dark brown smudging and streaks on foreneck/breast and dark brown flanks. Best separated from Great by size, shape, much thinner bill, dark ear-coverts, less extensive and duller gular skin, darker breast. HABITAT Various freshwater and saline wetlands; lowlands. RANGE Sc/lc **R** (some movements) S Myanmar, C,SE Thailand, Cambodia, Cochinchina. **Rc** in winter (status?) N Myanmar.

4 GREAT CORMORANT *Phalacrocorax carbo* 80–100 cm
(**a,b**) **Adult non-breeding** *sinensis*: Black head/neck/underparts, prominent white on head-sides/upper throat, browner scapulars/wings than other cormorants, with black fringing, extensive yellow facial/gular skin. In flight, apart from size, relatively thick-necked, large-winged and short-tailed, squarish head, slightly kinked neck. (**c**) **Adult breeding**: White streaks form sheen across crown-/neck-sides, more orange facial skin, darker gular skin, larger white area on ear-coverts/throat, greenish-glossed scapulars/wings, large white thigh-patch. (**d**) **Juvenile**: Much browner above than non-breeding adult, mostly whitish head-sides/underparts, with dark brown streaks on foreneck and upper breast, dark brown flanks/thighs. Apart from size and bill, differs from Indian by more extensive, yellower facial and gular skin, whitish ear-coverts, sparser/bolder breast markings. VOICE Deep guttural calls at breeding colonies. HABITAT Various freshwater and saline wetlands; up to 1,830 m. RANGE Sc/lo **R** Cambodia. **FR** (currently?) S Myanmar, SE Thailand, Cochinchina. Ra/sc **WV/NBV** N,C Myanmar, W,NW,C Thailand, E Tonkin, S Annam; formerly S Thailand, western Pen Malaysia. **FWV/FNBV** (currently?) Myanmar (except N,C), N Laos, C Annam. **Rc** (escapees?) Singapore.

5 GREAT FRIGATEBIRD *Fregata minor* 86–100 cm
(**a**) **Male** *minor*: All blackish. Lesser with dull whitish 'armpits' can cause confusion. (**b**) **Female**: Pale greyish throat, black belly, black inner underwing-coverts. (**c**) **Juvenile**: All-black inner underwing-coverts. (**d**) **Immature**: Gradually loses breast-band and attains blackish plumage parts of respective adults. HABITAT Open seas, islets. RANGE Sc offshore **NBV** west S Thailand. Coastal/offshore **V** W Thailand, south-east Pen Malaysia, Singapore, C Annam. Inland **V** N Laos.

6 LESSER FRIGATEBIRD *Fregata ariel* 71–81 cm
(**a,b**) **Male** *ariel*: Blackish with whitish 'armpits'. Dull birds resemble Great at long distance. Red gular pouch. (**c**) **Female**: Black hood/belly/lower flanks, white on rest of underparts, extending onto inner underwing-coverts. (**d**) **Juvenile**: Similar to female but rufous/brownish-white head, black breast-band enclosing white collar. Apart from size, possibly not separable from Christmas Island, unless black mottling on belly present. (**e**) **Immature second stage**: Gradually loses black breast-band and acquires blackish of respective adults. HABITAT Open seas, islets. RANGE Sc/lc offshore **NBV** S Thailand, Pen Malaysia, Cambodia. Coastal/offshore **V** Singapore, Cochinchina.

7 CHRISTMAS ISLAND FRIGATEBIRD *F.andrewsi* 92–102 cm
(**a**) **Male**: Blackish with white belly-patch. (**b**) **Female**: Larger than Lesser, white belly, black bar extending from forewing-base to breast-side. (**c**) **Juvenile**: Apart from size, possibly not safely separable from Lesser; always has white belly, possibly has broader black breast-band and broader white spur on inner underwing. (**d**) **Immature second stage**: Gradually loses black breast-band and acquires blackish of respective adults. HABITAT Open seas, islets. RANGE Sc/lfc offshore **NBV** S Thailand, Pen Malaysia, Cambodia; rarely straying inland. Coastal/offshore **V** C Thailand, Singapore, E Tonkin.

PLATE 69 EGRETS & POND HERONS

1 LITTLE EGRET *Egretta garzetta* 55–65 cm
(**a,b**) **Adult non-breeding/juvenile** *garzetta*: Mostly blackish bill, blackish legs with yellow feet. (**c**) **Adult breeding**: Long nape, back- and breast-plumes, reddish facial skin, blackish bill, black legs, yellowish to redder feet. **Other subspecies** *E.g.nigripes* (sc **NBV** Pen Malaysia, Singapore?): Blackish feet. **VOICE** Hoarse, grating *kgarrk* or longer *aaahk* when flushed. Various guttural calls at breeding colonies. **HABITAT** Various open freshwater and coastal wetlands, cultivation; up to 800 m. **RANGE** Sc/lc **R** (local movements) C,SE,W(coastal),S Thailand, Pen Malaysia, Cambodia, Cochinchina. **FR** (currently?) Myanmar. Un/co **WV** throughout. Also **PM** Laos. **Rc** in summer Singapore.

2 CHINESE EGRET *Egretta eulophotes* 68 cm
(**a,b**) **Adult non-breeding/juvenile**: Dull flesh/yellowish basal two-thirds of lower mandible, greenish/greenish-yellow legs. (**c**) **Adult breeding**: Yellow bill, shaggy nuchal crest, blue facial skin, blackish legs, greenish-yellowish/yellow feet. **HABITAT** Mudflats, mangroves. **RANGE** Lo **WV** west S Thailand, west Pen Malaysia, Singapore. Ra/sc **PM** S Thailand, Pen Malaysia, Singapore, E Tonkin, S Annam, Cochinchina (probably winters).

3 PACIFIC REEF EGRET *Egretta sacra* 58 cm
(**a**) **Adult dark morph non-breeding** *sacra*: Slaty-grey overall. (**b**) **Adult dark morph breeding**: Plumes on nape, back and breast. (**c,d**) **Adult white morph non-breeding**: All-white, bill relatively thick and blunt, mostly pale greenish to yellowish, upper mandible usually darker, legs greenish to yellowish. Very like Chinese but legs shorter (tarsus always shorter than bill), bill somewhat thicker and less pointed, typically with paler upper mandible (darker on culmen) and less contrasting dark tip to lower mandible. In flight, only feet and small amount of legs project behind tail-tip. **Adult white morph breeding**: Differs as dark morph. **Juvenile**: Like adult non-breeding. Dark morph somewhat paler smoky-grey. **VOICE** Grunting *ork*; harsh *squak* when flushed. **HABITAT & BEHAVIOUR** Rocky shores, islets, beaches, sometimes mudflats. Usually found singly or in pairs. **RANGE** Un/co coastal **R** (except N,C Annam).

4 GREAT EGRET *Casmerodius albus* 85–102 cm
(**a,b**) **Adult non-breeding/juvenile** *modestus*: Large size, long snake-like neck (sharply kinked when retracted), long sharply pointed yellow bill, blackish legs. (**c**) **Adult breeding**: Blackish bill, reddish legs, long back-plumes, short breast-plumes. Cobalt-blue facial skin. **Juvenile**: Similar to adult non-breeding. **VOICE** Harsh high rolling *krr'rr'rr'rra* when flushed. Guttural calls at colonies. **HABITAT** Various wetlands, mangroves; up to 800 m. **RANGE** Ra/lo **R** (some movements) C,W(coastal) Thailand, west Pen Malaysia, Cambodia, Cochinchina. **FR** (currently?) Myanmar. Fc/co **WV** throughout. Also **PM** Laos.

5 INTERMEDIATE EGRET *Mesophoyx intermedia* 65–72 cm
(**a,b**) **Adult non-breeding/juvenile**: Size between Little and Great (nearer former), bill shorter/blunter than Great, neck shorter, less kinked, looks somewhat rounder-crowned and heavier-jowled. (**c**) **Adult breeding**: Bill often shows dark on tip and ridge of upper mandible (blacker during courtship),

long breast-/back-plumes, blackish legs. **VOICE** Harsh croaking *kwark* or *kuwark* when flushed. Buzzing sounds during courtship display. **HABITAT & BEHAVIOUR** Various wetlands; up to 800 m. Wingbeats more rapid than Great Egret, slower and more graceful than Cattle. Often raises crown feathers. **RANGE** Sc/lo **R** (local movements) Cambodia, Cochinchina. **FR** (currently?) Myanmar. Un/fc **WV** (except W Myanmar, SE Thailand, W Tonkin). Also **PM** Laos. **Rc** (status?) SE Thailand (may breed).

6 CATTLE EGRET *Bubulcus ibis* 48–53 cm
(**a,b**) **Adult non-breeding** *coromandus*: Smallish, short yellow bill, short neck, heavy-jowled, shortish dark legs. (**c**) **Adult breeding**: Rufous-buff on head/neck/back/breast. Short nape-/breast-plumes, long back-plumes. **Juvenile**: As non-breeding adult but sometimes blackish legs/feet, grey tinge. **VOICE** Quiet croaking *ruk* in flight. Low rattling at roosts. **HABITAT & BEHAVIOUR** Various wetlands, cultivation (usually avoids salt water); up to 800 m. Often feeds near cattle. **RANGE** Sc/lo **R** (some movements) S Myanmar, W(coastal),C,SE,S Thailand, Cambodia, Cochinchina. **FR** (currently?) elsewhere Myanmar. Fc **WV** (except W,SE Thailand, W Tonkin). Also **PM** Pen Malaysia, Laos.

7 INDIAN POND HERON *Ardeola grayi* 45 cm
(**a**) **Adult breeding**: Brownish-buff head/neck/breast, rich brownish-maroon mantle/scapulars. Long white head-plumes. **Adult non-breeding/juvenile**: Indistinguishable from other pond herons? **VOICE** Gruff rolling *urrb urrb urrb..* and abrupt hollow *okb* in flight. Conversational *wa-koo* at breeding sites. **HABITAT** Various freshwater wetlands, sometimes coastal pools; lowlands. **RANGE** Un/lc **R** Myanmar. **V** (regular **WV**?) C,S (coastal),S Thailand, north-west Pen Malaysia.

8 CHINESE POND HERON *Ardeola bacchus* 45–52 cm
(**a,b**) **Adult non-breeding**: Rather small, stocky and nondescript, but in flight shows white wings/tail. Brown-streaked head/neck/breast. Possibly indistinguishable from other pond herons but may tend to have more obvious dusky tips to outermost primaries than Javan. (**c**) **Adult breeding**: Chestnut-maroon head/neck/breast, blackish-slate mantle and scapulars. **Juvenile**: Rather more spotted below than streaked (markings fainter), brownish markings on tail, brown inner primaries, grey-washed upperwing-coverts. **VOICE** High harsh squawk when flushed. **HABITAT** Various freshwater wetlands, also mangroves, tidal pools; up to 1,450 m. **RANGE** Sc/lo **R** (some movements) N Tonkin; possibly N Laos. Un/co **WV** (except SW Myanmar). Also **PM** Laos, E Tonkin, C Annam.

9 JAVAN POND HERON *Ardeola speciosa* 45 cm
(**a**) **Adult non-breeding/juvenile**: Possibly not distinguishable, but may show less obvious dusky tips to outermost primaries than Chinese. (**b**) **Adult breeding**: Buffish head and neck, deep cinnamon-rufous breast, blackish-slate mantle and scapulars, white head-plumes. **VOICE** Similar to other pond herons. **HABITAT** Various wetlands, particularly along coast; lowlands. **RANGE** Co **R** C Thailand, Cambodia, Cochinchina. **Rc** (status?) Tenasserim. **V** S Thailand, Pen Malaysia, Singapore.

146

PLATE 70 HERONS, SPOONBILLS & PELICANS

1 GREY HERON *Ardea cinerea* 90–98 cm
(**a,b**) **Adult non-breeding** *jouyi*: Grey above, mostly white head/neck with black markings, black nape-plumes, yellowish bill; grey coverts contrast with dark flight feathers. (**c**) **Adult breeding**: Orange to reddish bill. (**d**) **Juvenile**: Dark crown, grey neck-sides, short nape-plumes, duller bill. VOICE Loud, harsh, abrupt *krahnk* in flight. Deep grating *raark* in alarm. HABITAT Various wetlands, mangroves; up to 1,000 m. RANGE Sc/lo **R** (some movements) western Pen Malaysia, Singapore, Cambodia, Cochinchina. **FR** (currently?) C,S Myanmar, C Thailand. Un/fc **WV** (except Pen Malaysia, Singapore).

2 GOLIATH HERON *Ardea goliath* 135–150 cm
(**a,b**) **Adult**: Huge size, black bill, plain rufous-chestnut crown and hindneck, dark chestnut belly, blackish legs; rather plain upperwing, chestnut underwing-coverts. **Juvenile**: Blackish crown, paler hindneck, rufous fringes above, fainter foreneck markings, grey and pale chestnut streaks on belly/vent, dark grey underwing-coverts. VOICE Loud harsh deep *kowoorrk-kowoorrk-woorrk-work-worrk* in flight. HABITAT & BEHAVIOUR Various wetlands, mainly large lakes/rivers. Usually solitary. RANGE **V** S Myanmar (one old record).

3 WHITE-BELLIED HERON *Ardea insignis* 127 cm
(**a,b**) **Adult**: Large; very long neck, mostly greyish with clean white throat, whitish belly/vent; contrasting whitish underwing-coverts. **Juvenile**: Grey of plumage browner. VOICE Loud deep, croaking *ock ock ock ock urrrrrr*. HABITAT Shingle banks, shores of larger rivers, nearby wetlands; up to 1,135 m. RANGE Ra/sc **R** N Myanmar. **FR** (currently?) SW,W,C,S Myanmar.

4 GREAT-BILLED HERON *Ardea sumatrana* 114–115 cm
(**a,b**) **Adult breeding** *sumatrana*: Shorter neck than White-bellied, browner; less defined pale throat, dull greyish belly and vent, dark underwing-coverts. **Adult non-breeding**: Duller plumes on scapulars/breast. **Juvenile**: Warmer than adult non-breeding, buff/rufous-buff feather-tips above, vina-ceous-tinged neck/underparts, broader whitish streaks on lower foreneck and breast. VOICE Loud harsh croaks. Unnerving loud deep guttural roars during breeding season. HABITAT & BEHAVIOUR Mangroves, islets, undisturbed beaches, sometimes upstream along large rivers. Solitary or in pairs. RANGE Ra and lo coastal **R** SW Myanmar, Tenasserim, S Thailand, Pen Malaysia, Singapore, Cambodia. **FR** (currently?) SE Thailand, Cochinchina.

5 PURPLE HERON *Ardea purpurea* 78–90 cm
(**a,b**) **Adult** *manilensis*: Black crown and nape-plumes, mostly rufous-chestnut neck with black lines down side/front, dark chestnut-maroon belly/flanks/vent, yellow bill; upperwing pattern not sharply contrasting, underwing-coverts mostly chestnut-maroon. (**c,d**) **Juvenile**: Brownish above, neck duller with less distinct markings. Gradually attains adult plumage; mature at 3–5 years. VOICE Flight call thinner/higher than Grey's. Loud, hoarse *raanka* and *raank* at roosts. HABITAT & BEHAVIOUR Well-vegetated freshwater wetlands, large rivers, sometimes coastal wetlands; up to 1,000 m. More secretive than Grey. RANGE Sc/lo

R (some movements) W,C,NE,SE,S Thailand, Pen Malaysia, Singapore, Cambodia, S Laos, Cochinchina, probably E Tonkin. **FR** (currently?) S Myanmar. Sc/lfc **WV** (except W Myanmar, W Tonkin, N Annam).

6 EURASIAN SPOONBILL *Platalea leucorodia* 82.5–89 cm
(**a**) **Adult non-breeding** *major*: Larger than Black-faced, all-white forehead/cheeks, pale fleshy-yellow patch on bill 'spoon'. (**b**) **Adult breeding**: As Black-faced as non-breeding adult; also yellow-orange gular skin. (**c,d**) **Juvenile**: Dull pinkish bill and loral skin; similar wing markings to Black-faced. HABITAT Marshes, lakes, tidal mudflats; lowlands. RANGE Ra **WV** SW,S Myanmar. **V** NW Thailand, Cambodia, E Tonkin.

7 BLACK-FACED SPOONBILL *Platalea minor* 76 cm
(**a**) **Adult non-breeding**: All-blackish bill, black face encircles bill-base. (**b**) **Adult breeding**: Yellowish to buffish nuchal crest/breast-patch. (**c**) **Juvenile**: Like adult non-breeding but blackish edges to outer primaries, small blackish tips to flight feathers and primary coverts. HABITAT & BEHAVIOUR Tidal mudflats, coastal pools. Usually in flocks. RANGE Lo **WV** E Tonkin, rarely C Annam, Cochinchina. **V** NE,C,S Thailand, Cambodia.

8 GREAT WHITE PELICAN *Pelecanus onocrotalus* 140–175 cm
(**a,b**) **Adult non-breeding**: Huge; mostly whitish plumage, yellowish pouch, pinkish legs; black underside of flight feathers contrast with whitish underwing-coverts. (**c**) **Adult breeding**: White plumage tinged pinkish, bright deep yellow pouch, tufted nuchal crest, yellowish-buff patch on lower foreneck/breast. (**d,e**) **Juvenile**: Head, neck and upperside predominantly greyish-brown; dark brownish leading edge to underwing, dark underside of flight feathers. VOICE Quiet deep croaking notes in flight. At breeding colonies, low-pitched grunting and growling sounds. HABITAT Various inland and coastal wetland habitats; lowlands. RANGE **FR** (no recent records) Cochinchina. Ra/sc **WV** (at least formerly) S Myanmar. **V** Tenasserim, west Pen Malaysia, C Annam. **V** (former status unclear) Cambodia.

9 SPOT-BILLED PELICAN *P. philippensis* 127–140 cm
(**a,b**) **Adult breeding**: Huge, mostly whitish; yellowish-pink bill with dark spots along upper mandible, pinkish pouch with heavy purplish-grey mottling, dark bluish to purplish lores, tufted dusky nape/hindneck, blackish feet. Rump, tail-coverts and underwing-coverts variably washed cinnamon-pinkish, underparts variably flushed pink with faint yellowish-buff patch on lower foreneck and upper breast. In flight, dark greyish flight feathers (above and below), dull underwing-coverts with obvious whitish band along greater coverts. **Adult non-breeding**: Lacks pink/cinnamon plumage-washes, no yellowish-buff patch on lower foreneck/upper breast. (**c**) **Juvenile**: Head-sides, hindneck, upperparts and wing-coverts browner. Plain dull pinkish pouch. HABITAT Lakes, lagoons, large rivers, estuaries, mudflats; lowlands. RANGE Ra/lc **R** Cambodia, Cochinchina; formerly S Myanmar. Ra/sc **NBV** N,S Myanmar, north Tenasserim, W,C,NE Thailand, C,S Laos, E Tonkin, N Annam; formerly NW Thailand. **FNBV** (currently?) SW,W,C Myanmar. **V** (formerly more abundant) S Thailand, Pen Malaysia.

PLATE 71 LITTLE HERON, NIGHT HERONS & BITTERNS

1 LITTLE HERON *Butorides striatus* 40–48 cm
(a,b) Adult *javanicus*: Greyish; black crown and cheek-stripe, whitish/buffish-white streaks above; quite uniform in flight. Legs yellowish-orange. **(c,d) Juvenile:** Dull brown; darker crown and nape, all-streaked below, greenish to yellowish-green legs. **Other subspecies** *B.s.spodiogaster* (Coco Is, S Myanmar); *actophilus* (northern Myanmar to northern Indochina; exact distribution/status?); *amurensis* (VS, rc S Thailand southwards; ? E Myanmar). **VOICE** Harsh *skeow* or *k-yek* when flushed, high raspy *kitch-itch itch* in alarm. **HABITAT** Mangroves, tidal mudflats, offshore islands, rivers/streams in/near forest, lakes; up to 1,400 m. **RANGE** Sc/lc **R** (mostly coastal) Myanmar, W,C,SE,S Thailand, Pen Malaysia, Singapore, Cambodia, S Laos, E Tonkin, Cochinchina. Fc/co **WV** throughout. Also **PM** Pen Malaysia.

2 BLACK-CROWNED NIGHT HERON *Nycticorax nycticorax* 62 cm
(a,b) Adult non-breeding *nycticorax*: Grey; black crown/mantle/scapulars, whitish nape-plumes, yellow legs; wings broad, uniform. **Adult breeding:** Black parts glossed bluish-green, lores/legs go red for courtship. **(c) Juvenile:** Brown-streaked head to breast, dark brown above with buffish/whitish spots/streaks. **VOICE** Hollow croaking *kwok*, *quark*, or more sudden *guk*. **HABITAT & BEHAVIOUR** Marshes, rice paddies, mangroves. Mainly seen in flocks at dusk/dawn. **RANGE** Un/lc **R** (some movements) C,S Myanmar, W(coastal),C,NE(south-west),SE Thailand, north-west Pen Malaysia, Singapore, Cambodia, E Tonkin, S Annam, Cochinchina. **FR** (currently?) Myanmar (except C,S), C Annam. Un/co **NBV/WV** NW,NE,S(south-east) Thailand, Pen Malaysia, Singapore. **Rc** (status?) N Myanmar, Laos.

3 WHITE-EARED NIGHT HERON *Gorsachius magnificus* 55 cm
(a) Male: Black head with white markings, plain dark brownish above, rufescent neck-sides, dark streaks/scales below; legs green. **Female:** Less bold head/neck pattern, whitish streaks and spots above, shorter nape-plumes. **Juvenile:** Similar to female but blackish plumage browner, with heavier whitish to buff markings above. **HABITAT** Streams in broadleaved evergreen forest. **RANGE** Ra **R** (subject to movements?) E Tonkin.

4 MALAYAN NIGHT HERON *Gorsachius melanolophus* 48–51 cm
(a) Adult *melanolophus*: Chestnut-tinged brown above with blackish vermiculations, black crown/crest, blackish streaks on throat/foreneck, dark-marked belly, short bill. **(b) Juvenile:** Irregular white markings on crown/nape, heavy whitish/buffish and greyish vermiculations above/below, whitish throat with broken mesial streak. **VOICE** Deep *oo* notes (territorial) at night. **HABITAT & BEHAVIOUR** Swampy areas and streams in broadleaved forest, bamboo; up to 1,220 m. Very secretive, feeding mostly at night. **RANGE** Sc/un **R/BV** W,NW,NE,SE Thailand, Cambodia, Laos, C Annam. Sc **BV** E Tonkin. Sc **PM** C,S Thailand, Pen Malaysia. Probably also Sc **WV** southern S Thailand, Pen Malaysia. **Rc** (status?) SW,S,E Myanmar, Tenasserim, W Tonkin, Cochinchina. Sc **WV** and **PM** Singapore.

5 YELLOW BITTERN *Ixobrychus sinensis* 36–38 cm
(a,b) Male: Light buffish-brown, darker brown mantle, blackish crown/tail/flight feathers. Often a strong vinous-wash above and on head-/neck-sides (mainly when breeding). **Female:** More uniform warmer brown above (may look vaguely streaked), warm brown lines down foreneck, no vinous above. **(c,d) Juvenile:** Like female but bold streaks above and below. In flight, whitish underwing-coverts aid identification. **VOICE** Low *ou* notes (territorial); *kak-kak-kak* in flight. **HABITAT** Densely vegetated freshwater wetlands, sometimes rice paddies; up to 1,000 m. **RANGE** Sc/lc **R** Myanmar (except W,N), Thailand, Pen Malaysia, Singapore, Cambodia, E Tonkin, Cochinchina. Un/lc **WV** Thailand, Pen Malaysia, Singapore (at least). Also **PM** Pen Malaysia. Rc (status?) N Myanmar, N,S Laos, C,S Annam.

6 VON SCHRENCK'S BITTERN *I.eurhythmus* 39–42 cm
(a,b) Male: Dark chestnut above, blackish median crown-stripe; contrasting, mostly buffish coverts, dark grey flight feathers. **(c,d) Female/juvenile:** Bold white to buff speckles/spots above, blackish-grey flight feathers/tail. **HABITAT** Swampy areas or pools in/near lowland forest, sometimes more open vegetated wetlands. **RANGE** Ra/sc **PM** Tenasserim, W,NW,C,S Thailand, Pen Malaysia, Singapore, Laos, C Annam. **Rc** in winter Singapore, S Laos.

7 CINNAMON BITTERN *I.cinnamomeus* 38–41 cm
(a,b) Male non-breeding: Plain rich cinnamon-rufous above. **Male breeding:** Eyes/face-skin (like other *Ixobrychus*) turn red when breeding, bill turns more orange. **(c) Female:** Duller above with vague buffish speckles, brown streaking below; upperwing rather uniform warm brown in flight. **(d,e) Juvenile:** Duller than female, dense buffish markings above and on head-sides/darker streaks below. **VOICE** Throat *ukh-ukh-ukh-ukh-ukh-ukh..* (territorial). Clicky *ikh* or *ikh-ikh* in flight. **HABITAT** Various freshwater wetland habitats; up to 1,830 m. **RANGE** Fc/co **R**, subject to some movements (except W Myanmar). Also **PM** Pen Malaysia, E Tonkin, N Annam.

8 BLACK BITTERN *Dupetor flavicollis* 54–61 cm
(a,b) Male *flavicollis*: Blackish; whitish throat and breast with broad dark streaks, yellowish-buff neck-patch; all-dark upperwing. **(c) Female:** Dark parts browner, more rufescent breast-streaks. **(d) Juvenile:** Head/upperparts brown with paler fringing, breast washed buffish-brown. **VOICE** Territorial call is a loud booming. **HABITAT** Marshy freshwater wetlands, swamp forest, mangroves; up to 1,100 m (usually lowlands). **RANGE** Un **R** Cambodia. Un/fc **BV** Myanmar, W,NW,C,NE Thailand. Un/fc **PM** and un **WV** S Thailand, Pen Malaysia, Singapore. **Rc** (status?) SE Thailand, N,S Laos, E Tonkin, N,C Annam, Cochinchina.

9 GREAT BITTERN *Botaurus stellaris* 70–80 cm
(a,b) Adult *stellaris*: Large; cryptic pattern with blackish streaks and vermiculations, thick yellowish bill, plain rufous-buff head-sides; flight feathers barred black. **VOICE** Harsh nasal *kau* or *krau* in flight. Territorial boom (unlikely to be heard) is deep resonant far-carrying boom: *up-RUMBH*. **HABITAT** Well-vegetated freshwater marshes, reedy ditches. **RANGE** Ra/sc **WV** N,C,S,E Myanmar, Thailand (except SE,S), Cambodia, N,S Laos, E Tonkin, C Annam, Cochinchina. **V** south-west Pen Malaysia, Singapore.

PLATE 72 GREATER FLAMINGO, IBISES & ADJUTANTS

1 GREATER FLAMINGO *Phoenicopterus ruber* 125–145 cm
(**a**) **Adult** *roseus*: Large; mostly pinkish-white, very long neck, very long pinkish legs, broad, downward-kinked, deep pink bill with black tip. In flight, pinkish-red upper-/underwing-coverts, blackish flight feathers. (**b**) **Juvenile**: Mostly brownish-greyish, dark streaks on scapulars and coverts, browner flight feathers, pale greyish bill with blackish tip, dark brownish legs. Shorter neck/legs than adult, pink restricted to flush on underwing-coverts. **VOICE** Repeated goose-like honking *ka-ha* in flight; softer *kuk-kuk ke-kuk kuk-kuk..* when foraging. **HABITAT** Shallow, mainly brackish lowland lakes/lagoons, sometimes mudflats, saltpans. **RANGE FO** (status?) Cambodia (Tonle Sap).

2 GLOSSY IBIS *Plegadis falcinellus* 55–65 cm
(**a,b**) **Adult non-breeding** *falcinellus*: Mostly uniform dark brownish (slightly purplish-tinged), white-streaked head/neck, green-glossed scapulars/coverts. Pale brownish bill, dark brownish legs, dark facial skin bordered above and below by white lines. In flight, bulbous head, thin neck, all-dark wings. (**c**) **Adult breeding**: Mostly deep chestnut head/neck/body, green-glossed forecrown, purplish tinge to much of plumage, no head/neck-streaks, bolder white facial lines; bill mostly flesh-coloured. **Juvenile**: Duller than adult non-breeding, dense whitish mottling on head/neck, whitish throat, no facial lines, little greenish gloss above. **VOICE** Low harsh *graa*, subdued grunting in flight. **HABITAT & BEHAVIOUR** Marshy wetlands; up to 800 m. Flies with rapid wingbeats, then glides. **RANGE** Ra/lc **R** Cambodia, Cochinchina. **FR** (currently?) C Myanmar. Ra/lo **WV/NBV** SW,S,E Myanmar. **V** C,S Thailand, Singapore.

3 BLACK-HEADED IBIS *Threskiornis melanocephalus* 75 cm
(**a,b**) **Adult non-breeding**: White; blackish bill, naked head, upper neck and legs. In flight, reddish skin shows through underwing-coverts. **Adult breeding**: Yellowish wash on mantle and breast, greyish wash on scapulars/tertials, white plumes extend from lower neck, longer tertials. **Juvenile**: Brownish to greyish-white feathers on head/neck, black edges/tips to outer primaries, blackish skin shows through underwing-coverts. **VOICE** Vibrant grunting at colonies. **HABITAT** Marshy wetlands, mudflats, mangroves; up to 800 m. **RANGE** Sc/lo **R** Cambodia, Cochinchina. **FR** C Thailand. Ra/lo **NBV/WV** Myanmar (except W,N), W,C,NE,SE,S Thailand, E Tonkin (breeds?). **V** west Pen Malaysia (formerly more frequent), C,S Laos, C Annam.

4 RED-NAPED IBIS *Pseudibis papillosa* 62–72 cm
(**a,b**) **Adult**: Smaller than White-shouldered, shorter bill, no collar, red patch on hindcrown/nape. (**c**) **Juvenile**: Like White-shouldered but head/neck uniform dark brown (feathered). **VOICE** Repeated loud, nasal scream. **HABITAT** Lakes, large rivers, open areas, cultivation; lowlands. **RANGE** Sc **R** SW Myanmar.

5 WHITE-SHOULDERED IBIS *Pseudibis davisoni* 75–85 cm
(**a,b**) **Adult**: Large, mostly dark brownish; long, downcurved greyish bill, dull red legs, white collar (faintly bluish). Naked blackish head, dark greenish-blue gloss on upperwing. In flight, white patch on inner lesser upperwing-coverts. **Juvenile**: Duller/browner, dirty white collar, less gloss on wings, shorter

bill, dull legs. Similar white wing-patch. **VOICE** Territorial calls include loud hoarse screams: *ERRRRRRH* or *ERRRRRRROH*, accompanied antiphonally by moaning, rhythmic *errb errb errb errb...* Screams mixed with honking: *errrrb OWK OWK OWK OWK..* and more subdued *ohhaaa ohhaaa..* and *errrr-ah*. **HABITAT** Pools, streams and marshy areas in open lowland forest. **RANGE** Ra **R** Cambodia, S Laos, Cochinchina; formerly NW,C,S Thailand, N,C Laos. **FR** (currently?) SW,S,C Myanmar, Tenasserim. **Rc** (status?) C Annam.

6 GIANT IBIS *Pseudibis gigantea* 102–106.5 cm
(**a,b**) **Adult**: Huge; long pale horn bill, bare greyish head/neck with black bars at rear, mostly blackish-slate body, grey wings with black feather-tips. Faint greenish gloss on body, deep red eyes/legs. In flight, contrasting upperwing, all-dark underwing. **Juvenile**: Short black feathers on back of head/neck, shorter bill, brown eyes. **HABITAT** Pools, streams and marshy areas in open lowland forest. **RANGE** Ra **R** Cambodia, S Laos, north-west S Annam; formerly C,W Thailand, Cochinchina. **FO** (status?) Thailand, C Laos.

7 LESSER ADJUTANT *Leptoptilos javanicus* 122.5–129 cm
(**a**) **Male non-breeding**: Very large; big bill, bare head/neck, black above. Mostly horn bill with straight culmen, head/neck-skin mostly yellowish, more vinous-tinged head-sides, pale forehead, dark greyish legs. In flight, all-blackish wings with white patch on inner underwing-coverts. (**b**) **Male breeding**: Oval coppery spots near median covert tips, thin whitish edges to lower scapulars, tertials and inner greater coverts; head-sides redder. **Female**: As male non-breeding but shorter, with less massive bill. **Juvenile**: Duller above, downier head/neck. **VOICE** Deep guttural sounds at nest. **HABITAT & BEHAVIOUR** Freshwater marshes and pools in or near open forest, freshwater swamp forest, mangroves, sometimes rice paddies and open areas including mudflats. Flies with neck retracted. **RANGE** Ra **R** Tenasserim, S Thailand, Pen Malaysia, Cambodia, S Laos, C,S Annam, Cochinchina; formerly C Laos. **FB** (currently?) S Myanmar. Ra/sc **NBV** C,SE Thailand. Sc (status?) N Myanmar. **FO** (status?) SW,C Myanmar. **V/ra NBV** Singapore (**FR**).

8 GREATER ADJUTANT *Leptoptilos dubius* 145–150 cm
(**a**) **Adult non-breeding**: Larger than Lesser, deeper bill (culmen convex), more uniform pinkish head/neck, large drooping neck-pouch, white neck-ruff, greyer above with still paler, greyer greater coverts/tertials; greyer underwing with more whitish markings on coverts, sooty-grey undertail-coverts. (**b**) **Adult breeding**: Blacker face, redder head/neck, paler, bluer-grey above, bright saffron-yellow neck-pouch. **Juvenile**: Bill narrower (more like adult Lesser), denser pale brownish to grey down on head/neck, wings all dark but soon with paler underwing-coverts and brown band across greater coverts/tertials. **VOICE** Loud grunting, croaking and roaring at nest. **HABITAT** Freshwater marshes/pools in or near open drier forests, swamp forest, sometimes rice paddies, open areas; lowlands. **RANGE** Ra **R** Cambodia; formerly NW,C,SE Thailand, S Annam, Cochinchina. **FB** (currently?) S Myanmar, Tenasserim. **FO** (status?) SW,N,C,E Myanmar. Ra **NBV** W,C,NE Thailand, S Laos, C Annam, Cochinchina. **V** S Thailand.

7 and 8 to different scale

PLATE 73 STORKS

1 MILKY STORK *Mycteria cinerea* 92–97 cm
(**a,b**) **Adult non-breeding**: Resembles Painted but all white, apart from blackish primaries, secondaries and tail, limited dark red head-skin. Bill pale pinkish-yellow, legs dull pinkish-red. (**c**) **Adult breeding**: White parts of plumage suffused very pale creamy-buffish, bill bright yellow to orange-yellow, bare head brighter red, legs deep magenta. (**d,e**) **Juvenile**: Similar to Painted but browner, more uniform head and neck, paler lesser and median upperwing-coverts (hardly contrasting with mantle), no defined darker breast-band, slightly less extensive naked head-skin. In flight, off-whitish tips to underwing-coverts create overall paler appearance. **HABITAT** Tidal mudflats, mangroves. **RANGE** Ra/lo **R** west Pen Malaysia, Cambodia. **FR** (currently?) Cochinchina. Ra **NBV** C Thailand. **V** (or escapee?) Singapore. **FO** (status?) extreme S(west) Thailand.

2 PAINTED STORK *Mycteria leucocephala* 93–102 cm
(**a,b**) **Adult non-breeding**: Mostly white with black-and-white median/lesser coverts and breast-band, pink-washed inner greater coverts/tertials, blackish flight feathers/tail. Long thick pinkish-yellow bill droops at tip, naked orange-red head, pinkish-/brownish-red legs. In flight, white-barred black underwing-coverts. (**c**) **Adult breeding**: Bare head redder, bill pinkish-peach, legs brighter reddish-magenta, brighter pink on tertials etc. (**d,e**) **Juvenile**: Head/neck pale greyish-brown with whitish streaks, head-skin dull yellowish, limited to patch around eye to throat, mantle/greater coverts pale greyish-brown with whitish fringes, lesser/median coverts clearly darker, with whitish fringes, back to uppertail-coverts creamy-whitish; faint but defined dusky breast-band. Often a slight pinkish suffusion on tertials. In flight, uniformly dark underwing-coverts. **HABITAT** Marshes, lakes, freshwater swamp forest, sometimes rice paddies; up to 1,000 m. **RANGE** Ra/lo **R** (some movements) S Thailand (**E**?), Cambodia; formerly C,S Annam, Cochinchina. **FR** (currently?) C Myanmar. Ra/sc **NBV** (mainly winter) SW,S,C,E Myanmar, Tenasserim, W,C,NE,SE Thailand, Laos, E Tonkin, C,S Annam, Cochinchina. Ra/sc **PM** W,C Thailand. **V** Pen Malaysia, E Tonkin.

3 ASIAN OPENBILL *Anastomus oscitans* 68–81 cm
(**a,b**) **Adult non-breeding**: Dull horn/greyish bill with gap between mandibles. Relatively small, mostly dull greyish-white (including head), contrasting glossy black lower scapulars, tertials, primaries, secondaries and tail. Legs pinkish to greyish-pink. **Adult breeding**: Whiter with redder legs at onset of breeding season. **Juvenile**: Like adult non-breeding but brownish-grey head/neck/mantle/scapulars/breast, brownish bill (initially shorter with no space between mandibles), duller legs. **HABITAT** Freshwater marshes, rice paddies, cultivation ditches. **RANGE** Sc/lo **R** (some movements) C Thailand, Cambodia, Cochinchina. Sc/lfc **NBV** Myanmar, W,NW,C,NE Thailand, S Laos. Also **PM** SW Myanmar. **V** S Thailand.

4 BLACK STORK *Ciconia nigra* 95–100 cm
(**a,b**) **Adult**: Glossy greenish-/purplish-black, with white lower breast to undertail-coverts and inner underwing-coverts. Bill, orbital skin and legs red. **Juvenile**: Patterned like adult but dark parts mostly dark brown, white parts somewhat duller. Pale

brown flecks on neck/breast, pale brown tips to scapulars and coverts, mostly dull greyish-olive bill, orbital skin and legs. **HABITAT** Freshwater marshes, pools, ditches, rivers, cultivation, open areas; up to 1,525 m. **RANGE** Ra/un **WV** W,N(lc),C,E,S Myanmar, NW Thailand, N,C Laos, E Tonkin. **V** Cambodia.

5 WOOLLY-NECKED STORK *Ciconia episcopus* 75–91 cm
(**a,b**) **Adult** *episcopus*: Glossy purplish-/greenish-black, with black cap and white neck and vent. Bill blackish with some dark red at tip and along culmen; facial skin dark grey, legs dull red, bronzy area along inner upperwing-coverts, short, forked black tail (looks white due to extended undertail-coverts). **Juvenile**: Dark parts of plumage mostly dull brown, feathered forehead, duller bill and legs. **HABITAT** Marshes, freshwater swamp forest, pools and streams in open forest. **RANGE** Ra/lfc **R** N,C,S Myanmar, W(south),SE,S(north) Thailand, Cambodia, S Laos, C,S Annam, Cochinchina; formerly NW,C,NE,S(southern) Thailand. **FR** (currently?) SW,E Myanmar, Tenasserim, N,C Laos. **Rc** (status?) W Tonkin. **FO** (status?) north-west Pen Malaysia (Langkawi I).

6 STORM'S STORK *Ciconia stormi* 75–91 cm
(**a,b**) **Adult**: Similar to Woolly-necked but bill bright red, facial skin dull orange with broad golden-yellow around eye, lower foreneck glossy black, no bronzy area along inner wing-coverts. **Juvenile**: Blackish parts browner, bill dark-tipped, facial skin and legs duller. **HABITAT & BEHAVIOUR** Freshwater swamp forest, rivers, streams and pools in broadleaved evergreen forest; lowlands. Solitary or in pairs; rarely in small loose groups. **RANGE** Ra/sc **R** S Thailand (**E**?), Pen Malaysia.

7 WHITE STORK *Ciconia ciconia* 100–115 cm
(**a,b**) **Adult** *asiatica*?: Like Milky and Asian Openbill but straight, pointed red bill, red legs. All white (including head and tail), apart from black lower scapulars, tertials, greater coverts and flight feathers. **Juvenile**: Browner greater upperwing-coverts, brownish-red bill and legs. **HABITAT** Marshes, rice paddies, open areas; recorded in lowlands. **RANGE** **V** C Thailand.

8 BLACK-NECKED STORK *Ephippiorhynchus asiaticus* 121–135 cm
(**a**) **Female** *asiaticus*: Huge and mostly white, with glossy black head, neck, back to tail, greater and median coverts, tertials and lower scapulars. Distinctly long black bill, very long red legs, strong blue to greenish and purplish gloss on black of plumage (particularly head/neck), bright yellow eyes. In flight, white wings with broad black central band (above and below). (**b**) **Male**: Brown eyes. (**c,d**) **Juvenile**: Head, neck and upperparts dull brown with whitish lower back to base of tail, flight feathers blackish-brown, rest of underparts whitish, bill dark olive-brown, legs dull olive. In flight, all-dark wings. Gradually attains adult plumage and soon shows suggestion of distinctive adult wing pattern. **HABITAT** Freshwater marshes, marshy areas and pools in open forest, rarely also mud-/sandflats; up to 1,200 m. **RANGE** Ra/sc **R** N Myanmar, west S Thailand (almost **E**), Cambodia, S Laos, north-west S Annam; formerly NW,C Thailand, C Annam, Cochinchina. **FR** (currently?) C,E,S Myanmar. **FO** (status?) SW Myanmar, N,C Laos.

PLATE 74 TROPICBIRDS, BOOBIES, PETRELS, SHEARWATERS & STORM-PETRELS

1 RED-BILLED TROPICBIRD *Phaethon aethereus* 46–51 cm (tail <56+ more) (**a,b**) **Adult** *indicus*: Barred black above, largely black primary coverts, orange-red bill. (**c**) **Juvenile**: Densely barred blackish above, diffuse blackish nuchal band, small black spots on tail-tip, yellowish-cream bill with dark tip. HABITAT Open seas, islets. RANGE Offshore/coastal **V** S Myanmar (including Coco Is), south Tenasserim; all old sight records (doubtful?). Rc (said to breed) Cochinchina (Con Dao Is).

2 RED-TAILED TROPICBIRD *Phaethon rubricauda* 47 cm (tail <35 more) (**a,b**) **Adult** *westralis*?: Red bill and tail-streamers, almost completely white plumage. Narrow black mask, blackish shafts-streaks on primaries, primary coverts, innermost wing-coverts, inner secondaries and outertail, black chevrons on tertials. Often flushed pink. (**c**) **Juvenile**: Greyish to blackish bill, no obvious black on primaries/primary coverts. HABITAT Open seas, islets. RANGE **V** west S Thailand.

3 WHITE-TAILED TROPICBIRD *Phaethon lepturus* 38–41 cm (tail <40 more) (**a,b**) **Adult** *lepturus*: White above with broad black bar across upperwing, white primary coverts. (**c**) **Juvenile**: Sparsely barred/scaled blackish above, some blackish spots/bars on crown, small black spots on tail-tip, yellowish-cream bill with faint dark tip. HABITAT Open seas, islets. RANGE Offshore/coastal **V** south-east S Thailand; Myanmar?

4 MASKED BOOBY *Sula dactylatra* 74–86 cm (**a**) **Adult** *personata*: White, with blackish face, flight feathers and tail, yellowish bill, greyish feet. (**b**) **Juvenile**: Head, neck and upperside warmish brown, flight feathers browner, white hind-collar, white underwing-coverts with defined dark central band. HABITAT Open seas, islets. RANGE Ra offshore/coastal **VS** Pen Malaysia (**FB** Pulau Perak). Offshore/coastal **V** W,S Thailand. Reported to breed Cochinchina (Con Dao Is).

5 RED-FOOTED BOOBY *Sula sula* 68–72.5 cm (**a**) **Adult white morph** *rubripes*: Light blue-grey and pinkish bill/facial skin, red feet, white tertials/tail. May have apricot flush (particularly hindcrown/-neck). (**b**) **Adult intermediate morph**: Brown mantle/back/coverts (above and below). **Adult brown morph**: Like juvenile but bill/facial skin/feet as adult white morph. May show apricot flush on crown/hindneck. (**c**) **Juvenile**: Dark greyish-brown overall, dark grey bill, purplish facial skin, yellowish-grey/pinkish feet. (**d**) **Immature white morph**: Untidy whitish areas on head/body/underwing-coverts, darker breast-band. HABITAT Open seas, oceanic islets; rarely coastal waters. RANGE Coastal/offshore **V** west S Thailand.

6 BROWN BOOBY *Sula leucogaster* 73–83 cm (**a,b**) **Adult** *plotus*: Dark brown with white lower breast/vent, yellowish bill, pale yellowish feet, white underwing-coverts with dark leading edge and broken diagonal bar. (**c**) **Juvenile**: Duller, browner belly/vent/underwing-coverts, pale bluish-grey bill, pinker feet. VOICE At breeding colonies, goose-like whistling hiss and *koe-el* calls (male); honking quacks and crow-like

growling (female). HABITAT Open seas, islets. RANGE Sc offshore **R** west Pen Malaysia (Pulau Perak), Cochinchina (Con Dao Is). Offshore/coastal **V** Tenasserim, SE,C,S Thailand, Pen Malaysia, Singapore, C,S Annam; formerly more frequent.

7 BULWER'S PETREL *Bulweria bulwerii* 26–27 cm (**a,b**) **Adult**: Larger than Swinhoe's Storm-petrel, longer wings and long, graduated tail (usually closed in flight), indistinct paler band across upperwing-coverts, otherwise all dark. HABITAT & BEHAVIOUR Open seas. Flight buoyant and erratic with wings usually held forward and slightly bowed, usually close to water surface; in windy conditions, flies with faster wingbeats and glides in shallow arcs. RANGE Offshore **V** south-east Pen Malaysia.

8 STREAKED SHEARWATER *Calonectris leucomelas* 48.5 cm (**a,b**) **Adult**: Relatively large; white head with dark streaking on crown, nape and ear-coverts, white underwing-coverts with dark patches on primary coverts. HABITAT & BEHAVIOUR Open seas; very rarely inland. During calm conditions, flight direct but rather languid, with outer wing slightly angled backward; often glides on bowed wings. RANGE **V** NE Thailand; offshore west S Thailand, west Pen Malaysia, C Annam, Cochinchina.

9 WEDGE-TAILED SHEARWATER *Puffinus pacificus* 43.5 cm (**a,b**) **Adult pale morph**: All-dark crown and face, dark above, mostly white underwing-coverts, tail rather pointed. (**c**) **Adult dark morph**: Broad-winged, longish pointed tail, rather uniformly dark underwing, pinkish feet. HABITAT & BEHAVIOUR Open seas. In calm weather, flight rather lazy, with much gliding and banking, wings held forward and bowed. RANGE Offshore/coastal **V** C Thailand, west Pen Malaysia, Singapore.

10 SHORT-TAILED SHEARWATER *P.tenuirostris* 41–43 cm (**a,b**) **Adult**: Relatively small; short squarish tail (toes extend beyond tail-tip), dark overall, with pale chin, paler breast and belly and silvery underwing with dark base and surround; dark feet. HABITAT & BEHAVIOUR Open seas. Flight direct, consisting of a flapping rise followed by a long downward glide. RANGE Offshore **V** C, west S Thailand, Singapore (inland).

11 WILSON'S STORM-PETREL *Oceanites oceanicus* 17 cm (**a,b**) **Adult** *oceanicus*: Small and blackish; pale band across upperwing-coverts, white rump and uppertail-coverts to vent sides, fairly short square-cut tail, paler band along underwing-coverts. VOICE Occasional soft, rapid squeaking or chattering when feeding. HABITAT & BEHAVIOUR Open seas. Flight quite direct and purposeful but skips and bounds close to water surface when feeding. RANGE Offshore/coastal **V** Tenasserim, west Pen Malaysia.

12 SWINHOE'S STORM-PETREL *Oceanodroma monorhis* 20 cm (**a,b**) **Adult**: Small size, forked tail, all-dark body. Upperwing has contrasting paler diagonal bar across coverts and indistinct whitish shaft-streaks on base of primaries, underwing uniformly dark. HABITAT & BEHAVIOUR Open seas, sometimes inshore. Erratic swooping, bounding flight pattern. RANGE Sc/lc offshore **NBV** (spring and autumn) Pen Malaysia, Singapore. **V** S Thailand.

1–3 to different scale

7–12 to different scale

PLATE 75 PITTAS

1 EARED PITTA *Pitta phayrei* 20–24 cm
(**a**) **Male**: Blackish crown/head-sides/nape, elongated buffy-white supercilium; buffish below with dark scales. (**b**) **Female**: Browner head, heavier markings below. **Juvenile**: Duller than female, all-buffish crown-side/supercilium, short 'ears', no sub-moustachial, dark brown breast with rufous shaft-streaks. **VOICE** Airy whistled *wheeow-whit*. **HABITAT** Broadleaved evergreen and mixed deciduous forest, bamboo; up to 900 m, sometimes 1,500 m. **RANGE** Un R C,S,E Myanmar, north Tenasserim, W,NW,NE,SE Thailand, Cambodia, Laos, W,E Tonkin, C Annam.

2 BLUE-NAPED PITTA *Pitta nipalensis* 22–26 cm
(**a**) **Male** *nipalensis*: Rufous forehead/head-sides, no blue on lower back/rump. (**b**) **Female**: Green hindcrown/upper mantle; more rufescent forehead/head-sides than Blue-rumped. (**c**) **Juvenile**: Relatively pale/buffy covert-spots, weak/buffy crown markings, buffish ear-coverts. **Other subspecies** *P.n.bendeei* (north Indochina): Male has blue confined to neat nape-patch; female browner hindcrown, green confined to neat nape-patch. **VOICE** Clear *uk-WUIP* or *ip-WUI'IP* song. **HABITAT** Broadleaved evergreen forest, secondary growth; up to 1,400 m. **RANGE** Sc/un R SW,W,N,S Myanmar, N,C Laos, W,E Tonkin.

3 BLUE-RUMPED PITTA *Pitta soror* 20–22 cm
(**a**) **Male** *petersi*: Blue back/rump, pale blue crown/nape, mostly lilac-pinkish head-sides. (**b**) **Female**: Duller; greenish crown/nape, browner above. (**c**) **Juvenile**: Head-sides/throat buffier than Rusty-naped, richer marks above, lighter breast marks. (**d**) **Male** *tonkinensis* (north Tonkin): Green crown and nape (faintly blue). **Other subspecies** *P.s.flynnstonei* (SE Thailand, Cambodia); *annamensis* (S Laos, C Annam); *soror* (S Annam, Cochinchina). **VOICE** Full, slightly inflected *weaoe* or *weeya*. Short *ppew* or *cho*. **HABITAT** Broadleaved evergreen forest, sometimes mixed deciduous; up to 1,700 m (>900 m SE Thailand; <1,000 m Indochina [except W Tonkin]). **RANGE** Fc/co R SE Thailand (lo), Indochina (except N Laos).

4 RUSTY-NAPED PITTA *Pitta oatesi* 21–25 cm
(**a**) **Male** *oatesi*: Deep rufous head/underparts, thin blackish postocular stripe. **Female**: Duller; browner above, faint dark scales on lower throat/upper breast. (**b**) **Juvenile**: Dark brown above/on breast, whitish crown-streaks, whitish-buff spots elsewhere; whitish-buff supercilium, whitish head-sides/throat (faint dark streaks on former). **Other subspecies** *P.o.bolovenensis* (S Laos, ? S Annam): Bright blue on back/rump (sometimes mantle-wash), pinker below. *P.o.deborah* (Pen Malaysia, ? S Thailand): Blue rump, strongly pinkish below. *P.o.castaneiceps* (C Laos, W Tonkin, ? N Annam). **VOICE** Sharp *chow-whit*. **HABITAT** Broadleaved evergreen forest; 380–2,565 m. **RANGE** Un/fc R N,S,E Myanmar, Tenasserim, W,NW,NE,extreme S Thailand, Pen Malaysia, Laos, W,E Tonkin, N,S Annam.

5 GIANT PITTA *Pitta caerulea* 28–29 cm
(**a**) **Male** *caerulea*: Large; black crown-centre/nape/eyestripe, blue above. (**b**) **Female**: Base-colour of head warm buffish-brown, crown-centre scaled, rufescent-brown above, blue lower rump/tail. (**c**) **Juvenile**: Dark brown above, whitish below with

smudgy breast-band, faintly scaled head and upper breast. **VOICE** Song is loud, airy *hwoo-er* or *whee-er*. **HABITAT** Broadleaved evergreen forest, bamboo; up to 200 m. **RANGE** Ra/sc R south Tenasserim, S Thailand, Pen Malaysia.

6 BLUE PITTA *Pitta cyanea* 19.5–24 cm
(**a**) **Male** *cyanea*: Blue above, vivid red rear crown-side/nape, bluish-whitish below, spotted/barred black. (**b**) **Female**: Dull; browner above. (**c**) **Juvenile**: Buffish-brown crown/nape with darker scales and crown-/eyestripe, mostly dark brown body with warm buff streaks. **Other subspecies** *P.c.aurantiaca* (Thailand, south-west Cambodia): More yellowish-orange on head. *P.c.willoughbyi* (C Laos, S Annam): Brighter; often red on breast. **VOICE** Loud *peroo-whit* (*peroo* drawn-out, *whit* louder, sharper). Harsh *skyeew* in alarm. **HABITAT** Broadleaved evergreen and moister mixed deciduous forest; up to 1,890 m. **RANGE** Un/lc R SW,S,E Myanmar, Tenasserim, W,N,NE,SE, north S Thailand, Cambodia, Laos, E Tonkin, N,C,S Annam.

7 BANDED PITTA *Pitta guajana* 21–24 cm
(**a**) **Male** *irena*: Bright yellow to vivid orange-red supercilium to nape, blue-black breast/vent, white wing-band. (**b**) **Female**: Whitish below with narrow dark bars; less orange-red on nape. (**c**) **Juvenile**: Duller than female, dark brown breast with buff spots/streaks. **VOICE** Song is short *pouw* or *poww*. Sudden whirring *kirr* or *pprrr* in alarm. **HABITAT** Broadleaved evergreen forest, secondary forest; up to 610 m. **RANGE** Un/lc R S Thailand, Pen Malaysia.

8 BAR-BELLIED PITTA *Pitta elliotii* 19.5–21 cm
(**a**) **Male**: Green above, largely yellow below with narrow dark bars. (**b**) **Female**: Buffy-brown crown/breast, blackish head-sides with buffish streaks. (**c**) **Juvenile**: Brown, with darker head-sides, paler throat, pale buff spots above/on breast. **VOICE** Loud whistled *chawee-wu*. Harsh, shrill *jeeow* or *jow* in alarm. **HABITAT** Broadleaved forest, bamboo; up to 800 m. **RANGE** Fc/co R NE(south-east),SE Thailand (sc), Indochina.

9 GURNEY'S PITTA *Pitta gurneyi* 18.5–20.5 cm
(**a**) **Male**: Blue crown/nape, black forecrown/head-sides, black below, black-barred yellow sides. (**b**) **Female**: Buffy-rufous crown/nape, blackish-brown head-sides, mostly buffy-whitish below with dark bars. (**c**) **Juvenile**: Dark brown forehead to nape and dark brown breast/upper belly with buff streaks. **VOICE** Song is short, explosive *lilip*. Harsh falling *skyeew* in alarm. **HABITAT** Broadleaved evergreen forest, secondary forest, old rubber plantations; up to 160 m. **RANGE** Ra/lo R south Tenasserim, S Thailand.

10 GARNET PITTA *Pitta granatina* 14–16.5 cm
(**a**) **Adult** *coccinea*: Black head-sides/throat, scarlet crown and nape, crimson belly/vent. (**b**) **Juvenile**: Dark brown with paler throat, some red on nape/vent, duller coverts/tail. **VOICE** Clear whistle lasting c.1.5 s (swells in volume). Like Rail-babbler but upward inflection, sudden end. **HABITAT** Broadleaved evergreen forest; up to 300 m. **RANGE** Un/lc R south Tenasserim, extreme S Thailand, Pen Malaysia; formerly Singapore.

1a 1b 2a 2b 2c 3a 3b 3c 3d 4a 4b 5a 5b 5c 6a 6b 6c 7a 7b 7c 8a 8b 8c 9a 9b 9c 10a 10b

PLATE 76 PITTAS & BROADBILLS

1 HOODED PITTA *Pitta sordida* 16.5–19 cm
(**a,b**) **Adult** *cucullata*: Black head, brown crown/nape, green body. (**c**) **Juvenile**: Browner above, whitish throat, brownish below. **Other subspecies** *P.s.muelleri* (extreme S Thailand, north Pen Malaysia): Black crown, more white on primaries. **VOICE** Song is perky *whep-whep* or *whew-whew*. Short squeaky *skyew* in alarm. **HABITAT** Broadleaved forest, old plantations; up to 915 m. **RANGE** Fc **R** extreme S Thailand, north Pen Malaysia. Un/lc **BV** Myanmar, W,NE,SE,S Thailand, Cambodia, N,S Laos, W Tonkin. Un/fc **PM** NW,C Thailand, Pen Malaysia (also winters), Singapore. **Rc** (status?) Cochinchina.

2 FAIRY PITTA *Pitta nympha* 16–19.5 cm
(**a,b**) **Adult**: Smaller than Blue-winged, rufous crown-sides, thin whitish-buff supercilium. **VOICE** Clear *kwah-he kwa-wu*, longer/slower than Blue-winged. **HABITAT** Broadleaved forest; up to 1,000 m. **RANGE** Ra **PM/V** E Tonkin, N,C Annam, Cochinchina.

3 BLUE-WINGED PITTA *Pitta moluccensis* 18–20.5 cm
(**a,b**) **Adult**: Blackish head with buff crown-sides/supercilium and white throat, plain buff below with red vent. (**c**) **Juvenile**: Duller; scaled crown-sides/supercilium, whiter chin. **VOICE** Song is loud, *taew-laew taew-laew* (*laew* stressed). Harsh *skyeew* in alarm. **HABITAT** Relatively open broadleaved forests; also parks, gardens and mangroves on migration; up to 800 m. **RANGE** Fc/co **BV** (rarely winters) Myanmar (except W,N), Thailand (except C), north Pen Malaysia, Cambodia, Laos, C,S Annam, Cochinchina. Un/fc **WV** and **PM** Pen Malaysia, Singapore. Sc/fc **PM** W,C,S Thailand, Cambodia, E Tonkin.

4 MANGROVE PITTA *Pitta megarhyncha* 18–21 cm
(**a**) **Adult**: Bill longer than Blue-winged, drabber crown, slightly duller below, whitish chin. (**b**) **Juvenile**: Duller. From Blue-winged as adult. **VOICE** Like Blue-winged but more slurred, hurried: *wieuw-wieuw*. **HABITAT** Mangroves. **RANGE** Sc/lc coastal **R** Myanmar, west S Thailand, Pen Malaysia, Singapore.

5 GREEN BROADBILL *Calyptomena viridis* 15–17 cm
(**a**) **Male** *continentis*: Chunky; green with black ear-patch and bars on coverts. (**b**) **Female**: Duller, with no black. **Juvenile**: As female but breast paler, vent greenish-white. **VOICE** Bubbling trill, increasing in tempo: *toi toi-oi-oi-oi-oick*. Also *goik-goik*, frog-like bubbling *oo-turrr*, mournful whistles. **HABITAT** Broadleaved evergreen forest; up to 1,300 m. **RANGE** Un/lc **R** Tenasserim, W,S Thailand, Pen Malaysia; formerly Singapore.

6 BLACK-AND-RED BROADBILL *Cymbirhynchus macrorhynchos* 23 cm
(**a**) **Adult** *malaccensis*: Black and maroon-red; white wing-streak, bright bill. (**b**) **Juvenile**: Browner; spotted coverts. **Other subspecies** *C.m.affinis* (SW,S Myanmar): Smaller, redder; red tertial spots, more white at base of primaries (closed wing), dark rump-fringing; paler belly/vent. **VOICE** Accelerating cicada-like notes. Rasping *wiark* and rapid *pip* notes. **HABITAT** Broadleaved forests near water, mangroves; up to 300 m. **RANGE** Un/lc **R** SW,S Myanmar, Tenasserim, W,SE,S Thailand, Pen Malaysia, Cambodia, S Laos, Cochinchina; formerly NE(south) Thailand, Singapore.

7 LONG-TAILED BROADBILL *Psarisomus dalhousiae* 26 cm
(**a**) **Adult** *dalhousiae*: Mostly green; long blue tail, black and yellow/greenish-yellow head, blue on crown and nape. (**b**) **Juvenile**: Dark green crown/nape/ear-coverts, more uniformly green below. **Other subspecies** *P.d.psittacinus* (extreme S Thailand, Pen Malaysia); *cyanicauda* (SE Thailand, Cambodia, S Annam). **VOICE** Loud, high-pitched, piercing whistles, *tseeay* or *pseew*. Sometimes single sharp *tseeay* and rasping *psweep*. **HABITAT** Broadleaved evergreen forest; 500–2,000 m, locally to 50 m. **RANGE** Un/lc **R** (except C Thailand, Singapore, Cochinchina).

8 SILVER-BREASTED BROADBILL *Serilophus lunatus* 17 cm
(**a**) **Male** *lunatus*: Greyish-brown above, greyish-white below, black supercilium. (**b**) **Female**: Thin whitish necklace. (**c**) **Male** *rubropygius* (SW,W,N Myanmar): Grey crown to mantle, dark grey supercilium, less blue on wing. **Female**: Necklace broken in centre. **Other subspecies** *S.l.rothschildi* (extreme S Thailand southwards): Greyer crown/head-sides/throat/breast, more rufous-chestnut back to uppertail-coverts and tertials. *S.l.elisabethae* (E Myanmar, NE,SE Thailand, northern Indochina); *impavidus* (S Laos); *stolidus* (southern Tenasserim, northern S Thailand). **VOICE** Melancholy *pee-uu* (*uu* lower). Staccato trilled *kitikitikit...* **HABITAT** Broadleaved evergreen forest; 50–2,230 m. **RANGE** Un/lc **R** (except C Thailand, Singapore, Cochinchina).

9 BANDED BROADBILL *Eurylaimus javanicus* 22–23 cm
(**a**) **Male** *harterti*: Dull vinous-reddish head/underparts, dark above with yellow marks, blackish breast-band. (**b**) **Female**: No breast-band. (**c**) **Juvenile**: Paler and streaked below, browner crown/head-sides, yellow eyebrow, spots and streaks on mantle and tips to coverts. **VOICE** Sharp whistled *wheeoo*, followed by loud rising frantic notes. Brief, rather nasal *whee-u* (*ee* stressed), falling *kyeeow*, yelping *keek-eek-eek*. **HABITAT** Broadleaved forests; up to 1,100 m. **RANGE** Un/lc **R** S Myanmar, Tenasserim, Thailand (except C), Pen Malaysia, Cambodia, Laos, S Annam, Cochinchina; formerly Singapore.

10 BLACK-AND-YELLOW BROADBILL *Eurylaimus ochromalus* 15 cm
(**a**) **Male** *ochromalus*: Black head and breast-band, white collar. (**b**) **Female**: Broken breast-band. (**c**) **Juvenile**: Largely whitish throat, yellowish eyebrow, streaked breast. **VOICE** Frantic notes, starting slowly (downslurred), then accelerating. Lacks introductory note of Banded, ends abruptly. Has similar *kyeeow* and *keowrr* notes. **HABITAT** Broadleaved evergreen forest; up to 700 m. **RANGE** Fc/co **R** Tenasserim, W,S Thailand, Pen Malaysia.

11 DUSKY BROADBILL *Corydon sumatranus* 25–28.5 cm
(**a**) **Adult** *laoensis*: Blackish-brown, buffy bib, dull reddish bill with greyish tip. (**b**) **Juvenile**: Browner; paler bill. **Other subspecies** *C.s.sumatranus* (extreme S Thailand southwards): **VOICE** 6–8 shrill upward-inflected thin whistles: *hi-ky-ui ky-ui ky-ui...* or *ky-ee ky-ee ky-ee ky-ee...* Shrill thin falling *pseeoo* and piercing high *tsiu*; sometimes repeated quavering *ch wit* in flight. **HABITAT** Broadleaved forests; up to 1,220 m. **RANGE** Un **R** S Myanmar, Tenasserim, Thailand (except C), Pen Malaysia, Cambodia, Laos, Vietnam (except W,E Tonkin).

PLATE 77 LEAFBIRDS & IORAS

1 GREATER GREEN LEAFBIRD *Chloropsis sonnerati* 20–22 cm
(**a**) **Male** *zosterops*: Stout bill, all-green plumage apart from
black face and bib and purple-blue malar band. Blue shoulder-
patch (usually hidden in field). (**b**) **Female**: Sharply demarcated yellow throat and eyering. Blue malar band faint. (**c**) **Juvenile**: Similar to female but blue malar band may be absent; has
yellowish submoustachial band. VOICE Sings with liquid musical
whistles, mixed with chattering notes, ***wi-i chaka-wiu chi-
wiu..*** etc. HABITAT Broadleaved evergreen forest; up to 915 m.
RANGE Fc/co **R** south Tenasserim, W(south),S Thailand, Pen
Malaysia, Singapore (scarce).

2 LESSER GREEN LEAFBIRD *Chloropsis cyanopogon*
16–19 cm
(**a**) **Male** *septentrionalis*: Very like Greater Green but smaller,
much smaller-billed; yellowish forehead/bib surround, no blue
shoulder-patch. (**b**) **Female**: All-green with golden-green forehead and blue/purplish-blue malar band. Somewhat deeper
green than Blue-winged, no blue on shoulder/wings/tail. (**c**)
Juvenile: Smaller/smaller-billed than Greater Green, less defined
yellow throat, no obvious eyering. (**d**) **Male** *cyanopogon*
(extreme S Thailand southwards): Much less yellow on fore-
head/bordering bib (more like Greater). HABITAT Broadleaved
evergreen forest; up to 700 m. RANGE Co **R** south Tenasserim,
W(south),S Thailand, Pen Malaysia, Singapore (sc).

3 BLUE-WINGED LEAFBIRD *Chloropsis cochinchinensis*
16.5–18.5 cm
(**a**) **Male** *chlorocephala*: Obvious turquoise-blue on wing and
tail, extensive yellow-bronze on head/breast. (**b**) **Female**: Blue
on wings/tail (less than male); more golden-tinged crown/nape
than Lesser, fainter malar band. (**c**) **Juvenile**: Like female but
almost no blue on face/malar, greener crown/nape. (**d**) **Male**
C.c.moluccensis (extreme S Thailand southwards): Even yellower forecrown and bib surround, more defined golden nape.
Female: Usually more defined golden nape than *chlorocephala*. **Other subspecies** *C.c.serithai* (S Thailand, ? southern
Tenasserim): Intermediate between *chlorocephala* and *moluc-
censis*. *C.c.cochinchinensis* (SE,NE[south] Thailand, southern
Indochina); *kinneari* (rest of NE Thailand, Indochina). VOICE
Sings with musical liquid ***pli-pli-chu-chu, chi-chi-pli-i*** etc.
Also high ***chi-chi-chi*** and ***chi'ii*** and slightly rattling ***pridit***.
HABITAT Broadleaved forests; up to 1,500 m. RANGE Co **R**
throughout; sc (status?) Singapore.

4 GOLDEN-FRONTED LEAFBIRD *C.aurifrons* 18–19 cm
(**a**) **Adult** *pridii*: Golden-orange forecrown, purple-blue throat
and malar, rather slender/downcurved bill. Broad yellowish lower
border to bib. (**b**) **Juvenile**: All green; purple-blue and black
malar, blue on shoulder, duller golden forehead. **Other subspecies** *C.a.incompta* (W[south] Thailand, S Laos, C,S Annam)
and *inornata* (W,C,NE,SE Thailand, Cambodia, Cochinchina): No
obvious yellow bib border. *C.a.aurifrons* (SW,W,N,C,S[west]
Myanmar). VOICE Song is complex, squeaky and scratchy but
quite melodious, including mimicry. HABITAT Dry dipterocarp and
mixed deciduous forest, sometimes broadleaved evergreen/semi-
evergreen forest; up to 1,220 m. RANGE Co **R** (except S Thailand,
Pen Malaysia, Singapore, W,E Tonkin).

5 ORANGE-BELLIED LEAFBIRD *Chloropsis hardwickii*
18.5–20.5 cm
(**a**) **Male** *hardwickii*: Yellowish-orange breast and vent. (**b**)
Female: Yellowish-orange abdomen-centre/undertail-coverts,
broad purplish-blue malar. (**c**) **Juvenile**: Light green below, little blue on malar, no blue on shoulder. (**d**) **Female** *melliana*
(C Laos, E Tonkin, N,C Annam): Green below, turquoise-tinged
forecrown/ear-coverts. **Male**: Slightly duller than *hardwickii*,
greyish-blue-tinged crown, darker blue on shoulder, more
bluish-purple upper breast. **Other subspecies** *C.b.malayana*
(Pen Malaysia). VOICE Sings with jumpy phrases of ***chip, tsi,
chit*** and ***chi*** notes; monotonous shrill ***shrittitit*** and ***shrit***
notes; monotonous ***chit-wiu chit-wiu chit-wiu..*** and mono-
dious ***chip-chip-chip-chip-irr chirriwu-i pichu-pi*** etc.
Loud ***chissick*** in flight. HABITAT Broadleaved evergreen forest;
200–2,135 m. RANGE Un/lc **R** Myanmar, W,NW,NE Thailand, Pen
Malaysia, N,C Laos, Vietnam (except Cochinchina).

6 COMMON IORA *Aegithina tiphia* 12–14.5 cm
(**a**) **Male non-breeding** *philipi*: Yellow below, olive-washed
flanks, rather deep olive-green above, blackish wings/tail, two
white/yellowish-white wing-bars. **Male breeding**: More vivid yellow below, no olive on flanks. (**b**) **Male breeding variant**: May
show black on mantle to rump. (**c**) **Female non-breeding**:
Paler/duller body than male non-breeding, duller wings and wing-
bars. **Female breeding**: Darker/brighter yellow below. **Juvenile**: Body slightly paler than female non-breeding, upper wing-
bar fainter. (**d**) **Male breeding** *deignani* (W,N,C,S[north]
Myanmar): Often black crown to back with yellow mixed on mantle. **Other subspecies** *A.t.tiphia* (SW Myanmar): May have
black-mottled crown. *A.t.horizoptera* (S Myanmar to W Thailand
and south): Often black hindcrown and mantle (sometimes on
rest of upperparts). *A.t.cambodiana* (SE Thailand to S Annam,
Cochinchina): Sometimes black on crown/nape. VOICE Song is thin
drawn-out ***whiiiiii piu***. Also whistled ***di-di-dwiu*** and ***du-i
du-i*** etc., and low harsh chattering. HABITAT Open forest, mangroves, secondary growth, parks, gardens etc.; up to 1,500 m.
RANGE Co **R** throughout.

7 GREEN IORA *Aegithina viridissima* 12.5–14.5 cm
(**a**) **Male** *viridissima*: Dark olive-green body, yellow vent, dark
lores, yellow eyering. (**b**) **Female**: Greener than Common, faint
eyering, yellow wing-bars. **Juvenile** Duller than female. VOICE
Song is thin ***tsiiiu tsii-tu*** or ***itsu tsi-tu tsi-tu***. Chattering
tit-teeer, low ***chititititit***. HABITAT Broadleaved evergreen forest; up to 825 m. RANGE Un/co **R** south Tenasserim, W(south),S
Thailand, Pen Malaysia; formerly Singapore.

8 GREAT IORA *Aegithina lafresnayei* 15.5–17 cm
(**a**) **Male** *innotata*: Large size and bill, plain wings. Dark olive-
green above, bright yellow below. **Female**: Slightly paler above,
slightly duller below. (**b**) **Juvenile**: As female but duller and
washed olive below. (**c**) **Male** *lafresnayei* (S Thailand southward): Black above. (**d**) **Male variant**: Less black. **Other subspecies** *A.l.xanthotis* (Cambodia, southern Vietnam):
Paler/brighter green above. VOICE Clear ***chew chew chew
chew..*** song. HABITAT Broadleaf forest; up to 900 m. RANGE Co **R**
SW Myanmar, Tenasserim, Thailand, Pen Malaysia, Indochina.

PLATE 78 ASIAN FAIRY BLUEBIRD, SHRIKES & RAIL-BABBLER

1 ASIAN FAIRY BLUEBIRD *Irena puella* 24.5–26.5 cm
(**a**) **Male** *puella*: Shining deep blue and black. Eyes red. (**b**) **Female**: Dull turquoise-blue, blackish tail/flight feathers, reddish eyes. **Juvenile**: As female but duller, wings browner. **Other subspecies** *I.p.malayensis* (extreme S Thailand southwards). **VOICE** Loud liquid ***tu-lip wae-waet-oo***, and ***wi-it***, ***wait***, ***pip*** etc.; quavering ***u-iu***. **HABITAT** Broadleaved forest; up to 1,525 m. **RANGE** Fc/co **R** (except C Thailand).

2 TIGER SHRIKE *Lanius tigrinus* 17–18.5 cm
(**a**) **Male breeding**: Grey crown/nape, whitish below, rufescent above with blackish bars/scales, warm brown uppertail, no wing-patch. (**b**) **Female breeding**: Duller; bolder bars/scales above, buffy flanks with blackish scales, whitish loral-patch and thin supercilium. **Adult non-breeding**: Rather uniform brownish forehead to upper mantle, dull mask. (**c**) **Juvenile/first winter**: Duller than female, uniform warmish brown crown/head-sides with blackish bars/scales, pinkish-based lower mandible. Bolder dark scaling than on Brown, no obvious dark mask. **VOICE** Scolding chatter in alarm. Subdued sharp *tchick*. **HABITAT & BEHAVIOUR** Forest edge, secondary growth; up to 1,220 m. Skulks. **RANGE** Sc/un **PM** E Myanmar, south Tenasserim, Thailand (ra **WV** south W), Pen Malaysia (also **WV**), Singapore (also **WV**), Indochina (except C,S Laos, N Annam).

3 BULL-HEADED SHRIKE *Lanius bucephalus* 19.5–20.5 cm
(**a**) **Male** *bucephalus*: Rufescent-brown crown/nape, greyish mantle to uppertail-coverts with brown wash, white wing-patch. (**b**) **Female**: More uniform head, thinner supercilium, duller above, no wing-patch. (**c**) **First winter**: Like female but upperparts and body-sides more rufous, tail mid-brown, almost no mask. **VOICE** Noisy chattering *ju-ju-ju* or *gi-gi-gi*. **HABITAT** Forest edge, clearings; up to 750 m. **RANGE** V C Annam.

Laos + Cambodia

4 BROWN SHRIKE *Lanius cristatus* 19–20 cm
(**a**) **Male** *confusus*: Brown above, black mask, whitish supercilium, whitish below with buffish flank-wash. No wing-patch, greyish-white forehead, brighter rump/uppertail-coverts. (**b**) **Female**: Often slightly duller; cream-tinged supercilium, fine dusky vermiculations on breast/flanks. (**c**) **Juvenile**: Duller; narrow blackish and some buffish scales above, whiter below, dark scales/bars on sides, shorter supercilium, pink-based lower mandible. Brown base-colour above, pale supercilium, dark mask. (**d**) **Male** *superciliosus* (east and south): Rich chestnut above (crown brightest), defined white forehead and supercilium. (**e**) **Male** *lucionensis*: (widespread): Pale grey crown, less distinct supercilium, grey washed mantle/scapulars. **Other subspecies** *L.c.cristatus* (throughout). **VOICE** Harsh *chak-ak-ak-ak-ak* in alarm. High squawks. Song of rich varied chattering. **HABITAT** Open country, cultivation, gardens, secondary growth; up to 2,000 m. **RANGE** Co **WV** throughout. Also **PM** SW,S Myanmar, Pen Malaysia, Cambodia, E Tonkin.

5 BURMESE SHRIKE *Lanius collurioides* 19–21 cm
(**a**) **Male** *collurioides*: Slaty crown/nape, unbarred above, white wing-patch, white-edged blackish tail. (**b**) **Female**: Duller above, whitish lores. (**c**) **Juvenile**: Blackish-and-buff bars on head, dark scales above, wavy-barred breast and flanks. (**d**) *nigricapillus* (southern Vietnam): Blacker crown/nape, darker above. **Female**: Indistinct pale lores, slightly paler hindcrown/nape, often somewhat duller above. **VOICE** Song is quiet, rapid and scratchy, with repetition and mimicry. In alarm, chattering *chekoochekoochititititit*; *chetetetetet*; harsh *jao*. **HABITAT & BEHAVIOUR** Open areas in forest (mainly pine), cultivation; 600–1,995 m; locally winters in lowlands. **RANGE** Lfc/co **R** W,N,C,E,S(north-west) Myanmar, W,NW Thailand, Cambodia, Laos, Vietnam (except W,E Tonkin). Fc **WV** SW,E Myanmar, Tenasserim, W,NW,NE,C Thailand, E Tonkin (also **PM**).

6 LONG-TAILED SHRIKE *Lanius schach* 25–28 cm
(**a**) **Adult** *longicaudatus*: Black head with white throat. (**b**) **Juvenile**: Black bars/scales above, wavy dark bars below. (**c**) **Adult** *schach* (Vietnam): Grey crown to mantle, smaller wing-patch. **Juvenile**: Browner crown to mantle with indistinct bars/scales. (**d**) **Adult** *'fuscatus'* morph (E Tonkin): Blackish throat; brownish-grey crown/nape/body (paler below); mostly blackish scapulars. (**e**) **Juvenile**: Relatively plain, blackish throat. **Other subspecies** *L.s.bentet* (Pen Malaysia, Singapore): Like *schach* but smaller, varied black forecrown (may extend behind eye), paler crown to back, pale warm buff scapulars with whitish outer edges, rufous-buff rump/uppertail-coverts, whitish tertial fringes. *L.s.tricolor* (Myanmar, NW Thailand, N Laos). **VOICE** Sings with low scratchy warbling, including mimicry. Scolding *chaak-chaak* in alarm. **HABITAT** Open areas, cultivation, gardens, secondary growth; up to 2,135 m. **RANGE** Un/co **R** (except SW,S Myanmar, Tenasserim, S Thailand, Cambodia, S Annam, Cochinchina). **V** northern Cambodia. **Rc** (status?) SW,S Myanmar, Tenasserim.

7 GREY-BACKED SHRIKE *Lanius tephronotus* 22.5–25.5 cm
(**a**) **Adult** *tephronotus*: Grey scapulars, slight supercilium, no white wing-patch, pale wing-fringing. (**b**) **Juvenile**: Browner above with blackish-and-buffish scales/bars, warmer back to uppertail-coverts with black bars, buffier below with blackish scales, rufescent-fringed tertials and coverts. Greyish scapulars, no wing-patch. **First winter**: More like adult but mask duller, wings/underparts similar to juvenile, may have slightly paler mantle with brown tinge. **VOICE** Recalls Long-tailed. **HABITAT** Open country, cultivation, secondary growth; up to 2,135 m. **RANGE** Un **WV** Myanmar (except southern Tenasserim), W,NW,NE,C Thailand, Cambodia, Laos, W,E Tonkin, N Annam.

8 RAIL-BABBLER *Eupetes macrocerus* 29 cm
(**a**) **Adult** *macrocerus*: Slim, long neck/bill/tail; chestnut-red to warm brown, buffy-rufous forehead, long black and white head-/neck-bands; blue skin on neck-side inflates when calling. (**b**) **Juvenile**: Dull chestnut crown and hindneck, warmer above, somewhat duller head-/neck-stripes, orange-rufous foreneck and breast (no red), whitish throat, greyer belly. **VOICE** Thin, drawn-out monotone whistle, lasting 1.5–2 s. Like Garnet Pitta but purer and higher, not rising at end. Also, popping frog-like notes in alarm. **HABITAT & BEHAVIOUR** Broadleaved evergreen forest; up to 1,005 m. Walks, jerking head like chicken. **RANGE** Sc/lfc **R** S Thailand, Pen Malaysia.

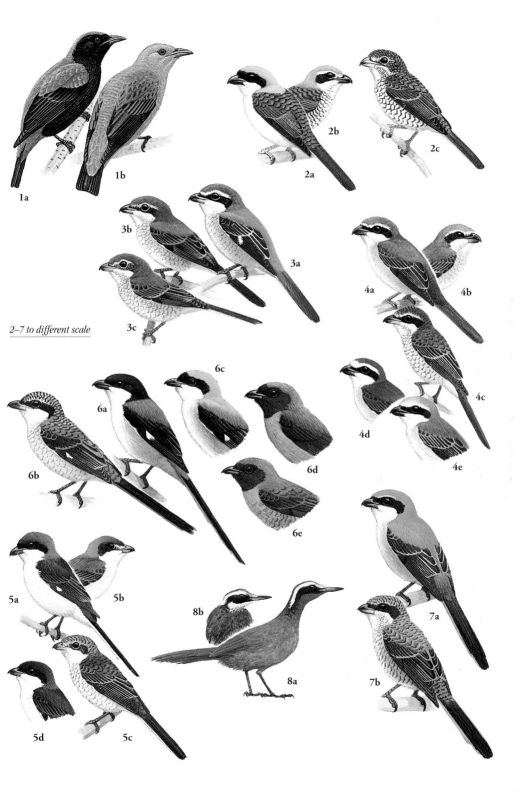

2–7 to different scale

PLATE 79 JAYS, MAGPIES & SPOTTED NUTCRACKER

1 CRESTED JAY *Platylophus galericulatus* 31–33 cm
(**a**) **Adult** *ardesiacus*: Black; white neck-patch, tall crest. (**b**) **Juvenile**: Tinged warm brown above, whitish bars below; warm buff covert-spots, short buff-tipped crest. (**c**) **Immature**: As adult but paler bars and streaks below. VOICE Song is fluty phrase, preceded by shrill high whistle: ***psssssiu HI-WU***. Call is grating metallic ***tit'it'it'it'it'it'it'it***... HABITAT Broadleaved evergreen forest; up to 1,220 m. RANGE Un/lc R south Tenasserim, S Thailand, W(south),S Thailand, Pen Malaysia.

2 BLACK MAGPIE *Platysmurus leucopterus* 39–41 cm
(**a**) **Adult** *leucopterus*: Black with white wing-band; fairly long, broad tail. VOICE Loud, discordant, metallic ***keh-eh-eh-eh-eh***, resonant, bell-like ***telope*** and ***kontingka-longk*** and xylophone-like ***tok-tok teklingk-klingk-klingk*** etc. HABITAT Broadleaved evergreen forest, sometimes mangroves; up to 215 m. RANGE Un R south Tenasserim, S Thailand, Pen Malaysia. Ra (status?) Singapore.

3 EURASIAN JAY *Garrulus glandarius* 31–34 cm
(**a**) **Adult** *leucotis*: Black cap and submoustachial, white head-sides/throat, buffish-grey above. (**b**) **Adult** *sinensis* (east N Myanmar): Warm pinkish-buff crown/nape/head-sides, more pinkish-buff mantle, pinker below. (**c**) **Adult** *oatesi* (northern W, north C Myanmar): Warm pinkish-buff crown with indistinct blackish streaks, slightly duller head-sides/throat. **Juvenile**: Darker, more rufescent body. **Other subspecies** *G.g.haringtoni* (southern W Myanmar): Like *sinensis* but more buffish-grey above. VOICE Sings with low musical notes, mimicry and clearer mewing. Call is screeching ***skaaaak skaaaak***... HABITAT Open forest, particularly pine and mixed evergreen/pine; up to 2,700 m. RANGE Fc/co R Myanmar, W,NW,NE Thailand, Cambodia, C,S Laos, S Annam, Cochinchina.

4 YELLOW-BILLED BLUE MAGPIE *Urocissa flavirostris* 64 cm
(**a**) **Adult** *flavirostris*: Yellow bill, black crown, small nuchal patch. (**b**) **Juvenile**: Initially browner on head/mantle/breast, duller nuchal patch, dull yellowish-olive bill, duller legs. **Other subspecies** *U.f.robini* (W Tonkin): When fresh, brighter olive wash above, yellowish wash below. *U.f.schaferi* (W Myanmar). VOICE Complex low squeaky chatter and whistles, raucous ***tsii-trrao tsii-trrao***.. and ***shitu-charrb shitu-charrb***... Scolding ***tcheb-be-be-be-be-be***.. and abrupt scratchy ***tcherr*** in alarm. HABITAT Broadleaved evergreen and open pine forest; 1,220–3,100 m. RANGE Lu/fc R W,N Myanmar, W Tonkin.

5 RED-BILLED BLUE MAGPIE *Urocissa erythrorhyncha* 67 cm
(**a**) **Adult** *magnirostris*: Red bill, black hood, white 'mane', blue above. (**b**) **Juvenile**: Dark of hood duller/browner, browner above (coverts pale-tipped). (**c**) **Adult** *erythrorhyncha* (N Indochina): More extensive, very pale bluish-grey 'mane', somewhat greyer above. **Other subspecies** *U.e.alticola* (N Myanmar): Like *erythrorhyncha*. VOICE Sharp raucous ***chweh-chweh-chweh***.. or ***chwit-wit-wit***.., shrill ***shrii*** and subdued ***kluk***. HABITAT Open broadleaved forest, secondary growth, conifer plantations; up to 1,940 m. RANGE Un/co R (except Tenasserim and S Thailand southwards).

6 WHITE-WINGED MAGPIE *Urocissa whiteheadi* 45–46 cm
(**a**) **Adult** *xanthomelana*: Dark brown hood/above, orange bill, large white wing/tail markings. (**b**) **Juvenile**: Paler greyer hood, greyish/brownish bill/eyes, pale of belly/vent/tail-sides washed yellowish. VOICE Hoarse rising ***shureek***, lower ***churree***, soft liquid rippling ***brrriii brrriii***.. and harsher rising ***errreep errreep***... HABITAT Broadleaved evergreen forest; up to 1,300 m. RANGE Lfc/co R Laos, W,E Tonkin, N,C Annam.

7 COMMON GREEN MAGPIE *Cissa chinensis* 37–40.5 cm
(**a**) **Adult** *chinensis*: Bright green, reddish-chestnut wings with black and whitish markings, black mask, red bill/eyering/legs. (**b**) **Adult worn**: May have strongly bluish plumage, browner wings. (**c**) **Juvenile**: Duller; paler lower breast/vent, smaller dark wing markings, duller bill/eyering/legs. (**d**) **Adult** *margaritae* (S Annam): Bright golden-yellow crown. **Other subspecies** *C.c.klossi* (C Laos, C Annam): Yellow forehead, yellowish-green crown. *C.c.robinsoni* (extreme S Thailand southwards). VOICE Penetrating high notes (sometimes followed by harsh note): ***wi-chi-chi jao***, ***wi-chi-chi jao wichitchit wi-chi-chi jao***... etc. Manic scolding ***chakakakakakak*** or ***chakakak-wi*** in alarm. Softer ***churrk chak-chak-chak*** and high ***weeer-wit*** and rising ***wieeee*** etc. HABITAT Broadleaved forest; up to 2,075 m. RANGE Co R (except Singapore, C,SE Thailand, Cochinchina).

8 INDOCHINESE GREEN MAGPIE *Cissa hypoleuca* 31–35 cm
(**a**) **Adult** *hypoleuca*: Only pale greenish wing marks, strongly yellow below. (**b**) **Adult** *concolor* (north Vietnam): Greener below, darker above, buffier tail-tips. **Juvenile**: Duller, paler vent, duller bill/eyering/legs. **Other subspecies** *C.h.chauleti* (C Annam): Yellower-green head, deeper yellow below, brownish-buff-washed outertail. VOICE Shrill ***peeeoo-peeeoo peeeoo-peeeoo***.., ***peu-peu-peu*** and clear whistles followed by harsh note: ***po-puueeee chuk*** and rising ***eeeooooeeep graak*** etc. Piercing falling ***peeeeooo*** and abrupt ***weep***. Harsh high scolding chatters in alarm. HABITAT Broadleaved evergreen and semi-evergreen forest; up to 1,870 m. RANGE Fc/co R SE Thailand, Indochina (except N Laos, W Tonkin).

9 BLACK-BILLED MAGPIE *Pica pica* 43–48 cm
(**a**) **Adult** *sericea*: Long tail, mostly black and white. **Juvenile**: Dark parts duller/browner. VOICE Harsh ***chak-chak-chak-chak-chak***... Enquiring ***ch'chack***, more squealing ***keee-uck***. HABITAT Forest edge, cultivation, plantations; up to 2,255 m. RANGE Ra/lc R N,C,E Myanmar, N Laos, Vietnam (except N Annam). FR (currently?) N Annam. V NW,C(or escapee?) Thailand.

10 SPOTTED NUTCRACKER *Nucifraga caryocatactes* 34 cm
(**a**) **Adult** *macella*: Brown head/body with extensive white streaks/spots, white vent, mostly white outertail. (**b**) **Juvenile**: Paler; thinner and buffier spots/streaks above, paler and mottled below. VOICE Sings with quiet musical piping, squeaking, clicking and whistling, mixed with mimicry. Harsh ***kraaaak***, sometimes extended to discordant rattle. HABITAT Open coniferous and mixed broadleaved/coniferous forest; 2,285–3,660 m. RANGE Un R N Myanmar.

PLATE 80 TREEPIES & CROWS

1 RUFOUS TREEPIE *Dendrocitta vagabunda* 46–50 cm
(**a**) **Adult** *kinneari*: Blackish-grey hood, deep buff below. (**b**) **Juvenile**: Paler; browner hood, buff-tippd greater coverts, tertials and tail. **Other subspecies** *D.v.saturatior* (Tenasserim, W Thailand) and *sakeratensis* (NE,SE Thailand, Indochina): Darker hood. *D.v.sclateri* (SW,W,S[west] Myanmar). **VOICE** Loud metallic flute-like *koku-lii*. Loud intermingled *kuki-uii*, *akuak* and *ekhekhekh* from pairs. Harsh *herb-herb-herb-herb bah-bah-bah herb-herb-herb..* etc. in alarm. **HABITAT** Deciduous forests, sometimes cultivation; up to 1,000 m, locally to 2,135 m. **RANGE** Lc R Myanmar, W,NW,NE,SE Thailand, Cambodia, C,S Laos, S Annam, Cochinchina.

2 GREY TREEPIE *Dendrocitta formosae* 36–40 cm
(**a**) **Adult** *assimilis*: Paler-naped than Rufous, blackish wings with small white patch, dull greyish below with deep rufous undertail-coverts. (**b**) **Juvenile**: Less black on face, paler head/breast with buffish tinge, whiter belly. (**c**) **Adult** *sinica* (E Tonkin): Darker brown above, whiter rump and uppertail-coverts, all-blackish tail. **Other subspecies** *D.f.himalayensis* (W,N,C,north E Myanmar). **VOICE** Loud, ringing, metallic *koh-kli-ka*, *koh-kli-koh-koh*, *ko-kiki* and *kuh'kuh'kuh'ki-kuh* etc. Harsh scolding chatters in alarm. **HABITAT** Broadleaved evergreen forest; 700–2,285 m, locally to 450 m. **RANGE** Fc/co R Myanmar, W,NW,NE Thailand, N,C Laos, W,E Tonkin, N Annam.

3 COLLARED TREEPIE *Dendrocitta frontalis* 38 cm
(**a**) **Adult**: Very pale grey hindcrown to upper belly, rufous rest of body (paler below), black forecrown to throat. **Juvenile**: Black of head duller, breast mixed with warm brown, coverts browner-grey. **VOICE** Throaty, clicking *u-wip*, and sudden shrill high metallic *drii* or *dreet*. **HABITAT** Broadleaved evergreen forest, bamboo; up to 1,220 m. **RANGE** Ra/lc R N Myanmar, W,E Tonkin.

Mangroves - H. village Camb.

4 RACKET-TAILED TREEPIE *Crypsirina temia* 30.5–32.5 cm
(**a**) **Adult**: Slim, all blackish; long spatulate-tipped tail. (**b**) **Juvenile**: Duller/browner, brown eyes, narrower tail-tip. **VOICE** Short, ringing *chu*, deep rasping *churg-churg*, harsh *chrrk-chrrrk*, more rising, questioning *churrk* etc. **HABITAT** Mixed deciduous woodland, open broadleaved forest (often near water), secondary growth, bamboo, mangroves; up to 915 m. **RANGE** Fc R E(south),S Myanmar, Tenasserim, Thailand, Indochina; formerly north-east Pen Malaysia.

5 HOODED TREEPIE *Crypsirina cucullata* 30–31 cm
(**a**) **Adult**: Pale greyish, black head/primaries/central tail feathers. (**b**) **Juvenile**: Paler/browner head, browner-tinged body. **VOICE** Calls include purring *drrrriiii'k*. **HABITAT** Open deciduous woodland, thorn-scrub jungle, bamboo, cultivation borders; up to 915 m. **RANGE** Un/lc R W,N,C,S Myanmar.

6 RATCHET-TAILED TREEPIE *Temnurus temnurus* 32–35 cm
(**a**) **Adult**: Broad tail with spikes. Greyish-black, black face, dark red/brown eyes. **First year**: Narrower tail feathers, blunter spikes (almost none on outer feathers). **VOICE** Loud ringing *clee-clee-clee..*, rhythmic grating *graak-graak-graak..*, short squeaky rising *eeup-eeup-eeup..*, short high, rasping,

rippling *rrrrrrrr* etc. **HABITAT** Broadleaved evergreen forest, bamboo; 50–1,500 m. **RANGE** Un/co R southern Tenasserim and south W Thailand (lo), north-east Cambodia, C Laos, W(south),E Tonkin, N,C,S Annam, north Cochinchina.

7 HOUSE CROW *Corvus splendens* 40–43 cm
(**a**) **Adult** *insolens*: Slender proportions, broad dull greyish collar. (**b**) **Adult** *protegatus* (feral range): Paler, more contrasting brownish-grey collar. (**c**) **Adult** *splendens* (SW Myanmar): Much paler collar. **Juvenile**: Duller/browner. **VOICE** Flat toneless dry *kaaa-kaaa*, rasping *ka* or down-turned *kow*, low *kowk*. **HABITAT** Open and urban areas, cultivation; up to 1,525 m. **RANGE** Co R Myanmar; formerly south W Thailand. Fc/co **FER** Pen Malaysia, Singapore. **V** (feral origin) west S Thailand.

8 SLENDER-BILLED CROW *Corvus enca* 43–47 cm
(**a**) **Adult** *compilator*: Slimmer with somewhat shorter, squarer-ended tail than Large-billed, relatively long slender bill with less strongly arched culmen; typically less glossy (lacks throat/breast gloss), no throat-hackles. **Juvenile**: Somewhat duller/browner, particularly body. **VOICE** Much higher and more nasal than Large-billed: *ka ka ka-a-a*, dry *ahk-ahk-ahk*, explosive, throaty, croaking *krok kok-kok* etc. When excited, series of *caaaw aaaaw* notes, mixed with unusual resonant twanging nasal *pe-yong* and *ne-awh*. **HABITAT** Broadleaved evergreen forest, sometimes mangroves; up to 520 m. **RANGE** Un R Pen Malaysia.

9 CARRION CROW *Corvus corone* 52–56 cm
(**a**) **Adult** *orientalis*: Bill shorter, slenderer and more pointed than Large-billed; shorter, squarer-ended tail. **VOICE** Calls usually longer, harsher and lower than Large-billed: vibrant dry *kraaa* (often repeated), hollower *konk-konk*. **HABITAT** Open country, cultivation; recorded at c.700 m. **RANGE** V E Tonkin.

10 LARGE-BILLED CROW *Corvus macrorhynchos* 48–59 cm
(**a**) **Adult** *macrorhynchos*: Bill rather long and arched (less so on females), steep forehead, rather wedge-shaped tail. (**b**) **Juvenile**: Duller and less glossy. (**c**) **Adult** *tibetosinensis* (N Myanmar): Largest and glossiest race. (**d**) **Adult** *levaillantii* (Myanmar, W,NW,NE,C Thailand): Smaller; squarer-ended tail, usually less arched culmen. **Other subspecies** *C.m.colonorum* (N Indochina): Roughly intermediate between *macrorhynchos* and *tibetosinensis*. **VOICE** Loud, deep, throaty, dry *khaa*, *kwaa*, *kaa kaa* or *kaaa-kaaa*, low harsh *kaak*, higher *awa awa awa...* Also low gargling noises. Nasal *quank quank quank* has been attributed to *C.m.levaillantii* only. **HABITAT** Open forest and woodland, open areas and cultivation, urban areas, mangroves; up to 3,660 m. **RANGE** Un/co R throughout.

11 COLLARED CROW *Corvus torquatus* 52–55 cm
(**a**) **Adult**: White collar. (**b**) **Juvenile**: Body browner and glossless, collar somewhat duller with dark feather-tips. **VOICE** Calls include loud *kaaarr* (often repeated), *kaar-kaar* and cawing, creaking and clicking sounds. **HABITAT** Open areas and cultivation with scattered trees (particularly near water), coasts, sometimes urban areas; lowlands. **RANGE** Ra R E Tonkin. **FR** (rarely?) N,C Annam.

PLATE 81 ORIOLES

1 DARK-THROATED ORIOLE *Oriolus xanthonotus* 20 cm (**a**) **Male** *xanthonotus*: Small; black hood and wings, white lower breast/belly with black streaks. Yellow and whitish fringing on flight feathers. (**b**) **Female**: Darker/greyer crown and head-sides, olive-green above with brighter rump/uppertail-coverts, whitish below with blackish streaks and yellow under-tail-coverts. **Juvenile**: Like female but dull duller; apparently has rufous fringes/tips to wing-coverts and sometimes also narrow tips to outer wing feathers. (**c**) **Immature male**: Yellower-green above than female, sooty crown/nape, greyish wash on throat. VOICE Song is fluty *phu phi-uu, phu-phu-phu wo, phu'phu-wiu-uu* etc. Call is high piping, relatively soft *kyew, pheeu* or *ti-u*. HABITAT Canopy of broadleaved evergreen forest; up to 1,220 m (mostly below 300 m). RANGE Un/co **R** south Tenasserim, S Thailand, Pen Malaysia; formerly Singapore.

2 BLACK-NAPED ORIOLE *Oriolus chinensis* 24.5–27.5 cm (**a**) **Male** *diffusus*: Large; golden-yellow body/coverts, broad black band from lores to nape. Black-and-yellow remainder of wing, thick fleshy-orange bill. (**b**) **Female**: Mostly olive-yellow upperparts/coverts. (**c**) **Juvenile**: Duller than female, no head-band, yellow head-sides with faint eyestripe, creamy/yellowish-white below with thin blackish streaks, yellow flank-wash and vent, mostly yellowish-green wings, mostly blackish bill. From Slender-billed mainly by thicker/shorter bill. (**d**) **Immature**: Gradually attains head-band. **Other subspecies** *O.c.maculatus* (west Pen Malaysia, Singapore). VOICE Sings with loud fluty *kwia-lu, u-dli-u*; and *u-liu* etc. Harsh rasping, nasal *kyehhr* call. HABITAT Open broadleaved forest, parks, gardens, plantations, mangroves; up to 1,525 m. RANGE Un/co **R** SW Myanmar, extreme S Thailand, Pen Malaysia, Singapore. Un **BV** N Laos, ? NE Thailand. Fc/co **WV** (except SW,W,N) Myanmar, Singapore, W,E Tonkin, N Annam). Fc **PM** W,E Tonkin.

3 SLENDER-BILLED ORIOLE *Oriolus tenuirostris* 23–26 cm (**a**) **Male** *tenuirostris*: Bill slightly longer and considerably thinner than Black-naped, nape-band narrower, roughly equal to width of black surrounding eye (obviously broader on Black-naped). (**b**) **Female**: Greener-tinged yellow than male, some indistinct narrow streaks below. (**c**) **Juvenile**: Hard to separate from Black-naped, except by longer, thinner bill. (**d**) **Immature**: See juvenile. **Other subspecies** *O.t.invisus* (S Annam). VOICE Sings with loud, fluty, quite hurried *wip-wi'u'wow'wow* or *wi wi'u-wu-wu* etc. Single fluty *tchew* or *tchi'u*. Harsh, slightly nasal, grating *kyerrrrh* or *ey'errrrh* in alarm. HABITAT Open pine forest, sometimes mixed pine/oak forest, also broadleaved evergreen forest in winter; 1,000–1,900 m; down to at least 600 m in winter. RANGE Fc/co **R** Myanmar (except N), N,S Laos, S Annam. Fc **WV** W,NW,NE Thailand (probably breeds locally). **Rc** (status?) W Tonkin, N Annam.

4 BLACK-HOODED ORIOLE *Oriolus xanthornus* 22–25 cm (**a**) **Male** *xanthornus*: Plain golden-yellow body, black hood. Black wings with much yellow, bill fleshy-orange. (**b**) **Female**: Lower mantle to rump washed olive, slightly paler and less rich yellow underparts/wing markings (latter slightly smaller).

(**c**) **Juvenile**: Black parts duller, crown often streaked olive, black-streaked yellowish forehead, yellowish-white eyering, whitish throat with blackish streaks (fading to breast), fainter wing markings, blackish bill. VOICE Song is clear fluty *h HWI'UU* and *h wu'CHI-WU* etc. Also mellow *tcheo* or *tchew* notes. Harsh *cheeeah* or *kwaaah* in alarm. HABITAT More open deciduous, semi-evergreen and swamp forest, mangroves; up to 915 m. RANGE Co **R** Myanmar, Thailand, north-west Pen Malaysia (Langkawi I), Indochina (except W,E Tonkin, N Annam).

5 BLACK-AND-CRIMSON ORIOLE *O.cruentus* 23–24.5 cm (**a**) **Male** *malayanus*: Black; dark crimson breast-/belly-patch and primary coverts, pale bluish bill and legs. (**b**) **Female**: No crimson, pale greyish lower breast/belly. **Juvenile**: Like female but initially has pale warmish brown streaks on lower breast and upper belly, some thin pale warmish brown wing-covert fringes. **First-winter male**: Like female. Gradually attains odd crimson feathers. VOICE Unusual thin strained *hhsssu* or *hsiiiu*. HABITAT Broadleaved evergreen forest; 915–1,280 m, occasionally down to 610 m. RANGE Un/fc **R** Pen Malaysia.

6 MAROON ORIOLE *Oriolus traillii* 24–28 cm (**a**) **Male** *traillii*: Dark maroon body, black hood and wings, pale dull maroon tail, grey bill, pale yellowish eyes. (**b**) **Female**: Blackish-brown crown, nape and head-sides, dark brown above with variable maroon tinge and dark reddish-chestnut rump/ uppertail-coverts, brownish-maroon tail (pale reddish-maroon below), whitish below with heavy dark streaks and pale reddish-maroon undertail-coverts. (**c**) **Female variant**: Darker and less distinctly streaked throat/upper breast (sometimes mostly blackish). (**d**) **Juvenile**: Like paler-throated female but pale-streaked forehead, rufescent covert-tips and scaling above, dark-streaked rump, narrower streaks below, washed-out undertail-coverts with dark streaks, browner eyes. Often has pale rufous wash on lower throat and upper breast. (**e**) **Immature male**: Attains black hood and variable maroon wash on body while underparts still streaked. (**f**) **Male** *nigellicauda* (visitor SE Thailand, N Indochina at least): Much redder body and tail. **Female**: Reddish wash on mantle and back, distinctly deep reddish rump, tail-coverts and tail. **Other subspecies** *O.t.robinsoni* (S Laos, C,S Annam). VOICE Song is fluty *pi-loi-lo* and *pi-oho-uu* etc. Call is long nasal *hwyerrrh*. HABITAT Broadleaved evergreen forest, sometimes deciduous forest; 450–2,710 m, locally down to 150 m. RANGE Fc/co **R** Myanmar, W,NW,NE Thailand, Cambodia, Laos, Vietnam (except Cochin-china). Un **WV** NE,SE Thailand, N Laos, W,E Tonkin, N Annam.

7 SILVER ORIOLE *Oriolus mellianus* 28 cm (**a**) **Male**: Silvery-whitish body, black hood and wings, dull maroon tail. Dull maroon body-feather centres (hard to see) and undertail-coverts (latter narrowly fringed silvery-whitish), silvery-whitish-edged tail feathers. (**b**) **Female**: Like Maroon but mostly greyish mantle to rump, paler pinkish undertail-coverts with whitish fringes; tends to have narrower streaks below. HABITAT Broadleaved evergreen and semi-evergreen forest; up to 800 m. RANGE Ra/sc **WV** W(south),NE,SE Thailand, south-west Cambodia. **V** NW Thailand.

PLATE 82 CUCKOOSHRIKES & PIED TRILLER

1 LARGE CUCKOOSHRIKE *Coracina macei* 27–30.5 cm [handwritten: Laos, Thailand]
(**a**) **Male** *siamensis*: Mostly quite pale grey, blackish lores, dark grey ear-coverts, whitish vent, grey/blackish tail with white tip. (**b**) **Female**: Paler; whiter breast/belly with grey bars, pale barring on rump/uppertail-coverts. (**c**) **Juvenile**: Heavily barred/scaled buffy-whitish and dusky-brownish, whitish rump, broad whitish wing-fringing. **Immature**: Like female but retains some juvenile coverts/tertials; ? more distinct bars below. (**d**) **Male** *rexpineti* (**rc** E Myanmar, N Indochina): Darker forehead, face and throat. **VOICE** Loud, shrill *kle-eep*. Varied chuckling. **HABITAT** Open broadleaved and pine forest; up to 2,710 m. **RANGE** Co R (except S Thailand, Pen Malaysia, Singapore). Also **PM** E Tonkin.

2 JAVAN CUCKOOSHRIKE *Coracina javensis* 27.5–29 cm
(**a**) **Male** *larutensis*: Darker grey than Large, blacker/more uniform primaries and primary coverts, less white on tail-tip. (**b**) **Female**: From Large as male. **VOICE** Loud thin nasal *yiee* or *yi'ik* and lower scratchier nasal *yerrk yerrk..* and *yererr'erk* etc. **HABITAT** Broadleaved evergreen forest; above 1,000 m. **RANGE** Co R extreme S Thailand, Pen Malaysia.

3 BAR-BELLIED CUCKOOSHRIKE *Coracina striata* 27.5–30 cm
(**a**) **Male** *sumatrensis*: Whitish/yellowish-white eyes, rather plain head, pale and some dark bars on rump/uppertail-coverts, faint grey bars on vent. (**b**) **Female**: Broad blackish and whitish bars on rump/uppertail-coverts and lower breast to undertail-coverts. (**c**) **Juvenile**: Heavily scaled whitish, blackish and dusky-brownish; whiter wing-fringing, blackish and whitish subterminal tertial markings, brownish eyes. **VOICE** Clear whinnying *kliu-kliu-kliu..* or shrill *kriiu-kriiu.* **HABITAT** Broadleaved evergreen and freshwater swamp forest, sometimes mangroves and old plantations; lowlands. **RANGE** Sc/lfc R southern S Thailand, Pen Malaysia; formerly Singapore.

4 INDOCHINESE CUCKOOSHRIKE *Coracina polioptera* 21.5–22 cm
(**a**) **Male** *indochinensis*: More pronounced pale wing-fringing than Black-winged, tail less graduated (central feathers <25 mm longer than outer), greyer above and with somewhat broader white tips below; whitish area on underside of primaries. (**b**,**c**) **Female**: Dark and pale bars/scales on head-sides/underparts; indistinct pale supercilium, broken whitish eyering. Usually more contrasting bars below than Black-winged; tail shape/pattern (as male); larger whitish underwing-patch. **Juvenile**: Best separated from Black-winged by tail shape/pattern and larger whitish underwing-patch. (**d**) **Male** *jabouillei* (N,C Annam): Much darker, more uniform, blacker wings, no whitish underwing-patch, only little grey at base of uppertail. **Other subspecies** *C.p.polioptera* (W Thailand, Cambodia, Cochinchina): Male a shade paler (paler, with paler wing-fringing, than any race of Black-winged). **VOICE** Sings with 5–7, mostly descending whistles: *wi-wi-wi-wi-wu*; *wi-wi-wi-wi-wiu-wu* etc. (quicker than Black-winged). Also, nasal chuntering *uh'uh'uh'uh-ik* and *uh'uh'uh'uh...* **HABITAT** Deciduous, semi-deciduous, pine, and locally peatswamp forest; up to 1,400 m. **RANGE** Fc R W,C,E,S Myanmar, Tenasserim, W,NW,NE Thailand, Indochina (except W,E Tonkin).

5 BLACK-WINGED CUCKOOSHRIKE *Coracina melaschistos* 23.5 cm
(**a**) **Male** *avensis*: Blackish wings, tail more graduated than Indochinese (central feathers >25 mm longer than outer), blackish above and with narrower white tips below; underwing-patch lacking/small. (**b**,**c**) **Female**: Throat to belly typically plainer than Indochinese, usually fainter pale wing fringing, less grey on tail, tail shape/pattern (as male); much smaller/no underwing-patch. (**d**) **Juvenile**: Paler; heavy buffish to whitish and dark sooty-brownish bars/scales. **Immature**: As female but scales/bars on rump/uppertail-coverts, clearer bars below. (**e**) **Male** *melaschistos* (**B** W,N Myanmar, **rc** NW Thailand): Darker. (**f**) **Male** *saturata* (**B** E Tonkin, N,C Annam, **rc** NW Thailand, Cambodia, S Laos): Very dark. **Other subspecies** *C.m.intermedia* (**VS** Tenasserim, W,C,NE,SE Thailand). **VOICE** 3–4 clear, well-spaced, high whistles: *wii-wii-jeeu-jeeu*, *wi'i-wii-wii-juu* etc.; slower than Indochinese. **HABITAT & BEHAVIOUR** Broadleaved evergreen forest; 300–1,920 m. Also more open lowland areas, deciduous forest etc. in winter. **RANGE** Fc R (some movements) W,N,E Myanmar, W,NW,NE Thailand, N Laos, W,E Tonkin, N,C Annam. Fc **WV** C,S Myanmar, Tenasserim, Thailand (except southern S), Indochina. Also **PM** E Tonkin.

6 LESSER CUCKOOSHRIKE *Coracina fimbriata* 19–20.5 cm
(**a**) **Male** *neglecta*: Smaller than Black-winged, less graduated tail (central feathers <25 mm longer than outer ones) with smaller white tips below. (**b**) **Female**: Like Indochinese but more uniform bars below, tends to show more obvious supercilium, dark eyestripe and pale ear-covert streaking, smaller white tips to undertail, usually no whitish underwing-patch. **Juvenile**: Best told from Indochinese by range, smaller size, tail shape/pattern. **Other subspecies** *C.f.culminata* (extreme S Thailand southwards). **VOICE** Sings with loud clear *whit-it-it-chui-choi* etc. Also quicker *whit-whit-whit-whit-whit-whit*. Squeaky nasal *wherrrh-wherrrh-wherrrh..* and high *whit-weei* in alarm. **HABITAT** Broadleaved evergreen forest, plantations; up to 975 m. **RANGE** Co R south Tenasserim, W(south),S Thailand, Pen Malaysia. Ra (status?) Singapore.

7 BLACK-HEADED CUCKOOSHRIKE *C.melanoptera* 19.5 cm
(**a**) **Male** *sykesi*: Black hood. (**b**) **Female**: Like Indochinese but with stronger pale wing-covert fringes, stronger black bars below, white vent. **Juvenile**: Like female but blackish and buffish-white scales above, dark subterminal covert/tertial markings, dark brown bill. **VOICE** Quick whistled *twit-wit-wee-twy-twy-twy-twy*, often followed by *pit-pit-pit*. **HABITAT** Open deciduous/semi-deciduous forest, sometimes orchards, gardens; up to 1,525 m. **RANGE** Sc **WV** SW,W Myanmar.

8 PIED TRILLER *Lalage nigra* 17–18 cm
(**a**) **Male** *nigra*: Black above, whitish supercilium, black eyestripe, grey back to uppertail-coverts, large white wing markings. (**b**) **Female**: Dark parts greyish-brown, tinged buffish with indistinct dark scales below. (**c**) **Juvenile**: Pale buff scales above, dark streaks on throat and breast. **VOICE** Disyllabic whistle with lower second note; descending series of nasal *chack* notes. **HABITAT** Coastal scrub, plantations, gardens; lowlands. **RANGE** Un/lc R S Thailand, Pen Malaysia, Singapore.

1c

1a

1b

2a

2b

3c

3a

3b

4d

4a

4b

4c

5c

5a

5b

5f

5e

5d

6a

6b

7b

7a

8b

8c

8a

PLATE 83 MINIVETS

1 SMALL MINIVET *Pericrocotus cinnamomeus* 14.5–16 cm
(**a**) **Male** *vividus*: Grey above, darker face/throat, reddish-orange rump/breast/flanks, orange-yellow vent, orange and yellow wing-patch. (**b**) **Female:** Paler/duller above, greyish-white throat/breast, pale yellow below. **Juvenile:** Browner above than female, pale yellowish/whitish bars/scales above, covert-tips and tertial fringes, faintly mottled breast. **First-winter male:** As female but often some orange on flanks. **Other subspecies** *P.c.sacerdos* (Cambodia, Cochinchina): Red-orange parts redder, more vivid (both sexes). *P.c.separatus* (west S Thailand): Female more washed-out below. *P.c.thai* (C,E Myanmar, NW,NE Thailand, Laos). VOICE Very thin, drawn-out, high *tswee-eet* and *swee swee..* etc. HABITAT Deciduous forest, more open areas with trees, parks, gardens, locally peatswamp forest, coastal scrub; up to 1,525 m. RANGE Co R (except N Myanmar, southern S Thailand, Pen Malaysia, Singapore, W,E Tonkin, N Annam).

2 FIERY MINIVET *Pericrocotus igneus* 15–15.5 cm
(**a**) **Male** *igneus*: Like miniature Scarlet but more orange, no isolated red on tertials/secondaries. (**b**) **Female:** Orange-yellow forehead-band, bright red-orange rump, yellow below. (**c**) **Juvenile:** Like female but browner above with dark and whitish markings, dark mottled breast. VOICE Very thin *swiiii* notes, and *tit tit swiiii*. HABITAT Broadleaved evergreen forest; up to 1,220 m, mostly below 610 m. RANGE Un R south Tenasserim, S Thailand, Pen Malaysia; formerly Singapore.

3 WHITE-BELLIED MINIVET *Pericrocotus erythropygius* 14.5–16 cm
(**a**) **Male** *albifrons*: Black above, white forehead/eyebrow and wing markings, white below, orange on rump and breast. (**b**) **Female:** Grey-brown above, white below, grey on breast. **Juvenile:** Like female but white scales/bars (mainly crown) and blackish subterminal markings above, white-tipped coverts, some dark speckles/mottling on breast. VOICE Spaced sweet high notes: *thi*, *tuee*, *chi*, *tschi* and *tchu-it* etc. Soft *tchip*. HABITAT Semi-desert, lowland dry cultivation with scrub/scattered trees, thorn scrub. RANGE Un R C,S(north) Myanmar.

4 GREY-CHINNED MINIVET *Pericrocotus solaris* 17–19 cm
(**a**) **Male** *rubrolimbatus*: Dark grey above, whitish chin, orange-yellow throat-wash, red parts are orange-tinged. (**b**) **Female:** Grey and olive-yellow, greyish-white chin, dark wings with yellow patch. (**c**) **Juvenile:** As female but yellow scales/bars and blackish subterminal markings above. (**d**) **Male** *deignani* (C,S Annam): More uniform lower head-sides and throat, yellowish-olive tint on throat, redder orange parts. (**e**) **Female:** Greyish-white throat, olive cast below, more olive rump. (**f**) **Male** *montanus* (Pen Malaysia, ? extreme S Thailand): Much redder, black above, dark throat. (**g**) **Female:** Blackish-slate above, orange-tinged yellow parts. **Other subspecies** *P.s.griseogularis* (N[east] Laos, northern Vietnam) and *nassovicus* (SW Cambodia): Males as *deignani* but former has paler, more contrasting yellowish-olive tint on throat and less red orange parts. Female *griseogularis* has uniform pale greyish-white throat, slight olive cast below, slightly more olive rump/uppertail-coverts. *P.s.solaris* (W,N,C,S Myanmar). VOICE Thin *tswee-seet* and more slurred *swirrririt*. Soft *trip* notes

and more sibilant *trii-ii*. HABITAT Broadleaved evergreen and sometimes pine forest; 300–2,350 m. RANGE Fc/co R (except SW Myanmar, C,SE Thailand, Singapore, Cochinchina).

5 LONG-TAILED MINIVET *Pericrocotus ethologus* 17.5–20.5 cm
(**a**) **Male** *ethologus* (WV/Rc range): Black with red rump and uppertail-coverts, underparts, wing-patch and outertail. (**b**) **Female:** Greyish-olive above, yellowish/greenish rump/uppertail-coverts; bright yellow below, paler lower throat, whitish chin. (**c**) **Juvenile:** As female but scaly above, yellowish-white covert-tips, scaly olive-greyish breast/flanks. (**d**) **First-summer male:** Darker above than female, yellowish parts mostly replaced by deep orange. (**e**) **Female** *annamensis* (S Annam): Grey above, yellow parts slightly orange-tinged, yellower forehead/cheeks/upper throat; may have forecrown and tail like Short-billed. Male may have wing and tail like Short-billed. **Other subspecies** *P.e.yvettae* (N,E[north] Myanmar): Female is more uniform grey above, often yellower on forehead. *P.e.mariae* (W Myanmar): Female is similar to *annamensis*, but yellower, forecrown and tail do not resemble Short-billed. *P.e.ripponi* (R E Myanmar, NW,? NE Thailand): Roughly intermediate between *mariae* and *ethologus*. VOICE Sweet, rolling *prrr'wi*, *prrr'i-wi* and *prrr'i-prrr'i* and thin *swii-swii swii-swii-swii...* HABITAT Broadleaved evergreen and pine forest; 900–3,100 m, down to 450 m in winter. RANGE Co R (some winter dispersal) W,N,E Myanmar, NW,NE Thailand, C,S Annam. Un/lc WV C,E,S Myanmar, NW,NE Thailand, E Tonkin. Rc (status?) N,C Laos, W Tonkin.

6 SHORT-BILLED MINIVET *Pericrocotus brevirostris* 17.5–19.5 cm
(**a**) **Male** *neglectus*: Like Long-tailed but only single red line extends from wing-patch, more red on outertail feathers, black throat extends lower. (**b**) **Female:** Like Long-tailed (*P.e.ethologus*) but forehead golden-yellow, forecrown washed yellow, mantle greyer, throat yellow, more yellow on outertail. **Juvenile:** Differs as Long-tailed. **Other subspecies** *P.b.affinis* (W,N Myanmar); *anthoides* (W,E Tonkin). VOICE Very thin sweet *tsuuuit tsuuuit tsuuuit...* Also dry *tup* notes. HABITAT Broadleaved evergreen and sometimes pine forest; 915–2,135 m, locally down to 750 m. RANGE Fc/lc R W,N,E Myanmar, N Tenasserim, W,NW Thailand, Laos, W,E Tonkin.

7 SCARLET MINIVET *Pericrocotus flammeus* 17–21.5 cm
(**a**) **Male** *semiruber*: Larger/shorter-tailed than Long-tailed, isolated red on tertials/secondaries. (**b**) **Female:** Size, build, yellow forecrown, slaty-grey above, all bright yellow below, isolated yellow on tertials/secondaries. (**c**) **Juvenile:** Like Long-tailed and Short-billed but yellower below. **Immature male:** Differs from female like Long-tailed. **Other subspecies** *P.f.elegans* (northern Myanmar, N Indochina and WV range): Larger, mostly black central tail feathers; *flammifer* (W,S Thailand, north-east/east Pen Malaysia) and *xanthogaster* (west/south Pen Malaysia): Smaller (range given). VOICE Loud piercing *sweeep-sweeep-sweeep..* and *weeep-weeep-weeep-wit-wip* etc. HABITAT Broadleaved forests; up to 1,700 m (below 915 m in Pen Malaysia). RANGE Co R (except C Thailand); sc Singapore. Un WV E Myanmar, NW Thailand.

174

PLATE 84 MINIVETS & DRONGOS

1 ROSY MINIVET *Pericrocotus roseus* 18–19.5 cm
(a) **Male** *roseus*: Greyish above, red on rump/wing/tail, largely pinkish below. (b) **Female**: Red replaced by pale yellow. (c) **Male** *'stanfordi'* (rc NE Thailand, Cambodia, Cochinchina): Recalls Swinhoe's but reddish/pinkish on forecrown, outertail, wing, rump and breast. (d) **Female**: Yellow on wing/tail and tinge to uppertail-coverts. **Juvenile/immature male**: Differ in similar way to other minivets. **VOICE** Similar to Ashy. **HABITAT** Open broadleaved forest (mainly deciduous); up to 1,525 m. **RANGE** Fc/co **R** Myanmar. **B** E Tonkin. Sc/fc **WV** Thailand, east Cambodia, N,S Laos, Cochinchina. Also **PM** E Tonkin. **Rc** (status?) W Tonkin.

2 SWINHOE'S MINIVET *Pericrocotus cantonensis* 19 cm
(a) **Male** Grey hindcrown, white behind eye, browner above than Ashy, pale brownish rump, vinous-brownish wash below; pale yellowish-buff wing-patch (or none). (b) **Female**: Paler above, yellower wing-patch (if present). **First winter**: Similar characters to Ashy. **HABITAT** Broadleaved forest; up to 1,200 m. **RANGE** Un **WV** S Myanmar, Tenasserim, Thailand, Cambodia, Laos, C Annam, Cochinchina. Sc **PM** Cambodia, E Tonkin.

3 ASHY MINIVET *Pericrocotus divaricatus* 18.5–20 cm
(a) **Male** *divaricatus*: Black head, whitish forecrown/under-parts, grey rump/uppertail-coverts. (b) **Female**: Pale grey above; blackish stripe across forehead. **First winter**: As female but white fringing and blackish subterminal marks on tertials, white-tipped greater coverts. **VOICE** Metallic jingling trill. Ascending *tchu-de tchu-dee-dee tchu-dee-dee* in flight. **HABITAT** Open forest, scattered trees, mangroves, plantations; up to 1,200 m. **RANGE** Un/lc **WV** (except SW,W,N,E Myanmar, W Tonkin, N Annam). Also **PM** Cambodia, E Tonkin.

Angkor Camb 2/13

4 BLACK DRONGO *Dicrurus macrocercus* 27–28.5 cm
(a) **Adult** *thai*: Blackish (slight gloss), often a white face-spot. **Juvenile**: Browner; paler breast/belly-scales. (b) **First winter**: Whitish-scaled uppertail-coverts and below. **Other subspecies** *D.m.cathoecus* (Myanmar [except W,N], northern Thailand, northern Indochina; and only **VS**)/*albirictus* (W,N Myanmar): Larger (latter 29–32 cm). **VOICE** Harsh *ti-tiu*, rasping *cheece*. **HABITAT** Open country, cultivation; to 1,220 m. **RANGE** Co **R** (some movements), except S Thailand southwards. Un/co **WV** SW,S Myanmar, Tenasserim, W,C,SE,S Thailand, Pen Malaysia, Singapore, Cambodia, Cochinchina. Also **PM** C,S Thailand, E Tonkin.

5 ASHY DRONGO *Dicrurus leucophaeus* 25.5–29 cm
(a) **Adult** *mouhoti* (B SW,W Myanmar to N,C Laos, C Annam; **VS** as far as S Thailand, Cambodia): Dark steely-grey (paler below). (b) **Adult** *nigrescens* (R Tenasserim and S Thailand southward): Blacker. (c) **Adult** *leucogenis* (widespread **VS** west to S Myanmar, south to Pen Malaysia): Pale grey, black forehead, whitish face. (d) **Adult** *salangensis*: (similar range to *leucogenis*): Darker than *leucogenis*, grey on ear-coverts. **Juvenile**: Dull; paler throat/vent. **Other subspecies** *D.l.bondi* (R W,NE(south),SE Thailand, S Indochina); *hopwoodi* (northern Myanmar/Indochina; **rc** in winter southern Myanmar, W,NE Thailand, S Laos). **VOICE** Thin wheezy *phuuuu* and *hieeeeeer*, repeated loud *tchik wu-wit* etc. Chattering, shrill whistles, harsh notes. **HABITAT** Open areas in forest; mangroves etc. in south. Up to 2,750 m. **RANGE** Co

R (except Singapore). Fc/co **WV** S Myanmar, Tenasserim, Thailand, Pen Malaysia, Singapore (sc), Laos, Cambodia, Cochinchina. Also **PM** C Thailand, E Tonkin, C Annam.

6 CROW-BILLED DRONGO *Dicrurus annectans* 27–32 cm
(a) **Adult**: Tail broad with shallow fork and strong upcurl, tail thick-based, longish. **Juvenile**: Browner. (b) **First winter**: White spots below. **VOICE** Musical whistles, churrs, chattering. **HABITAT** Broadleaved forest (mainly evergreen); migrants also in mangroves, plantations etc. Up to 1,445 m, rarely to 1,700 m. **RANGE** Lo **BV** C,W,NW(also **rc** winter) Thailand, C,S Laos, E Tonkin, N,C Annam. Un **WV** Tenasserim, SE,S Thailand, Pen Malaysia, Singapore. Un **PM** Tenasserim, Thailand, Pen Malaysia, Singapore, Cambodia, Cochinchina. **Rc** (status?) E,S Myanmar, S Annam.

7 BRONZED DRONGO *Dicrurus aeneus* 22–23.5 cm
(a) **Adult** *aeneus*: Small, very glossy. **Juvenile/first winter**: Less gloss. **Other subspecies** *D.a.malayensis* (south Pen Malaysia, Singapore). **HABITAT** Broadleaf forests; up to 2,135 m. **RANGE** Co **R** (except C Thailand, Singapore). **V** Singapore (**FR**).

8 LESSER RACKET-TAILED DRONGO *Dicrurus remifer* 25–27.5 cm
(a) **Adult** *tectirostris*: Short crest, square tail (shafts/straight pendants at 40 cm more). **Juvenile**: Duller, no tail extension. **Other subspecies** *D.r.peracensis* (south of 16°N, except *lefoli* range) and *lefoli* (south-west Cambodia): Thinner/longer pendants (longer on latter). **VOICE** Loud, musical and varied. Mimics. **HABITAT** Broadleaved evergreen/semi-evergreen forest; 140–2,590 m. **RANGE** Lc **R** (except C Thailand, Singapore).

9 SPANGLED DRONGO *Dicrurus hottentottus* 29–33 cm
(a) **Adult** *hottentottus*: Large, shiny; slender bill, unforked upcurled tail. **Juvenile**: Duller, flatter tail. **Other subspecies** *D.h.brevirostris* (R N Indochina; ? N Myanmar; only **VS**). **VOICE** Stressed *chit-wiii* and *wiii*. **HABITAT** Broadleaved forest; also parks, gardens (migrants). Up to 2,440 m. **RANGE** Un/lc **R** Myanmar, W,NW,NE,SE Thailand, Indochina. Sc/fc **WV** Thailand (except S). Also **PM** C Thailand. **Rc** (status?) E Tonkin.

10 ANDAMAN DRONGO *D.andamanensis* 31.5–33.5 cm
(a) **Adult** *dicruriformis*: Larger than Black, tail longer with shallower fork, upcurled tips. **Juvenile** Duller, tail initially squarer. **VOICE** Sharp metallic *tschew* notes. **HABITAT** Lowland broadleaved evergreen forest. **RANGE** **R** Coco Is, off S Myanmar.

11 GREATER RACKET-TAILED DRONGO *D.paradiseus* 30–37 cm
(a) **Adult** *rangoonensis*: Big crest, forked tail (shafts/twisted rackets to 30 cm more). **Juvenile** Duller; short crest, no tail extension. **First winter** White-speckled breast, white-barred belly/vent. (b) **Adult** *platurus* (Pen Malaysia except Tioman I): Smaller, short crest. **Other subspecies** *D.p.grandis* (north Myanmar/Indochina): Larger, longer crest. *D.p.hypoballus* (c.4–11°N): Intermediate with *platurus*. *D.p.microlophus* (Tioman I); *paradiseus* (Tenasserim to south Indochina). **VOICE** Varied whistles, screeching, churring and mimicry. **HABITAT** Broadleaved forest; up to 1,700 m. **RANGE** Co **R** throughout.

1–3 to different scale

PLATE 85 WOODSWALLOWS, FLYCATCHER-SHRIKES & FANTAILS ETC

1 ASHY WOODSWALLOW *Artamus fuscus* 16–18 cm
(**a,b**) **Adult**: Pale bluish bill, brownish-grey hood/upperparts, paler and browner below. Wings pale below, broad-based and pointed. (**c**) **Juvenile**: Duller bill; browner above with pale fringing, paler below with vague darker barring. VOICE Drawn-out twittering song, mixed with harsh *chack* notes. Sharp nasal *ma-a-a ma-a-a..* and repeated shrill, nasal *chreenk* and *chek* calls. HABITAT & BEHAVIOUR Open areas with scattered trees, cultivation; up to 2,135 m. Gregarious, often found perched in huddled groups. Spends much time gliding and circling. RANGE Fc/co R (some movements), except south Tenasserim, S Thailand, Pen Malaysia, Singapore.

2 WHITE-BREASTED WOODSWALLOW *A.leucorynchus* 18 cm
(**a,b**) **Adult** *leucorynchus*: Clean white below and on under-wing-coverts. (**c**) **Juvenile**: Whiter below than Ashy, whiter feather-tips above. **Other subspecies** *A.l.humei* (Coco Is, S Myanmar). VOICE Chattering song with avian mimicry. Rasping *wek-wek-wek..* and sharp, metallic *pirt pirt..* calls. HABITAT Open areas with scattered trees, cultivation. RANGE Un/fc R Coco Is, off S Myanmar, coastal west Pen Malaysia (lo).

Sum Reep Gooden

3 BAR-WINGED FLYCATCHER-SHRIKE *Hemipus picatus* 13 cm
(**a**) **Male** *picatus*: Black above, pale below with dusky/vinous wash, long white wing-patch. (**b**) **Female**: Brown above, paler below. (**c**) **Juvenile**: Buff bars/scales above, buffish wing-patch with dark bars/scales. (**d**) **Male** *capitalis* (N,C,E Myanmar, NW Thailand, N Laos, W Tonkin): Dark brown mantle/back/scapulars. **Other subspecies** *H.p.intermedius* (S Thailand southwards): Female blacker-brown above, darker below (more like male). VOICE Rapid thin musical *swit'i'wit-swit'i'wit..*, *sitti-wittit* and *sittititit* etc. HABITAT & BEHAVIOUR Broadleaved forests; up to 1,980 m. Usually in groups, often in bird-waves. RANGE Co R (except C Thailand, Singapore).

4 BLACK-WINGED FLYCATCHER-SHRIKE *H.hirundinaceus*
(**a**) **Male**: 13 cm. Like Bar-winged but no wing-patch. (**b**) **Female**: Browner above. (**c**) **Juvenile**: Paler/browner above than female with buff bars/scales, mostly buffish coverts with dark brown markings, whiter below with browner breast-wash. VOICE Coarse *tu-tu-tu-tu*, *bee-tee-tee-teet* and *bee-too-weet*, interspersed with high *cheet-weet-weet-weet* etc. HABITAT Broadleaved evergreen forest, freshwater swamp forest, sometimes mangroves, old plantations; up to 275 m. RANGE Sc/lc R south Tenasserim, extreme S Thailand, Pen Malaysia.

5 YELLOW-BELLIED FANTAIL *Rhipidura hypoxantha* 12 cm
(**a**) **Male**: Dull greenish above, long dark white-tipped graduated tail, blackish mask, bright yellow forehead, supercilium and underparts; whitish greater covert tips. (**b**) **Female**: Mask colour as crown. **Juvenile**: Duller above, yellow parts paler, less yellow on forehead and in front of eye. VOICE Sings with thin sweet *sewit*, *sweeit* and *tit* or *tsit* notes, followed by high-pitched trill. HABITAT & BEHAVIOUR Broadleaved evergreen forest; 1,500–3,655 m, locally down to 180 m in winter. Fans tail and twitches from side to side. RANGE Un/co R W,N,E,S(east) Myanmar, W,NW Thailand, N Laos, W Tonkin, N Annam.

6 WHITE-THROATED FANTAIL *R.albicollis* 17.5–20.5 cm
(**a**) **Adult** *celsa*: Dark greyish to blackish-slate, white supercilium and throat, fan-shaped white-tipped tail. (**b**) **Juvenile**: Browner above with warm brown scales/bars/tips, indistinct paler bars below, little white on throat, often buffier eyebrow. **Other subspecies** *R.a.cinerascens* (southern Indochina), *stanleyi* (W and northern Myanmar), *atrata* (S Thailand southwards). VOICE Sings with 4–8 unevenly spaced, clear, high whistles (sequence mostly descending): *tsu sit tsu sit sit sit sit-tsu* etc. Squeaky harsh *jick* or *wick*. HABITAT Broadleaved evergreen forest, locally cultivation, parks, gardens; 460–3,050 m, locally to sea level in Indochina. RANGE Co R (some movements?), except C Thailand, Singapore, Cochinchina.

7 WHITE-BROWED FANTAIL *Rhipidura aureola* 16–18.5 cm
(**a**) **Adult** *burmanica*: White supercilium, mostly whitish below. (**b**) **Juvenile**: Darker throat, browner above with pale warm brown scales, broad whitish to dull pale rufous covert tips. VOICE 6–7 spaced melodious whistles (usually first few ascending, rest descending): *chee-chee-cheweechee-vi* etc. Harsh *chuck*. HABITAT Deciduous forests; up to 1,065 m. RANGE Un/fc R Myanmar, W,NW,NE(south-west) Thailand, Cambodia, C,S Laos, C,S Annam.

8 PIED FANTAIL *Rhipidura javanica* 17.5–19.5 cm
(**a**) **Adult** *longicauda*: Pale below with blackish breast-band. **Juvenile**: Browner above with dull rufescent scales/bars, dull rufescent wing-feather tips/fringes, duller breast-band. VOICE Squeaky measured *chew-weet chew-weet chew-weet-chew* (last note falling). Squeaky chattering and squawking *chit* and *cheet* notes. HABITAT Mangroves, swamp forest, parks, gardens, plantations, secondary growth (usually near water); up to 455 m, locally 825 m. RANGE Co R (mostly coastal) Tenasserim, Thailand (except NW), Pen Malaysia, Singapore, Cambodia, N Laos (Mekong R), Cochinchina.

9 SPOTTED FANTAIL *Rhipidura perlata* 17–18 cm
(**a**) **Adult**: Blackish-slate, white vent and spots/streaks on throat/breast. **Juvenile**: Browner above, warm brownish tips to wing-coverts. VOICE Melodious *chilip pechilip-chi*, second phrase rising sharply. HABITAT Broadleaved evergreen forest; up to 1,130 m. RANGE Sc/lfc R southern S Thailand, Pen Malaysia.

10 GREY-HEADED CANARY FLYCATCHER *Culicicapa ceylonensis*
(**a**) **Adult** *calochrysea*: 12 cm. Grey hood, bright yellowish below. (**b**) **Juvenile**: Browner hood, duller above, paler below. **Other subspecies** *C.c.antioxantha* (southern Tenasserim, W[south] and S Thailand southwards): Darker head/breast, less bright green above, less bright yellow belly. VOICE Song is brief sharp *wittu-wittu-wit*; *chuit-it-ui* or *witti-wuti* etc. Calls with sharp metallic trills and twitters. HABITAT & BEHAVIOUR Broadleaved forest; migrants also in parks, gardens, mangroves. Up to 3,050 m (mainly breeds above 650 m), below 1,280 m Pen Malaysia. Often in bird-waves; sallies from perch. RANGE Co R (local movements) Myanmar, W,NW,NE(north-west),S Thailand, Pen Malaysia, Indochina (except Cochinchina). Un WV S Myanmar, C,NE,SE Thailand.

PLATE 86 WHISTLERS & MONARCHS TO WOODSHRIKES

1 MANGROVE WHISTLER *Pachycephala grisola* 15.5–17 cm
(a) **Adult** *grisola* (SW Myanmar to west S Thailand, Langkawi I): Drab brown above, greyer crown, white below, duller throat, greyish breast-wash. **Juvenile**: Rufescent-fringed tertials and secondaries, flesh/brown bill. **Other subspecies** *P.g.vandepolli* (elsewhere): Browner, slightly richer above. **VOICE** Song of loud high-pitched phrases introduced by 2–4 short notes: ***tit tit phew-whiu-whit***; ***chi chi chi wit-phew-chew***; ***tit tit tit too-whit*** etc. Last note often more explosive. **HABITAT & BEHAVIOUR** Mangroves and nearby areas, locally plantations, gardens, island forest. Unobtrusive and sluggish. **RANGE** Un/lc coastal **R** (except E Tonkin, N,C Annam); sc Singapore. Also inland Cambodia (Tonle Sap area), south-west S Laos.

Angkor Cambodia

2 BLACK-NAPED MONARCH *Hypothymis azurea* 16–17 cm
(a) **Male** *styani*: Blue with whitish belly/vent, black nuchal tuft and breast-band. (b) **Female:** Blue duller (mainly on head), warm-tinged greyish-brown above, no nuchal-patch or breast-band, greyer breast. **Juvenile:** Like female. **Other subspecies** *H.a.tytleri* (Coco Is) and *prophata* (Pen Malaysia, Singapore): Males deeper, more purplish-blue, less white below, *tytleri* with greyish (blue-tinged) vent. Females are deeper brown above, have deeper blue parts, particularly former which has greyish vent like male. *H.a.forrestia* (Mergui Archipelago), *montana* (W,NW,NE Thailand), *galerita* (W[south],SE Thailand). **VOICE** Song is clear ringing ***wii'wii'wii'wii'wii'wii..*** (c.3 notes per s). Harsh ***shweb-shweb*** or ***chwe-wi***, rasping ***tswit*** and ***tswit-wit***. **HABITAT** Broadleaved forest; up to 1,520 m (below 1,065 m Pen Malaysia). **RANGE** Co **R** (some movements), except C Thailand, E Tonkin; ra Singapore. Un/fc **WV** S Myanmar, C,NE,SE Thailand. Un **PM** C Thailand, E Tonkin.

3 ASIAN PARADISE-FLYCATCHER *Terpsiphone paradisi* 21 cm
(a) **Male** *indochinensis*: Tail <27 cm more. Rufous-chestnut upperside/tail, slaty-grey head/breast, crested black crown. (b) **Male white 'morph'**: Nearly all white, glossy black head. (c) **Female**: Like rufous male but no tail-streamers, crest shorter, eyering usually somewhat duller. (d) **Juvenile**: More rufous above, whitish below, initially scaled/mottled dull rufous on breast, brownish/pinkish bill, no eyering. (e) **Male** *incei* (VS E Myanmar, Tenasserim, Thailand and Cambodia southward): Black hood, grey breast, darker, deeper chestnut above. (f) **Female**: Throat darker than breast. **Other subspecies** *T.p.saturatior* (B N Myanmar), **WV** Tenasserim/S Thailand southwards) and *nicobarica* (Coco Is): Males duller, paler, more rufous above, buffy vent. *T.p.affinis* (**R** Pen Malaysia): Male typically richer, more chestnut above, darker throat/ breast. *T.p.burmae* (resident SW,S,C Myanmar). **VOICE** Song is clear rolling ***chu'wu'wu'wu'wu'wu...*** Typical call is harsh rasping ***whii***; ***whi-whu*** and ***whi-whu'whu*** etc. **HABITAT** Broadleaved evergreen forest, sometimes mangroves; migrants also in parks, gardens etc. Up to 1,500 m (below 1,220 m in Pen Malaysia). **RANGE** Fc/co. **R** (except N Myanmar, C Thailand, N Laos, W,E Tonkin, N Annam); formerly Singapore. **BV** (some may overwinter) N Myanmar, N Laos, W,E Tonkin, N Annam. **WV** C,S,E Myanmar, W,NE(south-west),SE Thailand. **PM** S Myanmar, N Laos, E Tonkin. **WV** and **PM** Tenasserim, C,S Thailand, Pen Malaysia, Singapore.

4 JAPANESE PARADISE-FLYCATCHER *T.atrocaudata* 19 cm
(a) **Male** *atrocaudata*: Tail <23 cm more. Black with whitish belly/vent, purplish above. (b) **Female/first winter**: Duller crown than Asian, breast and belly more demarcated, darker/browner tail. **HABITAT** Broadleaved evergreen forest, migrants also in mangroves, parks, gardens; up to 1,200 m. **RANGE** Ra/sc **WV** S Thailand, Pen Malaysia. Ra/sc **PM** W,NW,C,SE,S Thailand, Pen Malaysia, Singapore, C,S Laos, W,E Tonkin, C Annam.

5 RUFOUS-WINGED PHILENTOMA *Philentoma pyrhopterum* 17 cm
(a) **Male typical morph** *pyrhopterum*: Dull blue head/body, buffy-whitish belly/vent, reddish-chestnut greater coverts/tertials/ secondaries/tail. (b) **Male blue morph**: All dull blue, greyish vent (mixed whitish). (c) **Female**: Greyish-brown crown/head-sides (sometimes blue tinge), mid-brown above, buffy-whitish below, brown breast/flanks. **Juvenile**: Sexes said to soon be separable. **VOICE** Song is piping whistled ***tu-tuuu***. Harsh scoldings. **HABITAT** Middle/lower storey of broadleaved evergreen forest; up to 915 m. **RANGE** Fc/co **R** south Tenasserim, W(south),S Thailand, Pen Malaysia; formerly Singapore.

6 MAROON-BREASTED PHILENTOMA *P.velatum* 19–21 cm
(a) **Male** *caesium*: Dull blue, black face, dark maroon breast. (b) **Female**: Duller/darker; dull blackish lores/cheeks/throat/upper breast. **Juvenile**: Soon after fledging, males show some chestnut-maroon patches on breast. **VOICE** Bell-like whistled ***phu phu phu phu phu...*** Also quite powerful clear ***chut-ut chut-ut...*** **HABITAT** Middle/upper storey of broadleaved evergreen forest; up to 1,060 m. **RANGE** Sc/fc **R** Tenasserim, W,S Thailand, Pen Malaysia.

7 LARGE WOODSHRIKE *Tephrodornis gularis* 18.5–22.5 cm
(a) **Male** *jugans*: Greyish crown/nape, pale greyish-brown above, blackish mask, white rump. (b) **Female:** Duller, brown-streaked crown, browner mask and bill, buffier wash below. (c) **Juvenile**: Whitish/buffish shafts/tips/bars above. (d) **Male** *fretensis* (south-east S Thailand, Pen Malaysia [except northwest]): Smaller, more uniform bluish-slate above. Female has darker crown/throat/breast. **Other subspecies** *T.g.annectens* (south Tenasserim, S Thailand [except south-east], north-west Pen Malaysia): Male more greyish-washed, less contrasting above. *T.g.pelvicus* (SW,W,N,E,C,S Myanmar), *vernayi* (south E Myanmar, N Tenasserim, W Thailand), *mekongensis* (NE,SE Thailand, southern Indochina), *bainanus* (east N Laos, northern Vietnam). **VOICE** Song is airy ringing ***pi-pi-pi-pi-pi-pi...*** Harsh scolding ***chreek chreek chreek...*** **HABITAT & BEHAVIOUR** Broadleaved forest; up to 1,500 m. Usually in groups high in trees. **RANGE** Co **R** (except C Thailand); formerly Singapore.

Cambodia 2/13

8 COMMON WOODSHRIKE *T.pondicerianus* 14.5–17.5 cm
(a) **Adult** *pondicerianus*: Small, whitish eyebrow and outertail. (b) **Juvenile**: Whitish-buff spots/tips above, dusky mottling below. **Other subspecies** *T.p.orientis* (Cambodia, Vietnam). **VOICE** Accelerating trilled ***pi-pi-i-i-i-i-i***. Weak ***tue*** and ***tee*** notes and harsher, slightly ascending ***wih-wih-whee-whee*** etc. **HABITAT** Deciduous forests, dry areas with scattered trees; up to 1,100 m. **RANGE** Co **R** Myanmar, W,NW,NE,C Thailand, Cambodia, C,S Laos, C(south-west),S Annam, Cochinchina.

PLATE 87 MISCELLANEOUS THRUSHES & GRANDALA

1 BLUE-CAPPED ROCK THRUSH *Monticola cinclorhynchus* 19 cm
(**a**) **Male non-breeding**: Blue on throat, blackish lores; more rufous below than White-throated. (**b**) **Male breeding**: No fringing. (**c**) **Female**: Mostly plain above. **VOICE** Clear *rit-prileee-prileer*, *tew-li-di tew-li-di tew-li-di*. High *tri*, loud *goink*. **HABITAT** Open forest, cultivation. **RANGE** Rc (status?) SW Myanmar.

2 WHITE-THROATED ROCK THRUSH *M.gularis* 19 cm
(**a**) **Male non-breeding**: Chestnut lores/malar/rump/below (buffy-rufous vent), white throat-/wing-patch; pale fringes above. (**b**) **Male breeding**: No fringing. (**c**) **Female**: Heavy blackish bars/scales overall, white throat-patch. **VOICE** Sings with fluty whistles, 1–2 more complex phrases and *chat-at-at*. Soft *Quech*, *quack* and sharp *tack*. **HABITAT** More open broadleaved forest, plantations; to 1,220 m. **RANGE** Sc/un **WV** (except SW,N,S Myanmar, Tenasserim, C Thailand, Pen Malaysia, Singapore, W,E Tonkin). Un **PM** E Tonkin. **V** Pen Malaysia, Singapore.

3 CHESTNUT-BELLIED ROCK THRUSH *M.rufiventris* 23 cm
(**a**) **Male breeding**: Shiny blue above, dark face/throat, chestnut below. **Male non-breeding**: Pale fringing above/on throat. (**b**) **Female**: Dark-eared, buffy-white neck-patch, heavy scales below (few above). (**c**) **Juvenile female**: Broad buff to whitish spotting. **Juvenile male**: Wings/tail mostly blue, rump/upper-tail-coverts washed dull chestnut; warmer below than female. **VOICE** Sings with short warbling phrases. Sharp *quach*, rasping *chhrrr*. **HABITAT** Open evergreen/coniferous forest; 900–2,700 m. **RANGE** Un/co **R** (some movements) W,N,E Myanmar, NW Thailand (mainly **WV**), N Laos, W,E Tonkin.

4 BLUE ROCK THRUSH *Monticola solitarius* 21–23 cm
(**a**) **Male breeding** *pandoo*: Plainer/bluer than non-breeding. (**b**) **Male non-breeding**: Grey-blue with whitish-and-blackish bars/scales. (**c**) **Female non-breeding**: Plainer than other rock thrushes. **Female breeding**: Even plainer above. (**d**) **Juvenile**: Crown and mantle speckled buffish, paler below than female. (**e**) **Male non-breeding** *philippensis* (**WV** throughout): Dense scales, duller head/upperparts than Chestnut-bellied. (**f**) **Male breeding**: Cleaner; more like Chestnut-bellied. **Other subspecies** *M.s.madoci* (**R** S Thailand, Pen Malaysia). **VOICE** Sings with fluty *chu sree chur tee tee* and *wuchee-trr-trrt* etc. Low *tchuck* and high *tsee* or *tzick*, harsh *tak-tak* and *trr*. **HABITAT** Open areas, cultivation, cliffs, buildings; up to 1,830 m. **RANGE** Un R S Thailand, Pen Malaysia, W Tonkin; ? N Myanmar, N Laos. Co **WV** (except Singapore). Also **PM** SW Myanmar, E Tonkin. **V** Singapore.

5 MALAYAN WHISTLING THRUSH *Myophonus robinsoni* 26 cm
(**a**) **Adult**: Small; bright blue on shoulder, no spangling or whitish median covert tips. **Juvenile**: Duller. **VOICE** Softer song than Blue. Loud thin high *tseeee* call. **HABITAT & BEHAVIOUR** Broadleaved evergreen forest, usually near streams; 760–1,770 m. Shy, but on roads at dawn/dusk. **RANGE** Un R Pen Malaysia.

6 BLUE WHISTLING THRUSH *M.caeruleus* 30.5–35 cm
(**a**) **Adult** *eugenei*: Dark purple-blue with paler spangles, yellow bill. (**b**) **Juvenile**: Plainer/browner body/bill. (**c**) **Adult**

caeruleus (**WV**): Blackish bill; (**d**) **Adult** *dicrorhynchus* (south-east S Thailand, Pen Malaysia): Duller, whitish median covert tips, only vague spangling. **Other subspecies** *M.c.temminckii* (SW,W,N,C,E[north] Myanmar; **WV** NW Thailand), *crassirostris* (SE,S Thailand, north-west Pen Malaysia). **VOICE** Sings with fluty and scratchy notes. Harsh *scree*. **HABITAT** Broadleaved forest, usually near streams/waterfalls; up to 3,050 m, below 1,220 m in Pen Malaysia. **RANGE** Co **R** (except Thailand, Cochinchina). Un **WV** E Myanmar, NW,NE Thailand, Laos, W,E Tonkin, N Annam. Rc in winter (status?) Cochinchina.

7 CHESTNUT-CAPPED THRUSH *Zoothera interpres* 18 cm
(**a**) **Adult** *interpres*: Chestnut crown/nape, black throat/breast, white on wings. (**b**) **Juvenile**: Dull chestnut above with streaks, buffy face/breast, dark face-bars. **VOICE** Song of fluty whistles, chirrups, and sometimes grating and higher notes. Harsh, hard *tac*, thin high falling *tsi-i-i-i*. **HABITAT** Broadleaved evergreen forest; up to 760 m. **RANGE** Sc **R** S Thailand, Pen Malaysia.

8 ORANGE-HEADED THRUSH *Zoothera citrina* 20.5–23.5 cm
(**a**) **Male** *innotata* (NW Thailand to N Laos, S Indochina; winters to Pen Malaysia): Orange head/below, bluish-grey above. (**b**) **Female**: Duller; greyish-olive above. (**c**) **Juvenile**: Dark above, ear-covert bars, streaked/scaled. (**d**) **Male** *aurimacula* (north Indochina, C Annam): White median covert tips, dark ear-bars (both sexes). **Other subspecies** *Z.c.citrina* (**B** western and northern Myanmar)/*gibsonhilli* (**B** southern and eastern Myanmar, W Thailand; **VS** south to Pen Malaysia): White median covert tips. **VOICE** Sings with varied sweet rich musical notes. Low *tjuck* and thin *tsee* or *tzzeet*. **HABITAT** Broadleaved evergreen forest; thickets (mainly migrants); up to 1,525 m. **RANGE** Un **R** SW,W,S Myanmar, Tenasserim, W Thailand, Cambodia, C,S Annam. Un **BV** N Myanmar, NW,NE(north-west) Thailand. Un **WV** W,NE,S Thailand, Pen Malaysia, Cochinchina; S Myanmar? Also **PM** S Myanmar, C,S Thailand, Pen Malaysia. Rc (status?) C,E Myanmar, SE Thailand, Laos, E Tonkin, N Annam. **V** Singapore.

9 SIBERIAN THRUSH *Zoothera sibirica* 21.5–23.5 cm
(**a**) **Male** *sibirica*: Dark slaty; white supercilium and much of vent. (**b**) **Female**: Bold buffish supercilium, dark eyestripe and scales/mottling below, thin wing-bars. (**c**) **First-winter male**: Mixed male/female characters. **Other subspecies** *Z.s.davisoni* (widespread): Blacker; belly usually all dark. **VOICE** Song of hesitant, languid, rich 2–3 note phrases. Thin *tsit*, stronger *tseee*; soft *tsss* or *chrsss* in alarm. **HABITAT** Broadleaved evergreen forest; up to 2,565 m (**WV** mainly in mountains). **RANGE** Un/fc **WV** and **PM** Pen Malaysia, Singapore, W Tonkin, C,S Annam. Un **PM** (some winter?) Myanmar (except SW,W,N), Thailand (except C), N,C Laos, E Tonkin.

10 GRANDALA *Grandala coelicolor* 20.5–23 cm
(**a**) **Male**: Brilliant purplish-blue, black wings/tail. (**b**) **Female**: Brownish with whitish streaks, greyish-blue rump, white tips and patch on wings. **Juvenile**: Like female but more extensive/heavier streaks above. **VOICE** Conversational *dju-i*, *djew* and *djwi* notes. **HABITAT** Barren alpine areas, open forest; found at 1,830 m in winter. **RANGE** Rc (status?) N Myanmar.

182

PLATE 88 TYPICAL THRUSHES & COCHOAS

1 PLAIN-BACKED THRUSH *Zoothera mollissima* 26–27 cm
(a) Adult *mollissima*: Plainer wing with fainter bars than Long-tailed, warmer above. **Juvenile**: Differs like Long-tailed. **Other subspecies** *Z.m.griseiceps* (W Tonkin): Darker, greyer crown, warmer above. **VOICE** Song recalls Scaly (*Z.d.dauma*) but is slightly faster and more varied with rich melodious whistled phrases. Thin *chuck* and sharp rattle in alarm. **HABITAT** Rhododendron and conifer forest, thickets; 1,600–2,895 m. **RANGE** Sc **R** (minor movements) W Tonkin. **Rc** (R?) N Myanmar.

2 LONG-TAILED THRUSH *Zoothera dixoni* 25.5–27 cm
(a) Adult: Plain above, bold wing-bars, dark band across flight feathers. **(b) Juvenile**: Buff streaks and dark bars above. **VOICE** Quite slow *wu-ut-cheet-sher* or *wut-chet-shuur*, twittering *too-ee* etc.; sometimes rising *w'i-it*. **HABITAT** Broadleaved evergreen and coniferous forest; 2,135–3,655 m, to 1,000 m in winter. **RANGE** Un **R** N Myanmar. Sc/un **WV** E Myanmar, NW Thailand, N Laos. **Rc** (status?) W Myanmar, W Tonkin.

3 SCALY THRUSH *Zoothera dauma* 27–30 cm
(a) Adult *dauma*: Heavily marked with black and buff overall. **Juvenile**: Warmer above, diffuse markings. **Other subspecies** *Z.d.aurea* (**WV** N,E Myanmar, NW Thailand to northern Indochina, S Annam). **VOICE** Sings slow *pur-loo-tree-lay*, *dur-lee-dur-lee* and *drr-drr-chew-you-we-eeee* etc., after long pauses; *aurea* has whistled *weeeooooooon* or *pee-yuuuuu* (*pee* higher). Thin *tzeep*. **HABITAT** Broadleaved and rhododendron/coniferous forest; up to 2,590 m, **B** above 365 m. **RANGE** Sc/un lc **R** N,N Myanmar, W,NW,NE,S Thailand, N Laos, W,E Tonkin, S Annam. Sc/un **WV** (except C,SE,S Thailand, Pen Malaysia, Singapore, Cochinchina). Also **PM** E Tonkin. **V** S Thailand (away from **B** range), Pen Malaysia.

4 LONG-BILLED THRUSH *Zoothera monticola* 26.5–28 cm
(a) Adult *monticola*: Larger than Dark-sided; big bill, greyer and scaled above, spotted below. **Juvenile**: Colder above than Dark-sided, blacker, more spot-like markings below. **Other subspecies** *Z.m.atrata* (W Tonkin). **VOICE** Song is mournful slow whistled *te-e-uw* or *sew-a-tew-tew* etc.; sometimes with more rasping *rrraee ti tuu* or *trrray tya tyee* etc. Loud *zaaaaaaaa* alarm. **HABITAT** Broadleaved evergreen forest; 915–2,135 m. **RANGE** Sc **R** N,N Myanmar, W Tonkin.

5 DARK-SIDED THRUSH *Zoothera marginata* 23.5–25.5 cm
(a) Adult: Long bill, warmish above, dark flanks, scaly sides. **Juvenile**: Warm streaks/spots above, warmer breast with darker scales/mottling. **VOICE** Song is downward-inflected whistle (0.5 s). Soft *tchuck*. **HABITAT** Broadleaved evergreen forest, usually near water; 600–2,565 m. **RANGE** Un **R** Myanmar (except N,C), W,NW,NE,SE Thailand, Indochina (except Cochinchina).

6 WHITE-COLLARED BLACKBIRD *Turdus albocinctus* 27–28 cm
(a) Male: White collar. **(b) Female**: Brown; duller collar. **(c) Juvenile female**: Buffy streaks above, buffier below and scaly. Male is darker. **VOICE** Simple sad mellow song. Throaty *tuck-tuck...* **HABITAT** Broadleaved evergreen and coniferous forest, meadows; c.250 m (winter). **RANGE** Rc (status?) N Myanmar.

7 GREY-WINGED BLACKBIRD *Turdus boulboul* 27.5–29 cm
(a) Male: Pale greyish wing-patch. **(b) Female**: Brown with less subtle wing-patch. **(c) Juvenile female**: Buff streaks/spots above; buffish below with dark mottling. Male is darker. **VOICE** Rich melodious song (little repetition). Low *chuck* notes. **HABITAT** Broadleaved evergreen forest, clearings; 980–2,455 m. **RANGE** Un **R** N Laos, W Tonkin. Sc/un **WV** S Myanmar, NW Thailand. **V** NE Thailand. **Rc** (status?) N,E Myanmar, E Tonkin.

Laos, Luang Prabang

8 EURASIAN BLACKBIRD *Turdus merula* 28–29 cm
(a) Male *mandarinus*: All blackish. **(b) Female**: Browner; often paler, streaked throat. **First winter**: Dark bill. **VOICE** Leisurely mellow song, with little repetition. Deep *chup* notes, high *whiiiik*, soft *p'soook*. **HABITAT** Open forest, clearings, cultivation; up to 1,015 m. **RANGE** Sc/co **WV** Laos, W,E(also **PM**) Tonkin, N,C Annam. **V** N Myanmar, NW,NE Thailand, Cambodia.

9 CHESTNUT THRUSH *Turdus rubrocanus* 24–26.5 cm
(a) Male *gouldi*: Chestnut body; dark greyish hood. **(b) Female**: More rufous. **(c) Male** *rubrocanus* (W Myanmar): Paler hood, hint of collar. **(d) Female**: Duller/paler than male, more uniform hood. **VOICE** Sings with repeated short phrases. Deep *chuk*, and faster *kwik* notes. **HABITAT** Broadleaved evergreen forest; 200–2,900 m. **RANGE** Sc/un **WV** W,N,E Myanmar, NW Thailand, N Laos, W Tonkin. **V** C Laos, E Tonkin.

10 CHINESE THRUSH *Turdus mupinensis* 23 cm
(a) Adult: Smallish, spotted below; two buff wing-bars, no white on outertail. **First winter**: Faint darker fringing and pale buff streaks above; pale buff spots at wing-covert tips. **VOICE** Usually sings with measured, pleasant 3–5 note phrases. **HABITAT** Plantations, thickets; found at sea level. **RANGE** **V** E Tonkin.

11 PURPLE COCHOA *Cochoa purpurea* 26.5–28 cm
(a) Male: Brownish-purple with pale lavender-blue crown. **(b) Female**: Dark rufescent-brown above, deep buffish-rufous below. **(c) Juvenile male**: White-marked blackish crown, buff streaks above, buff below with blackish bars. Female differs similarly. **VOICE** Deeper and clearer than Green: *whiiiiii*. Very thin, thrush-like *sit* and *tssri* notes. **HABITAT & BEHAVIOUR** Broadleaved evergreen forest; 1,000–2,565 m, rarely down to 400 m. Forages on ground and visits fruiting trees. **RANGE** Sc N,C,E,S(east) Myanmar, north Tenasserim, NW Thailand, N Laos, W,E Tonkin.

12 GREEN COCHOA *Cochoa viridis* 27–29 cm
(a) Male: Green; blue crown and nape, silvery-blue markings on black wings, black-tipped blue tail. **(b) Female**: Wings washed brownish, no blue below. **(c) Juvenile**: White-marked blackish crown, spotted buff above, scaled below. **(d) First-summer male**: Whitish strip from chin to lower ear-coverts and neck-side, washed golden-buff below. Female differs similarly. **VOICE** Sings with loud pure, monotone whistles: *hiiiiiiii*, lasting c.2 s. **HABITAT** Broadleaved evergreen forest; 700–2,565 m, occasionally down to 400 m. **RANGE** Sc **R** east S,E Myanmar, W,NW,SE Thailand, south-west Cambodia, Laos, W,E Tonkin, N,C,S Annam.

PLATE 89 DIPPERS, TYPICAL THRUSHES & *RHINOMYIAS* FLYCATCHERS

1 WHITE-THROATED DIPPER *Cinclus cinclus* 19–20.5 cm
(**a**) **Adult** *przewalskii*: White throat/breast. **Juvenile**: Greyish with dark tips above, whitish with dark scales below, white tips on wing/tail. **First winter**: As adult but pale-scaled belly/vent. VOICE Sharp, rather rasping *zink* or *zrets*. HABITAT Rivers and streams; found at 2,835 m. RANGE Sc **WV** N Myanmar.

~~Luang Prabang (rwen)~~

2 BROWN DIPPER *Cinclus pallasii* 21.5 cm
(**a**) **Adult** *dorjei*: All brown. (**b**) **Juvenile**: Paler/greyer with dark scaling, pale greyish markings on throat/belly, whitish wing-fringing. **Other subspecies** *C.p.pallasii* (Indochina). VOICE High rasping *dzzit* or *dzit-dzit*. HABITAT Rivers and streams; 200–2,835 m (below 1,000 m Thailand). RANGE Un/co **R** W,N,E Myanmar, N,C Laos, W,E Tonkin, N Annam. Rc (status?) NW Thailand.

3 GREY-BACKED THRUSH *Turdus hortulorum* 24 cm
(**a**) **Male**: Bluish-grey; orange-rufous flanks, otherwise whitish below. (**b**) **Female**: From Black-breasted by brownish bill, paler and more olive-tinged head-sides/upperparts, paler breast with several rows of blackish arrowhead spots. **First-winter male**: Obvious throat-streaking, dark breast markings. VOICE Harsh *chack-chack* and shrill whistled *tsee* or *cheee* in alarm. HABITAT Broadleaved evergreen forest, more open woodland; up to 1,100 m. RANGE Un/fc **WV** E Tonkin, N Annam.

4 BLACK-BREASTED THRUSH *Turdus dissimilis* 23–23.5 cm
(**a**) **Male**: Black hood, orange-rufous lower breast and flanks. (**b**) **Female**: Yellowish bill, plain brown above, breast mixed grey and pale rufous with blackish blotches/spots, orange-rufous flanks. (**c**) **Juvenile**: As female but darker tips and buffy streaks/tips above, heavier markings below, duller flanks. VOICE Sings with sweet mellow, unhurried 3–8 note phrases. Throaty *tup-tup-tup..*, thin *seee*. HABITAT Broadleaved evergreen and coniferous forest; 1,220–2,500 m, to 200 m in winter. RANGE Un/fc **R** (local movements) W,N,E Myanmar. Sc/un **WV** NW Thailand, C Laos, E Tonkin. Rc (status?) N Laos, W Tonkin.

5 JAPANESE THRUSH *Turdus cardis* 22.5 cm
(**a**) **Male**: Blackish hood, white with dark spots below. (**b**) **Female**: Spotted flanks (/belly) with little orange-rufous, sometimes warm buff on throat/breast. (**c**) **First-winter male**: Paler; whiter throat with dark markings, grey breast with heavy markings. VOICE Thin *tsweee* or *tsuuu*. HABITAT Broadleaved evergreen forest, plantations; up to 1,100 m. RANGE Un/lc **WV** N,C Laos, W,E Tonkin, N,C Annam. **V** NW,NE Thailand, S Laos.

6 GREY-SIDED THRUSH *Turdus feae* 23.5 cm
(**a**) **Male**: Warmish above (mainly head), grey below with white chin and belly/vent. **Female**: Less grey below, warm breast-fringing, slight spots/streaks on throat/upper breast. (**b**) **First winter**: Warmer below than female, dark throat-streaks, pale wing-bar. VOICE *zeeee* or *sieee*, thinner than Eyebrowed. HABITAT Broadleaf evergreen forest; 520–2,565 m. RANGE Sc/un **WV** W,E Myanmar, north Tenasserim, W,NW Thailand, C Laos.

7 EYEBROWED THRUSH *Turdus obscurus* 22.5–24.5 cm
(**a**) **Male**: Grey hood, white eyebrow, orange-rufous breast and flanks. (**b**) **Female**: Browner, washed-out flanks. **First-winter**

female Pale buffish greater covert tips. Male hints at adult. VOICE Thin *tseee*, chuckling *dack-dack*, *tchuck*. HABITAT Forest, plantations etc.; to 3,100 m. RANGE Fc **WV** (except SW Myanmar, SE Thailand, Singapore, N Annam). Un **PM** Singapore, Cambodia.

8 DARK-THROATED THRUSH *Turdus ruficollis* 22.5–27.5 cm
(**a**) **Male breeding** *ruficollis* (Myanmar, Thailand): Rufous-red supercilium, throat, breast and outertail. **Male non-breeding**: Whitish fringing on supercilium to breast. (**b**) **Female**: Black-streaked throat-sides/breast, duller supercilium to breast. (**c**) **First-winter female**: Little rufous; black-streaked throat and breast. (**d**) **Male breeding** *atrogularis* 'Black-throated Thrush' (throughout): Black face to upper breast. (**e**) **Female**: Whiter throat and submoustachial, pale-scaled upper breast. (**f**) **First-winter female**: No rufous on tail or elsewhere. VOICE Calls include soft *tsak*, thin *seee* or *ziep* in flight; rapid *betetetet* and *wiwiwi*. Soft *which-which-which* from *ruficollis*. HABITAT Open broadleaved evergreen forest, cultivation; 150–2,565 m. RANGE Sc/un **WV** N,C,E Myanmar. **V** NW Thailand, E Tonkin.

9 DUSKY THRUSH *Turdus naumanni* 22.5–25 cm
(**a**) **Male** *eunomus*: Bold supercilium, much black on breast and flanks, rufescent wings. **Female**: Usually less black above and on ear-coverts/breast. (**b**) **First-winter female**: Like adult or duller, pale covert-tips. Male differs from adult similarly. **Other subspecies** *T.n.naumanni* (**V** N Myanmar): Greyer and plainer above on head-side, markings on head/underparts mostly reddish-rufous, rump to much of tail reddish-rufous. Male dappled reddish-rufous above, quite plain reddish-rufous on throat and breast. Females/first-winters have whiter head markings, some darker markings below (mainly malar), less reddish-rufous above. VOICE *chuk-chuk*, *chack-chack*, thin *shrree*, *swic*. HABITAT Open forest, cultivation; up to 2,900 m. RANGE Sc **WV** N,C,S Myanmar, W,NW Thailand, W,E Tonkin.

10 BROWN-CHESTED JUNGLE FLYCATCHER *Rhinomyias brunneata* 16 cm
(**a**) **Adult** *brunneata*: Yellowish lower mandible, faint throat-mottling. **First winter**: Dark lower mandible-tip, warm buff greater covert/tertial tips. HABITAT Broadleaf forest; to 395 m. RANGE Sc **WV** S Thailand southward. Sc **PM** W,NW,C,S Thailand, Pen Malaysia.

11 FULVOUS-CHESTED JUNGLE FLYCATCHER *Rhinomyias olivacea* 14–15.5 cm
(**a**) **Adult** *olivacea*: Dark bill, whitish throat, warm buffish-brown breast/flanks. (**b**) **Juvenile**: Brown tips and buff speckles above, mottled breast/flanks. VOICE Song recalls *Cyornis* but quite short/slurred phrases, some scratchy notes. Drawn-out *churr* or *trrt*, harsh *tac*. HABITAT Broadleaved evergreen forest; up to 885 m. RANGE Sc/lfc **R** south Tenasserim, S Thailand.

12 GREY-CHESTED JUNGLE FLYCATCHER *Rhinomyias umbratilis* 15.5–16.5 cm
(**a**) **Adult**: Grey breast, white throat, dark malar. (**b**) **Juvenile**: Greyer than Fulvous-chested, bolder spots. VOICE Song more varied than Fulvous-chested. Harsh *chrrr-chrrr-chrrr*, *trrrt'it'it'it*. HABITAT Broadleaved evergreen forest; up to 1,160 m. RANGE Sc/fc **R** extreme S Thailand, Pen Malaysia.

10–12 to different scale

PLATE 90 *MUSCICAPA* & *FICEDULA* FLYCATCHERS

1 GREY-STREAKED FLYCATCHER *Muscicapa griseisticta* 15 cm
(a) **Adult**: Clean whitish below (including undertail-coverts) with extensive, well-defined streaks across breast and flanks (often to belly). HABITAT Open forest, plantations, gardens; found in lowlands. RANGE V Singapore, C Annam, Cochinchina.

2 DARK-SIDED FLYCATCHER *Muscicapa sibirica* 11.5–13 cm
(a) **Adult** *rothschildi*: Dark smudgy-streaked breast/flanks, dark undertail-covert centres. (b) **Juvenile**: Blacker above with buff spots/tips, blackish-marked below. (c) **Adult** *sibirica* (widespread **VS**, except Myanmar): Whiter below, clearer breast-streaks. (d) **Adult (worn)**: Spring. Less streaking. **Other subspecies** *M.s.cacabata* (W Myanmar?). VOICE Weak sibilant *tsee* notes, then melodious trills/whistles. HABITAT Forest edge; plantations, gardens etc. on migration; up to 3,660 m (**B** above 2,135 m). RANGE Lfc **R** (some movements) W,N Myanmar. **Rc** (probably **B**) E Myanmar, W,E Tonkin. Un/fc **WV** (except SW,W,N Myanmar, N,C Laos, W,E Tonkin, N Annam). Un/fc **PM** W,C,S Thailand, Pen Malaysia, Cambodia, Laos, E Tonkin, N Annam. **Rc** (status?) SW Myanmar.

3 ASIAN BROWN FLYCATCHER *M.dauurica* 12.5–13.5 cm
(a) **Adult** *dauurica*: Brownish-grey upperparts/breast-wash (usually no defined streaks); pale-based lower mandible, whitish eyering/lores, pale greyish covert/tertial fringes. (b) **Adult (worn)**: Greyer; paler below. (c) **Adult** *siamensis* (**R** race): Browner above, duller/plainer below, mostly pale lower mandible, dull eyering. **Juvenile**: Whiter scapular/covert markings than Dark-sided, fine breast-scaling. **First winter** Paler greater covert tips/tertial fringes than adult. VOICE Song of short trills and 2–3 note whistled phrases. Calls with thin *tse-ti-ti-ti-ti*, short *tzi*. HABITAT Open forest, plantations, parks, gardens, mangroves; up to 1,585 m. **B** in open forest inland; 600–1,400 m. RANGE Sc/un **R** north Tenasserim, NW Thailand, S Annam. Co **WV** (except N,E Myanmar). Also **PM** C,S Thailand, Pen Malaysia, Singapore, Cambodia, Laos, E Tonkin.

4 BROWN-STREAKED FLYCATCHER *M.williamsoni* 13 cm
(a) **Adult**: Warmer/browner above than *M.d.dauurica*, yellowish lower mandible (tip dark), duller/buffier submoustachial, buffier lores/wing-fringing, usually distinct brownish streaks on breast/flanks. (a) **Adult (worn)**: Breeders have vaguer streaking below, plainer head/wing pattern. VOICE Thin sharp *tzi* and harsh slurred *cheititit*. HABITAT Edge of broadleaved forest, migrants also in parks etc.; to 1,295 m. RANGE Sc/un **R** (some movements) S Myanmar, S Thailand, north-west Pen Malaysia, Cambodia, Cochinchina. Sc/un **WV** Pen Malaysia, Singapore (ra). Sc **PM** C,W(coastal) Thailand. **Rc** (status?) NE Thailand.

5 BROWN-BREASTED FLYCATCHER *M.muttui* 13–14 cm
(a) **Adult (fresh)**: Autumn/early winter bird. Larger/largerbilled than Asian Brown, pale yellowish lower mandible, colder greyish-brown crown/head-sides contrast sharply with broad whitish eyering/lores, rufescent tinge above, enclosed white submoustachial patch, warm greyish breast/flanks, deep buff wing-fringing. Duller when worn. VOICE Complex weak high song. Thin *sit*. HABITAT Broadleaved evergreen forest; 1,220–1,645 m. RANGE Sc **BV** W Tonkin. Sc/un **PM** W,C Myanmar. **Rc** (breeds?) N,E Myanmar, NW Thailand, E Tonkin.

6 FERRUGINOUS FLYCATCHER *M.ferruginea* 12.5–13 cm
(a) **Adult (fresh)**: Richly rufescent, slaty-grey on head. (b) **Juvenile**: Blacker above with buff streaks/mottling, blackish-scaled breast. VOICE Very thin *tsit-tittu-tittu* phrases. Short sharp *tssit-tssit* and *tssit tssit tssit...* HABITAT Broadleaved evergreen forest; up to 2,135 m. RANGE Un/fc **BV** W Tonkin. Sc/un **WV** S Thailand, Pen Malaysia, S Annam, Cochinchina. Sc/un **PM** E,S Myanmar, Thailand (except C), Pen Malaysia, N,C Laos, C Annam. **V** Singapore. **Rc** (status?) W,N Myanmar.

7 YELLOW-RUMPED FLYCATCHER *Ficedula zanthopygia* 13 cm
(a) **Male winter**: White supercilium/long wing-patch, yellow on rump and below. (b) **Male spring**: Orange-flushed throat/breast. (c) **Female**: Greyish-olive above. Yellow rump, white wing-patch. **First-winter male**: From female by mostly blackish uppertail-coverts, white of wing only a bar on inner greater coverts. VOICE Rattled *tr'r'r't*. HABITAT Broadleaved forest, plantations, parks etc.; to 950 m. RANGE Sc/un **PM** Thailand, Pen Malaysia, Singapore, N Laos, W,E Tonkin, N,C Annam. Sc/un **WV** W(south),S Thailand, Pen Malaysia, Singapore.

8 NARCISSUS FLYCATCHER *Ficedula narcissina* 13–13.5 cm
(a) **Male** *narcissina*: Yellow supercilium, whiter belly than Yellow-rumped, small wing-patch. (b) **Female/first-winter male**: Browner above than Green-backed, whitish below with dark scales/mottling on throat-sides/breast, greyish/brownish breast-wash/flanks; sometimes faint yellowish tinge on belly. HABITAT Open woodland, plantations, parks, gardens; lowlands. RANGE **V** W(coastal) Thailand, E Tonkin, C Annam.

9 GREEN-BACKED FLYCATCHER *Ficedula elisae* 13–13.5 cm
(a) **Male**: Greyish olive-green above, bright yellow loral stripe, eyering, rump and below, white wing-patch. (b) **Female**: Duller above, rufescent-tinged uppertail-coverts/tail, no yellow on rump or white on wing, faint pale wing-bars; duller yellow below. HABITAT Broadleaved evergreen forest, migrants also in plantations, parks etc.; up to 1,295 m. RANGE Sc **WV** S Thailand, Pen Malaysia (also **PM**). **V** NE Thailand, Singapore, E Tonkin.

10 MUGIMAKI FLYCATCHER *F.mugimaki* 13–13.5 cm
(a) **Male**: White supercilium/wing-patch/tertial edges, rufousorange below. (b) **Female**: Greyish-brown above, buffy-orange throat/breast, wing-bars. (c) **First-winter male**: Greyer head-sides than female, stronger supercilium, brighter throat/breast. VOICE Rattled *trr'rr* or *trrrik*. HABITAT Broadleaved evergreen and pine forest, migrants also in plantations, parks, gardens; to 2,010 m (**WV** mainly above 800 m). RANGE Sc/lfc **WV** W,NE,SE,S Thailand, Pen Malaysia, Cambodia, Laos, C,S Annam. Sc/un **PM** NW,NE,C,S Thailand, Singapore, Cambodia, Laos, W,E Tonkin.

11 RUFOUS-CHESTED FLYCATCHER *F.dumetoria* 12 cm
(a) **Male** *muelleri*: Small; long supercilium/wing-streak, darker tertials than Mugimaki. (b) **Female**: Small; shortish tail, paler throat than Mugimaki, warm buff loral line/eyering, rusty-buffish covert-tips/tertial edges. VOICE Sings with thin wispy *sii'wi-sii* and *si-wi-oo* etc. HABITAT Understorey of broadleaved evergreen forest; up to 825 m. RANGE Sc/un **R** S Thailand, Pen Malaysia.

PLATE 91 *FICEDULA* FLYCATCHERS

1 SLATY-BACKED FLYCATCHER *Ficedula hodgsonii* 13 cm
(**a**) **Male**: Dark above, orange-rufous below. (**b**) **Female**: Dull olive-brown above, greyish throat/breast, rufescent uppertail-coverts, whitish eyering. **First winter**: Warmer above than female, clearer wing-bar. VOICE Song of rather short meandering, generally descending slurred-together whistled notes. Hard rattled *terrbt* or *tcbrt*. HABITAT Broadleaved evergreen forest, secondary growth; 600–2,750 m. RANGE Un/fc **R** (some movements) W,N,E Myanmar. Sc/fc **WV** C,S Myanmar, Tenasserim, W,NW,NE Thailand, south-west Cambodia, N,C Laos.

2 RUFOUS-GORGETED FLYCATCHER *Ficedula strophiata* 13–14 cm
(**a**) **Male** *strophiata*: Blackish face, whitish eyebrow, orangey gorget. (**b**) **Female**: Duller. (**c**) **Juvenile**: Blackish tips and rich buff spots above, buff with blackish scales below. **Other subspecies** *F.s.fuscogularis* (S Annam): Much larger gorget, warmer above. Male has greyer face; female a grey chin. VOICE Song is thin *zwi chir rri* (*zwi* sharp) etc. Low *tchuk-tchuk-tchuk*, harsh *trrt*, sharp *zwi*. HABITAT Broadleaved evergreen forest; 1,500–3,050 m, to 700 m in winter. RANGE Fc/co **R** W,N Myanmar, east S Laos, S Annam. Un/fc **WV** C,E,S(east) Myanmar, Tenasserim, NW,NE Thailand, N Laos, W,E Tonkin.

3 RED-THROATED FLYCATCHER *Ficedula parva* 13 cm
(**a**) **Male non-breeding/female** *albicilla*: Buffy-grey breast, blackish tail with white; dark bill. (**b**) **Male breeding**: Orange throat, bordered grey. **First winter**: As female but buffy greater covert/tertial tips. VOICE Rhythmic song is sharp/high, then clear, descending. Rattled *trrrt*, dry *tek* notes, harsh *zree*. HABITAT & BEHAVIOUR Open woodland, plantations, parks etc.; up to 2,135 m. Cocks tail. RANGE Co **WV** (except Pen Malaysia, Singapore). **V** Pen Malaysia. Also **PM** Cambodia, E Tonkin.

4 WHITE-GORGETED FLYCATCHER *Ficedula monileger* 12–13 cm
(**a**) **Adult** *leucops*: Small; clean white throat bordered black. **Juvenile**: Darker above with warm buff streaks, buff-tipped greater coverts, buffish below with diffuse dark brown streaks. **Other subspecies** *F.m.gularis* (SW Myanmar). VOICE Song of very high, wispy, slurred, rather forced scratchy phrases. Metallic *tik* or *trik* notes, sometimes with very thin, stressed *sii* or *siiu* notes. HABITAT Low vegetation in broadleaved evergreen forest, bamboo; 600–1,900 m. RANGE Un/lfc **R** SW,W,S,N,E Myanmar, NW,NE Thailand, Laos, W,E Tonkin, N,C Annam.

5 RUFOUS-BROWED FLYCATCHER *F.solitaris* 12–13 cm
(**a**) **Adult** *submonileger*: More rufescent than White-gorgeted, rufous spectacles; faint throat border. (**b**) **Adult** *malayana* (south of c.8°N): Richer rufous-chestnut. VOICE Similar to White-gorgeted. HABITAT Broadleaved evergreen forest, bamboo; 760–1,400 m, locally down to 395 m. RANGE Un/lc **R** Tenasserim, W,S Thailand, Pen Malaysia, east S Laos, S Annam.

6 SNOWY-BROWED FLYCATCHER *F.hyperythra* 11–13 cm
(**a**) **Male** *hyperythra*: Slaty-blue above, white eyebrow. (**b**) **Female**: Buffy lores/eyering/underparts, paler throat/vent, rufescent wings. (**c**) **Juvenile female**: Blackish fringes and warm buff

streaks/speckles above; heavily marked blackish below. Male has slaty-blue tail. (**b**) **Female** *annamensis* (S Annam): Crown washed bluish-grey, more orange-buff below. **Other subspecies** *F.h.sumatrana* (Pen Malaysia). VOICE Sings with thin wheezy *tsit-sit-si-sii* etc. Thin *sip*. HABITAT Broadleaved evergreen forest; 1,000–2,750 m, locally 400 m in winter. RANGE Fc **R**, some movements (except SW Myanmar, W,C,SE,S Thailand, Singapore, N Annam, Cochinchina). Also **PM** E Tonkin.

Laos Luang Prabang Jan

7 LITTLE PIED FLYCATCHER *F.westermanni* 11–12.5 cm
(**a**) **Male** *australorientis*: Black and white. (**b**) **Female**: Very grey, rufous uppertail-coverts, mostly white below. (**c**) **Juvenile female**: Blackish fringes/buff spots above, lightly scaled below. Male wing/tail blacker with white recalling adult. **Other subspecies** *F.w.westermanni* (S Thailand, Pen Malaysia): Female more slaty above. *F.w.langbianis* (S Laos, S Annam). VOICE Sweet thin song, often followed by rattled call. Sharp *swit* and rattling *trrrt*. HABITAT Broadleaved evergreen and pine forest; 200–2,565 m, above 1,065 m Pen Malaysia. RANGE Co **R** (except C,SE Thailand, Singapore, E Tonkin, C Annam, Cochinchina).

8 ULTRAMARINE FLYCATCHER *F.superciliaris* 12 cm
(**a**) **Male** *aestigma*: Dark blue breast-patches, white below. (**b**) **Female**: No rufous on uppertail-coverts, brownish-grey throat-/breast-side. (**c**) **Juvenile female**: Blackish tips and buff spots above, buffy-white with blackish scales below. Male shows some blue on wings/tail. (**d**) **First-winter male**: Like female but blue on wings/tail/mantle, buff wing-bar. VOICE Disjointed *tseep-te-e-te-e-te-e te-tib tseep tse-e-ep..* song. Rattled *trrrrt* and *chi trrrt*. HABITAT Open forest; 915–1,700 m, locally 150 m in winter. RANGE Sc/un **WV** NW Thailand. **Rc** (status?) C,E Myanmar.

9 SLATY-BLUE FLYCATCHER *Ficedula tricolor* 12.5–13 cm
(**a**) **Male** *diversa* (Thailand, Indochina): Buffy-white throat, buffy blue-grey breast, white in tail. (**b**) **Female/first-winter male**: Darker/warmer above than Slaty-backed, rufescent tail, buffish eyering/below. **Juvenile**: Large warm buff spots above, buffy with heavy blackish scales/streaks below. (**c**) **Male**; (**d**) **Female** *cerviniventris* (W Myanmar): Warm buff below. Other Myanmar races unclear. VOICE Song is high 3–4 note *chreet-chrr-whit-it* etc. Sharp *tic*, rolling *trrri* notes. HABITAT & BEHAVIOUR Secondary growth, scrub and grass; 1,500–2,750 m, to 450 m in winter. Skulks low down, cocks tail. RANGE Un/fc **R** (some movements) W,N,E,S(east) Myanmar, W Tonkin. Sc/fc **WV** NW Thailand, N Laos, E Tonkin. Also **PM** E Tonkin.

10 SAPPHIRE FLYCATCHER *Ficedula sapphira* 11–11.5 cm
(**a**) **Male breeding** *laotiana*: Recalls Ultramarine but orange-rufous throat-/breast-centre. (**b**) **Male non-breeding**: Brown on head/mantle/breast-sides. (**c**) **Female**: Shortish tail, rufescent uppertail-coverts, deep buffish-orange throat/breast. (**d**) **Juvenile**: Darker with rich buff spots above, buffier throat and breast with blackish scales. **First-winter male**: Like non-breeding but buff greater covert bar, pale tertial tips. **Other subspecies** *F.s.sapphira* (W Myanmar). VOICE Short hard rattles: *tssyi-tchrrrt; tchrrrt tchrrrt tchrrrt..* etc. HABITAT Broadleaved evergreen forest; 1,200–2,565 m. RANGE **Rc** (**R**?) N,E,S(east) Myanmar, N,C Laos, W Tonkin. Sc **WV** NW Thailand.

PLATE 92 BLUE-AND-WHITE & VERDITER FLYCATCHERS & NILTAVAS

1 BLUE-AND-WHITE FLYCATCHER *Cyanoptila cyanomelana* 18 cm
(**a**) **Male** *cyanomelana*: Large; azure to cobalt-blue above, blackish head-sides to breast, otherwise white. (**b**) **Female**: Clear-cut white belly/vent, no blue, no white at tail-base; rather uniform pale brownish throat/breast, usually buffish/whitish vertical/horizontal throat-patch. (**c**) **First-winter male**: As female but wings, tail, scapulars and back to uppertail-coverts like adult male. **Other subspecies** *C.c.cumatilis* (? widespread): More turquoise above, bluer/turquoise head-sides, throat and upper breast. A valid race? **VOICE** Low *tic* and *tac* notes. **HABITAT** Open broadleaved evergreen forest, plantations, parks etc.; up to 1,830 m (mostly lowlands). **RANGE** Sc/un **PM** south Tenasserim, Thailand, Pen Malaysia (some winter), Singapore, Indochina (except E Tonkin, N Annam).

2 VERDITER FLYCATCHER *Eumyias thalassina* 15–17 cm
(**a**) **Male breeding** *thalassina*: Turquoise-blue; black lores, white-tipped dark undertail-coverts. (**b**) **Male non-breeding**: Duller, more turquoise. (**c**) **Female breeding**: Duller/greyer-tinged than male, dusky lores. (**d**) **Female non-breeding**: Duller/greyer below. **Juvenile**: Greyer head/body than non-breeding female with buff/whitish speckling, buff/whitish covert-tips, dark scales below. **Other subspecies** *E.t.thallasoides* (S Tenasserim/S Thailand southward): Generally bluer, less turquoise. **VOICE** Sings with hurried high undulating musical notes, gradually descending. **HABITAT** More open broadleaved evergreen forest, also gardens, mangroves etc. on migration; up to 2,740 m (below 1,220 m in Pen Malaysia). **RANGE** Co **R** (except C,S Myanmar, C Thailand). Un **WV** C,NE,SE Thailand. Sc/un **PM** E Tonkin, S Annam. **Rc** (status?) C,S Myanmar.

3 LARGE NILTAVA *Niltava grandis* 20–21.5 cm
(**a**) **Male** *grandis*: Dark blue above, lighter crown/neck/rump, mostly blue-black below. (**b**) **Female**: Light blue neck-patch, brown below with buffish throat-patch. **Juvenile male**: Like juvenile female but mostly blue wings/tail, soon shows blue patches above. (**c**) **Juvenile female**: Black tips and buff to rufous-buff spots above, deep rich buff and narrowly scaled blackish below (paler throat-centre/vent). (**d**) **Female** *decorata* (S Annam): Darker blue neck-patch, shining blue crown and nape. **Other subspecies** *N.g.decipiens* (S Thailand, Pen Malaysia; N Laos[or unnamed race]): Recalls *decorata* but bluish-slate crown/nape. **VOICE** Ascending soft, whistled (usually 3–4 note): *uu-uu-du-di* or *uu'uu'di* etc. Rasping rattles and soft *chu-ii*, (*ii* higher). **HABITAT** Broadleaved evergreen forest; 900–2,565 m, locally to 450 m in winter (above 1,220 m in Pen Malaysia). **RANGE** F/c **R** (except SW,C Myanmar, C Thailand, Singapore, Cochinchina).

4 SMALL NILTAVA *Niltava macgrigoriae* 13.5–14 cm
(**a**) **Male** *signata*: Like miniature Large but throat/upper breast blue-black, grading to paler grey belly and whitish vent; lighter blue forehead/neck-patch. (**b**) **Female**: Like miniature Large but darker throat-centre, browner (less greyish) crown, generally greyer below with whitish abdomen-centre, buffy undertail-coverts. (**c**) **Juvenile female**: Much smaller than Large, throat concolorous with breast, centre of abdomen and vent whitish.

VOICE Song is very thin, high, rising/falling *swii-swii-ii-swii*, level *tsii-sii* or descending *tsii-sii-swi*. Harsh metallic churring and scolding. **HABITAT** Broadleaved evergreen forest; 700–2,565 m, locally to 275 m in winter. **RANGE** Un/fc **R** N,E,S(east) Myanmar, north Tenasserim, W,NW Thailand, Laos, W,E Tonkin, N,C Annam. Also **PM/V** coastal E Tonkin.

5 FUJIAN NILTAVA *Niltava davidi* 18 cm
(**a**) **Male**: Only front and side of crown shining blue, hind-crown hardly brighter than mantle, no shoulder-patch, breast duller/darker/more rufous than Rufous-bellied, usually contrasts with buffier belly/vent. (**b**) **Female**: A shade darker/colder above than Rufous-bellied, no bright rufous on wings/tail; usually slightly darker lower throat/upper breast/flanks, gorget contrasts more. **VOICE** Very thin high *sssseu* or *siiiii*. Sharp metallic *tit tit tit..* and *trrt trrt tit tit trrt trrt..* etc. **HABITAT** Broadleaved evergreen forest, also parks etc. on migration; up to 1,700 m. **RANGE** Un **R/BV** W Tonkin. Sc/fc **WV** SW Cambodia, Laos, E Tonkin, N,C Annam. **V** SE Thailand.

6 RUFOUS-BELLIED NILTAVA *Niltava sundara* 18 cm
(**a**) **Male** *sundara*: Very dark blue; paler shining blue crown, neck-/shoulder-patches and rump/uppertail-coverts, dark orange-rufous below. (**b**) **Female**: Strongly rufescent wings and tail, blue neck-patch, whitish gorget (sometimes absent). Greyish-olive below, buff chin, paler buffy-grey/whitish belly-centre/vent. **Juvenile**: Paler mantle than Large, much more rufous uppertail-coverts/tail, suggestion of gorget and whiter belly-centre/vent. Male soon shows orange-rufous below. **Other subspecies** *N.s.denotata* (**rc** N Myanmar, NW Thailand, N Laos). **VOICE** Calls with thin metallic *tsi tsi tsi tsi..*, hard *tic* and *trrt* notes, scolding rattles. **HABITAT** Broadleaved evergreen forest; 900–2,720 m, locally down to 450 m in winter. **RANGE** Fc/co **R** W,N,E,S(east) Myanmar. Un/fc **WV** C Myanmar, north Tenasserim, NW Thailand. **Rc** (status?) N,C Laos.

7 RUFOUS-VENTED NILTAVA *Niltava sumatrana* 15 cm
(**a**) **Male**: Shining blue duller than Rufous-bellied, no shoulder-patch, fainter neck-patch. (**b**) **Female**: Recalls Rufous-bellied but crown, nape and underparts greyer, undertail-coverts pale rufous. **VOICE** Song of monotonous, rather undulating clear whistles. Rapid scratchy slurred notes. **HABITAT** Broadleaved evergreen forest; above 1,525 m. **RANGE** Lc **R** Pen Malaysia.

8 VIVID NILTAVA *Niltava vivida* 18.5–19 cm
(**a**) **Male** *oatesi*: Like Rufous-bellied but orange-rufous forms wedge on centre of lower throat. (**b**) **Female**: No blue neck-patch. Otherwise like Large but somewhat paler/greyer below, belly-centre often paler still or buffy-tinged, undertail-coverts pale buff, wings/tail a shade paler/less rufescent. Lacks gorget. **Juvenile**: Spotting above and base-colour below typically paler and more buff than Large, plainer paler buff undertail-coverts, buff eyering. **VOICE** Song is slow mellow whistled *beu wii riu chrt-trrt beu wii tiu-wii-u..* (some scratchier notes). **HABITAT** Mid/upper levels of broadleaved evergreen forest; 750–2,565 m. **RANGE** Sc/un **WV** NW,NE,SE Thailand. **Rc** (status?) W,C,E,S(east) Myanmar, north Tenasserim, N Laos, W Tonkin.

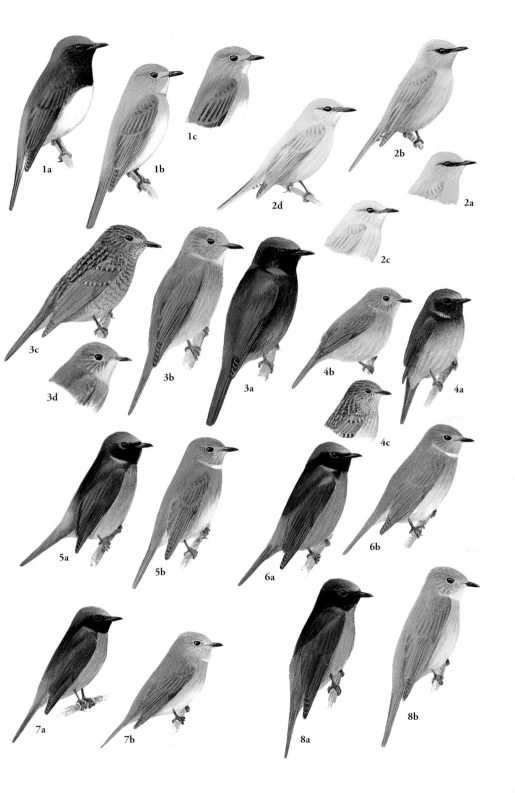

PLATE 93 *CYORNIS* FLYCATCHERS & PYGMY BLUE FLYCATCHER

1 WHITE-TAILED FLYCATCHER *Cyornis concretus* 19 cm
(**a**) **Male** *cyanea*: Blue head/body, white belly/vent, white tail-lines. (**b**) **Female**: White gorget/tail-lines. (**c**) **Female** *concretus* (S Thailand, Pen Malaysia): Warmer; whiter belly. **VOICE** Very variable song, often with mimicry. Typically high tuneful, 3–7 note: *pieu pieu pieu jee-oee*; *phi phi phi phi ju-rit* etc. Harsh *scree* notes. **HABITAT** Broadleaved evergreen forest; 100–1,360 m. **RANGE** Sc/lfc **R** N Myanmar, Tenasserim, W,S Thailand, Pen Malaysia, Laos, W,E Tonkin, N,C Annam.

2 HAINAN BLUE FLYCATCHER *Cyornis hainanus* 13.5–14 cm
(**a**) **Male**: Dark blue throat/breast, then grades to greyish-white. (**b**) **Male variant**: White throat-triangle. (**c**) **Female**: Duller than Blue-throated (*dialilaema*), brown on throat-/breast-side. **Juvenile**: Dark tips and buff streaks/spots above, dark-scaled breast. Male has blue on wings/tail. **VOICE** Weaker/simpler song than Hill Blue; rather short, hurried, slurred phrases. Light *tic* notes. **HABITAT** Broadleaved forest, bamboo; up to 1,020 m. **RANGE** Fc/co **R** C,S,E Myanmar, Tenasserim, Thailand (except C,S), Indochina (except S Annam). Also **PM** coastal E Tonkin.

3 PALE-CHINNED FLYCATCHER *Cyornis poliogenys* 15–17 cm
(**a**) **Adult** *poliogenys*: Greyish head, whitish throat, warm breast, pale buff spectacles. (**b**) **Juvenile**: Dark tips and buff spots above, dark-scaled breast. (**c**) **Adult** *cachariensis* (N Myanmar): Richer below. **VOICE** High, well-structured, slightly undulating song. **HABITAT** Broadleaved evergreen forest; up to 1,500 m. **RANGE** Un **R** SW,W,N,S(west) Myanmar.

4 PALE BLUE FLYCATCHER *Cyornis unicolor* 16–17.5 cm
(**a**) **Male** *unicolor*: Bluer (less turquoise) than Verditer, paler belly/vent. (**b**) **Female**: Rather greyish, rufous uppertail-coverts/tail. **Juvenile**: Blackish tips and buff spots above, uniformly dark-scaled below. Male has blue on wings/tail. **Other subspecies** *C.u.harterti* (S Thailand, Pen Malaysia): Greyer crown, warmer elsewhere. **VOICE** Relatively melodious, warbling song, phrases, often start with shorter *chi* and end with buzzy *chizz*. **HABITAT** Broadleaved evergreen forest; up to 1,600 m. **RANGE** Un **R** Myanmar (except SW,S), Thailand (except C,SE), Pen Malaysia, Cambodia, Laos, N,C Annam. **V** coastal E Tonkin.

5 BLUE-THROATED FLYCATCHER *Cyornis rubeculoides* 14–15 cm
(**a**) **Male** *dialilaema*: Dark blue throat with orange-rufous up centre. (**b**) **Female**: Paler, more buffy throat/breast than Hill Blue, paler lores and above. (**c**) **Juvenile female**: Paler than Hill Blue, light breast-scales, warmer tail. (**d**) **Male** *rubeculoides* (W Myanmar; **VS** SW,C,E,S Myanmar): All-blue throat. (**e**) **Male** *glaucicomans* (widespread **VS** west to N Myanmar and Tenasserim): Deeper blue than Hill Blue, contrasting shining azure shoulder-patch/uppertail-coverts, dark chin, brown flank-wash. (**f**) **Female**: Richer breast, pale throat, brown wash on flanks, warmer above. (**g**) **Male** *klossi* (south Indochina): Pale breast/throat-triangle. (**h**) **Male variant**: Whitish throat-triangle, very pale breast. **Other subspecies** *C.r.rogersi* (SW Myanmar). **VOICE** Song of sweet trills, slurred tinkling notes, fairly well-structured phrases. Faster/higher/more trilled than Tickell's Blue. Hard *tac* and *trrt*

notes. **HABITAT** Broadleaved forest, also non-forest on migration; up to 1,700 m. **RANGE** Un/fc **R** Myanmar, W,NW,NE Thailand, east Cambodia, S Laos, C,S Annam, Cochinchina. Un **WV** SW,C,E,S Myanmar, Tenasserim, W,S Thailand, Pen Malaysia. Un **PM** N Myanmar, NE,C,S Thailand, Pen Malaysia, S Laos. **V** Singapore.

6 HILL BLUE FLYCATCHER *Cyornis banyumas* 14–15.5 cm
(**a**) **Male** *whitei*: Like Tickell's but orange-rufous grades into white belly. (**b**) **Female**: Warm above, rufescent tail and wing-fringes, same gradation below. (**b**) **Juvenile female**: Dark tips and warm buff spots above; buff-and-dark scales below. Male has blue on wing/tail. **Other subspecies** *C.b.magnirostris* (**VS** Myanmar, Tenasserim, S Thailand, Pen Malaysia), *lekabuni* (**rc** NE Thailand) and *deignani* (**rc** SE Thailand): All bigger-billed. *C.b.coerulifrons* (**R** south of c.12°N). **VOICE** Sweet high, melancholy song. Quicker, longer, more complex than Tickell's. Similar calls. **HABITAT** Broadleaved evergreen forest, migrants in non-forest habitats; 400–2,515 m (below 1,220 m Pen Malaysia). **RANGE** Un/co **R** N,E Myanmar, Tenasserim, Thailand (except C), Pen Malaysia, N,C Laos, W,E Tonkin, N Annam. Un **WV** E Myanmar, Tenasserim, S Thailand, Pen Malaysia. Un **PM** C,S Thailand, Pen Malaysia. **Rc** (status?) C Myanmar, E Tonkin, Cambodia.

7 MALAYSIAN BLUE FLYCATCHER *Cyornis turcosus* 14 cm
(**a**) **Male** *rupatensis*: Bright deep blue throat, breast quite pale rufous-orange, relatively bright above. (**b**) **Female**: Warm buff throat (whiter chin/sides). **VOICE** Song of weak 5–6 note phrases. **HABITAT** Broadleaved evergreen forest, near rivers/streams; up to 760 m. **RANGE** Sc/un **R** extreme S Thailand, Pen Malaysia.

8 TICKELL'S BLUE FLYCATCHER *C.tickelliae* 13.5–15.5 cm
(**a**) **Male** *indochina*: Cleanly demarcated breast and belly. (**b**) **Female**: Greyish/bluish above, demarcated below. **Juvenile**: No rufous on tail, relatively greyish above, only thin crown-streaks. (**c**) **Female** *sumatrensis* (south of c.12°N): Bluer above. Male deeper blue above than *indochina*, paler/buffier throat. **Other subspecies** *C.t.tickelliae* (N,C Myanmar?): Male paler blue above than *indochina*; female much bluer. **VOICE** Slow, sweet, slightly descending/rising then descending song. Hard *tac* and *trrt* notes. **HABITAT** Broadleaved forest, bamboo; up to 915 m (below 600 m in Thailand). **RANGE** Co **R** (except SW Myanmar, C Thailand, Singapore, N Laos, W,E Tonkin).

9 MANGROVE BLUE FLYCATCHER *Cyornis rufigastra* 14.5 cm
(**a**) **Male** *rufigastra*: Relatively dark/dull, deep orange-rufous below, paler vent. (**b**) **Female**: Whitish face marks. **Juvenile**: Darker tips and dull buff streaks/speckles above, buffy below with dark-scaled throat-sides to upper belly. **VOICE** Song slightly slower/deeper than Tickell's. **HABITAT** Mangroves. **RANGE** Un/fc **R** S Thailand (local), Pen Malaysia, Singapore (ra/lo).

10 PYGMY BLUE FLYCATCHER *Muscicapella hodgsoni* 9 cm
(**a**) **Male** *hodgsoni*: Tiny, short tail; buffy rufous-orange below. (**b**) **Female**: Warmer above than Sapphire, buffy below. **Other subspecies** *M.h.sondaica* (Pen Malaysia). **VOICE** Song is high *sii-su'u-siiii* etc. **HABITAT** Broadleaf evergreen forest; 610–2,565 m. **RANGE** Un **R** W,N Myanmar, extreme S Thailand, Pen Malaysia, Laos, W Tonkin, N Annam. **Rc** (status?) E Myanmar, W,NW Thailand.

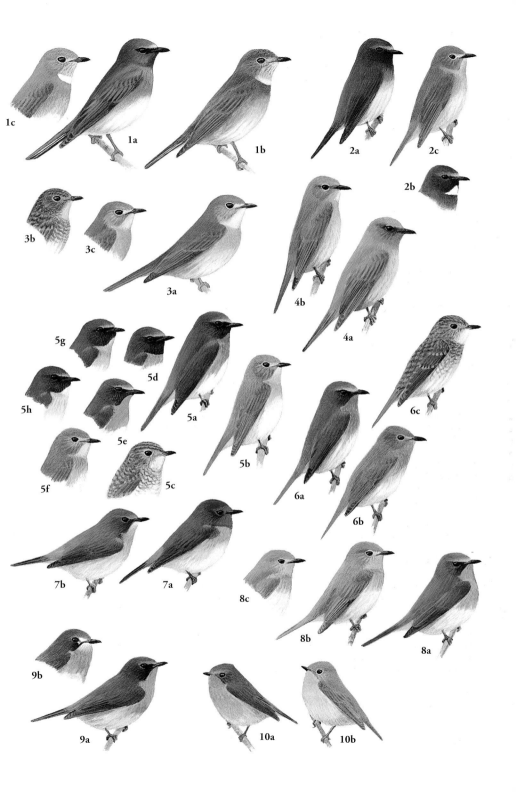

PLATE 94 *ERITHACUS* & *LUSCINIA* ROBINS

1 JAPANESE ROBIN *Erithacus akahige* 14–15 cm
(**a**) **Male** *akahige*: Rufous-orange head/breast, dark gorget, grey belly. (**b**) **Female**: Browner below, rufous-orange duller, no gorget. VOICE Simple spaced quavering song: *bi CH'H'H'H'H'H bi-tu CH'T'T'T'I bi CH'H'H'H'H'H ts-ti CH'U'U'U'U'U tsi CHUK'CHUK'CHUK..* etc. Metallic *tsip*. HABITAT & BEHAVIOUR Broadleaved evergreen forest, sometimes parks, gardens; up to 1,525 m. Skulks on/near ground. RANGE Ra WV/V NW,NE,C,SE Thailand, C Laos, E Tonkin, C Annam.

2 RUFOUS-TAILED ROBIN *Luscinia sibilans* 14 cm
(**a**) **Adult**: Like female Siberian Blue but rufescent rump/tail, distinct scales below (no buff). VOICE Song is accelerating, silvery trill: *tiuuuuuuuuuuuwwwww*. Low *tuhk* or *tupp* notes. HABITAT Broadleaved evergreen/semi-evergreen forest; up to 1,200 m. RANGE Sc/un WV NW,NE Thailand, Laos, Vietnam.

3 SIBERIAN RUBYTHROAT *Luscinia calliope* 15–16.5 cm
(**a**) **Male non-breeding**: Brilliant red throat, white supercilium and submoustachial. **Male breeding**: Breast more solidly grey, bill all black. (**b**) **Female**: Throat white, less distinct supercilium/submoustachial. **First winter**: As non-breeding adults but some buff-tipped coverts. Male's breast usually browner than adult, female rarely shows pink on throat. VOICE Song is scratchy varied warble, with mimicry. Calls include clear *ee-uh* or *se-ic* and deep *tschuck*. HABITAT & BEHAVIOUR Grass, scrub, thickets, sometimes gardens; up to 1,555 m, rarely 2,375 m on passage. Skulks in dense vegetation, cocks tail. RANGE Fc/co WV (except S Thailand, Pen Malaysia, Singapore). Also PM E Tonkin. V Pen Malaysia, Singapore.

4 WHITE-TAILED RUBYTHROAT *Luscinia pectoralis* 15–17 cm
(**a**) **Male breeding** *tschebaiewi*: Black breast, slaty above, white at base/tip of blackish tail. (**b**) **Male non-breeding**: Browner above, whitish-scaled breast. (**c**) **Female**: Greyer than Siberian, white spots on outertail-tips. (**d**) **Juvenile**: Pale buffish streaks/tips above, brownish-grey scales on buffish-white throat/breast, buffish tail-spots. **First-winter**: Buff-tipped greater coverts/tertials. Male has white at tail-base; often darker head-side/breast. VOICE Song of complex undulating trills/twitters. Deep *tchuk* and sparrow-like *tchink*. HABITAT Scrub above tree-line; grass and scrub (often near water) in winter. Up to 4,420 m. RANGE Sc R N Myanmar. V NW,C Thailand.

5 BLUETHROAT *Luscinia svecica* 13.5–15 cm
(**a**) **Male non-breeding** *svecica*: Scaly blue/black/rufous-red breast, white supercilium, rufous at tail-base. (**b**) **Male breeding**: Solid blue/black/red throat/breast. (**c**) **Female**: Blackish malar stripe and gorget. **First winter**: As non-breeding adults but buffish greater covert tips. VOICE Sings with rapid varied ringing notes, call-notes and mimicry. Calls with twanging *dzyink* and low *tuck* etc. HABITAT Grass/thickets near water; up to 760 m. RANGE Un/lc WV Myanmar, NW,NE,C Thailand, Indochina (except W Tonkin, N,S Annam). Also PM E Tonkin.

6 RUFOUS-HEADED ROBIN *Luscinia ruficeps* 15 cm
(**a**) **Male**: Grey above, orange-rufous crown/ear-coverts, black mask and throat-border. (**b**) **Female**: All-dark bill, no blue, warm-edged outertail. VOICE Well-spaced powerful rich song phrases: *ti CHO CHUK'UK'UK ti TCH-WR'RR'RR ti CHI-WRU-W'R'R'R'R ti CHR'R'R'R ti CHR'RIU'IU'IU...* Calls with deep *tuc* or *toc*, and soft thin *si*. HABITAT Found in montane scrub at 2,010 m. RANGE V Pen Malaysia (once; G. Brinchang).

7 BLACKTHROAT *Luscinia obscura* 12.5–14.5 cm
(**a**) **Male**: Black throat/upper breast, much white on outertail-base, dark legs. (**b**) **Female**: Like Siberian Blue but tail warm, legs dark, no obvious scales below. VOICE Sings with rather shrill, laid-back, phrases: *whr'ri-whr'ri,chu'ti-chu'ti (ri/ti* higher), and purring trills, *hdrriiii-ju'ju* and *uu ji'uu* etc. Soft *tup* notes. HABITAT Dense thickets, grass, scrub, bamboo; 300–395 m. RANGE V NW Thailand.

8 FIRETHROAT *Luscinia pectardens* 14 cm
(**a**) **Male breeding**: Bright orange-red throat/breast, white neck-patch. (**b**) **Male non-breeding**: Female-like head-sides/below; hint of neck-patch. (**c**) **Female**: Relatively plain warm, dark legs. (**d**) **First-winter male**: Some slaty-blue on scapulars/back. VOICE Simple spaced phrases (some husky, buzzy notes): *wiu-wihui'wi wi'chu-wi'chu whiiiii wi-chudu'chudu t'sii-sii wi'chu-wi'chu-wi'chu chu-tsri'sri...* HABITAT Broadleaved forest, bamboo, thickets; found at 150 m. RANGE Rc in winter N Myanmar.

9 INDIAN BLUE ROBIN *Luscinia brunnea* 13.5–14.5 cm
(**a**) **Male** *wickhami*: White supercilium, bright orange-rufous below, white vent. (**b**) **Female**: Plain rich buff breast/flanks, no blue above. (**c**) **Juvenile**: Dark and streaked buffish above, heavily brown-mottled breast and flanks. **First-winter male**: Duller above than adult, buff-tinged supercilium, duller lower throat/breast. VOICE Sweet but quite short, hurried/jumbled song, introduced by 2–4 thin whistles. Hard *tek* notes. HABITAT Bamboo, secondary growth, thickets, broadleaved evergreen forest; 1,480–2,040 m. RANGE Lc R W Myanmar.

10 SIBERIAN BLUE ROBIN *Luscinia cyane* 13.5–14.5 cm
(**a**) **Male** *cyane*: All blue above, white below, black-bordered throat/breast. (**b**) **Female**: Greyish-brown above, often dull blue on rump/uppertail-coverts (sometimes tail), variably mottled/scaled throat-sides/breast, distinctly pinkish legs. (**c**) **First-winter female**: Like adult but rufous-buff-tipped outer greater coverts, often no blue above. **First-winter male**: Like female but dull blue rump to uppertail, usually some blue on scapulars/coverts (sometimes most of upperparts/coverts). **Other subspecies** *L.c.bochaiensis* (rc Indochina?). VOICE Song is a loud, rapid, rather explosive *tri-tri-tri-tri, tjuree-tiu-tiu-tiu-tiu* etc., usually introduced by spaced *sit* notes. Calls with a low hard *tuk*, *tak* or *dak* and louder *se-ic*. HABITAT & BEHAVIOUR Broadleaved forest, secondary growth, bamboo; parks, gardens and mangroves etc. on migration; up to 1,830 m (mainly below 900 m). Skulks on or near ground, quivers tail. RANGE Fc WV (except N Myanmar, Cambodia). Also PM C Thailand, Pen Malaysia, Singapore, E Tonkin.

PLATE 95 SHORTWINGS, BUSH ROBINS, ORIENTAL MAGPIE ROBIN & SHAMAS

1 GOULD'S SHORTWING *Brachypteryx stellata* 13–13.5 cm (**a**) **Adult** *stellata*: Chestnut above, grey-and-black vermiculations and white stars below. (**b**) **Juvenile**: Blackish-brown with warm streaks, greyer below with arrow shapes on belly. **Other subspecies** *B.s.fusca* (W Tonkin). **VOICE** Song is very thin *tssiu tssiu tssiu tssiu-tsitsitssiutssiutssiutssiutsit-sitssiu…* **HABITAT** Rocky gullies in rhododendron and conifer forest, bamboo, broadleaved evergreen forest in winter; 1,800–2,450 m (winter). **RANGE** Sc **R** N Myanmar, W Tonkin.

2 RUSTY-BELLIED SHORTWING *Brachypteryx hyperythra* 12 cm (**a**) **Male**: Short white eyebrow, dark slaty-blue above, orange-rufous below. (**b**) **Female**: Duller below than male, dark brown above, no eyebrow. **VOICE** Song like Lesser but faster/longer/more musical. **HABITAT** Thickets and grass near broadleaved evergreen forest; 980–1,050 m. **RANGE** **Rc** in winter (status?) N Myanmar.

3 LESSER SHORTWING *Brachypteryx leucophrys* 12 cm (**a**) **Adult** *carolinae* (and other race females): Brown above, buffier below, whiter throat/vent. Concealable white brow. (**b**) **Juvenile**: Darker; rufous streaks/tips above, mottled/scaled buff/blackish below. (**c**) **Male** *langbianensis* (S Laos, S Annam): Greyer below. (**d**) **Male** *wrayi* (south of c.6°N): Slaty-blue above, bluish-grey on breast and flanks. Female warmer above than other races. **Other subspecies** *B.l.nipalensis* (Myanmar): Similar to *wrayi*. *B.l.leucophrys* (rest of S Thailand?). **VOICE** Song is brief, high, melodious; pauses after first note and ends with rapid jumble. Low *tuck*, thin high whistle. **HABITAT & BEHAVIOUR** Broadleaved evergreen forest; 380–2,550 m (mostly montane). Skulks on or near ground. **RANGE** Fc **R** (except SW,C Myanmar, C Thailand, Singapore, Cochinchina).

4 WHITE-BROWED SHORTWING *B.montana* 12.5–13.5 cm (**a**) **Male** *cruralis*: Dark blue, white supercilium. (**b**) **Female**: Rufous lores/eyering/supercilium. (**c**) **Juvenile**: Plainer than Lesser. (**d**) **First-winter male**: As female but dark lores, white supercilium. **VOICE** Monotone meandering warble, usually preceded by 1–3 *wheez* notes. Hard *tack*. **HABITAT** Broadleaved evergreen forest; 1,400–2,745 m, locally 305 m in winter, Myanmar. **RANGE** Un/fc **R** W,N,E,S(east) Myanmar, W,NW Thailand, N Laos, W Tonkin, N,C,S Annam.

5 ORANGE-FLANKED BUSH ROBIN *Tarsiger cyanurus* 14–15 cm (**a**) **Male** *rufilatus*: Dark blue throat/breast-side and above, rufous-orange flanks. (**b**) **Female/first winter**: Brown above, blue rump to uppertail. (**c**) **Juvenile**: Buff speckles/streaks, richer buff flanks, mostly blue uppertail-coverts/tail. (**d**) **Male** *cyanurus* (VS NW Thailand, north Indochina): Lighter, almost turquoise, duller below. **VOICE** Song is clear *didiu-diu dew dew dew dew*. Nasal *agag* or *rug* and high *uist*. **HABITAT** Open broadleaved evergreen and coniferous forest; up to 3,655 m. **RANGE** Rc (probably **B** at higher levels N Myanmar. Un **WV** W,C,E Myanmar, NW,NE Thailand, Laos, W,E Tonkin, N,C Annam. Also **PM** E Tonkin. **V** S Annam.

6 GOLDEN BUSH ROBIN *Tarsiger chrysaeus* 13–14 cm (**a**) **Male** *chrysaeus*: Largely rufous-yellow, blackish head-side and tail-centre/tip. (**b**) **Female**: Greenish-olive above, browner

tail, yellowish eyebrow/eyering/below. (**c**) **Juvenile**: Recalls Orange-flanked but tail like adults. **VOICE** Wispy *tze'du'tee'tse* etc., then rolling *tew'r'r'r*. Purring *trrr'rr* and harder *tcheck*. **HABITAT & BEHAVIOUR** Open broadleaved evergreen and coniferous forest, thickets; B 3,050–3,655 m down to 1,050 m, in winter. Usually skulking. **RANGE** Un **R** W,N Myanmar. Sc WV E Myanmar, NW Thailand. Rc (status?) W Tonkin.

7 WHITE-BROWED BUSH ROBIN *Tarsiger indicus* 13.5–15 cm (**a**) **Male** *yunnanensis*: Recalls Indian Blue but longer supercilium, slatier above, longer tail, dark legs. (**b**) **Female/first-summer male**: No blue above, buffy-brownish below. **Juvenile**: Best told from other bush robins by brown tail. **VOICE** Song is wispy slurred *whi-wi'wich'u-wi'rr* etc. Calls with *trrrr* notes. **HABITAT** Rhododendron and conifer forest, bamboo; 2,000–3,355 m. **RANGE** Sc **R** N Myanmar, W Tonkin.

8 RUFOUS-BREASTED BUSH ROBIN *Tarsiger hyperythrus* 13–14 cm (**a**) **Male**: Like Orange-flanked but orange-rufous below. (**b**) **Female**: Much darker than Orange-flanked, notably throat and breast/flanks. (**c**) **Juvenile**: Much darker above than Orange-flanked, buffier below. **VOICE** Song is lisping warbled *zeew zee zwee zwee…* Low *duk* calls. **HABITAT** Broadleaved evergreen and coniferous forest; found at 1,105–1,525 m in winter. **RANGE** Rc (probably **B**) N Myanmar.

9 ORIENTAL MAGPIE ROBIN *Copsychus saularis* 19–21 cm (**a**) **Male** *erimelas*: Glossy blackish; white belly, wing-stripe and outertail. (**b**) **Female**: Black parts greyer. **Juvenile**: Duller; brown wing-fringing, buffier wing-stripe, dark-scaled coverts; paler/buffier throat/breast with dark scales. Male darker above, soon shows black. **Other subspecies** *C.s.musicus* (south of c.12°N). **VOICE** Varied musical warbling song, with churrs and sliding whistles. Clear rising whistle, harsh rasping *che'e'e'e'e* in alarm. **HABITAT** Gardens, parks, cultivation, open woodland etc.; up to 1,830 m. **RANGE** Co **R** throughout.

10 WHITE-RUMPED SHAMA *C.malabaricus* 21.5–28 cm (**a**) **Male** *interpositus*: Blue-black; orange-rufous below, white rump, long blackish tail with white outer feathers. (**b**) **Female**: Dark parts greyer, paler below, tail shorter. (**c**) **Juvenile**: Buff speckles/tips/fringing above, dark-scaled buffish throat/breast. **Other subspecies** *C.m.pellogynus* (Tenasserim, S Thailand), *mallopercnus* (south of c.6°N). **VOICE** Highly varied melodious song, with mimicry. Harsh *tschack*. **HABITAT** Broadleaved forest, bamboo; up to 1,525 m. **RANGE** Fc/co **R** (sc Singapore).

11 RUFOUS-TAILED SHAMA *Trichixos pyrropyga* 21–22 cm (**a**) **Male**: Rufous rump/uppertail-coverts and most of shortish tail; white brow-spot. (**b**) **Female**: Grey-brown above, buffy-rufous throat/breast, whitish belly. (**c**) **Juvenile**: As female but bold rich buff markings above, buff throat/breast with broad streaks. **VOICE** Sings with loud well-spaced whistles: *whi-ii* and *whi-uuu* etc. Scolding *tcherrr*. **HABITAT** Broadleaved evergreen and swamp forest; up to 915 m. Often sits motionless for long periods. **RANGE** Sc/un **R** extreme S Thailand, Pen Malaysia.

PLATE 96 REDSTARTS, ROBINS, CHATS & ISABELLINE WHEATEAR

1 WHITE-CAPPED WATER REDSTART *Chaimarrornis leucocephalus* 19 cm
(a) **Adult**: Black and chestnut, white crown. (b) **Juvenile**: Browner. **VOICE** Weak undulating song. Sharp *peeeiii*. **HABITAT** Rocky rivers/streams/waterfalls; 215–4,265 m. **RANGE** Un/fc R (local movements) N Myanmar, N,C Laos, W,E Tonkin. **Rc** (status?) SW,W,C,S,E Myanmar, NW,NE Thailand, N Annam.

2 PLUMBEOUS WATER REDSTART *Rhyacornis fuliginosus*
(a) **Male** *fuliginosus*: 15 cm. Slaty-blue, chestnut tail-coverts and tail. (b) **Female/first-year male**: Blue-grey, mottled/scaled grey-and-whitish below, whitish wing-bars, dark tail with white at base. **Juvenile**: Brown with buffy-white spots/streaks above, buffy/whitish and broadly mottled below (plainer vent). **VOICE** Sings with insect-like *streee-treee-tree-treeeh*. Strident *peet*. **HABITAT** Rocky rivers, streams and waterfalls; 300–2,285 m. **RANGE** Sc/lc R (some movements) W,N Myanmar, NW Thailand, Laos, W,E Tonkin, N,C,S Annam. **Rc** (status?) elsewhere Myanmar.

3 WHITE-BELLIED REDSTART *Hodgsonius phaenicuroides* 18 cm
(a) **Male** *ichangensis*: Slaty-blue, whitish vent, long tail with orange-rufous patches. (b) **Female**: Brown; buffy below, duller tail. **Juvenile**: As female but blackish fringes and buff spots and streaks above, dark-scaled throat/breast. **First-winter male**: Brighter tail-patches than female. **Other subspecies** *H.p.phaenicuroides* (W Myanmar): Paler blue. **VOICE** Song is whistled *teuuh-tiyou-tuh* etc. Low *tuk* and grating *chack* notes. **HABITAT & BEHAVIOUR** Open forest, thickets; 150–2,565 m (B above 2,075 m). Very skulking. **RANGE** Un R (local movements) W,N Myanmar, N Laos, W Tonkin. Un **WV** E Myanmar, NW Thailand.

4 WHITE-TAILED ROBIN *Myiomela leucura* 17.5–19.5 cm
(a) **Male** *leucura*: Blackish; blue brow/shoulder, white tail-lines. (b) **Female**: Cold brown, buffier below, pale throat/vent. **Juvenile female**: Warmer above with dark and buff tips/streaks/spots, warm buff with blackish-brown scales/streaks below. (c) **Juvenile male**: Darker than female, notably below. **Other subspecies** *M.l.cambodianum* (Cambodia): Male almost without blue brow and shoulder; female much darker/colder. **VOICE** Song is quite hurried, sweet, thin, quavering warble. Thin whistles and low *tuc*. **HABITAT** Broadleaved evergreen forest, bamboo; 1,000–2,480 m, locally 150 m (winter only?). **RANGE** Un R (except SW,C Myanmar, C Thailand, Singapore, Cochinchina); minor movements.

5 BLUE-FRONTED ROBIN *Cinclidium frontale* 18–20 cm
(a) **Male** *orientale*: Longer tail than White-tailed with no white; ashier-blue. (b) **Female**: Longer plain tail, more russet-brown below than White-tailed. **Juvenile**: From White-tailed by lack of white in tail. **VOICE** Sings with short melodic *tuuee-be-tue* and *tuu-buudy-doo* etc. Buzzy *zshwick* alarm. **HABITAT** Bamboo, broadleaved evergreen forest; 1,850–2,100 m. **RANGE** Rc (probably R) NW Thailand, N Laos, W Tonkin.

6 SIBERIAN STONECHAT *Saxicola maura* 14 cm
(a) **Male non-breeding/first winter** *stejnegeri*: Black head-flecking. (b) **Male breeding**: Black hood/above, whitish neck, wing-patch and rump, bright rufous breast. (c) **Female non-**

breeding: Rump/tail-tip buff to rufous-buff. **Female breeding**: Greyer, paler below, duller rump/tail-tip. (d) **Male breeding** *przewalskii* (R race): Rufous-chestnut to belly. (e) **Juvenile**: Dark brown above, spotted buff, all buffy below, dark-streaked breast. **VOICE** Scratchy twittering, warbling song. Hard *chack* or *tsak*, thin *hweet*. **HABITAT** Grass, scrub, various open areas; to 2,470 m. **RANGE** Lo/fc R N Myanmar, NW Thailand, N,S Laos, W,E Tonkin. Un/co **WV** throughout. **PM** NW Thailand, E Tonkin.

7 WHITE-TAILED STONECHAT *Saxicola leucura* 14 cm
(a) **Male non-breeding**: Best told by tail pattern. (b) **Male breeding**: As Siberian but much white on tail, whiter, more cut-off belly. (c) **Female non-breeding/breeding** (former illustrated): Paler/plainer than Siberian, paler-fringed tail. **Juvenile** Best told by tail. **HABITAT** Lowland grassland, nearby scrub/cultivation, often by larger rivers. **RANGE** Lfc R N,C,E,S Myanmar.

8 PIED BUSHCHAT *Saxicola caprata* 14 cm
(a) **Male non-breeding** *burmanica*: Blackish fringed brownish, whitish rump/tail-coverts/wing-streak. (b) **Male breeding**: Black and white. (c) **Female non-breeding**: Darker than Siberian, dark streaks below, rusty tail-coverts/belly, plain wings. (d) **Female breeding**: Plainer, broad streaks. **Juvenile** Resembles non-breeding female but body speckled pale buffish. Male with blacker wings and white wing-streak. **VOICE** Sings with brisk whistled *hiu-hiu-hiu u'wee'wipee'chiu* etc. Clear *chep*; *chek chek trweet* and *hew*. **HABITAT** Open areas, cultivation, grass, scrub; up to 1,600 m. **RANGE** Un/co R (except SE,S Thailand, Pen Malaysia, Singapore, W,E Tonkin, N Annam).

9 JERDON'S BUSHCHAT *Saxicola jerdoni* 15 cm
(a) **Male**: Glossy black and white. (b) **Female**: No supercilium, longer/plainer/darker tail than Grey. **VOICE** Short wispy sweet song. Short clear whistle; muffled husky rising *dr'iit*. **HABITAT & BEHAVIOUR** Tall grass, thickets, mainly riverine; to 1,650 m. Quite skulking. **RANGE** Ra/sc R (some movements) N,C,E,S Myanmar, NW,NE Thailand, N,C Laos, E Tonkin. **Rc** (status?) C Thailand.

10 GREY BUSHCHAT *Saxicola ferrea* 14–15.5 cm
(a) **Male non-breeding**: Browner than breeding. (b) **Male breeding**: Grey, black and white. (c) **Female non-breeding**: Autumn. Warmer/browner/plainer than breeding. (d) **Female breeding**: Streakier than non-breeding male, no wing-streak. **Juvenile**: Broad buff/rufous streaks/mottling above, blackish-brown breast-scalloping. **VOICE** Song is brief *tree-toooh tu-treeeh-t't't-tuhr* etc. Soft *churr*, clear *hew*, harsh *bzech*. **HABITAT** Open pine and broadleaved evergreen forest, scrub, grass, cultivation; 1,220–3,054 m, locally lowlands in winter. **RANGE** Co R Myanmar (except C and Tenasserim), NW Thailand (lo), W Tonkin, S Annam. Un/fc **WV** C Myanmar, W,NW,NE,C Thailand, Laos, E Tonkin. **Rc** (status?) Cambodia, Cochinchina.

11 ISABELLINE WHEATEAR *Oenanthe isabellina* 16.5 cm
(a) **Adult**: Robust, short tail, longish legs, sandy-brown, white uppertail-coverts, white-based blackish tail. **VOICE** Calls include clear *cheep* and clicking *chick* or *tshk* in alarm. **HABITAT** Dry open habitats; lowlands. **RANGE** V C Myanmar, south W Thailand.

PLATE 97 REDSTARTS & FORKTAILS

1 BLACK REDSTART *Phoenicurus ochruros* 16 cm
(a) **Male non-breeding** *rufiventris*: Brownish-grey crown to back (some black), blackish head-sides and throat/breast with brownish-grey scales, blackish wings with buff fringing. (b) **Male breeding**: More uniformly black hood/upperparts. (c) **Female/first-year male**: Like Daurian but no wing-patch, duller below, less distinct eyering. VOICE Song is scratchy trill, then short wheezy jingle. High-pitched *tseep* or *tsip* (repeated when agitated), scolding *tak* or *tuc* and rapid rattling *tititik*. HABITAT Open country, semi-desert; lowlands. RANGE Sc/un WV W,N,C,E Myanmar. V NW Thailand, W Tonkin.

2 HODGSON'S REDSTART *Phoenicurus hodgsoni* 16 cm
(a) **Male**: Resembles Daurian but grey mantle and wings, black upper breast, thin wing-patch. (b) **Female/first-year Male**: Similar to Black but paler and greyer above, more obvious pale eyering, creamy-whitish below with broad greyish wash across breast to throat-side (sometimes most of throat and flanks). Can appear to have large white belly-patch. VOICE Rattling *prit* and *trr* or *tschrrr* when alarmed. HABITAT Open, often rocky areas, scrub; found at 150–1,830 m. RANGE Un WV N Myanmar.

3 WHITE-THROATED REDSTART *P.schisticeps* 16 cm
(a) **Male non-breeding**: Crown, mantle and breast feathers fringed pale brownish. (b) **Male breeding**: Mostly light blue crown, white throat-patch, extensive white wing-patch, extending to tertial fringes, blackish tail with rufous-chestnut only on basal third of outer feather. (c) **Female**: Told by white throat-patch, wing and tail pattern (similar to male). **Juvenile**: Like female (similar wings/tail) but dark scales and buff spots above and below. VOICE Drawn-out *zieh* followed by rattling note. HABITAT Open forest, low vegetation above tree-line, rocky areas; 2,285–3,230 m. RANGE Rc (status?) N Myanmar.

4 DAURIAN REDSTART *Phoenicurus auroreus* 15 cm
(a) **Male non-breeding** *leucopterus*: Crown to upper mantle mostly brownish-grey, broad brown fringing on lower mantle, pale greyish fringing on blackish throat/breast. (b) **Male breeding**: Grey crown to upper mantle, black lower mantle and throat, broad white wing-patch. (c) **Female**: Rather uniform brown, paler and warmer below, broad white wing-patch, obvious pale buffy eyering. **Juvenile**: Resembles female (including wings/tail) but dark-scaled and buff-spotted above and below. VOICE Song is scratchy trill followed by short wheezy jingle. High *tseep* or *tsip* (repeated in alarm), scolding *tak* or *tuc* notes, rapid rattling *tititik*. HABITAT Forest edge, orchards, thickets; up to 2,565 m. RANGE Sc/fc WV Myanmar (except SW and Tenasserim; R N?), NW Thailand, Laos, W,E Tonkin, N,C(ra)S(ra) Annam.

5 BLUE-FRONTED REDSTART *Phoenicurus frontalis* 16 cm
(a) **Male non-breeding**: Broadly fringed pale brown. (b) **Male breeding**: Dark blue hood (brighter eyebrow), mantle and back, blackish tail-tip. (c) **Female**: Told by tail pattern (as male), lack of white wing-patch, buffy wing-bar and tertial fringes. (d) **Juvenile**: Recalls female but mostly blackish, with buff speckles/streaks/mottling, buff vent, wing-bars and tertial/secondary fringes. VOICE Song of 1–2 quite harsh trilled warbles followed by short whistled phrases. Calls include thin

ee-tit, *ee-tit-tit* etc. and clicking *tik*. HABITAT Open forest, forest edge, cultivation, thickets; 800–2,750 m. RANGE Sc WV E Myanmar, NW Thailand. Rc (status?) W,N Myanmar, N Laos, W Tonkin. B at high levels N Myanmar at least?

6 LITTLE FORKTAIL *Enicurus scouleri* 12.5–14.5 cm
(a) **Adult** *scouleri*: Small; tail short with white restricted to sides. (b) **Juvenile**: Browner above, no white on forehead, sooty-scaled white throat/breast. VOICE Song described as loud, thin *ts-youeee*. HABITAT Rocky rivers and streams, waterfalls; 450–2,590 m. RANGE Sc/lfc R W,N Myanmar, W,E Tonkin.

7 CHESTNUT-NAPED FORKTAIL *Enicurus ruficapillus* 19.5–21 cm
(a) **Male**: Chestnut crown/upper mantle, dark-scaled white breast. (b) **Female**: Chestnut crown to back. (c) **Juvenile**: Duller above than female, white submoustachial and throat, ill-defined breast markings. VOICE Thin shrill metallic whistles and high *dir-tee*. HABITAT Rivers and streams, waterfalls; up to 915 m. RANGE Un R Tenasserim, W,S Thailand, Pen Malaysia.

8 BLACK-BACKED FORKTAIL *Enicurus immaculatus* 20.5–23 cm
(a) **Adult**: Like Slaty-backed but black crown and mantle. (b) **Juvenile**: Duller/browner above; no white on forehead, white throat, faint sooty breast-scales. VOICE Short high *zeee* (slightly higher-pitched than Slaty-backed); sometimes preceded by hollow *huu*. HABITAT Rivers and streams, waterfalls; up to 1,135 m. RANGE Un/fc R Myanmar (except Tenasserim), NW Thailand.

9 SLATY-BACKED FORKTAIL *E.schistaceus* 22.5–24.5 cm
(a) **Adult**: Slaty-grey crown, nape and mantle, white forehead-band. (b) **Juvenile**: Tinged brown above, no white on forehead, white throat with greyish flecks, dull greyish scales/streaks on breast. VOICE Thin shrill sharp metallic *teenk*. HABITAT Rivers, streams, waterfalls; 400–2,200 m, lower locally (above 610 m in Pen Malaysia). RANGE Fc R (except SW Myanmar, C Thailand, Singapore, Cochinchina).

10 WHITE-CROWNED FORKTAIL *E.leschenaulti* 28 cm
(a) **Adult** *indicus*: Size, white forecrown, black mantle/breast. (b) **Juvenile**: Browner; initially no white on forehead/crown, faint white streaks on throat and breast. **Other subspecies** *E.l.frontalis* (S Thailand, Pen Malaysia): 20.5 cm, shorter-tailed; white crown goes further back, smaller wing-patch. VOICE Song is elaborate high whistled *tsswi'i'i-lli'i'i* etc. Harsh shrill whistled *tssee* or *tssee chit-chit-chit* etc. HABITAT Rivers, streams and adjacent areas; up to 2,400 m (*frontalis* below 760 m). RANGE Fc R (except SW,C Myanmar, C,SE Thailand, Singapore, Cambodia, Cochinchina).

11 SPOTTED FORKTAIL *Enicurus maculatus* 25–28.5 cm
(a) **Adult** *guttatus*: White mantle-spots. (b) **Juvenile**: Like White-crowned but white tips on outer webs of tertials/secondaries. **Other subspecies** *E.m.bacatus* (W Tonkin), *robinsoni* (S Annam). VOICE Very high, thin *tsueee*. HABITAT Rivers, streams; 915–2,560 m. RANGE Sc/lfc R SW,W,N,E,S(west) Myanmar, W,E Tonkin, S Annam.

PLATE 98 STARLINGS

1 SPOT-WINGED STARLING *Saroglossa spiloptera* 19–20 cm
(**a,b**) **Male**: Greyish, dark-scaled upperparts, rufescent upper-tail-coverts, breast and flanks, blackish ear-coverts, dark chestnut throat. Pale yellow to whitish eyes, small white patch at base of primaries. (**c,d**) **Female**: Distinguished by slightly scaly brown upperparts, pale underparts with darker throat-streaking and breast-scaling, pale eyes, slender bill. In flight, upperparts and upperwing rather uniform, apart from small white wing-patch. **Juvenile**: Similar to female but more streaked below. **VOICE** Song is continuous, harsh, unmusical jumble of dry discordant notes and some melodious warbling. Calls include scolding **kwerrh**, nasal **schaik** or **chek** notes and noisy chattering from flocks. **HABITAT & BEHAVIOUR** Open areas with scattered trees, open deciduous woodland, cultivation; lowlands. Gregarious; habitually feeds on nectar in flowering trees. **RANGE** Ra/un **WV** N,E,C,S Myanmar, W,NW Thailand.

2 CHESTNUT-TAILED STARLING *Sturnus malabaricus* 18.5–20.5 cm
(**a,b**) **Adult** *nemoricola*: Blue-based yellowish bill, greyish-white hood, rufous-chestnut outertail feathers. Greyish above, with blacker primaries and primary coverts and small white area on wing-bend, often shows rufous-chestnut tinge on rump and uppertail-coverts; pale below with variable salmon-buff (usually restricted to belly/flanks). **Juvenile**: Similar to adult but has browner fringes to upperwing-coverts, tertials and secondaries, less rufous-chestnut in tail. (**c**) **Adult** *malabaricus* (rc north W Myanmar, S Thailand): Usually very pale chestnut below (sometimes throat) with deeper chestnut vent; usually less white at wing-bend. **VOICE** Sharp disyllabic metallic notes and mild tremulous single whistles. **HABITAT & BEHAVIOUR** Open forest of various types, open country with scattered trees; up to 1,450 m. Gregarious; often feeds on nectar in flowering trees. **RANGE** Fc **R** (some movements) Myanmar, W,NW Thailand, Laos, Vietnam (except W Tonkin). Un/co **WV** Thailand (except southern S), Cambodia. **V** southern S Thailand.

3 RED-BILLED STARLING *Sturnus sericeus* 24 cm
(**a**) **Male**: Light slaty-greyish body, whitish hood (sometimes yellowish-tinged), dark-tipped red bill. Rump and uppertail-coverts paler than rest of upperparts, wings and tail black with white on primary coverts and bases of primaries, legs orange. Easily separated from White-shouldered and Chestnut-tailed by bill and leg colour and all-dark wings/tail (apart from white wing-patch). (**b**) **Female**: Body paler and brown-tinged. (**c**) **Juvenile**: Browner than female, browner wings/tail, slightly less distinct wing-patch, yellower bill. **HABITAT & BEHAVIOUR** Scrub, cultivation, open areas; lowlands. Usually in flocks, sometimes large. **RANGE** Sc/un **WV** E Tonkin, C Annam (ra). **Rc** (**V** or escapee) Singapore.

4 PURPLE-BACKED STARLING *Sturnus sturninus* 17–19 cm
(**a,b**) **Male**: Pale greyish head and underparts, glossy dark purplish nape-patch and upperparts, glossy dark green upperwing, with whitish to pale buff scapular band and tips of median and greater coverts and tertials. Blackish bill and legs, pale buff uppertail-coverts and vent, glossy dark green tail, buff flight-feather fringing. (**c,d**) **Female**: Glossy purple and green

of male replaced by brown, crown duller and browner. **Juvenile**: Similar to female. **VOICE** Soft drawn-out **chirrup** or **prrrp** when flushed. **HABITAT & BEHAVIOUR** Secondary growth, forest edge, open areas, cultivation; lowlands. Highly gregarious, often associates with Asian Glossy. **RANGE** Sc/un **PM** S Myanmar, Tenasserim, Thailand (except NW), Pen Malaysia, Singapore, Cambodia, N Laos, E Tonkin, N Annam, Cochinchina. Lo **WV** C,S Thailand, Pen Malaysia, Singapore. **V** NW Thailand.

5 CHESTNUT-CHEEKED STARLING *Sturnus philippensis* 17 cm
(**a,b**) **Male**: Resembles Purple-backed but head pale (tinged yellowish-buff to brownish) with chestnut patch on ear-coverts and neck-side, darker grey below, whitish fringing on secondaries, no whitish tips to scapulars/greater coverts/tertials. (**c,d**) **Female**: Like Purple-backed but whitish fringing on secondaries, no whitish tips to scapulars/greater coverts/tertials. **Juvenile**: Similar to female. **VOICE** Song is described as simple babbling sequence. Calls include **airr** or **tshairr** notes, penetrating **tshick** when alarmed and soft, melodious **chrueruchu** in flight. **HABITAT & BEHAVIOUR** Secondary growth, open areas, cultivation; lowlands. May be found in association with other starlings. **RANGE** **V** S Thailand, Pen Malaysia, Singapore.

6 WHITE-SHOULDERED STARLING *Sturnus sinensis* 19.5 cm
(**a,b**) **Male**: Mostly grey plumage, contrasting black wings (glossed dark green), blackish tail with white border, wholly white upperwing-coverts and scapulars. Has whiter rump and uppertail-coverts, mostly bluish-grey bill; whiter plumage parts occasionally washed salmon-buff. (**c**) **Female**: Wings almost glossless with smaller white patch, rump and uppertail-coverts duller. (**d,e**) **Juvenile**: Similar to female but initially lacks white wing-patch; upperparts, rump and uppertail-coverts more uniform, grey of plumage tinged brown, pale tail-feather tips duller, bill duller. Bare-part colour, all-dark upperwing and pale-bordered dark tail rule out similar starlings. **VOICE** Soft **preep** when flushed, harsh **kaar** when agitated. **HABITAT** Open areas with scattered trees, scrub, cultivation, coastal habitats; up to 400 m. **RANGE** Lc **R** E Tonkin, N,C Annam. Sc/fc **WV** (except SW,W,N,C,E Myanmar, Tenasserim). Also **PM** Cambodia.

7 WHITE-CHEEKED STARLING *Sturnus cineraceus* 24 cm
(**a,b**) **Male**: Blackish head and breast with mostly white forehead and ear-coverts. Rest of plumage mostly dark with white band across uppertail-coverts, paler centre of abdomen and vent, whitish-fringed secondaries, whitish tail-border; orange bill with dark tip. (**c**) **Female**: Upperparts somewhat paler, throat paler and mixed with whitish, base colour of breast and flanks paler and browner. (**d,e**) **Juvenile**: Paler and browner than female, greyish-brown overall with whitish ear-coverts and throat and darker crown and submoustachial stripe; bill duller, lacking obvious dark tip. From other starlings by bare-part colours, rather uniform plumage and contrasting whitish ear-coverts, uppertail-covert band and tail border. **VOICE** Monotonous creaking **chir-chir-chay-cheet-cheet...** **HABITAT** Open country; lowlands. **RANGE** Un **WV** E Tonkin. **V** N Myanmar, NW,C Thailand.

PLATE 99 ASIAN GLOSSY STARLING & MYNAS

1 ASIAN GLOSSY STARLING *Aplonis panayensis* 19–21.5 cm **(a) Adult** *strigata*: Overall glossy blackish-green (sometimes slightly bluish-tinged), red eyes. **(b) Juvenile**: Greyish-brown above, whitish to dull buffish-white below, with bold dark streaks; eyes often paler. **Other subspecies** *A.p.affinis* (SW Myanmar), *tytleri* (Coco Is, off S Myanmar). **VOICE** Shrill sharp ringing whistles: *tieuu, tseu* etc. **HABITAT** Coastal scrub, secondary growth, cultivation, plantations, urban areas; lowlands. **RANGE** Co (mostly coastal) **R** (local movements) SW,S Myanmar, Tenasserim, S Thailand, Pen Malaysia, Singapore.

Laos, Cambodia

2 COMMON MYNA *Acridotheres tristis* 24.5–27 cm **(a,b) Adult** *tristis*: Brown; greyish-black hood, whitish vent, yellow bill and facial skin. In flight, shows large white patch on primary coverts and bases of primaries and white underwing-coverts. **(c) Juvenile**: Hood paler and more brownish-grey. Very similar to Jungle but upperparts, lower breast and belly warmer brown, shows some yellow facial skin, much larger white wing-patch, white underwing-coverts. **VOICE** Song consists of repetitive tuneless, whistled, chattering and gurgling notes: *bee bee chirk-a chirk-a chirk-a* and *krr krr krr ci ri ci ri krrup krrup krrup chirri chirri chirri weeu weeu..* etc.; often combined with skilled avian mimicry. Typical calls include harsh, scolding *chake-chake..* when alarmed and weak *kwerrh* when flushed. **HABITAT** Open areas, scrub, cultivation, urban areas; up to 1,525 m. **RANGE** Co **R** throughout.

3 JUNGLE MYNA *Acridotheres fuscus* 24.5–25 cm **(a,b) Adult** *fuscus*: Similar to White-vented but bill orange with bluish base, eyes yellow, very short crest; blackish head contrasts with greyer body, which grades to dull whitish under-tail-coverts. In flight, smaller white wing-patch (above and below) and mostly greyish underwing-coverts. **(c) Juvenile**: Browner overall, head less contrasting, centre of throat or whole throat slightly paler, no obvious crest, bill yellowish. From Common by greyer-brown upperparts, lower breast and belly, lack of yellow facial skin, smaller white wing-patch, mostly dark underwing-coverts. **VOICE** Song similar to Common. Repeated *tiuck-tiuck-tiuck* and high *tchieu-tchieu* calls. **HABITAT** Open dry and grassy areas, often near wetlands/rivers, cultivation, roadsides; occasionally forest clearings, mangroves; up to 1,525 m (mostly lowlands). **RANGE** Un/lc **R** Myanmar (except N), C(coastal),W(coastal),S Thailand, Pen Malaysia.

4 WHITE-VENTED MYNA *Acridotheres grandis* 24.5–27.5 cm **(a,b) Adult**: Yellow bill, floppy tufted crest, uniform slaty-black plumage with contrasting white undertail-coverts. Eyes reddish-brown. In flight, large white wing-patch, mostly blackish underwing-coverts, broad white outertail-tips. **(c) Juvenile**: Browner, no obvious crest, dark brown undertail-coverts with pale scaling, little/no white on tail-tip, duller bill. Best told from Crested by yellower bill and leg, somewhat paler undertail-coverts, smaller wing-patch. **VOICE** Song is a disjointed jumble of repeated tuneless phrases, perhaps coarser/harsher than Common. High *chuur-chuur..*, harsh *kaar* in alarm, soft *piu* when flushed. **HABITAT** Open country, cultivation, urban areas; up to 1,525 m (mostly lowlands). **RANGE** Co **R** (except SW Myanmar,

Pen Malaysia, Singapore). Un/lo **FER** Pen Malaysia (Kuala Lumpur).

5 JAVAN MYNA *Acridotheres javanicus* 24–25 cm **(a,b) Adult**: Recalls Jungle but dark slaty-grey (apart from crown/ear-coverts) with clean white undertail-coverts, yellow bill, blacker underwing-coverts, broader white tail-tip. **(c) Juvenile**: Greyer body than Jungle, including belly. **VOICE** Very like Common. **HABITAT** Urban areas, open country, cultivation; lowlands. **RANGE** Co **FER** southern Pen Malaysia, Singapore.

6 COLLARED MYNA *Acridotheres albocinctus* 25.5–26.5 cm **(a,b) Adult**: Broad white half-collar (buff-tinged in winter), blackish-grey underbird-coverts with broad white tips, short crest, pale blue eyes. Similar wing pattern to Jungle. **(c) Juvenile**: Browner; less obvious neck-patch. **VOICE** Continuous shrill, slurred, harsh and sweet chattering. **HABITAT** Open country, grassy areas, cultivation; to 1,525 m. **RANGE** Un/lc **R** W,N,C,E Myanmar.

7 CRESTED MYNA *Acridotheres cristatellus* 25.5–27.5 cm **(a,b) Adult** *brevipennis*: Like White-vented but bill ivory-coloured with rosy-red flush at base of lower mandible, eyes pale orange, crest shorter/fuller, undertail-coverts black with narrow white fringes. In flight, very large white wing-patches, narrow white outertail-tips. **(c) Juvenile**: Paler/duller bill and legs than White-vented, darker undertail-coverts, larger wing-patch. **Other subspecies** *A.c.cristatellus* (rc E Myanmar). **VOICE** Similar to Common. **HABITAT** Open areas, scrub, cultivation, rice paddies, urban areas; lowlands. **RANGE** Un/co **R** W,N Laos, Vietnam (except Cochinchina). **Rc** (status?) N(south),E Myanmar. Sc/lo **FER** Pen Malaysia (Penang I, Kuala Lumpur), Singapore. **Rc** (V or escapee) C Thailand.

8 GOLDEN-CRESTED MYNA *Ampeliceps coronatus* 22–24 cm **(a,b) Male**: Yellow crown/face/throat and wing-patch. Wing-patch can look white at distance. **(c) Female**: Yellow on head restricted and patchy. **(d) Juvenile**: Duller and browner; no yellow on crown, yellowish-white lores, throat and wing-patch, faint streaking below. **VOICE** Higher and more metallic than Hill, with bell-like notes. **HABITAT & BEHAVIOUR** Broadleaved forest, clearings; up to 800 m. Gregarious; often perches in exposed tree-tops. **RANGE** Sc/lc **R** WC,S Myanmar, Tenasserim, Thailand (except C), Cambodia, Laos, Vietnam (except W Tonkin). **Rc** (status?) north-west Pen Malaysia.

9 HILL MYNA *Gracula religiosa* 27–31 cm **(a,b) Adult** *intermedia*: Glossy black, heavy deep orange bill (tip often yellower), connected yellow head-wattles, prominent white wing-patch. **Juvenile**: Duller; naked pale yellow areas on head where wattles develop, duller bill. **(c) Adult** *religiosa* (S Thailand southwards): 29–34.5 cm, thicker bill, separated head-wattles. **Other subspecies** *G.r.andamanensis* (Coco Is). **VOICE** Very varied, with piercing whistles, screeches, croaks and wheezes. **HABITAT & BEHAVIOUR** Broadleaved forest, clearings; up to 1,370 m (mostly below 600 m). Often in pairs; regularly perches in exposed tree-tops. **RANGE** Un/fc **R** (except C Thailand). **Rc** (V or escapee) C Thailand.

PLATE 100 STARLINGS, NUTHATCHES & WINTER WREN

1 BRAHMINY STARLING *Sturnus pagodarum* 19–21 cm
(a) **Adult**: Blackish crown/nape, salmon-pinkish head-sides, breast and belly, lighter breast-streaking, blue-based yellow bill. (b) **Juvenile**: Duller; browner/shorter crown feathers, paler below with plainer breast. **VOICE** Song is drawn-out gurgling sound followed by louder bubbling yodel: roughly *gu-u-weerh-kwurti-kwee-ah*. **HABITAT** Dry open country; lowlands. **RANGE** V W,S Thailand.

2 ROSY STARLING *Sturnus roseus* 21–24 cm
(a) **Adult non-breeding**: Buffish-pink with contrasting blackish hood, glossy greenish-black wings, blackish tail. Brownish-pink bill, paler-scaled vent, shaggy crest. (b) **Adult breeding**: Cleaner and pinker, glossy purplish-black hood, pink bill with black base. (c) **Juvenile**: Pale sandy greyish-brown with darker wings and tail and paler rump and underparts; yellowish bill. Similar to White-shouldered but paler bill and legs, paler wings, paler tail with no whitish tip, slight crown/breast-streaking. **VOICE** Song of bubbling, warbling and whistled phrases. Loud clear *ki-ki-ki..* in flight, harsh *shrr* and rattling *chik-ik-ik-ik..* when foraging. **HABITAT** Open areas, scrub; lowlands. **RANGE** V W,NW,C,S Thailand, Singapore, E Tonkin.

3 COMMON STARLING *Sturnus vulgaris* 20.5–23 cm
(a) **Adult non-breeding** *poltaratskyi*: Blackish with extensive heavy white to buff speckling/spotting; bill blackish. (b) **Adult breeding**: More uniform glossy purplish to greenish-black, only sparse pale buffish speckling; bill yellow. **Juvenile**: Rather uniform dusky-brown with paler throat and vent, indistinct dark streaking below, buffish wing-fringing; dark bill and legs. (c) **Juvenile/first winter (transitional)**: Dusky-brown hood. **VOICE** Sings with complex chirps, twittering, clicks, drawn-out whistles and mimicry. Calls with soft *prurrp* in flight, short metallic *chip* in alarm, *scree* notes when foraging. **HABITAT** Open country, cultivation; lowlands. **RANGE** V/ra WV N Myanmar, NW,NE Thailand, E Tonkin, C Annam.

4 ASIAN PIED STARLING *Sturnus contra* 22–25 cm
(a,b) **Adult** *floweri*: Black and white, long red-based yellowish bill, forecrown streaked white. (c) **Juvenile**: Duller/browner, brown forecrown, paler to whitish throat, brownish bill. (d) **Adult** *superciliaris* (Myanmar): Pale grey below, more black on crown. **Other subspecies** *S.c.contra* (rc SW Myanmar): Duller, greyer-tinged below, almost no white on forehead. **VOICE** Song recalls Common Myna but more melodious. Myna-like *cheek-cheurk*, descending *treek-treek-treek*, various high musical liquid notes. **HABITAT** Open areas, particularly near water, cultivation, towns; lowlands. **RANGE** Fc/co R Myanmar, W,NW,NE,SE,C,S(north) Thailand, Cambodia, west N Laos.

5 BLACK-COLLARED STARLING *Sturnus nigricollis* 27–30.5 cm
(a) **Adult**: Large; black and whitish, broad blackish collar, yellowish facial skin. (b,c) **Juvenile**: Dull brownish hood, no collar, white parts duller. **VOICE** Loud, shrill, harsh *tcheeuw, tcheeuw-tchew* and *tcheeuw-tchew-trieuw* etc. **HABITAT** Open country, scrub, cultivation; up to 1,525 m. **RANGE** Co R (except SW,S Myanmar, Pen Malaysia, Singapore). V (or escapee) Pen Malaysia.

6 VINOUS-BREASTED STARLING *Sturnus burmannicus* 22–25.5 cm
(a) **Adult** *leucocephalus*: Whitish head, naked black mask, yellow/orange-yellow bill, pale vinous-brownish below, buff rump/uppertail-coverts/tail-tip. (b,c) **Juvenile**: Browner overall with dull mask and bill and buffish-fringed wing feathers. (d) **Adult** *burmannicus* (Myanmar, except Tenasserim): 19.5–24 cm), blackish-based red bill, paler above, darker below, whiter tail-tip. **VOICE** Harsh *tchew-ii; tchew'iri-tchew'iri-tchieuw* etc. **HABITAT** Dry open habitats, scrub, cultivation, forest clearings; up to 1,500 m. **RANGE** Fc/co R Myanmar, W,C,NE,SE,S Thailand (spreading south), Cambodia, C,S Laos, C,S Annam, Cochinchina. V (or escapee) Pen Malaysia, Singapore.

7 BLACK-WINGED STARLING *Sturnus melanopterus* 23 cm
(a) **Adult** *melanopterus?*: White with black wings and tail, yellowish bill/facial skin/legs. (b) **Juvenile**: Crown to scapulars brownish-streaked grey, duller wings/tail. **VOICE** Falling *cha* notes, throaty *tok* or *chok*, harsh *kaar* and *keeer*; high-pitched *tsoowit* or *tsoowee* in flight. **HABITAT** Open areas, scrub; lowlands. **RANGE** Un FER Singapore (may have died out).

8 BLUE NUTHATCH *Sitta azurea* 13.5 cm
(a) **Adult** *expectata*: Blackish, whitish throat/breast, bluish-white eyering, silver-blue and black wings. **Juvenile**: Blackish bill with some pink at base, brown-tinged crown and ear-coverts, whitish fringing on undertail-coverts. **VOICE** Thin squeaky *zhe* notes, nasal *sniew*, mellow *tup*, thin *sit*, harder *chit*. Rapid *chi-chit chit-chit-chit*, trilled *titititititititik* or rattling *tr'r'r'r'r'r't* in alarm. **HABITAT** Broadleaved evergreen forest; 820–2,180 m. **RANGE** lfc R extreme S Thailand, Pen Malaysia.

9 GIANT NUTHATCH *Sitta magna* 19.5 cm
(a) **Male** *magna*: Large; broad head-bands, pale grey crown-centre, greyish flanks/belly. (b) **Female**: Buff wash below, head-bands duller. **Juvenile**: Duller. **VOICE** Chuntering *gd-da-da* or *dig-er-up*, more melodic *kid-der-ku*, harsher *gu-drr gu-drr gu-drr*, trumpet-like *naa*, piping *keep* notes. **HABITAT** Open mature pine and mixed oak/pine forest; 1,200–1,830 m. **RANGE** Sc/lc R C,E,S(east) Myanmar, NW Thailand.

10 BEAUTIFUL NUTHATCH *Sitta formosa* 16.5 cm
(a) **Adult** Black above, streaked/edged blue and white, rufous-buff below with paler throat/face. **VOICE** High shrill tremulous *chit'it'it'it'it'it'it'it...* Shorter *chit-it chit-it chit-it..* and *chit'it-it, chirririt-it* etc. **HABITAT** Broadleaved evergreen and semi-evergreen forest; 950–2,290 m. **RANGE** Sc/un R S(west),N,E Myanmar, NW Thailand, N,C Laos, W Tonkin.

11 WINTER WREN *Troglodytes troglodytes* 9.5–10 cm
(a) **Adult** *talifuensis*: Short tail; warm dark brown, paler below, dark-barred lower body/wings/tail; buffish supercilium. **Juvenile**: Darker throat, heavier dark bars below. **VOICE** Song of loud prolonged rapid vibrant notes. Dry *chek*, rolling *cherr*, often extended to hard rattle. **HABITAT** Open broadleaved evergreen and coniferous forest, clearings, rocky areas, cultivation edges; 1,830–2,800 m. **RANGE** Lo R N Myanmar.

208

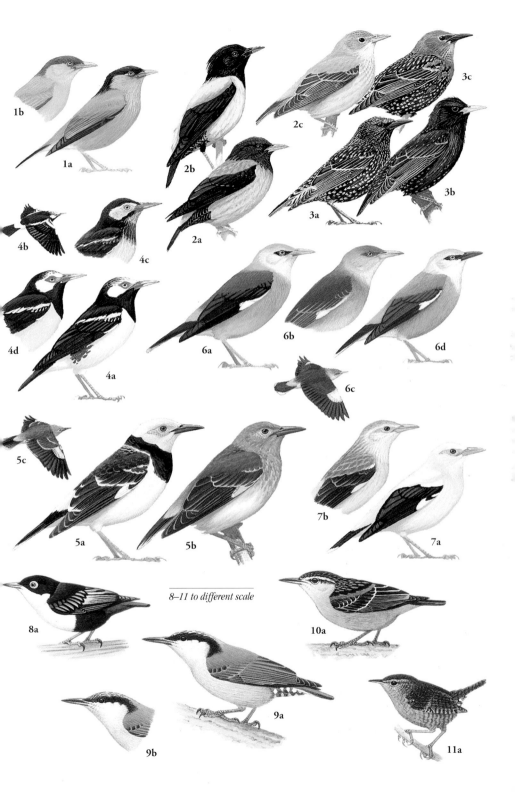

8–11 to different scale

PLATE 101 NUTHATCHES, WALLCREEPER & TREECREEPERS

1 CHESTNUT-VENTED NUTHATCH *Sitta nagaensis* 13 cm
(**a**) **Male** *montium*: Pale greyish-buff below, reddish-chestnut lower flanks/vent (latter marked white). **Female**: Lower flanks more rufous-chestnut, may be slightly duller buff and less grey below. **Other subspecies** *S.n.nagaensis* (W,N Myanmar). *S.n.grisiventris* (W Myanmar, S Annam; S Laos?). **VOICE** Song is tremolo or rattle: *chichichichichi..* or *trr'r'r'r'r'r'r'r'ri..*, or much slower *diu-diu-diu-diu-diu..* etc. Slightly squeaky *sit* notes and drier *chit*, often extended to *chit'it'it'it'it...* Whining nasal *quir* or *kner* and hard metallic *tsit* notes in alarm. **HABITAT** Broadleaf evergreen and coniferous forest, pine forest; 1,000–2,800 m. **RANGE** Co **R** W,N,C(east),E Myanmar, NW Thailand, S Laos, W Tonkin, S Annam, north Cochinchina.

2 CHESTNUT-BELLIED NUTHATCH *Sitta castanea* 13 cm
(**a**) **Male** *neglecta*: Pale buffish-chestnut below, white cheeks, dark grey and white undertail-coverts. (**b**) **Female**: Pale orange-buff below, whiter cheeks. (**c**) **Male** *tonkinensis* (NW Thailand [lo], N Indochina): Darker above, deep reddish-chestnut below, black-barred cheeks, darker grey on undertail-coverts. (**d**) **Female**: Pale chestnut below. **Other subspecies** *S.c.cinnamoventris* (N Myanmar): Like *tonkinensis* but white cheeks, chestnut, grey and white undertail-coverts. **VOICE** Song is whistled *wheeu*, trilling *trililililili..* and flatter *tutututu-tu..* etc. Sparrow-like *cheep-cheep-cheep..*, mellow *tui-tui-tui*, high *seet*, squeakier *vit*, rattling *sitit sidititit* etc. **HABITAT** Deciduous and pine, sometimes broadleaved evergreen forest; 305–1,525 m, to 1,700 m (? 2,200 m) N Indochina. **RANGE** Lc **R** Myanmar, W,NW,NE Thailand, Indochina.

3 WHITE-TAILED NUTHATCH *Sitta himalayensis* 12 cm
(**a**) **Male**: Plain cinnamon-orange undertail-coverts; white at tail- base. **Female**: Slightly paler/duller below. **VOICE** Song is fast *tiu-tiu-tiu..*, *dwi-dwi-dwi..*, slow *tui-tui-tui..* etc. High *nit*, rattled *chik-kak-ka-ka-ka..*, thin *tsik* and *sisisit*, quavering *kreeeeeeeeeee..* etc. **HABITAT** Broadleaved evergreen and mixed broadleaved/coniferous forest; 1,800–2,900 m, to 980 m in winter. **RANGE R** (local movements) W,N,E Myanmar, N Laos, W Tonkin.

4 WHITE-BROWED NUTHATCH *Sitta victoriae* 11.5 cm
(**a**) **Adult**: Whitish lores/supercilium, orange-rufous ear-patch and flank-band. **VOICE** Song is crescendo: *whi-whi-whi-whi-whi-whi-whi-whi...* Low *pit* or *plit* notes, insistent *pee pee pee pee pee...* **HABITAT** Oak and oak/rhododendron forest; 2,285–2,800 m. **RANGE** Lfc **R** W Myanmar (south Chin hills).

5 VELVET-FRONTED NUTHATCH *Sitta frontalis* 12–13.5 cm
(**a**) **Male** *frontalis*: Red bill, violet-blue above, black forehead and postocular line, whitish throat, pale dull beige/lavender below. (**b**) **Female**: No postocular line, cinnamon tinge below. (**c**) **Juvenile**: Dark bill, greyer above, cinnamon-orange wash below. **Other subspecies** *S.f.saturatior* (S Thailand southward): Deeper cinnamon-/pinkish-buff below, washed lilac. **VOICE** Song of repeated *sit* notes, sometimes a fast hard rattle. Hard *chit* and thin *sit* notes. **HABITAT** Broadleaved forest, mixed oak/pine forest; up to 1,800 m (below 1,450 m S Annam). **RANGE** Co **R** (except Singapore). Rc (status?) Singapore.

6 YELLOW-BILLED NUTHATCH *S.solangiae* 12.5–13.5 cm
(**a**) **Male** *fortior*: Yellow bill, pale below, vague nuchal collar. (**b**) **Female**: No postocular stripe. (**c**) **Male** *solangiae* (W Tonkin): Paler, more violet, less blue crown, slightly paler/greyer blue above, duller below. **VOICE** Fast *sit'ti'ti'ti'ti'ti..* song. Calls with *chit-it-it-it-it..*; single *chit* and *sit*. **HABITAT** Broadleaved evergreen forest; 900–2,500 m. **RANGE** Sc/un east S Laos, W Tonkin, C,S Annam.

7 WALLCREEPER *Tichodroma muraria* 16.5 cm
(**a,b**) **Adult non-breeding** *nepalensis*: Grey; whiter throat and upper breast, thin curved dark bill, pale-tipped undertail-coverts/tail, crimson and black on wings, white primary spots in flight. (**c**) **Male breeding**: Black face to breast. **Female breeding**: Whitish chin, variable blackish on throat/upper breast. **Juvenile**: Paler, more uniform grey below, straighter bill. **VOICE** High *ti-tiu treeb* phrases, increasing in speed/volume. Thin piping *twee* and *tuweeht* etc. **HABITAT** Cliffs, rocks, stony riverbeds in winter; found in plains. **RANGE** V N Myanmar.

8 EURASIAN TREECREEPER *Certhia familiaris* 12.5–14 cm
(**a**) **Adult** *khamensis*: Plain tail, shortish bill, white supercilium, whitish below. **Juvenile**: Slightly duller below, some dark fringing, more spotted mantle. **VOICE** Song is thin silvery *tsee-tsee-tsi-tsi-si-si-si-sisisisisi-tsee* etc. Thin *srrih* and sharp *ziih* notes, clear *teeeh*, quiet *sit*. **HABITAT** Broadleaved evergreen and coniferous forest, mixed oak and rhododendron forest; recorded at 3,960 m. **RANGE** Lo **R** N Myanmar.

9 BAR-TAILED TREECREEPER *C.himalayana* 15–16 cm
(**a**) **Adult** *ripponi*: Dark-barred greyish-brown tail, relatively long curved bill. **Juvenile**: Plainer mantle, some dark fringing below, more contrasting white throat, shorter bill. **Other subspecies** *C.b.yunnanensis* (N Myanmar). **VOICE** Song is trilled *tsee tsui-tsui-tsui-tsui-tsui-tsui-tsui-tsui-tsui-tsuip* or *tsee'tsu-tsu'tsut'tut'tut'ti'tee* etc. Thin *tsiu* notes, rising *tseeet*, sharp *tsit* etc. **HABITAT** Coniferous and broadleaved evergreen forest; 2,135–3,000 m. **RANGE** Lc **R** W,N Myanmar.

10 RUSTY-FLANKED TREECREEPER *C.nipalensis* 15.5 cm
(**a**) **Adult**: Rusty breast-sides/flanks/vent; supercilium encircles dark ear-coverts. (**b**) **Juvenile**: Duller below with dark fringing. **VOICE** Short high, accelerating trilled *si-si-sit-st't't't*. Thin *sit* call. **HABITAT** Broadleaved evergreen and mixed broadleaved/coniferous forest; 2,285–3,050 m. **RANGE** Lo **R** N Myanmar.

11 BROWN-THROATED TREECREEPER *C.discolor* 15–16 cm
(**a**) **Adult**: *shanensis*: Drab greyish below, buffy vent, indistinct supercilium. **Juvenile**: Faint darker scales on throat/breast. (**b**) **Adult** *manipurensis* (W Myanmar): Deep buffish below. (**c**) **Adult** *meridionalis* (S Annam): Darker/greyer below, warmer/darker above. **Other subspecies** *C.d.laotiana* (N Laos): Similar to *meridionalis*. **VOICE** Song is monotonous hesitant *tchi-tchi tchi-tchi tchi-tchi tchi-tchi tchichip* etc. Loud *chit* or *tchip*, sometimes rattling *chi'r'r'it*; thinner *tsit* or *seep*. **HABITAT** Broadleaved evergreen and mixed broadleaved/pine forest; 1,370–3,000 m. **RANGE** Un/lc **R** W,N,S,E Myanmar, W,NW Thailand, N Laos, W Tonkin, S Annam.

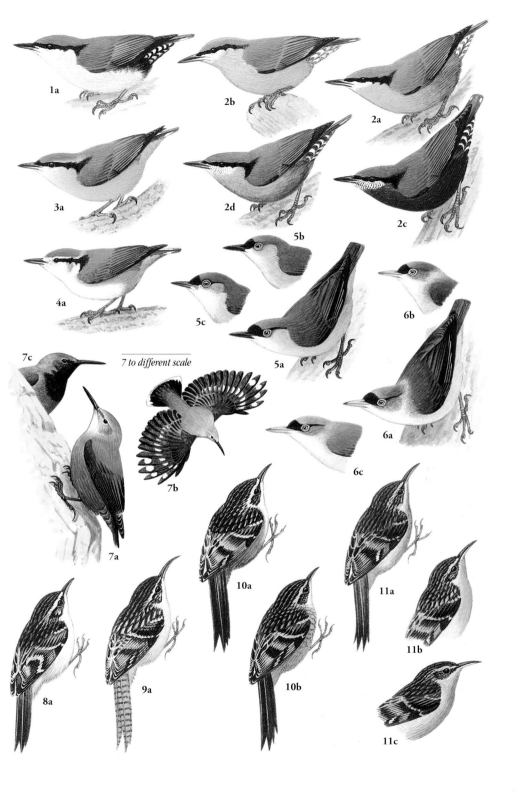

7 to different scale

PLATE 102 TYPICAL TITS, YELLOW-BROWED TIT & *AEGITHALOS* TITS

1 BLACK-BIBBED TIT *Parus hypermelaena* 11.5 cm
(a) Adult: Browner above than Coal, no crest or wing-bars. **(b) Juvenile**: Browner on head, warmer above, buff-tinged headsides, smaller bib. VOICE Thin *stip*, *si-si* and explosive *psiup*; *si-si psiup* etc. Chattering *chrrrrr*, scolding *chay*. HABITAT Open broadleaved evergreen and pine forest, scrub; 2,200–3,000 m. RANGE Lo **R** W Myanmar (Mt Victoria).

2 RUFOUS-VENTED TIT *Parus rubidiventris* 12 cm
(a) Adult *beavani*: Crest; greyish below with rufous vent. **(b) Juvenile**: Duller; white of head washed buff, shorter crest. **Other subspecies** *P.r.saramatii* (Mt Saramati, N Myanmar): Buffy-olive tinge above, deep olive-grey below, duller vent. VOICE Song is stony rattled *chi-chi-chi-chi...* or *chip-chip-chip-chip..* etc. Thin *seet*, sharp *psit*, clear *pee*, clicking *chip* etc., scolding *chit'it'it'it*. HABITAT Broadleaved evergreen and coniferous forest; 2,745–3,660 m. RANGE Lc **R** N Myanmar.

3 COAL TIT *Parus ater* 11 cm
(a) Adult *aemodius*: Pinkish/buffy-white below, wing-bars. **(b) Juvenile**: Duller; short crest, head-sides washed yellowish. VOICE *chip-pe chip-pe*; *peechoo-peechoo-peechoo*; *sit'-tui-sit'tui-sit'tui..* songs. Calls with clear *pwi*, cheerful *tsueet*, explosive twitters. Thin *sisisi* and hoarse *szee* notes in alarm. HABITAT Coniferous and mixed coniferous and broadleaved forest; 2,745–3,445 m. RANGE Lc **R** N Myanmar.

4 GREY-CRESTED TIT *Parus dichrous* 12 cm
(a) Adult *wellsi*: Greyish crest, pale buffish throat, half-collar and underparts. **Juvenile**: Faint darker tips above, paler below. VOICE Simple *whee-whee-tz-tz-tz* song. High *zai*, *ti-di* or *ti-ti-ti-ti-ti*; *cheea cheea* in alarm. HABITAT Coniferous and broadleaved evergreen forest; 2,745–3,200 m. RANGE Lo **R** N Myanmar.

5 GREAT TIT *Parus major* 14 cm
(a) Male *ambiguus*: Grey above, black head and ventral stripe, large white cheek-patch, small nape-patch and single wing-bar. **Female**: Thinner ventral stripe, black parts may be duller. **(b) Juvenile**: Dark of head duller, tinged olive above, reduced ventral stripe. **(c) Male** *nubicolus* (north-east Myanmar, NW Thailand, N Laos, W Tonkin): Yellowish-green on upper mantle, blue-grey on wing, more white on tail. **Other subspecies** *P.m.subtibetanus* (east N Myanmar?): Similar to *nubicolus*. *P.m.commixtus* (northern Vietnam): Intermediate between *nubicolus* and *ambiguus*. *P.m.nipalensis* (SW,W,N,C,S Myanmar); *templorum* (NE Thailand, southern Laos/Vietnam). VOICE Sings with *chew-a-ti chew-a-ti chew-a-ti..*, *wheat-ear wheat-ear..* etc. Metallic *pink*, thin *tsee*, lower *pee*, nasal *tcha-tcha-tcha*. Low *chich-ich-ich-ich..* and *chur'r'r'r'ribihi* alarm. HABITAT Open broadleaved forest, mangroves, coastal scrub, plantations, gardens; up to 2,135 m. Coastal in south. RANGE Lc **R** (except Tenasserim, W,C,SE Thailand, Singapore).

6 GREEN-BACKED TIT *Parus monticolus* 12.5–14.5 cm
(a) Male *legendrei* (S Annam): Greenish above, pale yellow below, very broad ventral stripe, two wing-bars. **Female**: Bib and ventral stripe narrower/duller. **(b) Juvenile**: Duller yellowish

nuchal patch/wing-bars. **(c) Male** *yunnanensis* (rest of range): Greener and yellower, thinner ventral stripe, broader wing-bars. VOICE Sings with *seta-seta-seta..*; *tu-weeh tu-weeh..*; *tsing-tsing pi-diu..*; *pli-pli-pli..* etc. Thin *si-si-si-si-li*, harsh *shick-shick-shick*, clear *te-te-whee* calls. HABITAT Broadleaved evergreen and pine forest; 915–2,650 m, locally 315 m in winter; **R** 220–500 m C Laos. RANGE Co **R** W,S Myanmar, C Laos, north E Tonkin, S Annam.

7 YELLOW-CHEEKED TIT *Parus spilonotus* 13.5–15.5 cm
(a) Male *subviridis*: Black and yellow crested head, scaly above, big wing-bars. **(b) Female**: Plainer above, olive-yellow bib/ventral stripe. **(c) Juvenile male**: Duller; shorter crest, yellowish wing-bars. **(d) Male** *rex* (N Indochina): Blue-grey above, broader bib/ventral stripe, greyish below. **(e) Female**: Greyer below. **Other subspecies** *P.s.basileus* (S Indochina): Male between *subviridis* and *rex*. Female has paler, yellower tinge above than *rex*, yellower belly. *P.s.spilonotus* (W,N Myanmar). VOICE Song is ringing *chee-chee-piu chee-chee-piu chee-chee-piu..*, *dzi-dzi-pu dzi-dzi-pu..* etc. Thin *sit si-si-si*, lisping *tsee-tsee-tsee* and *witch-a-witch-a-witch-a*. HABITAT Broadleaved evergreen forest; 600–2,745 m. RANGE Fc/co **R** Myanmar (except SW,C), W,NW,NE Thailand, Laos, W,E Tonkin, N,C,S Annam.

8 YELLOW-BROWED TIT *Sylviparus modestus* 9–10 cm
(a) Adult *modestus*: Small, short tail, dull olive above, paler below, slight crest, short pale yellowish eyebrow, narrow wing-bar. **Other subspecies** *S.m.klossi* (S Annam): Brighter/yellower overall. VOICE Ringing *pli-pli-pli-pli..* or mellower *tiu-tiu-tiu-tiu...* Thin emphatic *psit* and *tchup* notes. Trilled *sisisisisi*. HABITAT Broadleaf evergreen forest; 1,450–3,350 m (1,100 m in winter N Myanmar). RANGE Un/fc **R** W,N,E Myanmar, NW Thailand, N,S(east) Laos, W Tonkin, S Annam.

9 BLACK-THROATED TIT *Aegithalos concinnus* 11–11.5 cm
(a) Adult *pulchellus*: Black throat-patch, rufous-chestnut on breast to flank. Drab greyish crown. **(b) Juvenile**: Whitish throat, dark necklace. **(c) Adult** *talifuensis* (N Myanmar, north Indochina): Rufescent crown. **(d) Adult** *annamensis* (south Indochina): Dull grey crown, mostly grey breast to flank. **Other subspecies** *A.c.manipurensis* (W Myanmar): Like *talifuensis*. VOICE Song is twittering *tir-ir-ir-ir-ir* mixed with chirping etc. Thin *psip psip*, *si-si-si-si..*; rattling *churr trrrt trrrt* in alarm. HABITAT Broadleaved evergreen and mixed broadleaved/pine forest; 900–2,600 m (lo 490 m Indochina). RANGE Lc **R** W,N,E,S(east) Myanmar, NW Thailand, east Cambodia, Laos, W,E Tonkin, N,C,S Annam, north Cochinchina.

10 BLACK-BROWED TIT *Aegithalos bonvaloti* 11–12 cm
(a) Adult *bonvaloti*: Broader head-bands than Black-throated, pale cinnamon-rufous neck, speckled throat, broader breast-band. **(b) Juvenile**: Paler below with greyish mottling. **(c) Adult** *sharpei* (W Myanmar): White lower throat/neck, brownish breast-band, buffish below. VOICE Continuous *see-see-see-see..* and *tup* or *trrup*. Shrill *zeet* and *trr-trr-trr* in alarm. HABITAT Open broadleaved evergreen and coniferous forest; 1,830–3,110 m. RANGE Lfc **R** W,N Myanmar.

PLATE 103 CHINESE PENDULINE, FIRE-CAPPED & SULTAN TITS, & MARTINS

1 CHINESE PENDULINE TIT *Remiz consobrinus* 10.5 cm
(a) **Male non-breeding**: Pointed bill, greyish-brown crown, white-bordered black mask. Mostly buffish-brown; dull chestnut upper mantle-band, buffish wing-fringing. **Male breeding**: Crown plainer drab mid-grey, thinner white mask-border, buffier above with thinner/bolder mantle-band, darker flight feathers. (b) **Female non-breeding**: Duller than male; browner mask/above. **Female breeding**: May show dark-mottled upper mantle/breast-sides. **First-year male**: Duller than non-breeding adult, browner crown/nape, pale-mottled mask, less distinct mantle-band. (c) **First-year female**: Pale mask (hardly contrasts with crown). **VOICE** Calls with high soft thin penetrating *tseee* or *pseee*. Also fuller *piu* and fast *siu-siu-siu-siu...* **HABITAT** Reedbeds, marshes, scrub; lowlands. **RANGE** V E Tonkin.

2 FIRE-CAPPED TIT *Cephalopyrus flammiceps* 10 cm
(a) **Male breeding** *olivaceus*: Yellowish-green above (yellower rump), yellowish below, reddish-orange forehead-patch, faint reddish throat-wash. (b) **Female breeding**: Like breeding male but forehead-patch golden-olive, throat dull olive-yellow. (c) **Adult non-breeding**: Like breeding female but throat whitish. Greener and yellower than Yellow-browed Tit, pointed bill, no crest. (d) **Juvenile**: Whitish below. Daintier, thinner-billed than Green Shrike Babbler. **VOICE** Song is high *pis-su-psisu-pissu-pissu..*, *tink-tink-tink-tink*, ringing *psing-psing-psing..* or sweet *tsui tsui-tsui..* etc. High *tsit* notes and weak *whitoo-whitoo*. **HABITAT & BEHAVIOUR** Broadleaved evergreen/semi-evergreen forest; 1,400–2,135 m. Often in flocks. **RANGE** Ra **WV** E Myanmar, NW Thailand, N Laos.

3 SULTAN TIT *Melanochlora sultanea* 20.5 cm
(a) **Male** *sultanea*: Large; black and yellow, yellow crest. (b) **Female**: Duller/browner above, washed green, yellowish-olive throat/upper breast. **Juvenile**: Duller than female, shorter crest, whitish greater covert tips, sooty-olive throat/upper breast. (c) **Male** *gayeti* (S Laos, C Annam): Black crest (both sexes). **Other subspecies** *M.s.flavocristata* (S Myanmar to SE Thailand and southward). **VOICE** Clear *piu-piu-piu-piu-piu..* song. Rattling *tji-jup*, shrill squeaky *tria-tria-tria*, *tcheery-tcheery-tcheery* and *squeasy-squear-squear* etc. **HABITAT** Broadleaved forest; up to 1,680 m (below 1,200 m in Thailand and Pen Malaysia). **RANGE** Un/lc **R** (except C Thailand, Singapore, Cambodia, southern S Annam, Cochinchina).

4 SAND MARTIN *Riparia riparia* 11.5–13 cm
(a) **Adult** *ijimae*: Larger than Plain, whitish below with broad brown breast-band, tail-fork somewhat deeper. (b) **Juvenile**: Upperparts fringed buffish, throat tinged buff, rest of underparts often less white. **VOICE** Dry rasping *trrrsh*, higher *chiir* in alarm. Harsh twittering *trrrsh trre-trre-trre-rrerrerre..* etc. may be song. **HABITAT** Lakes, rivers, marshes, sometimes open areas away from water; up to 1,830 m. **RANGE** Un **WV** Myanmar, W,NW Thailand, N,C Laos, Cambodia, C Annam, Cochinchina.

5 PALE MARTIN *Riparia diluta* 11–12.5 cm
(a) **Adult** *fokienensis*: Slightly smaller/smaller-billed than Sand, slightly shallower tail-fork, paler and greyer above, less

clean white below, with creamy wash on belly/vent, paler but neater breast-band, no dark smudging on breast or upper belly. **Juvenile**: Differs from adult like Sand. **HABITAT** Lowland lakes, rivers, marshes. **RANGE** Rc in winter (status?) E Tonkin.

6 PLAIN MARTIN *Riparia paludicola* 10.5–12 cm
(a,b) **Adult** *chinensis*: Similar to Sand but smaller and daintier, shallower tail-fork, no breast-band, throat and breast sullied greyish-brown, rump/uppertail-coverts clearly paler than rest of upperparts. Throat often paler than breast. **Juvenile**: Fringed warm buffish above (except crown), buffier throat and breast. **VOICE** Song is weak high twitter. Low spluttering *chrr'r*, short, slightly explosive *chit* or *chut* notes. **HABITAT** Large rivers, lakes; up to 1,220 m. **RANGE** Lc **R** Myanmar, NW,NE Thailand, Cambodia, Laos, W Tonkin.

7 DUSKY CRAG MARTIN *Hirundo concolor* 13–14 cm
(a,b) **Adult**: Dark brown, slightly paler throat/breast (thin dark streaks on former), barely forked tail with whitish spots (visible when tail spread). **Juvenile**: Rufous-grey fringing above, throat paler with no streaks. **VOICE** Song of soft twittering sounds. Usually calls with soft *chit* notes. **HABITAT** Open areas, mainly near cliffs, caves or buildings; up to 2,000 m. **RANGE** Lo **R** C,E,S (south-east) Myanmar, Tenasserim, Thailand (except SE), Pen Malaysia, Laos, W Tonkin, E Tonkin, N,S Annam.

8 NORTHERN HOUSE MARTIN *Delichon urbica* 13–14 cm
(a,b) **Adult** *lagopoda*: Like Asian but glossier above, whiter and larger rump-patch, whiter below, greyish-white underwing-coverts, deeper tail-fork. (c) **Juvenile**: Browner above, greyish-washed below, often with duller breast-sides; some dark scaling on vent and tail-coverts. **VOICE** Sings with unstructured, chirpy twittering. Calls include sharp *d-gitt*, scratchy, dry twittering *prrit* notes and emphatic, drawn-out *chierr* when agitated. **HABITAT** Over forests and open areas; up to 2,565 m. **RANGE** Sc/un **WV** N,C,E,S Myanmar, Tenasserim, NW,NE Thailand, Laos, C,S Annam, Cochinchina.

9 ASIAN HOUSE MARTIN *Delichon dasypus* 12–13 cm
(a,b) **Adult** *dasypus*: Smallish; shallow tail-fork, black above, greyish-white rump (faintly streaked) and underside, darkish underwing-coverts. (c) **Juvenile**: Browner above, tail less deeply forked. **Other subspecies** *D.d.cashmiriensis* (rc Myanmar, NW Thailand). **VOICE** Song similar to Northern. Calls include reedy *screeeel*. **HABITAT** Over forests and open areas; up to 3,100 m. **RANGE** Un/fc **WV** W,N,C,S Myanmar, Thailand, Pen Malaysia, Singapore, Cambodia, Laos, C,S Annam.

10 NEPAL HOUSE MARTIN *Delichon nipalensis* 11.5–12.5 cm
(a,b) **Adult** *nipalensis*: Like Asian but tail almost square-cut, throat mostly dark, undertail-coverts black, rump-band narrower. (c) **Juvenile**: Browner above; throat and undertail-coverts mixed with whitish, breast greyish. **Other subspecies** *D.n.cuttingi* (rc N Myanmar). **VOICE** Calls with high-pitched *chi-i*. **HABITAT** Over forested and open areas, often near cliffs; up to 1,830 m. **RANGE** Un **R** SW,W,N Myanmar, NE Thailand, Laos, W Tonkin.

4–10 to different scale

PLATE 104 WHITE-EYED RIVER MARTIN, SWALLOWS & WHITE-EYES

1 WHITE-EYED RIVER MARTIN *Pseudochelidon sirintarae* 15 cm (**a**) **Adult**: Robust; big yellow bill, white eyes/broad eyering, dark below, white rump-band; tail-streamers <9 cm. (**b**) **Juvenile**: Browner with paler throat; no tail-streamers. HABITAT In lakeside reeds during night (roosting?). RANGE Frc C Thailand (Bung Boraphet) in winter (last definite record 1980).

2 BARN SWALLOW *Hirundo rustica* 15 cm (tail <5 more) (**a,b**) **Adult breeding** *gutturalis*: Blue-black above/on breast-band, chestnut-red forehead/throat, whitish below, deeply forked tail with streamers. (**c**) **Juvenile**: Browner above/on breast-band, duller forehead/throat (latter may be whitish); short tail-fork. (**d**) **Adult non-breeding** *tytleri* (rc SW,N,E,C,S Myanmar, C,SE Thailand, Pen Malaysia, C Annam): Pale rufous below (seasonally lacking tail-streamers). **Other subspecies** *H.r.mandschurica* (rc NW Thailand). VOICE Song is rapid twittering with croaking sound that extends to dry rattle. High-pitched sharp *vit* notes, and louder, anxious *vheet vheet..* or *flitt-flitt* in alarm. HABITAT Open areas, often near water and habitation; up to 2,000 m. RANGE Lo R/BV NW,NE Thailand, N Laos, W,E Tonkin. Co WV and PM throughout. Rc in summer Pen Malaysia, S Laos, Cochinchina.

3 PACIFIC SWALLOW *Hirundo tahitica* 13–14 cm (**a,b**) **Adult** *abbotti*: Upper breast chestnut-red (no blue-black band), belly tinged greyish-brown, dark-mottled vent, dusky underwing-coverts, shallower tail-fork with no streamers. (**c**) **Juvenile**: Browner above, paler throat/upper breast. **Other subspecies** *H.t.javanica* (Coco Is, off S Myanmar). VOICE Short, high, slightly explosive *swi* or *tswi; tswi-tswi-tswi* etc. Lower *swoo*. HABITAT Coastal habitats, often near habitation; also over forested/open areas inland, up to 2,010 m (Pen Malaysia). RANGE Co coastal R (except C Thailand, E Tonkin, N,C,S Annam). Inland (minor movements) Pen Malaysia.

4 WIRE-TAILED SWALLOW *Hirundo smithii* 13.5 cm (tail <12.5 more) (**a**) **Adult** *filifera*: Chestnut crown, snowy-white below (including throat), very blue above, square tail with very long streamers. (**b**) **Juvenile**: Browner above, paler crown, vaguely buffish throat, no streamers. VOICE Twittering song. Calls include *chit-chit*, and *chirrik-weet chirrik-weet..* and *chichip chichip..* when alarmed. HABITAT Large rivers, lakes and nearby areas; up to 1,980 m. RANGE Ra/un R (local movements) Myanmar, NW,NE Thailand, Cambodia, Laos, C,S Annam.

5 RED-RUMPED SWALLOW *H.daurica* 16.5 cm (tail <3 more) (**a,b**) **Adult** *japonica*: Hard to tell from Striated (*mayri*) but slightly smaller, almost complete orange-rufous nuchal collar (narrowly broken on nape-centre), somewhat narrower streaks on rump and underparts. Breast-streaks possibly tend to be slightly heavier than belly-streaks. **Juvenile**: Duller; paler nuchal collar/rump/underparts, browner and pale-tipped tertials, short tail-streamers. **Other subspecies** *H.d.nipalensis* (widely rc?): Thinner, more even underpart-streaking. VOICE Sings like Barn but lower, harsher, slower and shorter. Nasal *djuit* or *tveyk*; sharp *kiir* alarm notes. HABITAT Open areas, often near water; up to 2,440 m. RANGE Un/fc WV throughout. Also PM W Tonkin.

6 STRIATED SWALLOW *H.striolata* 18–19 cm (tail <3 more) (**a**) **Adult** *stanfordi*: Like Red-rumped but slightly larger, lacks orange-rufous nuchal collar, much broader streaks on rump and underparts. Only little reddish-rufous behind ear-coverts. (**b**) **Juvenile**: Differs as Red-rumped. (**c**) **Adult** *mayri* (B west N Myanmar, and WV range): Narrower streaks (only slightly broader than Red-rumped). (**d**) **Adult** *badia* (R S Thailand southward): Larger; deep rufous-chestnut underparts/underwing-coverts. **Other subspecies** *H.s.vernayi* (R north Tenasserim, W Thailand): Like *stanfordi* but base-colour of lores, ear-coverts, upper breast, flanks and undertail-coverts reddish-rufous (rest of underparts with paler reddish-rufous wash), underpart streaks shorter (more like spot-streaks on throat/breast). VOICE Sings with soft twittering notes. Loud metallic *cheenk*, long drawn-out *quitsch*, short *pin* and repeated *chi-chi-chi* when alarmed. HABITAT Open areas (often near water), cliffs; up to 2,565 m. RANGE Co R N,C,E,S Myanmar, Tenasserim, N,NW,NE,S Thailand, Pen Malaysia, Singapore, Cambodia, Laos, N,S Annam, Cochinchina. WV N,E,S[east] Myanmar east to E Tonkin, C Annam. Rc (status?) W Tonkin.

7 CHESTNUT-FLANKED WHITE-EYE *Zosterops erythropleurus* 11.5 cm (**a**) **Adult**: Chestnut flanks, green forehead. HABITAT & BEHAVIOUR Open and secondary forest; up to 2,590 m, mostly above 800 m. Often in flocks with Japanese. RANGE Un/lc WV W,C,S,E Myanmar, W,NW,NE Thailand, Cambodia, N,C Laos, W,E Tonkin.

8 ORIENTAL WHITE-EYE *Zosterops palpebrosus* 10.5–11 cm (**a**) **Adult typical morph** *siamensis*: Yellowish-white ventral stripe, yellow forehead. (**b**) **Adult yellow morph**: All-yellow below. (**c**) **Adult** *williamsoni* (C,W,S[east] Thailand): Faint ventral stripe, paler below, duller above. (**d**) **Adult** *auriventer* (Tenasserim and west S Thailand southward): Clear yellow ventral stripe, less yellow on forehead. VOICE Short thin wispy song of slurred call notes. Wispy sibilant *jeww* or *cheuw* call. HABITAT & BEHAVIOUR Broadleaved forest, secondary growth, mangroves, plantations, parks etc.; up to 1,525 m, locally 1,830 m (*williamsoni/auriventer* mainly coastal). Highly gregarious. RANGE Co R (except E Tonkin, N Annam, Singapore). Sc (probably now originating from captivity) Singapore.

9 JAPANESE WHITE-EYE *Zosterops japonicus* 10–11.5 cm (**a**) **Adult** *simplex*: Darker above than Oriental, no ventral stripe; defined yellow loral band. (**b**) **Juvenile**: Faint eyering. VOICE Like Oriental. HABITAT Forest, secondary growth, plantations, parks, gardens; up to 2,590 m (B lowlands). RANGE Co R E Tonkin. Co WV C,S,E Myanmar, north Tenasserim, NW(also rc summer),NE Thailand, Laos, W,E Tonkin, N,C Annam.

10 EVERETT'S WHITE-EYE *Zosterops everetti* 11–11.5 cm (**a**) **Adult** *wetmorei*: Green forehead, deep grey sides, deep yellow throat/ventral stripe. **Juvenile**: Duller, paler, less pronounced ventral stripe, greener wing-fringing. **Other species** *Z.e.tahanensis* (extreme S Thailand southward): VOICE Thinner and higher calls than Oriental: *tsieu* or *tschew*. HABITAT Broadleaved evergreen forest; up to 2,010 m. RANGE Un/lfc R SE,W(south),S Thailand, Pen Malaysia.

1b

1a

2a

3a

3c

3b

2c

2b

2d

6b

4b

4a

5a

6c

6a

7–10 to different scale

5b

6d

7a

8c

8b

8a

8d

9b

9a

10a

PLATE 105 *PYCNONOTUS* BULBULS

1 BLACK-HEADED BULBUL *Pycnonotus atriceps* 18 cm
(**a**) **Adult** *atriceps*: Mostly yellowish-green, black head and sub-terminal tail-band, blackish primaries. (**b**) **Adult**: Greener variant. (**c**) **Adult grey morph**: Grey neck, breast and belly. (**d**) **Juvenile**: Duller; largely dull greenish head. VOICE Sings with short, spaced, tuneless whistles. Loud chipping *chew* or *chiw* calls. HABITAT Broadleaved forest; up to 1,600 m (rarely 2,440 m). RANGE Un/co **R** (except N Myanmar?, W,E Tonkin, N Annam).

2 BLACK-CRESTED BULBUL *Pycnonotus melanicterus* 18.5–19.5 cm
(**a**) **Adult** *caecilli* (south of c.12°N): Black head, crest, yellow below. (**b**) **Juvenile**: Duller, short crest. (**c**) **Adult** *johnsoni* (C,NE,SE Thailand, S Indochina): Red on throat, deeper yellow (often orangey) breast. **Other subspecies** *P.m.flaviventris* (SW,W,N,C,S Myanmar), *vantynei* (E Myanmar, north Thailand and Indochina), *xantbops* (S,E Myanmar to W(north),NW(south) Thailand), *auratus* (north NE Thailand, C Laos), *elbeli* (islands off SE Thailand), *negatus* (central Tenasserim, south W Thailand). VOICE Song is quick *whitu-whirru-wheet* and *whit-whaet-ti-whaet* etc. HABITAT Broadleaved forest; up to 2,565 m. RANGE Co **R** (except Singapore). Un **FER** (established?) Singapore.

3 SCALY-BREASTED BULBUL *Pycnonotus squamatus* 14–16 cm
(**a**) **Adult** *weberi*: Black head, white throat, white-scaled black breast and flanks, yellow undertail-coverts. VOICE Calls with sharp high chinking *wit* or *tit* notes. HABITAT & BEHAVIOUR Broadleaved evergreen forest; up to 1,000 m. Often in canopy. RANGE Un/fc **R** south Tenasserim, S Thailand, Pen Malaysia.

4 GREY-BELLIED BULBUL *Pycnonotus cyaniventris* 16.5 cm
(**a**) **Adult** *cyaniventris*: Grey head/underparts, yellow under-tail-coverts. VOICE Clear *pi-pi-pwi-pwi..*, low *wit wit wit...* Bubbling trilled whistle: *pi-pi-pi-pi-pi...* HABITAT Broadleaved evergreen forest; up to 1,000 m. RANGE Un/fc **R** south Tenasserim, S Thailand, Pen Malaysia; formerly Singapore.

5 PUFF-BACKED BULBUL *Pycnonotus eutilotus* 23 cm
(**a**) **Adult**: Brown and whitish; short crest. VOICE Song is quavering *tchui'uui tch'i-iwi'iwi*; *iwu'iwi i'wu-u* etc. HABITAT Broadleaf evergreen forest; to 210 m. RANGE Un/fc **R** south Tenasserim, S Thailand, Pen Malaysia; formerly Singapore.

6 STRIPE-THROATED BULBUL *Pycnonotus finlaysoni* 19–20 cm
(**a**) **Adult** *eous*: Yellow head-streaks, yellow vent. (**b**) **Juvenile**: Browner, little streaking. (**c**) **Adult** *davisoni* (S Myanmar): No yellow streaks on forecrown and ear-coverts, greener crown and rump, pale eyes. **Other subspecies** *P.f.finlaysoni* (south of c.12°N). VOICE Song is throaty measured *whit-chu whic-ic* and *whit whit-tu-iwhit-whitu'tu* etc. HABITAT Secondary growth, scrub, forest edge; up to 1,300 m. RANGE Co **R** (minor movements), except W,N,C Myanmar, C Thailand, Singapore.

7 FLAVESCENT BULBUL *Pycnonotus flavescens* 21.5–22 cm
(**a**) **Adult** *vividus*: Yellowish below, greyish head, blackish crown/lores, whitish eyebrow. (**b**) **Juvenile**: Browner/plainer

head and above, paler bill. **Other subspecies** *P.f.flavescens* (south-western Myanmar), *sordidus* (S Laos, S Annam). VOICE Song is jolly, rather quick *joi whiti-whiti-wit*; *ti-chi whiti-whiti-whit-tu*; *chi whiti-whiti-whi-tu chitiwit* etc. Harsh buzzy *djo djo drrrrrt*, *dreet dreet drrrr dreet-dreet..* etc. in alarm. HABITAT Edge of broadleaved evergreen forest, scrub and grass; 900–2,590 m. RANGE Co **R** Myanmar, W,NW,NE Thailand, Laos, W,E Tonkin, C,S Annam.

8 YELLOW-VENTED BULBUL *P.goiavier* 20–20.5 cm
(**a**) **Adult** *personatus*: White supercilium/throat, dark crown and lores, yellow vent. (**b**) **Juvenile**: Washed out. **Other subspecies** *P.g.jambu* (C Thailand eastwards). VOICE Bubbling *chic-chic-chic..* and *tiddloo-tiddloo-tiddloo..*, sharp harsh *chwich-chwich*. HABITAT Lowland scrub, mangroves, plantations, cultivation (to 1,830 m Pen Malaysia). RANGE Co **R** (minor movements) south Tenasserim, W,C,SE,S Thailand, Pen Malaysia, Singapore, Cambodia, C,S Laos, Cochinchina.

9 OLIVE-WINGED BULBUL *P.plumosus* 20–20.5 cm
(**a**) **Adult** *plumosus*: Weak ear-covert streaks, red eyes, dark bill; yellowish-green wing-fringes. (**b**) **Juvenile**: Browner overall. **Other subspecies** *P.p.chiroplethis* (Pulau Tinggi, Pen Malaysia). VOICE Song is simple *whip wi-wiu wu-wurri'i* etc. Throaty *whip-whip..* and *wrrb wrrb wrrb...* HABITAT Secondary growth, mangroves; up to 610 m. RANGE Co **R** south Tenasserim, S Thailand, Pen Malaysia, Singapore.

10 STREAK-EARED BULBUL *P.blanfordi* 17.5–19.5 cm
(**a**) **Adult** *conradi*: Nondescript, yellowish vent, whitish ear-covert streaks, pale eyes. (**b**) **Juvenile**: Paler, fainter ear-covert streaks, brown eyes. **Other subspecies** *P.b.blanfordi* (W,C,E,S Myanmar): Less yellow vent. VOICE Harsh rasping *which-which-which...*, piping *brink-brink-brink...* HABITAT Semi-desert, scrub, cultivation, gardens, open deciduous forest; up to 915 m. RANGE Co **R** Myanmar (except N), Thailand, north Pen Malaysia, Cambodia, Laos, C,S Annam, Cochinchina.

11 CREAM-VENTED BULBUL *Pycnonotus simplex* 18 cm
(**a**) **Adult** *simplex*: Whitish eyes. (**b**) **Juvenile**: Warmer, brown eyes. VOICE Quavering *whi-whi-whi-whi-whi..* and low *pru* and *prrr* notes. HABITAT Broadleaved evergreen forest; up to 1,220 m. RANGE Un/co **R** S Thailand, Pen Malaysia, Singapore.

12 RED-EYED BULBUL *Pycnonotus brunneus* 19 cm
(**a**) **Adult** *brunneus*: Nondescript, red eyes. (**b**) **Juvenile**: Paler/warmer, brownish eyes, paler bill. **Other subspecies** *P.b.zapolius* (Pulau Tioman, Pen Malaysia). VOICE High throaty bubbling *pri-pri-pri-pri-pri-pit-pit*. HABITAT Broadleaved evergreen; up to 1,000 m. RANGE Fc/co **R** south Tenasserim, S Thailand, Pen Malaysia, Singapore (sc).

13 SPECTACLED BULBUL *P.erythropthalmos* 16–18 cm
(**a**) **Adult** *erythropthalmos*: Orangey eyering, paler throat/vent than Red-eyed. (**b**) **Juvenile**: Paler, brown eyes, duller eyering. VOICE Quite high *wip-wip-wi'i'i'i*. HABITAT Broadleaved evergreen forest; up to 900 m. RANGE Fc/co **R** south Tenasserim, S Thailand, Pen Malaysia; formerly Singapore.

PLATE 106 FINCHBILLS, *PYCNONOTUS, HEMIXOS* & *HYPSIPETES* BULBULS

1 CRESTED FINCHBILL *Spizixos canifrons* 21.5 cm
(**a**) **Adult** *ingrami*: Thick pale bill, erect crest. (**b**) **Juvenile**: Greener head, shorter crest. **Other subspecies** *S.c.canifrons* (W,N Myanmar). **VOICE** Bubbling *purr-purr-prruit-prruit-prruit..* etc. **HABITAT** Second growth, thickets; 1,065–2,720 m. **RANGE** Lc **R** W,N,C,E Myanmar, NW Thailand, N Laos, W Tonkin.

2 COLLARED FINCHBILL *Spizixos semitorques* 23 cm
(**a**) **Adult** *semitorques*: No crest, white face-patch and streaks, whitish half-collar. (**b**) **Juvenile**: Browner head. **HABITAT** Scrub, secondary growth; 1,200–1,500 m. **RANGE** Lo **R** W,E Tonkin.

3 STRIATED BULBUL *Pycnonotus striatus* 23 cm
(**a**) **Adult** *paulus*: Streaked yellowish-white, throat/undertail-coverts yellow. **Other subspecies** *P.s.striatus* (Myanmar, except N,C); *arctus* (N Myanmar). **VOICE** *chu-wip* and *chi'pi-wi* song phrases. Harsh *djrrri*. **HABITAT** Broadleaved evergreen forest; 1,200–2,900 m. **RANGE** Un/fc **R** SW,W,N,E,S Myanmar, north Tenasserim, W,NW,NE Thailand, N,C Laos, W Tonkin.

4 BLACK-AND-WHITE BULBUL *Pycnonotus melanoleucos* 18 cm
(**a**) **Male**: Blackish; mostly white coverts. **Female**: Browner, slightly less white on coverts. (**b**) **Juvenile**: Cold brownish; darker centres above, dark breast-streaks. **VOICE** Tuneless *pet-it*. **HABITAT** Broadleaved evergreen forest; up to 1,830 m. **RANGE** Ra/un **R** S Thailand, Pen Malaysia; formerly Singapore.

5 RED-WHISKERED BULBUL *P.jocosus* 18–20.5 cm
(**a**) **Adult** *pattani*: Black crest, red ear-patch and vent. (**b**) **Juvenile**: Browner, no ear-patch, vent pinkish to orangey. (**c**) **Adult** *monticola* (N Myanmar): Larger; darker ear-patch. **Other subspecies** *P.j.emeria* (southern Myanmar, W Thailand): Larger red ear-patch. *P.j.hainanensis* (northern Indochina): Like *monticola*. **VOICE** Lively song phrases: *wit-ti-waet*; *queep kwil-ya*; *queek-kay* etc. Rolling *prroop*. **HABITAT** Secondary growth, scrub, cultivation, parks, gardens; up to 1,800 m. **RANGE** Co **R** (except southern Pen Malaysia, Singapore, where un **FER**).

6 BROWN-BREASTED BULBUL *P.xanthorrhous* 20 cm
(**a**) **Adult** *xanthorrhous*: Brownish ear-coverts/breast/upper-parts, little white on tail. (**b**) **Juvenile**: Browner and plainer. **VOICE** Song is simple *chirriwu'i whi'chu whirri'ui* etc. Harsh *chee* notes, thinner *ti-whi*. **HABITAT** Secondary growth, thickets; 1,020–2,290 m; sometimes to 610 m. **RANGE** Lc **R** N,E,C(east),S(east) Myanmar, NW Thailand, N Laos, W Tonkin.

7 LIGHT-VENTED BULBUL *Pycnonotus sinensis* 19 cm
(**a**) **Adult** *hainanus* (**R** and **VS** Vietnam): Whitish vent, yellowish-grey breast, whitish ear-patch. (**b**) **Juvenile**: Paler; largely greyish-brown head, faint breast-band. (**c**) **Adult** *P.s.sinensis* (**VS**): White head-streak. **VOICE** *jhieu* and *jhoit* notes. **HABITAT** Lowland cultivation, scrub, mangroves. **RANGE** Un **R** E Tonkin. Co **WV** E Tonkin, N,C Annam. **V** NW,NE Thailand, C Laos.

8 RED-VENTED BULBUL *Pycnonotus cafer* 23 cm
(**a**) **Adult** *melanchimus* (S Myanmar): Dark with whitish scales, white rump, red undertail-coverts. **Juvenile**: Browner

above. **Other subspecies** *P.c.stanfordi*. **VOICE** Cheerful *be care-ful* or *be quick-quick* etc. Calls with *peep-peep-peep.., peep-a peep-a-lo* etc. **HABITAT** Semi-desert, thickets, cultivation; up to 1,910 m. **RANGE** Co **R** SW,W,N,C,E,S Myanmar.

9 SOOTY-HEADED BULBUL *Pycnonotus aurigaster* 19–21 cm
(**a**) **Adult** *klossi*: Black cap, white rump, red vent. **Juvenile**: Browner cap, paler vent. (**b**) **Adult** *thais* (C to SE Thailand, C Laos)/*germani* (NE Thailand, S Indochina): Yellow vent. **Other subspecies** *P.a.latouchei* (E Myanmar and north NW Thailand to W Tonkin); *resurrectus* (E Tonkin, N Annam); *dolichurus* (C Annam); *schauenseei* (central Tenasserim, W Thailand). **VOICE** Chatty *whi wi-wiwi-wiwi* song. Whistled *u'whi'hi'hu* etc. **HABITAT** Secondary growth, cultivation; up to 1,830 m. **RANGE** Fc/co **R** E,S Myanmar, Tenasserim, Thailand (except S), Indochina.

10 ASHY BULBUL *Hemixos flavala* 20.5–21 cm
(**a**) **Adult** *hildebrandi*: Black crown/face, brown ear-coverts, grey above, yellowish on wing. (**b**) **Adult** *flavala* (SW to northern Myanmar): Grey crown. (**c**) **Adult** *remotus* (S Laos, S Annam): Paler and browner. (**d**) **Adult** *cinereus* (S Thailand southwards): Much plainer and browner above. **Juvenile**: Browner-tinged above. **Other subspecies** *H.f.davisoni* (Tenasserim, W Thailand); *bourdellei* (NE Thailand, N Laos). **VOICE** Song is high *ii-wit'ti-ui* etc. Ringing *tree-tree-tree...* **HABITAT** Broadleaved evergreen forest; up to 2,100 m. **RANGE** Fc/co **R** Myanmar, Thailand (except C,SE), Pen Malaysia, E Cambodia, Laos, W Tonkin, N,C,S Annam. Ra **NBV** Singapore.

11 CHESTNUT BULBUL *Hemixos castanonotus* 21.5 cm
(**a**) **Adult** *canipennis* (**rc** north E Tonkin): Chestnut head-side and above, pale greyish wing-fringing. (**b**) **Juvenile**: Duller. **Other subspecies** *H.c.castanonotus* (**R** E Tonkin): Yellow-green wing-fringing. **VOICE** Sings simple jolly *whi i-wu* etc. **HABITAT** Broadleaf evergreen forest; up to 1,000 m. **RANGE** Lo **R** (and **WV**?) E Tonkin.

12 BLACK BULBUL *Hypsipetes leucocephalus* 23.5–26.5 cm
(**a**) **Adult** *concolor*: Blackish, red bill and legs. (**b**) **Juvenile**: Browner. (**c**) **Adult** *stresemanni* (VS NW Thailand to S Laos, E Tonkin): White head, greyer rump/below. (**d**) **Adult** *leucotho-rax* (VS W Myanmar to S Annam and north): White head/breast. **Other subspecies** *H.l.ambiens* (N Myanmar), *perniger* (E Tonkin?) and *sinensis* (VS NE Thailand, E Tonkin, S Laos): Blacker. *H.l.leucocephalus* (VS N Myanmar to N Indochina): White head. *H.l.nigrescens* (south/west Myanmar): **VOICE** Song is simple *trip wi tit-i-whi* etc. Mewing *hwieeer*. **HABITAT** Broadleaved forests; 500–3,000 m, to 120 m in winter. **RANGE** Fc/co **R** Myanmar, W,NW,NE Thailand, Indochina (except Cochinchina). Un/lc **WV** W,N,C,E Myanmar, NW,NE Thailand, Cambodia, C,S Laos, W,E Tonkin, N,C Annam. **V** S Thailand.

13 WHITE-HEADED BULBUL *Hypsipetes thompsoni* 20 cm
(**a**) **Adult**: Size; no crest, grey body, rufescent vent, black lores. (**b**) **Juvenile**: Browner overall. **VOICE** Squeaky song phrases, including *chit-chiriu chit-chiriu...* **HABITAT** Forest edge, secondary forest 900–2,135 m. **RANGE** Un/lc **R** N,C,E,S(east) Myanmar, north Tenasserim, W,NW Thailand.

220

PLATE 107 MISCELLANEOUS (MAINLY FOREST) BULBULS

1 STRAW-HEADED BULBUL *Pycnonotus zeylanicus* 29 cm
(a) Adult: Large; golden-yellowish crown, blackish eye-stripe/moustache. **Juvenile**: Duller/browner head. **VOICE** Long song bursts of loud melodious warbling. **HABITAT** Forest edge, secondary growth, plantations, cultivation, rarely mangroves; usually along larger rivers/streams. Up to 245 m. **RANGE** Ra/lo **R** south Tenasserim, S Thailand (**E**?), Pen Malaysia, Singapore.

2 FINSCH'S BULBUL *Alophoixus finschii* 16.5–17 cm
(a) Adult: Brownish-olive, short dark bill, yellow throat/vent. **VOICE** Harsh *scree* notes. **HABITAT** Broadleaved evergreen forest; up to 760 m. **RANGE** Sc/un **R** extreme S Thailand, Pen Malaysia.

3 WHITE-THROATED BULBUL *Alophoixus flaveolus* 21.5–22 cm
(a) Adult *burmanicus*: Whitish-grey face, white throat, yellow below; long crest. **(b) Juvenile**: Brown above, yellow below is suffused brown. **Other subspecies** *A.f.flaveolus* (SW,W,N,C Myanmar). **VOICE** *Chi-chack chi-chack chi-chack* and nasal *cheer* etc. **HABITAT** Broadleaved evergreen forest; up to 1,525 m. **RANGE** Un/lc **R** Myanmar, W,NW Thailand.

4 PUFF-THROATED BULBUL *Alophoixus pallidus* 22–25 cm
(a) Adult *henrici*: Darker below than White-throated and Ochraceous, strong greenish-olive tinge above. **(b) Adult** *griseiceps* (Pegu Yomas, S Myanmar): Whiter ear-coverts, yellower below. **(c) Adult** *annamensis* (N,C Annam): Darker breast/flanks, slaty cheeks. **Other subspecies** *A.p.robinsoni* (Tenasserim): Intermediate between *henrici* and *griseiceps*. *A.p.khmerensis* (south Indochina): Similar to *annamensis*. *A.p.isani* (NE Thailand). **VOICE** Raucous *churt churt churt..; chutt chutt chick-it chick-it..* etc. **HABITAT** Broadleaved evergreen forest; to 1,450 m. **RANGE** Co **R** S,E Myanmar, Tenasserim, NW,NE Thailand, Indochina (except south-west Cambodia, Cochinchina).

5 OCHRACEOUS BULBUL *Alophoixus ochraceus* 19–22 cm
(a) Adult *sacculatus*: Browner than Puff-throated, no obvious yellow/olive. **Juvenile**: Warmer wings/tail. **(b) Adult** *hallae* (S Annam, Cochinchina): Tinged yellow below. **Other subspecies** *A.o.cambodianus* (SE Thailand, south-west Cambodia); *ochraceus* (central Tenasserim, south W Thailand); *sordidus* (south of c.12°N). **VOICE** Raucous *chrrt chrrt chrrt chrrt.., chik-chik-chik-chik* and *chit'it-chit'it-chit'it-it* and nasal *eeyi* etc. **HABITAT** Middle storey of broadleaved evergreen forest; up to 1,525 m. **RANGE** Co **R** southern Tenasserim, W,SE,S Thailand, Pen Malaysia, Cambodia, S Annam, Cochinchina.

6 GREY-CHEEKED BULBUL *Alophoixus bres* 21.5–22 cm
(a) Adult *tephrogenys*: No obvious crest, grey head-sides, olive breast-wash. **Juvenile**: Warmer wings, browner head-sides. **VOICE** Mournful *whi'u wiu iwi* and *iiu you yuwi* etc., often followed by shriller high *ii-wi tchiu-tchiu* or *whii wi witchi-witchi-witchi* etc. **HABITAT** Broadleaved evergreen forest; up to 915 m. **RANGE** Un/co **R** Tenasserim, S Thailand, Pen Malaysia.

7 YELLOW-BELLIED BULBUL *A.phaeocephalus* 20–20.5 cm
(a) Adult *phaeocephalus*: Blue-grey head, pale lores, bright yellow below. **VOICE** Low buzzy *whi'ee whi'ee whi'ee...* **HABI-**

TAT Broadleaf evergreen forest; to 915 m. **RANGE** Fc/co **R** south Tenasserim, S Thailand, Pen Malaysia; formerly Singapore.

8 HAIRY-BACKED BULBUL *Tricholestes criniger* 16.5–17 cm
(a) Adult *criniger*: Broad yellowish orbital area, breast mottled greyish-olive, vent yellow. **VOICE** Scratchy chattering, warbles and quavering *whirrrh*. High rising *whiiii*. **HABITAT** Broadleaved evergreen forest; up to 915 m. **RANGE** Fc/co **R** south Tenasserim, W(south),S Thailand, Pen Malaysia.

9 OLIVE BULBUL *Iole virescens* 19 cm
(a) Adult *virescens*: Dark eyes, more olive and yellow than Grey-eyed. **Juvenile**: Warmer above, paler vent. **Other subspecies** *I.v.myitkyinensis* (N,E Myanmar): Less yellow below. **VOICE** Musical *whe-ic*. **HABITAT** Broadleaved evergreen forest; up to 915 m. **RANGE** Lc **R** Myanmar, W,NW Thailand.

10 GREY-EYED BULBUL *Iole propinqua* 17–19 cm
(a) Adult *propinqua*: Yellowish below, rufous-buff vent. **(b) Adult** *cinnamomeoventris* (south Tenasserim, S Thailand): Smaller; browner above, less yellow below. **Other subspecies** *I.p.aquilonis* (E Tonkin, N Annam): As yellow as northern Olive races. *I.p.innectens* (Cochinchina): Very similar to *cinnamomeoventris*. *I.p.simulator* (SE Thailand to S Annam); *lekhakuni* (north Tenasserim, W Thailand). **VOICE** Nasal *uuu-wit*; *whii-it* (Cochinchina); less nasal *prrrit* (S Thailand). **HABITAT** Broadleaved evergreen forest; to 1,525 m. **RANGE** Co **R** E,S Myanmar, Tenasserim, Thailand (except C), Indochina.

11 BUFF-VENTED BULBUL *Iole olivacea* 20–20.5 cm
(a) Adult *cryptus*: Greyer below than Grey-eyed, buffish vent. **VOICE** Musical *er-whit; wher-it; whirr*. **HABITAT** Broadleaved evergreen forest; up to 825 m. **RANGE** Co **R** south Tenasserim, W,S Thailand, Pen Malaysia. Ra (status?) Singapore.

12 STREAKED BULBUL *Ixos malaccensis* 23 cm
(a) Adult: Olive above, greyish throat and breast with whitish streaks. **(b) Juvenile**: Warm brown above, plainer breast. **VOICE** Sings with simple, slightly descending *chiri-chiri-chu* and *chiru-chiru* etc. Call is a loud harsh rattle. **HABITAT** Broadleaved evergreen forest; up to 915 m. **RANGE** Fc/co **R** south Tenasserim, S Thailand, Pen Malaysia. **V** Singapore.

13 MOUNTAIN BULBUL *Hypsipetes mcclellandii* 21–24 cm
(a) Adult *tickelli*: Greenish-olive above, whitish streaks on shaggy crown/throat/upper breast, yellow vent. **Juvenile**: Browner above (including wings), less shaggy crown. **(b) Adult** *similis* (east N Myanmar, N Indochina): Greyish-brown above, pinkish-chestnut ear-coverts/breast. **Other subspecies** *H.m. mcclellandii* (west N Myanmar)/*ventralis* (SW,W,S[west] Myanmar): As *similis* but greenish-olive above. *H.m.canescens* (Cambodia): Duller/plainer than *tickelli*. *H.m.loquax* (NW [east],NE[north-west] Thailand, S Laos); *griseiventer* (S Annam); *peracensis* (S Thailand, Pen Malaysia). **VOICE** Shrill squawking *tscheu* and *tchi-chitu*. **HABITAT** Broadleaved evergreen forest; 800–2,590 m. **RANGE** Co **R** Myanmar, Thailand (except C,SE), Pen Malaysia, south-west Cambodia, Laos, W,E Tonkin, N,C,S Annam.

PLATE 108 PRINIAS & STRIATED GRASSBIRD

1 STRIATED PRINIA *Prinia criniger* 15.5–20 cm
(a) **Adult non-breeding** *catharia*: Large, long-tailed; heavily streaked above, speckled on throat/breast. (b) **Adult breeding**: Darker above, streaks less defined, breast more mottled, bill black (male only?). (c) **Juvenile**: Warmer above than non-breeding adult, fainter streaks, less speckled below. VOICE Sings with a monotonous wheezy scraping *chi'sireet-chi'sireet-chi'sireet-chi'sireet-chi'sireet-chi'sireet...* Harsh *tchak-tchak...* HABITAT & BEHAVIOUR More open areas with grass and scrub; up to 1,525 m. Skulking. RANGE Lc R W,N Myanmar.

2 BROWN PRINIA *Prinia polychroa* 14.5–18 cm
(a) **Adult non-breeding** *cooki*: Resembles Plain but larger, indistinct supercilium, dark streaks on crown/mantle. Brown bill. (b) **Adult breeding**: Greyer and less distinctly streaked above. Bill black (male only ?). (c) **Juvenile**: Much more uniform and warmer above than breeding, faint streaking restricted to forecrown or almost absent. Slight yellowish tinge below. **Other subspecies** *P.p.rocki* (C,S Annam): Non-breeders are buffier below, richer buff on lower flanks than *cooki*. VOICE Song is monotonous wheezy *ts'weu-ts'weu-ts'weu-ts'weu-ts'weu..* or *tis'iyu-tis'iyu-tis'iyu...* Loud *chii* or *chiu* and *hu'ee*. HABITAT Grass, undergrowth in dry dipterocarp and pine forest; up to 1,450 m. RANGE Un/lc R S(north),C,E Myanmar, W,NW,NE,C Thailand, Cambodia, C,S Laos, C,S Annam.

3 HILL PRINIA *Prinia atrogularis* 15–20.5 cm
(a) **Adult breeding** *erythropleura*: Large, long-tailed; plain above, white supercilium, greyish head-sides, sparse breast-spots/streaks. (b) **Adult non-breeding**: More extensive and prominent breast-streaks. **Juvenile**: Like non-breeding but warmer above, breast-streaking diffuse. (c) **Adult non-breeding** *khasiana* (W Myanmar): Rufescent above, paler and browner head-sides, few breast-streaks. (d) **Adult breeding**: Black throat merges to scales on breast, white submoustachial. (a) **Adult breeding** *waterstradti* (Pen Malaysia): Darker above, thin supercilium, smudgy breast-streaks. **Other subspecies** *P.a.superciliaris* (N Indochina); *klossi* (S Indochina). VOICE Sings with clear *thew thew thew..* and faster *thew-thew-thew-thew-thew..* and *cher-cher-cher-cher-cher...* Also high *twi twi twi-chew twi twi-chew..* and *twi-twi-twi..* etc. HABITAT & BEHAVIOUR Grass, scrub, bracken, thickets; 760–2,750 m. Skulking. RANGE Co R W,N,E,S(east) Myanmar, north Tenasserim, W,NW,NE Thailand, Pen Malaysia (G. Tahan), Laos, W,E Tonkin, C,S Annam, north Cochinchina.

4 RUFESCENT PRINIA *Prinia rufescens* 10.5–12.5 cm
(a) **Adult non-breeding** *beavani*: Small; plain rufescent mantle, graduated tail with pale tips. Bill slightly thicker than Grey-breasted, buffier flanks/vent, longer supercilium. (b) **Adult breeding**: Distinctly slaty crown/nape/ear-coverts. **Juvenile**: Crown more olive than non-breeding adult, yellow tinge below, warmer wing-fringing. **Other subspecies** *P.r.objurgans* (SE Thailand), *peninsularis* (south Tenasserim, S Thailand), *extrema* (extreme S Thailand, Pen Malaysia) and *dalatensis* (S Annam): Slightly darker grey crown/nape, darker above. *P.r.rufescens* (western and northern Myanmar): VOICE Song is a

rhythmic *ti'chew-ti'chew-ti'chew-ti'chew..* or more rapid *chewp'chewp'chewp'chewp...* Buzzing *peez-eez-eez-eez* and *tchi* calls. HABITAT & BEHAVIOUR Undergrowth in open broadleaved forest, grass, scrub; up to 1,675 m. Often in lively parties. RANGE Co R (except C Thailand, Singapore).

5 GREY-BREASTED PRINIA *Prinia hodgsonii* 10–12 cm
(a) **Adult non-breeding** *erro*: Like Rufescent (which see for differences); often greyish on neck-sides/breast. (b) **Adult breeding**: Dark grey head and broad breast-band, whitish throat and belly. (c) **Juvenile**: Like non-breeding adult but more rufescent above, bill pale. **Other subspecies** *P.h.rufula* (N Myanmar): Non-breeders typically warmer above. *P.h.hodgsonii* (SW,W,C,S[west] Myanmar); *confusa* (N Indochina). VOICE Song is repeated *ti swii-swii-swii-swii* (each *swii* gets louder). Rapid scratchy warbling with thin *tee-tsi* and *tir tir tir...* Calls include high *ti-chu* and laughing *bee-bee-bee-bee*. HABITAT & BEHAVIOUR Dry grassland, scrub, secondary growth; up to 1,525 m. Usually in hyperactive parties. RANGE Co R (except Tenasserim, S Thailand, Pen Malaysia, Singapore).

6 YELLOW-BELLIED PRINIA *Prinia flaviventris* 12–14.5 cm
(a) **Adult** *delacouri*: Greyish head, greenish mantle, whitish throat/breast, then yellow. (b) **Juvenile**: Plain rufescent olive-brown above, pale yellow supercilium/below, buffier flanks. (c) **Adult** *sonitans* (E Tonkin): More rufescent above, light buffish throat/breast, deep buff belly/vent. (d) **Juvenile**: Whiter than to abdomen-centre, duller head. **Other subspecies** *P.f.flaviventris* (SW,W,N,C,S[west] Myanmar), *rafflesi* (south Tenasserim and S Thailand southwards). VOICE Song is rhythmic, descending, chuckling *didli-idli-u didli-idli-u didli-idli-u...* Mewing *pzeeew* call. HABITAT Grassland, mainly in marshes, coastal scrub; up to 1,450 m. RANGE Co R throughout.

7 PLAIN PRINIA *Prinia inornata* 13.5–15 cm
(a) **Adult** *herberti*: Clear whitish supercilium. Larger/longer-tailed than Rufescent and Grey-breasted, smaller/plainer above than Striated and Brown. (b) **Juvenile**: Warmer above, washed yellowish below. (c) **Adult non-breeding** *extensicauda* (N Indochina): Deep buff below, warmer above, long tail. **Other subspecies** *P.i.blanfordi* (Myanmar [except Tenasserim], NW Thailand): Similar to *extensicauda*. VOICE Song is rattling buzzing *jit-it-it-it-it-it-it* or *jirt'jirt'jirt'jirt'jirt...* Calls include clear *tee-tee-tee* and nasal *beep*. HABITAT Grass, reeds and scrub, usually in marshy areas; up to 1,450 m. RANGE Co R (except W,S Thailand, Pen Malaysia, Singapore).

8 STRIATED GRASSBIRD *Megalurus palustris* M 26.5, f 23 cm
(a) **Adult (female)** *toklao*: Size; long graduated tail, buffish-brown above with heavy streaks, white supercilium, fine dark streaks on breast/flanks. (b) **Juvenile**: Supercilium and underparts washed yellow, fainter breast/flank-streaks, bill paler. VOICE Song of loud, rich, fluty warbling notes. Explosive *pwit*. HABITAT & BEHAVIOUR Clumps of tall grass, reeds, scrub, usually in marshes; up to 1,525 m. High soaring and parachuting song-flight. RANGE Lc R Myanmar, C,NW,NE(south-west),SE Thailand, Indochina (except C,S Laos, S Annam).

1c
1a
1b
2a
2b
2c
3a
3b
3e
3d
4a
4b
5b
3c
5a
5c
6d
6b
6a
6c
7a
7b
7c
8a
8b

PLATE 109 CISTICOLAS, ASIAN STUBTAIL & *CETTIA* BUSH WARBLERS

Laos Mekong Jan 13

1 ZITTING CISTICOLA *Cisticola juncidis* 10.5–12 cm
(**a**) **Adult non-breeding** *malaya*: Supercilium whiter than non-breeding Bright-headed, nape duller, tail-tips whiter. (**b**) **Adult breeding**: Crown/mantle quite uniform with broader dark streaks, tail paler/warmer, slightly shorter. (**c**) **Juvenile**: Upperparts intermediate between non-breeding and breeding adult, washed light yellow below. **Other subspecies** *C.j.cursitans* (SW,W,N,E,C Myanmar); *tinnabulans* (Indochina). VOICE Song is monotonous, clicking *dzip dzip dzip dzip...* Calls with *chipp* or *plit*. HABITAT Rice paddies, marshes, grassland (mainly wet); up to 1,220 m. RANGE Co R throughout.

2 BRIGHT-HEADED CISTICOLA *Cisticola exilis* 9.5–11.5 cm
(**a**) **Male breeding** *equicaudata*: Plain golden-rufous crown, rich buff breast. (**b**) **Female breeding**: Broad dark streaks on crown/mantle, plain warm supercilium/nape. **Non-breeding**: Male's tail longer than female's. From Zitting by rufescent supercilium/nuchal collar/neck-sides, brownish-white tail-tips. (**c**) **Juvenile**: Browner above, pale yellow below, buff-washed flanks. (**d**) **Male non-breeding** *tytleri* (SW,N Myanmar): Heavier streaking above. (**e**) **Male breeding**: Creamy-buffish crown, bolder mantle-streaks. VOICE Song is buzzy wheeze, then 1–2 comical jolly doubled notes: *bzzzeeee joo-ee, bzzzeeee joo-ee di-di* and *bzzzeeee-dji-shiwi joo-ee* etc. HABITAT Grassland (often marshy), bushes, sometimes dry croplands; up to 1,450 m. RANGE Lc R SW,W,N,S Myanmar, Thailand (except S), Cambodia, N(south),C,S Laos, C,S Annam, Cochinchina.

3 ASIAN STUBTAIL *Urosphena squameiceps* 9.5–10 cm
(**a**) **Adult**: Very small, short tail; long buffy-whitish supercilium, black eyestripe, pale pinkish legs. VOICE Song is insect-like *si'i'i'i'i'i'i...* Slower *si-si-si-si-si-si..*, rising in volume. Sharp *sit* notes in alarm. HABITAT & BEHAVIOUR Undergrowth in broadleaved forest; up to 2,285 m. On/near ground. RANGE Un/fc WV W,C,E,S Myanmar, Tenasserim, W,NW,N,SE,C,S(north) Thailand, Indochina (except Cochinchina).

4 PALE-FOOTED BUSH WARBLER *Cettia pallidipes* 11–12 cm
(**a**) **Adult** *laurentei*: Striking supercilium, blackish eyestripe, square tail-end, whitish below, pale pink legs. VOICE Sings with explosive jumbled *wi wi-chi'ti'ti'chi* etc. Spluttering *twip* and *tup* notes and *tid-ip*. HABITAT Grass, scrub, bracken, sometimes in open forest; 200–2,135 m. RANGE Un R C,E,S(east) Myanmar, NW Thailand, N,C Laos, E Tonkin, S Annam.

5 MANCHURIAN BUSH WARBLER *Cettia canturians* M 18, f 15 cm
(**a**) **Male**: Large size, broad dark eyestripe, buffy-white supercilium, rufous forecrown. Warm brown above, pale buffish below, faintly greyer-washed ear-coverts and flanks, whiter throat/belly. (**b**) **Female**: Smaller. Bulkier and stouter-billed than Brownish-flanked, warmer overall, rufescent forecrown; often buffier breast (than *davidiana*). VOICE Song is loud short fluty warble, introduced by liquid crescendo: *wrrrrrr-whuchi-uchi* etc. Stony *tchet tchet tchet..*, sometimes with rattling *trrrt* notes. HABITAT Scrub, secondary growth, bamboo, forest edge; up to 1,525 m. RANGE Un/fc WV NW Thailand, N,C Laos, Vietnam (except Cochinchina).

6 BROWNISH-FLANKED BUSH WARBLER *Cettia fortipes* 12 cm
(**a**) **Adult** *fortipes*: Deep rufescent-tinged brown above, paler supercilium and underparts, dark eyestripe, deep buffy-brownish flanks/vent/breast-wash. Relatively shorter-tailed than Aberrant and Yellowish-bellied, stouter than former, larger, and larger-billed than latter, darker and warmer above than Aberrant but usually less rufescent than Yellowish-bellied; darker, warmer flanks/vent than both, no obvious yellowish below. **Juvenile**: Warmer wing-fringing, possibly warmer above, may be yellowish-tinged below. (**b**) **Adult** *davidiana* (N Laos, W,E Tonkin): Whiter throat to belly-centre, less buff on breast/flanks. VOICE Sings with long clear rising whistle, then short explosive phrase: *wheeeeee chiwiyou* etc. Short metallic *tit* and *trrt* notes. HABITAT & BEHAVIOUR Scrub, grass, edge of broadleaved evergreen forest, bamboo; 900–2,135 m, locally to 215 m in winter. Flicks wings in alarm, flashing pale underwing-coverts. RANGE Fc R W,N Myanmar, N Laos, W,E Tonkin.

7 CHESTNUT-CROWNED BUSH WARBLER *C.major* 13 cm
(**a**) **Adult**: From smaller Grey-sided by rufescent lores, buffier supercilium, whiter underparts. VOICE Sings with rather hurried, shrill, slightly slurred *i i-wi-wi-wirri-wi*. Call similar to Grey-sided. HABITAT Grass and scrub near wet areas, sometimes in open forest; 1,500–2,200 m. RANGE V NW Thailand.

8 ABERRANT BUSH WARBLER *Cettia flavolivacea* 12–13 cm
(**a**) **Adult** *intricata*: Paler, more olive above than Brownish-flanked, faint pale yellowish wash below, paler, more olive flanks. **Juvenile**: More uniform buffy-yellow below. (**b**) *weberi* (W Myanmar): More rufescent above, slightly yellower below, buffier flanks (lightly across breast). **Other subspecies** *oblita* (N Indochina): Brighter olive above, more yellow-washed below, warmer flanks. VOICE Song is wispy *it-it-uee'uee*, (*uee* rising). Calls like Brownish-flanked. HABITAT & BEHAVIOUR Scrub and grass in or bordering broadleaved evergreen forest, bamboo; 1,200–2,700 m (breeds at higher levels). Behaves like Brownish-flanked. RANGE Fc R W,N,E,S(east) Myanmar, N Laos, W Tonkin. Un/fc WV NW Thailand.

9 YELLOWISH-BELLIED BUSH WARBLER *Cettia acanthizoides* 11.5 cm
(**a**) **Adult** *acanthizoides*: Small, short-tailed; rufescent above, yellowish belly, dull throat/breast. VOICE Sings with long thin high notes, ascending scale until barely audible, then long descending trill. HABITAT Bamboo, undergrowth in/near broadleaved evergreen and mixed broadleaved/coniferous forest; 1,350–3,660 m (Indian subcontinent). RANGE Rc E Myanmar? (specimen misidentified?).

10 GREY-SIDED BUSH WARBLER *C.brunnifrons* 10.5–11.5 cm
(**a**) **Adult** *umbraticus*: Smaller than Chestnut-crowned, whiter supercilium, greyer breast/flanks. (**b**) **Juvenile**: Crown like mantle, drab brownish-olive below, buffish supercilium. VOICE Song is rapid thin *ti si'si'si'swi* or *ti sisisi'swi*, followed by buzzing wheeze. High metallic *tizz* or *tiss* in alarm. HABITAT Scrub and grass bordering broadleaved evergreen and mixed broadleaved/coniferous forest; above 2,100 m Winters down to 460 m. RANGE Un R W,N Myanmar. Sc/un WV SW Myanmar.

1a

1b

1c

2a

2b

2c

2d

2e

3a

4a

5a

5b

6a

6b

7a

8a

8b

9a

10a

10b

PLATE 110 *BRADYPTERUS* & *LOCUSTELLA* WARBLERS & GRASSBIRDS

1 SPOTTED BUSH WARBLER *Bradypterus thoracicus* 13.5 cm (a) Adult *suschkini* (syn. *shanensis*): Cold dark brown above (slightly rufescent), dark-speckled lower throat/upper breast, greyish breast-sides, dark undertail-coverts with contrasting white tips, shortish tail. Whitish supercilium, dark-tipped pale lower mandible. (b) Adult variant: Weakly spotted individual. (c) Adult *thoracicus* (N Myanmar): More rufescent above, greyer supercilium/breast-sides, heavier spotting below, all-blackish bill. (d) Adult variant: Weakly spotted individual. (e) Juvenile: Obvious yellowish wash on supercilium, head-sides and under-parts, browner-grey breast/flanks, vague breast markings. VOICE Sings with monotonous *dzzzzr dzzzzr dzzzzr dzzzzr...* Harsh low *tuk* and *rrtuk* notes. Song of *thoracicus* is rhythmic *trr-tri'tri'tree trr-tri'tri'tree trr-tri'tri'tree trr-tri'tri'tree*. HABITAT & BEHAVIOUR Tall grass, scrub and weeds in open areas, often near water; up to 1,400 m (winter). Low vegetation bordering broadleaved evergreen and coniferous forest; 3,050–3,655 m (summer). Very skulking, on or close to ground. RANGE Un **R** (minor movements) N Myanmar. Lc **WV** W(north),C,E Myanmar, W,NW,NE,C Thailand, N Laos.

2 CHINESE BUSH WARBLER *Bradypterus tacsanowskius* 14 cm (a) Adult: Relatively long tail; greyish-olive above, plain-looking undertail-coverts (faintly darker centres may be visible), pale lower mandible, no speckling on throat or breast. (b) First winter: Supercilium and underparts washed yellow, often light speckling on throat/upper breast. VOICE Song is husky crackling insect-like *hhhhhht hhhhhht hhhhhht hhhhhhht...* HABITAT Tall grass, reeds and scrub, mainly in alluvial plains; up to 1,500 m. RANGE Sc **WV** S Myanmar, NW Thailand, N Laos, S Annam.

3 BROWN BUSH WARBLER *Bradypterus luteoventris* 14–14.5 cm (a) Adult: Dark rufescent above, buffy-rufous flanks, plain throat/breast and undertail-coverts, pale lower mandible. (b) Juvenile: More rufous-chestnut above, washed yellow below. VOICE Song is sewing-machine-like *tutututututututututut..* or *hehehehehehehehe...* Calls with deep *thuck thuck thuck..*, sharp *tink tink tink..*, harsh grating *tchrrrrk tchrrrrk...* HABITAT Low vegetation in clearings and along forest edge, grass and scrub; 1,830–2,590 m, down to 800 m in winter. RANGE Lc **R** W,N Myanmar, W Tonkin. Sc **WV** S Myanmar, NW,NE Thailand.

4 RUSSET BUSH WARBLER *Bradypterus mandelli* 13–14 cm (a) Adult *mandelli*: Similar to Brown but dark brown undertail-coverts with broad whitish tips, all-blackish bill, usually speckled on throat/ breast. More rufescent above and on flanks than Spotted. (b) Adult variant: Little or no spotting on throat and breast. (c) Juvenile: Like adult variant but tinged yellowish below. Other subspecies *B.m.idoneus* (S Annam). VOICE Song is monotonous metallic buzzing *zree-ut zree-ut zree-ut zree-ut zree-ut...* Calls are very similar to those of Brown. HABITAT Low vegetation in clearings and along forest edge, grass and scrub; 400–2,500 m (mainly above 1,000 m). RANGE Lc **R** W,N Myanmar, NW Thailand, N Laos, W,E Tonkin, S Annam.

5 LANCEOLATED WARBLER *Locustella lanceolata* 12–13.5 cm (a) Adult (worn): Small and heavily streaked; streaked on rump, throat, breast, flanks and undertail-coverts. (b) Adult (fresh): Warmer above and on flanks. Juvenile: Somewhat less heavily and boldly streaked; looser, fluffier plumage. VOICE Song is sustained shuttling trill: *zizizizizizizizizizizizi...* Rather subdued *tack*, thin clicking *chick* or *pit* and trilled *rit-tit-tit-tit*. HABITAT & BEHAVIOUR Grass, weeds and scrub, often in marshy areas; up to 1,800 m. Very skulking, on or near ground, difficult to flush. RANGE Co **WV** (except SW,W,N,C Myanmar, W Tonkin). Also **PM** Pen Malaysia, Cambodia, E Tonkin.

6 RUSTY-RUMPED WARBLER *Locustella certhiola* 14–15 cm (a) Adult *certhiola*: Largish; dark rufescent above, whitish-tipped tail, rufescent rump, unstreaked below. (b) Juvenile: Washed yellowish-buff below, faint throat/breast-streaks. (c) Adult *rubescens* (rc C,E Myanmar; ? NW Thailand): Darker above, less heavily and contrastingly streaked. VOICE Sings with rapid, well-structured musical warbling phrases: *tri-tri-tri-tri*; *prt-prt*; *srrrrt*; *sivih-sivih-sivih* etc. Calls with metallic *pit* notes, clicking *chick*, dry *trrrrt* and rattling *rit-tit-tit-tit...* HABITAT & BEHAVIOUR Tall reeds, grass and other vegetation in marshes or freshwater wetlands; up to 610 m. Slightly less skulking than Lanceolated. RANGE Fc/co **WV** (except SW,W,N Myanmar, Tenasserim, C Laos, W Tonkin, C,S Annam). Also **PM** NW,C,S Thailand, Pen Malaysia, Cambodia.

7 PLESKE'S WARBLER *Locustella pleskei* 15–16 cm (a) Adult: Larger and bulkier than Rusty-rumped, much longer bill. Plain-looking, greyish-brown above (no rufous). Relatively indistinct supercilium, but obvious pale cream eyering (broken at front/rear). Whitish below with greyish-brown flanks and to lesser extent breast. Can show vague spots/mottling on lower throat/upper breast and darker shaft-streaks on creamy-brownish undertail-coverts; only thin pale tail feather tips. Resembles Oriental Reed. VOICE Sings like Rusty-rumped, but much thinner and reedier. HABITAT Mangrove scrub and other low coastal vegetation. RANGE Ra/sc **WV** E Tonkin (Red River Delta).

8 RUFOUS-RUMPED GRASSBIRD *Graminicola bengalensis* 17 cm (a) Adult *striata*: Resembles Rusty-rumped Warbler but larger, tail blackish with broad white crescent-shaped tips (prominent from below), undertail-coverts much shorter; broader blackish mantle-streaks contrast with plain rufous rump and uppertail-coverts, white streaks on neck- and nape-side, relatively shorter, thicker bill. (b) Juvenile: Warmer buff streaks on crown and mantle, duller dark streaking on upperparts, paler rufous wing-fringing. VOICE Song is high *er-wi-wi-wi* or *bzz-wi-wi-wi you-wuoo yu-wuoo*, then call notes or *er-wit-wit-wit* and, finally, odd wheezy sounds. Calls with scolding *err-err-err-errrr* and *jjjerrreah* etc. HABITAT & BEHAVIOUR Tall emergent vegetation in or bordering freshwater marshes and swamps, or along banks of rivers; lowlands. Skulking, typically perches on grass-/reed-stems in upright posture. RANGE **FR** (currently?) Tenasserim, C Thailand, E Tonkin.

PLATE 111 *ACROCEPHALUS* WARBLERS

1 BLACK-BROWED REED WARBLER *Acrocephalus bistrigiceps* 14 cm
(**a**) **Adult (worn)**: Paler, more greyish-olive than fresh. (**b**) **Adult (fresh)**: Broad buffy-white supercilium, blackish lateral crown-stripes, warm olive-brown above, whitish below with warm buff breast-sides/flanks. VOICE Sings with quickly repeated short phrases, mixed with dry rasping and churring notes. Calls with soft, clucking *chuc* notes. HABITAT Emergent vegetation and scrub in and around marshes, rice paddy margins, sometimes drier areas on passage; up to 800 m. RANGE Fc/co WV (except SW,W,N,C Myanmar, W Tonkin, S Annam). Also PM Cambodia.

2 PADDYFIELD WARBLER *Acrocephalus agricola* 13–14.5 cm
(**a**) **Adult (worn)**: Slightly greyer above and less rufescent on rump than fresh adult. (**b**) **Adult (fresh)**: Like Blunt-winged but supercilium extends further behind eye, and often bordered above by a faint dark line, bill shorter with dark tip to lower mandible, has longer primary projection. VOICE Song is series of rich warbling phrases, interspersed with squeakier higher-pitched notes; clearly richer, more musical and varied than Black-browed, and slightly slower and less forced. Calls with soft *dzak* or *tack*, fairly gentle *trrrr* notes and rather harsh, nasal *cheeer*. HABITAT Reedbeds, emergent vegetation in freshwater marshes, lake borders; lowlands. RANGE Ra WV/V SW,N Myanmar, NW Thailand, N Laos.

3 MANCHURIAN REED WARBLER *Acrocephalus tangorum* 13–14.5 cm
(**a**) **Adult (worn)**: Like Black-browed but has longer bill, darker greyish-brown upperparts, thin dark line above supercilium. Darker above than Paddyfield, with more prominent dark line above supercilium. (**b**) **Adult (fresh)**: Like Paddyfield but longer bill usually has completely pale lower mandible, stronger blackish line on crown-side, usually more rufescent above. VOICE Similar to Paddyfield. HABITAT Reedbeds and emergent vegetation in freshwater marshes, lake borders; lowlands. RANGE Lo WV S(east) Myanmar, SE,C,W(coastal) Thailand, Cambodia, S Laos. Ra PM E Tonkin, Cochinchina.

4 BLUNT-WINGED WARBLER *Acrocephalus concinens* 14–14.5 cm
(**a**) **Adult (worn)** *concinens*: Greyer above than fresh adult (rump warm-tinged). (**b**) **Adult (fresh)**: Told from other small reed warblers (except Blyth's) by relatively long bill with all-pale lower mandible (occasionally with darker shadow near tip), short whitish supercilium (ending just behind eye), lack of dark line on crown-side, longer primary projection (beyond tertial tips). **Other subspecies** *A.c.stevensi* (Myanmar). VOICE Song is relatively slow and deep-throated (rhythm and quality may almost recall miniature Oriental Reed), broken into short repeated phrases and including some fairly deep churring notes. Calls are short, quiet *tcheck* and soft drawn-out *churrr*. HABITAT Tall grass and reeds, usually near water; up to 1,525 m. RANGE Un WV S,E Myanmar, north Tenasserim, W(coastal),NW,NE,C Thailand, N,C Laos, E Tonkin. Sc PM E Tonkin.

5 BLYTH'S REED WARBLER *Acrocephalus dumetorum* 13.5–15.5 cm
(**a**) **Adult (worn)**: Greyer-olive and plainer above than Blunt-winged. (**b**) **Adult (fresh)**: Difficult to separate from Blunt-winged but slightly longer-billed and shorter-tailed, noticeably colder, less rufescent above, less contrasting tertial fringes, slightly longer primary projection, duller flanks. VOICE Song of pleasant, varied, well-spaced phrases, each repeated 2–10 times and typically beginning with 1–3 'tongue-clicking' notes. Phrases include a *trek-trek CHUEE, chrak-chrak CHU-EE-LOO* and *trek-trek see-ee-hue*. Often includes avian mimicry. Soft *chek* or *teck* (slightly softer than Paddyfield), *chek-tchr* and harsh, scraping *cherr* or *trrrr* notes when agitated. HABITAT Scrub and rank vegetation in wet and dry areas, cultivation borders; lowlands. RANGE Un WV SW,C,S,E Myanmar.

6 ORIENTAL REED WARBLER *Acrocephalus orientalis* 18–20 cm
(**a**) **Adult (worn)**: Greyish streaks on lower throat and upper breast more obvious than fresh adult, colder above. (**b**) **Adult (fresh)**: From Clamorous by somewhat stouter bill, more prominent supercilium (particularly behind eye), slightly longer primary projection, shorter tail with whitish tips; usually less buffish below. VOICE Song consists of deep guttural churring and croaking notes interspersed with repeated warbling phrases: *kawa-kawa-kawa-gurk-gurk eek eek gurk kawa..* etc. Calls with loud *chack* notes, soft churring notes. HABITAT Emergent vegetation in marshes, rice paddies, borders of cultivation, grass and scrub in less wet areas; up to 950 m. RANGE Un/co WV and PM (except SW,W,E Myanmar, W Tonkin, N Annam). Rc in summer C Thailand.

7 CLAMOROUS REED WARBLER *Acrocephalus stentoreus* 18.5–20.5 cm
(**a**) **Adult (worn)** *brunnescens*: Very like Oriental but narrower bill, shorter supercilium, slightly shorter primary projection, longer tail without whitish tips. (**b**) **First winter (fresh)**: Warmer than worn adult. Differs from Oriental similarly. VOICE Song is like Oriental but more tentative, following less regimented pattern (relatively melodious): *track track track karra-kru-kih karra-kru-kih chivi tru chivi chih..* etc. Calls with rather loud, deep *track* and hard, rolling *trrrrr* when agitated. HABITAT Emergent vegetation in marshes; up to 915 m. RANGE Un R SW,C,E Myanmar. Rc (status?) NW,C Thailand, N Laos, C Annam.

8 THICK-BILLED WARBLER *A.aedon* 18.5–21 cm
(**a**) **Adult (worn)** *stegmanni*: Like Oriental and Clamorous Reed but relatively short/stout bill, distinctly round-headed, no supercilium or eyestripe, pale-faced (paler area on lores), relatively short-winged/long-tailed. (**b**) **First winter (fresh)**: Rufescent tinge above and on flanks. **Other subspecies** *A.a.aedon* (rc Indochina). VOICE Song is fast loud stream of avian mimicry, interspersed with twittering and excitable sounds (many calls repeated 2–3 times). Calls include hard clicky *teck* notes and a harsh wheezy *verrrb* when agitated. HABITAT Scrub and grass in relatively dry areas, forest clearings and edge; up to 1,525 m. RANGE Co WV (except southern S Thailand, Pen Malaysia, Singapore, W Tonkin). V Pen Malaysia.

PLATE 112 GOLDEN-BELLIED GERYGONE, TESIAS & TAILORBIRDS

1 GOLDEN-BELLIED GERYGONE *Gerygone sulphurea* 10 cm
(a) **Adult** *sulphurea*: Most likely to be confused with warblers and female sunbirds. Rather short straight blackish bill, plain greyish-brown above, pale yellow below, whitish lores and sub-terminal tail-spots. Darker cheeks/head-sides contrast sharply with yellow throat. (b) **Juvenile**: Narrow whitish eyering, plain greyish-brown head-sides, slightly paler below, pinkish bill-base. **VOICE** Song of up to 10 high musical, wheezy, glissading, rising/descending whistles: *zweee*, *zrriii* and *zriii'i'i'uu* etc. Call is musical rising *chu-whee*. **HABITAT** Mangroves, coastal scrub, also inland in swamp forest, rubber plantations etc., sometimes other types of forest, secondary growth, parks and gardens up to 915 m. **RANGE Co R** (sc inland) coastal and S Thailand, Pen Malaysia, Singapore, Cambodia, Cochinchina.

2 CHESTNUT-HEADED TESIA *Tesia castaneocoronata* 9 cm
(a) **Adult** *castaneocoronata*: Almost tail-less, chestnut head, mostly yellow below, whitish patch behind eye. (b) **Juvenile**: Darker and browner above, dark rufous below. **Other subspecies** *T.c.abediei* (Tonkin). **VOICE** Sings with fairly quick *ti tisu-eei* and simpler *si tchui* etc. (no introductory notes). Shrill explosive *whit* (often doubled) and sharp *tit* notes. **HABITAT** Broadleaved evergreen forest undergrowth, mainly near streams; 950–2,810 m, to 450 m in winter. **RANGE Un/lc R** W,N,E,S(east) Myanmar, NW Thailand, N Laos, W,E Tonkin.

3 SLATY-BELLIED TESIA Hotel Chrang Mi *Tesia olivea* 9 cm
(a) **Adult**: Dark olive-green above, crown washed golden-yellow, dark slaty-grey below, orange lower mandible. **Juvenile**: Said to be more uniform dull olive-green below than Grey-bellied. **VOICE** Song recalls Grey-bellied but phrases longer, more tuneless, with 4–11, more spaced, irregular introductory notes. Spluttering: *trrrrt trrrrt trrrrt...* **HABITAT** Undergrowth in broadleaved evergreen forest, mainly near streams; 700–2,565 m, locally to 455 m in winter. **RANGE Co R** W,N,E,S Myanmar, W,NW Thailand, N,C Laos, W,E Tonkin, N Annam.

4 GREY-BELLIED TESIA *Tesia cyaniventer* 8.5–10 cm
(a) **Adult**: Olive-green crown, yellowish supercilium, paler below than Slaty-bellied, dull yellowish lower mandible. (b) **Juvenile**: Dark brown above, duller supercilium and eyestripe, drab olive below. **VOICE** Loud rich slurred short song phrases, introduced by high spaced notes: *ji ji ju ju ju-chewit*; *ji ji ji'wi-jui* etc. Rattling *trrrrrrk*. **HABITAT** As Slaty-bellied; 1,000–2,565 m, locally down to 60 m (winter only?). **RANGE Co R** W,N,E,S Myanmar, NW Thailand (sc), south-west Cambodia, N,S Laos, W,E(sc) Tonkin, S Annam.

5 MOUNTAIN TAILORBIRD *Orthotomus cuculatus* 12 cm
(a) **Adult** *coronatus*: Rufous forecrown, yellowish-white super-cilium, dark eyestripe, yellow belly/vent. (b) **Juvenile**: Uniform dull green above, grey of hindcrown/nape duller, head-side pattern fainter, yellower supercilium, more uniform/duller yellow below. **Other subspecies** *O.c.malayanus* (Pen Malaysia, ? extreme S Thailand): Rufous-chestnut on forecrown, more extensive darker grey on hindcrown/nape, deeper green above. *O.c.thais* (S Thailand). **VOICE** Sings with 4–6 very high notes, glissading up and down the scale. Thin *trrit* notes in alarm. **HABITAT**

Undergrowth in broadleaved evergreen forest, bamboo, scrub; 1,000–2,200 m, locally to 450 m N Myanmar. **RANGE Co R** Myanmar (except SW,C), W,NW,NE,S Thailand, Pen Malaysia, south-west Cambodia, Laos, Vietnam (except Cochinchina).

6 COMMON TAILORBIRD *Orthotomus sutorius* 11–13 cm
(a) **Male breeding** *inexpectatus*: Rufescent forecrown, pale below (including vent), long bill/tail. (b) **Male non-breeding/female**: Shorter tail. **Juvenile**: Crown initially all green. (c) **Adult** *maculicollis* (southern S Thailand southward): Darker above, darker grey nape, ear-coverts and streaks on breast-sides. **Other subspecies** *O.s.longicauda* (north Indochina; E Myanmar?). **VOICE** Explosive *chee-yup chee-yup chee-yup...*, *pitchik-pitchik-pitchik..* or *te-chi te-chi te-chi te-chi..* etc. Calls with *pit-pit-pit..* and quick *cheep-cheep...* **HABITAT** & **BEHAVIOUR** Gardens, scrub, bamboo clumps, cultivation borders, open woodland, mangroves; up to 1,525 m. Quite skulking, frequently cocks tail. **RANGE Co R** throughout.

7 DARK-NECKED TAILORBIRD *Orthotomus atrogularis* 10.5–12 cm
(a) **Male breeding** *nitidus*: No supercilium, solidly dark lower throat/upper breast, yellow vent. **Male non-breeding**: Like female but stronger throat-/breast-streaks. (b) **Female**: Weakly streaked throat/breast. (c) **Juvenile**: Duller above than female, initially no rufous on crown. **Other subspecies** In E Tonkin and N Annam shows darker rufous crown, darker green above (undescribed race?). *O.a.atrogularis* (S Thailand southwards), *annambensis* (Pulau Tioman, Pen Malaysia). **VOICE** Nasal high *kri'i'i'i'i* and *tew* notes. Trilled *churrrit churrrit churrrit-churrrit* and *titttrrrt titttrrrt* etc.; ringing *prrrp-prrrp*. **HABITAT** & **BEHAVIOUR** Broadleaved forest, secondary growth, mangroves, rarely parks, gardens; up to 1,200 m. Behaves like Common. **RANGE Co R** (except SW Myanmar).

8 RUFOUS-TAILED TAILORBIRD *Orthotomus sericeus* 12–13.5 cm
(a) **Adult** *hesperius*: Rufous-chestnut crown, dull rufous tail, pale below. (b) **Juvenile**: Plainer and browner above, yellowish tinge below, tail with dark centres turning blackish subterminally. **VOICE** Song of rapidly repeated loud couplets: *chop-wir*; *chik-wir*, *tu-twik* and *prui-chir* etc. Partner often adds monotonous *u'u'u'u'u...* Also high wheezy *tzee-tzee-tzee...* **HABITAT** Forest edge, secondary growth, locally edge of cultivation and mangroves, dense gardens; up to 400 m. **RANGE Un/fc R** Tenasserim, S Thailand, Pen Malaysia, Singapore.

9 ASHY TAILORBIRD *Orthotomus ruficeps* 11–12 cm
(a) **Male** *cineraceus*: Rufous face, dark grey throat, breast and flanks. (b) **Female**: Mostly whitish centre of underparts. (c) **Juvenile**: Browner above without rufous, like washed-out female below. **VOICE** Song is repetitive *chip-wii-chip chip-wii-chip..* (*chip* brief, *wii* stressed) and *chu-iip chu-iip chu-iip* (*iip* stressed) etc. Calls with spluttering trilled *prrrrt*, rolling *prii'u* and harsh *thieu* notes etc. **HABITAT** Mangroves, coastal scrub, peatswamp forest, rarely inland forest; also all habitats on certain offshore islands. **RANGE Co R** Tenasserim, S Thailand, Pen Malaysia, Singapore, Cochinchina.

PLATE 113 *PHYLLOSCOPUS* WARBLERS & LESSER WHITETHROAT

1 COMMON CHIFFCHAFF *Phylloscopus collybita* 12 cm
(**a**) **Adult (fresh)** *tristis*: Recalls Dusky and Buff-throated but grey-brown above, whitish below with buffy-washed breast and flanks, olive-green wing-fringing, slight pale wing-bar, blackish bill/legs. (**b**) **Adult (worn)**: Greyer and whiter, duller wings, no wing-bar. VOICE Song is *ch-ch-chewy-chewy-chewy-chewy-ch*, followed by pause. Calls with weak *peu*, *sie-u*, *peeep* or *vii(e)p*. HABITAT & BEHAVIOUR Low vegetation and smaller trees in wooded/open areas; found at c.1,500 m. Forages actively at all levels. RANGE V W Tonkin.

2 DUSKY WARBLER *Phylloscopus fuscatus* 12–12.5 cm
(**a**) **Adult (fresh)** *fuscatus*: Smaller/slimmer than Radde's, bill finer (lower mandible usually dark-tipped), legs thinner, supercilium narrower, whiter and more defined in front of eye, usually distinctly buffish behind. (**b**) **Adult (worn)**: Paler greyish-brown above. (**c**) **Adult variant**: More olive-tinged bird. VOICE Song higher and slower than Radde's, fewer syllables per phrase, no strong rattling trills or *ty-ty* introductions; often begins with thin *tsirit*. Hard *tett* or *tak* calls. HABITAT Low vegetation and small trees in open areas, often near water, mangroves; lowlands (migrants up to 1,830 m). RANGE Fc/co WV (except S Thailand southwards). Ra WV/V S Thailand, Pen Malaysia, Singapore. Also PM Cambodia, E Tonkin.

3 TICKELL'S LEAF WARBLER *Phylloscopus affinis* 11–11.5 cm
(**a**) **Adult (fresh)**: Greener above than Buff-throated, lemon-yellow-washed supercilium/ear-coverts/below, typically better-defined supercilium (often whiter to rear), slightly bolder eye-stripe, little/no dark tip to lower mandible. Wings more pointed, tail shorter/squarer than Aberrant Bush Warbler. (**b**) **Adult (worn)**: Washed out, less distinctly yellow. VOICE Song is short *chip whi-whi-whi-whi*; *chit* or *sit* call notes. HABITAT & BEHAVIOUR Low vegetation, grass; up to 2,135 m. Very active and conspicuous. RANGE Un/fc WV Myanmar (except Tenasserim).

4 BUFF-THROATED WARBLER *Phylloscopus subaffinis* 11–11.5 cm
(**a**) **Adult (fresh)**: Browner above than fresh Tickell's Leaf, more yellowish-buff supercilium, ear-coverts and underparts, typically less defined, more uniform buffish-yellow supercilium (only slightly yellower than below), duller eyestripe, usually extensive dark tip to lower mandible. VOICE Song slower/weaker than Tickell's (no introductory *chip*); may be introduced by low *trr* or *trr-trr*. Call is cricket-like *trrup* or *tripp*. HABITAT Low vegetation in open areas; 200–2,565 m (breeds above c.1,800 m). RANGE Lo R W Tonkin. Sc/fc WV N,E Myanmar, NW Thailand, N Laos, E Tonkin. V south-west NE Thailand, C Annam.

5 YELLOW-STREAKED WARBLER *P.armandii* 13–14 cm
(**a**) **Adult (fresh)**: From Radde's (close up) by finely yellow-streaked breast/belly, slightly more defined supercilium in front of eye; slightly smaller and smaller-headed, thinner bill/legs (slightly thicker than Dusky). (**b**) **Adult (worn)**: Less obvious yellow streaking. **First winter**: As fresh adult but buffish throat (paler than breast) with fine yellow streaks. VOICE Song of short rapid undulating, slurred phrases, after call notes. Call is bunting-like *tzic*. HABITAT & BEHAVIOUR Low vegetation, scrub

and small trees in forest borders and clearings. Up to 2,500 m. breeds 1,220–3,355 m. Often 2–3 m up in small trees. RANGE Lo R N Myanmar. Sc/lc WV W,C,S,E Myanmar, NW Thailand, N Laos, E Tonkin. Also PM E Tonkin. V NE,SE Thailand, E Tonkin.

6 RADDE'S WARBLER *Phylloscopus schwarzi* 13.5–14 cm
(**a**) **Adult (fresh)**: Like Yellow-streaked (see that species). More olive above than Dusky, broader supercilium, often bordered darkish above, ill-defined/buffish in front of eye, rusty-buff undertail-coverts. (**b**) **Adult (worn)**: No olive tinge above. VOICE Sings with outbursts of fast trilling: *tydydydydydydyd ty-tytyrrrrrrrrrrrrr ty-ty suisuisuisuisuisuisui tuee-tuee-tuee-tuee-tuee..* etc. Calls with low soft *tyt* or *tuc* notes. HABITAT & BEHAVIOUR Low vegetation in open forest, forest edge, road and track verges, sometimes more open areas; up to 2,135 m. Quite skulking, usually near ground. RANGE Fc/co WV (except SW,N Myanmar, S Thailand, Pen Malaysia, Singapore, W Tonkin). V west Pen Malaysia.

7 YELLOW-BROWED WARBLER *Phylloscopus inornatus* 11–11.5 cm
(**a**) **Adult (fresh)**: Smaller/shorter-tailed than Two-barred, tertials whitish-tipped, wing-bars broader, bill weaker (usually darker-tipped). (**b**) **Adult (worn)**: Narrower wing-bars. VOICE Song is high *tsitsitsui itsui-it seee tsi tsi-u-eee* etc. High, slightly rising *tswee-eep* or *tsweet* calls. HABITAT All kinds of wooded areas; up to 2,440 m. RANGE Co WV throughout; sc Pen Malaysia, Singapore. Also PM Pen Malaysia, Cambodia, E Tonkin.

8 HUME'S WARBLER *Phylloscopus humei* 11–11.5 cm
(**a**) **Adult (fresh)** *mandellii*: From Yellow-browed by grey wash above, darker lower mandible/legs; median covert bar usually slightly less distinct than greater covert bar, slightly duller throat/breast. (**b**) **Adult (worn)**: Greyer above, weaker wing-bars. VOICE Song is thin falling *zweeeeeeeeeoooo*, preceded by call notes. Thin *we-soo* and *tschu'is*, *tschui* or *tschuit* (first syllable stressed). HABITAT Forest, wooded areas, secondary growth; 1,000–2,780 m. RANGE Sc/lc WV W,S(north-west) Myanmar, NW Thailand, N Laos, W,E Tonkin. V S Thailand.

9 PALE-LEGGED LEAF WARBLER *P.tenellipes* 12.5–13 cm
(**a**) **Adult** *tenellipes*: Crown dark greyish, rump paler/browner than Arctic and Greenish, legs pale greyish-pink; two narrow wing-bars. VOICE Song similar to Arctic but faster/thinner: *sres-resresresresre...* Very high *tib* or *tip* call. HABITAT & BEHAVIOUR Broadleaved forest, also mangroves, gardens on migration; up to 1,500 m (mainly winters below 1,000 m). Usually near ground. RANGE Co WV C,S Myanmar, Tenasserim, Thailand, Pen Malaysia (ra), Cambodia, Laos, Cochinchina. Un/fc PM C Thailand, E Tonkin (ra WV), N,C Annam. V Singapore.

10 LESSER WHITETHROAT *Sylvia curruca* 14 cm
(**a**) **Adult** *blythi*: Grey crown, darker lores/ear-coverts, white on outertail feathers. (**b**) **First winter**: Crown sullied brownish, duller head-sides, narrow pale supercilium. VOICE Song is rather low scratchy warble, often followed by dry throbbing rattle. Low dry *tett*, similar to Dusky Warbler. HABITAT Thickets in more open areas; up to 1,300 m. RANGE V NW,C Thailand.

234

PLATE 114 GOLDCREST & *PHYLLOSCOPUS* WARBLERS

1 GOLDCREST *Regulus regulus* 9 cm
(a) Male *yunnanensis*: Bright yellowish-orange median crown-stripe with blackish border, broad pale orbital area, blackish and whitish flight-feather markings. **Female**: Median crown-stripe yellow. **Juvenile**: Somewhat browner above, crown unmarked. **VOICE** Song is very high undulating *seeh sissisyu-see sissisyu-see siss-seeitueet* etc. Thin *see-see-see* call. **HABITAT** Coniferous and broadleaved evergreen forest; 2,200–2,800 m. **RANGE** Rc in winter (status?) N,E Myanmar.

2 BUFF-BARRED WARBLER *Phylloscopus pulcher* 11 cm
(a) Adult (fresh) *pulcher*: Broad orange-buff wing-bar, yellowish rump, extensively white outertail. **(b) Adult (worn)**: Wing-bar narrower, buffier. **VOICE** Song is high twitter, preceded by/ending with drawn-out trill. Sharp thin *swit* or *sit*, sharper/more strident than Ashy-throated. **HABITAT** Broadleaved evergreen forest; 1,050–3,655 m (breeds above 2,135 m). **RANGE** Lc R W,N Myanmar, N Laos, W Tonkin. Un/lc **WV** S Myanmar, north Tenasserim, NW Thailand. **Rc** (status?) E Myanmar.

3 ASHY-THROATED WARBLER *Phylloscopus maculipennis* 9–9.5 cm
(a) Adult *maculipennis*: Like Lemon-rumped, but supercilium white, throat greyish, much white on tail. **Juvenile**: Olive-washed crown/throat, brighter buffish-tinged wing-bars. **VOICE** Sings like White-tailed Leaf but shorter, with repeated *sweechoo* and *sweeti* notes. Sharp *zip* or *zit* calls. **HABITAT** Broadleaved evergreen forest; 1,525–3,050 m, locally 610 m in winter N Myanmar (breeds above c.1,800 m). **RANGE** Lc R W,N,E,S(east) Myanmar, NW Thailand (Doi Inthanon), N,S Laos, W Tonkin, S Annam.

4 PALLAS'S LEAF WARBLER *P.proregulus* 10 cm
(a) Adult (fresh): As Lemon-rumped, but supercilium and median crown-stripe much yellower, mantle greener. **(b) Adult (worn)**: Duller above with narrower wing-bars, less strongly marked yellow. **VOICE** Song is loud, rich and varied, its clear whistles and trills recalling Canary *Serinus canaria*. Calls with subdued, squeaky *chuit* or *chui*. **HABITAT** Broadleaved evergreen and semi-evergreen forest; 900–1,700 m. **RANGE** Lc **WV** NW Thailand (sc), N Laos, W,E Tonkin. Also **PM** E Tonkin.

5 LEMON-RUMPED WARBLER *P.chloronotus* 10 cm
(a) Adult *chloronotus*: Pale yellow rump, supercilium, median crown-stripe and double wing-bar, no white on tail. Duller head-stripes/wing-bars/mantle than Pallas's. **VOICE** Two songs: (1) rapid even notes, then thin rattle: *tsirrrrrrrrrrr-tsi-tsi-tsi-tsi-tsi-tsi-tsi-tsi..*; (2) varied endless stuttering: *tsi tsi-tsi tsi-tsi tsu-tsu tsi-tsu tsi-tsi tsi-tsi tsi-tsi tsi-tsi tsirrp tsi-tsi...* Sunbird-like *twit* or *tuit*. **HABITAT** Broadleaved evergreen forest; 450–2,500 m. **RANGE** Sc **WV** E Myanmar, north Tenasserim, NW Thailand, W Tonkin. **Rc** (status?) W,N Myanmar.

6 CHINESE LEAF WARBLER *P.sichuanensis* 10 cm
(a) Adult: Like Lemon-rumped but crown-sides slightly paler, median crown-stripe fainter, eyestripe slightly paler and fairly straight, no pale spot on ear-coverts; slightly larger, more elongated and longer-billed. **VOICE** Song is monotonous *tsiridi-tsiridi-tsiridi-tsiridi-tsiridi...* Calls with loud *tueet*, and irregular

scolding whistles *tueet-tueet-tueet tueet-tueet tueet-tueet-tueet tueet tUEE tuee-tuee-tuee-tuee-tuee..* etc., and hammering *tueet tuee-tee-tee-tee-tee-tee-tee..* **HABITAT** Broadleaved evergreen forest; 400–1,800 m. **RANGE** Sc/fc **WV** east C Myanmar, W,NW,NE Thailand, N Laos, W,E Tonkin.

7 ARCTIC WARBLER *Phylloscopus borealis* 11.5–13 cm
(a) Adult (fresh) *borealis*: Slightly larger and longer-/heavier-billed than Greenish/Two-barred, supercilium falls short of bill-base, ear-coverts more mottled, legs browner/yellower, breast-sides greyer/slightly streaked. **(b) Adult (worn)**: Duller, with narrower wing-bars. **(c) Adult** *xanthodryas* (**rc** Pen Malaysia, E Tonkin): Yellower below (more when fresh). **VOICE** Song is fast trilled *dyryryryryryryr..* or *dererererererererererere..* (pitch/speed varies). Sharp *dzip* or *dzrt* call. **HABITAT & BEHAVIOUR** Lowland broadleaved forest, gardens, mangroves; up to 1,800 m on migration. Sluggish compared to Greenish and Two-barred. **RANGE** Sc/co **WV** E Myanmar, Tenasserim, W,C,SE,S Thailand, Pen Malaysia, Singapore, S Laos, S Annam, Cochinchina; commoner in south. Un/co **PM** Thailand, Pen Malaysia, Singapore, Indochina (except C Laos, W Tonkin).

8 GREENISH WARBLER *Phylloscopus trochiloides* 12 cm
(a) Adult (fresh) *trochiloides*: Like Two-barred but usually one wing-bar on greater coverts. **(b) Adult (worn)**: Greyer above, narrower wing-bar/s. **Other subspecies** *P.t.obscuratus* (widely claimed wintering). **VOICE** Song is simple hurried repetition of call-type notes: *chiree-chiree-chiree-chiree-chee-chee witchu-witchu-witchu-witchu* etc. Calls with fairly high slurred *chiree* or *chir'ee*. **HABITAT** Broadleaved evergreen forest; up to 2,565 m (mainly mountains). **RANGE** Fc **WV** Myanmar, W,NW,NE Thailand, N Laos, W,E Tonkin.

9 TWO-BARRED WARBLER *Phylloscopus plumbeitarsus* 12 cm
(a) Adult (fresh): As Greenish but two broader yellowish-white wing-bars. Larger/longer-billed than Yellow-browed, no whitish tertial fringes. **(b) Adult (worn)**: Often worn in winter, with narrower wing-bars (may lack upper one). **VOICE** Song faster/more jumbled than Greenish. Sparrow-like *chireewee* or *chir'ee'wee*. **HABITAT** Deciduous, semi-evergreen and sometimes broadleaved evergreen forest, also parks etc. on migration; up to 1,295 m. **RANGE** Fc/lc **WV** Myanmar, Thailand (except extreme S), Cambodia, S Laos, C,S Annam, Cochinchina. Un/fc **PM** C Thailand, N Laos, E Tonkin, N Annam. **V** Pen Malaysia, Singapore.

10 LARGE-BILLED LEAF WARBLER *P.magnirostris* 12.5 cm
(a) Adult (fresh): Stockier and larger-/darker-billed than Greenish/Two-barred, greener-olive above, broader eyestripe, longer supercilium, darker crown, greyish-mottled ear-coverts, rather dirty and streaky below. Somewhat darker above than Arctic, more dark on lower mandible, duller legs. **(b) Adult (worn)**: Duller above, narrower wing-bars. **VOICE** Song is sweet high descending *si si-si su-su*. Calls with tit-like *duu-ti* or *dir-tee* (*ti* higher). **HABITAT** Broadleaved evergreen forest, near mountain streams when breeding; up to 2,745 m. **RANGE** Un R/BV N Myanmar. Sc/un **WV** C,S Myanmar.

PLATE 115 *PHYLLOSCOPUS, TICKELLIA* & *ABROSCOPUS* WARBLERS

1 EASTERN CROWNED WARBLER *Phylloscopus coronatus* 13 cm
(a) **Adult**: Like Arctic but pale crown-stripe, yellow vent; lower mandible pale. **VOICE** Clear song ends with harsh squeaky note: *tuweeu tuweeu tuweeu tuweeu tswi-tswi zueee* etc.; or short *psit-su zueee*. Harsh *zweet* (quieter than Arctic). **HABITAT** Broadleaved forest, migrants also in mangroves, parks etc.; up to 1,830 m (mainly lowlands). **RANGE** Un/co **WV** Tenasserim, S Thailand, Pen Malaysia, Singapore, S Laos. Un/fc **PM** S Myanmar, Thailand, Pen Malaysia, Singapore, Laos, W,E Tonkin, N Annam. **Rc** (status?) Cambodia, Cochinchina.

2 EMEI LEAF WARBLER *Phylloscopus emeiensis* 11.5 cm
(a) **Adult**: As Blyth's (particularly *claudiae*) but greenish-grey (not blackish) rear of lateral crown-stripes, duller median stripe (contrasts most at rear). In hand, narrower whitish margins to inner webs of two outer pairs of tail feathers, faint or lacking at tip of outermost and lacking (or very nearly so) at tip of penultimate feather. Limited white on tail rules out most white-tailed races; *ogilviegranti* has bolder crown pattern, greener/yellower plumage; *davisoni* is similar but with much white on tail. **VOICE** Song is slightly quivering trill (c.3–4 s), recalling Arctic. Call is soft *tu-du* or *tu-du-du-du* etc. **HABITAT** Broadleaved evergreen forest; found at 305 m. **RANGE** Rc in winter (status?) east S Myanmar.

3 BLYTH'S LEAF WARBLER *P.reguloides* 11.5–12 cm
(a) **Adult** *assamensis*: Like White-tailed but less yellow, less white on tail (thinner fringe to inner web of two outermost feathers). (b) **Juvenile**: Duller/plainer crown, duller below. (c) **Adult** *ticehursti* (S Laos, S Annam, ? SE Thailand): Yellower, slightly greener above; **Other subspecies** *P.r.claudiae* (**VS** [**R?**] W Tonkin): Similar/slightly less white on tail. *P.r.fokiensis* (**VS** Vietnam?): Least white in tail (more than Emei), yellower than *ticehursti*? *P.r.reguloides* (**VS** Myanmar?). **VOICE** Sings with strident, undulating, alternating phrases: *wit tissu-tissu-tissu wit tewi-tewi-tewi-wit chewi-chewi-chewi..*; *wit-chuit wit-chuit wit chuit chi-tewsi chi-tewsi chi..* etc. High *pit-chee* and *pit-chee wi'chit* (*pit* stressed). **HABITAT & BEHAVIOUR** Broadleaved evergreen forest; up to 2,700 m (breeds above 1,500 m). Creeps on trunks/branches. Flicks wings one by one (territorial). **RANGE** Lc **R** W,N,E Myanmar, W,NW Thailand, S Laos, W Tonkin, S Annam. Fc/co **WV** C,S Myanmar, north Tenasserim, Thailand (except S), Laos, W,E Tonkin, N,C Annam.

4 WHITE-TAILED LEAF WARBLER *P.davisoni* 11–11.5 cm
(a) **Adult** *davisoni*: Daintier than Blyth's, yellower, more white on tail. (b) **Adult** *klossi* (C,S Annam): Brighter yellow, less white on tail (also yellower). **Other subspecies** *P.d.ogilviegranti* (**VS?** E Myanmar, Vietnam): Less yellow than *klossi*, little white in tail. *P.d.disturbans* (**VS?** E Myanmar to N Indochina): Least white in tail/yellow in plumage (like *assamensis* Blyth's). **VOICE** Faster/more slurred song than Blyth's: *itsi-itsi-chee-wi itsi-itsi-chee-wi itsi-itsi-chee-wi..*; *seechewee-tisseechewee-tiss seechewee-tisseechewee-tiss..* etc. High *ti'chee-wi* (*ti/chee* stressed) and *wit-chee*. **HABITAT** Broadleaved evergreen and pine forest; 50–2,565 m (breeds above 900 m). **RANGE** Co **R** (except SW,W Myanmar, C,S Thailand, Pen Malaysia, Singapore, Cochinchina). Sc/un **WV** E Tonkin.

5 YELLOW-VENTED WARBLER *Phylloscopus cantator* 11 cm
(a) **Adult** *cantator*: Bright yellow on head/vent, whitish lower breast/belly. **Other subspecies** *P.c.pernotus* (N,C Laos). **VOICE** Fast high song: roughly *sit siri'sii si-chu*; *sit weet'weet-weet'weet si-chu-chu* etc. **HABITAT** Broadleaved evergreen/semi-evergreen forest; 500–1,700 m. **RANGE** Sc **WV** Myanmar (except Tenasserim), W,NW Thailand, west N Laos. **Rc** (status?) N(east),C Laos, W Tonkin.

6 SULPHUR-BREASTED WARBLER *P.ricketti* 11 cm
(a) **Adult**: Bright yellow below, blackish head-stripes, narrow wing-bars. (b) **Adult R** population (C Laos, C Annam): Perhaps paler yellow, greyer above, narrower crown-stripe, slightly bigger bill. **VOICE** Song is very high *sit'ti si-si-si-si'chu* and *sit si-si'si-chu* etc. Residents give quicker, slower-ended *sit-ititu-ititu-wetu*; *sit-it ti'wetu-wetu*; *sit-it si-we'chu-we'chu* etc. Low *wi'chu* or *pit-choo* from residents. **HABITAT** Broadleaved forest, rarely more open places on migration; up to 1,520 m (lowland breeder). **RANGE** Lo **R** northern C Laos, north C Annam. Un/lfc **WV** Thailand (except C,S), S Laos, W,E Tonkin, N Annam. Un **PM** Laos, E Tonkin. **V** C Thailand.

7 MOUNTAIN LEAF WARBLER *P.trivirgatus* 11.5 cm
(a) **Adult** *parvirostris*: Yellowish below, plain wings. (b) **Juvenile**: Duller, washed olive below. **VOICE** Slurred, high song recalls white-eyes. **HABITAT** Broadleaved evergreen forest; above 1,220 m. **RANGE** Co **R** extreme S Thailand, Pen Malaysia.

8 BROAD-BILLED WARBLER *Tickellia hodgsoni* 10 cm
(a) **Adult** *hodgsoni*: Dark rufous crown, grey throat/breast, yellow belly. **Other subspecies** *T.h.tonkinensis* (W Tonkin). **VOICE** Song is very thin *si seeee-ee-eee si seeee-ee-eee siiiiiiiiii-ii siiiiiiiiiii..* etc., often becoming hard to hear. Excited rapid *chitiwichitiwit-chit-chitiwichitiwit-chit-chitiwichitiwit..* etc. **HABITAT** Bamboo, broadleaved evergreen forest; 1,050–2,650 m. **RANGE** Un **R** W,N Myanmar, W Tonkin.

9 BLACK-FACED WARBLER *Abroscopus schisticeps* 10 cm
(a) **Adult** *ripponi*: Slaty crown/nape/upper breast, dark mask, yellow supercilium, dark-centred yellow throat. **Juvenile**: Crown/nape washed greenish, yellow of throat paler. (b) **Adult** *flavimentalis* (W Myanmar): All-yellow throat. **VOICE** Song is very thin, tinkling *tirririr-tsii tirririr-tsii tirririr-tsii..* and *tit sirriri-sirriri sirriri tit sirriri-sirriri..* etc. Subdued *tit* notes. **HABITAT** Broadleaved evergreen forest; 1,525–2,350 m. **RANGE** Fc **R** W,N,E Myanmar, W,E Tonkin.

10 YELLOW-BELLIED WARBLER *Abroscopus superciliaris* 9.5–11.5 cm
(a) **Adult** *superciliaris*: Greyish head, whitish supercilium, throat and breast, yellow belly. **Juvenile**: Paler below. **Other subspecies** *A.s.smythiesi* (C,S Myanmar): Grey of crown paler and more limited to forehead, yellower above. *A.s.sakaiorum* (south of c.8°N): White on belly-centre. *A.s.drasticus* (SW,W Myanmar), *bambusarum* (northern S Thailand), *euthymus* (Vietnam). **VOICE** Song is thin tinkling *uu-uu-ti* and *uu-uu-ti-i* etc. (*ti* higher). Low thin twittering. **HABITAT** Bamboo; up to 1,525 m. **RANGE** Co **R** (except C,SE Thailand, Singapore).

PLATE 116 *SEICERCUS* WARBLERS & RUFOUS-FACED WARBLER

1 GREY-CROWNED WARBLER *Seicercus tephrocephalus* 11–12 cm
(a) **Adult**: Greyish crown with black lateral stripes, yellow eyering, usually no wing-bar, much white on tail. (b) **Juvenile**: Duller; weaker crown-stripes. VOICE Song differs from Plain-tailed and Bianchi's by its tremolos and trills; higher than latter, with greater frequency range. Call is sibilant *ch'rr*, *chrr'k* or *trr'uk*, recalling Buff-throated. HABITAT & BEHAVIOUR Broadleaved evergreen forest, secondary growth; up to 2,500 m (breeds above 1,400 m). Quite skulking, in low vegetation. RANGE Co **R** (some movements) W,N Myanmar, W Tonkin. Sc/fc **WV** S Myanmar, Tenasserim, NW,NE Thailand, N,C Laos, E Tonkin, N Annam, Cochinchina; ? C,E Myanmar.

OMEI WARBLER *Seicercus omeiensis* 11–12 cm
Adult: Roughly intermediate between Grey-crowned and Plain-tailed. White on two outermost tail feathers also intermediate (Grey-crowned shows much, Plain-tailed very little); sometimes a little on tip of next pair inwards? (never on Plain-tailed, often on Grey-crowned). VOICE Call is diagnostic wholesome *chup* or *chut* and *chu-du*, *chu-tu*. HABITAT As Grey-crowned; 600–2,075 m. RANGE Un/fc **WV** W,NW,NE,SE Thailand, SW Cambodia. NOTE Only recently described (Martens *et al.* 1999); not illustrated.

2 PLAIN-TAILED WARBLER *Seicercus soror* 10.5–11 cm
(a) **Adult**: Little white on tail, greenish forehead, relatively short greyish-black crown-stripes. VOICE Song higher than Bianchi's, covering wider frequency range, and preceded by soft *chip*. Call is high thin *tsrit* or *tsi-dit*. HABITAT Broadleaved evergreen forest, secondary growth; to 1,500 m. RANGE Un/fc **WV** S Myanmar, Tenasserim, Thailand (except NW), Cambodia, S Annam.

3 WHISTLER'S WARBLER *Seicercus whistleri* 11.5–12 cm
(a) **Adult** *nemoralis*: Green median crown-stripe with little grey, no grey on rear supercilium. Wing-bar usually distinct (very rarely lacking); lateral crown-stripes often fade above eye, much white on tail. VOICE Song like Bianchi's, short phrases with <10 short soft whistled notes, usually preceded by short introductory note. Soft low *tiu'du* call. HABITAT Broadleaved evergreen forest, secondary growth; 2,000–2,740 m. RANGE Co **R** W Myanmar.

4 BIANCHI'S WARBLER *Seicercus valentini* 12 cm
(a) **Adult** *valentini*: Crown-stripes blacker and more extensive than Plain-tailed, much white on tail, wing-bar usually distinct. VOICE Song like Whistler's but introduced by soft *chu*. Call is soft deflected *tiu* or *heu* (sometimes doubled). HABITAT Broadleaf evergreen forest, secondary growth; 200–1,900 m (breeds above 1,760 m). RANGE Fc/co **R** W Tonkin. Un/fc **WV** NW Thailand, N Laos, E Tonkin; ? C,E,S Myanmar, north Tenasserim.

5 GREY-HOODED WARBLER *S.xanthoschistos* 9.5–11 cm
(a) **Adult** *tephrodiras*: Grey crown/nape/head-sides, dark head-stripes, whitish supercilium. **Juvenile**: Duller above, slightly paler below. **Other subspecies** *S.x.flavogularis* (N Myanmar). VOICE Song is incessantly repeated high *ti-tsi-ti-wee-ti* or *tsi-weetsi-weetsi-weetu-ti-tu* etc. High *psit-psit* and clear *tyee-tyee..* calls. HABITAT Broadleaved evergreen and broadleaved/pine forest; 1,065–2,105 m. RANGE Co **R** W,N,S(west) Myanmar.

6 WHITE-SPECTACLED WARBLER *Seicercus affinis* 11–12 cm
(a) **Adult** *affinis*: Grey crown to head-side, white eyering, yellow lores/chin. (b) **Juvenile**: Washed-out/faded. (c) **Adult** *intermedius* (**VS**): Crown less pure grey, broad yellow eyering (broken above eye), sometimes two wing-bars. VOICE Song is rather sweet, variable: *sweet-sweet-sweet-sweet-sweet-sweet-sweet*, *tutitutitutituti*, *sweet-sweet-switititit*, *tit-twi-twi-twi-twi*, *tu-swit-switititititit* and *tu-swit-swee-sisisisisi* etc. Calls with hurried tremulous *chri-chri-chri..* (S Annam). HABITAT Lower/mid-storey of broadleaved evergreen forest; 1,375–2,285 m, down to 450 m in winter. RANGE Lc **R** N Myanmar, C,S Annam. Sc **WV** W Tonkin, ? N Laos.

7 GREY-CHEEKED WARBLER *Seicercus poliogenys* 9–10 cm
(a) **Adult**: Like White-spectacled but darker grey head, greyish-white lores/chin, tear-drop eyering. VOICE Thinner, less melodic, more slurred song phrases than White-spectacled, lacking tremolos and trills: *titsi-titsi-chi*; *chi-chi-chi-chi-chi*; *titwi-titwi-titwi-titwi*; *tewchi-chewchi-chew*; *switu-switu-switu-switu* etc. Thin *tsew tsew tsew..* call and rather explosive *twit twit...* HABITAT Broadleaved evergreen forest; 700–2,135 m. RANGE Lfc **R** N Myanmar, Laos, W,E Tonkin, N,C,S Annam. Rc (status?) NW Thailand.

8 CHESTNUT-CROWNED WARBLER *S.castaniceps* 9–10 cm
(a) **Adult** *collinsi*: Rufous crown with blackish lateral stripes, yellow rump/vent/wing-bars, grey throat/breast. (b) **Adult** *butleri* (Pen Malaysia): Darker crown, darker grey, no yellow rump-patch. **Juvenile**: Crown/nape duller, throat/breast sullied yellowish-olive, paler below. **Other subspecies** *S.c.youngi* (S Thailand): More rufous crown than *butleri*, more grey above (paler on rump), less yellow below. *S.c.sinensis* (N Indochina) and *annamensis* (S Annam): Yellow belly demarcated from grey breast, green up to lower mantle. *S.c.castaniceps* (W,N Myanmar); *stresemanni* (S Laos). VOICE Song is extremely thin *wi si'si'si-si'si'si* etc. Soft *chit* notes. HABITAT Broadleaved evergreen forest; 825–2,500 m, to 450 m N Myanmar (winter only?). RANGE Fc/co **R** W,N,E Myanmar, W,NW,S Thailand, Pen Malaysia, Indochina (except Cochinchina). Also **PM** E Tonkin

9 YELLOW-BREASTED WARBLER *S.montis* 9.5–10 cm
(a) **Adult** *davisoni*: Like Chestnut-crowned but rufous head-sides, greenish mantle, all-yellow below. (b) **Juvenile**: Duller head, less intense below. VOICE Song very like Chestnut-crowned: *wi si'si-si'si*; *wi si-si-si'si'si* etc. HABITAT Broadleaved evergreen forest; 1,160–2,185 m. RANGE Un/lc **R** Pen Malaysia.

10 RUFOUS-FACED WARBLER *Abroscopus albogularis* 9 cm
(a) **Adult** *hugonis*: Dull crown, rufous head-sides, dark throat, whitish below, yellow breast-band/vent. (b) **Juvenile**: Washed-out head-sides, no crown-stripes, less obvious throat-streaks. (c) **Adult** *fulvifacies* (Indochina): Less rufescent crown, very faint breast-band. **Other subspecies** *A.a.albogularis* (Myanmar). VOICE Sibilant high whistles: *titiriiiii titiriiiii titiriiiii titiriiiii...* HABITAT Broadleaved evergreen forest, bamboo, secondary growth; 450–1,800 m. RANGE Ra/lo **R** W,N Myanmar, NW Thailand, N,C Laos, W,E Tonkin, N,C Annam.

PLATE 117 LAUGHINGTHRUSHES

1 MASKED LAUGHINGTHRUSH *Garrulax perspicillatus* 30 cm (**a**) **Adult**: Grey-brown, blackish mask, orange-buff vent. (**b**) **Juvenile**: Duller/browner, mask fainter. VOICE Loud *jhew* or *jhow* notes, harsh chattering. HABITAT Scrub, bamboo, cultivation borders; lowlands. RANGE Fc **R** E Tonkin, N,C Annam.

2 WHITE-THROATED LAUGHINGTHRUSH *Garrulax albogularis* 30 cm (**a**) **Adult** *eous*: Bold white throat/upper breast, grey-brown breast-band, buffy below. **Juvenile**: Warmer above, less rufous forehead, fainter breast-band, whitish belly-centre. VOICE Thin shrill wheezy *tsu'ueeeee* and *hsiii*, gentle *chrrr*, low chattering, forced *chrrr-chrrr-chrrr..* in alarm. HABITAT Broadleaved evergreen forest, secondary growth, bamboo; above 1,600 m (down to 600 m in winter). RANGE Un **R** W Tonkin.

3 WHITE-CRESTED LAUGHINGTHRUSH *Garrulax leucolophus* 29 cm (**a**) **Adult** *diardi*: Broad white crest, black mask, white below, rufescent flanks/vent. **Juvenile**: Short crest, warmer above. (**b**) *patkaicus* (western/northern Myanmar): Chestnut mantle/ lower breast/belly. **Other subspecies** *G.l.belangeri* (eastern/southern Myanmar, W Thailand): Between other races. VOICE Outbursts of loud cackling laughter, often started by low *ow* or *u'ah* notes. HABITAT & BEHAVIOUR Broadleaved forest; to 1,600 m, rarely 2,135 m. In flocks. RANGE Co **R** (except C,S Thailand, Pen Malaysia, Singapore). Co/lo **FER** C Thailand (Bangkok), Singapore.

4 LESSER NECKLACED LAUGHINGTHRUSH *Garrulax monileger* 29 cm (**a**) **Adult** *mouhoti*: Dark lores, whitish throat/breast, pale primary coverts. (**b**) **Adult variant**: Blacker ear-coverts. (**c**) **Adult** *pasquieri* (C Annam): Small, dark; dark line above supercilium, rufous breast. **Juvenile**: Warmer above, less distinct gorget, buffier belly, smaller pale tail-tips. **Other subspecies** *G.m.monileger* (Myanmar; except next races): Paler rufous collar, white tail-tips. *G.m.stuarti* (E Myanmar to W,NW Thailand) and *fuscatus* (central Tenasserim, south W Thailand): Intermediate between *mouhoti* and *monileger*. *G.m.tonkinensis* (W,E Tonkin, N Annam): Between *mouhoti* and *pasquieri*. *G.m.schauenseei* (E Myanmar, to northern Thailand, N Laos). VOICE Repeated mellow *u-wi-uu* and more quickly repeated *ui-ee-ee-wu* etc. Low flock-calls, harsh and continuous in alarm. HABITAT Broadleaved forest; up to 1,675 m. RANGE Co **R** (except C,S Thailand, Pen Malaysia, Singapore).

5 GREATER NECKLACED LAUGHINGTHRUSH *Garrulax pectoralis* 31 cm (**a**) **Adult** *subfusus*: Pale lores, black line under cheeks and ear-coverts, buff throat/breast, dark primary coverts. (**b**) **Adult** *melanotis* (W,N,E,C,S Myanmar): More solid gorget. (**c**) **Adult variant** Black ear-coverts. (**d**) **Adult** *robini* (N Indochina): Rufous-chestnut collar, grey and black neck-side, broken gorget. **Juvenile**: Warmer above, faint gorget. VOICE Loud quavering nervous *wee'i'i*, *wee'u* and *wee'ee'u* phrases. Low gruff calls. HABITAT Broadleaved forests; up to 1,830 m. RANGE Un/co **R** Myanmar, W,NW Thailand, N,C Laos, W,E Tonkin, N Annam.

6 BLACK LAUGHINGTHRUSH *Garrulax lugubris* 25.5–27 cm (**a**) **Adult**: Blackish; bluish-white postocular skin, orange-red bill. **Juvenile**: Duller and browner. VOICE Sings with loud hooping *huup-huup-huup..* and rapid *ohk-okh-okh-okh..*, with harsh *aak* notes. HABITAT Broadleaved evergreen forest; 800–1,500 m. RANGE Un **R** extreme S Thailand, Pen Malaysia.

7 STRIATED LAUGHINGTHRUSH *G.striatus* 29.5–34 cm (**a**) **Adult** *cranbrooki*: Rounded crest, rich brown with pale streaks, broad blackish supercilium. (**b**) *brahmaputra* (W Myanmar): Narrower supercilium, whitish shaft-streaks on forehead and above eye. **Juvenile**: Lighter/warmer above, narrower/fainter streaks below. VOICE Song is loud, vibrant, rolling *prrrit-you prrit-pri-prii'u*. Low grumbling *aawh aawh aawh'o aawh aawh...* HABITAT Broadleaved evergreen forest, secondary growth; 800–2,500 m. RANGE Un/lc **R** N Myanmar.

8 WHITE-NECKED LAUGHINGTHRUSH *G.strepitans* 30 cm (**a**) **Adult**: Brown crown, blackish-brown face to breast, rufous ear-coverts, white neck-patch. (**b**) **Adult variant**: Browner upper breast. VOICE Flock vocalisations recall White-crested, but faster, with longer, rapid rattling calls. Outbursts preceded by/mixed with clicking *tick* or *tekh* contact calls. HABITAT Broadleaved evergreen forest; 500–1,800 m. RANGE Fc **R** E Myanmar, Tenasserim, W,NW,NE Thailand, west N Laos.

9 CAMBODIAN LAUGHINGTHRUSH *G.ferrarius* 28–30 cm (**a**) **Adult**: Browner hood than Black-hooded, darker upper mantle/belly, isolated white neck-patch. HABITAT Broadleaved evergreen forest; 800–1,450 m. RANGE Sc/un **R** SW Cambodia.

10 BLACK-HOODED LAUGHINGTHRUSH *G.milleti* 29 cm (**a**) **Adult** *milleti*: Brownish-black hood bordered by whitish band. **Other subspecies** *G.m.sweeti* (C Annam, S Laos): Greyer; blacker hood, darker wings/tail. VOICE Similar to White-necked. HABITAT Broadleaved evergreen forest; 800–1,650 m. RANGE Sc/lc **R** east S Laos, C,S Annam.

11 GREY LAUGHINGTHRUSH *Garrulax maesi* 28–30.5 cm (**a**) **Adult** *maesi*: Greyish, black face/chin, whitish ear-/neck-patch. **Juvenile**: Browner above, greyish-brown throat and breast. VOICE Similar to White-necked. HABITAT Broadleaved evergreen forest; 380–1,700 m. RANGE Lc **R** W(north),E Tonkin.

12 RUFOUS-CHEEKED LAUGHINGTHRUSH *G.castanotis* 29 cm (**a**) **Adult** *varennei*: Large orange-rufous ear-patch, greyish crown, white rear supercilium. VOICE Like White-necked. HABITAT Broadleaved evergreen forest; 400–1,700 m. RANGE Lc **R** N(east),C Laos, E Tonkin (Mt Ba Vi), N,C Annam.

13 RUFOUS-NECKED LAUGHINGTHRUSH *G.ruficollis* 24 cm (**a**) **Adult**: Smallish; grey crown, blackish face to upper breast, light rufous-chestnut neck-patch/vent. **Juvenile**: Paler and browner. VOICE Song of fairly quickly repeated, jolly whistled phrases: *wiwi'wi-whu whi-yi-ha* etc. (hurried at beginning); also longer, slurred, scratchy outpourings. Calls with harsh high shrill *ch'yaa* or *cher* and harsh *whit'it* notes and slow short rattles. HABITAT Broadleaved evergreen forest, secondary growth, scrub and grass, bamboo; 150–1,220 m. RANGE Un **R** W,N,E(north) Myanmar.

PLATE 118 LAUGHINGTHRUSHES

1 CHESTNUT-BACKED LAUGHINGTHRUSH *Garrulax nuchalis* 24–27 cm
(**a**) **Adult**: Rufous-chestnut on mantle, paler breast than Black-throated. **VOICE** Song recalls Black-throated. **HABITAT** Secondary growth, scrub, bamboo; 305–915 m. **RANGE** Un **R** N Myanmar.

2 BLACK-THROATED LAUGHINGTHRUSH *Garrulax chinensis* 28 cm
(**a**) **Adult** *lochmius*: Olive-brown above, black face to breast, large white cheek-patch. (**b**) **Adult dark morph** ('lugens'): Grey to blackish cheek-patch (intergrades occur). Only occurs in *G.c.chinensis* (northern Indochina), which typically resembles *lochmius*. (**c**) **Adult** *germaini* (S Annam, Cochinchina): Rufescent body. **Other subspecies** *G.c.propinquus* (C,S Myanmar to W Thailand): Between *lochmius* and *germaini*. **VOICE** Repetitive fluty thrush-like song, with harsh *wraaah* notes and squeaky whistles. Husky *how* notes. **HABITAT** Broadleaved forest, secondary growth; up to 1,525 m. **RANGE** Fc/co **R** C,E,S Myanmar, Tenasserim, W,NW,NE Thailand, Indochina.

3 WHITE-CHEEKED LAUGHINGTHRUSH *Garrulax vassali* 28 cm
(**a**) **Adult**: Recalls Black-throated but black upper ear-coverts, white mostly on throat-side, narrow black throat-stripe only, paler below, black tail-band, white tail-tips. **VOICE** Simple *whii-u whii-u whii-u...* Continuous rattles and quick *whi* notes from flocks. **HABITAT & BEHAVIOUR** Broadleaved evergreen forest, secondary growth, scrub, grass; 650–1,900 m. In large flocks. **RANGE** Un/lc **R** east Cambodia, S Laos, C,S Annam.

4 YELLOW-THROATED LAUGHINGTHRUSH *Garrulax galbanus* 24 cm
(**a**) **Adult** *galbanus*: Olive-grey crown/nape, black mask and chin, pale yellow below, greyish tail with black band and white tips. **VOICE** Flocks utter feeble chirping. **HABITAT & BEHAVIOUR** Scrub, grass, secondary growth, edge of broadleaved evergreen forest; 610–1,800 m. In large flocks. **RANGE** Ra **R** W Myanmar.

5 RUFOUS-VENTED LAUGHINGTHRUSH *G.gularis* 25 cm
(**a**) **Adult**: Larger/heavier than Yellow-throated, plain brown tail, yellow chin, rufous vent. **Juvenile**: Warmer wings, grey of breast-sides mixed with rusty-brown, perhaps some brown fringing on crown. **VOICE** Flocks utter harsh rattling churrs, and rather nasal, discordant, high whistled phrases. **HABITAT & BEHAVIOUR** Broadleaved evergreen forest; 300–1,220 m. In large flocks. Shy. **RANGE** Lo **R** N Myanmar, N,C Laos, N Annam.

6 MOUSTACHED LAUGHINGTHRUSH *G.cineraceus* 23 cm
(**a**) **Adult** *cineraceus*: Sandy-brown, black crown and tail-band, greyish-white head-sides with frayed submoustachial stripe, black, grey and white wings. (**b**) **Adult** *strenuus* (E Myanmar): Buffier-brown overall. **HABITAT** Edge of broadleaved evergreen and mixed broadleaved/coniferous forest, scrub and grass, bamboo; 1,220–2,500 m. **RANGE** Un **R** W,E(north) Myanmar.

7 RUFOUS-CHINNED LAUGHINGTHRUSH *Garrulax rufogularis* 24 cm
(**a**) **Adult** *rufiberbis*: Warm olive above with black crown/scaling/wing-bands/tail-band; whitish below, pale rufous-chestnut chin/vent, dark-spotted breast. (**b**) **Juvenile**: Reduced dark markings, paler chin. (**c**) **Adult** *intensior* (W Tonkin): Deeper

rufous, more black on head-/neck-side, larger spots below, paler chin. **VOICE** Song is loud, slightly husky *whi-whi-whu-whi* or *whi-whi-whi-whi* etc. Harsh low notes and grating rattles. **HABITAT** Broadleaved evergreen forest, secondary growth; 915–1,600 m. **RANGE** Un **R** N Myanmar, W Tonkin.

8 CHESTNUT-EARED LAUGHINGTHRUSH *Garrulax konkakinhensis* 24 cm.
(**a**) **Adult**: Like Rufous-chinned (*intensior*) but ear-coverts chestnut, lacks rufous chin and dark band across flight feathers, tail-tip buffish-white, forehead and supercilium mostly grey. **HABITAT** Broadleaved evergreen forest, bamboo; 1,600–1,700 m. **RANGE** Lo **R** C Annam (Kon Ka Kinh); ? east S Laos.

9 SPOTTED LAUGHINGTHRUSH *Garrulax ocellatus* 31–33.5 cm
(**a**) **Adult** *maculipectus*: Large; mostly chestnut above, with black-and-white spots, black crown/lower throat, black-and-white breast-bars. **Juvenile**: Browner crown and throat, fewer/smaller white spots. **VOICE** Sings with mellow fluty phrases: *wu-it wu-u wu-u wi-u wi-u*; *w'you w'you uu-i w'you uu'i* and *w'you uu-wi'ii uwa* etc. **HABITAT** Light broadleaved evergreen and mixed broadleaved/coniferous forest, rhododendron scrub; 2,135–2,745 m. **RANGE** Fc **R** N Myanmar.

10 GREY-SIDED LAUGHINGTHRUSH *G.caerulatus* 27–28 cm
(**a**) **Adult** *latifrons*: Warm above, white below, grey flanks, black face, white ear-patch. **Juvenile**: No crown-scales, browner flanks. **Other subspecies** *G.c.livingstoni* (south-west N Myanmar); *kaurensis* (south-east N Myanmar). **VOICE** Sings with clear whistled phrases: *wii'u wii'u wiii-uu whitwitwit witwitwit whi'i whii'u whii'uu whii'it..* etc. Harsh *grrrh* and *grrititit* in alarm. **HABITAT** Broadleaved evergreen forest, secondary growth; 1,525–2,620 m. **RANGE** Un **R** N,E(north) Myanmar.

11 CHESTNUT-CAPPED LAUGHINGTHRUSH *Garrulax mitratus* 23 cm
(**a**) **Adult** *major*: Greyish; chestnut crown/vent, white eyering. **Juvenile**: Duller/browner. **VOICE** Song of clear, quite shrill phrases: *wi wu-wi-wu-wi* (*wi* stressed), *wi-wu-wiu-wu-wi* (*wiu* stressed) etc. Sibilant *ju-ju-ju-ju-ju* and squirrel-like *wikakakaka* calls. **HABITAT** Broadleaved evergreen forest; above 900 m. **RANGE** Co **R** extreme S Thailand, Pen Malaysia.

12 SPOT-BREASTED LAUGHINGTHRUSH *G.merulinus* 25 cm
(**a**) **Adult** *merulinus*: Blackish spots on buffy-white throat and breast, thin buff supercilium. (**b**) **Adult** *obscurus* (east N Laos, W Tonkin): Richer buff below, heavier spots. **Juvenile**: More rufescent. **Other subspecies** *G.m.laoensis* (NW Thailand). **VOICE** Recalls Black-throated but much richer/more varied, no harsh notes or squeaky whistles. **HABITAT & BEHAVIOUR** Broadleaved evergreen forest edge, overgrown clearings, bamboo; 800–2,000 m. Usually in pairs; very skulking. **RANGE** Sc/un **R** W,N Myanmar, NW Thailand, N Laos, W,E Tonkin, N Annam.

13 ORANGE-BREASTED LAUGHINGTHRUSH *Garrulax annamensis* 25 cm
(**a**) **Adult**: Like Spot-breasted but black throat, heavy black streaks on deep orange-rufous breast, pale orange-rufous supercilium. **VOICE** Very similar to Spot-breasted. **HABITAT** As Spot-breasted; 915–1,510 m. **RANGE** Un **R** S Annam.

PLATE 119 LAUGHINGTHRUSHES & RED-FACED LIOCICHLA

1 HWAMEI *Garrulax canorus* 23 cm
(a) **Adult** *canorus*: Warm brown; dark streaks above/on breast, white spectacles. **VOICE** Rich varied, quite high song, with much repetition; slowly increases in volume/pitch. **HABITAT** Secondary growth, thickets, bamboo; to 1,450 m. **RANGE** Fc **R** N,C,S(northeast) Laos, W,E Tonkin, N,C(north) Annam. Un **FER** Singapore.

2 WHITE-BROWED LAUGHINGTHRUSH *Garrulax sannio* 23 cm
(a) **Adult** *comis*: Plain; buffish-white supercilium/cheek-patch, rufescent vent. **VOICE** Loud emphatic *jhew* and *jhew-jhu*. Harsh buzzy *dzwee* alarm notes. **HABITAT** Scrub, grass, secondary growth, bamboo, cultivation; 600–1,830 m, locally to 215 m. **RANGE** Lc/co **R** N,C,E Myanmar, NW Thailand, N Laos, W,E Tonkin.

3 STRIPED LAUGHINGTHRUSH *G.virgatus* 23 cm
(a) **Adult**: Rufescent; narrowly streaked whitish, broad whitish supercilium and submoustachial. **VOICE** Clear, hurried *chwi-pieu, pi-pweu* or *wiwi-weu*. Loud staccato rattling trilled *cho-prrrrrt* or *chrrru-prrrrrrt*. Calls with mixed harsh *chit* and *chrrrrrr* notes. **HABITAT** Scrub and grass, secondary growth, forest edge; 1,400–2,400 m. **RANGE** Fc/co **R** W Myanmar.

4 BROWN-CAPPED LAUGHINGTHRUSH *G.austeni* 24 cm
(a) **Adult** *victoriae*: White-streaked neck, brown-and-whitish scales below. **VOICE** Sings with clear jolly *whit-wee-wi-weeoo*; *whichi-wi-chooee*; *whiwiwi-weeee-weeoo* etc. Low harsh *grrrret-grrrret-grrrret...* **HABITAT** Oak and rhododendron forest, bamboo; 1,975–3,050 m. **RANGE** Co **R** W Myanmar.

5 BLUE-WINGED LAUGHINGTHRUSH *G.squamatus* 24 cm
(a) **Adult**: White eyes, black supercilium, scaled body, largely rufous-chestnut wings, black tail with reddish tip. **Juvenile**: Brown eyes. **VOICE** Song of thrice rising whistles: *pwuuuuu-wit* and *weeuwiiiii-it* etc., and lower *pwiiiieeu* and *phwiiiiu* etc. Low buzzy *jrrrrr-rrr-rrr..* etc. and harsh, rather liquid *jo-jorrrru*. **HABITAT** Broadleaved evergreen forest, bamboo; 900–2,200 m. **RANGE** Un **R** W,N,C(east),E Myanmar, W Tonkin.

6 SCALY LAUGHINGTHRUSH *G.subunicolor* 23–25.5 cm
(a) **Adult** *griseatus*: Dark-scaled as Blue-winged, but dark eyes, no supercilium, yellowish-olive wings, golden-brown tail with white tips. **Juvenile**: Warmer, fainter scaling, smaller tail-tips. (b) **Adult** *fooksi* (W Tonkin): Slatier crown, much dark on throat. **VOICE** Sings with rather shrill high whistled *whiu-whiiiu* and *whi'ii'i whi'ii'i* etc. Low buzzing *thriiii* notes and high squeaks. **HABITAT** Broadleaved evergreen forest, scrub, bamboo; 1,600–3,960 m. **RANGE** Un **R** N,E(north) Myanmar, W Tonkin.

7 BLACK-FACED LAUGHINGTHRUSH *G.affinis* 24–26 cm
(a) **Adult** *oustaleti*: Blackish head with whitish patches, rufescent-brown body, grey and yellowish-olive wings/tail. **Juvenile**: Crown brown, no neck-patch, more uniform brown body. **Other subspecies** *G.a.saturatus* (W Tonkin). **VOICE** Song of loud, shrill, rather high phrases: *wiee-chiweeoo, wiee-chweeiu* and *wiee-weeoo-wi* etc. Continuous high rattling call. **HABITAT** Broadleaved evergreen and coniferous forest, scrub, bamboo; 1,705–3,660 m. **RANGE** Lc **R** N Myanmar, W Tonkin.

8 CHESTNUT-CROWNED LAUGHINGTHRUSH *Garrulax erythrocephalus* 25.5–28.5 cm
(a) **Adult** *schistaceus* (east E Myanmar, north NW Thailand): Rufous-chestnut crown, yellowish-olive wing/tail-fringing, mostly olive-greyish with silvery ear-coverts. (b) **Adult** *erythrolaema* (W,S[west] Myanmar): Rufous head-sides/below, dark mantle and breast-spots. (c) **Adult** *woodi* (N Myanmar): Black-streaked silvery forehead, dark mantle/breast-spots. (d) **Adult** *peninsulae* (south of 9°N): Plain rufescent, darker ear-coverts. **Other subspecies** *G.e.melanostigma* (south E Myanmar, north Tenasserim, NW Thailand): Warmer. *G.e.ramsayi* (south-east Myanmar, west of *melanostigma*): Much warmer, strongly rufous below. *G.e.subconnectens* (east NW Thailand)/*connectens* (east N Laos, W Tonkin): As *melanostigma* but grey/whitish breast-scales. **VOICE** *weeaa-ao* and *aoaaaa*. Rattling *grrrt-grrrt-grrrt..* and *greet-greet...* **HABITAT** Broadleaved evergreen and broadleaf/conifer forest; 610–3,050 m. **RANGE** Co **R** Myanmar (except C), W,NW,S Thailand, Pen Malaysia, N,C Laos, W Tonkin, N Annam.

9 GOLDEN-WINGED LAUGHINGTHRUSH *G.ngoclinhensis* 27 cm
(a) **Adult**: Dark head/body, silvery breast-scaling, golden to orange wing/tail-fringing. **HABITAT** Broadleaved evergreen forest; 2,000–2,200 m. **RANGE** Un lo **R** C Annam (Mt Ngoc Linh).

10 COLLARED LAUGHINGTHRUSH *G.yersini* 27 cm
(a) **Adult**: Black hood, silvery ear-coverts, deep orange-rufous collar and breast. **VOICE** Song of loud, quite high rising whistles: *wueeeeoo*; *uuuu-weeoo* or *wiu-weeeu* etc. Low mewing *wiaaah* or *ohaaaah*. Low harsh *grreet-grreet-grreet-grreet-grreet-grrr-rr...* etc.; **HABITAT** Broadleaved evergreen forest, secondary growth; 1,500–2,440 m. **RANGE** Lc **R** S Annam.

11 RED-WINGED LAUGHINGTHRUSH *G.formosus* 27 cm
(a) **Adult** *greenwayi*: Very brown, grey forecrown/ear-coverts, largely red wings/tail. **VOICE** Song is loud clear whistled *chu-weewu* or *chiu-wee* etc. *chiu-wee-u-weeoo* and *u-weeoo-wueeoo* are duets? **HABITAT** Broadleaved evergreen forest, secondary growth, bamboo; 2,400–2,800 m. **RANGE** Un **R** W Tonkin.

12 RED-TAILED LAUGHINGTHRUSH *G.milnei* 27 cm
(a) **Adult** *sharpei*: Rufous crown, red wings/tail. **Other subspecies** *G.m.vitryi* (S Laos)/*ssp.* (C Annam, ? east S Laos): Dark-marked pale breast. **VOICE** *uuu-weeoo* and *uuuu-hiu-hiu* songs. **HABITAT** Broadleaf evergreen forest, bamboo; 800–2,500 m. **RANGE** Un **R** N,E Myanmar, NW Thailand, Laos, W,E Tonkin, N,C Annam.

13 RED-FACED LIOCICHLA *Liocichla phoenicea* 22 cm
(a) **Adult** *ripponi*: Quite small; striking red head-/throat-side, red on wing. (b) **Adult** *bakeri* (W,north E Myanmar): Warmer brown; darker red on head. **Juvenile**: Duller, shows less red. **Other subspecies** *L.p.wellsi* (N Indochina). **VOICE** Loud clear cheerful song phrases: *chewi-ter-twi-twitoo*; *chi-cho-chooee-wi-chu-chooee*; *chiu-too-ee* etc. Rasping *chrrrt-chrrrt..*, mewing *ji-uuuu*. **HABITAT** Secondary growth, scrub, grass, broadleaved evergreen forest; 800–2,500 m. **RANGE** Fc **R** W,N,C,E,S(east) Myanmar, NW Thailand, N Laos, W Tonkin.

PLATE 120 JUNGLE BABBLERS & STRIPED & WEDGE-BILLED WREN BABBLERS

1 WHITE-CHESTED BABBLER *Trichastoma rostratum* 15.5 cm
(a) **Adult** *rostratum*: Clean white below, grey-washed breast-side, narrow bill, cold brown above. VOICE Song is quite high clear *wi-ti-tiu*, *chui-chwi-chew* or *chwi-chi-cheei* etc. Harsh scolding rattles. HABITAT River/stream-sides in broadleaved evergreen and swamp forest, mangroves; up to 200 m. RANGE Lc **R** south Tenasserim, S Thailand, Pen Malaysia, Singapore.

2 FERRUGINOUS BABBLER *Trichastoma bicolor* 16–18.5 cm
(a) **Adult**: Bright rufous above, creamy-/buffy-whitish below. **Juvenile**: More orange above. VOICE Sings with loud clear sharp *u-wit* or *u-wee* (*wit/wee* higher). Low harsh, dry, rasping and sharp, explosive *wit* notes. HABITAT Understorey of broadleaved evergreen forest, secondary forest; up to 200 m. RANGE Un/fc **R** south Tenasserim, S Thailand, Pen Malaysia.

3 ABBOTT'S BABBLER *Malacocincla abbotti* 15–16.5 cm
(a) **Adult** *abbotti*: As Horsfield's but paler, shaft-streaked crown coloured as upperparts, less contrasting supercilium, unstreaked breast. (b) **Juvenile**: Dark rufescent-brown above. **Other subspecies** *M.a.alterum* (N[south],C Laos, C Annam); *williamsoni* (NE Thailand, north-west Cambodia); *obscurius* (coastal SE Thailand); *olivaceum* (south of c.6°N). VOICE Loud jolly song: *chiu-woo-wooi*, *wiu-wuoo-wiu* and *wi-wu-yu-wi* etc. Explosive *cheu* and nervous *wer* notes. HABITAT Broadleaved evergreen forest, secondary growth; up to 1,100 m. RANGE Fc/co **R** SW,S Myanmar, Tenasserim, W,NE,SE,S Thailand, Pen Malaysia, Singapore, Cambodia, Laos, N,C Annam, Cochinchina.

4 HORSFIELD'S BABBLER *M.sepiarium* 14–15.5 cm
(a) **Adult** *tardinatum*: See Abbott's; crown darker than mantle, breast vaguely streaked. **Juvenile**: More rufescent above. VOICE Song is strident spaced *wi-cho-teuu* (*wi* sharp, *cho* short, *teuu* high/shrill). Explosive *whit-whit-whit..* and quieter *wer* notes. HABITAT Broadleaved evergreen forest, often near water; up to 700 m. RANGE Ra/fc **R** S Thailand, Pen Malaysia.

5 SHORT-TAILED BABBLER *M.malaccensis* 13.5–15.5 cm
(a) **Adult** *malaccensis*: Short tail, black moustachial, grey ear-coverts, white throat. **Juvenile**: Browner head-sides, rusty primary fringes. VOICE Song is dry trill, then loud descending whistles: *pi'pi'pi'pi'pi pew pew pew pew pew pew*. Harsh rattles and mechanical *chutututut..*; soft *yer* notes. HABITAT Understorey of broadleaved evergreen forest; up to 915 m. RANGE Fc/co **R** south Tenasserim, S Thailand, Pen Malaysia, Singapore.

6 BUFF-BREASTED BABBLER *Pellorneum tickelli* 14.5 cm
(a) **Adult** *fulvum*: Buff head-side/breast (latter faintly streaked), paler vent and longer tail than Abbott's. (b) **Juvenile**: Very rufescent above. (c) **Adult** *assamense* (N Myanmar): Darker, more rufous above. **Other subspecies** *P.t.annamense* (southern Laos/Vietnam)/*tickelli* (Tenasserim/W Thailand southward): More rufous. *P.t.grisescens* (south-west Myanmar). VOICE Song is rapidly repeated *wi-twee* or *wi-choo*. High laughing *swi-tit-tit-titchoo* etc. Rattling *prrree* and explosive *whit* notes. HABITAT Broadleaved forest, secondary growth, bamboo; up to 1,550 m. RANGE Co **R** (except W,C Myanmar, C,SE Thailand, Singapore).

7 SPOT-THROATED BABBLER *P.albiventre* 13–14.5 cm
(a) **Adult** *cinnamomeum*: Dark-spotted whitish throat, shortish, rounded tail, shortish bill, greyish head-sides. **Juvenile**: Rufescent wing-fringing. (b) **Adult** *albiventre* (W Myanmar): More white below, duller flanks. **Other subspecies** *P.a.pusillum* (N Indochina): has much darker rufous underparts, particularly breast and flanks. VOICE Complex, quickly delivered rich thrush-/chat-like song. with much repetition. Harsh *chrrr* and slightly explosive *tip* notes. HABITAT Understorey of open broadleaved evergreen forest, secondary growth, thickets; 500–2,135 m, locally down to 280 m. RANGE Fc/co **R** W,N,E,S(east) Myanmar, NW Thailand, Laos, W,E Tonkin, C,S Annam.

8 PUFF-THROATED BABBLER *P.ruficeps* 16–18 cm
(a) **Adult** *chthonium* (NW Thailand): Rufescent crown, buffy-white supercilium, whitish below with streaked breast/flanks. (b) **Juvenile**: Warmer above, weaker streaks below. (c) **Adult** *stageri* (N Myanmar): Bold nuchal streaks. (d) **Adult** *minus* (SW,S Myanmar): No nuchal streaks, thin breast-streaks. (e) **Adult** *acrum* (W Thailand southward): No nuchal streaks, neat light breast-streaks. **Other subspecies** *P.r.subochraceum*, *insularum* (Myanmar south of 20°N [except *minus* range]); *euroum*, *smithi*, *ubonense*, *deignani*, *dilloni* (eastern Thailand, southern Indochina): No dark nuchal streaks. *P.r.chthonium* and races below are intermediate with *stageri*. Southern forms also buffier below with narrow breast-streaks. *P.r.shanense* (E Myanmar); *bilarum* (C Myanmar); *victoriae* (W Myanmar [Chin Hills]); *indistinctum* (north NW Thailand); *elbeli* (north-west NE Thailand); *oreum* (N Laos, W Tonkin); *vividum* (E Tonkin, N,C Annam). VOICE Song is loud shrill high *wi-chu* or *wi-ti-chu*. Jolly, rapid, descending *tuituitititi-twititi-tititi..* etc. Nasal *chi* and *erb* notes and rasping *rrrrrit*. HABITAT Understorey/floor of broadleaved forest, secondary forest, bamboo; up to 1,800 m. RANGE Co **R** (except south Pen Malaysia, Singapore).

9 BLACK-CAPPED BABBLER *P.capistratum* 17–18.5 cm
(a) **Adult** *nigrocapitatum*: Deep rufous below, black crown and moustachial, white throat. (b) **Juvenile**: Less distinct head pattern, warmer above. VOICE Sings with loud high *teeu*. Low *bekbekbekbek..* and nasal *nwit-nwit-nwit...* HABITAT Understorey/floor of broadleaved evergreen forest; up to 760 m. RANGE Co **R** south Tenasserim, S Thailand, Pen Malaysia.

10 STRIPED WREN BABBLER *Kenopia striata* 15 cm
(a) **Adult**: White streaks on dark crown/mantle/coverts/breast-sides, white head-sides/below, buff lores/flanks. (b) **Juvenile**: Browner crown/breast-side, buffier streaks, mottled breast. VOICE Short whistled *chuuii* song, sometimes *chiuuu*. HABITAT Understorey of broadleaved evergreen forest; up to 750 m. RANGE Un **R** S Thailand, Pen Malaysia; formerly Singapore.

11 WEDGE-BILLED WREN BABBLER *Sphenocichla humei* 17 cm
(a) **Adult** *roberti*: Heavy white chevron-scaling, dark-barred wings/tail, conical, dark-barred head. **Juvenile**: Warmer overall, scaling duller. VOICE Low *brrrb brrrb brrr'it brrrb brrrh..* in alarm. HABITAT Understorey of broadleaved evergreen forest, secondary growth, bamboo; 915–1,525 m. RANGE Sc **R** N Myanmar.

1a

2a

3b

3a

4a

5a

6b

6a

6c

7a 7b

9a 9b

8a

8b

8d

8c

8e

11a

10b

10a

PLATE 121 SCIMITAR BABBLERS & LONG-BILLED WREN BABBLER

1 LARGE SCIMITAR BABBLER *Pomatorhinus hypoleucos* 27 cm
(**a**) **Adult** *tickelli*: Large, dull bill; chestnut neck-patch, white-streaked grey sides. (**b**) **Adult** *hypoleucos* (western and N Myanmar): Whiter breast-sides, rufous supercilium/neck-patch. (**c**) **Adult** *wrayi* (south of c.6°N): Darker above, scaly supercilium. **Juvenile**: Very warm above, diffusely marked. **Other subspecies** *P.h.brevirostris* (southern Indochina). **VOICE** Usually 3 hollow piping notes (pairs duet): *wiu-pu-pu..wup-up-piu*; *wiu-pu-pu..wo-hu*; *whiu-pu-pu..whip-up-up* etc. Grating *whit-tchtchtchtch*; *hekhekhekhekhek...* **HABITAT** Broadleaved forest, bamboo; up to 1,550 m (915–2,135 m Pen Malaysia). **RANGE** Fc/co **R** (except C,E Myanmar, C,S Thailand, Singapore).

2 SPOT-BREASTED SCIMITAR BABBLER *Pomatorhinus erythrocnemis* 23 cm
(**a**) **Adult** *odicus*: As Rusty-cheeked but has blackish breast-spots. (**b**) **Adult** *mcclellandi* (W Myanmar): Brown flanks/breast-spots. **Juvenile**: Fainter breast markings. **VOICE** Pairs duet: fluty two-note phrase is answered by sharp *pi, ju* or *jrr*: *wi-wru-pi-wi-wru..*; *wip-uip-ju-wip-uip..*; *wi-wu-jrr-wi-wu..* etc. In alarm, quick high notes or loud frog-like sound, followed by rattle: *wi-wi-chitit*; *whoip-tutututututut*. **HABITAT** Scrub and grass, open forest; 1,000–1,830 m. **RANGE** Co **R** W,N,E(north) Myanmar, N Laos, W,E Tonkin.

3 RUSTY-CHEEKED SCIMITAR BABBLER *Pomatorhinus erythrogenys* 24 cm
(**a**) **Adult** *celatus*: Orange-rufous head-side to vent, white throat to belly. **Juvenile**: Rufous below, little white on throat/belly. **Other subspecies** *P.e.imberbis* (south-east Myanmar). **VOICE** Song like Spot-breasted: *whi-u-ju-whi-u..*, *iu-chu-ip-iu-chu..* and *yu-u-yi-yu-u..* etc. Rattling *whib-whihihihi*, harsh *whoi-whititititit*. **HABITAT** As Spot-breasted; 915–2,000 m. **RANGE** Co **R** C(east),E,S(east) Myanmar, NW Thailand.

4 WHITE-BROWED SCIMITAR BABBLER *Pomatorhinus schisticeps* 22 cm
(**a**) **Adult** *olivaceus*: Yellow bill, white below. (**b**) **Adult** *ripponi* (C Myanmar to west N Laos): Greyer above, broad rufous-chestnut collar/flanks. (**c**) **Adult** *mearsi* (SW,W,C,S Myanmar): Dark crown, chestnut flanks with streaks. **Other subspecies** *P.s.schisticeps* (N[north-west] Myanmar), *cryptanthus* (N Myanmar?) and *annamensis* (south Vietnam): Like *mearsi*. *P.s.nuchalis* (E,S Myanmar): As *ripponi* but more rufous-chestnut on flanks. *P.s.klossi* (SE Thailand, south-west Cambodia); *difficilis* (north Tenasserim to NW Thailand); *fastidiosus* (south of c.12°N); *humilis* (east NW Thailand to C Annam). **VOICE** Hollow piping *hu-hu-hu-hu-hu*; *whi-hu-wi*; *whuhuhuhuhuhu*. Harsh *whihihihihi* and *whichitit* etc. **HABITAT** Broadleaved forest, bamboo; up to 2,600 m. **RANGE** Fc/co **R** Myanmar, Thailand (except C,SE), Cambodia, N(west/south),C,S Laos, C,S Annam, Cochinchina.

5 CHESTNUT-BACKED SCIMITAR BABBLER *Pomatorhinus montanus* 19 cm
(**a**) **Adult** *occidentalis*: Like White-browed but black crown, dark chestnut above. **VOICE** Clear resonant *whu-whoi*, *woi-woip* and *yu-hu-hu* etc. **HABITAT** Broadleaved evergreen forest; up to 1,370 m. **RANGE** Fc **R** extreme S Thailand, Pen Malaysia.

6 STREAK-BREASTED SCIMITAR BABBLER *P.ruficollis* 18 cm
(**a**) **Adult** *reconditus*: Shortish, yellowish bill, chestnut streaks below. (**b**) **Juvenile**: Warmer; dull mask, plain buffish-brown below. (**c**) **Adult** *bakeri* (W,N Myanmar): Fewer/duller streaks. (**d**) **Adult** *beaulieui* (N[southern],C Laos): Much duller streaks, whiter-centred breast/belly. **Other subspecies** *P.r.similis* (N Myanmar): Much duller streaks. *P.r.albipectus* (south-east N Myanmar, northern N Laos): Between *reconditus* and *beaulieui*. **VOICE** Song is quick *u-hu-hu* or *wu-wee-wu* etc. Scolding rattles. **HABITAT** Open broadleaved evergreen forest, bamboo, thickets; 900–2,750 m, locally 50 m Indochina. **RANGE** Un/co **R** W,N Myanmar, N(east),C Laos, W,E Tonkin, N,C(north) Annam.

7 RED-BILLED SCIMITAR BABBLER *P.ochraceiceps* 23 cm
(**a**) **Adult** *ochraceiceps*: Thin orange-red bill; breast/belly white. (**b**) **Adult** *stenorhynchus* (north N Myanmar): Breast/belly buff. **Other subspecies** *P.o.austeni* (W,N Myanmar): Duller above. *P.o.alius* (NE Thailand to S Annam). **VOICE** Piping *wu-wu-wu* and *wu-wu-whip*. Scratchy *whi-chutututut*. **HABITAT** Broadleaf evergreen forest, bamboo; 600–1,800 m. **RANGE** Un **R** Myanmar (except SW), W,NW,NE Thailand, Laos, W,E Tonkin, N,C,S Annam.

8 CORAL-BILLED SCIMITAR BABBLER *P.ferruginosus* 22 cm
(**a**) **Adult** *albogularis*: Thick red bill, black line over supercilium, broad mask. **Juvenile**: Warmer. (**b**) **Adult** *phayrei* (SW,W Myanmar): Orange-buff below. **Other subspecies** *P.f.stanfordi* (N Myanmar) and *orientalis* (N Laos, Tonkin): Warmer buff below; latter darker/warmer above. *P.f.dickinsoni* (C Annam, ? S Laos): Buff only on flanks, no line over supercilium. **VOICE** Harsh *whit whit-tchrrrt* and *whitchitit*, dry *krrrrt*. **HABITAT** Broadleaved evergreen forest, bamboo; 800–2,000 m. **RANGE** Un **R** Myanmar (except C), W,NW Thailand, Laos, W,E Tonkin, N,C Annam.

9 SLENDER-BILLED SCIMITAR BABBLER *Xiphirhynchus superciliaris* 20 cm
(**a**) **Adult** *forresti*: Very long dark bill, blackish crown and head-side, rufous below. **Other subspecies** *X.s.rothschildi* (N Myanmar): Paler crown, weaker supercilium. *X.s.intextus* (W Myanmar?). **VOICE** Hollow piping *wuwuwuwuwuwu* and slower *put-put-put-put-put-put*. **HABITAT** Bamboo, broadleaved evergreen forest; 915–2,745 m. **RANGE** Un **R** W,N Myanmar, W Tonkin.

10 SHORT-TAILED SCIMITAR BABBLER *Jabouilleia danjoui* 19 cm
(**a**) **Adult** *parvirostris*: Shortish tail, double moustache, rufescent breast with dark streaks. (**b**) **Adult** *danjoui* (S Annam): Brown breast-streaks, paler rufous, longer bill. *J.d.ssp.* (C Annam highlands): Darker brown, duller/paler rufous, intermediate bill. **VOICE** Sings with short clear monotone high whistles (0.5–0.75 s long). Scolding *chrrr-chrrr-chrrr...* **HABITAT** Broadleaved evergreen forest, bamboo. 50–2,100 m (above 1,500 m in south). **RANGE** Un **R** C Laos, E Tonkin, N,C,S Annam.

11 LONG-BILLED WREN BABBLER *Rimator malacoptilus* 12 cm
(**a**) **Adult** *malacoptilus*: Long, slightly curved bill, very short tail, all streaky. (**b**) *pasquieri* (W Tonkin): Darker; whiter throat and streaks. **VOICE** Sings with loud, clear, c.1 s long whistle: *thiiw* or *thii'uu* (*thii* stressed). **HABITAT** Broadleaved evergreen forest, bamboo; 1,220–2,000 m. **RANGE** Sc **R** N Myanmar, W Tonkin.

PLATE 122 WREN BABBLERS

1 LARGE WREN BABBLER *Napothera macrodactyla* 20 cm (**a**) **Adult** *macrodactyla*: Black-and-white lores/mask, white throat, blue eyering; faint pattern below. (**b**) **Juvenile**: Warmer, plainer, buff streaks above. **VOICE** Clear whistled *chuu-chreeh*; *chu-chiii*; *phuu-wiii*; *uuurr-wi'wi'wi'wi'wrriiu* etc. **HABITAT** Understorey/floor of broadleaved evergreen forest; up to 700 m. **RANGE** Un/fc **R** S Thailand, Pen Malaysia; formerly Singapore.

2 MARBLED WREN BABBLER *N.marmorata* 21.5 cm (**a**) **Adult** *grandior*: Longish tail, rufous ear-coverts, white-scaled blackish below. **Juvenile**: Rufous-streaked above. **VOICE** Song recalls Large: *puuu-chiiii*, *pyuuu-jhiiii* or *puuui-jhiiii*, (*puuu* higher, rising; *chiiii* lower, buzzier etc.). Also *piuuu-whiiii*, *uuuui-jhiii* and *piuuu*. **HABITAT** Broadleaved evergreen forest; 610–1,220 m. **RANGE** Ra lo **R** Pen Malaysia.

3 LIMESTONE WREN BABBLER *N.crispifrons* 18–20.5 cm (**a**) **Adult** *crispifrons*: Larger than Streaked, longer tail, no covert-spots, bolder throat-streaks, whiter belly-centre. (**b**) **Adult white-throated morph**: White face/throat. (**c**) **Adult** *calcicola* (NE Thailand): Rufescent below. (**d**) **Adult** *annamensis* (Indochina): Grey-er crown/mantle/breast/belly. **VOICE** Sudden loud, rapid, slurred, jumbled chattering. Scolding *chrrr-chrrr-chrrr..* etc. in alarm. **HABITAT** Forest on limestone, vicinity of limestone rocks/outcrops; up to 915 m. **RANGE** Lc **R** south-east S Myanmar, Tenasserim, W,NW,NE Thailand, N Laos, W,E Tonkin, N Annam.

4 STREAKED WREN BABBLER *N.brevicaudata* 14–14.5 cm (**a**) **Adult** *brevicaudata*: Whitish wing-spots, rufescent below, streaked throat/breast, grey face. (**b**) **Juvenile**: Plainer/browner, pale streaks above, dull wing-spots. (**c**) **Adult** *stevensi* (northern Indochina): Bigger, colder brown below. (**d**) **Adult** *leucosticta* (S Thailand southwards): Very broad streaks below. **Other subspecies** *N.b.striata* (W,N,S[west] Myanmar) and *griseigularis* (SE Thailand, south-west Cambodia): Duller, paler-centred belly; latter with greyer throat/breast. *N.b.proxima* (S Laos, C Annam): Like *stevensi* but smaller. *N.b.rufiventer* (S Annam). **VOICE** Clear ringing *peee-oo*; *pu-ee*; *chiu-ree* etc. Rattling *chrrreerrrrt* etc. **HABITAT** Broadleaved evergreen forest, limestone rocks/boulders; up to 1,620 m. **RANGE** Co **R** (except SW,C Myanmar, C Thailand, Singapore, Cochinchina).

5 EYEBROWED WREN BABBLER *N.epilepidota* 10–11.5 cm (**a**) **Adult** *davisoni*: Small, short tail, long buff supercilium, dark eyestripe, large whitish covert-spots. (**b**) **Juvenile**: Plain rufescent brown, vague supercilium/covert-spots. (**c**) **Adult** *roberti* (N Myanmar): Duller above, blackish streaks below. (**d**) **Adult** *amyae* (east N Laos, north Vietnam): Larger; colder above, whiter throat and supercilium. **Other subspecies** *N.e.clara* (S Annam): Whiter throat/supercilium/underpart-streaks (latter also broader). *N.e.granti* (S Thailand southward): Paler-centred breast/abdomen. **VOICE** Song is clear falling whistled *cheeeoo* or *piiiiiu*. Rattled *prrrt-prrrt-prrrt* and *chrrut-chrrut-chrrut* etc. in alarm. **HABITAT** Understorey of broadleaved evergreen forest; 50–2,135 m. **RANGE** Fc/co **R** N,C,E,S(east) Myanmar, Tenasserim, Thailand (except C,SE), Pen Malaysia, Laos, Vietnam (except Cochinchina).

6 SCALY-BREASTED WREN BABBLER *Pnoepyga albiventer* 9.5 cm (**a**) **Adult dark morph** *albiventer*: Small, tail-less, dark brown with buff scales below. Pale speckling on head. In some populations (i.e. W Myanmar) throat often white. (**b**) **Adult pale morph**: White instead of buff below (except lower flanks). (**c**) **Juvenile (dark morph?)**: Rather plain above, mottled dark brown and dark buff below. (**d**) **Juvenile (pale morph?)**: Mottled pale and dark below. **VOICE** Rapid high jumbled warbler-like song: roughly *wisisitititiwi* or *wiswisiwitwisititui*. Call is loud, explosive *tschik* or *tchik*. **HABITAT** Understorey/floor of broadleaved evergreen forest; 2,200–3,000 m (to 1,200 m in winter). **RANGE** Fc **R** W,N Myanmar, W Tonkin.

7 PYGMY WREN BABBLER *Pnoepyga pusilla* 8.5 cm (**a**) **Adult dark morph** *pusilla*: Smaller/slimmer than Scaly-breasted, unspeckled head. (**b**) **Adult pale morph**: From Scaly-breasted as dark morph. **Other subspecies** *P.p.annamensis* (S Annam; ? Cambodia, S Laos) and *harterti* (south of c.9°N): Plainer throat/belly-centre, warmer above/on lores. **VOICE** Very high *ti tu*; *ti ti tu* in north of region. Sharp *tchit* call. **HABITAT** Broadleaf evergreen forest; 750–2,565 m (locally to 180 m winter). **RANGE** Co **R** Myanmar (except SW,C), NW,S Thailand, Pen Malaysia, Indochina (except C Annam, Cochinchina).

8 SPOTTED WREN BABBLER *Spelaeornis formosus* 10 cm (**a**) **Adult**: Brown, peppered white, black bars on rufescent wings/tail. **Juvenile**: Blackish-brown with more prominent spots. **VOICE** Song is extremely high tinkling *ti-ti-ti-i tit-si-ii ti-ti-ti-i tit-si-ii..* or *tit-tit-ti-i tit-tsii-ii tit-tit-ti-i tit-tsii-ii*. **HABITAT** Broadleaved evergreen forest, weedy gullies; 480–1,975 m. **RANGE** Un **R** W,N Myanmar, N,C Laos, W Tonkin, N Annam.

9 BAR-WINGED WREN BABBLER *S.troglodytoides* 13 cm (**a**) **Adult** *souliei*: Dark-barred wings/tail, largely rufescent with black-tipped pale streaks. (**b**) **Juvenile**: Duller and plainer head/body. **VOICE** Song is husky rolling *chi'whi-whi'whi-whi'whi-whi'whi* or *ch-whi-whi-whi-whi*. **HABITAT** Undergrowth of broadleaved evergreen forest, bamboo; 2,440–2,895 m. **RANGE** Sc **R** N Myanmar.

10 LONG-TAILED WREN BABBLER *S.chocolatinus* 11.5 cm (**a**) **Male** *reptatus*: Plain wings/longish tail, dark scaling above, grey head-sides, mostly white throat, brownish below with black-and-white scales. (**b**) **Female**: Washed rufescent-buff below. (**c**) **Male** *kinneari* (W Tonkin): Darker moustachial line, stronger scales below. (**d**) **Female**: Buffier throat, browner breast/flanks, stronger breast-scales. (**e**) **Adult** *oatesi* (W Myanmar): Less grey on head-side, white throat to belly-centre with black spots, brown-washed throat-sides to flanks. **VOICE** *S.c.reptatus* sings with decelerating trill: *puwrriii'i'i'i'i* or *puwrree'e'e'e'e*; *kinneari* with trills that slow towards end: *chwi'i'i'i'witchu-wit* and *churrrrr'r'r-rt-rt-yut-yut-yut-yut* etc.; *oatsei* with abrupt undulating *chiwi-chiwi-chiwi-chew* and *witchi-witchi-witchi-wu* etc. Soft *tuc tuc tuc..*, very quiet *ik ik ik..* etc. **HABITAT** Undergrowth in broadleaved evergreen forest, secondary growth; 1,400–2,800 m. **RANGE** Lc **R** W,N,E Myanmar, W Thailand, W,E Tonkin.

PLATE 123 *STACHYRIS* BABBLERS

1 RUFOUS-FRONTED BABBLER *Stachyris rufifrons* 12 cm
(a) **Adult** *rufifrons*: Greyish over/around eye, duller crown than Rufous-capped, buffier below. **Juvenile**: Paler overall. (b) **Adult** *poliogaster* (Pen Malaysia): Darker above, paler lower underparts. **Other subspecies** *S.r.obscura* (c.12°N to c.6°N): Roughly between *rufifrons* and *poliogaster*. *S.r.pallescens* (SW,W Myanmar); *planicola* (N Myanmar); *adjuncta* (east NW Thailand, northern Indochina); *insuspecta* (S Laos). **VOICE** Song is usually quite quick, piping, 5–7 note *tub tub-tub-tub-tub-tub* (sometimes no pause after first note), lasting 1.25–1.75 s. Querulous *wirrrri* alarm. **HABITAT** Secondary growth, bamboo, broadleaved evergreen forest; up to 2,100 m. **RANGE** Co **R** Myanmar, Thailand (except C,SE), Pen Malaysia, Laos, W Tonkin, N Annam.

2 RUFOUS-CAPPED BABBLER *Stachyris ruficeps* 12.5 cm
(a) **Adult** *pagana*: Paler/more olive above than Rufous-fronted, orange-rufous crown, yellowish lores/head-sides/below; usually pinker bill. (b) **Juvenile**: Crown paler, washed-out below. (c) **Adult** *bhamoensis* (N[east],E Myanmar): Darker/warmer above, greyer flanks. **Other subspecies** *S.r.rufipectus* (west N Myanmar): Warmer above, buffy-yellow below (whiter throat-/belly-centre), flanks more greyish-olive. *S.r.davidi* (N Indochina): As *bhamoensis*; also yellower lores to upper breast. **VOICE** Song slower than Rufous-fronted? Scolding *trrrrt-trrrrt-trrrrt*. **HABITAT** Broadleaved evergreen forest, bamboo; 455–2,195 m. **RANGE** Co **R** N,E Myanmar, N,S(east) Laos, Vietnam (except Cochinchina).

3 GOLDEN BABBLER *Stachyris chrysaea* 10–12 cm
(a) **Adult** *assimilis*: Bright yellow forehead/below, black face, dark crown-streaks. **Juvenile**: Washed out below, dull eyes. (b) **Adult** *binghami* (W Myanmar): Grey ear-coverts, bolder crown-streaks. **Other subspecies** *S.c.chrysaea* (N Myanmar): Brighter; bolder crown-streaks. *S.c.aurata* (east E Myanmar to northern Indochina); *chrysops* (south of c.12°N). **VOICE** Song like Rufous-fronted but shorter, notes often more spaced, with longer pause after first note. Scolding *chrrrrr-rr-rr*. **HABITAT** Broadleaved evergreen forest; 450–2,600 m. **RANGE** Co **R** (except SW,C Myanmar, C,SE Thailand, Singapore, Cambodia, S Annam, Cochinchina).

4 SOOTY BABBLER *Stachyris herberti* 18 cm
(a) **Adult**: Sooty dark brown, whiter throat, pale bill/eyering. **VOICE** Soft *tip* and *tu-tip* notes; hard *wittitit* in alarm. **HABITAT** Broadleaved evergreen forest on limestone, usually close to limestone outcrops; 50–610 m. **RANGE** Lfc **R** C Laos, C Annam.

5 GREY-THROATED BABBLER *Stachyris nigriceps* 12.5–14 cm
(a) **Adult** *spadix*: Black-and-silver crown-streaks, grey throat with white patch, warm buffish below. (b) **Juvenile**: Warmer; plain hindcrown. (c) **Adult** *coltarti* (N Myanmar) Darker throat, warmer below. (d) **Adult** *rileyi* (C,S Annam): Pale; all-grey throat, less crown-streaking. (e) **Adult** *dipora* (c.12°N to c.6°N)/*davisoni* (south of c.6°N): Duller/thinner crown-streaks. **Other subspecies** *S.n.yunnanensis* (E Myanmar, east NW Thailand, northern Indochina): Darker. **VOICE** Song is high quavering, rising *ti tsuuuuuuuueee*. Scolding *chrrrrrr-rrr-rrt*. **HABITAT** Broadleaf evergreen forest, secondary growth; up to 1,830 m. **RANGE** Co **R** (except C,SE Thailand, Singapore, Cambodia).

6 GREY-HEADED BABBLER *Stachyris poliocephala* 14–15 cm
(a) **Adult**: Silver-streaked greyish head, pale eyes, rufous-chestnut below. (b) **Juvenile**: Duller; paler below, fainter head-streaks, duller eyes. **VOICE** Song is clear, quite high *chit-tiwi-wioo-iwee* and *chu-chi-chiee* etc. Scolding *chrrrrttutut* in alarm. **HABITAT** Broadleaved evergreen forest, secondary growth; up to 760 m. **RANGE** Un/fc **R** S Thailand, Pen Malaysia.

7 SNOWY-THROATED BABBLER *Stachyris oglei* 16 cm
(a) **Adult**: Recalls Spot-necked but bold white supercilium, broad black mask, clean white throat, grey breast. **VOICE** Rapid metallic rattling in alarm. **HABITAT** Broadleaved evergreen forest, bamboo; 450–800 m. **RANGE** Un lo **R** N Myanmar.

8 SPOT-NECKED BABBLER *Stachyris striolata* 16–16.5 cm
(a) **Adult** *guttata*: White throat, blackish malar, white-flecked supercilium/neck. **Other subspecies** *S.s.nigrescentior* (S Thailand): Deeper rufous-chestnut below. *S.s.tonkinensis* (northern Vietnam); *helenae* (east NW Thailand, northern Laos). **VOICE** Song is high *tub tih tub* or *tub tih*. Also high rising note and hard rattle: *whiiii-titititititi*. Scolding *tirrrrirrirr*. **HABITAT** Broadleaved evergreen forest, secondary growth, thickets; 50–1,525 m. **RANGE** Un/lc **R** N Myanmar, Tenasserim, W,NW,S Thailand, N,C Laos, W,E Tonkin, N,C Annam.

9 WHITE-NECKED BABBLER *Stachyris leucotis* 14–15 cm
(a) **Adult** *leucotis*: White-spotted supercilium/neck, grey ear-coverts, black throat, pale covert-tips. (b) **Juvenile**: Duller; dark brown below. **VOICE** Song is simple whistled *uu-wi-u-wi, uu-wi-u-wi-u* or *uui-wi-oi-wi*. **HABITAT** Broadleaved evergreen forest; up to 800 m. **RANGE** Ra/sc **R** S Thailand, Pen Malaysia.

10 BLACK-THROATED BABBLER *S.nigricollis* 15.5–16 cm
(a) **Adult**: Black face to upper breast, white eyebrow/cheek-patch/necklace. (b) **Juvenile**: Sooty-brown below/on head, white brow/cheek-patch. **VOICE** Song is spaced, quite weak piping *pu-pu-pu-pu-pu-pu* and faster *pupupupupupupu*. Also hollow *puwut-puwut-puwut-puwut* and *chu-chuwu-chu-chu-chu-chu..* etc. Slow rattled *tchrrr-rrt* and *chrrrt-trrerrt-trrerrt*. **HABITAT** Broadleaved evergreen forest; up to 455 m. **RANGE** Un/fc **R** S Thailand, Pen Malaysia; formerly Singapore.

11 CHESTNUT-RUMPED BABBLER *S.maculata* 17–18.5 cm
(a) **Adult** *maculata*: Large; rufous-chestnut rump, broad blackish streaks on whitish breast/belly. **VOICE** Loud full *wup wup wup wup..*; *wuhup-wuhup*; tremulous *t'u'u'u'u'u'u* and *tik-tik-wrrrrrrrr* etc. **HABITAT** Broadleaved evergreen forest; up to 200 m. **RANGE** Co **R** S Thailand, Pen Malaysia; formerly Singapore.

12 CHESTNUT-WINGED BABBLER *S.erythroptera* 13 cm
(a) **Adult** *erythroptera*: Mostly greyish head/breast, blue spectacles. (b) **Juvenile**: More rufescent above, much paler grey, duller spectacles. **VOICE** Song is soft, quite quick, piping *hu-hu-hu-hu-hu-hu*, tremulous *hu hu'u'u'u'u'u'u'u* or slow *chu hu-hu-hu-hu*. Harsh scolding *trrrrrt-trrrrrt..* **HABITAT** Broadleaved evergreen forest; up to 800 m. **RANGE** Co **R** south Tenasserim, S Thailand, Pen Malaysia, Singapore.

PLATE 124 *MALACOPTERON* BABBLERS, TIT BABBLERS & GRASS BABBLERS

1 MOUSTACHED BABBLER *Malacopteron magnirostre* 17 cm
(a) Adult *magnirostre*: Greyish head-sides, dark moustachial, whitish below with greyish wash/streaks. **(b) Juvenile**: Indistinct moustachial, pinkish lower mandible. VOICE Song is clear sweet whistled *tii-tu-ti-tu* or *ti-tiee-ti-ti-tu* etc. (may descend slightly towards end). Soft but quite explosive *whit* and buzzing *bzzii* notes. HABITAT Middle storey of broadleaved evergreen forest; up to 900 m. RANGE Co **R** south Tenasserim, S Thailand, Pen Malaysia, Singapore (ra).

2 SOOTY-CAPPED BABBLER *M.affine* 15–16.5 cm
(A) Adult *affine*: Smaller than Moustached, slenderer bill, sooty crown, no moustache. **(b) Juvenile**: Crown paler, lower mandible dull flesh. VOICE Song of rising/falling shistles; *phu-phi-phu-phoo-phu-phi-phu* etc. Sub-song is variable *whi-whi-whui* and faster *chut-whi-whi-whi-whu-whi-whu* etc. Calls with sharp **which-it** and harsh rattles. HABITAT Broadleaved, evergreen forst, often near water, forest edge; up to 455m. RANGE Ra/lc **R** S Thailend, Pen Malaysia.

3 SCALY-CROWNED BABBLER *M.cinereum* 14–17 cm
(a) Adult *cinereum*: Smaller than Rufous-crowned, no breast-streaks, pinkish legs. **(b) Adult** *indochinense* (SE,NE Thailand, Indochina): Brown nape, paler above, buffier below. VOICE Four-part song (variously combined). Rapid *dit-dit-dit-dit-dit..* etc. Rapid *du-du-du-du-du-du..* (usually descends). More spaced, ascending *phu-phu-phu-phu*; *phu-pu-pi-pee* etc. High, even *wiwiwiwiwi-wi-wi-wi-wu* etc. Sharp **chit**, **tcheu** and **titu** calls. HABITAT Lower/middle storey of broadleaved evergreen forest; up to 800 m. RANGE Co **R** NE,SE,S Thailand, Pen Malaysia, Cambodia, C,S Laos, south E Tonkin, N,C,S Annam, Cochinchina.

4 RUFOUS-CROWNED BABBLER *M.magnum* 17.5–19.5 cm
(a) Adult *magnum*: Larger than Scaly-crowned, bigger bill, greyish breast-streaks/legs. VOICE Three-part song. Well-spaced clear *phu-phu-phi-phi* etc. (usually not descending). Well-spaced *chuwee-chuwee-chuwee-chuwu-chuwu*; *chu-chi-chi-chi-chi-chu-chu-chu-chu-chu* etc. (may descend slightly/hurry towards end). Well-spaced, even *chut-chut chut-chut-chut-chut-chut-chut* etc. HABITAT Broadleaved evergreen forest; up to 455 m. RANGE Un/fc **R** south Tenasserim, S Thailand, Pen Malaysia.

5 GREY-BREASTED BABBLER *M.albogulare* 13.5–15 cm
(a) Adult *albogulare*: Slaty-grey head, white eyebrow/throat, grey breast-band. VOICE Sings with low discordant ascending *whu-whi*, *whit-whu* and *uu-whi-u* phrases, sometimes short *chit* notes. HABITAT Lower storey of lowland freshwater swamp and broadleaved evergreen forest. RANGE Sc lo **R** Pen Malaysia.

6 STRIPED TIT BABBLER *Macronous gularis* 12.5–14 cm
(a) Adult *sulphureus*: Rufous crown, yellow supercilium, narrow throat/breast-streaks. **(b) Juvenile**: Plainer/paler. **(c) Adult** *chersonesophilus* (c.12° to 5°N): Bolder throat/breast-streaks, darker/more chestnut above. **(d) Adult** *gularis* (south of c.4°N): Bolder throat/breast-streaks, much darker (less contrasting) above. **Other subspecies** *M.g.lutescens* (east E Myanmar to northern Indochina): Brighter below. *M.g.archipelagicus* (Mergui Archipelago): More rufous-chestnut below, yellower below, bold-

er streaks. *M.g.kinneari* (C Annam), *versuricola* (east Cambodia, south Vietnam), *connectens* (south Tenasserim to Cambodia), *inveteratus* (SE Thailand/Cambodia islands): Roughly intermediate between *sulphureus* and *gularis*. *M.g.condorensis* (Con Dao Is, Cochinchina): Darker above than last group, like *gularis* below. *M.g.ticehursti* (SW,W Myanmar); *saraburiensis* (south NE Thailand, west Cambodia). VOICE Song (northern Vietnam) is loud bouncing *ti chut-chutut-chut* or *tit-chutut-chutut-chutut..*; or (C Annam and Thailand) even *chut-chut-chut-chut-chut...* Harsh *chrrt-chrr* and *tititit-chrreeoo* etc. HABITAT Open broadleaved forest, mangroves, secondary growth, thickets, bamboo; up to 1,525 m. RANGE Co **R** (except C Thailand).

7 GREY-FACED TIT BABBLER *Macronous kelleyi* 14 cm
(a) Adult: Plainer above than Striped, grey supercilium/head-sides, paler and barely streaked below. **Juvenile**: Greyer/less yellow below, diffuse throat-streaks. VOICE Song is soft, even *tuh-tuh-tuh-tuh-tuh-tuh-tuh-tuh...* Calls include harsh *chrrrrii-chrrruu-chrrrii-chru* and *chit-chrrerr*. HABITAT Broadleaved evergreen forest, secondary forest; 50–1,165 m. RANGE Fc **R** E Cambodia, C,S Laos, N,C,S Annam, Cochinchina.

8 FLUFFY-BACKED TIT BABBLER *Macronous ptilosus* 16.5 cm
(a) Adult *ptilosus*: Rufous crown, black throat, blue spectacles. **Juvenile**: Paler crown, darker mantle, dull throat, warmer breast. VOICE Song is low *puh puh puh-puh-puh* or *wuh wu-hu wu-hu* etc. Forced husky *hherrh herr hherr herr*. Creaking *aahk-eeah-oh*. HABITAT Edge of broadleaved evergreen forest; up to 200 m. RANGE Sc/fc **R** S Thailand, Pen Malaysia; formerly Singapore.

Cambodia Garden

9 CHESTNUT-CAPPED BABBLER *Timalia pileata* 16–17 cm
(a) Adult *smithi*: Chestnut cap, black mask, white supercilium, cheeks/throat/breast. **(b) Juvenile**: Warmer/plainer above, paler bill. **Other subspecies** *T.p.bengalensis* (western Myanmar) and *patriciae* (south-west Thailand): More greyish-olive above (warm buffish tinged in latter), less buffy below, greyer flanks; *intermedia* (C,S Myanmar to W Thailand)/*dictator* (NE Thailand to S Indochina) are intermediate. VOICE Husky *wher-wher witch-it-it* etc. Metallic *tzit*, harsh *chrrt*. HABITAT Grassland, thickets; up to 1,500 m. RANGE Co **R** (except S Thailand, Pen Malaysia, Singapore).

10 YELLOW-EYED BABBLER *Chrysomma sinense* 18 cm
(a) Adult *sinense*: Short black bill, white face/breast, orange-yellow eyes, orange eyering. **Other subspecies** *C.s.hypoleucum* (western Myanmar). VOICE Clear high *wi-wu-chiu*; *wi-tchwi-wi-tchiwi* etc. Trilled *chrr-chrr-chrr..*; *chr'r'r'r'r'r*. HABITAT Grassland, thickets; up to 1,830 m. RANGE Co **R** (except S Thailand, Pen Malaysia, Singapore, Cambodia, W Tonkin, C Annam).

11 JERDON'S BABBLER *Chrysomma altirostre* 16–17 cm
(a) Adult *altirostre*: Grey over eye, greyish throat/breast greyer, pale lower mandible, brown eyes, greenish-yellow eyering. **Juvenile**: Warmer. **(b) Adult** *griseigularis* (N Myanmar): Greyer throat/breast, richer buff belly/vent. VOICE Sings with *ih-ih-ih-ih chew chitit chew i'wwiuu* etc. Short *tic* calls. HABITAT Tall grass; lowlands. RANGE Sc lo **R** N,S Myanmar.

PLATE 125 CUTIA & SHRIKE BABBLERS

1 CUTIA *Cutia nipalensis* 17–19.5 cm
(**a**) **Male** *melanchima*: Black and bluish-grey head/wings, rufous-chestnut above, whitish below, black flank-bars. (**b**) **Female** More olive-brown above with blackish streaks, dark brown head-sides. **Juvenile**: Duller; browner crown, fainter bars. (**c**) **Male** *legalleni* (S Annam): All-barred below. (**d**) **Female**: All-barred below, brown crown, paler greyish-brown above. **Other subspecies** *C.n.cervinicrissa* (Pen Malaysia): Male darker, more chestnut above, buffier flanks/vent. *C.n.boae* (C Annam; ? east S Laos): Much narrower bars below, going further towards centre. *C.n.nipalensis* (W Myanmar). **VOICE** *C.n.nipalensis* sings with rather high *yuip-yuip-yuip-yuip-yuip-yuip jiw-jiw-jiw-jiw yuip-yuip-yuip-yuip-yuip-yuip..* and *jorrri-jorrri-jorrri-ip-ip-ip-ip-ip-ip..* etc. *C.n.cervinicrissa* gives loud, quite shrill series of notes that change in pitch: *chip'chip'chip'chip'chip'chip piuu chu'chu'chu'chu'chu* etc. *C.n.legalleni* utters *wuyeet wu wi wi wi wi woo* and high strident *wiii-chiwu-wipwi-weei-weei..* and *wipwi-weei-weei-weei* mixed with *wii chiwi-chiwi...* Calls with light *chick chick chick..*, sharper *chit*, and harsh low *jert jert..*; *yeet-u yeet-u yeet-yeet yeet-u..* in alarm (*cervinicrissa*). **HABITAT & BEHAVIOUR** Broadleaved evergreen and mixed broadleaved/pine forest; 1,200–2,500 m, locally 850 m N Myanmar. Often in bird-waves, foraging methodically. **RANGE** Sc/fc R W,N,E,S(east) Myanmar, NW Thailand, Pen Malaysia, N,C,S(east) Laos, W Tonkin, C,S Annam.

2 BLACK-HEADED SHRIKE BABBLER *P.rufiventer* 21 cm
(**a**) **Male** *rufiventer*: Black head/wings/tail, pale grey throat and breast, deep pinkish belly/vent. (**b**) **Female**: Grey crown-scales/ear-coverts, mostly olive-green above, darker below. **Juvenile**: Similar to female. (**c**) **Immature male**: Duller/browner crown/nape than adult, yellowish-green above with blackish bars. **Other subspecies** *P.r.delacouri* (W Tonkin). **VOICE** Song is rather mellow *wip-wiyu* (*yu* slightly stressed) and *wip wu-yu*. Also more even, slightly descending *yu-wu-uu*. Calls with nervous, tremulous *ukuk-wrrrrii-yiwu* (*wrrrrii* long and high); scolding gruff *rrrrt-rrrrt-rrrr-rrrrt-rrrrt...* in alarm. **HABITAT** Broadleaved evergreen forest; 1,220–2,600 m. **RANGE** Sc/un R W,N Myanmar, W Tonkin.

3 WHITE-BROWED SHRIKE BABBLER *Pteruthius flaviscapis* 16.5 cm
(**a**) **Male** *aeralatus*: Black head with white supercilium, grey rest of upperparts, black tail and wings, pale grey throat and underparts, chestnut tertials with black tips. (**b**) **Female**: Head greyish, supercilium duller, upperparts greyish-brown, wings and tail mostly golden-olive, underparts creamy-buffish, throat paler. (**c**) **Juvenile male**: Like juvenile female but nape to uppertail-coverts more rufescent-tinged, lores and ear-coverts blacker, wings similar to adult male but with golden-olive fringing on median and greater coverts. **Juvenile female**: Quite uniform grey-brown above with buffish-white streaks, whiter below. (**d**) **Male** *ricketti* (NW[east] Thailand, N Indochina): Greyer ear-coverts, grey below. (**e**) **Female**: Grey throat and upper breast. (**f**) **Male** *validirostris* (W,N Myanmar): Whiter below, all-chestnut tertials. (**g**) **Female**: All-chestnut tertials, dark grey head, whiter throat and upper breast. **Other subspecies** *P.f.schauenseei* (S Thai-

land) and *cameranoi* (Pen Malaysia): Females have browner crown/nape/head-sides, almost no chestnut on tertials. *P.f.annamensis* (S Annam): Similar to *validirostris*; female with less chestnut on tertials. **VOICE** Sings with loud strident rhythmic *ip ch-chu ch-chu* or *itu chi-chu chi-chu* (W Myanmar/NW Thailand); *ip chip chip ch-chip* (Pen Malaysia) and *ip chu ch-chu* (S Annam). Calls with short *pink*, grating churring sounds in alarm. **HABITAT** Broadleaved evergreen and mixed broadleaved/coniferous forest; 700–2,500 m. **RANGE** Co R (except SW Myanmar, C Thailand, Singapore, Cochinchina).

4 GREEN SHRIKE BABBLER *Pteruthius xanthochlorus* 12–12.5 cm
(**a**) **Male** *hybridus*: Stout bill, greyish crown/head-sides, white eyering, greyish-white throat/breast, yellowish-buff flanks/vent, narrow pale wing-bar. (**b**) **Female**: Paler, less obvious grey on head, more brownish-olive above. (**c**) **Male** *pallidus* (N Myanmar): Slaty-grey head to upper mantle, broad eyering, brighter lower flanks/vent, largely grey wing-fringing. **Female**: Slightly paler above than male, with vague brownish tinge, mostly greenish-olive wing-fringing. **VOICE** Song is monotonously repeated, fairly high and well-spaced *whitu-whitu-wheet*; *wheet-wheet-wheet*; *chuwi-chuwi*; faster *whituwbituwhitwhit..* and *chiwichiwichiwichiwi..* etc. Calls include tit-like *jerr* and higher *jerri* notes. **HABITAT & BEHAVIOUR** Broadleaved evergreen forest; 1,700–2,800 m. Often in bird-waves; rather slow, heavy movements. **RANGE** Co R W,N Myanmar.

5 BLACK-EARED SHRIKE BABBLER *P.melanotis* 12 cm
(**a**) **Male** *melanotis*: Like Chestnut-fronted but forehead yellowish, paler throat, slate-grey nape, broad black rear ear-covert border, slaty-grey wing-fringing. (**b**) **Female**: Rufous-buff wing-bars, all-yellowish below, pale chestnut malar. (**c**) **Juvenile**: Like female but weaker head pattern, brown nape, much paler below. (**d**) **Male** *tahanensis* (extreme S Thailand, Pen Malaysia): Chestnut restricted to throat. (**e**) **Female**: Whitish-yellow below. **Juvenile**: Whiter below than *melanotis*, warm buff malar area. **VOICE** Monotonous *twi-twi-twi-twi-twi..*, slower *dwit-dwit-dwit-dwit-dwit..* and rattling *dr'r'r'r'r'r'r'r*. Rapid *whiwhiwhiwhi-whi..* and *jujujujujuju..* from *tahanensis*. Short *chid-it* call. **HABITAT** Broadleaved evergreen forest; 1,050–2,200 m, locally 700 m N Myanmar. **RANGE** Un R W,N,E,S(east) Myanmar, NW Thailand, Pen Malaysia, Laos, W,E Tonkin, N,C Annam.

6 CHESTNUT-FRONTED SHRIKE BABBLER *P.aenobarbus* 12 cm
(**a**) **Male** *intermedius*: Chestnut and yellow forehead, white eyering/wing-bars, grey supercilium, dark chestnut throat-centre/breast-wash, greyish-white primary edges. (**b**) **Female**: Rufous-chestnut forehead and throat-wash, yellowish-white below, rufescent wing-bars/primary edges. (**c**) **Male** *indochinensis* (S Annam): Reduced chestnut on breast. **VOICE** Sings with monotonous *chip-chip-chip-chip-chip..*, *wheet-wheet-wheet-wheet..*, *whit-whit-whit-whit-whit..* and *wchip-wchip-wchip-wchip..* etc. Calls with series of buzzy *jer* and *jerri* notes, chattering *chr'r'r'r'uk* and sharp *pwit*. **HABITAT** Broadleaved evergreen forest; 700–2,500 m. **RANGE** Fc R Myanmar (except SW,W), W,NW,NE Thailand, Laos, W Tonkin, N,C,S Annam.

PLATE 126 BARWINGS, MINLAS & FULVETTAS

1 RUSTY-FRONTED BARWING *Actinodura egertoni* 22.5 cm
(a) Adult *ripponi*: Slim, long-tailed; brownish-grey hood, chestnut face, mostly rufous-buff below. **Juvenile**: Crown/nape washed warm brown. **VOICE** Song is fairly quick, clear, rather high *ti-wi-wi-wu ti-wi-wi-wu* or *ti-wi-wi-woi ti-wi-wi-woi*. Calls with low harsh *grrit*, *grrrrrrit* and *gwah* notes. **HABITAT** Broadleaved evergreen forest, secondary growth; 1,220–2,600 m, locally down to 215 m in winter (N Myanmar). **RANGE** Co **R** SW,W,S(west),N,E(north),C(east) Myanmar.

2 SPECTACLED BARWING *Actinodura ramsayi* 23.5–24.5 cm
(a) Adult *ramsayi*: Greyish-olive above, buffy-rufous forehead, white eyering, blackish lores, deep buff below. **(b) Adult** *yunnanensis* (W,E Tonkin): Rufous crown, narrow throat-streaks. **Other subspecies** *A.r.radcliffei* (north E Myanmar): Intermediate between other races and also rich dark brown lores/cheeks. In south-east N Laos (undescribed race?), like *yunnanensis* but greyer above, deep rufous only on forehead. **VOICE** Song is rather mournful, high, bouncing, descending *iee-iee-iee-iuu*. Calls with low harsh *baoh* or *berrh* notes. **HABITAT** Broadleaved evergreen forest, secondary growth, scrub, grass; 1,000–2,500 m, locally to 610 m Myanmar. **RANGE** Co **R** C(east),E,S(east) Myanmar, NW Thailand, N,C Laos, W,E Tonkin.

3 BLACK-CROWNED BARWING *Actinodura sodangorum* 24 cm
(a) Adult: Black crown, olive-brown above, mostly black wings. (Eyering broader than shown.) **VOICE** Like Spectacled. **HABITAT** Broadleaved evergreen forest, grass and scrub bordering pine forest; 1,100–2,400 m. **RANGE** Lo **R** east S Laos, southern C Annam.

4 STREAK-THROATED BARWING *Actinodura waldeni* 20–22 cm
(a) Adult *poliotis*: Bulky; relatively short tail; no eyering, streaked dark on crown and light below. **(b) Adult** *waldeni* (west N Myanmar): Paler on head, darker rufescent below with less distinct streaking. **(c) Adult** *saturatior* (east N Myanmar): More strongly contrasting streaks. **VOICE** Song is loud strident, slightly wavering and rising phrase, starting with slight rattle: *tchrrrr-jo-jwiee* or *dddrrt-juee-iwee*; sometimes shorter *jorr-dwidu*. Calls include low, rather nasal grumbling *grrr-ut grrr-ut..* and *grr-grr-grr-grr-grr...* **HABITAT & BEHAVIOUR** Broadleaved evergreen forest; 1,700–3,300 m. Often in small slow-moving parties; joins bird-waves. **RANGE** Fc **R** W,N Myanmar.

5 STREAKED BARWING *Actinodura souliei* 21–23 cm
(a) Adult *griseinucha*: Like Streak-throated but plainer ear-coverts/nape, plumpish body with broad blackish streaks (above and below). **VOICE** Calls recall Streak-throated. **HABITAT & BEHAVIOUR** Broadleaved evergreen forest; 1,950–2,500 m. Behaves like Streak-throated. **RANGE** Un **R** W Tonkin.

6 BLUE-WINGED MINLA *Minla cyanouroptera* 14–15.5 cm
(a) Adult *sordida*: Slim, long tail; violet-blue wing/tail-fringing and lateral crown-/forehead-streaks, whitish supercilium, greyish-white below, warmish above. **(b) Adult** *aglae* (W Myanmar): Bluer crown, warmer above, greyer throat/breast. **(c) Adult** *orientalis* (S Annam): Brownish above, dull wings/tail (no blue), whiter

below. **Juvenile**: Browner crown/nape. **Other subspecies** *M.c.wingatei* (N,E Myanmar, north-east NW Thailand, N Indochina): Intermediate between *sordida* and *aglae*. *M.c.sordidior* (S Thailand, Pen Malaysia): Much plainer/browner above. *M.c.rufodorsalis* (SW Cambodia): Chestnut wash above (rump and uppertail-coverts brighter), darker blue on wing/tail. **VOICE** Song is very thin high *psii sii-suuu* (*suuu* falling) or rising/falling *tsuit-twoo* etc. Short *whit* and *bwik* notes. **HABITAT & BEHAVIOUR** Edge of broadleaved evergreen forest; 900–2,600 m locally to 460 m N Myanmar. Usually in small flocks. **RANGE** Co **R** (except SW,C Myanmar, C Thailand, Singapore, Cochinchina).

7 CHESTNUT-TAILED MINLA *Minla strigula* 16–18.5 cm
(a) Adult *castanicauda*: Golden-rufous crown, blackish eye-brow/submoustachial, scaly throat; olive-greyish above, yellowish below, multi-coloured wings/tail. **(b) Adult** *malayana* (Pen Malaysia): Duller; broader throat-scales. **(c) Adult** *traii* (C Annam): Solid black and white face, bright crown, greyer above. **Juvenile**: Washed out; less distinct throat-bars. **Other subspecies** *M.s.yunnanensis* (northern Myanmar and Indochina): Warmer above, darker chestnut on tail. **VOICE** Song with high, quavering *tui-twi ti-tu* or *twi-twi twi twi* (third note higher) etc. **HABITAT** Broadleaved evergreen forest; 1,600–3,000 m. **RANGE** Lc/co **R** W,N,E,S(east) Myanmar, Tenasserim, W(lo),NW Thailand, Pen Malaysia, N,C Laos, W Tonkin, C Annam.

8 RED-TAILED MINLA *Minla ignotincta* 13–14.5 cm
(a) Male *mariae*: Black crown/head-sides, broad white supercilium, pale yellow below, olive-brownish above, black, white and red on wings, much red on tail. **(b) Female**: Little/no red on wings, pinker tail-fringes/-tip. **(c) Male** *ignotincta* (Myanmar): Darker, chestnut-tinged above. **VOICE** Song is fairly high, quite quickly repeated *wi ti wi-wu* (first two notes higher). Calls with low harsh *wih-wih-wih-wih..*, louder *yih-yih-yih-yih..*, short *wit* and *wih* notes etc. **HABITAT** Broadleaved evergreen forest, secondary forest; 1,100–2,800 m (locally to 470 m in winter N Myanmar). **RANGE** Co **R** W,N,S(east),E Myanmar, N,C,S(east) Laos, W,E Tonkin, N,C Annam.

9 GOLDEN-BREASTED FULVETTA *Alcippe chrysotis* 11 cm
(a) Adult *forresti*: White median crown-stripe, silvery ear-coverts, black and grey throat, orange-yellow below. **(b) Adult** *amoena* (W Tonkin): All-blackish throat, yellow eyering. **Juvenile**: Mostly yellowish throat. **Other subspecies** *A.c.robsoni*: Drab olive-grey above (darker lateral and whitish median crown-stripes), yellow throat and eyering. **VOICE** Song is rather rapid, very thin, high *si-si-si-si-suu*. Calls with low rattling *witrrrit*, *wit* and *wittit* etc. **HABITAT & BEHAVIOUR** Bamboo, broadleaved evergreen forest; 1,765–2,650 m. Often in small flocks. **RANGE** Fc/co **R** N Myanmar, W Tonkin, southern C Annam.

10 YELLOW-THROATED FULVETTA *A.cinerea* 9.5–10 cm
(a) Adult: Tiny; greyish-olive above, yellow supercilium and most of underparts. **VOICE** Song of very thin high notes, starting slowly, but ending in complex jumble: *titz titz-tsi-si-si tititutitu* etc. Thin high *si-si-si-si-si'si'si* and sharp *titz* notes. Rapid *tit* notes. **HABITAT** Understorey of broadleaved evergreen forest; 900–2,745 m. **RANGE** Un **R** N Myanmar, N Laos, N Annam.

PLATE 127 FULVETTAS

1 RUFOUS-WINGED FULVETTA *Alcippe castaneceps* 10.5–12 cm
(a) **Adult** *castaneceps*: Chestnut crown, black and white face, blackish and rufous on wing. (b) **Adult** *klossi* (S Annam): Blackish crown, plain wings. **Other subspecies** *A.c.exul* (eastern Thailand to W Tonkin): Darker crown/wing. *A.c.soror* (south of c.6°N): Darker wing/flanks. *A.c.stepanyani* (C Annam): Blacker crown, buffier below, darker wing. **VOICE** Song is descending *si tju-tji-tju-tji-tju*. **HABITAT** Broadleaved evergreen forest; 1,000–3,505 m, to 760 m N Myanmar. **RANGE** Co **R** Myanmar (except C), W,NW,NE,S Thailand, Pen Malaysia, Laos, W,E Tonkin, N,C,S Annam.

2 WHITE-BROWED FULVETTA *A.vinipectus* 11.5–12.5 cm
(a) **Adult** *perstriata*: Warm crown, white supercilium, dark headside, throat-streaks. (b) **Adult** *ripponi* (W Myanmar): Warm headside/throat-streaks. (c) **Adult** *austeni* (Mt Saramati, west N Myanmar): Supercilium behind eye, head-side darker than *ripponi*. (d) **Adult** *valentinae* (W Tonkin): Much greyer. **VOICE** *A.v.ripponi* sings with thin *si wi-su*. **HABITAT** Bamboo, thickets, open forest; 1,830–3,355 m. **RANGE** Co **R** N,W N Myanmar, W Tonkin.

3 INDOCHINESE FULVETTA *Alcippe danisi* 13 cm
(a) **Adult** *danisi*: Streaked head-sides/upper breast, plainer wings than Streak-throated. **Other subspecies** *A.d.bidoupensis* (C,S Annam, ? S Laos): Browner crown, no whitish on wing. **HABITAT** Broadleaved evergreen forest, bamboo, scrub; 1,800–2,440 m. **RANGE** Lc **R** N(south-east),C,S(east) Laos, C(southern),S Annam.

4 STREAK-THROATED FULVETTA *A.cinereiceps* 11.5–12.5 cm
(a) **Adult** *manipurensis*: Greyish above, paler head-side, streaked throat. **Other subspecies** *A.c.tonkinensis* (W Tonkin). **VOICE** Thin *ti ti si-su* song. **HABITAT** Broadleaved evergreen forest edge, bamboo; 1,525–2,800 m. **RANGE** Co **R** N Myanmar, W Tonkin.

5 LUDLOW'S FULVETTA *Alcippe ludlowi* 11.5–12.5 cm
(a) **Adult**: Dark above, plain-looking crown/head-side, bold throat-streaks. **HABITAT** More open broadleaved evergreen forest, bamboo; found at 2,900 m. **RANGE** Un **R** north N Myanmar.

6 RUFOUS-THROATED FULVETTA *A.rufogularis* 12–14 cm
(a) **Adult** *major*: Rufescent crown, white supercilium, dark rufous throat-band. (b) **Adult** *collaris* (N Myanmar): Broader throat-band. (c) **Adult** *stevensi* (east N Laos; northern Vietnam): Duller/buffier on head, paler rufous throat-band. **Other subspecies** *A.r.khmerensis* (SE Thailand): Darker above. *A.r.kelleyi* (C Annam): Darker throat-band. **VOICE** Loud shrill song: *wi-chuw-i-chewi-cheeu* and *chuu-chu-wichu-chi-chu* etc. **HABITAT** Broadleaved evergreen forest; to 1,100 m. **RANGE** Sc/lc **R** N Myanmar, NW,NE,SE Thailand, N,C Laos, W,E Tonkin, N,C Annam.

7 RUSTY-CAPPED FULVETTA *Alcippe dubia* 13.5–15.5 cm
(a) **Adult** *genestieri*: White supercilium/throat. (b) **Adult** *mandellii* (W Myanmar): Darker ear-coverts, bold neck-streaks. **Other subspecies** *A.d.intermedia* (N,C,E Myanmar): Between *genestieri/mandellii*. *A.d.dubia* (rest of Myanmar): Warmer/buffier. *A.d.cui* (C Annam; ? S Laos): Colder/darker above, very buff below. **VOICE** Recalls Rufous-throated: *wi-chi-chu-chiu* etc. **HABITAT** Broadleaf evergreen forest, bamboo; 1,000–2,600 m. **RANGE** Fc/co **R** Myanmar (except SW), W Thailand, Laos, W Tonkin, C Annam.8

8 BROWN FULVETTA *Alcippe brunneicauda* 14–15.5 cm
(a) **Adult** *brunneicauda*: Rather plain greyish head, whiter throat, dull below. **VOICE** Sings with slowish high, slightly undulating *hi-tu-tu ti-tu ti-tu* etc. **HABITAT** Broadleaved evergreen forest; up to 900 m. **RANGE** Un/fc **R** S Thailand, Pen Malaysia.

9 BROWN-CHEEKED FULVETTA *Alcippe poioicephala* 15.5–16.5 cm
(a) **Adult** *haringtoniae*: Greyish-buff head-sides, buff below, narrow crown-stripes. (b) **Adult** *phayrei* (SW,W Myanmar): Paler; no crown-stripes. (c) **Adult** *karenni* (south-east Myanmar): Between preceding races. **Other subspecies** *A.p.fusca* (north W,C,E Myanmar): Only suggestion of crown-stripes. *A.p.davisoni* (Tenasserim, S Thailand): Similar to *karenni* *A.p.alearis* (north-east Thailand, N Indochina): Duller. **VOICE** Pleasant song phrases usually rise at end: *chu'uwi-uwi-uwee; yi'chiwi-wi-uwuuee* etc. **HABITAT** Broadleaf forest; to 1,520 m (mainly lowlands). **RANGE** Co **R** Myanmar, W,NW,NE,north S Thailand, N,C Laos, W,E Tonkin.

10 BLACK-BROWED FULVETTA *Alcippe grotei* 15.5–16.5 cm
(a) **Adult** *grotei*: Rufescent above, brown-washed head-side, vague eyering, largely whitish below. (b) **Juvenile**: Warmer, plainer. **Other subspecies** *A.g.eremita* (SE Thailand). **VOICE** Song usually rises less at end than Brown-cheeked: *yu-chi-chiwi-chu-woo*; *yi-yuii-yui-uwee-uwee* etc. **HABITAT** Broadleaved evergreen forest; up to 1,000 m. **RANGE** Co **R** SE Thailand, east Cambodia, C,S Laos, E Tonkin, N,C,S Annam, Cochinchina.

11 MOUNTAIN FULVETTA *Alcippe peracensis* 14–15.5 cm
(a) **Adult** *peracensis*: Bold crown-stripes, grey head-sides, white eyering, whitish below. **Juvenile**: Duller, plainer. (b) **Adult** *annamensis* (Indochina): Paler; olivey above. **VOICE** Sings with *iti-iwu uwi-u wheer wheer* and *it'iti-iwu wi-wui wheer wheer* etc. (*annamensis*); similar *iti iwu-wi-wi* etc., apparently without buzzy notes (*peracensis*). Faster/shorter than Grey-cheeked. **HABITAT** Broadleaved evergreen forest; 900–2,100 m. **RANGE** Co **R** extreme S Thailand, Pen Malaysia, C,S Laos, C,S Annam.

12 GREY-CHEEKED FULVETTA *A.morrisonia* 13–15 cm
(a) **Adult** *fraterculus*: Buff below, dark crown-stripes, white eyering. **Juvenile**: Warmer/browner. (b) **Adult** *schaefferi* (Tonkin): Faint crown-stripes, paler below, faint throat-streaks. (c) **Adult** *laotianus* (N[south-east],C Laos): Dark crown-stripes, throat-streaks. **Other subspecies** *A.m.yunnanensis* (N Myanmar): Fainter crown-stripes, buffier below. **VOICE** Sings with *it-chi wi-wi* or *ii yu yu-wi wi-you* (*fraterculus*) and *it'i u-iwi-u-i-ii* (*schaefferi*), then buzzy *eerb* sounds. **HABITAT** Broadleaved evergreen forest; 600–2,565 m. **RANGE** Co **R** N,E,C,S Myanmar, Tenasserim, W,NW,NE Thailand, N,C Laos, W,E Tonkin, N Annam.

13 NEPAL FULVETTA *Alcippe nipalensis* 13.5–14 cm
(a) **Adult** *commoda*: Brown-tinged crown, whitish centre to underparts, broad eyering. **Other subspecies** *A.n.stanfordi* (elsewhere Myanmar). **Juvenile**: Warmer. **VOICE** Sings with quite slow *chu-chui-chiwi; ew-ew-ui-iwi* etc. **HABITAT** Broadleaved evergreen forest; 440–2,400 m. **RANGE** Co **R** SW,W,N,S(east) Myanmar.

PLATE 128 *TURDOIDES* & *GAMPSORHYNCHUS* BABBLERS, BABAXES & SIBIAS

1 STRIATED BABBLER *Turdoides earlei* 21–22 cm
(a) **Adult** *earlei*: Long tail, blackish streaks above, thinly streaked throat/breast. **Juvenile**: Shows less distinct streaking above. **VOICE** Loud *tiew-tiew-tiew-tiew* and *quip-quip-quip*. **HABITAT & BEHAVIOUR** Grassland and scrub, usually near water; lowlands. In small flocks. **RANGE** Un **R** SW,N,C,S Myanmar.

2 WHITE-THROATED BABBLER *Turdoides gularis* 25.5 cm
(a) **Adult**: Very long tail, white throat, rich buff below, streaked pale forehead, black lores. **Juvenile**: Washed buffish above, with slightly fainter streaks. **VOICE** Sibilant low *trrrr trrrr trrrr..*, louder, incessant *whir'r'r'r'r'r'r*. **HABITAT** Scrub in semi-desert, cultivation borders; up to 600 m. **RANGE** Co **R** SW,C,S Myanmar.

3 SLENDER-BILLED BABBLER *T. longirostris* 20–21 cm
(a) **Adult**: Plain; slightly downcurved bill, pale eyes, whitish throat/upper breast, buff below. (b) **Juvenile**: More rufescent overall. **VOICE** Songs are: strident high, shrill *yi chiwiyu chi-wiyu'chiwiyu'chiwiyu'chiwiyu..*; and rather clear high *wiii-wii-jiu-di* or *wi-yu-ii* etc. Also even, fairly strident *chiu-chiu-chiu-chiu..* and discordant high *tiu-tiu-tit-tit-tu-tu..* etc. **HABITAT & BEHAVIOUR** Tall grass; lowlands. Usually in small, skulking groups. **RANGE** Sc lo **R** SW Myanmar.

4 CHINESE BABAX *Babax lanceolatus* 22.5–26 cm
(a) **Adult** *lanceolatus*: Large and boldly streaked. (b) **Juvenile**: Buffier; fainter streaks, plainer crown. **Other subspecies** *B.l.woodi* (W Myanmar): Black submoustachial and streaking above, dark shaft-streaks on throat. **VOICE** *B.l.lanceolatus* sings with high clear whistled *pi–pu–pyu–wii*; *woodi* with full clear whistled *pu-i pu-i pu-i pu-i pu-i pu-i..*, or faster *pui-pui-pui-pui...*. Chuntering *witchawitchawitcha-wit* and *whit* notes. **HABITAT** Open broadleaved evergreen forest, thickets, bamboo; 1,200–2,800 m. **RANGE** Un **R** W,N,C,E Myanmar.

5 WHITE-HOODED BABBLER *Gampsorhynchus rufulus* 25 cm
(a) **Adult** *torquatus*: . White hood, warm brown/buff elsewhere, dark neck/breast-mark. (b) **Juvenile**: Rufous crown/ear-coverts. (c) **Adult** *rufulus* (SW,N,C,west S Myanmar): More olive above, paler below, white shoulder-slash (median and some lesser coverts) and neck/breast. (d) **Adult** *saturatior* (south of c.6°N): More obvious collar. (e) **Adult** *luciae* (northern Indochina): Blackish hindcrown/necklace, rufescent nape. **VOICE** Harsh stuttering, rattling, cackling *krrrrrut* or *krrrrutut* etc. More structured *u'u'YER-yrrrt* from *rufulus*. **HABITAT** Bamboo in/near broadleaved evergreen/semi-evergreen forest; 50–1,800 m. **RANGE** Lc **R** (except C,SE Thailand, Singapore, Cambodia).

6 GREY-CROWNED CROCIAS *Crocias langbianis* 22 cm
(a) **Adult**: Grey crown/nape, blackish mask, rufescent with dark streaks above, bold flank-streaks. (b) **Juvenile**: Browner above, smaller flank-streaks. **VOICE** High loud *wip'ip'ip'ip'ip'ip..*; *wu-tu-ti'ti'ti'ti'ti'ti..*; *uee'uee'uee'uee'uee'uee..*; ocellating *wi'wi'wi'wi'wi'wi'wi'..*; with grumbly, buzzy *bidu-bidu-bidu-bidu..* and *bidi-wi-di-di-di* etc. **HABITAT & BEHAVIOUR** Broadleaved evergreen forest; 910–1,450 m. Forages slowly in denser middle storey. **RANGE** Sc lo **R** S Annam.

7 RUFOUS-BACKED SIBIA *Heterophasia annectens* 19–20 cm
(a) **Adult** *mixta*: Black crown/head-side, rufous-chestnut back to uppertail-coverts, buff vent. (b) **Adult** *saturata* (E Myanmar, NW Thailand [except north/east]): More black above, then chestnut. (c) **Adult** *davisoni* (north Tenasserim, ? W Thailand): Nearly all-black mantle/scapulars. **Other subspecies** *H.a.annectens* (western/northern Myanmar): Paler rufous-chestnut above, darker vent. *H.a.roundi* (C Annam, ? S Laos): Like *saturata*. *H.a.eximia* (S Annam): Similar to *davisoni*. **VOICE** Sings with clear, slightly descending *wip'i-iu-iu-ju* (*annectens*); *wii-wii-wii-er-yu* (*eximia*), slower, more even *it wi-wiu-jui* (*saturata*). **HABITAT** Mid/upper storey of broadleaved evergreen forest; 1,000–2,300 m, to 215 m in winter (N Myanmar). **RANGE** Fc **R** Myanmar, W,NW Thailand, N,S(east) Laos, W Tonkin, N,C,S Annam.

8 GREY SIBIA *Heterophasia gracilis* 22.5–24.5 cm
(a) **Adult** *dorsalis*: Much grey on wing/tail, buff vent. **Juvenile**: Paler; duller/browner above. (b) **Adult** (N Myanmar): Greyer above. **VOICE** Song is high shrill whistled (usually descending) *tu-tu-ti-ti-ti-tu*, and *ti-ti-titi-ti-ta* etc. **HABITAT** Broadleaved evergreen forest; 1,400–2,800 m. **RANGE** Co **R** W,N Myanmar.

9 DARK-BACKED SIBIA *H.melanoleuca* 21–23 cm
(a) **Adult** *radcliffei*: Blackish above, white below, whitish tail-tips. (b) **Adult** *melanoleuca* (N Tenasserim, ? W Thailand): Browner above. (c) **Adult** *castanoptera* (south-western E Myanmar): Rufous on coverts/tertials. **VOICE** Sings with loud, high, wavering, whistled *hrrrr'rrr'r'r'i-u*; *hrrrr'r'r'r'i-i* etc. **HABITAT** Broadleaved evergreen forest; 1,000–2,565 m. **RANGE** Co **R** C,E,S(east) Myanmar, north Tenasserim, W,NW Thailand, west S Laos.

10 BLACK-HEADED SIBIA *H.desgodinsi* 21.5–24.5 cm
(a) **Adult** *desgodinsi*: Black head/wings/tail, greyish above, mauvish-grey on flanks. (b) **Adult** *engelbachi* (Bolovens Plateau, S Laos): Dark brown lower mantle/scapulars/back, white eyering. (c) **Adult** *robinsoni* (S Annam): Broad white eyering, white ear-covert streaks. **Juvenile**: Duller; slightly darker breast. **Other subspecies** *H.d.kingi* (east S Laos, C Annam): Drab brown wash above, white eyering. *H.d.tonkinensis* (W Tonkin). **VOICE** Slower, less descending song than Dark-backed: *hi wi-wi wi wi* etc. **HABITAT** Broadleaved evergreen forest; 800–2,290 m. **RANGE** Co **R** east N Myanmar, S Laos, W,E Tonkin, C,S Annam.

11 BEAUTIFUL SIBIA *Heterophasia pulchella* 23.5 cm.
(a) **Adult** *pulchella*: Blue-grey, black mask/coverts, brown on tertials/tail. **Juvenile**: Lower body browner. **VOICE** Slightly descending *ti-ti-titi-tu-ti*. **HABITAT** Broadleaf evergreen forest; 1,830–2,745 m, down to 900 m in winter. **RANGE** Un **R** N Myanmar.

12 LONG-TAILED SIBIA *Heterophasia picaoides* 28–34.5 cm
(a) **Adult** *cana*: All grey; very long whitish-tipped tail, white wing-patch. (b) **Adult** *wrayi* (Pen Malaysia): Browner; smaller wing-patch. **Other subspecies** *H.p.picaoides* (W,N Myanmar): Slightly browner. **VOICE** Thin metallic notes and dry rattling: *tsittsit-tsic-tsic-tsic-tsic chrrrrrrrrt..* etc. **HABITAT** Broadleaved evergreen forest; 900–2,285 m, to 460 m in winter. **RANGE** Lc **R** Myanmar (except SW,C), W,NW Thailand, Pen Malaysia, Laos, W,E Tonkin.

PLATE 129 LEIOTHRIXES, YUHINAS & FIRE-TAILED MYZORNIS

1 SILVER-EARED MESIA *Leiothrix argentauris* 16.5–18 cm
(**a**) **Male** *galbana*: Yellow forehead, black head, silvery ear-coverts, rich yellow throat/breast, reddish wing-patch/tail-coverts. (**b**) **Female**: Duller nape/tail-coverts. **Juvenile**: Generally washed out. (**c**) **Male** *cunhaci* (S Indochina): Larger forehead-patch. (**d**) **Male** *ricketti* (N Indochina): Orange-red throat/breast (shadowed on female). **Other subspecies** *L.a.tahanensis* (south of c.9°N): More orange throat-side/breast, paler wing-patch. *L.a.aureigularis* (W Myanmar); *vernayi* (N Myanmar). **VOICE** Song is cheerful loud, descending *che tchu-tchu che-rit* etc. Piping *pe-pe-pe-pe-pe*. **HABITAT** Edge of broadleaved evergreen forest; 450–2,000 m, locally 175 m in winter. **RANGE** Co **R** (except SW,C Myanmar, C,SE Thailand, Singapore, Cochinchina).

2 RED-BILLED LEIOTHRIX *Leiothrix lutea* 15.5–16 cm
(**a**) **Male** *kwangtungensis*: Red bill, yellowish face, golden-olive crown, dark submoustachial, orange-rufous breast, patterned wing. (**b**) **Female**: Greener crown, greyer face, paler below. (**c**) **Juvenile**: Greyish crown, olive-grey to whitish below, pale bill. (**d**) **Male** *yunnanensis* (N Myanmar): Dull crown, greyer above, redder breast; both sexes with more black on wing. **Other subspecies** *L.l.calipyga* (W Myanmar): Roughly intermediate between other races. **VOICE** Sings with fluty, thrush-like warble. Scolding buzzy rattles. **HABITAT** Open broadleaf evergreen forest, secondary forest; 800–2,135 m. **RANGE** Co **R** W(sc),N Myanmar, W,E Tonkin.

3 STRIATED YUHINA *Yuhina castaniceps* 11.5–14 cm
(**a**) **Adult** *striata*: Short crest, whitish eyebrow, thin pale streaks above, white-edged tail. **Juvenile**: Duller; shorter crest. (**b**) **Adult** *castaniceps* (W Myanmar): Pale-fringed warmer crown, rufous-chestnut nape. (**c**) **Adult** *plumbeiceps* (N Myanmar): Plainer above, more rufous ear-coverts. (**d**) **Adult** *torqueola* (east NW Thailand, Indochina): Chestnut ear-coverts/collar with bold whitish streaks, greyer crown. **VOICE** Sings with simple high shrill *tchu* or *tchi* notes; double *di-duit* from *torqueola*. Loud chattering and squeaky notes. **HABITAT** Broadleaved evergreen forest,; 610–1,800 m, locally 180 m in winter. **RANGE** Co **R** SW,W,N,E,S(east) Myanmar, north Tenasserim, W,NW Thailand, Laos, W,E Tonkin, N,C Annam.

4 WHITE-NAPED YUHINA *Yuhina bakeri* 12.5–13 cm
(**a**) **Adult**: Dark rufous head, white ear-covert streaks/nape-patch. **Juvenile**: Browner mantle, fainter streaks below. **VOICE** Piercing high *tsit*, *tssu* and *tsidit* notes. **HABITAT** Broadleaved evergreen forest; 800–1,400 m. **RANGE** Un **R** N Myanmar.

5 WHISKERED YUHINA *Yuhina flavicollis* 12.5–13.5 cm
(**a**) **Adult** *rouxi*: Crest, white eyering, blackish moustache, golden-yellow collar, white-streaked olivey flanks. **Juvenile**: Duller. **Other subspecies** *Y.f.rogersi* (east NW Thailand): Greyer above, paler/duller collar, browner flanks. *Y.f.constantiae* (south-east N Laos): Plain rufous collar, warmer flanks. **VOICE** Song is shrill high *tzii-jhu ziddi* (*tzii* stressed). Nasal *jhoh*. **HABITAT** Broadleaved evergreen forest, secondary growth; 1,000–2,620 m, locally 215 m in winter N Myanmar. **RANGE** Co **R** W,N,E Myanmar, NW Thailand (lo), N,C Laos, W,E Tonkin, N Annam.

6 BURMESE YUHINA *Yuhina humilis* 13 cm
(**a**) **Adult** *clarki*: From Whiskered by greyish-brown crown/ear-coverts, grey collar/flanks. **Other subspecies** *Y.h.humilis* (north Tenasserim, W Thailand). **HABITAT** Broadleaf evergreen forest, secondary growth; 1,065–2,285 m. **RANGE** Un/lc **R** E(south),S(east) Myanmar, north Tenasserim, W(north),NW(south-west) Thailand.

7 STRIPE-THROATED YUHINA *Yuhina gularis* 14–15.5 cm
(**a**) **Adult** *gularis*: Crest, throat-streaks, orange and black on wing. (**a**) **Adult** *uthaii*.(C Annam): Broad throat-streaks, colder above, greyer head-side. **Juvenile**: Warmer above, crest short. **VOICE** Nasal *mherr* and *wiht* notes, and *whu'whu'whu'whi'whi'whi*. **HABITAT** Broadleaved evergreen and mixed broadleaved/coniferous forest, secondary growth; 1,675–3,200 m. **RANGE** Co **R** W,E Myanmar, N Laos, W Tonkin, C Annam (lo).

8 WHITE-COLLARED YUHINA *Y.diademata* 17.5–18 cm
(**a**) **Adult**: Greyish, darker face/tall crest, white nuchal patch. **Juvenile**: Tinged warm. **VOICE** Low *wi wrrr'i wrrr wrrr'i*. **HABITAT** Open broadleaved evergreen forest, secondary growth; 1,250–2,745 m. **RANGE** Fc **R** N,north E Myanmar, W Tonkin.

9 RUFOUS-VENTED YUHINA *Yuhina occipitalis* 13 cm
(**a**) **Adult** *obscurior*: Greyish crest, white eyering, black whisker, rufous on nape/vent. **Juvenile**: Nuchal patch paler, breast duller, crest shorter. **VOICE** Song is simple high *swi'si'si su'su'su swi'si'si si'si'si su'su'su..* etc. Nasal, buzzy *bee* notes. **HABITAT** Broadleaved evergreen forest, secondary growth; 1,830–2,500 m, locally to 800 m in winter. **RANGE** Co **R** N Myanmar.

10 BLACK-CHINNED YUHINA *Y.nigrimenta* 10.5–11.5 cm
(**a**) **Adult** *intermedia*: Black and red bill, black face/chin. **Juvenile**: Browner above. **VOICE** Song is high ringing *uu ii uui ii uui uu ii uui ii uui uu ii uui ii uui..* (*ii* higher). Nervous harsh *whrr'rr'ik*. **HABITAT & BEHAVIOUR** Broadleaved evergreen forest, secondary growth; 450–2,135 m. **RANGE** Lc **R** N Myanmar, Indochina (except S Laos, Cochinchina).

11 WHITE-BELLIED YUHINA *Y.zantholeuca* 12–13.5 cm
(**a**) **Adult** *zantholeuca*: Yellowish-green above, short crest, pale greyish below with whiter throat, yellow vent. (**b**) **Juvenile**: Crest shorter, unscaled. (**c**) **Adult** *tyrannula* (eastern Thailand, N Indochina): Greener above, darker grey below. (**d**) **Adult** *canescens* (SE Thailand, west Cambodia): Pale grey wash above. **Other subspecies** *Y.z.interposita* (south of c.12°N): Like *tyrannula*. *Y.z.sordida* (south-east NE Thailand, S Indochina): Slightly paler below, possibly duller above. **VOICE** High descending trill: *si'i'i'i'i*. Nasal *nher-nher* and *nhi*. **HABITAT** Broadleaved forest; up to 2,000 m, rarely 2,650 m N Myanmar (below 1,220 m Pen Malaysia). **RANGE** Co **R** (except C Thailand).

12 FIRE-TAILED MYZORNIS *Myzornis pyrrhoura* 12.5 cm
(**a**) **Male**: Mostly green, black mask, reddish throat/breast, multi-coloured wings/tail. (**b**) **Female**: Bluer tinge below (and often above), duller throat/breast/vent. (**c**) **Immature male**: Greener below than female, more faint of male's throat/breast. **VOICE** Thin *si* notes. **HABITAT** Open broadleaved evergreen forest, thickets; 2,440–3,660 m, to 1,800 m in winter. **RANGE** Un **R** N Myanmar.

PLATE 130 PARROTBILLS

1 GREAT PARROTBILL *Conostoma oemodium* 27.5–28.5 cm
(a) **Adult**: Large; quite pointed bill, greyish-white forehead, blackish eye-patch. **VOICE** Sings with loud full *whip whi-uu*; *uu-chip uu-chip*; *eep whu-eep*; *ee-uu braah* etc. **HABITAT** Open broadleaved evergreen forest, bamboo, scrub; 2,775–3,660 m, down to 2,285 m in winter. **RANGE** Un **R** N Myanmar.

2 BROWN PARROTBILL *Paradoxornis unicolor* 21 cm
(a) **Adult**: Greyish-brown: blackish lateral crown-stripe. **VOICE** Song is loud, quite high *it'ik'ik II-WUU-IIEW*. Also high *hee-hew*. Calls with shrill whining *whi-whi-whi*, crackling *churrrh* and *churr'rr'rr*. **HABITAT** Bamboo, open broadleaved evergreen forest; 2,135–3,660 m. **RANGE** Un **R** N Myanmar.

3 GREY-HEADED PARROTBILL *P.gularis* 15.5–18.5 cm
(a) **Adult** *transfluvialis*: Greyish head, white around eye, long black lateral crown-stripes, black throat. (b) *margaritae* (S Annam, east Cambodia): Black crown, mottled ear-coverts, darker above, white below. **Juvenile**: Warmer above, duller crown/throat. **Other subspecies** *P.g.rasus* (W Myanmar): White throat. *P.g.laotianus* (extreme E Myanmar, east NW Thailand, N Indochina): Paler grey crown/ear-coverts, whiter below. **VOICE** Song (*margaritae*) is loud, slightly husky *jhiu-jhiu-jhiu* or *jchew-jchew-jchew*. Quite harsh *jiow* and weaker *djer* notes. Rattling alarm call. **HABITAT** Broadleaved evergreen forest, secondary growth, bamboo; 1,000–1,830 m, locally to 610 m. **RANGE** Lc **R** W,N,E,S(east) Myanmar, NW Thailand, Indochina (except west Cambodia, Cochinchina).

4 SPOT-BREASTED PARROTBILL *P.guttaticollis* 18–22 cm
(a) **Adult**: White head-side/throat/breast with black patches and pointed spots. **Juvenile**: Paler crown, warmer above. **VOICE** Loud staccato *whit-whit-whit-whit..*, jollier *wui-wui-wui-wui* and *dri-dri-dri-dri..* etc. Longer *ju-ju-jiu-witwitwitwit witwitwitwit* etc. when excited. Coarse *ee-cho-cho-cho-cho, jieu-jieu-jieu-jieu* etc. **HABITAT** Tall grass, scrub, secondary growth; 1,050–2,135 m. **RANGE** Co **R** W,N,C(east),S(east),E Myanmar, NW Thailand, N Laos, W,E Tonkin.

5 VINOUS-THROATED PARROTBILL *P.webbianus* 11–12.5 cm
(a) **Adult** *suffusus*: Warm above, brown-streaked throat/upper breast. (b) **Adult** *elisabethae* (north W Tonkin): Slightly duller, fainter streaks. May just be worn examples of *suffusus*? **VOICE** Song is high *rit rit piwee-you wee-ee-ee* (*you* higher; short tripping introductory notes). Rapid harsh chattering, and odd thin high notes from flocks. **HABITAT** Scrub, grass, bamboo thickets; up to 1,500 m. **RANGE** Fc **R** W(north),E Tonkin.

6 BROWN-WINGED PARROTBILL *P.brunneus* c.12–13 cm
(a) **Adult** *brunneus*: Dull brown wings, more vinous throat and upper breast with darker chestnut streaks. **HABITAT** Thickets and grass; 1,525–2,375 m. **RANGE** Fc **R** N(east),C(east) Myanmar.

7 ASHY-THROATED PARROTBILL *P.alphonsianus* 12.5–13 cm
(a) **Adult** *yunnanensis*: Brownish-grey head- and neck-side, whitish throat and breast with faint greyish streaks. **VOICE** Flock calls similar to Vinous-throated. **HABITAT** Grass and thickets; 1,100–1,500 m. **RANGE** Lfc **R** north W Tonkin.

8 FULVOUS PARROTBILL *P. fulvifrons* 12–12.5 cm
(a) **Adult** *albifacies*: Rather uniform buff head/breast, dark brownish-grey lateral crown-stripes. **Juvenile**: Duller, particularly below. **VOICE** Thin high *si-si'ssuuu-juuu* (*ssuuu* rising, *juuu* harsh) or *si-si-sissu-suu-u* (thin end-notes). **HABITAT** Bamboo, edge of broadleaved evergreen forest; 2,895–3,660 m, sometimes to 2,440 m in winter. **RANGE** Un **R** N Myanmar.

9 BLACK-THROATED PARROTBILL *P.nipalensis* 11.5 cm
(a) **Adult** *feae*: Black crown-stripes/throat, grey head-side/breast, thin rufous supercilium. (b) **Adult** *ripponi* (W Myanmar): Broader crown-stripes, mostly white supercilium/eyering, rufous-buff breast. (c) **Adult** *beaulieui* (N Indochina, ? NE Thailand): Shorter, broader crown-stripes, white supercilium, black ear-coverts, greyish and buff breast. (d) **Adult** *kamoli* (S Laos, C Annam): As *beaulieui* but rufous rear supercilium, grey rear ear-coverts, thin crown-stripes. **Other subspecies** *P.n.poliotis* (N Myanmar): Head differs as *ripponi*, also blacker throat. **VOICE** Song is very thin, steadily rising *ssu-ssu-si-si*. Rapid thin short notes. **HABITAT** Bamboo, broadleaved evergreen forest; 1,200–2,650 m, locally 980 m N Myanmar. **RANGE** Un **R** W,N,E(south),S(east) Myanmar, W,NW,NE Thailand, N,C,east S Laos, N,southern C Annam.

10 GOLDEN PARROTBILL *P.verreauxi* 11.5 cm
(a) **Adult** *craddocki*: No crown-stripes, warm buff ear-coverts, black throat. **VOICE** Thin high *ssii-ssii-ssu-ssii*. Flocks utter rattling *trr'r, trrr'it* and shorter, higher notes. **HABITAT** Bamboo, edge of broadleaved evergreen forest; 1,500–2,590 m. **RANGE** Un/lc **R** extreme E Myanmar, northern N Laos, W,E Tonkin.

11 SHORT-TAILED PARROTBILL *P.davidianus* 10 cm
(a) **Adult** *thompsoni*: Short tail, thick bill, chestnut head, black throat. **Other subspecies** *tonkinensis* (north Vietnam). **VOICE** Song is thin, high, rapid, rising whistled *ih'ih'ih'ih'ih'ih*. Low twittering. **HABITAT** Bamboo and grass in/near broadleaved evergreen forest; 50–1,200 m. **RANGE** Un/lo **R** E Myanmar, NW,NE Thailand, N Laos, E Tonkin, N Annam.

12 LESSER RUFOUS-HEADED PARROTBILL *Paradoxornis atrosuperciliaris* 15 cm
(a) **Adult** *atrosuperciliaris*: Buffy-rufous peaked head, black eyebrow, buffish-white below. **VOICE** Long series of sharp chipping *tik, chit* and *tsu* notes etc. Low rapid chattering with harsher series of *chut* or *chip* notes. **HABITAT** Bamboo in/near broadleaved evergreen forest; 550–2,000 m, locally to 215 m in Myanmar. **RANGE** Un **R** N,S(east) Myanmar, NW Thailand, N,C Laos, W,E Tonkin.

13 GREATER RUFOUS-HEADED PARROTBILL *P.ruficeps* 19 cm
(a) **Adult** *bakeri*: Rounder head than Lesser, more rufous face, no black eyebrow. **Juvenile**: Paler crown/head-side, more rufescent above. **Other subspecies** *P.r.magnirostris* (E Tonkin). **VOICE** Song is loud jolly *wup chip wi-wiwii wi-wuuuuu* (quick introductory notes). Spluttering *trrrrrrrrrrrt..*; twangy *jhaowh*. **HABITAT & BEHAVIOUR** Bamboo in/near broadleaved evergreen forest; 500–1,850 m. Often with White-hooded Babbler. **RANGE** Sc/un **R** N,E,S(east) Myanmar, N Laos, E Tonkin.

PLATE 131 LARKS & ACCENTORS

1 AUSTRALASIAN BUSHLARK *Mirafra javanica* 14–15 cm (**a**) **Adult** *williamsoni*: Weak streaks on warm breast, all-whitish outermost tail feathers. (**b**) **Juvenile**: Less clearly streaked above, crown darker, with pale scaling, breast paler with diffuse streaking. **VOICE** Song recalls Oriental Skylark, but slower/less continuous. Sharp *pitsi pitsi pitsipipipipi* in alarm. **HABITAT & BEHAVIOUR** Short grassland with bushes, rice-paddy stubble; up to 915 m. Sings from perch or in song-flight. **RANGE** Un/lc **R** C,E Myanmar, north Tenasserim, W,NW,NE,C Thailand, Cambodia, N,C Laos, C,S Annam, Cochinchina.

2 BENGAL BUSHLARK *Mirafra assamica* 15–16 cm (**a**) **Adult**: Larger than Burmese, much greyer above, less boldly streaked, richer buff belly. (**b**) **Juvenile**: Greyer and less boldly patterned above than Burmese, narrower (less bold/spot-like) breast markings (less bold than illustrated). **VOICE** Sings with monotonous thin, slightly hoarse, squeaky *uu-eez* notes; or slow jingle of thin notes and mimicry. Calls with thin, rather explosive *tzrep-tzi'tzee'tzee'tzee* or *tzep-tzi'tzi'tzi'tzu'tz-i'tzi'tzu* etc. **HABITAT & BEHAVIOUR** Dry scrub, edge of open forest, cultivation. First song typically delivered during display-flight; second from ground or low perch. **RANGE** Co **R** SW Myanmar.

3 BURMESE BUSHLARK *Mirafra microptera* 14 cm (**a**) **Adult**: Warmer and more boldly streaked above than Indochinese, breast more spotted. **VOICE** Three songs. (1) 3–10 short, high, squeaky, jingling notes, at almost explosive pace. (2) Similar but much longer, with more phrases; only during high song-flight and leading (during descent) to type 3. (3) Rather high *tsi'tsi'tsiu'tsui'tsuu'tsi'ee'tsuu'tsi'eee'tsuu't-si'eee'tsi'tsuu'tsiu* etc. High *beep* notes, and *tsi-tsi-tsi-tsi-tsi-tsi...* **HABITAT & BEHAVIOUR** Scrubby semi-desert, cultivation; up to 1,310 m. Often perches on trees/telephone wires etc. First song usually from elevated perch, third during short display-flight. **RANGE** Co **R** C,E(west),S(north) Myanmar.

4 INDOCHINESE BUSHLARK *Mirafra marionae* 14–15 cm (**a**) **Adult**: Heavier-marked breast than Australasian, no white on tail. (**b**) **Juvenile**: Scaled buff above, breast-streaks more diffuse. **VOICE** Song is thin *tzu'eeez'eezu-eeez'eezu-eeez'eezu-eeez'eezu-eeez'eezu-eeez'-eeez' eez'piz'piz-eez'piz'piz-eeez'piz'piz-eeez'piz'piz-eeez'piz'piz-tzueeez'piz'piz-tzueeez'piz'piz-tzueeez'piz'piz-tzueee z pizeeeu-pizeeeu-pizeeeu-pizeeeu-pizeeeu...* Thin rattling *tirrrrrrrr..*, hammering *tzet-tzet-tzet-tzet-tzet...* **HABITAT & BEHAVIOUR** Dry scrubby areas, edge of open forest, cultivation; up to 900 m. Flies short distance when flushed. Sings from ground or elevated perch, sometimes short parachuting song-flight. **RANGE** Lc **R** E Myanmar, Tenasserim, Thailand (except S), Cambodia, Laos, N,C,S Annam, Cochinchina.

5 GREATER SHORT-TOED LARK *Calandrella brachydactyla* 16 cm (**a**) **Adult** *dukhunensis*: Patch on breast-side. From Asian also by browner, streakier upperparts, longer tertials. **VOICE** Calls (usually in flight) with dry *trrrip*, *triep* or *prrit*, often in combination with short soft *dju* or *djyp* notes: *trriep-dju* etc. **HABITAT** Dry open habitats; lowlands. **RANGE** Ra **WV/V** N,S Myanmar.

6 ASIAN SHORT-TOED LARK *Calandrella cheleensis* 16 cm (**a**) **Adult** *kukunoorensis*: Paler/greyer above than Greater, fine breast-streaks. Primaries protrude beyond tertials. Larger, more buffish above, more distinctly streaked and shorter-billed than Sand Lark. **VOICE** Calls with dry rolling *trrrrt* or *prrrt-up*. **HABITAT** Dry open lowland areas. **RANGE** V N Myanmar, E Tonkin.

7 SAND LARK *Calandrella raytal* 14 cm (**a**) **Adult** *raytal*: Small, short-tailed, very pale greyish above, white below, slender bill, fine breast-streaks. (**b**) **Juvenile**: Whitish tips and dark subterminal markings above. **VOICE** Sings with short bursts of disjointed tinkling notes (often with mimicry), usually in flight. Calls with low dry *chrrru*, *chrrt chu* and *chirrru* etc. **HABITAT** Dry banks/sand-bars along larger rivers, rarely dry open areas; lowlands. **RANGE** Co **R** C,S Myanmar.

8 ORIENTAL SKYLARK *Alauda gulgula* 16.5–18 cm (**a**) **Adult** *herberti*: Slender bill, crest, dark streaks above/on breast, buffy-whitish below. (**b**) **Juvenile**: Paler above with narrow whitish fringing, whitish covert-tips, diffuse breast-streaks. (**c**) **Adult** *inopinata* (**VS**): More contrasting streaks above, whiter below, warmer wing-fringing. **Other subspecies** *A.g.vernayi* (W,N Myanmar): Broader, blacker markings above. *A.g.gulgula* (rest of Myanmar): Less boldly marked above than *herberti*. *A.g.coelivox* (Vietnam). **VOICE** Incessant high sweet song (delivered in song-flight). Dry twangy *chizz*, *baz baz* and *baz-terrr* etc. **HABITAT** Various open habitats, cultivation; up to 2,805 m. **RANGE** Un/fc **R** (except southern Tenasserim, S Thailand, Pen Malaysia, Singapore, C,S laos, W Tonkin). Un **WV** N,E Myanmar.

9 ALPINE ACCENTOR *Prunella collaris* 18 cm (**a**) **Adult** *nipalensis*: Robust; brownish-grey head and breast, chestnut flank-streaks, black-and-white throat-bars. (**b**) **Juvenile**: Duller/plainer; brownish flank-streaks. **VOICE** Song is varied chattering warble. Calls with clear, rippling *truiririp* and *turrr*, shorter *zuju* and *tju-tju-tju* etc. **HABITAT** Rocky places, stony gullies, sparsely vegetated open areas; above 2,440 m. **RANGE** Rc (status?) N Myanmar.

10 RUFOUS-BREASTED ACCENTOR *Prunella strophiata* 15 cm (**a**) **Adult** *strophiata*: Pipit-like but with orange-rufous supercilium/breast, dark face, rufous-buff flanks. (**b**) **Juvenile**: No orange-rufous. From pipits by small size, streaked throat, rufescent wing-fringing. **VOICE** Melodious song recalls Winter Wren, but less shrill and vehement, with some pretty trills and warbling. Calls with penetrating rattling *trrrrrt* and *trrr'rit*. **HABITAT** Forest edge, scrub and thickets, borders of cultivation; 2,135–2,590 m. **RANGE** Rc (status?) N Myanmar.

11 MAROON-BACKED ACCENTOR *P.immaculata* 16.5 cm (**a**) **Adult**: Dark grey head, whitish eyes, dark chestnut scapulars and wings with grey greater coverts, brownish-olive above, dull grey below with rufescent flanks/vent. (**b**) **Juvenile**: Olive-greyish head, dark-streaked warm brownish above, whitish-buff below with dark brown streaks. **VOICE** Calls with feeble, thin, metallic *tzip* and *zieh-dzit*. **HABITAT** Forest edge, scrub; 1,675–2,135 m. **RANGE** Rc (status?) N Myanmar.

PLATE 132 FLOWERPECKERS

1 YELLOW-BREASTED FLOWERPECKER *Prionochilus maculatus* 10 cm
(a) **Adult** *septentrionalis*: Greenish above, with orange crown-patch, yellowish below with broad olive-green streaks. **Juvenile**: No crown-patch, pinkish bill with darker culmen, paler yellow below with fainter streaks. **Other subspecies** *P.m.oblitus* (Pen Malaysia, Singapore). **VOICE** Sibilant high silvery *tisi-sisit*. **HABITAT** Lower/middle storey of broadleaved evergreen forest; up to 1,600 m. **RANGE** Co **R** south Tenasserim, W(south),S Thailand, Pen Malaysia; formerly Singapore.

2 CRIMSON-BREASTED FLOWERPECKER *P.percussus* 10 cm
(a) **Male** *ignicapilla*: Slaty-blue above, bright yellow below, red crown-/breast-patches, white submoustachial. (b) **Female**: Dull orange crown-patch, greyish-olive below with yellow centre, whitish submoustachial. (c) **Juvenile**: Duller and more uniform olive than female, bill mostly pinkish. **VOICE** Sharp high *teez tit-tit* (*teez* stressed), and buzzy *whit-whit* or *vit-vit*. **HABITAT** Broadleaved evergreen forest, forest edge; up to 1,200 m. **RANGE** Un/fc **R** south Tenasserim, S Thailand, Pen Malaysia.

3 SCARLET-BREASTED FLOWERPECKER *P.thoracicus* 10 cm
(a) **Male**: Black head/breast with red patches, yellowish body, black wings/tail. (b) **Female**: Greyish head, whitish throat/submoustachial, yellowish below, greyish-mottled reddish-orange breast-wash. (c) **Juvenile**: More greyish-olive below than female. **HABITAT** Broadleaved evergreen and swamp forest; up to 1,280 m. **RANGE** Ra/un **R** southern S Thailand, Pen Malaysia.

4 THICK-BILLED FLOWERPECKER *Dicaeum agile* 10 cm
(a) **Adult** *modestum*: From Brown-backed by reddish/orange eyes, malar line, greener above, paler below, darker streaks, whitish tail-tips. **Juvenile**: Bill pinker, fainter streaks. **Other subspecies** *D.a.remotum* (Pen Malaysia, Singapore). **VOICE** Thin *pseeou*. **HABITAT & BEHAVIOUR** Broadleaved evergreen forest; up to 1,500 m. Wags tail from side to side. **RANGE** Un/co **R** (except SW,W,N Myanmar, Singapore, W,E Tonkin). Sc **NBV** Singapore.

5 BROWN-BACKED FLOWERPECKER *D.everetti* 10 cm
(a) **Adult** *sordidum*: Earth-brown above, pale buffy-brown below with faint streaks, pale yellowish eye. **HABITAT** Edge of lowland broadleaved evergreen/swamp forest. **RANGE** R **R** Pen Malaysia.

6 YELLOW-VENTED FLOWERPECKER *D.chrysorrheum* 10 cm
(a) **Adult** *chrysochlore*: Narrow, slightly curved bill, whitish loral stripe, white below with bold blackish streaks, orange-yellow undertail-coverts; yellowish-olive above. **Juvenile**: Greyer below with duller streaks, pale yellow undertail-coverts. **Other subspecies** *D.c.chrysorrheum* (S Thailand southwards). **VOICE** Short harsh *dzeep*. **HABITAT** Broadleaved forest, gardens; up to 1,100 m. **RANGE** Fc **R** throughout; ra Singapore.

7 YELLOW-BELLIED FLOWERPECKER *D.melanoxanthum* 13 cm
(a) **Male**: Large; upper body black with white throat/ breast-centre, rest of underparts yellow. (b) **Female**: Pattern like male but dull olive-greyish head/breast-sides, dull greyish-brown above, duller/paler belly. **Juvenile male**: Similar to female but brighter

yellow below, blue-black cast to mantle and back. **VOICE** Agitated *zit* notes. **HABITAT & BEHAVIOUR** Broadleaved evergreen forest; 1,200–2,500 m. Often sits upright on exposed perch; sallies for insects. **RANGE** Sc/un **R** W,E Myanmar, NW,north-west NE Thailand, N Laos, W Tonkin.

8 ORANGE-BELLIED FLOWERPECKER *D.trigonostigma* 9 cm
(a) **Male** *rubropygium*: Slaty-blue crown/nape/wings/tail, grey throat/upper breast, orange lower breast/mantle/back, yellower uppertail-coverts/vent. (b) **Female**: Slender, slightly curved bill, plain olive head, orange-yellow rump, greyish throat/upper breast, dull yellow belly-centre/vent. **Juvenile**: As female but throat/breast more olive. **Other subspecies** *D.t.trigonostigma* (south of c.8°30'N). **VOICE** Song is high, slightly descending *tsi-si-si-si-sew*. Harsh *dzip*. **HABITAT** Edge of broadleaved evergreen forest, gardens, cultivation; up to 915 m, locally 1,525 m. **RANGE** Fc/co **R** SW,S,E(south) Myanmar, Tenasserim, W(south),S Thailand, Pen Malaysia, Singapore.

9 PALE-BILLED FLOWERPECKER *D.erythrorynchos* 8.5 cm
(a) **Adult** *erythrorynchos*: Like Plain but bill pinkish. **Juvenile**: Greyer; yellowish bill. **VOICE** Sharp *chik* and *pseep* notes. **HABITAT** Open lowland broadleaved forest, plantations, gardens. **RANGE** Fc **R** SW,W Myanmar.

10 PLAIN FLOWERPECKER *Dicaeum concolor* 8.5 cm
(a) **Adult** *olivaceum*: Greenish-olive above, pale olive-greyish below, cream belly-centre (sometimes throat), dark bill, quite pale head-sides. (b) **Juvenile**: Bill pinkish with darker culmen. **Other subspecies** *D.c.borneanum* (Pen Malaysia). **VOICE** Sings with high *tsit tsi-si-si-si-si*. Monotonous *tu-wit tu-wit tu-wit...* **HABITAT** Open broadleaved forest; up to 1,700 m. **RANGE** Fc **R** (except S Thailand, Cochinchina); formerly Singapore.

11 FIRE-BREASTED FLOWERPECKER *D.ignipectus* 8.5 cm
(a) **Male** *ignipectus*: Dark greenish-blue above, buffish below, red breast-patch and black line, black head-/breast-sides. (b) **Female**: Dark bill, greenish-olive upperparts and head-sides, uniform buffish below with olive-tinged flanks. **Juvenile**: Paler-based lower mandible, no buff below, appears greyish across breast, yellower belly-centre. (c) **Male** *cambodianum* (SE Thailand, western Cambodia): No red breast-patch. **Other subspecies** *D.i.dolichorhynchum* (S Thailand, Pen Malaysia). **VOICE** Song is high shrill *tissit tissit tissit tissit..* or *titty-titty-titty-titty...* Sharp *dik* or *chip* notes. **HABITAT** Broadleaved evergreen forest; 450–2,565 m. **RANGE** Co **R** (except SW Myanmar, C Thailand, Cochinchina).

12 SCARLET-BACKED FLOWERPECKER *Dicaeum cruentatum* 8.5 cm
(a) **Male** *cruentatum*: Red above, blackish head-/breast-sides, blue-blackish wings. (b) **Female**: Bright red rump and uppertail-coverts, pale below. (c) **Juvenile**: Mostly red-pink- based lower mandible, uniform above with orange-tinged uppertail-coverts, more uniform greyish throat/breast. **VOICE** Song is thin *tissit tissit tissit...* Hard metallic *tip* and thin metallic *tizz* and *tsi* notes. **HABITAT** Open forests, secondary growth, parks, gardens etc.; up to 1,220 m. **RANGE** Co **R** throughout.

PLATE 133 SUNBIRDS

1 PURPLE-THROATED SUNBIRD *Nectarinia sperata* 10 cm (a) **Male** *brasiliana*: Small, dark: green crown, purple throat, deep red belly. (b) **Female**: Dull olive above, plain head, dull yellow below, olivey throat/breast. **Other subspecies** *N.s.emmae* (Indochina). **voice** Sings with high, discordant *psweet, psit-it* and *trr'rr* notes. Also high *ti-swit titwitwitwitwitit..* and *si-si-si-si-si-si..* etc. **habitat** Open broadleaved evergreen forest, secondary growth, gardens; up to 1,200 m. **range** Un/fc **R** SW,S Myanmar, Tenasserim, C,NE,SE,S Thailand, Pen Malaysia, Singapore, Cambodia, S Laos, S Annam, Cochinchina.

2 COPPER-THROATED SUNBIRD *N.calcostetha* 14 cm (a) **Male**: Dark; longish tail, green crown/shoulder/uppertail-coverts, copper-red throat. (b) **Female**: Greyish head, white throat, white outertail-tips. **habitat** Mangroves, coastal scrub, rarely away from coast. Up to 915 m. **range** Un/lc **R** S Tenasserim, SE,S Thailand, Pen Malaysia, Singapore, Cambodia, Cochinchina.

3 PURPLE SUNBIRD *Nectarinia asiatica* 10.5–11.5 cm (a) **Male** *intermedia*: Plain dark bluish/purplish. (b) **Male eclipse**: Dark blue on coverts, darker wings than Olive-backed. (c) **Female**: Pale yellow/whitish below, less white on tail than Olive-backed. **Juvenile**: All-yellow below. **voice** Descending *swee-swee-swee swit zizi-zizi* song. Buzzing *zit*, high *swee*. **habitat** Deciduous woodland, bushy semi-desert, coastal scrub, gardens, cultivation; up to 1,525 m. **range** Co **R** Myanmar, Thailand (except SE,S), Cambodia, Laos, C,S Annam, Cochinchina (lo).

4 MRS GOULD'S SUNBIRD *Aethopyga gouldiae* 11–16.5 cm (a) **Male** *dabryii*: Red above/on breast, yellow rump/belly. **Male eclipse**: As female but red on breast, yellow belly. (b) **Female**: Rump-band/belly brighter than Black-throated. (c) **Male** *annamensis* (S Indochina): Yellow breast, blue rump. (d) **Female**: Greyish hood, indistinct yellowish rump. **Juvenile**: Like female; male yellower below. **Other subspecies** *A.g.isolata* (W Myanmar): Male's breast yellow. **voice** Sings with monotonous high *twit* or *tzip* notes. Lisping *squeeeeee*. **habitat** Broadleaved evergreen forest, secondary growth; 1,000–2,565 m. **range** Co **R** Myanmar (except SW), Laos, W,E Tonkin, southern C Annam. Fc **WV** W(lo),NW,NE Thailand. **Rc** (status?) N Annam.

5 GREEN-TAILED SUNBIRD *A.nipalensis* 11–13.5 cm (a) **Male** *koelzi* (N,E Myanmar, W Tonkin): Green crown/throat and tail, dark red mantle, red-streaked yellow breast. (b) **Female**: White undertail-tips, no rump-band. Yellowish belly. **Juvenile**: As female but squarer tail with less white; male's breast may be washed orange. (c) **Male** *karensis* (south E Myanmar): Yellow breast, little red above. (d) **Female**: Like Mrs Gould's (*annamensis*) but greener above, less yellow rump, more olive-green breast, graduated tail. **Other subspecies** *A.g.angkanensis* (NW Thailand): Male has scarlet breast-patch. *A.n.victoriae* (W Myanmar); *australis* (S Thailand); *blanci* (south-east N Laos); *ezrai* (C,S Annam). **voice** Sings with high *wit-iritz wit-iri wit-iritz wit-iritz wit-iri wit-iritz...* High *chit* notes. **habitat** Broadleaved evergreen forest, secondary growth; 1,400–2,745 m, down to 1,140 m in winter (above 915 m S Thailand). **range** Lo **R** W,N,E,S(east) Myanmar, W,NW,S Thailand, Laos, W Tonkin, N,C,S Annam.

6 FORK-TAILED SUNBIRD *Aethopyga christinae* 10–12 cm (a) **Male** *latouchii*: Green crown/tail, olive mantle, yellow rump-band, dark crimson throat/upper breast. (b) **Female**: Like Crimson but crown greyish, belly/vent yellowish (paler than breast), white undertail-tips. **voice** Calls with sharp, metallic *tswit* or *twis* notes and nervous *wi'wi'wi'wi'wi'i'i'i* and *ts-wi'i'i'i'i'i'i'i*. **habitat** Broadleaved evergreen/semi-evergreen forest, secondary growth; up to 1,400 m. **range** Fc **R** C,S(east) Laos, W,E Tonkin, N,C,S Annam, north Cochinchina.

7 BLACK-THROATED SUNBIRD *A.saturata* 11–15 cm (a) **Male** *petersi*: Black throat/upper breast, whitish-yellow belly/rump. (b) **Female**: Greyer than Mrs Gould's, paler/narrower rump-band. (c) **Male** *johnsi* (S Annam): Redder mantle, reddish breast. (d) **Male** *assamensis* (W,N Myanmar): Black breast, grey belly. **Other subspecies** *wrayi* (Pen Malaysia) and *anomala* (S Thailand): Between *petersi/assamensis*, latter without rump-band. *A.s.galenae* (southern NW Thailand); *sanguinipectus* (south E,east S Myanmar, Tenasserim; *ochra* (S Laos, C Annam); *cambodiana* (south-west Cambodia). **voice** Sings with uneven sharp *swi*, *tis* and *tsi* notes and metallic trilled *swi'it'it'it'it'it* etc. High thin *tit* and *tiss-it* etc. **habitat** Broadleaved evergreen forest, forest edge; 200–1,700 m. **range** Un/co **R** W,N,C(east),E,S(east) Myanmar, Tenasserim, Thailand (except C), Pen Malaysia, Indochina (except Cochinchina).

8 CRIMSON SUNBIRD *Aethopyga siparaja* 11–13.5 cm (a) **Male** *seheriae*: Red hood/mantle, dark green crown/tail, greyish belly. (b) **Male eclipse**: Like female but throat/breast red. (c) **Female**: Dull olive-coloured, slightly yellower below; no paler rump-band or white on tail. **Juvenile**: Like female; males with red-washed throat/breast. **Other subspecies** *A.s.siparaja* (south of c.6°30'N), *tonkinensis* (E Tonkin), *mangini* (south-east NE Thailand, southern Indochina), *cara* (C,S,E[south] Myanmar to NW[east],C,NE,SE Thailand), *trangensis* (W[south],S Thailand), *insularis* (Phu Quoc Is, Cochinchina). **voice** Sings with rapid, tripping, sharp *tsip-it-sip-it-sit* etc. Sharp *whit* and *wit-it*. **habitat** Broadleaved forest, secondary growth, gardens; up to 1,370 m. **range** Co **R** (except C Thailand). Mostly coastal Pen Malaysia, Singapore.

9 TEMMINCK'S SUNBIRD *A.temminckii* 10–12.5 cm (a) **Male** *temminckii*: Like Crimson but head-sides, nape, mantle, wing-coverts, throat, breast and tail scarlet. (b) **Female**: Like Crimson but yellowish-olive below, wings and tail fringed reddish-rufous. **voice** Song is rhythmic *tit-it tit-it tit-it tit-it...* **habitat** Broadleaved evergreen forest, secondary growth; up to 1,525 m. **range** Sc/fc **R** S Thailand, Pen Malaysia.

10 FIRE-TAILED SUNBIRD *A.ignicauda* 11.5–19 cm (a) **Male** *ignicauda*: Very long red tail. **Male eclipse**: As female but red on uppertail-coverts/tail-side. (b) **Female**: As Green-tailed but yellower rump, squarer plain tail. **Other subspecies** *A.i.flavescens* (W Myanmar). **voice** Sings with high *it'i'tit-tit'tut'tutututut* etc. **habitat** Broadleaved evergreen and coniferous forest, secondary growth; 2,745–3,960 m, to 1,200 m, locally 700 m in winter. **range** Co **R** W,N Myanmar. **V** C Myanmar, NW Thailand.

PLATE 134 SUNBIRDS & SPIDERHUNTERS

1 PLAIN SUNBIRD *Anthreptes simplex* 13 cm
(a) **Adult**: Shortish/straightish bill, dark blue-green forehead. Greyish throat/breast. (b) **Female**: Olive forehead. HABITAT & BEHAVIOUR Middle storey of broadleaved evergreen forest, rarely mangroves; up to 915 m. Slow, methodical. RANGE Un/fc **R** south Tenasserim, W(south),S Thailand, Pen Malaysia, Singapore (sc).

2 BROWN-THROATED SUNBIRD *A.malacensis* 14 cm
(a) **Male** *malacensis*: Stocky; green and purple above, brownish head-side/throat. (b) **Female**: Straightish bill, yellow below, yellowish eyering. VOICE Song is monotonous ***wrick-wrick-wrick wrah wrick-wrick-wrick wrick-wrick wrah...*** Sharp ***too-wit.*** HABITAT Forest edge, mangroves, swamp forest, coastal scrub, plantations etc.; lowlands. RANGE Co **R** (mostly coastal) SW,S Myanmar, Tenasserim, Thailand (except NW,NE), Pen Malaysia, Singapore, Cambodia, N(south),S Laos, S Annam, Cochinchina.

3 RED-THROATED SUNBIRD *A.rhodolaema* 12.5–13 cm
(a) **Male**: Pale brick-red throat, maroon-red head-side, mostly chestnut-maroon coverts. (b) **Female**: Greyish-tinged eyering, greener breast-sides than Brown-throated, duller below, sometimes orange-tinged throat/breast. VOICE Rising high ***uu'is*** or ***tsu-u'i.*** HABITAT Broadleaved evergreen forest, forest edge; to 790 m. RANGE Sc/un **R** south Tenasserim, S Thailand, Pen Malaysia.

4 RUBY-CHEEKED SUNBIRD *A.singalensis* 10.5–11 cm
(a) **Male** *assamensis*: Green above, orangey throat/breast. (b) **Female**: Greenish-olive above. **Juvenile**: Yellower below than female. **Other subspecies** *A.s.koratensis* (NE,SE Thailand, Indochina): Orange-rufous sharply demarcated. *A.s.singalensis* (Pen Malaysia, Singapore); *internotus* (south-west Thailand, ? Tenasserim); *interpositus* (S Thailand). VOICE Song is high ***switi-ti-chi-chu tusi-tit swit-swit switi-ti-chi-chu...*** HABITAT Broadleaved forest, mangroves; up to 1,370 m. RANGE Co **R** (except E Myanmar, C Thailand, Singapore). **Rc** (status?) Singapore.

5 PURPLE-NAPED SUNBIRD *Hypogramma hypogrammicum* 14 cm
(a) **Male** *H.b.lisettae*: Purple-blue on nape/rump/uppertail-coverts, streaked below. (b) **Female**: No purple-blue. **Other subspecies** *H.b.nuchale* (south of c.12°N): Bluer patches. *H.b. mariae* (Cochinchina). VOICE Song is tinkling trill mixed with call notes. High ***chip*** or ***tchu*** notes. HABITAT Lower storey of broadleaved evergreen forest; up to 1,160 m. RANGE Un/fc **R** (except SW,W,S,E Myanmar, C,NE,SE Thailand, Singapore).

6 PURPLE-RUMPED SUNBIRD *Nectarinia zeylonica* 11.5 cm
(a) **Male** *flaviventris*: Maroon and yellow, green crown/shoulder, purple throat/rump. (b) **Female**: Pale greyish-white throat/upper breast/flanks, shortish dark tail. **Juvenile**: As female but all yellow below. VOICE Song is twittering ***tityou tityou tityou trr-r-r-tit tityou...*** High ***ptsee*** or ***sisisuwee***, and metallic ***chit.*** HABITAT Lowland forest edge, cultivation. RANGE Fc **R** SW Myanmar.

7 OLIVE-BACKED SUNBIRD *Nectarinia jugularis* 11.5 cm
(a) **Male** *flamaxillaris*: Blue-black forehead to breast (latter with reddish), yellow belly/vent. (b) **Male eclipse**: Blue-black gular stripe. (c) **Female**: All yellow below, white on tail. **Other**

subspecies *N.j.ornata* (Pen Malaysia): Yellower, no reddish on male's breast. *N.j.rhizophorae* (N Vietnam): Whitish belly. *N.j.andamanica* (Coco Is, S Myanmar). VOICE Sings with thin ***tswi-tswit-titititit; tswi-switswitswitswitswit; tuit-tuittuittuit; tswit-tswit-tswit-tswit*** etc. Rising ***sweet.*** HABITAT Open forest, mangroves, gardens; up to 915 m. RANGE Co **R** (except N Myanmar).

8 LITTLE SPIDERHUNTER *Arachnothera longirostra* 16 cm
(a) **Adult** *longirostra*: Slaty head, whitish around eye/on throat. **Juvenile**: Throat yellowish-olive. **Other subspecies** *A.l.sordida* (east NW Thailand to N Indochina); *pallida* (SE Thailand, Cambodia); *cinereicollis* (S Thailand southward). VOICE Monotonous ***wit-wit-wit-wit-wit-wit..*** song. Sharp, abrasive ***itch*** or ***chit.*** HABITAT Broadleaved evergreen/semi-evergreen forest, cultivation; up to 1,670 m. RANGE Co **R** (except C Thailand).

9 THICK-BILLED SPIDERHUNTER *A.crassirostris* 17 cm
(a) **Adult**: Greyish-olive throat/upper breast, yellowish around eye. VOICE Song is monotonous ***whit whit whit whit whit...*** Chattering ***chit*** notes and nervous ***ut-u-it-it-it-it-it-it.*** HABITAT Broadleaved evergreen forest, forest edge; up to 1,220 m. RANGE Un **R** S Thailand, Pen Malaysia. **Rc** (status?) Singapore.

10 LONG-BILLED SPIDERHUNTER *A.robusta* 21.5–22 cm
(a) **Adult** *robusta*: Very long bill, plain head, streaked throat/breast. **Juvenile**: No streaks. VOICE Series of loud, deepish ***chut*** or ***chit*** notes. HABITAT Broadleaved evergreen forest; up to 1,280 m. RANGE Sc/un **R** south S Thailand, Pen Malaysia.

11 SPECTACLED SPIDERHUNTER *A.flavigaster* 21.5–22 cm
(a) **Adult** Large shortish, thick broad-based bill, broad yellow eyering, prominent yellow ear-patch. VOICE Loud, rather deep ***chit'it*** or ***chut'ut.*** HABITAT Broadleaved evergreen forest, forest edge, secondary growth; up to 610 m. RANGE Fc/co **R** W(south),S Thailand, Pen Malaysia; formerly Singapore.

12 YELLOW-EARED SPIDERHUNTER *A.chrysogenys* 18 cm
(a) **Adult** *chrysogenys*: Smaller than Spectacled, slenderer bill, thin eyering, drooping splayed ear-patch. **Juvenile**: Smaller/no ear-patch. VOICE Harsh ***tchick.*** HABITAT Broadleaved evergreen forest, secondary growth; up to 1,830 m. RANGE Fc/co **R** S Tenasserim, W(south),S Thailand, Pen Malaysia. **FR** (currently?) Singapore.

13 GREY-BREASTED SPIDERHUNTER *A.affinis* 18 cm
(a) **Adult** *modesta*: Greyish below with thin streaks. **Juvenile**: No streaks. VOICE Harsh ***chititick***; chattering ***tchitititew*** and ***tchew-tew-tew*** alarm. HABITAT Broadleaved evergreen forest, secondary growth; up to 1,130 m. RANGE Fc/co **R** Tenasserim, W(south),S Thailand, Pen Malaysia; formerly Singapore.

14 STREAKED SPIDERHUNTER *A.magna* 17–20.5 cm
(a) **Adult** *musarum*: Heavily streaked. **Other subspecies** *A.m.magna* (SW,W,N Myanmar, Pen Malaysia); *aurata* (central C,S Myanmar); *pagodarum* (central Tenasserim, south W Thailand); *remota* (S Annam). VOICE Chattering song. Strident ***chit-ik.*** HABITAT Broadleaved forest; up to 1,830 m (sc in lowlands). RANGE Co **R** (except C,SE Thailand, Singapore).

PLATE 135 WAGTAILS

[handwritten: 22/1/13 Bangkok river]

1 WHITE WAGTAIL *Motacilla alba* 19 cm (a) **Male non-breeding** *leucopsis*: White head and underparts, black hindcrown, nape and isolated gorget, black above with broad white fringes to wing-coverts and tertials, and white outertail feathers. (b) **Male breeding**: Black gorget extends up to lower throat and joins black of mantle. (c) **Female non-breeding**: Slaty-grey above, narrower gorget. (d) **Juvenile**: Like female but crown and nape grey, gorget more diffuse. (e) **Male non-breeding** *alboides* (only B race; VS C,S Myanmar, Tenasserim, NW Thailand, Indochina): Black ear-coverts and neck-sides join broader gorget, less white on forehead (supercilium well defined). (f) **Male breeding**: All-black throat. (g) **Female non-breeding**: Greyer above than male. (h) **Juvenile**: Appears more like very washed-out adult than *leucopsis*. (i) **Male non-breeding** *personata* (VS N Myanmar): Black hood with white forecrown, eyering and upper throat, grey above. (j) **Male breeding**: All-black throat. (k) **Female non-breeding**: Greyer hindcrown/nape than male. (l) **Male non-breeding** *baicalensis* (VS Myanmar [except SW,W], NW,NE Thailand): Grey above, larger black gorget. (m) **Female non-breeding**: Crown duller than male, much paler grey above than *leucopsis* (n) **Male non-breeding** *ocularis* (VS N,C,S Myanmar, NW,NE,C Thailand, Indochina, Pen Malaysia): Like *baicalensis* but has black eyestripe. (o) **Male breeding**: Black lower throat and upper breast. (p) **Female non-breeding**: Black of crown/nape greyer and less contrasting than male. (q) **Male non-breeding** *lugens* (rc SE Thailand, E Tonkin): Like *ocularis* but blackish above, wing-coverts look all-white. (r) **Male breeding**: More solid black areas. (s) **Female non-breeding**: Less black but differs from *ocularis* in similar way to male. VOICE Simple twittering and chattering song. Calls with clear harsh *tsli-vitt*. HABITAT Various open habitats, often near water; up to 2,000 m. RANGE Un **R/BV** N Myanmar, N Laos, W,E Tonkin. Co **WV/PM** (except S Thailand, Singapore); ra Pen Malaysia. V S Thailand, Singapore.

[handwritten: Laos + Luang Prabang]

2 MEKONG WAGTAIL *Motacilla samveasnae* 19 cm (a) **Male**: Black forehead, broad white supercilium, white throat and enclosed neck-patch. (b) **Female**: Distinctly paler and greyer above. (c) **Juvenile**: Washed-out; less distinct head pattern, pale throat with dark malar stripe, smudgy dark breast. VOICE Short sharp *dzeer* (sometimes doubled) flight-call; thin soft *tsip*, *tseeup* and *tsriu* etc. HABITAT Sandy and rocky banks and islands with bushland, grass etc., in Mekong R and its tributaries. RANGE Lo **R** north-east Cambodia, S Laos, north-west S Annam. Rc (status?) south-east NE Thailand.

3 CITRINE WAGTAIL *Motacilla citreola* 18–19 cm (a) **Male breeding** *citreola*: All-yellow head and underparts, black nuchal band, grey mantle, back and rump. (b) **Male non-breeding/female**: Resembles female Yellow but yellow lores, supercilium, throat and breast, grey above, whitish undertail-coverts; ear-coverts have dark border and paler centre (often washed yellow) and are encircled by yellow. Usually prominent white wing-bars. (c) **First winter**: Usual-

ly purer grey above than Yellow, supercilium goes behind ear-coverts (or slightly broken), often a blackish lateral crown-line; buff-washed forehead, pale lores, all-dark bill, usually bolder wing-bars. (d) **Male breeding** *calcarata* (SW,S,N Myanmar; NW Thailand?): Black mantle to uppertail-coverts. VOICE Song is simple repetition of sounds resembling call notes. Usually calls with harsh *dzeep* or *brrzreep*, very similar to Yellow. HABITAT Marshes, banks of lakes and larger rivers, wet cultivation; up to 450 m. RANGE Un/lc **WV** Myanmar, NW,NE,C Thailand, N Laos. **V** coastal W Thailand, Singapore, E Tonkin, Cochinchina.

4 YELLOW WAGTAIL *Motacilla flava* 18 cm (a) **Male breeding** *thunbergi* (incl. *angarensis, plexa*): Olive-green above, blue-grey head, thin whitish supercilium, yellow below with whiter throat. **Male non-breeding**: Much duller head, whiter below. Subspecific identification can be impossible. From female Grey by obvious pale fringes and tips to wing-coverts, lack of bright yellow on rump, uppertail-coverts and vent, and less pure grey above. (b) **Female**: Duller than breeding male, dull greyish- to brownish-olive above, duller and less extensive yellow below. (c) **First winter**: Like female but upperparts tend to be greyer, underparts whiter. ~~(d) **Male breeding** *macronyx* (widespread): Dark~~er bluish-slate crown and nape, darker head-sides, no supercilium, yellower lower throat. (e) **Male breeding**: *simillima* (Pen Malaysia, Singapore, E Tonkin, Cochinchina): Darker bluish-slate crown, nape and head-sides, more pronounced whitish supercilium. **Female**: Typically more prominent supercilium than *thunbergi*. (f) **Male breeding** *taivana* (widespread): Olive-green crown and head-sides, broad yellow supercilium. (g) **Female**: Broad, clear-cut, yellowish supercilium. VOICE Song is very simple, typically consisting of 2–3 scraping notes, the last usually stressed. Calls with harsh, drawn-out *chrzeep*. HABITAT & BEHAVIOUR Various open habitats, particularly near water. Roosts communally, often in large numbers. RANGE Fc/co **WV/PM** (except W Myanmar).

5 GREY WAGTAIL *Motacilla cinerea* 19 cm (a) **Male non-breeding/female** *cinerea*: Slaty-grey crown, ear-coverts and upperparts, narrow whitish supercilium, bright yellow vent. Females may show blackish throat-mottling in spring. Resembles female and non-breeding male Yellow but slatier-grey above, more uniform blackish wing-coverts, yellowish rump and uppertail-coverts; in flight white bar along base of secondaries and inner primaries. (b) **Male breeding**: Underparts all yellow with black throat and upper breast. **Juvenile**: Similar to female/non-breeding male but browner-tinged above, supercilium buff-tinged, dark mottling on breast-sides. VOICE Song is short mechanical series of sharp notes: *ziss-ziss-ziss-ziss..*, often alternated with higher *si si si siu* etc. Calls with loud disyllabic *tittick* or *tzit-tzit*, recalling White but clearly sharper and higher. HABITAT Various open habitats and open forest, often near flowing streams; up to 2,565 m. RANGE Fc/co **WV/PM** throughout.

278

PLATE 136 FOREST WAGTAIL & PIPITS

1 FOREST WAGTAIL *Dendronanthus indicus* 17–18 cm
(**a**) **Adult**: Double breast-band, strongly contrasting blackish and whitish wing. VOICE Song is intense see-sawing *dzi-chu dzi-chu dzi-chu dzi-chu...* Low metallic *pink* or *dzink-dzzt* in flight. HABITAT Open broadleaved forest, gardens etc.; up to 1,500 m. RANGE Un/lc WV (except N Myanmar, N,C Laos, W,E Tonkin, N Annam). Un/fc PM SW,S Myanmar, Thailand, Pen Malaysia, Cambodia, N,C Laos, E Tonkin, N Annam.

2 RICHARD'S PIPIT *Anthus richardi* 18–20.5 cm
(**a**) **Adult** *richardi*: Slightly longer bill/legs/tail than Blyth's, less contrasting streaks above, more pointed/less clear-cut dark median covert centres; longer, straighter, less arched hindclaw. Much larger than Paddyfield, longer bill/tail, usually more, bolder (less fine/neat) breast-streaks. (**b**) **Adult worn**: Greyer above, bolder streaking, paler below. (**c**) **First winter**: Whiter-fringed coverts than adult (like Blyth's). **Other subspecies** *A.r.sinensis* (Thailand, Indochina): Very slightly smaller, less heavily streaked above (hard to see in field). VOICE Loud, harsh *schree-ep* or *shreep* flight call. HABITAT & BEHAVIOUR Open country, grassy areas, cultivation; up to 1,830 m. Often hovers before landing (Blyth's rarely does); more upright than Blyth's. RANGE Fc WV and PM (except Pen Malaysia, Singapore); ra S Thailand. V Singapore.

3 PADDYFIELD PIPIT *Anthus rufulus* 15–16 cm
(**a**) **Adult** *rufulus*: Less well-marked above than Blyth's (crown being most obviously streaked), more rufescent below (particularly flanks), throat often buffy. Lower mandible more yellow-horn than Richard's/Blyth's. See Richard's for differences. (**b**) **Adult worn**: Differs as Richard's. (**c**) **Juvenile**: More scalloped and spotted. **Other subspecies** *A.r.malayensis* (S). **Other subspecies** *A.r.malayensis* (south of c.12°N and S Indochina). VOICE Simple repetitive *chew-ii chew-ii chew-ii chew-ii...* song. Explosive but relatively subdued *chip*, *chup* or *chwist*, usually in flight. HABITAT & BEHAVIOUR Open areas, drier cultivation; up to 1,500 m. Weaker, more fluttering flight than Richard's. Undulating and parachuting song-flights. RANGE Co R throughout.

4 BLYTH'S PIPIT *Anthus godlewskii* 17 cm
(**a**) **Adult**: Slightly shorter/more pointed bill than Richard's, squarer/bolder median covert centres; white on penultimate outertail feather usually a wedge on terminal third (mostly white on Richard's). (**b**) **First winter**: Only separable from Richard's when adult median-coverts present. VOICE Quieter than Richard's. Short *tchu*, *dju*, *chep* or *tchupp* (may be doubled), softer *chewp* or *cheep*; slightly nasal *tchii* and shriller *psheet* or *pshreu* in alarm. HABITAT Open country, dry cultivation; up to 3,050 m. RANGE Un WV W,C,S Myanmar, north Tenasserim, V NE Thailand.

5 LONG-BILLED PIPIT *Anthus similis* 20.5 cm
(**a**) **Adult** *yamethini*: Large; long bill/tail; relatively very plain/warm, outertail fringed buffish. (**b**) **Juvenile**: Pale scalloping above, more strongly streaked. VOICE Song is *ureee-tsur*. Flat *chup*, *chip* or *klup* etc., slightly lower *djup* notes. HABITAT & BEHAVIOUR Scrubby semi-desert with ravines, dry open areas/cultivation; lowlands. Bounding flight; undulating song-flight. RANGE Fc/co R W,C,S,E Myanmar.

6 TREE PIPIT *Anthus trivialis* 15–16.5 cm
(**a**) **Adult** *trivialis*?: Buffier/greyer above than Olive-backed with heavy streaks, plainer head-sides. (**b**) **Adult (worn)**: Browner above, whiter below. VOICE Flight call is short incisive *zeep* or *spzeep*, sometimes harsher *speez*. Soft *syt* alarm. HABITAT Open woodland, scrub and grass; up to 1,000 m. Grassier habitats than Olive-backed. RANGE V S Myanmar.

7 OLIVE-BACKED PIPIT *Anthus hodgsoni* 16–17 cm
(**a**) **Adult** *yunnanensis*: Rather plain greenish-olive above, broad whitish supercilium (buffier in front of eye), whitish spot and blackish patch on rear ear-coverts, bold blackish streaks/spots on buff breast/flanks. Greyer above and whiter below when worn. (**b**) **Juvenile**: Initially browner, more boldly streaked above. (**c**) **Adult** *hodgsoni* (widely **rc** N Myanmar to Indochina): Heavier streaks above/on flanks, more streaks on lower underparts. VOICE Sings with rapid high sweet slurred-together notes, mixed with shortish trills/rattles. Thin hoarse *teez* or *spiz* in flight. Quiet short *tsi tsi..* alarm. HABITAT Open forest, secondary growth, wooded cultivation; up to 2,860 m. RANGE Un **R/BV** N Myanmar; W Myanmar? Co **WV** (except S Thailand, Singapore); ra Pen Malaysia. Also **PM** SW,S Myanmar, Cambodia, E Tonkin. V S Thailand.

8 RED-THROATED PIPIT *Anthus cervinus* 15–16.5 cm
(**a**) **Adult**: Brick-/pinkish-red head-sides and throat. (**b**) **Adult variant (dull female)**: Autumn/winter birds and females tend to have less reddish on head. (**c**) **First winter**: No red. Bold dark-streaks above (including rump), pronounced whitish/pale buff 'braces', whitish wing-bars, bold blackish streaks below. VOICE Rhythmic ringing song of sharp drawn-out notes and dry buzzing sounds. Long high *pseeoo* or *pssiib* in flight. Short *chupp* alarm. HABITAT Open areas, drier cultivation, often near water; up to 1,500 m. RANGE Un/lc WV (except W Myanmar, Pen Malaysia, W Tonkin); ra Singapore. V Pen Malaysia.

9 ROSY PIPIT *Anthus roseatus* 16.5 cm
(**a**) **Adult non-breeding**: Greyer-brown above (more olive when fresh) than Red-throated, darker head-sides, bold supercilium, no obvious 'braces', more olive wing-fringing (mainly when fresh), quite plain rump/uppertail-coverts, darker bill. (**b**) **Adult breeding**: Plain vinous-pinkish supercilium/throat/breast. (**c**) **Juvenile**: Browner above, less heavy streaks below. VOICE Sings in flight: twittering *tit-tit-tit-tit-tit teedle teedle*, and fading *tsuli-tsuli-tsuli-tsuli..* or *sweet-sweet-sweet* during descent. Thin *tsip tsip tsip..* or *seep-seep...* HABITAT Open short-grass areas (often marshy), rice paddies. Up to 1,300 m (winter). RANGE Un WV SW,N (breeds at high levels?),C,E Myanmar, NW Thailand, W,E Tonkin. V north Tenasserim, C Thailand, Cochinchina.

10 BUFF-BELLIED PIPIT *Anthus rubescens* 16.5 cm
(**a**) **Adult non-breeding** *japonicus*: Plain-looking cold greyish-brown above (a little more boldly streaked when worn), quite pale lores, whitish to pale buffish base-colour below. (**b**) **Adult breeding**: Greyer above, plainer/buffier below, fine streaks on breast only. VOICE Frequently repeated thin high *tseep* or *zzeeep* in flight. HABITAT Marshy areas, wetland fringes, cultivation; up to 2,440 m. RANGE V N Myanmar, NE Thailand, W Tonkin.

PLATE 137 SPARROWS, WEAVERS & PLAIN MOUNTAIN FINCH

1 HOUSE SPARROW *Passer domesticus* 15 cm
(a) Male breeding *indicus*: Grey crown, whitish head-sides, big black bib. Chestnut from eye to nape-side, streaked mantle, brownish-grey rump/uppertail-coverts. **(b) Male non-breeding**: Browner crown, greyer mantle, pale-tipped bib and crown-/nape-sides, pale bill. **(c) Female**: Nondescript; paler supercilium/ underparts, dark streaks above, pale horn bill. **Juvenile**: Paler/plainer above than female, often bolder supercilium, paler bill. **VOICE** Sings with monotonous *chirrup cheep chirp..* etc. Calls include *chirrup*, *chissick*, shrill *chree*, and rolling *chur'r'r'it'it'it*. **HABITAT** Towns/villages, cultivation, scrub, mainly in dry areas. **RANGE** Lc/co **R** Myanmar, W,NW,NE,C Thailand, Cambodia, N,S Laos, west Cochinchina. Un **FER** Singapore.

2 RUSSET SPARROW *Passer rutilans* 13.5–14 cm
(a) Male *intensior*: Rufous-chestnut above, dingy pale yellowish to pale greyish head-sides/underparts, narrow black bib. **(b) Female**: Dark eyestripe, bold supercilium, rufescent rump, bold white wing-bar, creamy-yellowish throat with dusky central stripe. **Juvenile**: Like female but warmer above, supercilium buffier, bill paler. **First-winter male**: Duller than adult, mixed greyish-brown above, dusky bib mixed black. **VOICE** Song is simple *cheep-chirrup-cheweep* or *chwe-cha-cha* etc.; *cheeep* or *chilp* calls, more musical than House; *swee swee* in alarm. **HABITAT** Open forest, cultivation; 1,100–2,680 m, locally to 700 m in winter. **RANGE** Fc **R** W,N,E,S(east) Myanmar, N Laos, W,E Tonkin. Ra **WV** NW,NE Thailand. Rc (status?) SW Myanmar.

3 PLAIN-BACKED SPARROW *Passer flaveolus* 13.5–15 cm
(a) Male: Unstreaked; rufous-chestnut edge of crown/upperparts, greenish-grey crown/upper mantle and back to uppertail-coverts, yellowish cheeks/vent. **(b) Female**: Unstreaked; pale yellowish tinge below. **Juvenile**: Like female but slightly darker crown/lower mantle, duller throat. **VOICE** Loud clear *filip* or *chirrup*, less harsh/more metallic than Eurasian Tree; *chu-chu-weet* in alarm. **HABITAT** Open woodland, coastal scrub, dry open areas, edge of cultivation; up to 1,525 m (below 800 m Thailand). **RANGE** Lc/co **R** SW,W,C,E,S Myanmar, Thailand, Pen Malaysia, Cambodia, Laos, C,S Annam, Cochinchina.

4 EURASIAN TREE SPARROW *Passer montanus* 14–14.5 cm
(a) Adult *malaccensis*: Whitish head-sides with black patch, chestnut, crown/nape, small bib. **(b) Juvenile**: Duller; crown paler with dark forecrown markings, fainter ear-covert patch/bib, pale bill-base. **VOICE** Sings with call-notes and *tsooit*, *tsreet* and *tswee-ip* notes. Harsh *chip* and *chissip* calls, sharp *tet* and *tsooit*, dry *tet-tet-tet...* **HABITAT** Urban areas, human habitation, cultivation; up to 1,830 m. **RANGE** Co **R** throughout.

5 BLACK-BREASTED WEAVER *Ploceus benghalensis* 14 cm
(a) Male breeding: Yellow crown, blackish breast-band. **(b) Male non-breeding**: Like female but buffish-scaled blackish breast-band. **(c) Female**: Like Streaked but crown/nape plainer and greyer, breast unstreaked, rump plainer. **VOICE** Song is barely audible *tsi tsi tsisik tsisik tsik tsik*. Soft *chit* call notes. **HABITAT** Marshes and grassland near water, cultivation; lowlands. **RANGE** Doubtful historical records from S Myanmar.

6 STREAKED WEAVER *Ploceus manyar* 13.5 cm
(a) Male breeding *williamsoni*: Yellow crown, streaked breast/flanks. **(b) Male non-breeding/female**: Dark head-sides, yellowish-white supercilium, submoustachial and neck-patch. Boldly streaked crown/nape, finely streaked breast. **(c) Male breeding** *P.m.peguensis* (Myanmar): Broader blackish streaking. **VOICE** Sings with soft continuous trill: *see-see-see-see-see..*, ending with *o-chee*. Also *tre tre cherrer cherrer*. Loud *chirt* notes. **HABITAT** Grassland, marshes, cultivation, often near water; up to 915 m. **RANGE** Lc **R** Myanmar (except Tenasserim), NW,C,W(coastal) Thailand, Cambodia, C,S Annam, Cochinchina. Un **FER** Singapore.

7 BAYA WEAVER *Ploceus philippinus* 15 cm
(a) Male breeding *angelorum*: Yellow crown, plain buffish-brown breast. **(b) Male non-breeding/female**: Rather plain head-sides, quite plain warm brown breast, sometimes faintly dark-streaked at sides (no obvious streaks); whitish throat and vent. **(c) Juvenile**: Like female but breast and flanks rather deeper buff, crown-streaking broader and more broken. **(d) Male breeding** *infortunatus* (south of c.12°N; ? C Annam, Cochinchina): More rufescent base-colour above, darker/more rufescent breast/flanks. **Other subspecies** *P.p.burmanicus* (Myanmar, except Tenasserim). VOICE Sings with chattering notes, then wheezy *cher-wiu*. Harsh *chit* notes. **HABITAT** Cultivation, grassland, open areas, secondary growth; up to 1,220 m. **RANGE** Un/lc **R** (except C Laos, W,E Tonkin, N Annam).

8 ASIAN GOLDEN WEAVER *Ploceus hypoxanthus* 15 cm
(a) Male breeding *hymenaicus*: Yellow head/body, black head-side/throat/upperpart-streaks. **Male non-breeding**: Like female but often tinged yellow on supercilium/below (sometimes above). **(b) Female**: Like Baya but bill as deep as long, no obvious forehead, no mottling on breast, broader crown-streaks. **HABITAT** Lowland marshes, grassland, rice paddies, usually near water. **RANGE** Sc/lc **R** SW,C,S Myanmar, Tenasserim, NW,NE,C Thailand, Cambodia, S Laos, S Annam, Cochinchina.

9 JAVA SPARROW *Padda oryzivora* 16 cm
(a) Adult: Grey with black head and rump to tail, white ear-coverts, red bill, pinkish belly. **(b) Juvenile**: Brownish; darker crown/tail, pale ear-coverts, dull buffish below, breast streaked. **VOICE** Sings with soft bell-like notes, then trilling and clucking sounds, often ending with whining metallic *ti-tui*. Soft liquid *tup*, *ch-luk* and sharp *tak*. **HABITAT** Cultivation, rice paddies, margins of human habitation; lowlands. **RANGE** Lo **FER** C,S Thailand (Bangkok, Phuket I), Pen Malaysia, Singapore; formerly (still?) SW Myanmar, Tenasserim, S Annam, Cochinchina.

10 PLAIN MOUNTAIN FINCH *Leucosticte nemoricola* 17 cm
(a) Adult *nemoricola*: Brownish above with broad streaks, wing with black patches and whitish bars, greyish-brown below with whiter vent, whitish outertail-fringes. **(b) Juvenile**: Warmer; plainer head. **VOICE** Sings with sharp twittering *rick-pi-vitt* or *dui-dip-dip-dip*. Soft *chi-chi-chi-chi...* **HABITAT & BEHAVIOUR** Open, often rocky areas, cultivation; 1,830–2,285 m (winter). Usually in flocks. **RANGE** Rc (status?) N Myanmar.

PLATE 138 PARROTFINCHES & MUNIAS

1 RED AVADAVAT *Amandava amandava* 10 cm
(**a**) **Male breeding** *punicea*: Bright red with white spotting.
Male non-breeding: As female but white-spotted uppertail-coverts, large wing-spots. (**b**) **Female**: Greyish-brown, paler below; red rump/uppertail-coverts/bill, small covert-spots. (**c**) **Juvenile**: Like female but no red, buff wing-bars. **Other subspecies** *A.a.flavidiventris* (Myanmar): Whitish-orange/yellowish-buff belly, less deep red head/breast-sides. **VOICE** Song is feeble, very high warble, with sweeter twittering. Calls with thin *pseep*, *teei* or *tsi*. **HABITAT** Grassland, marshes, thickets, open areas; up to 1,525 m (mainly lowlands). **RANGE** Sc/lc **R** Myanmar (except Tenasserim), NW,C,NE(south),SE Thailand, Cambodia, W,E Tonkin, Cochinchina. Sc **FER** Singapore.

2 TAWNY-BREASTED PARROTFINCH *Erythrura hyperythra* 10 cm
Male *malayana*: Undescribed. Male of extralimital nominate race is like female but brighter green above, with black patch on extreme forehead and more extensive, brighter/paler blue on forecrown. (**a**) **Female**: Short green tail, warm buff head-sides and uppertail-coverts, dark brown then blue on forehead. (**b**) **Juvenile**: Paler; all-green crown, pale yellowish/pinkish bill with dark tip. **VOICE** Sings with very quiet soft notes, then 4 musical/bell-like notes. High hissing *tzit-tzit* or *tseet-tseet*, mainly in flight. **HABITAT & BEHAVIOUR** Bamboo, edge of broadleaved evergreen forest; 1,065–1,830 m. Skulking. **RANGE** Ra **R** Pen Malaysia.

3 PIN-TAILED PARROTFINCH *Erythrura prasina* 12.5–16 cm
(**a**) **Male** *prasina*: Green above, blue face/throat, warm buff below, bright red lower rump to long pointed tail. Often a pale red belly-patch and pale bluish breast-wash. (**b**) **Female**: Much shorter tail, often pale powder-blue on head-side but no blue face, washed-out buffish below. (**c**) **Juvenile**: As female but lower rump to tail orange-/brownish-red, lower mandible mostly yellowish/pinkish. **VOICE** Less musical song than Tawny-breasted, more clinking/chirping notes. High *zit*, *tseet-tseet* or *tsit-tsit* and sharp *teger-teter-terge* calls. **HABITAT & BEHAVIOUR** Bamboo, open forest, secondary growth; up to 1,500 m. Semi-nomadic, depending on seeding bamboo. **RANGE** Sc/lc **R** (unpredictable movements) Tenasserim, Thailand (except C), Pen Malaysia, east Cambodia, N,C Laos, C,S Annam, north Cochinchina.

4 WHITE-RUMPED MUNIA *Lonchura striata* 11–11.5 cm
(**a**) **Adult** *subsquamicollis*: Dark brownish with contrasting whitish rump/belly. (**b**) **Juvenile**: Dark parts paler/browner, buffy-tinged rump/belly. **Other subspecies** *L.s.acuticauda* (Myanmar [except Tenasserim], north NW Thailand, N Laos, W Tonkin); *swinhoei* (E Tonkin). **VOICE** Song is twittering *pit pit pit spee boyee* or *prt prt prt spee boyee* (*boyee* downturned). Tinkling metallic *prrrit*, *pirit* or *tr-tr-tr* calls. **HABITAT** Clearings, secondary growth, scrub and grass, cultivation; up to 1,830 m. **RANGE** Co **R** throughout; local Singapore.

5 JAVAN MUNIA *Lonchura leucogastroides* 11.5 cm
(**a**) **Adult**: Rich dark brown above, blackish face, throat, upper breast and tail, white belly. (**b**) **Juvenile**: Brownish throat and

upper breast, dark-barred undertail-coverts, pale buffish belly. **VOICE** Sings with pleasant purring or *prreet* notes. Shrill *pi-i* and *pee-ee-eet* or *tyee-ee-ee*. **HABITAT** Secondary growth, scrub, gardens; lowlands. **RANGE** Un **FER** Singapore.

6 SCALY-BREASTED MUNIA *Lonchura punctulata* 12–12.5 cm
(**a**) **Adult** *topela*: Drab above, yellowish-olive on rump/tail, chestnut-tinged head-sides, brown-scaled below. (**b**) **Juvenile**: Paler and plain above, slightly buffish drab brown below, lower mandible paler than upper. (**c**) **Adult** *subundulata* (Myanmar [except southern S and Tenasserim]): Bolder, blacker scaling below, slightly paler/warmer above. **Other subspecies** *L.p.fretensis* (south of c.7°N): Similar to *subundulata*. *L.p.yunnanensis* (north E Myanmar). **VOICE** Song is very quiet series of high flute-like whistles and low slurred notes. Calls include sibilant piping *ki-dee ki-dee..* or *kitty-kitty-kitty*, rapidly repeated harsh *chup* or *tret* notes and *kit-eeeeee* or *ki-ki-ki-ki-ki-teeee* in alarm. **HABITAT** Cultivation, scrub, secondary growth; up to 1,915 m. **RANGE** Co **R** throughout.

7 WHITE-BELLIED MUNIA *Lonchura leucogastra* 11–11.5 cm
(**a**) **Adult** ~~leucogastra: Very dark brown, olive-yellow tail-~~ fringes, whitish belly, no whitish rump. **Juvenile**: Dark parts browner, unstreaked above, duller tail, buffier belly. **VOICE** Song is *di-di-ptcheee-pti-pti-pti-pteep*. Calls with piping *prrip prrip..*, soft *chee-ee-ee*. **HABITAT** Open broadleaved evergreen forest, nearby secondary growth and cultivation; up to 455 m. **RANGE** Lc **R** south Tenasserim, S Thailand, Pen Malaysia.

8 BLACK-HEADED MUNIA *Lonchura malacca* 11–11.5 cm
(**a**) **Adult** *deignani*: Rufous-chestnut with black hood, blackish vent, blue-grey bill. (**b**) **Juvenile**: Plain brown above, buff below, bluish bill, crown darker than White-headed, underparts buffer. (**c**) **Adult** *atricapilla* (Myanmar [except Tenasserim]): Orange-yellow on tail, blacker vent. (**d**) **Adult** *ferruginosa* (introduced Singapore, ? established): Whitish head, black throat and lower breast-centre to vent. **Other subspecies** *L.m.sinensis* (Tenasserim and south-west Thailand southwards). **VOICE** Song is very quiet series of bill-snapping sounds, followed by 'silent' singing (no sound audible), then faint drawn-out whistles. Weak reedy *pee pee..* call. **HABITAT** Grassland, marshes, scrub, cultivation; up to 1,525 m (mostly lowlands). **RANGE** Lc **R** (except NE Thailand, C,S Laos, W,E Tonkin, N Annam).

9 WHITE-HEADED MUNIA *Lonchura maja* 11.5 cm
(**a**) **Adult** *maja*: White head, broad pale vinous-brown collar. (**b**) **Juvenile**: Like Black-headed but crown duller and paler (though often slightly darker than upperparts), head-sides paler, underparts duller buff. **Other subspecies** *L.m.vietnamensis* (Indochina): Mostly pale brownish head with white around eye only. **VOICE** Song involves bill-clicking, then high, tinkling *weeeeee heeheeheeheehee*. Calls with thin piping *puip*, *peekt* and *pee-eet* (mainly in flight); higher and less reedy than Black-headed. **HABITAT** Grassland, cultivation, rice paddies; scrub; up to 500 m. **RANGE** Un/lfc **R** S Thailand, Pen Malaysia, Singapore. Sc **R** S Annam, Cochinchina.

PLATE 139 *FRINGILLA* & *CARDUELIS* FINCHES, BULLFINCHES & GROSBEAKS

1 CHAFFINCH *Fringilla coelebs* 16 cm
(a) Male non-breeding *coelebs*?: Mostly blue-grey crown, vinous-pinkish face/below, grey-green rump. **(b) Male breeding**: Crown/nape smooth blue-grey, forehead black, more rufescent face/below. **(c) Female**: Duller than Brambling; no orange, grey-buff to whitish below, vague head-bands; green-grey rump. **Juvenile**: Like female but browner nape/rump. **VOICE** Song is loud rattling phrase, introduced by sharp notes: *zitt-zitt-zitt-zitt-sett-sett-chatt-chiterii-dia*. Loud sharp *fink*, low *yupp* in flight (softer than Brambling), sharp *ziih* notes in alarm. **HABITAT** Open forest, secondary growth, cultivation; lowlands. **RANGE** V NW Thailand.

2 BRAMBLING *Fringilla montifringilla* 15.5–16 cm
(a) Male non-breeding: Black head/mantle with grey/brown scaling, pale orange throat/breast/flanks/scapulars, white rump. **(b) Male breeding**: Black and orange more solid, blackish bill. **(c) Female**: Like non-breeding male but crown and ear-coverts plainer greyish-brown. **(d) Juvenile**: Like female but head buffier. **VOICE** Simple buzzing *rrrrhuh* song. Hard nasal *te-ehp*, slightly nasal *yeck*, rasping *zweee* or *tsweek* and silvery *slitt* notes. **HABITAT** Open forest, cultivation; found at c.1,400–1,500 m. **RANGE** V NW Thailand, W Tonkin.

3 GREY-CAPPED GREENFINCH *Carduelis sinica* 14 cm
(a) Male *sinica*: Yellow on wing/vent/tail-sides, greyish crown and nape, rich brown mantle/scapulars, warm brownish breast and flanks. **(b) Female**: Duller/washed out; plainer greyish-brown head. **(c) Juvenile**: Relatively pale body/coverts/tertials, pale greyish fringing on secondaries. **VOICE** Song phrases incorporate call notes; usually begin with dry nasal trill and include *kirr* and *korr* notes. Calls with nasal *dzweee*, twittering *dzi-dz-i-dzi-i...* **HABITAT** Parks, gardens, casuarinas; lowlands. **RANGE** Lo coastal R S Annam. **Rc** (status?; probably **R**) E Tonkin.

4 YELLOW-BREASTED GREENFINCH *Carduelis spinoides* 14 cm
(a) Male *heinrichi*: Blackish crown/head-sides, yellow supercilium/underparts/wing-bars. **(b) Female**: Duller, paler; nape to back streaked. **(c) Juvenile**: Paler/browner than Black-headed, thinner yellow wing-slash. **VOICE** Song is said to recall extralimital European Greenfinch *C. chloris*, but higher. Calls with light twittering and harsh *dzwee*, *beez* or *zeez* notes and drawn-out *sweee-tu-tu*. **HABITAT** Forest edge, secondary growth, alder groves, cultivation; 1,220–2,550 m. **RANGE** Lc **R** W Myanmar.

5 BLACK-HEADED GREENFINCH *C.ambigua* 13–13.5 cm
(a) Male *ambigua*: Dull olive-green above, mottled dull olive-green throat to flanks, blackish crown/ear-coverts, greyish-white greater covert bar. **(b) Female**: Lacks obvious supercilium of Yellow-breasted, plainer above, greyish wing-bars. **(c) Juvenile**: Darker/greener than Yellow-breasted, broader yellow wing-slash. **VOICE** Sings with long wheezes: *wheeeeeu* or *jiiiiii*, punctuated by call notes. Jumbled jingling *titutitu* and *titu-titu titu-tittrititititit* etc., with harder *chututut*, quiet rising buzzy *jieuu* and soft *chu-chu* etc. **HABITAT** Open forest, secondary growth, cultivation; 1,010–2,565 m. **RANGE** Lc **R** N,E,S(east) Myanmar, N Laos (sc), W Tonkin. Sc **WV** NW Thailand.

6 VIETNAMESE GREENFINCH *Carduelis monguilloti* 13.5 cm
(a) Male: Black head, blackish-green above, yellow below with mottled breast. **(b) Female**: Duller/paler; streaked above, more mottling below. **(c) Juvenile**: Paler/duller than female. **VOICE** Song is rising *seeuuu-seeuuu-seeuuu*, followed by dry nasal *weeeee*. Twittering *chi-chi-chi..*, nasal *zweee*. **HABITAT** Open pine forest; 1,050–1,900 m. **RANGE** Lc **R** S Annam.

7 EURASIAN SISKIN *Carduelis spinus* 12 cm
(a) Male: Black forehead/chin, yellow supercilium/breast, white belly, streaked flanks. **(b) Female**: Whiter below than Tibetan and juvenile greenfinches, broad wing-bars. **(c) Juvenile**: Browner above than female, more streaked. **VOICE** Sings with flowing twitters, trills, mimicry, and odd drawn-out choking/wheezing notes. Clear ringing *tluib* and *tilu*, dry *tet* notes, trilling *tittereee* and sharp *tsooeet* in alarm. **HABITAT** Open forest, secondary growth; found at c.1,500 m. **RANGE** V W Tonkin.

8 TIBETAN SISKIN *Carduelis thibetana* 12.5 cm
(a) Male: Small, unstreaked, greenish-yellow. **(b) Female**: Darker above with blackish streaks, streaked below and whiter-vented. **(c) Juvenile**: Duller/paler than female, buffish covert fringes, more streaked below. **VOICE** Song is nasal buzzing *zeezle-eezle-eeze* etc., with trills. Twittering from flocks. **HABITAT** Open forest, forest edge; 610–2,135 m. **RANGE** Rc (status?) N Myanmar.

9 BROWN BULLFINCH *Pyrrhula nipalensis* 16.5 cm
(a) Adult *waterstradti*: Grey-brown; whitish ear-coverts/vent/rump-band. **(b) Juvenile**: No dark face, buffier body/covert-bar. **(c) Adult** *P.n.ricketti* (N Myanmar, W Tonkin): Blacker crown, darker ear-coverts. **Other subspecies** *P.n.victoriae* (W Myanmar): Similar to *ricketti*. *P.n.ssp.* (S Annam): Head appears mostly whitish (apart from throat). **VOICE** Song is mellow *u'iib pi-huu*; *ip-pr'ipi-piru* from *victoriae*, quick mellow *ip'ipi-you* in S Annam. Calls (S Annam) with *pirr-pirru*, hurried *per-you*. **HABITAT** More open broadleaved evergreen and mixed broadleaved/coniferous forest; 1,050–2,520 m. **RANGE** Sc/un **R** W,N Myanmar, Pen Malaysia, W Tonkin, S Annam.

10 GREY-HEADED BULLFINCH *Pyrrhula erythaca* 15 cm
(a) Male *erythaca*: Mid-grey above, white-bordered face, deep orange breast/belly. **(b) Female**: Body mostly suffused pinkish-buff. **(c) Juvenile**: Head plainer buffish-brown than female, no black on forehead. **First-winter male**: Dull yellow-orange below (also splashed on throat). **VOICE** Soft *soo-ee* or *poo-ee*. **HABITAT** Open broadleaved evergreen forest, forest edge, secondary growth, scrub; 2,135–3,655 m. **RANGE** Un **R** N Myanmar.

11 YELLOW-BILLED GROSBEAK *Eophona migratoria* 20 cm
(a) Male *migratoria*: Dark-tipped yellow bill, greyish-brown with black hood/tail/wings (latter tipped white). **(b) Female**: Brownish-grey head, less white on wing. **Juvenile**: Buffier-brown on head/below than female, whitish throat, browner above; two narrow buffish wing-bars. **VOICE** Song of various whistles and trills. Loud *tek-tek*. **HABITAT** Open woodland, secondary growth, scrub, cultivation, parks and gardens; up to 800 m. **RANGE** V N Myanmar, NE Thailand, N Laos, E Tonkin.

PLATE 140 FINCHES & RED CROSSBILL

1 DARK-BREASTED ROSEFINCH *Carpodacus nipalensis* 16 cm. (a) **Male** *intensicolor*: Dark brownish-red above/on breast, pinkish-red supercilium, throat and belly. (b) **Female/juvenile**: Unstreaked drab brown, vague mantle- streaks, brown wing-bars and tertial fringes. VOICE Song of monotonous chipping notes. Calls with clear double whistle, sparrow-like twittering and *cha'a'rrr* in alarm. HABITAT Underbrush in open broadleaved evergreen forest, forest edge, secondary growth, scrub, cultivation borders; 1,525–2,900 m, rarely down to 500 m in winter. RANGE Rc (status?) N Myanmar (probably R), W Tonkin. Ra WV E Myanmar, NW Thailand.

2 COMMON ROSEFINCH *Carpodacus erythrinus* 16–16.5 cm (a) **Male breeding** *roseatus*: Red head, wing-bars and underparts, darker eyeline; darker above. (b) **Male nonbreeding/female**: Greyish-brown above, whitish below, finely streaked; two buffy-whitish wing-bars, plain head-sides. (c) **Juvenile**: Browner and darker-streaked above and below than female, broader/buffier wing-bars. (d) **Male breeding** *erythrinus* (VS N Myanmar, NW Thailand, ? Indochina): Greyer above, paler lower breast and belly. VOICE Song is slowly rising whistle: *weeeja-wu-weeeja* or *te-te-weechew*. Typically calls with clear whistled *ooeet* or *too-ee* and sharp nasal *chay-eeee* in alarm. HABITAT Forest edge, secondary growth, scrub, cultivation; up to 2,565 m. RANGE Lc WV Myanmar, W,NW,NE Thailand, N Laos, W Tonkin.

3 PINK-RUMPED ROSEFINCH *Carpodacus eos* 15 cm (a) **Male**: Pink-tinged greyish above with blackish streaking, reddish-pink rump, supercilium and underparts. (b) **Female**: Resembles juvenile Common but defined paler supercilium, greyer above and whiter below, with denser, regular, darker streaking overall; wing-bars and tertial fringes indistinct, bill narrower. From Dark-rumped and Spot-winged by overall paler coloration, whiter underparts with broader dark streaks, no tertial markings. VOICE Calls with assertive *pink* or *tink* and bunting-like *tsip* or *tsick*. Sometimes harsh *piprit* or tinny rattling *tvitt-itt-itt-itt*. HABITAT Forest edge, secondary growth, scrub, cultivation borders; found in lowlands. RANGE V NW Thailand.

4 VINACEOUS ROSEFINCH *Carpodacus vinaceus* 15 cm (a) **Male** *vinaceus*: Body almost uniform dark red, pink supercilium, paler red rump, whitish tertial spots. (b) **Female**: Rather dull dark brown above with darker streaks, rather plain rump and uppertail-coverts; underparts dull, deep, dark buffy-brown with dark streaking, mainly on throat and breast. From Dark-rumped and Spot-winged by plainer head-sides (without dark ear-coverts and contrasting supercilium), less distinctly dark-streaked upper- and underparts. (c) **Juvenile**: Like female but more boldly streaked. VOICE Song is simple *pee-dee* or *do-do*. Calls with hard assertive whiplash-like *pwit* or *zieh* (often introducing song), thin high *tip*, faint *tink*, *pink* and bunting-like *zick*. HABITAT Edge of broadleaved evergreen forest, secondary growth, scrub, bamboo; 1,830–2,745 m. RANGE Sc/un R N,E(north) Myanmar.

5 DARK-RUMPED ROSEFINCH *C.edwardsii* 17 cm (a) **Male** *rubicunda*: Recalls Dark-breasted but paler/streakier above, complete pale pink supercilium, pinker belly. (b) **Female/juvenile**: Larger/bulkier than Spot-winged, no whitish-buff mantle streaks, deeper buffish-brown below. **First-summer male**: Similar to female but dark red tinge above, paler, pinker supercilium/face; breast washed deep pink. VOICE Call is abrupt, rather shrill, high metallic *zwiiib* or *tswii*. HABITAT Undergrowth in more open broadleaved evergreen forest, secondary growth; 1,980–3,050 m. RANGE Lo R N Myanmar.

6 SPOT-WINGED ROSEFINCH *C.rodopeplus* 16.5 cm (a) **Male** *verreauxii*: Plain dark reddish crown, narrow pinkish streaks on mantle and tertials, pink rump, supercilium and darker-mottled underparts. (b) **Female/juvenile**: Smaller than Dark-rumped, some thin whitish-buff streaks on mantle, paler below with broader streaks on lower throat/breast. VOICE Call is nasal *wu'eee* (*eee* higher) in Nepal. HABITAT Edge of evergreen forest, secondary growth, bamboo; 2,135–2,895 m. RANGE Un R N,E(north) Myanmar.

7 CRIMSON-BROWED FINCH *Propyrrhula subhimachala* 20 cm. (a) **Male**: Warm to reddish-brown above, greenish wing-fringing, red rump/forehead, greyish below with pinkish-speckled red throat/breast. (b) **Female/juvenile**: Dull green and grey, yellowish rump/forehead/upper breast, grey-streaked whitish throat. (c) **First-year male**: Rufous and orange tinges where red on adult. VOICE Song is bright, varied warble. Simple *ter-ter-tee* call. HABITAT Broadleaved evergreen and coniferous forest, thickets; 1,830–3,050 m. RANGE Un R N Myanmar. Rc in winter (status?) W Myanmar.

8 SCARLET FINCH *Haematospiza sipahi* 19 cm (a) **Male**: Uniform bright red head and body, pale yellowish bill. Black wings/tail with scarlet fringing. (b) **Female/juvenile**: Rather uniform scaly brownish-olive, paler below, pale bill, sharply defined bright yellow rump. (c) **First-year male**: Differs from female by orange-rufous tinge to head, upperparts and wing-feather fringes, more rufous-tinged below, bright orange rump. VOICE Song is clear liquid *par-ree-reeeeeee*. Calls with loud clear *too-eee* or *pleeau* and *kwee'i'iu* or *chew'we'auh*. HABITAT More open broadleaved evergreen forest, secondary growth; 1,160–2,100 m. RANGE Un R W,N Myanmar. Rc (status?) NW Thailand, N Laos, W Tonkin.

9 RED CROSSBILL *Loxia curvirostra* 16.5–17.5 cm (a) **Male** *meridionalis* (S Annam): Heavy bill, crossed mandibles, largely red body, brownish wings/tail. (b) **Female**: Dull, dark-streaked greenish-grey, paler and yellower rump, breast and belly. (c) **Juvenile**: Paler and darker-streaked than female. (d) **Male** *himalayensis* (Myanmar): 15 cm. Mandible tips overlap more. VOICE *L.c.meridionalis* typically calls with clear double *whit-whit*, recalling Rain Quail. Also lower, slower *whic-whic* and extended series of *whit*, *twit* and *whic* notes. Elsewhere, call is described as hard *chip-chip*. HABITAT Mature pine forest, sometimes alder woods; 1,370–2,900 m. RANGE Lc R (some movements) N Myanmar, S Annam.

1a
1b
2a
2b
2c
2d
3a
3b
4a
4b
4c
5a
5b
6a
6b
7a
7b
7c
8a
8b
8c
9a
9b
9c
9d

7–9 to different scale

PLATE 141 *MYCEROBAS* GROSBEAKS, GOLD-NAPED FINCH & BUNTINGS

1 COLLARED GROSBEAK *Mycerobas affinis* 24 cm
(**a**) **Male**: Black hood/wings/tail, yellow nape, back, rump and underparts, orange-rufous-washed nape/rump. (**b**) **Female**: Grey head, pale greyish-green above (greener upper mantle, rump and uppertail-coverts), yellowish-olive below, blackish primaries/tail. (**c**) **Juvenile male**: As adult but olive-tinged yellow plumage, duller head, greyish-brown throat-mottling. **Juvenile female**: Paler chin/throat than adult, duller below, variable yellow on rump. **VOICE** Song is loud piping *ti-di-li-ti-di-li-um* etc. Loud creaky sounds, mixed with musical notes. Rapid mellow *pip-pip-pip-pip-pip-pip-ugh*. Sharp *kurr* notes. **HABITAT** Broadleaved evergreen and mixed broadleaved and coniferous forest, secondary growth; 2,500–3,655 m. **RANGE** Un **R** N Myanmar. **V** NW Thailand.

2 SPOT-WINGED GROSBEAK *Mycerobas melanozanthos* 23 cm
(**a**) **Male**: Black, with yellow breast to vent, whitish-tipped greater coverts/secondaries/tertials. (**b**) **Female**: Paler; yellow-streaked crown/mantle, streaky yellow head-sides/lower head-sides, yellow below, with blackish malar line/streaking. Buffy-white wing-bars/tips. (**c**) **Juvenile**: Dark parts a shade paler than female, head-sides, throat, breast and flanks tinged buffish. **VOICE** Oriole-like *tew-tew-teeeu*, *tyop-tiu* or *tyu-tio*, rising *ah*. Rattled *krrr* or *charrarauk*. **HABITAT** Broadleaved evergreen and mixed broadleaved/coniferous forest, secondary growth; 1,400–2,440 m, locally to 300 m in winter. **RANGE** Un **R** W,N,E Myanmar, NW Thailand, N Laos, W Tonkin.

3 WHITE-WINGED GROSBEAK *Mycerobas carnipes* 24 cm
(**a**) **Male** *carnipes*: Sooty-black with greenish-yellow back, rump, belly and vent, white primary patch. (**b**) **Female**: Paler, greyer; less demarcated below, whitish streaks on ear-coverts to upper breast, reduced wing markings, greener rump to uppertail-coverts. **Juvenile**: Browner than female, pale fringing on head/mantle. Male gradually attains dark patches. **VOICE** Usual song is *add-a-dit un-di-di-di-dit* or *add-a-dit dja-dji-dji-dju* etc. Calls include soft nasal *shwenk* or *chwenk*, squawking *wit* or *wet* notes, and *wet-et-et* and *add-a-dit* etc. **HABITAT** Stunted vegetation at high altitudes, scrub, cultivation; found at 3,655 m. **RANGE** Un **R** N Myanmar.

4 GOLD-NAPED FINCH *Pyrrhoplectes epauletta* 15 cm
(**a**) **Male**: Small, blackish; golden-orange hindcrown/nape and shoulder-spot, white tertial fringes. (**b**) **Female**: Drab rufescent-chestnut, olive-green hindcrown/nape, grey face/upper mantle, dark flight feathers/tail, white tertial fringes. (**c**) **Juvenile**: Richer brown than female, greyer nape. **VOICE** Song is rapid high *pi-pi-pi-pi*. Usual calls are thin high *teeu*, *tseu* or *peeuu*, *purl-ee* and squeaky *plee-e-e*. **HABITAT** Undergrowth in open broadleaved evergreen forest, secondary growth, scrub; 1,705–2,135 m. **RANGE** Un **R** N Myanmar.

5 YELLOW-BREASTED BUNTING *Emberiza aureola* 15 cm
(**a**) **Male non-breeding** *ornata*: Yellow below, warm brown breast-band, white median/lesser coverts. Pale buffish supercilium and ear-coverts, the latter with broad dark border, indistinctly streaked above and on flanks. (**b**) **Male breeding**: Chestnut upperparts and breast-band, blackish forehead, face and upper throat. (**c**) **Female**: Duller than non-breeding male, no breast-band, paler below, darker streaks on breast-sides and flanks, duller/paler above, dark-streaked crown with paler median stripe. Often has paler mantle 'braces'. (**d**) **Juvenile**: Less yellow than female, fine breast-streaks/malar line. Pale brownish rump with darker streaks. **Other subspecies** *E.a.aureola* (Myanmar): Only little black on forehead, all-chestnut breast-band. **VOICE** Song is fairly slow, high *djuu-djuu weee-weee ziii-zii* etc. Call is short, metallic *tic*. **HABITAT & BEHAVIOUR** Grass and scrub, cultivation, open areas, often near water; up to 1,370 m. Often roosts in large numbers, particularly in reedbeds. **RANGE** Sc/lc **WV** (except N,S Annam). Also **PM** Cambodia, N Laos, E Tonkin.

6 CHESTNUT BUNTING *Emberiza rutila* 14–14.5 cm
(**a**) **Male non-breeding**: Duller than breeding male, with pale fringes to chestnut feathers. (**b**) **Male breeding**: Bright chestnut plumage with yellow breast and belly. (**c**) **Female/juvenile**: Similar to juvenile Yellow-breasted but plain rufous-chestnut rump and uppertail-coverts, rather plain ear-coverts, no 'braces', almost no white on outertail. **VOICE** Song is rather high *wiie-wiie-wiie tzrree-tzrree-tzrree zizizitt* etc. Call is *zick*, similar to Little. **HABITAT** Underbrush in open forest, scrub and grass, bamboo, cultivation; up to 2,590 m. **RANGE** Un/lc **WV** Myanmar, W,NW,NE Thailand, N,C Laos, Vietnam.

7 BLACK-HEADED BUNTING *Emberiza melanocephala* 16–18 cm
(**a**) **Male non-breeding**: Pattern as breeding male but very washed out, pale fringes above, duller and buffier below. (**b**) **Male breeding**: Black crown and head-sides, rufous-chestnut above, all-yellow below. (**c**) **Female**: Large; washed-out look, no white on outertail, whitish wing-fringing, pale yellow undertail-coverts. (**d**) **First winter**: As female but streakier above, pinkish-buff breast-wash; may show sparse streaking on breast and flanks. **VOICE** Song is melodious, quite harsh *zrt zrt preep-ree chu-chiwu-chiwu ze-treeurr*. Sparrow-like *chleep* or *chlip* calls, metallic *tzik* or *plutt*. Deep *tchup* in flight. **HABITAT** Open country, scrub, cultivation; lowlands. **RANGE** **V** S Thailand (market specimen), Singapore, N Laos.

8 BLACK-FACED BUNTING *Emberiza spodocephala* 14–15 cm
(**a**) **Male** *sordida*: Greenish-olive hood (may be paler-fringed on non-breeders), blackish face, yellow below. (**b**) **Female breeding**: Lacks dark face, yellowish throat and breast, dark malar line and streaking below. Dull birds (illustrated) resemble non-breeders, which are like first winter but with buffier head and pale buffish-yellow wash below. (**c**) **First winter**: No obvious rufous or yellow in plumage, greyish ear-coverts, neck-side and lesser coverts, grey-brown rump, clear streaking below, whitish submoustachial stripe. Lores and neck-sides of some males resemble adult. **VOICE** Song is variable, lively series of ringing chirps and trills: *chi-chi-chu chirri-chu chi-zeee-chu chi-chi* etc. Sibilant sharp thin *tzii* call. **HABITAT** Scrub and grass, cultivation, often near water; lowlands. **RANGE** Sc/un **WV** W,N Myanmar, NW Thailand, N Laos, W,E Tonkin, N Annam.

PLATE 142 BUNTINGS

1 CRESTED BUNTING *Melophus lathami* 16.5–17 cm
(**a**) **Male non-breeding**: Blackish with buffish-grey edgings; chestnut wings/tail, crest. **Male breeding**: Blacker, no buffish-grey edgings. (**b**) **Female non-breeding**: Less chestnut wings/tail, short crest. Olive-brown above, with dark streaks; paler below with faint breast-streaks. **Female breeding**: Paler than non-breeding, mantle more boldly streaked. (**c**) **Juvenile**: Darker than breeding female, buffier below. VOICE Song is brief, falling *tzit dzit dzit see-see-suee* or *tzit dzit tzit-tzitswe-e-ee-tiyuh* etc. Soft *tip* or *tup*. HABITAT Cultivation, scrub, tall grass; up to 2,565 m. RANGE Un/lc **R** (local movements) Myanmar, N,C Laos, W,E Tonkin. Lc **WV** W,NW Thailand.

2 GODLEWSKI'S BUNTING *Emberiza godlewskii* 16.5–17 cm
(**a**) **Male** *yunnanensis*: Chestnut and black stripes on grey hood. (**b**) **Female**: Less rufous-chestnut on scapulars, paler below, streaky flanks. (**c**) **Juvenile**: Buffish-brown head/breast with streaks; no prominent head markings. VOICE Song is fairly high *chit-chit-chu-chitu-tsi-chitu-chu-chitrru* etc. Thin drawn-out *tzii*, hard *pett pett*. HABITAT Open country with bushes, cultivation; 745–2,285 m. RANGE Un (status?) N,E(north) Myanmar.

3 TRISTRAM'S BUNTING *Emberiza tristrami* 15 cm
(**a**) **Male non-breeding**: Duller head than breeding, white parts buffier, larger ear-spot. (**b**) **Male breeding**: Bold black and white head. (**c**) **Female/juvenile**: Recalls non-breeding male but throat buffish-white, head-sides/lores pale brownish; breast and flanks streaked brown. From Rustic by complete medial crown-stripe, greyer neck, fainter breast/flank-streaks; unscaled rufous-chestnut rump/uppertail-coverts. VOICE Song is simple *hsiee swee-swee swee-tsirririri* etc. Explosive *tzick*. HABITAT Thickets in open forest, secondary growth; 900–2,565 m. RANGE Ra **WV** N Myanmar, NW Thailand, N Laos, W,E Tonkin.

4 CHESTNUT-EARED BUNTING *Emberiza fucata* 15–16 cm
(**a**) **Male breeding** *fucata*: Dark-streaked grey crown/nape, chestnut ear-coverts, black and rufous-chestnut breast-bands. **Male non-breeding/first-winter male**: As adult female but buffier supercilium, whitish base to throat and breast contrasts more with buffy flanks/upper belly. (**b**) **Female**: Like breeding male but duller crown/nape/below, fainter gorget/breast-band. (**c**) **Juvenile**: Duller than female, ear-coverts dull greyish-brown, with pale centre and broad dark border. (**d**) **First-winter female**: Buffy crown/nape/breast/flanks. Dull birds (illustrated) have browner head-sides. Darker malar and streaks below than juvenile Godlewski's, whitish submoustachial, much less white on tail. **Other subspecies** *E.f.arcuata* (rc W,N Myanmar): More solid black gorget, broader breast-band (also on female), extending to flanks. VOICE Sings with rapid twittering *zwee zwiz-wezwizizi trup-trup* etc. Explosive *pzick* call. HABITAT Open country, cultivation; up to 1,890 m. RANGE Un/lc **WV** Myanmar, W,NW,NE Thailand, Laos, W,E Tonkin, C,S Annam. **V** Pen Malaysia.

5 LITTLE BUNTING *Emberiza pusilla* 12–14 cm
(**a**) **Adult non-breeding**: Fine streaks below, blackish lateral crown-stripe, eyestripe and border to rufous-chestnut ear-coverts. Buffy median crown-stripe/supercilium/submoustachial/ear-spot; rufescent face, whitish eyering. (**b**) **Adult breeding**: Chestnut-

flushed head; solid black crown-stripes. (**c**) **Juvenile**: Like non-breeding adult but duller head, browner below with coarser streaks. VOICE Song is quite metallic *zree zree zree tsutsutsut-su tzriiitu* etc. Hard *tzik* or *zick*. HABITAT Secondary growth, scrub, grass, cultivation; up to 2,610 m. RANGE Fc/co **WV** Myanmar, NW,NE Thailand, N,C Laos, W,E Tonkin. Also **PM** E Tonkin.

6 RUSTIC BUNTING *Emberiza rustica* 14–15 cm
(**a**) **Male non-breeding** *rustica*: Less black on head than breeding, less solid breast-band/collar. (**b**) **Male breeding**: Bold black and white head, dark reddish-chestnut collar, rump/uppertail-coverts, lesser coverts and breast/flank-streaks. (**c**) **Female non-breeding**: Less black on crown and ear-coverts than breeding, crown more uniformly streaked. **Female breeding**: Similar to non-breeding male. (**d**) **First-winter female**: Buffier than non-breeding, browner neck/rump, some dark throat-/breast-streaks. Pale hindcrown-/ear-spot. VOICE Song is mellow *dudeleu-dewee-deweea-weeu* etc. Short, piercing *zit* or *tzik*. HABITAT Secondary growth, thickets, cultivation; found at c. 900 m. RANGE **V** E Tonkin.

7 YELLOW-THROATED BUNTING *Emberiza elegans* 15 cm
(**a**) **Male non-breeding** *elegantula*: Duller than breeding, black replaced by dark greyish. (**b**) **Male breeding**: Black (crested) crown, ear-coverts, chin and breast-band, yellow supercilium and throat. **Female non-breeding**: Breast-band replaced by dark brown streaks. (**c**) **Female breeding**: Like male non-breeding but crown, ear-coverts and solid breast-band dark warmish brown, supercilium/throat light yellowish-buff. (**d**) **Juvenile**: Broad pale supercilium, rufescent wing-fringing, pale below. VOICE Twittering *tswit-tsu-ri-tu tswee witt tsuri weee-dee tswit-tsuri-tu*. Sharp, rather liquid *tzik*. HABITAT Forest edge, nearby scrub, cultivation; 1,010–2,135 m. RANGE **Rc** (status?) N Myanmar.

8 PALLAS'S BUNTING *Emberiza pallasi* 13 cm
(**a**) **Male non-breeding** *pallasi?*: Like non-breeding female but some black on head. (**b**) **Male breeding**: Bold black and white head, mostly white collar/below; bold streaks above, white rump and uppertail-coverts. (**c**) **Female non-breeding/first winter**: Pale warm brown crown/ear-coverts, white submoustachial/throat, only vague streaks below, pale rump/uppertail-coverts, brownish-grey lesser coverts. **Female breeding**: Duller and greyer. (**d**) **Juvenile**: More boldly streaked than female. VOICE Song is simple shrill *srih-srih-srih-srih-srih...* Fine sparrow-like *chleep*, *tschialp*, *tsilip* or *tschirp*. HABITAT Grass and scrub near water, cultivation; found at c.900 m. RANGE **V** C Myanmar.

9 REED BUNTING *Emberiza schoeniclus* 16–17 cm
(**a**) **Male non-breeding** *pyrrhulina*: Much thicker bill than Pallas's, rufous wing-fringing (including lesser coverts), streakier flanks, usually warmer above. (**b**) **Male breeding**: From Pallas's as non-breeding. (**c**) **Female non-breeding** and (**d**) **Female breeding** and **First winter**: Best told from Pallas's by thick dark bill, rufescent lesser/median covert tips, plainer crown and particularly hindneck. VOICE Song is hesitant *zritt zreet zreet zritt zriuu* etc. Thin falling *seeoo*, hoarse *brzee*. HABITAT Grass and scrub, cultivation; lowlands. RANGE **V** E Tonkin (race not certain).

SELECTED BIBLIOGRAPHY

Duckworth, J.W., Alström, P. Davidson, P., Evans, T.D., Poole, C.M., Setha, T. and Timmins, R.J. (2001) A new species of wagtail from the lower Mekong basin. *Bull. B.O.C.* 121(3): 152–182.

Duckworth, J.W., Davidson, P., Evans, T.D., Round, P.D. and Timmins, R.J. (2002) Bird records from Laos, principally the Upper Lao/Thai Mekong and Xiangkhouang Province, in 1998–2000. *Forktail* 18: 11–44.

Eames, J.C., and Eames, C. (2001) A new species of Laughingthrush (Passeriformes: Garrulacinae) from the Central Highlands of Vietnam. *Bull. B.O.C.* 121(1): 10–23.

Eames, J.C. (2002) Eleven new subspecies of babbler (Passeriformes: Timaliinae) from Kon Tum Province, Vietnam. *Bull. B.O.C.* 122(2): 109–141.

Eames, J.C., Steinheimer, F.D. and Bansok, R. (2002) A collection of birds from the Cardamom Mountains, Cambodia, including a new subspecies of *Arborophila cambodiana. Forktail* 18: 67–86.

Evans, T.D. (2001) Ornithological records from Savannakhet Province, Lao PDR, January–July 1997. *Forktail* 17: 21–28.

Evans, T.D., Towll, H.C., Timmins, R.J., Thewlis, R.M., Stones, A.J., Robichaud, W.G. and Barzen, J. (2000) Ornithological records from the lowlands of southern Laos during December 1995–September 1996, including areas on the Thai and Cambodian borders. *Forktail* 16: 29–52.

Inskipp, T., Lindsey, N. and Duckworth, W. (1996) An annotated checklist of the birds of the Oriental region. Sandy, U.K.: Oriental Bird Club.

King, B.F. (2002) The *Hierococcyx fugax*, Hodgson's Hawk Cuckoo, complex. *Bull. B.O.C.* 122(1): 74–80.

King, B., Buck, H., Ferguson, R., Fisher, T., Goblet, C., Nickel, H. and Suter, W. (2001) Birds recorded during two expeditions to north Myanmar (Burma). *Forktail* 17: 29–40.

Parry, S.J., Clark, W.S. and Prakash, V. (2002) On the taxonomic status of the Indian Spotted Eagle *Aquila hastata. Ibis* 144: 665–675.

Martens J., Eck, S., Packert, M., and Sun, Y-H. (1999)

The Golden-spectacled Warbler *Seicercus burkii* – a species swarm (Aves: Passeriformes: Sylviidae), part 1. *Zool. Abhandl. Mus. Dresden* 50: 281–327.

Rasmussen, P.C., and Parry, S.J. (2001) The taxonomic status of the 'Long-billed' Vulture *Gyps indicus. Vulture News* 44: 18–21.

Robson, C. (1999–2003) From the field. *Oriental Bird Club Bull.* 30: 52–56; 31: 49–57; 32: 66–76; 33: 68–78; 34: 83–93; 35: 83–93; 36: 61–71; 37: 77–87.

Round, P.D. (2000) *Field Check-List of Thai Birds.* Bangkok: Bird Conservation Society of Thailand.

Round, P.D. and Robson, C. (2001) Provenance and affinities of the Cambodian Laughingthrush *Garrulax ferrarius. Forktail* 17: 41–44.

Round, P.D. (2003) BCST Records Committee: Review of additions to the list of Thai birds since June 2000. *Bird Conserv. Soc. of Thailand Bull.* 20(1): 16–19.

Treesucon, U. (2000) *Birds of Kaeng Krachan: Check-List and Guide to Birds Finding.* Bangkok: Bird Conservation Society of Thailand.

van der Ven, J. (2000) Myanmar Expedition 1999–2000. Report, visit January 2000. Unpublished.

van der Ven, J. (2001) Myanmar Expedition 1999–2000. Report. Second expedition, December 2000–January 2001. Unpublished.

van der Ven, J. (2002) Myanmar Expedition 2001. Report. Third expedition, December 2001. Unpublished.

Wink, M., Sauer-Gürth, H., and Gwinner, E. (2002) Evolutionary relationships of stonechats and related species inferred from mitochondrial-DNA sequences and genomic fingerprinting. *Brit. Birds* 95: 349–355.

Yésou, P. (2001) Phenotypic variation and systematics of Mongolian Gull. *Dutch Birding* 23(2): 65–82.

Yésou, P. (2002) Trends in systematics. Systematics of *Larus argentatus-cachinnans-fuscus* complex revisited. *Dutch Birding* 24(5): 271–298.

For a more detailed bibliography, please refer to the original work (*A Field Guide to the Birds of South-East Asia* (Robson 2000)).

BIRD STUDY AND CONSERVATION ORGANIZATIONS

NATIONAL

CAMBODIA

Wildlife Protection Office
40 Norodom Boulevard, Phnom Penh
Email: wildlifedfw@online.com.kh

Cambodia Bird News
c/o Wildlife Conservation Society, Cambodia Program,
PO Box 1620, Phnom Penh
Email: cambodia@wcs.org

LAOS

Wildlife Conservation Society (Lao programme)
P.O. Box 6712, Vientiane, Lao PDR
Email: wcslao@laonet.net

WWF Lao Programme
c/o Department of Forestry, Vientiane, Lao PDR
Email: wwflao@laonet.net / wwflao@loxinfo.co.th

MYANMAR

Myanmar Bird and Nature Society
69 Myaynigone Zay Street, Sanchaung Township,
Yangon 11111, Myanmar
Email: SST@mptmail.net.mm

PENINSULAR MALAYSIA

Malaysian Nature Society
JKR 641, Jalan Kelantan, Bukit Persekutuan, 50480
Kuala Lumpur
Email: natsoc@po.jaring.my

SINGAPORE

Nature Society (Singapore)
510 Geylang Road, # 02-05, The Sunflower,
Singapore 389466
Email: nss@nss.org.sg

THAILAND

Bird Conservation Society of Thailand
69/12 Ramintra 24, Jarakheebua, Lardprao,
Bangkok 10230
Email: bcst@box1.a-net.net.th

VIETNAM (also Myanmar)

BirdLife International *in Indochina*
4, Lane 209, Doi Can, Ba Dinh, Hanoi, Vietnam
Email: birdlife@birdlife.netnam.vn

INTERNATIONAL

BirdLife International
Wellbrook Court, Girton Road, Cambridge CB3 0NA,
U.K.
Email: birdlife@birdlife.org.uk
Website: www.birdlife.org

Oriental Bird Club
c/o The Lodge, Sandy, Bedfordshire SG19 2DL, U.K.
Email: mail@orientalbirdclub.org

TRAFFIC Southeast Asia
Unit 9–3A, 3rd Floor, Jalan SS23/11, Taman SEA, 47400
Petaling Jaya, Selangor, Malaysia
Email: tsea@po.jaring.my

Wetlands International–Asia Pacific
3A39, Block A, Kelana Centre Point, Jalan SS7/19, 47301
Petaling Jaya, Selangor, Malaysia
Email: wiap@wiap.nasionet.net

302